# PENNSYLVANIA GERMAN IMMIGRANTS, 1709-1786

# PENNSYLVANIA GERMAN IMMIGRANTS, 1709-1786

*Lists Consolidated from Yearbooks of The Pennsylvania German Folklore Society*

Edited by
DON YODER

CLEARFIELD

Excerpted from *Yearbooks of*
*The Pennsylvania German Folklore Society*,
Volume One (1936); Volume Ten (1945);
Volume Twelve (1947); Volume Sixteen (1951)


Reprinted by arrangement with
The Pennsylvania German Society
Successor to The Pennsylvania German Folklore Society
With a new Foreword and Indexes


Reprinted by Genealogical Publishing Co., Inc.
3600 Clipper Mill Rd., Suite 260
Baltimore, MD 21211-1953
1980, 1984, 1989, 1998, 2006
Library of Congress Catalogue Card Number 80-50502
ISBN-13: 978-0-8063-0892-0
ISBN-10: 0-8063-0892-3
*Made in the United States of America*

Reprinted for Clearfield Company by
Genealogical Publishing Company
Baltimore, Maryland, 2012

# CONTENTS

# FOREWORD

he story of the German migration to the United States has been told many times in its general details. When I began my studies of the eighteenth-century emigration, in the 1940s, I was convinced that what was needed was more detail on the individual side of emigration, more genealogical and social-historical particulars. Such details had been amassed for ethnic groups like the Poles and the Norwegians and a few others, but never in enough detail for the German-speaking groups, except perhaps the Swiss. As an historian of the Pennsylvania German culture I determined to remedy this deficiency through the translation of source materials which were already in print in Germany but practically unknown on this side of the Atlantic.

I began with Adolf Gerber's Württemberg materials, published in two rare pamphlets in the 1920s. Through the kindness of Professor Otto Springer, then head of the German Department of the University of Pennsylvania, and one of my oldest friends and colleagues there, I borrowed the only copies of the Gerber pamphlets that I was able to locate, those of the University of Pennsylvania library. I was a graduate student at the University of Chicago at the time, and the translation and editing was done both in Chicago and at various Pennsylvania libraries.

Dr. Preston A. Barba, head of the German Department at Muhlenberg College, and Editor of the Pennsylvania German Folklore Society yearbooks, for whom I had written articles for *'S Pennsylfawnisch Deitsch Eck* in the Allentown *Morning Call,* commissioned me to finish my edition of the Gerber Lists for inclusion in Volume Ten (1945) of the Society's yearbook. I did so with pleasure and continued with the similar materials in Otto Langguth's Wertheim Lists, which appeared in Volume Twelve (1947). In 1951 I published Friedrich Krebs's transcription of the second Zweibrücken List, 1750-1771, and Ernst Steinemann's Schaffhausen List, 1734-1752.

The Gerber and Langguth Lists, in particular, did for American readers what I had hoped they would do: they brought before them detailed materials in English on individual emigrants and their experiences in leaving their homelands in Europe, which involved manumission in the home territories, the disposition of property, sailing down the Rhine to Rotterdam, boarding ship there, and, after many weeks on the Atlantic, arriving at Philadelphia. The materials included personal financial details, moral characterizations of the emigrants by the authorities, copies of emigrant passports, shipping contracts, and other papers. They gave the reader a glimpse at the relationship of individual emigrants to the cultural matrix which produced them—the *Dorf* or agricultural village, the Protestant church and its pastor, and the local government with its range of offices and petty authorities. Materials were included also on the trades or occupations of most individuals. In some cases nicknames were given by which the emigrant was known in the close-knit village structure in which he grew up.

While the emigrants in all five lists settled principally in Southeastern Pennsylvania and hence became a component part of the Pennsylvania German ethnic group, a minority settled in colonies extending from Nova Scotia to the Carolinas. That the geographical knowledge on the part of emigrant and government alike was not always precise is seen in the frequent statement that an emigrant left for "the island of Pennsylvania." In most cases the official recorded the emigrant's destination as "the New Land," or "America."

The Pennsylvania Germans settled in Southeastern Pennsylvania and parts of Central and Western Pennsylvania over a region roughly the size of Switzerland, but some soon migrated to other areas. Before the Revolution a considerable channel of migration had opened up to the south, and migrants travelling this route settled parts of Western Maryland, the Shenandoah Valley of Virginia, and portions of North and South Carolina, from which secondary settlements were later planted in Kentucky, Tennessee, Missouri, and elsewhere. After the Revolution many Pennsylvania Germans, particularly of the pacifist sects such as the Mennonites, headed northward for the Niagara Country and Ontario, where their descendants still preserve many aspects of Pennsylvania German culture. But the big push of the Pennsylvanians, also after the Revolution, was directly west from Pennsylvania into Ohio, Indiana, Illinois, and eventually Iowa, Nebraska, Kansas, and other midwestern and plains states. Into all these areas the Pennsylvania Germans carried elements of culture which had been adapted from various Continental and British Isles sources. In short, their influence on religion, architecture, language, cookery, and foodways reshaped the cultural map in every region the Pennsylvania Germans settled.

The religious dimensions of the lists are important to note, since in most cases the emigrants identified in America with the denomination in which they had been born, baptized, and confirmed in the old homeland across the Atlantic. The Württembergers, for example, were Lutherans, and formed one strong component of Pennsylvania's colonial Lutheran congregations. There was an ethnic and religious minority in Württemberg, however. These were the Waldensians, Protestant refugees from France, who bore French names: *Armingeon, Balme, Bonnet, Brun, Caffarel, Chapelle, Gautier, Morel, Ozias, Paris, Peirot, Richardon, Rochon, Talmon,* and *Tiers.* The County of Löwenstein-Wertheim was also Lutheran, as was the Duchy of Zweibrücken. The Canton of Schaffhausen in Switzerland was largely Reformed, with a minority of Separatists (Mennonites), among them in our lists: *Heinrich Irmel, Georg Meyer, Samuel Peyer,* and *Michael* and *Hans Russenberger.* In addition, there were a few Catholic converts to Protestantism–*Pancratius Lengenfelder,* for example, with his unforgettable name (Gerber Lists). Finally, a few emigrants were converted to the Moravian Church in Pennsylvania, such as *Johann Matthias Spohn* and *Ludwig Stotz,* again in the Gerber Lists.

Not all of the emigrants listed were registered as arriving in the port of Philadelphia, as recorded in Strassburger and Hinke's *Pennsylvania German Pioneers.* Some undoubtedly entered via New York or Baltimore, and according to the original European sources, some sailed for the Carolinas or Nova Scotia. The identifications of emigrants in the Pennsylvania source materials, at least in the case of unusual names, are accurate. Where there were several emigrants of the same name, I generally provided settlement data on all of them. The materials drawn together from the *Pennsylvania Archives* and other Pennsylvania sources were intended to make it easier for descendants to discover their ancestry. Since my original editing of the lists some additional material has turned up on certain individuals, placing them definitely in the Pennsylvania German world. For example, *Friedrich Schienle* (Gerber Lists) of Steinenbronn, an emigrant of 1754, married Elizabeth Kolb in 1761 at Red Hill in Montgomery County and is buried at New Hanover (Swamp). *Maximilian Speidel* of Ofterdingen (Gerber Lists), an emigrant of 1749, turns up in the Sand Hill Lutheran records of Derry Township, Lancaster (now Dauphin) County, Pennsylvania. And an emigrant with the unmistakable name of *Philipp Jacob Gruendler* of Ostelsheim (Gerber Lists), who arrived in 1754, turns up as sponsor at a baptism at St. Michael's Lutheran Church at Strasburg in Lancaster County in 1756. But the trail of the emigrants is sometimes complex, involving settlement in several Pennsylvania communities and in some cases migration to other colonies. The work of identification goes forward, and the Editor will be pleased to receive from descendants working on their families additional identifications of emigrants in American sources.

This book has not one hero but a multitude of heroes—the eighteenth-century forefathers who left the Old World for the New, the familiar for the unknown. The sources portray them with all their human shortcomings and all their faith and hope. I have quoted many times in my classes the statement of one of them, Johannes Schlessmann of Oxford, Philadelphia County. In a letter he wrote to his relatives in his home village in the Main Valley soon after his arrival in America, in 1753, he makes this statement: "I and my children and my wife thank and praise God a thousand times, that we are in this healthy country. We expect to support ourselves much better here than in Germany, for this is a free country." And while the journey across the ocean is long and tedious, "time, day and hours, sun and moon, stars, day and night, summer and winter, and all creatures under heaven appear here as they do in Germany. Winter comes just as soon in the Pennsylvania country as in Germany—on Simon and Jude's Day, we had such a deep snow, with cold and cutting winds." It was one world even then, one transatlantic world with a common culture and a common goal.

In looking back on these products of my earlier academic career, I wish again to call to memory the persons who assisted me along the way; first of all, a long chain of friendly librarians, archivists, and professors; second, the authors of the works I include in this volume: Adolf Gerber, Otto Langguth, William John Hinke, John Baer Stoudt, Friedrich Krebs, and Ernst Steinemann. None of these is among the living today, but I treasure their memories. I knew most of them personally, and their families, in particular the Hinkes, Stoudts, and Langguths. In addition, I have pleasant memories of working closely with Preston A. Barba of Muhlenberg College, whose expertise in American-German studies, wit, and humanity will always remain fresh in my mind. Finally, I wish to thank the Board of the Pennsylvania German Society, successor to the Pennsylvania German Folklore Society, for permission to reprint these articles in permanent book form. I dedicate them, with affection, to my fellow Pennsylvanians, in state and out, who are working on the history and genealogy of the Commonwealth.

University of Pennsylvania
10 February 1980

DON YODER

# EMIGRANTS

## FROM

# WUERTTEMBERG

## THE ADOLF GERBER LISTS

Edited by

Don Yoder

Union Theological Seminary

# Introduction

The student of our Pennsylvania German folk-culture will find much of interest in a study of Württemberg, the delightful old "Schwabenland" in South Germany, whose pleasant rural life in the past has been portrayed in song and story by Berthold Auerbach and others. The land and its people, their customs and speech, bear striking resemblance to our own, a natural consequence of the fact that, after the Palatinate and Switzerland, it was the little duchy of Württemberg that sent the largest number of our Pennsylvania German pioneers to America.[1] This large Württemberg element in German Pennsylvania has never been properly evaluated. The standard histories of our people, in dealing with European backgrounds, play up the contribution of the largely Reformed Palatinate almost to the point of over-emphasis, leaving Lutheran Württemberg, references to which meet the research student at every hand in Pennsylvania church records, to an underserved obscurity.[2]

So we are delighted to present to Pennsylvania German readers an American edition of two lists of eighteenth-century

[1] Cf. William J. Hinke (ed.), *Pennsylvania German Pioneers* (Norristown, Pa.: The Pennsylvania German Society, 1934), published by Ralph Beaver Strassburger, I, *passim,* for many references to Württembergers accompanying Palatines and Swiss to America. A typical reference is that for the ship *Dragon,* landing at Philadelphia, October 17, 1749, whose passengers were "Palatines, Wirtembergers, and Alsatians" [I, 423].

[2] The wide distribution of birthplaces of emigrants to Pennsylvania, as well as the relative importance of Württemberg and the Palatinate as emigration centers, is well illustrated in a list of about 200 continental European origins of emigrants to Pennsylvania, culled from the Lutheran, Moravian, and Reformed Church Records of York County, Pennsylvania, by the staff of the Historical Society of York County, and sent the editor to aid him in preparing a complete list of all such available unpublished references to birthplaces of German emigrants, from church records, tombstones, passports, Bible records and other sources. This York County list credits the Palatinate with 58 emigrants, Württemberg with 27, Alsace with 15, Switzerland and the Hesses each with 12, with 7 from Baden, 5 each from Saxony and Anspach, 4 from Wittgenstein, 3 each from Ysenberg and Wetterau, 2 each from Franconia, Brandenburg, Denmark, and Hungary, and 1 each from Waldeck, Upper Lusatia, Thuringia, and Hanover.

emigrants from Württemberg to America, published in pamphlet form by Dr. Adolf Gerber, a German-American scholar, two decades ago.[3] The first of these, a booklet of thirty-two pages, is entitled *Beiträge zur Auswanderung nach Amerika im 18. Jahrhundert aus Altwürttembergischen Kirchenbüchern* (Stuttgart: J. F. Steinkopf, n.d.); the second, of forty-four pages, bears the title *Neue Beiträge zur Auswanderung nach Amerika im 18 Jahrhundert aus Altwürttembergischen Kirchenbüchern unter Hinzuziehung anderer Quellen* (Stuttgart: J. F. Steinkopf, [1928]). For the genealogist these lists, extracted from original Württemberg parish registers and furnishing genealogical records of over six hundred emigrating families, will be the key to the European background of many a Pennsylvania German family. To the general historian the information here presented as to the emigrants' occupations, economic status, conduct, and reasons for emigration, will provide the means of drawing a truer picture of the eighteenth-century emigration, and when further similar materials have been culled from the available governmental and ecclesiastical archives in Germany, the definitive study of German emigration to colonial America can be written.

A word to what has been accomplished in this field of research before we pass to a discussion of Gerber's results. In the past three or four decades there has been a veritable renaissance of interest not only in things Pennsylvania German, but in the continental German background of our culture. Research on the background of the German emigration to colonial Pennsylvania has been done partly by our own scholars, partly by native Germans. To German scholarship we are indebted for the basic bibliography

---

[3]Adolf Gerber, Ph.D., German-American historian and genealogist, sometime member of the faculty of Earlham College (1886-1904), contributing editor of German American Annals, returned to Germany in the early years of the century, where he engaged in historical research. In addition to his *Beiträge zur Auswanderung nach Amerika im 18. Jahrhundert aus Altwürttembergischen Kirchenbüchern,* he compiled similar ones for Nassau-Dillenburg. He also prepared the sections on Emigrants from Canton Basel, Switzerland, for Faust and Brumbaugh's *Lists of Swiss Emigrants in the Eighteenth Century to the American Colonies (Vol. I, 1921; Vol. II, 1925).* To Adolf Gerber, for his careful research in the German backgrounds of the Pennsylvania Germans, and for his publication of these lists, is due the gratitude of all who find these results of his labors of value for historical and genealogical research.

of our people and their influence in America, namely to Emil Meynen's monumental *Bibliographie des Deutschtums der Kolonialzeitlichen Einwanderung in Nordamerika, Insbesondere der Pennsylvanien-Deutschen und Ihrer Nachkommen 1683-1933* (Leipzig: Otto Harrassowitz, 1937). Of historical accounts of emigration, Daniel Häberle's *Auswanderung und Koloniegründungen der Pfälzer im 18. Jahrhundert* (Kaiserslautern: Kgl. Bayer. Hofbuchdruckerei, 1909), dedicated to the Palatines "in the homeland and abroad", takes up the American Palatine settlements as well as those in Hungary and Russia. Martin Lohmann's valuable *Die Bedeutung der deutschen Ansiedlungen in Pennsylvanien* (Stuttgart: Deutsches Ausland-Institut, 1923), is Volume XII of the excellent series of historical publications of the *Deutsches Ausland-Institut* at Stuttgart, which American scholars have come to know through the splendid intercultural contributions of Heinz Kloss. As to names of the eighteenth-century emigrants, Gerber's pamphlets are the chief source of information on Württemberg. He has also published another on the emigration from Nassau-Dillenburg, entitled *Die Nassau-Dillenburger Auswanderung nach America im 18. Jahrhundert* [,] *Das Verhalten der Regierungen dazu und die späteren Schicksale der Auswanderer* (Flensburg: Flensburger Nachrichten, 1930).

On this side of the Atlantic, the most notable contribution has been the publication of the ship lists of immigrants, kept by the provincial authorities. These were first, and then only partially, published in the *Colonial Records,* Volumes III-IV (1852); and again by Israel Daniel Rupp in 1856. The Rupp edition, reprinted by Ignatius Kohler of Philadelphia in 1876, by Leary, Stuart and Company of Philadelphia in 1927, and by Ernst Wecken in Leipzig, in 1931, bears the title *A Collection of Thirty Thousand Names of German, Swiss, Dutch, French, Portuguese and Other Immigrants in Pennsylvania; Chronologically Arranged from 1727 to 1776.* In 1892, William H. Egle, State Librarian, reissued the lists in the *Pennsylvania Archives,* Series II, Volume XVII. The fourth, and definitive, edition appeared at Norristown, Pennsylvania, in 1934, in the magnificent three-volume work, *Pennsylvania German Pioneers,* published by Ralph Beaver Strassburger and edited by William John Hinke. The first attempt by Americans to publish emigrant lists from European archives, was the work of Albert Bernhardt Faust, entitled *Lists of Swiss Emigrants in the Eighteenth Century to the American Colonies,* Volume I (Washington, D. C.; The National Genealogical Society, 1920), covering the Zürich archives; and Volume II (Washington, D. C., 1925), in collaboration with Gaius Marcus Brumbaugh, covering Cantons Bern and Basel. A second valuable contribution of this kind is William John Hinke and John Baer Stoudt's editing of *A List of German Immigrants to the American Colonies from Zweibruecken in the Palatinate 1728-1749,* published in Volume I (1936) of the Pennsylvania German Folklore Society Yearbook.

# The Wuerttemberg Emigration

UERTTEMBERG, from medieval times a South German duchy, later a kingdom, and since 1871 part of the German Empire, is about one-sixth the size of Pennsylvania, and lies in the heart of South Germany, bordering Baden, Bavaria, and Switzerland. Like other parts of South Germany, Württemberg suffered untold hardships during the Thirty Years' War, and during the later seventeenth-century struggles for empire between France and Austria. We need not enter into a discussion of these underlying causes of emigration to America—they have been well covered by earlier historians. Suffice it to say that with this background of war, destruction, and heartache, it is not strange to find that Württemberg contributed to the first great mass-emigration from South Germany, that of 1709. At least three emigrants in the Gerber Lists started for Pennsylvania in 1709. The pastor of Steinenberg wrote August 19, 1709, that *"Leonhardt Koser* and *Caspar Auperle,* both citizens of Michelau, each with wife and three children . . . left Michelau for the faraway island of Pennsylvania," and added the prayer, "May God the Lord of Heaven and Earth take them into His protection and accompany them to the place where He wants them to go." However, he was forced to add later, "These pilgrims came as far as Koblenz on the Rhine and could not go any farther. On that account Auperle settled here again, but Koser remained at Neuenstadt on the Linden. These people are experiencing the truth of the 37th Psalm, 'Remain in the country, and support yourself honestly.' "[4] *Ludwig David Eberhardi,* a preacher's son from Hirschlanden, was the third of our emigrants who set forth in 1709 for the New World. An account of this emigration and a list of some of those who left South Germany for New York at the time, can be found in a rare pamphlet by Ulrich Simmendinger, published at Reutlingen, Württemberg, in 1717. Simmendinger was a native of Reutlingen, who came to America in 1709, with his wife, Anna Maria Schnabel of Cannstatt, near Stuttgart, and their two children, and returning in 1717, published his list of "persons still living, by God's grace, who in the year 1709, under the wonderful providences of the Lord, journeyed from Germany to America or the New World, there to seek their bread at various places."[5]

By 1717 a worried ducal government issued a rescript showing displeasure over the fact that "different ones of our subjects, indeed whole families in rather large numbers, and among them not only those laden with debts, but according to report, even the propertied class, have made the ill-considered and dangerous decision, to leave our Duchy and lands and go to Pennsylvania

[4]Adolf Gerber, *Beiträge zur Auswanderung nach Amerika im 18. Jahrhundert aus Altwürttembergischen Kirchenbüchern* (Stuttgart: J. F. Steinkopf, n.d.), 26-27. Hereafter Gerber will not be cited, unless the reference is from his historical introductions, since all the materials relating to individual emigrants are contained in the present edition of the lists.

[5]The German title of this work is *"Wahrhaffte und glaubwürdige Verzeichnüss, jeniger, durch die Gnade Gottes, annoch im Leben sich befindenden Personen, Welche sich Anno 1709 unter des Herren wunderbarer Führung aus Deutschland in Americam oder Neue Welt begeben, und allda an verschiedenen Orten ihr Stücklein Brods suchen. Allen Liebhabern, insonderheit aber deroselben Familien und nahen Freunden zur freudigen Nachricht gestellet. Von Ulrich Simmendinger, siebenjährigen Nord Americanern, in der Provintz Neu-York, anjetzo aber wieder in seiner Vatter-Stadt Reuttlingen.* An English translation by Herman F. Vesper appeared in print at St. Johnsville, N. Y., in 1934.

and Carolina in America."[6] But the great exodus did not come until the 'forties, when, due to a series of economic causes which will presently be outlined, thousands left the homeland for America and other settlements of the German diaspora in Eastern Europe. From June, 1747, to June, 1750, out of sixty-eight of the ninety-two admnistrative districts, 4049 people emigrated, of whom 2480 went to America, 1512 to Pomerania, and 57 to Hungary and elsewhere. The official report of this emigration added, somewhat disappointedly no doubt, that of these "only a third were worthless, lazy people, of whom we may well be rid."[7]

Gerber's researches reveal that the greatest emigration came in the years 1749-1754.[8] It came both as a result of the unsettled political conditions in Europe in mid-century, and of unfavorable economic conditions in Württemberg, including (1) a series of crop failures in the vineyards along with severe damage done what crops there were, by wild game, (2) the revocation of former grazing and wood-gathering rights in the ducal forests, with severe penalties for trespassing, (3) the oppressive and annoying compulsory service to the overlords, a hangover from medieval feudalism, and (4) the mounting taxes, which rested on the propertied classes alone, with the result that many sold their lands to emigrate.[9] A statesman of the period wrote, "These days the farmer is the most miserable of all creatures—he is being annoyed constantly with compulsory service, running errands, game beatings (battues), work on fortifications, and the like. What is rescued from the wild game, a rough official may take to pay outstanding taxes. The barns are empty, the dwellings threaten col-

[6]Gerber, *op. cit.*, 1.

[7]*Op. cit., loc. cit.*

[8]*Op. cit.*, 3.

[9]*Op. cit.* 2. For a concise account of all the political, religious, economic, and social causes involved in emigration from Germany in the eighteenth century, see John Duncan Brite, "The Attitude of European States Toward Emigration to the American Colonies, 1607-1820" (Typed Ph.D. dissertation, The University of Chicago, 1937), Chapter II, "The Causes of Emigration," 33-70.

lapse, the inhabitants appear miserable and ruined."[10] In the accounts of the emigration of several in the present lists, reference is made to small means, debts, bankruptcy. Several others, on being refused citizenship in a new village, came to America for the cheap land promised by the colonial governments. A report from Mayor Matthess Dammel of Grötzingen to his superiors, telling of emigration from the village in 1746, reflects the poverty of some of the emigrants, whose departure depended on begging traveling expenses from friends and neighbors.

> The following report is herewith subserviently submitted to Your Worship: that the following local people, who intend to journey to the Indies [*Indien*], namely, *Philip Ziegler,* tilemaker, with wife and three children, and *Hans Jerg Schnirring,* with wife and three children, have made their departure on last Wednesday, the 23d. Also *Hans Jerg Dannenhawer,* tailor, with his wife and one child, along with *Danniel Kinckhele,* who is still single, left here on Friday the 25th, making a total of sixteen persons. The above-mentioned Dannenhawer and his brother-in-law Danniel Kinckhele, had to remain here longer, because, on account of their poverty, they were soliciting traveling expenses [ein *Reisspfening*] from some goodhearted people. Serving as my due report, March 27, 1746,
>
> Your faithful servant, Mayor Matthess Dammel.[11]

Religious reasons as such do not enter into the picture. Württemberg was Lutheran, and most of our present emigrants

---

[10]Paul Kapff, *Schwaben in Amerika seit der Entdeckung des Weltteils* (Stuttgart: D. Gundert, 1893), 10; published as Number 10 of the *Württembergische Neujahrsblätter.* A similar passage, written by a Württemberg village pastor in the eighteenth century, suggest that these conditions led the oppressed to seek comfort in pietistic religion: "If a man beats his dog the whole day it will run away and seek another master that will treat it better. Now every one beats the common people. The duke beats them, the soldiers beat them, the huntsmen beat them. This they will not endure, but run away and seek another master, namely, Christ; and he who seeks Christ is a pietist," quoted from Ritschl, *Geschichte des Pietismus,* II, 8, in Kerr D. Macmillan, *Protestantism in Germany* (Princeton, N. J., Princeton University Press, 1917), 270.

[11]Adolf Gerber, *Neue Beiträge zur Auswanderung nach Amerika im 18. Jahrhundert aus Altwürttembergischen Kirchenbüchern unter Hinzuziehung anderer Quellen* (Stuttgart: J. F. Steinkopf, [1928]), 16, quoted from the Nürtingen Documents.

were members of that church.[12] Four Catholic and ex-Catholic emigrants are referred to, *Anna* and *Christian Weyh,* children of *Hans Weyh,* a Catholic from the village of Täbingen, "of scandalous conduct"; *Philipp Eyler,* a "Catholic stocking-weaver" of Oberboihingen; and one ex-Catholic, *Pancratius Lengenfelder* of Sillenbuch, listed as a "convert from the Diocese of Bamberg or Würzburg." The only other non-Lutherans in the Gerber Lists are the several families of French Waldensians from the villages of Dürrmenz, Pinache, Gross- and Kleinvillars, Knittlingen, and Diefenbach. These, writes the historian Weiss, were descendants of about three thousand Waldenses, for the most part natives of the valleys of Pragela and Perouse, which by the Treaty of Ryswick had been incorporated into France, who left their homes in 1698 to escape persecution by the Catholic state-church of France.[13] In 1699 they were granted extensive privileges by the Duke of Württemberg, and given land on the eastern slope of the Schwarzwald, an area left uncultivated during the wars of the seventeenth century. Here were founded the colonies of Villar[s], Pinache, LaSerre, Lucerne, Queyras, Perouse, Bourset, Mentoule, LaBalme, and Muriers, named after the exiles' homes in France. These settlements remained Reformed in religion and French in culture until the nineteenth century, though intermarriage with German families began almost immediately. From these Waldensian refugees who came to Pennsylvania after a sojourn in hospitable Württemberg, are descended such Pennsylvania German families as the Schappells [Chappelles] of Berks County, and the Armingeons of Lancaster County.

---

[12]Several of the families listed in Gerber became Moravians; cf. Baur, Christe, Heer, and Stotz. At least one of them, Rudolph Christe, was "awakened" in 1744, while still living in Germany, and made repeated visits to the Moravian community at Herrnhaag, but there is no record of persecution by the Lutheran authorities. It was a different story with the emigration of the Rappites, Württemberg separatists from the Lutheran state church, who, under the leadership of Johann Georg Rapp (1770-1847, settled in Western Pennsylvania in 1803, establishing colonies at Harmony and Economy in Pennsylvania, and New Harmony in Indiana. For a recent treatment of these religious communists, setting them against the background of other similar movements in America, see Alice Felt Tyler, *Freedom's Ferment/Phases of American Social History to 1860.* (Minneapolis: The University of Minnesota Press, c1944), 121-125.

[13]Charles Weiss, *History of the French Protestant Refugees, From the Revocation of the Edict of Nantes to Our Own Days* (New York: Stringer & Townsend, 1854), I, 216-217.

Although according to the Treaty of Tübingen in 1514, following a peasant rebellion, the ducal authorities could not forbid emigration, they did their best to hinder it by (1) revoking forever the citizenship of emigrants, so that those who for various reasons had to return home were denied renaturalization, and (2) by withholding, until they reached their majority, the inheritances of minors who emigrated. But despite these sinister threats, which may have frightened a few of the weak-hearted, letters from kinsmen or friends who had emigrated, or, better still, visits from prosperous Pennsylvania farmers to their old homes—stimulated further emigration. Of this an interesting case occurs in the Lists. Hans Balthass Bitzer and Matthäus Mauthe, had emigrated from Laufen/Eyach in 1746, and settled in Pennsylvania. In the summer of 1749, a "Newlander" named Landenberger, from the village of Ebingen, who made frequent trips between Germany and America, brought back favorable letters from both. According to a report made in 1749 by Mayer Venninger of Laufen, the letters are said to have "made such an impression among different families, that even now they appear to be intent on leaving next Spring." This bit of personal stimulation resulted in the large emigration from Laufen in the year 1750.

A document from this period, which illustrates the size of emigration from typical villages, as well as the requirement of renunciation of citizenship, is the rescript of the Duke, written to Magistrate Christoph Heinrich Sattler, in reply to his report on emigration from villages of Reudern, Neckartenzlingen, Grötzingen, and Aich:

CARL, BY THE GRACE OF GOD

Duke of Württemberg and Teck, Count of Montbeliard, Lord of Heidenheim, Knight of the Golden Fleece and General Field-Marshal of the Honorable Swabian Circle, Etc.

Dear and Faithful Servant!

As to your most dutiful report, telling that *Hanns Jerg Bössmer, Jacob Haussmann, Johannes Hausch's* children, and *Johannes Haussmann,* all from Reudern; likewise *Hanns Jerg Conzelman, Christoph Letsch, Michael Jung, Michael Bauknecht, Johannes Hemminger, Hanns Martin Löll, Friedrich*

*Mauz, Matthes Blieninger, Hanns Martin Schmid,* and *Christoph Rommel's* son, all from Neckartenzlingen; likewise *Augustin Gentner, Hanns Jerg Hoffses, Conrad Raisch, Michael Pfrang, Johannes Nübling, Michael Laub, Barbara Mayer,* and *Matthes Weiss's* widow, from Grötzingen; also *Christoph Oster* of *Aich*—want to go to Pennsylvania, it is our command herewith that you shall let the aforesaid go, after they have properly renounced their citizenship and have signed the usual written declaration thereof, but make it clear to them, that if, sooner or later, they ever have regrets and want to return, they shall never be re-admitted. Besides which, you are to make the arrangements, concerning the Hausch children of Reudern and Hanns Martin Löhl's daughter of Neckartenzlingen, to have their property, which came to them by the law of inheritance, put under administration. This is our opinion of the matter.

Stuttgart, April 11, 1749.

PFLUG MYLIUS.[14]

The emigration continued unabated throughout the 'fifties, until the Seven Years' War (1756-1763) cut it off temporarily. The exodus resumed in the 'seventies, though in the last quarter of the century, the chief objective point for Württemberg emigration was the newly acquired Polish lands, and the frontier Volga settlements in Russia. In closing this brief discussion of eighteenth-century emigration from Württemberg to America, we cannot do better than to place this movement in its proper setting as part of the larger eighteenth-century German diaspora.[15] Especially in Eastern Europe—in Siebenbürgen or Transylvania, in the Rumanian Banat, and in the Volga Valley of Russia — were planted colonies of German farmers and tradesmen, who left Germany for the same reasons whch impelled the emigration of

---

14Gerber, *Neue Beiträge,* 4-5, from the Nürtengen Documents.

15The literature on *Auslanddeutschtum* is voluminous, but unfortunately few libraries in this country have sizable collections in this field. The chief German depository for such materials is the library of the *Deutsches Ausland-Institut* at Stuttgart, which, I have been informed, was moved during the war to escape the bombings, and is now safe in a small hotel at Marbach, Württemberg.

our own Pennsylvania German pioneers.[16] They were not sent by the authorities in the homeland, but were, very often, invited by the governments of their new fatherlands. A case in point is the great cultural island of Volga-Germans [*Wolga-Deutschen*], which, until the breakup of the Volga German Republic by the Soviets in the 1930's, was a sizable German-speaking farming community. The ancestors of these people had been invited to the Volga frontier in 1763 by Catherine the Great, who, promising liberal land grants, exemption from military service, and religious freedom, induced over 23,000 German farmers and tradesmen to found 104 German villages in the area, from 1764 to 1768. In 1871, when these exemptions were revoked, thousands began coming to America, where today, through the middle and farther west, especially in Nebraska and the Dakotas, are to be found large colonies of *Russlanddeutschen* [Russian or Volga Germans], who have preserved German dialects, a folk literature and a proverbial lore which closely resembles the Pennsylvania German.[17]

---

[16]Johannes Künzig, writing in 1935, before many of the *Volksdeutschen* were uprooted from the lands they had tilled for several centuries, states that "wer heute das von den Donauschwaben besiedelte Banat besucht, trifft ein wohlhabendes, überaus strebsames und tüchtiges Bauerntum an, treu seiner angestammten, aus der zumeist süddeutschen Heimat mitgebrachten Art, Sitte und Sprache." There, as in many parts of the world, German farmers, in their more than two centuries of residence, had made a fruitful area out of swamp and waste land. The folklore of these people had preserved some interesting memories of their South German origin; cf. the gay song,

I bin e Schwob vom Schwobeland,
I han fünf Finger an jeder Hand,
Esse un Trinke kann ich gut
Und rede tu ich wie's mer kummt.

For this and other bits of folklore reminiscent of the Pennsylvania German variety, see Johannes Künzig, *Deutsche Volkslieder aus dem rumänischen Banat* (Berlin u. Leipzig: Walter de Gruyter & Co., 1935), 69-70.

[17]The standard history of the Volga Germans is Gerhard Bonwetsch, *Geschichte der deutschen Kolonien an der Wolga* (Stuttgart: J. Engelhorn, 1919), Volume II in the series *Schriften des Deutschen Ausland-Instituts Stuttgart*. A valuable treatment of the religion of the Volga Germans has recently appeared—George J. Eisenach's "Pietism and the Russian Germans in the United States," (Typed Ph.D. dissertation, The University of Chicago, 1945), which shows how this group, influenced in the eighteenth century by Moravian revivalists and in the nineteenth by Württemberg Stundists, developed a pietistic lay religious movement of the "brotherhood" variety, outside of, yet not interfering with, the Lutheran and Reformed Churches, to which the majority of Volga Germans belonged.

## DOCUMENTS BROUGHT OVER BY THE EMIGRANTS

An emigrant who complied with the regulations by selling his property, making the proper application for permission to emigrate before the ducal authorities, and renouncing his citizenship, was usually supplied with a certificate of good conduct [*Leumundszeugniss*] or passport from the ducal or local authorities, or a family record and certificate of church membership, from the village pastor. Two of these will suffice for examples. The first is the letter of recommendation granted to Antonius Bourrell in 1752, by the village authorities of Dornstetten, Württemberg; the second is the family record and certificate of church membership of Sebastian Schweicker (t) of Bodelshausen, who emigrated to Pennsylvania in 1772. The Bourrell passport, the German original of which is unfortunately not available, reads as follows:

> We, the graciously appointed magistrate of His Serene Highness, the Duke of Wittenburg [Württemberg], in the princely borough and ducal village of Dornsletter [Dornstetten], hereby announce and affirm to all whom it may concern to read this that—Whereas *Antonius Bourrell,* burger and tailor of said borough, and legitimate son of *Paul Bourrell,* late burger of Perrose, duly declared to us that he was determined, with the help of God and in the hope of a fairer fortune, to emigrate to the territories of America, there to settle in domestic life, and—Whereas he confirmed testimony as to his legitimacy with freedom and conduct and in due form requires us to give him the necessary certificate therefor; and—Whereas we deem his desire to be fully justified and in account with the most recent laws of the Kingdom—Therefore, for the sake of truth and for the love of it by means of this open and public letter, and in virtue of our present office we declare of the aforesaid *Antonius Bourrell* from evidence placed before us, from the Church and Baptismal register [,] that he was begotten in lawful wedlock of the aforementioned *Paul Bourrell* and of his lawful wife, *Anna Felicetas,* as true and natural parents, that he was born into the world on the 5th of May, in the year 1716, and was brought to holy baptism here. Thus, that no reproach can be brought against his family, and its posterity, but rather that a true and honorable birth is his, and that he was never held in servitude by any man. Furthermore as far as we know he has conducted himself in daily life and deed in such wise

that we can testify all things kind, honorable and good of him. To all magistrates, high and low, our humble and dutiful request is that they will be pleased to receive *Antonius Bourrell* kindly and graciously together with his 25-year-old wife, *Anna Maria Barbara Hindemachin,* and their three children, *Johannes,* aged ten; *Christina* seven, and *Elizabeth* seven years, professors of the Lutheran faith, and in servitude to no man. In consequence of these presents we desire that they (the family) be indeed permitted to enjoy prosperity. Such service we will requite gladly, and as in duty bound in all cases of a similar, or of any other nature, and further testimony whereof we have begged and interested the worthiest, the most learned and venerable of His Serene Highness' bailiffs, Mr. *Ludwig Achatius Wohren,* openly to affix hereunto his seal of office. Given in Dornstetter [Dornstetten], the 12th of May, 1752. Ducal Württemburgisch, bailiff and officer in Dornstetter.

[Signed] LUDWIG ACHATIUS WOHREN.[18]

The second document is the "Baptismal, Marriage, and Burial Certificate for Sebatian Schweicker, Citizen and Joiner in Bodelshausen, in the District of Tübingen [*Tauf- Ehe- und Toden-Schein vor Sebastian Schweicker, Bürger und Schreiner in Bodelshausen, Tübinger Ober-Amts*"]. It reads as follows:

In the year 1736, on the 15th of November, at Mössingen in the District of Tübingen, in the Duchy of Württemberg, was born in lawful wedlock and baptized by Christian ordinances

SEBASTIAN SCHWEICKER,
Citizen and Joiner in Bodelshausen.

His father is SEBASTIAN SCHWEICKER, Citizen and Joiner in Mössingen, his mother's name was AGNES, née SPEIDEL.

This man was joined in matrimony

In the year 1760, the 27th of November, to AGNES MARIA, who was born in lawful wedlock and baptized in Bodelshausen the 22d of December, 1743. Her father was the late FELIX KELLER, Citizen and Joiner here; her mother, who is still living, is named AGNES, née SCHLOTTERER.

From this marriage were born
Legitimately, four children:

---

[18]*Commemorative Biographical Record of Central Pennsylvania, Including the Counties of Centre, Clearfield, Jefferson and Clarion, Containing Biographical Sketches of Prominent and Representative Citizens, And of Many of the Early Settled Families* (Chicago: J. H. Beers & Co., 1898), 247. Descendants spelling their name Burrell settled in Shamokin, and later in George's Valley, Centre Co., Pa., where in 1898 they were still adherents of the Lutheran Church.

lein

von

Sebastian Schwicker,

Bürger und Schreiner

in

hausen,

Tübinger Ober-Amt.

2 fl.

N. 5.

Anno 1736 den 15ten Nov. ist zu Mössingen, Tübinger Ober-Amt, in dem Herzogthum Würtemberg gelegen, ehelich erzeugt und christl. getauft worden

Sebastian Schweicker,
Bürger und Schreiner in Dreißigacker.

Dessen Vatter ist Sebastian Schweicker, Bürger und Schreiner in Mössingen, die Mutter aber hatte geheißen Agnes geb. Thudalin.

Dieser hat sich in den Ehestand begeben.

Anno 1764 den 27ten Nov. mit Anna Maria, welche ehelich gebohren und getauft worden in Dreißigacker den 22ten Dec. 1743. deren Vatter war weyl. Felix Zeller, Bürger und Schreiner allhier und noch lebende Mutter heißet Agnes, geb. Schlotterin.

Und diesem Ehestand sind bis dato 4. Kinder ehelich erzeugt worden.

1.) Anna Maria geb. den 26ten Nov. 1765
2.) Felix geb. den 10ten Jul. 1766

3.) Anna Margaretha, geb. am 12.ten Mart. 1769.

4.) Anna Barbara, geb. am 10.ten Nov. 1770.

welche alle noch im leben sind.

Daß alles vorstehende aus dem Tauf- Ehe- und Todten-Buch fideliter extrahirt worden, wird unter vorgedrucktem Pfarrl. Insiegel eigenhändig bezeuget, [illegible], am 12.ten Maji. 1772.

Pfarrer daselbsten

M. Joh. Alexander Luz.

[illegible] [illegible] starb den 16ten Tag März Anno Domini 1808, ein Alter von 71 Jahr und 4 Monat 4 Tage

Agnes Maria entschlief selig in dem Herrn am 25sten Tag Aprilis Jahr Anno Domini 1812. brachte ihr Alter auf 68 Jahr 4 Monat und 3 Tage

1.) AGNES MARIA, born the 26th of November, 1762.
2.) FELIX, born the 18th of July, 1765.
3.) ANNA MARGARETHA, born the 12th of March, 1769.
4.) ANNA BARBARA, born the 18th of November, 1770.

All of whom are still living.

That all of the above has been faithfully extracted from the Baptismal, Marriage, and Burial Registers, Witness my hand, Bodelshausen, the 12th of May, 1772.

M[agister]
JOHANNES ALEXANDER LUZ,
*Pastor Loci*[19]

### WUERTTEMBERG INFLUENCE ON THE PENNSYLVANIA GERMANS

Despite the large emigration from Württemberg and the natural influence of Swabian customs upon our own,[20] at the present day the average Pennsylvania German's knowledge of the Swabian homeland is limited to our folklore, in which the

---

[19]For this document, a facsimile of which accompanies our introduction, the editor is indebted to a descendant of Sebastian Schweicker, Mrs. M. Luther Heisey, of Lancaster, Pennsylvania, wife of the editor of *Papers Read Before the Lancaster County Historical Society.*

Reference to a similar Family Record given by the pastor of Altdorf "im Herzogtum Württemberg, Babenhauser Kloster Ober-Amt" to Christoph Heinrich Bissinger, a master joiner emigrating with his family to the Batschka, can be found in Friedrich Lotz, "Die deutsch-protestantische Besiedlung der Batschka (Jugoslawien)", in *Auslanddeutschtum und evangelische Kirche,* Jahrbuch 1938 (München: Chr. Kaiser, 1938), 235. The record closes with the prayer: "Der Herr erhalte Eltern und Kinder bei unverrückter Treue in diesem Bunde eines guten Gewissens mit Gott, bewahre sie vor allem Uebel und leite sie mit seinen Augen und bringe sie dereinst in dem rechten Vaterland zum ewigen Frieden alle wieder zusammen! Solches wünscht ihr bisheriger Seel-Sorger, bezeugt auch zugleich die Richtigkeit dieses Extractes als/dermalige Pfarrer des Orts/
M. L. P. Kling."

[20]Such influence is, of course, impossible to estimate accurately at the present time, without fuller knowledge of the folk-culture of both Württemberg and German Pennsylvania. Kapff (*op. cit.,* 28) names many Pennsylvania customs reminiscent of the Swabian homeland: "das fröhliche Treiben beim Mostbereiten, das heitere Fest der Metzelsuppe mit 'Knackwurscht un Leberwurscht', der Speisezettel bei der 'Hochzig' mit 'Sauerkraut' und 'Schweinefleisch' un 'Krumbiere'." The short work-coat or jacket known in Pennsylvania as a "Wammes" may possible reflect the Swabian farmer's jacket told of in the Württemberg folksong:

Was bringen uns die Schwaben?
Nix als kurze Röck, nix als kurze Röck!
Kurze Röckle hant sie an,
Hint und vorne Bändel dran!
Schwabenland, das ist bekant,
Weil sie kurze Röckle hant!

quoted in August Lämmle, *Württembergische Volkslieder* (Heilbronn: Eugen Salzer, 1929), 107-108; though this, as well as some of the customs suggested above, is common to a larger area of South Germany.

Swabian [PG *Schwob*] of folk-humor, "big and dumb" to describe him briefly, figures prominently.[21] According to Albrecht Keller, the historian of the Swabian in popular humor, the "stupid Swabians," in much the same way that the Yankee-type, or hayseed farmer was caricatured on our stage years ago, have been the scapegoat for the whole German people in laughing at themselves, for the so-called "Swabian characteristics" are often common to other areas of Germany. [22] It is interesting, though natural, that in remembering this we have forgotten the great men produced by this little German land. Philip Schaff, who as a boy attended the Pietistic school at Kornthal, in Württemberg, mentions as products of this little kingdom, the poets Schiller, Uhland, and Wieland; the philosophers Schelling and Hegel; the Protestant theologians Andreae, Bengel, and Dorner; and the rationalists Paulus, Baur, and Strauss. "Five years," Schaff writes, I spent among this genial people, whose country became to me a second fatherland." "The people," he continues, "are good-natured, kind-hearted, plain, and economical in their habits, somewhat slow and heavy as compared with the people of Northern Germany, but reliable, intelligent and well informed, industrious and persevering,

---

[21]For some Pennsylvania versions of the *Schwabenstreiche*„ see J. W. Frey (ed.), *Der Pennsylvaanisch Deitsch Eileschpiggel* (Lancaster, Pa.), Numbers 1 and 4, 1944; also Thomas R. Brendle and Claude W. Unger, *Pennsylvania German Folk Tales, etc.* (Proceedings of the Pennsylvania German Society, Vol. L).

[22]Albrecht Keller, *Die Schwaben in der Geschichte des Volkshumors* (Freiburg/Baden: J. Bielefeld, 1907), 104-105. Among the characteristics of the Swabian farmer, as transmitted by the jokes and folksongs, are *Gefrässigkeit, Geschwätzigkeit and Gemütlichkeit,* in all of which the Pennsylvania Germans make a rather good showing! Hans Sachs could write in the sixteenth century (*Ibid.,* 89):

> So sind die suppen der Schwaben schatz,
> Darzu die klapperey und schwatz.

One of the folksongs (*Württembergische Volkslieder,* 97) well describes the Swabian love of sauerkraut and dumplings *(Spätzle),* in words:

> Solang's no Kraut und Spätzle git,
> Solang verderbet d' Schwobe nit.

And best of all is the proverb, quoted in Keller, 166: "Ein Schwabe hat kein Herz, aber zwei Magen."

fond of philosophy and poetry, and possessed of a harmless humor of their own."[23]

For our Pennsylvania German culture, the most important of those Württembergers who settled in Pennsylvania—with the exception of Conrad Weiser, the Indian agent, who, thanks to Dr. Graeff's biography of him which appeared last year, is no stranger to the members of the Pennsylvania German Folklore Society—were the leaders of the German churches, particularly the Lutheran and Moravian. These men, through their lives and works spent serving frontier communities, transmitted the fervent though not fanatic Pietism of Württemberg, to their German countrymen in America. Among the colonial German ministers in Pennsylvania who were Württembergers by birth, were Pastors Wagner, Gerock, Hausihl, and Schertlin; and even the Patriarch Muhlenberg, though a native of Hannover, married the daughter of Conrad Weiser, who was born at Astaet in Württemberg.[24] Prominent colonial Moravian leaders from Württemberg were Bishop Johannes Ettwein (1721-1802),[25] a native of Freudenstadt, who was the spokesman for the Unitas Fratrum during the trying days of the Revolutionary War; and Bishop Matthäus Gottfried Hehl (1705-1787), a native of Ebersdorf, who was a graduate of the University of Tübingen, and an outstanding preacher and hymnist.[26] Such men, spiritual and cultural leaders of our people in the eighteenth century, are examples of the influence of Württemberg in America.

Württemberg influences upon our Pennsylvania German culture continued throughout the nineteenth century as well. Again

[23]David S. Schaff, *The Life of Philip Schaff In Part Autobiographical* (New York: Charles Scribner's Sons, 1897), 9-10. Of interest also is Martin Luther's statement: "Wenn ich viel reisen sollte, wollte ich nirgends lieber, denn durch Schwaben und Baierland ziehen; denn sie sind freundlich und gutwillig, herbergen gerne, gehen Freunden und Wandersleuten entgegen, und thun den Leuten gütlich, und gute Ausrichtung um ihr Geld", quoted in Philpi Schaff, *History of the Christian Church,* VI (New York: Charles Scribner's Sons, 1888), 127.

[24]For these and other Württembergers in Pennsylvania, see Kapff, *op. cit.,* 40-47.

[25]See Kenneth Gardiner Hamilton, *John Ettwein and the Moravian Church During the Revolutionary Period* (Bethlehem, Pennsylvania: 1940).

[26]Abraham Reinke Beck, "The Moravian Graveyards of Lititz, Pa., 1744-1905," in *Transactions of the Moravian Historical Society,* VII, 243.

it was in religious circles that the connection with the old homeland was kept up.[27] Many Pennsylvania ministers subscribed to German religious periodicals, many bought copies of German religious books. Among the classics of nineteenth-century German Pietism which had wide circulation in America were the sermons and devotional books by the famous Württemberg preachers, Ludwig Hofacker and Karl Gerok. Hofacker's *Predigten* appeared in an American edition at Philadelphia in the 1860's, published by the Lutheran Ignatius Kohler, who by his publishing mediated between German and American Christianity. The Gerok poems and hymns often appeared in such papers as *Der Pilger,* or the *Reformirter Hausfreund,* and an edition of the Gerok *Palmblätter* was brought out by Kohler in 1894.

Another source of continuing contact with Württemberg was the influx of German preachers from South Germany, particularly Württemberg, to America in the nineteenth century.[28]

Many of these were welcomed by parishes in the German settlements in Eastern Pennsylvania. Chief among them was Dr. Wilhelm Julius Mann (1819-1892), a native of Stuttgart, who came to America in 1845. After a few years in the Reformed ministry, to which he was attracted by his friend Philip Schaff, he became assistant to Dr. Carl Rudolph Demme at Zion's Luth-

---

[27]The famous *Gemeinschaftliches Gesangbuch* of the Lutheran and Reformed union churches, which appeared first in 1817 and ran through at least twenty-two editions until 1884, contained some of the pietistic hymns of the Württemberger Philipp Friedrich Hiller, whose *Geistliches Liederkästlein* was carried by Württemberg emigrants to many parts of the world. The hymnal of the Lutheran state church of Württemberg was also drawn on for the preparation of later Pennsylvania Lutheran hymnbooks.

[28]In the early part of the nineteenth century, there were also several outstanding native Pennsylvania German religious leaders of Württemberg ancestry; cf. Johannes Stauch (1762-1845), the first Lutheran minister to officiate in Ohio and Kentucky, who was a native of York Co., Pa., son of a Württemberg emigrant and his wife, who was a native of Hannover [*The Lutheran World Almanac and Encyclopedia 1931-1933* (New York: The National Lutheran Council, 1932), 144]. Another was the pioneer bishop of the Evangelical Association, Johannes Seybert (1791-1860), whose mother was Susanna Kreuzer, daughter of Stephen Kreuzer from Württemberg, who died on the way across the ocean in 1771. [S(olomon) Neitz, *Das Leben und Wirken des seligen Johannes Seybert, Ersten Bischofs der Evangelischen Gemeinschaft* (Cleveland, Ohio: Evangelical Association, 1862), 17-18].

eran Church in Philadelphia, later editing Schaff's *Kirchenfreund* (1854-1859), and teaching in the Philadelphia Lutheran Seminary. Mann was in general an outstanding leader in the Lutheran Ministerium of Pennsylvania, and later in the Lutheran General Council. The universal respect in which he was held by his Pennsylvania German colleagues in the ministry, is well expressed in a statement by Pastor William Weicksel, on the flyleaf of a copy of the German biography of Dr. Mann, now in the editor's library: "Dr. Mann was our Luther, rough, earnest & true, loving & sympathetic, plain and far from deceitfulness—An honest German plain & true."[29] So much for Pennsylvania German contacts with Württemberg in the eighteenth and nineteenth centuries.

---

[29]The biography referred to is Adolph Späth, *D. Wilhelm Julius Mann, ein deutsch-amerikanischer Theologe. Erinnerungsblätter* (Reading, Pa.: Pilger-Buchhandlung, 1895); for Mann's accounts of the Swabian homeland, see pp. 1-4.

# The Adolf Gerber Lists

A brief word is here necessary as to the sources used by Gerber. They were the records of the local parishes, including, in addition to the Membership Registers [*Seelenregister*], the Baptismal Registers [*Taufbücher*], the Communicant Registers [*Kommunicantenregister*], the Marriage Registers [*Ehebücher*], and the Burial Registers [*Totenbücher*]. The names found represent some 2000 emigrants from at least 150 Württemberg communities. Two-thirds of the clergymen whom Gerber requested to furnish such information, did so, but only sixty or seventy could state positive results. The Church Registers were used as a last resort, since in the nineteenth century, by executive order, the early lists of emigrants kept by the Württemberg government, along with reports on the property of the emigrants, sent to the authorities by the local village-mayors, were destroyed. The only governmental records still extant which contain information on eighteenth-century emigrants, are (1) the Protocol of the Ludwigsburg Council [*Ludwigsburger Oberrats-Protocol*], cited in the Lists as the "Ludwigsburg Protocol," and (2) the Nürtingen Documents [*Nürtinger Dokumente*], papers preserved at Nürtingen relating to those who received the ducal permission to emigrate. Unfortunately the Ludwigsburg Protocol occasionally registers all the emigrants from one village under such a phrase as, for example, "Morell and associates [*und Consorten*]," without specifically naming the others.

Only those individuals in the local church records who are identified as emigrants in the Ludwigsburg Protocol and specifically noted in the record book themselves as going to America, have been included. There were probably many others who left secretly for the New World. But those with whom we are concerned are those to whose records in the church registers the village pastor affixed the legend "went to America" [*nach Amerika gezogen*], or some similar phrase. The names given to the American goal of the emigration are interesting. They include Carolina, South Carolina, "New Georgia", America, "New America", the "New Land", the "New World", the "Indies", the "West Indies", and "New Scotland" (Nova Scotia). Pennsylvania, however, was the chief objective point. In a few references it is delightfully referred to as "the faraway British *island* of Pennsylvania." Occasionally the pastor, displaying his erudition, wrote a flowery record in Latin, as for instance the record of the emigration of the Krämer family of Malmsheim, who, the pastor wrote, *"d. 16 Maji* [*1754*] *Patriae valedixerunt, Pennsylvaniam petierunt."*

The occupations of the emigrants make an interesting study. Among those listed are Daylaborers, Masons, Vinedressers, Farmers, Weavers, Shoemakers, Carpenters, Joiners, Clothmakers, Cartwrights, Tailors, Innkeepers, Dyers, Bakers, Coopers, Stockingweavers, Butchers, Blacksmiths, Miners, Cowherds, Shepherds, Barbers, Stonecutters, Soldiers, Judges, Mayors, and Lawyers. Of these, Gerber has estimated that in Volume I, farmers and workers on the land in general, made up only 20 per cent of the whole. The remainder of the occupations can be divided up into weavers of various sorts, 14 per cent; tailors and shoemakers, 14 per cent; masons and carpenters, 9 per cent; cabinetmakers, coopers and cartwrights, 8 per cent; smiths of various sorts, 7 per cent; and butchers and bakers, 6 per cent. In Volume II, a higher percentage of farmers is given. The value of such information, available nowhere else, for the economic background of the Pennsylvania immigrants, is self-evident.

A few individual references will be of interest at this point. Johann Georg Klingenmayr of Höfingen was listed as a "deserted Württemberg soldier." Baltas Däsch of Sulz am Neckar was a "Baker and Beer-brewer." Christianus Pfingstag of Altenriet was the village Grave-digger. Eberhart Bürcklin of Weil im Schönbuch was a "Peddler and farmer"; Knobloch of Kusterdingen, a "Night Watchman" and Häberle of Maichingen, a "Weaver and Field-Ranger." Of the politicians and professional men, there were Johann Caspar Gajer of Schlaitdorf, who was the Mayor of his village; the same is true for Paulus Achatius Daser of Nagold. Johannes Weiss of Gechingen, was a "Judge"; Hofelin of Steinheim am Albach, a "Lawyer". Among the doctors or surgeons were Degele, Hailer, Crämer, and Stuber. Schoolmasters included Pfaff of Steinheim an der Murr, a preacher's son; and Fissler of Lossburg. And, most interesting of all is the versatile *Johannes Siglin* of Neckartenzlingen—"Butcher, Landlord of the Stag Inn, Judge, Senator, and Farmer."

Just a few more "crumbs" from the rich store of comments on individuals in the Gerber Lists. As would be expected, neighbors from the same or neighboring villages set out together, and can often be found in the same shiplists, arriving at Philadelphia. The relationships outlined will explain why certain families settled together in Pennsylvania, or stand sponsor to each other's children in the Pennsylvania church records. For example, Hans Georg Knödler of Niederhofen was the son-in-law of Christian Heussler of the same village; they came to America on the same ship, the *Osgood*, arriving at Philadelphia on September 29, 1750; and they are found in records of Berks and neighboring Lehigh County.[30] Several cases of "spur of the moment" marriage are recorded of young couples who decided to emigrate with friends or older rela-

[30]Cf. the records of the Weisenberg Church, Pennsylvania State Library, Harrisburg; also the Genealogical Society of Pennsylvania's transcript of the private ministerial record of the Reverend Daniel Schumacher, covering various churches in Lehigh and Berks Counties during the period following 1754. It is of interest that these emigrants came to America on the same ship with the Württemberger, Gottlieb Mittelberger of Enzweihingen in the District of Vaihingen, who spent nearly four

tives. Usually the church ordinances were administered immediately before departure—children were baptized, or youngsters confirmed under age, by special permission, so that they could accompany their parents to America. The many references to taking the Lord's Supper in common before leaving, are proof of the strong hold the things of religion had on many of our ancestors. The pastor at Grünwettersbach even prepared baptismal certificates [*Taufscheine*] for the emigrants from his parish, or sent copies after them to America.

Not that they were all religious, however! A few references to "scandalous lives" occur. Several of the young unmarried women brought illegitimate children to America. Hans Jerg Fischer of Neckartenzlingen, was according to the record of his pastor, "very much given to stealing." We are often in danger of idealizing the Pennsylvania Germans, and lists like these will show us that among the emigrants there were both the deeply religious and the indifferent, the industrious and the shiftless. If you doubt the latter, read the description of Johann Heinrich Brand of Neckartailfingen, whose occupation was that of "peddler and fisherman." In his request to emigrate, Brand described himself as a "poor soldier's son", who Gerber writes had never learned a trade, and had to support himself by "peddling notions." Or take the case of Johannes Mack of Neckartenzlingen, who, as Gerber states, was "always somewhat frivolous, didn't like to work, but kept trying in vain to get rich by other schemes"! Or Christoph Lenz, "a restless fellow here", who left Beutelsbach in 1746 for Pennsylvania, without farewell either to his father or his pastor.

---

years in Pennsylvania as organist and schoolmaster, and has left us a lively account of the province at midcentury in his *Gottlieb Mittelberger's Journey to Pennsylvania in the Year 1750 and Return to Germany in the Year 1754, Containing Not Only a Description of the Country According to its Present Condition, But Also a Detailed Account of the Sad and Unfortunate Circumstances of Most of the Germans that Have Emigrated, or are Emigrating to That Country,* (tr. Carl Theodore Eben) (Philadelphia: John Joseph McVey, 1898). Another interesting account, more particularly of the journey across the ocean rather than of the New World itself, is the journal of a well-to-do and apparently well-educated lady from Herrenberg, Württemberg, who came to America in 1786, to seek her husband, a merchant in Carolina who had come several years previously, and, after investigating conditions here, to return for their children. The name of the writer is not disclosed, but the document, quoted in Kapff, *op. cit.*, pp. 19-24, presents a most intimate picture of life on an immigrant ship.

These, I say, are exceptions to the rule, but they were "among us" nevertheless. We hope the majority deserved the tribute the pastor of Aich paid to Franz Kuhn and wife, in calling them "especially God-fearing, pious, dutiful, upright, honest, and honorable."

---

## Emigrants from Wuerttemberg

NOTE ON THE EDITING: The German edition of the Gerber lists is in two volumes, with the emigrants listed chronologically under the villages from which they came, while the present edition makes one alphabetical list of the 735c names. The numbers "1" and "2" after each name signify which volume of Gerber the information is from, "1" standing for his *Beiträge* and "2" for his *Neue Beiträge.* An attempt has been made to identify the date of emigration and the place of settlement in Pennsylvania. Dr. Gerber used Rupp's *Immigrants,* but for identification of the emigrants only in Volume II. The American editor collated the names with certain basic Pennsylvania source materials, resulting in the more or less positive identification of some 435 of the names. The sources used for collation are (1) the ship lists, cited as "Hinke"; (2) the provincial tax lists and records of warrantees of land, in the *Pennsylvania Archives,* Series III, volumes XI-XXVI, cited as "3PA"; and (3) the Abstracts of Wills of Philadelphia, Berks, Northampton, Lancaster and Northumberland Counties, available at the Genealogical Society of Pennsylvania, at Philadelphia, cited as "———*County Will Abstracts,* [Volume]——, [Page]——, GSP." The lists have been further collated with the Moravian burial records for Bethlehem, Nazareth and Lititz, published in (1) Augustus Schultze, "Guide to the Old Moravian Cemetery of Bethlehem, Pa., 1742-1910" in the *Proceedings of the Pennsylvania German Society,* Volume XXI; Edward T. Kluge, "The Moravian Graveyards at Nazareth, Pa., 1744-1904", in *Transactions of the Moravian Historical Society,* Volume VII; and Abraham Reinke Beck, "The Moravian Graveyards of Lititz, Pa., 1744-1905", ibid., volume VII. Lastly, the editor has used Edward W. Hocker's helpful *Genealogical Data Relating to the German Settlers of Pennsylvania and Adjacent*

*Territory from Advertisements in German Newspapers Published in Philadelphia and Germantown 1743-1800* (Typescript, Germantown, Philadelphia, Pa., 1935), 300 pages, copies of which are available at the Historical Society of Pennsylvania in Philadelphia, and the Newberry Library in Chicago. The editor's collated material always follows upon the sign //. Additions or corrections to any part of these lists will be welcomed by the editor.—D.Y.

---

# A

ADAM, HANS JACOB (1)—Schlaitdorf

Village watchman [*Dorfschütz*]. To Pennsylvania 1753 with his daughter ANNA BARBARA KUHN and husband, JOHANNES KUHN (q.v.), of Schlaitdorf. // HANS JACOB ADAM, RICHARD and MARY, September 17, 1753, Hinke, I, 531. 3PA, 26, 241: JACOB ADAM, 330 acres, Berks County, survey November 15, 1776. 3PA, 22, 735: JACOB ADAM, single, Fallowfield Tp., Washington Co., Pa., 1781.

ADAM, JOHANN JACOB (1)—Schlaitdorf

Cartwright [*Wagner*]. Wf: ANNA née KUMMERLIN of Dörnach. Ch: (1) Anna Magdalena, b. 4-9-1743; (2) Margaretha, b. 1-23-1745; (3) Maria, b. 7-10-1747; (4) Barbara, b. 1-9-1750. // JACOB ADAM, with JOHANN CASPER GAJER of Schlaitdorf, RICHARD and MARY, September 30, 1754, Hinke, I, 604,606. Cf. *supra.* HANS JACOB ADAM.

AICHELE, ANNA MARIA (1)—Lomersheim

Ch: (1) Maria Margaretha, b. (illegitimate) 4-11-1742. To "Pennsylvania."

AICHELE, JACOB (1)—Döffingen

Tailor [*Schneider*]. B. 10-3-1725. Wf: ANNA BARBARA née VELLNAGEL. Ch: (1) Johann Jacob, b. 9-21-1752; (2) Johannes, b. 3-1-1754. "Parents and children to America, May 21, 1754" [*21. Mai. 1754 Eltern u. K. Amer.*] // JACOB EYGLE (EICHELY), aged 28, BARCLAY, September 14, 1754, Hinke, I, 595, 600.

AISENBREY, PETER (2)—Gündelbach

B. 1716. Emigrated after 1752, with wife and their one son, along with an illegitimate daughter of the wife. // PETER ISINGBRID (*Eysenbreit*), age 27, *Brothers,* September 26, 1753, Hinke, I, 551, 553. 3PA 14, 295: PETER ISINBREY, tavern keeper, City of Philadelphia, Pa., 1774. The will of PETER EISINBRY, City of Philadelphia, Tavernkeeper, dated January 26, 1774, administration September 9, 1778, mentions wife DOROTHY, child JOHN, and DOROTHY RIFIN, stepdaughter's child; also a brother SIMON, in Germany. Executors: DOROTHY EISINBRY, JOHN LORENTZ, HENRY KAMMERER. Witnesses: PHILIP HALL, GEORGE GOTTFRIED WHELPPER. *Philadelphia County Will Abstracts,* VII (1777-1790), 2031-2032. Cf. also the will of JOHN EISENBRY, of Philadelphia, Innkeeper, made and probated 1783, Book W, 359, witnessed by HENRY K. HELMUTH.

## AMMON, JOHANN GEORG (2)—Sternenfels (1743)

Wf: ROSINA. Ch: (1) Christian, b. 8-25-1741. The family perhaps did not move into the village until shortly before the son's birth, since the Ludwigsburg Protocol, 4-30-1743, describes Hans Jerg Ammann as the father of six children. // HANS GEO. AMENT (HANS GERG AMON), age 38, (with ERNEST AMON), *St. Andrew,* October 7, 1743, Hinke, I, 349-350. 3PA, 17, 856: GEORGE AMEND, Donegal Tp., Lancaster Co., 1782.

## ARMBRUSTER, FRIEDRICH (1)—Schlaitdorf

Farmer [*Bauer*]. Wf: ANNA MARIA, *née* VOEGLIN. Ch: (1) Johann Jacob, b. 1-3-1747; (2) Jacob Friedrich, b. 11-13-1749.

## ARMBRUSTER, MARTIN (1)—Weil im Schönbuch.

Wf: AGNES. Ch: (1) Barbara, b. 3-4-1736.

## ARMINGEON, PIERRE (2)—Grossvillars (1753)

Wf: MADELEINE (*Vincent*). Ch: (1) Pierre, b. 10-16-1744; (2) Jaques, b. 2-17-1747; (3) Godefroy, b. 7-8-1749; (4) Jean Daniel, b. 5-29-1752. From the Waldensian Church Register [*Waldenser Kirchenbuch*] for Gross- and Kleinvillars, including also Knittlingen and Diefenbach. Ludwigsburg Protocol, 4-27-1753, "Armegnon" to "New England" [*Neu Engelland*]. // PIERRE ARMESON (*Armingeon*), age 40, *Patience,* September 15, 1753, Hinke, I, 526-7. 3PA, 24, 353: PETER ARMESHON, 32 acres, Lancaster County, survey September 25, 1767. 3PA, 17, 211: PETER ARMINION, Warwick Tp., Lancaster Co., Pa., 1772. 3PA, 17, 477: FREDERICK ARMENSHON, freeman, Warwick Tp., Lancaster Co., Pa., 1773.

## AUPERLE, CASPAR (1-2)—Steinenberg (1709)

According to a reference in the Church Register, by Pastor Brecht, who served 1699-1724, dated August 19, 1709: "LEONHARDT KOSER and CASPAR AUGERLE [corrected in Vol. II to "Auperle"], both citizens of Michelau, each with wife and three children, therefore two wives and six children, left Michelau for the faraway island of Pennsylvania, at the time subject to the dominion of England—their names and children are frequently found in this baptismal, marriage, and burial record-book. May God the Lord of Heaven and earth take them into his protection and accompany them to the place where He wants them to go.

"NB. These pilgrims came as far as Koblenz on the Rhine and couldn't get any farther. On that account Augerle settled here again, but Koser remained at Neuenstadt on the Linden. These people are experiencing the truth of the 37th Psalm, 'Remain in the country, and support yourself honestly.'"

[Den 19. August sind Leonhardt Koser, und Caspar Augerle, beide verbürgerte zu Michelau, mit Weib und jegl. 3 Kinder, also 2 Weibern u. 6 Kindern, von Michelau walfart und aussgezogen in die weitentlegene Insel *Pensylvania,* derzeit dem *Dominio* Engellands unterworfen—deren Namen u. Kinder vielfältig in diesem Tauf-, Ehe- u. Totenbuch gefunden wirdt. Gott der Herr Himmels u. der Erden müsse sie in Seinen Schutz nehmen u. sie an den Ort begleiten, wohin Er sie haben will.

"NB. Diese Walbrüder seind kommen bis gen Cobolenz am Rhein u. haben nicht weiter kommen können, darob der Augerle sich auch wieder hierher gesetzt, der Koser aber ist um Neuenstadt an d. Linden behangen blieben. Diese erfahren die Wahrheit des 37 Ps. bleibe im Land u. nähre dich redlich."]

AYRER, JACOB HEINRICH (1)—Plüderhausen

Wf: ANNA MARGARETHA, *née* WOEHRLE. Ch: (1) Johann Friedrich, b. 3-26-1744. "To New England." "Married outside Württemberg". From the records of Johann Melchior Kapff, pastor 1725-1770.

## B

BADER, JOHANN GEORG (2)—Stammheim, Ludwigsburg (1749)

Winedresser [*Weingärtner*]. Wf: ANNA MAGDALENA (*Marquard*) of Sindelfingen. Ch: (1) Eva Catharina, b. 9-1-1723, and others who died young. Eva Catharina had an illegitimate daughter, *Anna Maria,* 1749, giving as father a soldier in the Honorable Infantry Guard [*in löbl. Guarde zu Fuss*]; she had already been twice punished for adultery [*Ehebruch*]. With this record the family disappears from the Church Register. Ludwigsburg Protocol, 5-6-1749, with wife and daughter, who was sentenced to the house of correction [*Zuchthaus*], to "New England." // JOHAN GERG BADER, *Patience,* August 11, 1750, Hinke, I, 427; others in 1752 and 1754. GEORG BADER, Maxatawny, Berks Co., Pa., mentioned in Sower's newspaper, November 11, 1758, quoted in Hocker, 77. 3PA, 18, 635: GEO. BADER, Maxatawny Tp., Berks Co., Pa., 1784. 3PA, 19, 410: GEORGE BADER, Penns Tp., Northumberland Co., Pa., 1778-1780.

BADER, MATTHAEUS (2)—Jettenburg (1752)

Shepherd [*Hirt*]. Wf: ANNA MARIA. Ch: (1) Johann Georg, b. 7-31-1733; (2) Hans Martin, b. 10-12-1741; (3) Anna Margaretha, b. 8-28-1745; (4) Matthäus, b. 1-26-1749; (5) Michael, b. 11-3-1751. Ludwigsburg Protocol, 4-13-1752, *venia emigrandi.* // MATTEAS BADER and HANS GERG BADER, *Forest,* October 10, 1752, Hinke, I, 494. 3PA, 17, 603: MATH'S BADER, Lancaster Borough, Lancaster Co., Pa., 1779. Cf. also Hocker, 12: "HANSZ ADAM BADER, at Gottschalk's mill, Skippack, seeks his brothers, PETER and MATHEUS, with whom he came to the country last year," from Sower's newspaper, September 1, 1748.

BAEDER, MATTHAEUS (2)—Geradstetten (1760)

B. 1708. Wf: ANNA MARGARETHA (*Schaal*). Ch: (1) Matthäus, b. 1736; (2) Catharina Margaretha, b. 1738. According to the Church Register, 1760. "This family left here November 8, 1760, for the home of their son, who married in South Carolina in the English territory and lives there." Year of son's emigration not indicated.

BAERLE, CASPAR (1)—Steinheim an der Murr (1750)

Glazier [*Glaser*]. Wf: SARA. Ch: (1) Justina Magdalena, b. 11-13-1730; (2) Johann Caspar, b. 7-28-1734; (3) Sophia Catharina, b. 9-3-1742. All three children "went to America, May 28, 1750, with their parents." // *Staatsbote,* Philadelphia, December 5, 1775, quoted in Hocker, 158: "JACOB GEIGER, living with Nicolaus Weber, Third street, Philadelphia, seeks information of JOHANN CASPAR BERLEN, who came to America in 1750 from Steinheim an der Murr and left his three children in New York—Justinia Magdalena, who married Seckler Falkenhan; Sophia Catharina, who married Dreher Wohlhaupt, and a son, Johann Caspar, a shoemaker. The father's sister, Eva Agnes Durstin, died in 1774."

BAHNMAIER, JOHANN CHRISTIAN (2)— Gündelbach

B. 1768, emigrated after 1794, leaving his family behind.

BAITENMANN, JOHANN GEORG (1)—Dagersheim

Clothmaker [*Zeugmacher*]. Wf: MARGARETHA née EULENFUSS. Ch: (1) Georg Friedrich, b. 1-10-1730; (2) Rosina, b. 8-25-1735. To the "New Land.'" // HANS JERG BEYTENMAN, with JOHANN JACOB BEITENMAN and GEORG FRIEDERIGH BEITTENMAN, *Nancy*, August 31, 1750, Hinke, I, 443. 3PA, 15, 390: GEORGE BIDEMANN, Douglass Tp., Philadelphia Co., Pa., 1780. 3PA, 16, 627: GEORGE BEITENMAN, New Hanover Tp., Philadelphia Co., Pa., 1783.

BALME, JAQUES (2)—Pinache (1753)

Wf: MARIE (*Costebel*). Ch: (1) Susanne Maria, b. 1-14-1747; (2) Catherine, b. 1-6-1749. // JACOB BALD (*Jaques Balme*), age 35, *Patience*, September 15, 1753, Hinke, I, 526-7. 3PA, 18, 51: JOHN PALM, Heidelberg Tp., Berks Co., Pa., 1767. 3PA, 17, 136: JNO. BALM, Lebanon Tp., Lancaster Co., Pa. 1771.

BAPP, MARIA MARGARETHA (2)—Dürrmenz (1750)

B. 11-20-1713, daughter of MATTHEIS and DOROTHEA BAPP. To "Pennsylvania", with sister MARIA BARBARA ROMANN, wife of ANDREAS ROMANN (q.v.). Ludwigsburg Protocol 4-30-1750, Maria Barbara Romann and Margaretha Papp ask for manumission and permission to go to Pennsylvania. From the German and Waldensian Church Registers for Dürrmenz-Schönenberg. // Others in Hinke.

BARDAU (BARTHAU), JOHANN GEORG (2)—Aurich (1752)

B. 4-22-1729, son of the late BARTHOLOMAEUS BARDAU. Wf: CATHARINA (*Widmayer*), shoemaker's daughter [*Schuhmacherstochter*] of Abstatt. Married 1753. Ludwigsburg Protocol, 5-4-1752, to "Pennsylvania." // 3PA, 14, 212; GEORGE BARTHO, Mulberry Ward, City of Philadelphia, Pa., 1769.

BARET(H), JOHANNES (1-2) — Beihingen, Oberamt Ludwigsburg (1744)

B. 5-4-1720. "To Pennsylvania, May 4, 1744." In the years 1752-1757, "JOHANNES BARET from Pennsylvania visited his home and attended communion." // Others in Hinke.

BA(T)Z, BARBARA (2)—Mockmühl (1751)

Ludwigsburg Protocol, 1-22-1751, to "Pennsylvania." // Others in Hinke.

BAUER, EVA (1)—Plüderhausen

Children: (1) Johann Georg, b. 12-8-1745. "To New England."

BAUKNECHT, MICHAEL (2)—Neckartenzlingen (1749)

Tailor's son [*Schneidersohn*]. Wf: MARIA MARGARETHA (*Stöcklin*), linenweaver's daughter [*Leineweberstochter*]. Children: (1) Johann Georg, b. 1-11-1742.

BAUMANN, DANIEL (1)—Grünwettersbach (1751)

Day laborer [*Taglöhner*]. Wf: CATHARINA née KNODLIN. Ch: (1) Johann Daniel, b. 12-28-1740; (2) Catharina Barbara, b. 9-16-1748; (3) Eva Maria, b. 4-12-1750. Baptismal Certificate made May 24, 1751, for the three children. // DANIEL BAUMANN, *Duke of Wirtenberg,* October 16, 1751, Hinke, I, 476.

BAUMANN, ROSINA BARBARA (1) — Grünwettersbach (1753)

B. 8-18-1719, posthumous daughter of DANIEL BAUMANN. Baptismal certificate made June 8, 1753, for "Yburg"; probably Pennsylvania is meant; cf. the Grünwettersbach emigrants of 1751.

BAUR, MARTIN (1)—Unterjesingen (1753)

Wf: ANNA BARBARA. Ch: (1) Michael, b. 9-30-1745; (2) Anna, b. 12-4-1746; (3) Georg Heinrich, b. 9-5-1749; (4) Johann Gottlieb, b. 4-17-1751; (5) Anna Maria, b. 2-11-1753. Ludwigsburg Protocol, 1753. To "Pennsylvania." // MARTIN BOWER (*Bauer*), age 44, heading the list, *Peggy,* September 24, 1753, Hinke, I, 545, 547, c The Moravian records supply information in two of the children: (1) "GEORGE HENRY BAUER, 1741-1836, from Jessingen in Württemberg, Germany; a farmer; lived mostly at Emmaus, where he married A. R. Demuth, and after her death E. Fleckser. [Schultze, 40]. (2) ANNA BAUER, unmarried, born in "Usingen," Württemberg, December 4, 1746, died at Nazareth, Pa., July 31, 1834. "In 1752 came with her parents, Martin and Anna Bauer, to America. In 1762 all united with the congregation in Emmaus. In 1766 moved to Nazareth. 1784 into the new Sisters' House." [Kluge, 135].

BAYHA, GEORG (2)—Sielmingen (1754)

Wf (2): ANNA MARIA (*Schweizer*). Ch: (1) Catharine, b. 12-1-1732; (2) George, b. 8-13-1734; (3) Johann Martin, b. 12-1-1737. Ludwigsburg Protocol, 2-5-1754 to "New York" [Marriage Register, to "Pennsylvania"], requesting that his property may be transferred and that his three children, besides his daughter's husband, may go with him. The daughter, CATHARINA BAYHA, married 1751 JOHANN JACOB RUESS (q.v.) GEORGE BAYHA, JR., married 1754, without banns, BARBARA ARNOLD (q.v.)

BECK (BECC), ANDREAS (1)—Ebingen

Dyer [*Färber*]. Wf: CHRISTINA DOROTHEA née KRIMMEL. Ch: (1) Andreas, b. 11-4-1740; (2) Johannes, b. 7-15-1743. To "Pennsylvania." // ANDREAS BECKH, with BERNHARDT BECK and JOHANN JACOB BECK, *Edinburg,* September 14, 1753, Hinke, I, 521-2. Sower's newspaper, August 19, 1758, quoted in Hocker, 75, mentions ANDREAS BECK, Skippack, near Bernhart Rap. ANDREAS BECK married CATHARINA BUCHER, July 30, 1754, ceremony by Pastor Heinzelman, according to the *Records of Augustus Lutheran Church, Trappe, Pa.,* 268, GSP.

BECKH, JOHANN BERNHARD (2)—Linsenhofen (1753)

Wf: ANNA MARIA (ROTHWEILER). Ch: (1) Johannes, b. 7-5-1731; (2) Rosina Barbara, b. 12-22-1733; (3) Andreas, b. 11-30-1737; (4) Anna Maria, b. 3-17-1743; (4) Ursula, b. 6-20-1747. Register of Convocation [*Kirch. Konv. Register*], 1752, complaint against this couple for giving much offense; thus evidently identical with the Beck who according to the Ludwigsburg Protocol, 5-2-1753, prevailed upon the authorities for release from the penitentiary [*Schellenwerkstraf*] and for permission to go to "Pennsylvania." // BERNHART BECK, with ANDREAS BECKH and JOHANN JACOB BECK, *Edinburg,* September 14, 1753, Hinke, I, 521-2. 3PA, 18, 74: BERNHARD BECK, Tulpehocken Tp., Berks Co., Pa., 1767. 3PA, 26, 245: BERNHART BECK, 30 acres, Berks Co., Pa., survey December 3, 1770.

BELTZHUBER, (CHRISTIAN) MELCHIOR (2)—Metterzimmern (1752)

Wf: ANNA MARIA. "Married at Schnaitheim" [*Nuptias habuere Schnaithii*]. Ch: (1) Melchior, b. 1-27-1740; (2) Georg Eduard, b. 11-8-1741; (3) Johann Jacob, b. 2-8-1746; (4) Johann Martin, b. 11-3-1747; (5) Thomas, b. 9-27-1749; (6) Anna Maria Dorothea, b. 10-3-1751. Ludwigsburg Protocol, 4-12-1752, *venia emigrandi* only. // MELCHER BELZHUBER, *President,* September 27, 1752, Hinke, I, 490.

BENTZ, HANS (1)—Steinenberg

Journeyman [*Gesell*] from Miedelsbach. Wf: CATHARINA. Ch: (1) Christina Barbara, baptized 12-25-1711; "went from Rudersberg to Pennsylvania."

BERNER, ANDREAS (1)—Lomersheim

Wf: BARBARA. Ch: (1) Andreas, b. 6-[?]-1748. To "Pennsylvania." // ANDREW BARNER, witness to will of JOHN CUNRADS, Creesham, Philadelphia Co., Pa., shoemaker (1756-1758), *Philadelphia County Will Abstracts,* V, 1251, GSP. 3PA, 14, 341: ANDREW BARNER, Germantown, Philadelphia Co., Pa., 1774.

BERNOTH, MARTIN (1)—Täbingen (1749)

B. 2-12-1724. Wf: ELISABETHA née SULLINGER of Sondelfingen. "Emigrated April 16, 1749, with his wife." To "New England."

BETTINGER, ANDREAS (1)—Döffingen (1750)

Cartwright [*Wagner*]. B. 12-11-1709. Wf: DOROTHEA née GOTTSCHALL. Ch: (1) Maria Dorothea, b. 12-20-1736; (2) Johann Jacob, b. 5-15-1739; (3) Andreas, b. 8-14-1741; (4) Johann Michael, b. 5-17-1744; (4) Georg Heinrich, b. 3-1-1747. "To America 1750 with wife and five children, and two children of his father-in-law." The in-laws referred to were AGATHA GOTTSCHALL (q.v.) and HEINRICH GOTTSCHALL (q.v.). // ANDREAS BITINGER, with CHRISTIAN NAGEL of Döffingen, *Nancy,* September 16, 1751, Hinke, I, 463.

BICKELER, THOMAS (1)—Söhnstetten

Weaver [*Weber*]. Wf: ANNA MARIA. Ch: (1) Johann Friedrich, b. 9-24-1743, who "went with his parents to the English island of Carolina in 1752" [*m. Elten n. d. engelländ, Insul Carolina abgegangen 1752.*]

BIRCKMAYER (BURCKMAYER), MARIA CATHARINA (2)—Neuffen (1749)

To "Pennsylvania" with eight children, 1749. Ludwigsburg Protocol, 3-21-1749.

BIRKMAIER, JOHANN DANIEL (2)—Neuffen (1749)

"Went to Pennsylvania", after communion on Palm Sunday, 1749. // 3PA, 14, 558: DANIEL BURKMIRE, Upper Delaware Ward, Philadelphia, Pa., 1779.

BIRKMAIER, LUDWIG (2)—Neuffen

"Went to Pennsylvania." Perhaps this refers also to the three sisters, CATHARINA BARBARA, ANNA CATHARINA, and ANNA MARIA BIRKMAIER, whose names precede his, since the Ludwigsburg Protocol, 3-21-1749, speaks of eight brothers and sisters. Cf. *supra,* MARIA CATHARINA BIRCKMAYER.

BISINGER, HANS (JOHANN) JERG (GEORG) (1)—Altenriet

Wf: ANNA née WEISS. Ch: (1) Anna Magdalena, b. 5-7-1741; (2) Johann Jacob, b. 10-25-1748. To "Pennsylvania."

BI(T)ZER, HANS (JOHANN) BALTES (BALTHAS) (1-2)—Dürrwangen (1746)

Innkeeper of the Little Horse Inn [*Rösslinswirt*]. Wf: DOROTHEA, daughter of JOHANN HAERTER, Judge and Miller [*Richter u. Müller*] at Oberdigesheim. Ch: (1) Anna Maria, b. 12-6-1735; (2) Sibylla, b. 2-26-1740; (3) Dorothea, b. 3-10-1743; (4) Ursula, b. 2-4-1745. "With wife and three children to Pennsylvania"; note, however, that none of the children are listed in the Burial Register. Ludwigsburg Protocol, left the village 1773 [1743?-ed.], emigrated 1746; in 1749 were settled eighteen German miles [*Stunden*] from Philadelphia. // 3PA, 17, 890: BALTZER BITZER, inmate, Earl Tp., Lancaster Co., Pa., 1782.

BITZER, HANS BALTHASS (2)—Laufen/Eyach (1746)

Son of HANS BALTHASS BITZER and wife ANNA MARIA née WOLFER. "To Pennsylvania, 1746." Bitzer and MATTHAEUS MAUTTE (q.v.) went to Pennsylvania in 1746. In the summer of 1749, *Landenberger* (q.v.) of Ebingen, who made frequent trips between Germany and America, brought back favorable letters from both. According to a report made 1749 by Mayor Venninger of Laufen, preserved at Ludwigsburg, the letters are said to have "made such an impression among different families, that they even now appear to be intent on leaving next Spring" [*bey verschiedenen Familien solchen Eindruck gemacht haben, dass sie schon jezo zu ihrem Abzug auf das künfftige Frühjahr bedacht zu seyn anscheinen*]. This resulted in the large Laufen emigration of 1750.

BITZER, JOHANN JACOB (2)—Tailfingen (Balingen)

Shoemaker [*Schuhmacher*], son of the farmer [*Bauer*] JOHANN BALTHAS BITZER. Wf: CATHARINA née BITZER, daughter of the baker [*Beck*] CONRAD BITZER. Ch: (1) Johann Jacob, b. 9-6-1750. Both of the parents died 1750.

BITZER, JOHANNES (1)—Dürrwangen (1750)

B. 12-4-1732, son of HANS BALTES BITZER (q.v.) of Dürrwangen and his [first] wife BARBARA, who died 10-15-1733. Ludwigsburg Protocol, 1750, to "Pennsylvania." // JOHANNES BITZER, with LUDWIG BITZER, *Osgood*, September 29, 1750, Hinke, I, 445; a fellow-passenger was Gottlieb Mittelberger. 3PA, 17, 272: JOHN BITZER, Earl Tp., Lancaster Co., Pa., 1772.

BITZER, LUCIA (2)—Laufen/Eyach (1750)

B. 11-20-1714, daughter of the magistrate [*Vogt*] MARTIN BITZER and his wife MARIA (FETZER). // LUCIA (BIEZER) SPOHN (1714-1788), born at Lauffen, Württemberg, wife of MATTHEW SPOHN (q.v.) The two were employed on the farm at Christiansbrunn, near Nazareth, until the husband's death. Buried at Bethlehem, Pa. [Schultze, 68].

BITZER, LUDWIG (2)—Laufen/Eyach (1750)

B. 11-11-1703, brother of HANS BALTHASS BITZER (q.v.) of Laufen/Eyach. Called "Big Ludwig" [*der Grosse*]. Wf: ANNA MARIA. Ch: (1) Agnes, b. 7-13-1733; (2) Ludwig, b. 3-21-1740; (3) Johannes, b. 8-9-1742; (4) Friedrich, b. 1-16-1745; (5) Anna Maria, b. 8-2-1747; (6) Anna, b. 9-6-1749. // LUDWIG BITZER, with JOHANNES BITZER, *Osgood*, September 29, 1750, Hinke, I, 445; a fellow-passenger was Gottlieb Mittelberger.

BIX, JOHANNES (1)—Grünthal

B. 11-4-1727, son of HANS JERG BIX, weaver [*Weber*], and wife CHRISTINA. "To the New World."

BLAENCKLE, MICHAEL (1)—Mägerkingen

Mason [*Maurer*]. Wf: ANNA MARIA née HIPP. Ch: (1) Anna Maria, b. 3-23-1759. According to the record kept by Pastor Hauff, who served Mägerkingen 1770-1809, "parents and child went to America."

BLAICH, (JOHANN) LEONHARD (2)—Stammheim (Calw) (1754)

Farmer [*Bauer*]. Wf: MAGDALENA née MANN, clothmaker's daughter [*Zeugmacherstochter*] from Holzbronn. Married 1716. Ludwigsburg Protocol, 3-29-1754, *venia emigrandi*. Neither is in Burial Register, so it is presumed they emigrated.

BLOCHER (PLOCHER), MICHAEL (2)—Holzhausen (1753)

Two by this name, of whom no later reference is to be found in the Church Register. (1) b. 9-13-1724 son of MICHAEL PLOCHER; (2) b. 4-7-1730 son of CHRISTINA PLOCHER. Ludwigsburg Protocol, 4-13-1753, to "Pennsylvania." // MICHAEL PLOCHER, *Louisa*, October 3, 1753, Hinke, I, 583. 3PA, 14, 552: MICHAEL BLOCKER, Mulberry Ward, West Part, City of Philadelphia, Pa., 1779.

BODAMER (BODEMER), MARGARETHA MAGDALENA (1)—Grünwettersbach (1752)

B. 10-30-1719, daughter of PHILIP and BARBARA BODAMER (BODEMER); sister of JUSTINA CATHARINA (BODAMER) SCHWEICKART, wife of GEORG CONRAD SCHWEICKART (q.v.). "May 2, 1752, a baptismal certificate sent for her to Pennsylvania, whither she went from Berghausen."

BOESSMER (BESSMER), HANS JERG (1-2)—Reudern

Wife: ANNA BARBARA. Ch: (1) Johann Caspar, b. 1-25-1739, "emigrated with parents"; (2) Maria Elisabetha, b. 11-15-1740; (3) Cordula, b. 10-22-1744; (4) Dorothea, b. 6-12-1746; (5) Christina, b. 7-25-1748. To "Pennsylvania," *ca.* 1750. // HANS JERG BOESMER, with JOHANN CHRISTOPH BESMER, Snow *Good Intent,* November 9, 1749, Hinke, I, 426.

BOETZ, ANDREAS (1)—Ochsenbach

B. 5-14-1730, son of Hans Jerg Bötz, vinedresser [*Weingärtner*], and wife CATHARINA. "Said to be buried in Philadelphia." 3PA, 17, 677: //ANDREW BETZ, tavern, Manheim Town, Rapho Tp., Lancaster Co., Pa., 1779; MARTIN BETZ also had a tavern there.

BOGER, JOSEPH (1-2)—Lomersheim (1754)

Wf: SUSANNA. Ch: (1) Maria Margaretha, b. 6-8-1748; (2) Anna Maria, b. 4-24-1750, to the "New Land" [Pennsylvania]; (3) Jacob Friedrich, b. 7-27-1752. "Arrived at Philadelphia, October 16, 1754." // Jos[EPH] POUGER (BOGER), *Peggy,* October 16, 1754, Hinke, I, 637, 639.

BO(H)NACKER, DAVID (2)—Sonderbuch (1752)

Day laborer [*Taglöhner*], and day laborer's son from Feldstetten. Wf: ANNA DURST, shepherd's daughter [*Hirtentochter*]. Married 10-23-1742. Ch: six, born November 1744 to October 1751, of whom only Elisabetha b. 9-4-1747, lived. Ludwigsburg Protocol, 3-28-1752, to "Nova Scotia" [*Neu Schottland*].

BOLAY, LAURENTIUS (2)—Tailfingen (Balingen) (1752)

Son of the late shepherd [*Schäfer*] HANS BOLAY. Wf: ANNA BARBARA née JETTER, daughter of the herdsman [*Hirt*] JOHANN JETTER at Onstmettingen. Ch: (1) Anna Martha, b. 10-15-1749. Listed as communicants up to Palm Sunday, 1752; none of the family appears later in the Baptismal or Burial Registers. Ludwigsburg Protocol, 5-3-1752, to "Pennsylvania."

BONNET, JEAN (2)—Kleinvillars (Grossvillars Parish)

B. 7-1-1753, son of ABRAHAM and CATHERINE (SOULIER) BONNET. Died single in America before February, 1819, "when the family tree [*Stammbaum*] was made." From the Waldensian Church Register for Gross- and Kleinvillars, including also Knittlingen and Diefenbach.

BONNET, JEAN, JR. (2)—Kleinvillars (Grossvillars Parish) (1753)

Wf: MADELEINE (GERMANET). Ch: (1) Marguerite, b. 6-21-1733; (2) Madeleine, b. 2-11-1738 (3) Jean, b. 4-29-1740; (4) Judith, b. 7-22-1742; (5) Catherine, b. 1-2-1745. Ludwigsburg Protocol, 4-13-1753, to "Pennsylvania." From the Waldensian Church Register for Gross- and Kleinvillars, including also Knittlingen and Diefenbach. // JOHN (JEAN) BONNET, *Patience,* September 15, 1753, Hinke, I, 526, 528. 3PA, 17, 754: JOHN BONNET, Lancaster Borough, Lancaster Co., Pa., 1782. 3PA, 22, 159: JOHN BONNET, Bedford Tp., Bedford Co., Pa., 1779.

BORELL, ANNA MARIA (2)—Laufen/Eyach (1750)

B. 2-16-1730, daughter of ANTONIUS BORELL and ANNA MARIA BORELL. To "Pennsylvania." // ANNA MARIA HUELLER, née BOREL, 1730-1789, from Lauffen, Württemberg. "She was married to Henry Mueller, tailor and brickmaker, who died in 1779, leaving a widow and several children." [Schultze, 68]. See introduction, for the passport of another ANTONIUS BOURRELL, of Dornstetten (1752).

BOSCH, JOHANNES (HANS MARTIN?) (2) — Onstmettingen

Wf: MARGARETHA (GOMERINGER). Ch: (1) Catharina, b. 7-10-1743; (2) Johann Michael, b. 10-20-1745; (3) Conrad, b. 12-24-1748; (4) Jacob, b. 9-29-1750. "Went to New England." Ludwigsburg Protocol, 5-3-1752, mentions emigrants from Onstmettingen to Pennsylvania, without giving names. // Sower's newspaper, December 1, 1752, quoted in Hocker, 37, "PETER SCHMITT, on Little Swatara Creek, advertises that his German servant, JOHANNES BUSCH, ran away." *Ibid.*, June 16, 1754, quoted in Hocker, 43, "JOHANNES BUSCH, near PETER SCHMITT, on Little Swatara Creek." 3PA, 17, 136: MARTIN BUSH, Lebanon Tp., Lancaster Co., Pa., 1771.

BRAND, JOHANN HEINRICH (2)—Neckartailfingen (1764)

Peddler and Fisherman [*Krämer und daneben Fischer*]. According to the Marraige Register, he was from Kirchheim unter Teck, b. 1-13-1727, son of JOHANN BRAND, former sergeant-major in the Württemberg Cavalry Guard [*Wachtmeister in d. Württ. Garde zu Pferd*]. Wf: MARIA MAGDALENA (HOERZ), b. 8-27-1732. Ch: (1) Johanna Catharina, b. 6-23-1754; (2) Johann Heinrich, b. 10-19-1758; (3) Elisabetha Christina, b. 2-13-1761; (4) Maria Barbara, b. 7-4-1763. By Brand's name is the reference: "went to Mississippi 1764; returned 1768" [*Anno* 1764 *nach Misisipi fortgezogen. Anno* 1768 *wieder gekommen*]. By his wife's name in the Baptismal Register: "Left again 1772" [1772 *wieder fortgezogen*]. Corresponding references by the children's names for 1764, 1768, and 1772, except that the last is lacking for MARIA BARBARA, who died 1770.

According to Gerber, "Brand, in a request for emigration dating from 1764, calls himself a 'poor soldier's son', who, because he had learned no trade, had to support himself with peddling notions and in different other ways. Neither his means, which already had increased to 530 gulden, nor the personal counsel of the Duke, could dissuade him from emigration, but conditions in Mississippi (which we encounter nowhere else in this volume), drove him back to the old world, where he found refuge in Alsace. In his request for readmission to Württemberg, written in Alsace, he says among other things, 'Like many others who for this reason did not find the expected conditions—since almost all who came there were taken by death—I and my own therefore found it necessary to return, where in Alsace I now find myself in the service of the father of the local magistrate von Hügel.' The readmission into the Fatherland succeeded, partly perhaps through the intercession of von Hügel, and even his home community, thanks to his good conduct earlier, had no objection to his return. However, four years later, during the hard times of 1771-2, he was again so taken with the emigration fever, that he again left the country, despite two denials of his request to emigrate. This time he wanted to go to his only brother's (well-to-do and childless), who lived in New York."

BRAUN, JOHANN JACOB (2)—Bietigheim (1754)

Vinedresser [*Weingärtner*]. Son of the late vinedresser CASPAR BRAUN at Pleidelsheim. Wf: MARIA ELISABETHA, widow of the vinedresser

MICHAEL KOERBER. Married 11-13-1742. Ludwigsburg Protocol, 4-26-1754, Maria Braun, for her husband, asks permission to go to the New World.

BREITENBUECHER, ABRAHAM (1)—Plüderhausen (1765-6)

Farmer [*Bauer*]. B. 3-14-1731, son of MATTHAEUS BREITENBUCHER. Wf: CATHARINA, *née* FRIZ. Married April, 1754. "To America" in 1765 or 1766." // ABRAHAM BREITENBUECHER, with BALTHAS BREITENBUECHER, *Chance,* September 9, 1765, Hinke, I, 705-6. *Staatsbote,* Philadelphia, July 9, 1771, quoted in Hocker, 114, "WILLIAM RIEGEL, Albany [Township], advertises that his German servant, ABRAHAM BREITENDUCHER, 40 years old, ran away." 3PA, 22, 168, ABRAHAM BRIDENBURGH, Brothers Valley Tp., Bedford Co., Pa., 1779.

BRENNENSTUHL, JOHANN MICHAEL (1)—Weil im Schönbuch (1754)

Linenweaver [*Leineweber*]. Wf: (MARIA) MAGDALENA née SCHILLING. Ch: (1) Johann Michael, b. 10-21-1742; (2) Christina b. 7-31-1744; (3) Maria Magdalena, b. 3-30-1746; (4) Johann Ulrich, b. 10-19-1748. Ludwigsburg Protocol, 1754.

BRENZIGHOFER, GEORG CHRISTOPH (2)—Sersheim

B. 4-20-1782, son of JOHANN GEORG BRENZIGHOFER, b. 11-24-1749.

BRENZIGHOFER, JACOB FRIEDRICH (2)—Sersheim

B. 5-25-1776, son of JOHANN GEORG BRENZIGHOFER, b. 11-24-1749. "Went with his property to Philadelphia", or "to America." Evidently before 1801, according to the Family Register.

BREYMAJER, JOHANN GEORG (1)—Mundingen

Smith [*Schmied*]. Wf: ANNA MARIA. Ch: (1) Johann, b. 5-16-1745. To "America." // JOHANN GEORG BREYMEYER, *Anderson,* September 27, 1752, Hinke, I, 489.

BRIGEL (?), JACOB (1)—Beihingen, Oberamt Ludwigsburg (1744)

B. 9-15-1716, son of JOSEPH and CATHARINA BRIGEL. Emigrated May 4, 1744.

BRODBECK, HANS JERG (1)—Schlaitdorf

Farmer [*Bauer*]. Wf: ANNA. Ch: (1) Georg Friedrich, b. 4-23-1742. // HANS JERG BRODBECK (two), *Leslie,* October 7, 1749, Hinke, I, 420. 3PA, 14, 532, FREDERICK BROADBECK, Mulberry Ward (East Part), City of Philadelphia, Pa., 1779.

BROISCH (BREUSCH), JOSEPH (2)—Neckartenzlingen (1764)

Fisherman [*Fischer*]. Son of the late baker and fisherman [*Beck. u. Fischer*] MATTHAEUS BROISCH. Wf: ANNA BARBARA (KURZ), weaver's daughter [*Weberstochter*]. Ch: (1) Johann Michael, b. 2-1-1749; (2) Johannes, b. 2-3-1752, "went to the New World, 1764"; (3) Joseph, b. 3-14-1755, "went to the New World"; (4) Maria Catharina, b. 12-17-1757; (5) Anna Barbara, b. 8-18-1760; (6) Jacob Friedrich, b. 4-13-1762, "went away." Ludwigsburg Protocol, 5-2-1764, to "Pennsylvania."

According to Gerber's digest of the available references, "Breusch and his wife and his six children were poor and had no prospect of inheriting anything. Although he worked industriously at his trade of fisherman and conducted himself well toward magistrates and fellow-citizens, he went back instead of forward, and, with the exception of his fishing outfit, he had only a little old house and two bad little pieces of property, which were so loaded with debts, that he could not count on a saving of more than 31 gulden. With the result that he and his wife had their hopes so firmly set on America, that even the personal endeavors of the Duke could not change their minds. They arrived in Philadelphia, along with [FRANZ] KUHN of Aich, in October of the same year [1764]." // JOSEPH BREISCH with JACOB BREISCH *Richmond* October 20, 1764, Hinke, I, 695.

BRONNER, JOHANN MICHAEL (2)—Dürrmenz (1753)

B. 5-31-1720, son of MICHAEL BRONNER, JR., and wf. MARIA MARGARETHA (HILTWEIN) BRONNER. Uncertain whether it was father or son who emigrated. From the German and Waldensian Church Registers for Dürrmenz-Schönenberg.

BRONNJ, CATHARINA (1)—Schlaitdorf

Single daughter of the cooper [*Kiefer*] JOHANN JACOB BRONNJ. Ch: (1) Catharine, b. (illeg.), 8-4-1748.

BROSS, HANS JERG (2)—Dürrmenz (1753)

B. 6-5-1729, son of HANS JERG and MARGARETHA (ALBRECHT) BROSS. Uncertain whether father or son emigrated. // HANS YERR'K BROSS (HANS JERG BROSS), age 21, *Patience,* September 15, 1753, Hinke, I, 528. 3PA, 18, 211: GEORGE BROSS, single freeman, Bethel Tp., Berks Co., Pa,, 1779. GEORGE BROS, witness to will of BARTHOLOMEW ZIEBACH, Bethel Tp., 1775, *Berks County Will Abstracts,* I, 208, GSP.

BRUDER, MATTHESS (1)—Lossburg

Wf: CHRISTINA. Ch: (1) Johann Georg, b. 8-20-1749. To "Pennsylvania." // MATHEIS BRUDER, *Duke of Wirtenburg,* October 20, 1752, Hinke, I, 497. Estate of MATHIAS BRUDER, Longswamp Tp., Berks Co., Pa., November 3, 1762, administration of CHRISTINA BRUDER, the widow, *Berks County Will Abstracts,* I, 69, GSP. 3PA, 18: 373: MATHEW BROTHER, weaver, Longswamp Tp., Berks Co., Pa., 1780; spelled MATHIAS BRUDER, *ibid.,* 1784.

BRUMM, MICHAEL (2)—Siglingen (1752)

Ludwigsburg Protocol, 4-21-1752, to "Pennsylvania", with three associates (Consorten).

BRUN, ETIENNE (2)—Dürrmenz (1753)

Wf: MARIE (SINQUETTE). Ch: (1) [?], b. 12-10-1730; (2) Marie, b. 12-23-1731. From the German and Waldensian Church Registers for Dürrmenz-Schönenberg. // Cf. STEPHEN BRAUN (STEFFE BRUN), age 37, *Glasgow,* September 9, 1738, Hinke, I, 205, 208. Several STEPHEN BROWNS in PA taxlists.

BUCK, JACOB (1)—Hülben (1751)

Day laborer [*Taglöhner*]. Wf: MAGDALENA née RAUTENB[—] of Zainingen. Ch: (1) Johann, b. 7-25-1739; (2) Sofia, b. 5-25-1745; (3) Christian, b. 12-8-1749. "Emigrated" [*demigrarunt*]. // JACOB BUC(H)S, (two) *Neptune*, September 24, 1751, Hinke, I, 469, with CHRISTOPH COTZ, ALBRECHT SHLEPPY, DAVID KULLING, and UHLLERICH SHWENKEL, all from Hülben.

BUERCKLIN, EBERHARD (1)—Weil im Schönbuch

Peddler and farmer [*Krämer und Rusticus*]. Wf: MARGARETHA née HOFF. Ch: (1) Eberhard, b. 10-15-1740; (2) Johann Jacob, b. 10-8-1742; (3) Christian, b. 12-25-1745; (4) Joachim, b. 5-20-1747; (5) Johann Jacob, b. 7-13-1748; (6) Heinrich Adam, b. 7-11-1750. // 3PA, 22, 130: JACOB BERKLY and LUDWICK BERKLEY, Brothers Valley Tp., Bedford Co., Pa., 1776. 3PA, 21, 696: JACOB BERCKLE, Windsor Tp., York Co., Pa., 1783.

BURCKHARD, JOACHIM (1)—Plattenhardt

Wf: ELISABETHA née ROTH. Ch: (1) Jacob, b. 3-27-1755. "Died in Hagerstown in North America."

BUTZ, JOHANN FRIEDRICH (2)—Hirschlanden (1751)

B. 5-6-1725, son of the cooper [*Küfer*] HANS GEORG BUTZ, Ludwigsburg Protocol, 7-13-1751, to "Pennsylvania." // JOHANNES BUTZ, *Nancy*, September 27, 1752, Hinke, I, 491.

# C

CAFFAREL, PAUL (2)—Dürrmenz (1753)

Wf: LUCRESSE (CHAPELLE). Ch: (1) Antoine, b. 4-6-1731; (2) Suzanne, b. 4-25-1732; (3) Catherine, b. 1-16-1734; (4) Marguerite, b. 5-19-1741; (5) Lucresse, b. 12-18-1743. From the German and Waldensian Church Registers for Dürrmenz-Schönenberg. Ludwigsburg Protocol, 5-8-1753, to "Pennsylvania." // PAUL CAUFFEREL (CAFFARAL, CAFFAREL), age 45, *Patience*, September 15, 1753, Hinke, I, 526.

CHAPELLE, EBERHARD (2)—Dürrmenz (1751)

B. 8-22-1753. son of SALOMON and MADELEINE (SIMON) CHAPELLE. // EBERHART CHAPELLE, *Patience*, September 9, 1751, Hinke, I, 455. 3PA, 18, 46: EBERHARD SHAPPEL, Windsor Tp., Berks Co., Pa., 1767. Executor of wills of GEORGE SNEIDER, of Windsor Tp., 1779-1781, and of VITUS HARTH, of Windsor Tp., 1784-1791, *Berks County Will Abstracts*, I, 273, 462, GSP.

CHAPELLE, (JEAN) PIERRE (2)—Pinache (1753)

Wf: CATHERINE (DON). Ch: (1) Jean Pierre, b. 1-21-1742; (2) Marguerite, b. 9-13-1744; (3) Madeleine, b. 3-8-1750; (4) Germain, b. 10-20-1752. Ludwigsburg Protocol, 4-10-1753, to "Pennsylvania." // (PETER SCHIBELT), JEAN PIERRE CHAPPELLE (age 30), *Patience*, September 15 [17], 1753, Hinke, I, 526-7. Cf. 3PA, 24, 10: JOHN CHAPPELL, city lots in Philadelphia, Philadelphia Co., Pa., survey December 24, 1744. PETER SCHAPPEL and ADAM GILBERT, witnesses to will of FREDERICK FISHER, of Windsor Tp., Berks Co., Pa., 1808-1808, *Berks County Will Abstracts*, II, 214, GSP.

CHAPELLE, JEREMIE (2)—Dürrmenz (1753)

Wf: CATHERINE (ROUCHON). Ch: (1) Jaques, b. 2-4-1744; Wf (2d): MADELEINE (ROUCHON). Ch: (2) Matthieu, b. 4-22-1746; (3) Jeremie, b. 3-14-1749; (4) Madeleine, b. 1-28-1752. Ludwigsburg Protocol, 4-10-

1753, to "Pennsylvania." From the German and Waldensian Church Registers for Dürrmenz-Schönenberg. // (JEREMIAS CHAPPEL), JEREMIE CHAPPELLE, age 25, *Patience,* September 15 [17], 1753, Hinke, I, 526-7. 3PA, 18, 46: JEREMIAH SCHAPPEL, Windsor Tp., Berks Co., Pa., 1767. JEREMIAH SHAPPEL, *creditor,* administrator to estate of the Rev. JOHN MANN of Windsor Tp., May 12, 1804. ELIZABETH the widow renouncing, *Berks County Will Abstracts,* II, 121. The will, in German, of JEREMIAH SHAPPELL, of Windsor Tp., Berks Co., Pa., dated February 11, 1803, probated January 7, 1805, mentions sons JACOB, MATHIAS, JEREMIAH, and daughters MAGDALENA and CATHARINE. Executor, son JACOB; witness: ADAM GILBERT, JEREMIAH SHAPPELL, JR., *Berks County Will Abstracts,* II, 131, GSP.

## CHRISTE (CHRISTI), RUDOLPH (2)—Laufen/Eyach (1750)

B. 5-23-1710, son of MELCHIOR and MARIA CHRISTE. Wf: ANNA. Ch: (1) Maria, b. 4-27-1738; (2) Johann Jacob, b. 10-8-1740; (3) Johann Peter, b. 3-24-1743; (4) Margaretha, b. 7-29-1747. // RUDOLPH CHRISTY, *Osgood,* September 29, 1750, Hinke, I, 445; a fellow-passenger was Gottlieb Mittelberger. According to Kluge, 100, RUDOLPH CHRIST died at Nazareth, Pa., May 22, 1763. He was "born in Lauffen, Württemberg, May 23 1710. Baptized in the Lutheran Church, 1733, July 21, married ANNA WOLFER. Having been awakened in 1744, he visited in Herrnhaag repeatedly. In 1750 moved to this country, with his wife and six children, and lived in Bethlehem. In 1755 united with the congregation." According to Kluge, 114, ANNA (WOLFER) CHRIST died December 4, 1788. She was "born in Lauffen, Württemberg, Oct. 1, 1711. In 1733 married Rudolph Christ. 1750, came with her six children to Pennsylvania, living in Bethlehem, uniting with that congregation. They resided in Friedensthal, Bethlehem and Gnadenthal. After the death of her husband, she lived, for some time, in the Bethlehem Widows' House, and since 1772 at Nazareth with her son JACOB. 'Her joy was in the Lord, by whose blood she had been redeemed.'" Records of the children can also be found in Kluge; especially interesting is the fact that JOHANNA MARIA CHRIST (b. 6-25, 1778, daughter of JOHN JACOB CHRIST (1740-1805), son of Rudolph and Anna, married ANDREW BENADE, Moravian Bishop. [*Ibid.,* 121.]

## CONZELMANN, HANS JERG (2)—Neckartenzlingen (1749)

Of Truchtelfingen. Wf: MARGARETHA (RAUSENBERGER), cobbler's daughter [*Schusterstochter*]. Married 1737. Ch: (1) a son, born before their marriage; (2) Catharina Barbara; (3) Johann Georg. // HANS JERG KUNTZELMAN, Snow *Good Intent,* November 9, 1749. Hinke, I, 426.

## CRAEMER, JOHANN DANIEL FRIEDRICH (1)—Rommelshausen (1750)

Surgeon [*Chirurg*]. Wf. (1st): ANNA CATHARINE, née WILHELM. Ch: (1) Philipp Bernhard, b. 10-19-1733, "went to America, single", "his living or death uncertain"; (2) Wilhelm Jacob, b. 8-12-1738. Wf. (2d): SOFIA née PFEIL of Leutenbach. Ch: (3) Johann Daniel, b. 5-22-1743. Ludwigsburg Protocol, 1750. "This surgeon went to America with his entire family." // DANIEL CRAMER, *Richard and Mary,* September 26, 1752, Hinke, I, 488. *Staatsbote,* Philadelphia, February 7, 1775, quoted in Hocker, 148, "DANIEL CRAMER, Manheim Tp., York

Co." 3PA, 18, 486, JOHN FREDERICK KREMER, Greenwich Tp., Berks Co., 1781, with John Frederick, Frederick Jr., George Jr., Godfrey, and Christoph Kremer.

# D

DAESCH, BALTAS (2)—Sulz am Neckar (1750)

Baker and brewer [*Beck u. Bierbrauer*]. B. 10-19-1727, son of BALTAS DAESCH. Wf: ANNA MARIA (GLEICHNER), farmer's daughter [*Bauerntochter*] from Weiden bei Sulz. Married 5-29-1750. "Emigrated to Pennsylvania, May 30, 1750. // Others in Hinke.

DAMMEL, JOHANNES (2)—Grötzingen

Wf (2d): ANNA MARIA. Ch: (1) Johannes, b. 5-17-1752. According to the Nürtingen Documents, he was allowed to take along the maternal inheritance of a child of his first marriage, to Pennsylvania. // (JOHN DAMER), JOHAN DAMMEL, *Peggy,* October 16, 1754, Hinke, I, 367, 639, 641.

DAMSON, JOHANN GOTTLIEB (1)—Plüderhausen

B. 11-6-1734, son of the surgeon [*Chirurgus*]. SAMUEL DAMSON and wf. ANNA MARIA née GREINER. "Married in America."

DAMSON, JOHANN SAMUEL (1)—Plüderhausen

B. 9-12-1733, son of the surgeon [*Chirurgus*]. SAMUEL DAMSON and wf ANNA MARIA née GREINER. "Married in America."

DAMSON, SIXT JACOB (1)—Plüderhausen

B. 11-11-1744, son of the surgeon [*Chirurgus*]. SAMUEL DAMSON and wf ANNA MARIA née GREINER. "Married in America."

DANNECKER, CHRISTIAN (1)—Mühlheim a. B.

B. 1-9-1724, son of BALTHASAR and MAGDALENA DANNECKER. "Came to America." // 3PA, 16, 796: CHRISTIAN DANAKER, "taylor", Middle Ward, City of Philadelphia, Pa., 1783. CHRISTIAN DANNECKER, executor of will of brother GEORGE DANNECKER, City of Philadelphia (1795-1795), *Philadelphia County Will Book, X,* 370.

DANNECKHER, JACOB (2)—Beutelsbach (1750)

Tailor [*Schneider*]. B. 4-21-1699. Wf: MARGARETHA née BURGER, b. 1715. Ch: (1) Johann Georg, b. 1-15-1736; (2) Elisabetha Margaretha, b. 9-2-1739; (3) Christian, b. 6-5-1749. "To Pennsylvania, 5-4-1750." // JACOB DANNCKHER, *Patience,* August 11, 1750, Hinke, I, 428.

The will of JACOB DANECKER, of Kensington, Northern Liberties, Philadelphia Co., Pa., dated May 23, 1768, recorded in *Will Book T,* 147, grants administration of the estate to CATHERINE HEIMER; executrix, wf MARGARET DANECKER; children: GEORGE, CATHERINE, MAGDALINE, JULIANA DOROTHY; Witnesses, ISAAC WILL and MATHEW HOHL.

DANNENHAUER, HANS JERG (1-2)—Grötzingen (1746)

Tailor [*Schneider*]. Wf: CATHARINA. Ch: (1) Rosina Catharina, b. 7-22-1745, "emigrated with parents, 1746".// HANS JERG DANNENHAUER, *Ann Galley,* September 27, 1746, Hinke, I, 360. Several by this name in Pennsylvania; cf. 3PA, 14, 90: GEORGE DONNEHOVER, mill, with

ABRAHAM DONNEHOVER, Germantown Tp., Philadelphia Co., Pa., 1769. 3PA, 16, 536: GEORGE DANNEHOWER's estate, Bristol Tp., Philadelphia Co., 1783. The will of GEORGE DONAHOWR, of Robeson Tp., Berks Co., Pa., dated December 5, 1769, probated December 20, 1769, mentions wife CHRISTIANA, sons JOHN and GEORGE, executors, and their younger brothers and sisters; witness: JACOB WRATZ, SAMUEL GRIFFITH, OWEN LONG, *Berks County Will Abstracts,* I, 137-8.

## DASER, PAULUS ACHATIUS (2)—Nagold (1753)

Former magistrate [*Vogt*]. Wf: MARGARETHA GRATIA née RAYMOND, daughter of the surgeon [*Chirurg*] JOHANN RAYMOND at *Berro* [Pérols] near Montpellier, b. 1-7-1709. Ch: (1) Johanna Margaretha, b. 2-22-1731; (2) Elisabetha Friederica, b. 4-20-1732; (3) George Achatius, b. [?]; (4) Regina Catharina, m. 12-12-1735; (5) Maria Christina, b. 3-19-1737; (6) Anna Dorothea, b. 5-17-1738; (7) Paul Friedrich Wilhelm, b. 12-29-1740; (8) Regina Margaretha b. 6-29-1743; (9) Anna Catharine, b. 11-3-1744; (10) Ludwig Heinrich, b. 5-14-1748; (11) Heinricke Charlotte, b. 6-9-1752. Ludwigsburg Protocol, 3-16-1753, "Margaretha Daser, with husband and children, to Pennsylvania"; *ibid.* 4-26-1753, claim for payment of 800 gulden to former magistrate Daser before his departure for Pennsylvania. // PAULUS DASSER (DASAR), age 45, with AGATIUS DASSER (age 17) (G. A. DASER), *Peggy,* September 24, 1753, Hinke, I, 548, 550. According to Siebmacher, *Wappenbuch,* VI, Pt. 2, 84, the Dasers were a distinguished Württemberg family, including the learned Councilor [*Oberrath*] WILHELM DASER (d. 1639), and his grandson PAUL ACHATIUS DASER (1626-1694), who was prelate of several cloisters, lastly in 1688 at Königsbronn. The PAUL ACHATIUS DASER appearing in our lists was magistrate at Nagold during the years 1737-1747. A third PAUL ACHATIUS DASER, who died 1795, was captain of the British East Indian Company in Bombay.

## DAST, JACOB (2)—Steinenbronn

B. 1724, son of CHRISTINA DAST, née ENTENMANN, of Weil im Scönbuch. "Went to America" [*abiit in Americam*]. // Sower's newspaper, February 1, 1750, quoted in Hocker, 17, "JACOB DAST, smith, Skippack, on Isaac Klein's place." 3PA, 25, 119: JACOB DAST, 290 acres, Northumberland Co., Pa., survey September 25, 1784.

## DEGELE, JOHANN DAVID (1)—Nordheim

Surgeon[*Chirurg*]. Wf: JULIANA. Ch: (1) Margaretha Barbara, b. 9-21-1747.

## DESSECKER, PETER (1)—Kayh

Smith [*Schmied*]. Ch: (1) Johann Jacob, b. 2-21-1740, "to America"; (2) Michael, b. 2-23-1742, "to America" (3) Peter, b. 12-25-1748, "to America with his father."

## DI(E)CHTEL, JOHANN GEORG (2)—Stammheim (Calw) (1752)

Baker's apprentice [*Beckenknecht*]. Farmer's son [*Bauernsohn*] from Gechingen. Wf: MAGDALEN, née BLAICH, daughter of JOHANN LEONHARD BLAICH (q.v.). Married 1742. Ch: three, died young. Ludwigsburg Protocol, 4-21-1752, to "Pennsylvania." Neither is listed in the Burial Register.

DIETERLIN, ANNA BARBARA (1)—Rötenberg

B. 1-25-1728.

DIEZ, HANS JERG ((1)—Wurmberg

Wf: ANNA MARIA. Ch: (1) Johann Caspar, b. 9-13-1737. To "Pennsylvania." // 3PA, 21, 600: GEORGE DIETZ, Hamilton's Bann Tp., York Co., Pa., 1782.

DIGEL (TIEGEL), HANS (JOHANN) JACOB (2)—Sickenhausen (1752)

Son of HANS JACOB and ANNA MARIA (HENES) DIGEL. Wf: URSULA. Ch: (1) Johann Jacob, b. 6-18-1748; (2) Anna Barbara, b. 5-1-1751. Ludwigsburg Protocol, 4-24-1752, to "Pennsylvania." // JACOB DIGEL, *Forest,* October 10, 1752, Hinke, I, 495. 3PA, 14, 273: JACOB DIGLE, painter, North Ward, City of Philadelphia, Pa., 1774.

DINGLER, JOHANNES (1)—Dagersheim

Clothmaker [*Zeugmacher*]. Wf: MARIA MAGDALENA, *née* GAERTNER. Ch: (1) Johannes, b. 9-5-1750. to the "New Land." // JOHN (JOHAN) DINGLER, *Queen of Denmark,* September 11, 1753, Hinke, I, 517, 519. 3PA, 16, 168: JOHN DENGLER, with JACOB and GEORGE DENGLER, Douglass Tp., Philadelphia Co., Pa., 1782. 3PA, 19, 81: JOHN DINGLER's estate, with GEORGE DINGLER (single), Easton Tp., Northampton Co., Pa., 1785.

DIRR, MATTHAEUS (2)—Bempflingen

Shepherd [*Schäfer*]. Known to have emigrated, but Church Register does not specify America. // MATHIAS DEER (MATTHAEUS DIR), with HANS MICHEL DIR, *Peggy,* October 16, 1754, Hinke, I, 637, 639, 640. 3PA, 19, 32: MATHIAS DERR, laborer, Lower Saucon Tp., Northampton Co., Pa., 1772.

DIRR, MICHAEL (2)—Bempflingen

Shepherd [*Schäfer*]. Known to have emigrated, but Church Register does not specify America. // MICHAEL TIERER (HANS MICHEL DIR), with MATTHAEUS DIR, *Peggy,* October 16, 1754, Hinke, I, 637, 639, 640. 3PA, 14, 722: MICHAEL DERR, Upper Salford Tp., Philadelphia Co., Pa., 1779. 3PA, 16, 714: MICHAEL DERR, Upper Hanover Tp., Philadelphia Co., Pa., 1783. 3PA, 26, 420: MICHAEL DERR, 150 acres, Westmoreland Co., Pa., survey January 19, 1785.

DITTUS, TOBIAS (1)—Ensingen

From Vaihingen Enz. Brother of the lakeside miller [*Seemüller*]. Ch: (1) one illegitimate child, b. 1738. "Went to the New World." // The will of TOBIAS DITTUS, baker, of Bethlehem, Northampton Co., Pa., dated December 29, 1775, probated May 17, 1779, mentions wife MAGDALENE, a maid SUPHIA FENCHEL, executor MICHAEL DIPER, and witnesses, BARTEL HOOVER, GOTTLIEB BOLTZIUS, and P. RHOADS, *Northampton County Will Abstracts,* No. 262, GSP.

DOBLER, JACOB CHRISTIAN (2)—Beutelsbach

B. 8-1-1776. "To America with two children."

DOCKENWADEL, AGNES (2)—Zazenhausen (1754)

Ludwigsburg Protocol, 4-9-1754 (some months after her husband's death), AGNES DOCKENWADLIN and son, to "Pennsylvania."

DOCKENWADEL, GEORG FRIEDRICH (2)—Zazenhausen (1754)

B. 3-24-1719, son of the vinedresser [*Weingärtner*]. NICOLAUS DOCKENWADEL and wife MARIA AGNES née SCHNEIDER. Wf: ANNA MARIA née MAJER, daughter of the grenadier [*Grenadier*] *Majer at* Strümpfelbach, b. 3-13-1720. Ch: (1) Matthäus, b. at Münster, 1743; (2) Philipp Friedrich, b. 1745; (3) Johann Georg, b. 4-3-1747; (4) Elisabetha Dorothea, b. 10-17-1749; (5) Ludwig, b. 7-9-1753. Ludwigsburg Protocol, 4-9-1754, to "Pennsylvania" with his mother. // (FRED'K DOCKWADEL), GEORG FRIEDRICH DOCKUSBADEL, *Richard and Mary,* September 30, 1754, Hinke, I, 605-6. *Staatsbote,* Philadelphia, June 29, 1773, quoted in Hocker, 132: "GEORG FRIEDRICH DOCKENWADEL, Upper Saucon." *Philadelphische Correspondenz,* November 2, 1784, quoted in Hocker, 182, "GEORG FRIEDRICH DOCKENWADEL, Berks County, one mile from the Warm Springs." Cf. also the marriage of MARIA MAGDALENA DOCKENWADLERIN, deserted wife of HANS JUERG RAMSBERGER, with MARTIN JAGER, April 17, 1757, *Records of Augustus Lutheran Church, Trappe, Pa.,* 281, GSP.

DOELCKER (DELGER), ADAM (1)—Dornhan (1751)

Farmer [*Bauer*]. Wf: EVA, *née* STORTZ. Ch: (1) Sara, b. 9-7-1748. Ludwigsburg Protocol, 1751. To "Pennsylvania." // The Will of ADAM DELCKER, of Derry Township, Lancaster Co., Pa., dated June 12, 1759, probated April 15, 1765, mentions wife EVE and children ABRAHAM and SARAH; executors: EVE DELCKER and GEORGE KLEIN, *Lancaster County Will Abstracts,* I, 204. According to Beck, 234, SARAH DELCKER, born in Dornhan, Württemberg, September 7, 1748, died at Lititz as an "unmarried Sister", November 24, 1774. Her brother ABRAHAM DELKER also died unmarried. March 13, 1772, *ibid.,* 232.

DOMINICK, ANDREAS (2)—Machtolsheim (1752)

Mercernary soldier's son [*Söldnersohn*]. B. 8-10-1720. Wf: BARBARA (REYLER), orphaned farmer's daughter [*Bauerntochter*]. Married 4-22-1752, with hastened procedure, omitting banns with magisterial permission, "on account of rapid departure for America" [*wegen schneller Abreise nach America*]. Ch: (1) Walpurga b. 7-24-1751. Ludwigsburg Protocol, 3-7-1752, *venia emigrandi* only.

DRES, CONRAD (1)—Aich

B. 3-4-1728, son of JOHANN GEORG and AGNES DRES. "Went to Pennsylvania" [*migravit in Pens.*] // CONRAD DRESS, *Ann Galley,* September 27, 1746, Hinke, I, 360. 3PA, 18, 244: CONRAD TRESS, Long Swamp Tp., Berks Co., Pa., 1779. The will of CONRAD DRESS, of Longswamp Tp., Berks Co., Pa., dated May 29, 1790, probated June 17, 1790, makes bequests to the Reformed Church in Longswamp and the Lutheran Church in Macungy, with the remainder of his estate given to his six children: DEOBALD, JOHN, MATHIAS, GEORGE, ELISABETH, and MICHAEL; executors: sons JOHN and MICHAEL; witness: JACOB REINER and JOHN WAGONER, *Berks County Will Abstract,* I, 442, GSP.

DRESCHER, HANS JERG (2)—Beihingen, Oberamt Ludwigsburg (1746)

Wf: ANNA MARIA. Ch: (1) Johann Georg, catechumen; (2) Georg Adam, catechumen, b. 11-24-1737; (3) Anna Maria, b. 1-19-1739; (4) Ursula, b. 8-5-1740. "Went to Pennsylvania, 1746." // HANS GEORGE TRASHER, *Ann Galley*, September 27, 1746, Hinke, I, 362. 3PA, 14, 446: GEORGE DRESHER, with ABRAHAM DRESHER, Towamencin Tp., Philadelphia Co., Pa., 1774. 3PA, 15, 546: GEORGE DRESHER, Springfield Tp., Philadelphia Co., Pa., 1780. 3PA, 16, 49: GEORGE DRESHER, miller, Upper Dublin Tp., Philadelphia Co., Pa., 1781.

DUEMMLER, GEORG PETER (1)—Nordheim

B. 11-8-1724, son of GEORG PETER DUEMMLER, Weaver [*Weber*] and wf ELISABETHA. // 3PA, 11, 94: PETER TIMLER, inmate, Pikeland Tp., Chester Co., Pa., 1765.

DULLNICK, MATTHAEUS (1)—Grünwettersbach (1751)

B. 1-9-1720, at Mutschelbach, son of MATTHAEUS and URSULA DULLNICK. Wf: JUSTINA CATHARINA. Ch: (1) Margaretha, b. 9-1-1748; (2) Catharina, b. 5-18-1750. "May 13, 1751, baptismal certificate made for him, his wife, and three children going with him to Pennsylvania." // MATTHEUS DULLNICK, *Duke of Wirtenberg*, October 16, 1751, Hinke, I, 476. 3PA, 26, 324: MATTHAIS TULLNECK, Lot 197 in Reading, Berks Co., Pa., surveyed October 8, 1753.

DUSS, CHRISTIAN JACOB (1)—Effringen

Tailor [*Schneider*]. Wf: ANNA MARIA, daughter of JACOB ROLLER, clothmaker and associate justice [*Zeugmacher u. Gerichtsverwandten*]. Ch: (1) Magdalena, b. 3-1-1749; (2) Anna Maria, b. 1-26-1751, "to the New Land with her parents."

DUTT, DAVID (2)—Weissach (1751)

B. 1-19-1729, son of DAVID DUTT, farmer [*rusticus*], *and* wf CATHARINA. Not in Marriage Register. // DAVID DUETTE, immediately following HANS GEORGE DUTE, *Duke of Wirtenberg*, October 16, 1751, Hinke, I, 475.

DUTT, JOHANNES (2)—Weissach (1751)

B. 10-20-1731, son of DAVID DUTT, farmer [*rusticus*], and wf CATHARINA. // 3PA, 17, 134, JOHN DUTT, Manheim Town, Lancaster Co., Pa., 1771. HANNES DUTH, son-in-law of JOHN EREMAN, mentioned in the latters will (1773-1773), Warwick Tp., Lancaster Co., Pa., *Lancaster County Will Abstracts*, I, 241, GSP.

DUTT, JOHANN GEORG (2)—Weissach (1751)

B. 12-19-1723, son of DAVID DUTT, farmer [*rusticus*], and wf CATHARINA. Not in Marriage Register. Ludwigsburg Protocol, 4-30-1751, HANS JERG DUTT with two brothers, to "Pennsylvania.' // HANS GEORGE DUTE, with DAVID DUETTE, *Duke of Wirtenberg*, October 16, 1751, Hinke, I, 475. 3PA, 19, 96, GEORGE DUTT, Upper Milford Tp., Northampton Co., Pa., 1785. 3PA, 26, 64: George Dutt, 100 acres, Northampton Co., Pa., survey March 11, 1789. GEORGE DUT, brother-in-law, executor of will of FREDERICK HABERKAM (1796-1796), of Warwick Tp., Lancaster Co., Pa., *Lancaster County Will Abstracts*, I, 467.

DUTT, JOHANN MICHAEL (2)—Weissach (1751)

B. 4-17-1720, son of DAVID DUTT, farmer [*rusticus*], and wf CATHARINA.

# E

EBERHARDI, LUDWIG DAVID (2)—Hirschlanden (1709)

Butcher [*Metzger*], preacher's son [*Pfarrersohn*]. Wf: ANNA (GWINNER). Ch: (1) Salome Gertraute, b. 12-27-1686; (2) Wilhelm Benedict, b. 5-9-1689; (3) Regina Barbara, b. 5-23-1695; (4) Catharina Susanna, b. 5-8-1698. Ludwigsburg Protocol, 7-30-1709, wants to go to America, property already sold. Not in Burial Register up to 1736.

EBERLEN, JOHANNES ()—Neuffen

Nailsmith [*Nagelschmied*]. Wf: ANNA BARBARA. Ch: (1) Johann Conrad, b. 1-10-1749. // JOHANNES EBERLE, *Dragon*, October 17, 1749, Hinke, I, 424. 3PA, 18, 27: JOHN EBELING, Alsace Tp., Berks Co., Pa., 1767. 3PA, 15, 526: JOHN EBERLY, tavern keeper, Passyunk Tp., Philadelphia Co., Pa., 1780. 3PA, 17, 292: JOHN EBERLY, with GEORGE EBERLY, Lancaster Borough, Lancaster Co., Pa., 1772.

EBINGER, JOHANN CASPAR (2)—Neckartailfingen (1752)

B. 10-12-1725, son of JOHANNES EBINGER. To "Pennsylvania", 1752.

ECKARDT, JEREMIAS (2)—Hausen/Zaber (1754)

Ludwigsburg Protocol, 5-3-1754, *venia emigrandi* Only the family name identified in the Church Register. // JEREMIAH ECKERT (JERIMIAS ECKERT), *Henrietta*, October 22, 1754, Hinke, I, 649, 650.

EGLER, MARGARETHA BARBARA (1)—Pfaffenhofen (1753)

"Went to America, 1753" [1753 *Amer. petiit*].

EISEBRAUN, MATTHAEUS (1)—Weiler

B. 8-12-1745, son of JOHANN MICHAEL EISEBRAUN. "Allegedly married in Carolina to a CATHARINA née KICHER[ER] and died there.

EISENHARDT, ANDREAS (2)—Deckenpfronn (1751)

Shoemaker [*Schuhmacher*], son of the farmer [*Bauer*] BALTHAS EISENHARDT at Dachtel. Wf: ANNA MARGARETHA (HERTER, HAERDER), daughter of the late clothmaker [*Zeugmacher*] SIMON HAERTER. Ch: (1) Johann Andreas, b. 4-3-1742; (2) Joseph, b. 3-19-1744; (3) Johann Jacob, b. 12-27-1745; (4) Catharina Barbara, b. 5-1-1747; (5) Lorenz Simon, b. 2-1-1749. No further entries in Church Register. Ludwigsburg Protocol, 4-23-1751, with wife and five children, to "Pennsylvania." //ANDREAS EISENHARDT, *Phoenix*, September 25, 1751, Hinke, I, 471. Sower's newspaper, July 8, 1758, quoted in Hocker, 74: "ANDREAS EISENHARDT, Macungie." 3PA, 19, 43: ANDREW EISENHARD, farmer, with JOSEPH EISENHARD (laborer) and JACOB EISSENHARD (single), Macungi Tp., Northampton Co., Pa., 1772. 3PA, 26, 71: ANDREW EISENHART, 200 acres, Northampton Co., Pa., survey December 9, 1767; *ibid.*, 100 acres, survey January 17, 1769. 3PA, 19, 110: JOHN ANDREW EISENHARD, Salisbury Tp., Northampton Co., Pa., 1785.

EISENMANN, HANS PHILIPP (1)—Nordheim

B. 3-26-1717, son of SIGMUND EISENMANN, weaver [*Weber*] in Nordhausen. // PHILIPP ISEMANN, *Hope*, October 1, 1773, Hinke, I, 754.

EITEL, ADAM (1)—Bodelshausen (1772)

B. 9-24-1739, son of HANS CUNRAD EITEL, mason [*Maurer*], and wf CATHERINA née EBERHARD. To America, May 14, 1772.

EITEL, JACOB (1)—Bodelshausen (1772)

B. 11-10-1731, son of HANS CUNRAD EITEL, mason [*Maurer*], and wf CATHARINA née EBERHARD. To America, May 14, 1772.

EITEL, MATTHIAS JOHANNES (1)—Bodelshausen

Mason [*Maurer*]. Wf: AGNES. Ch: (1) Margaretha, b. 3-23-1744; (2) Johann Bernhard, b. 5-1-1746; (3) Catharina, b. 7-8-1749. "Went to America," or "Pennsylvania."

ENGELBRECHT, GEORG MARTIN (1)—Nordheim

B. 6-17-1727. Son of BALTHASAR and CATHARINA MAGDALENA ENGELBRECHT. // MARTIN ENGELBRECHT, *Phoenix*, September 25, 1751, Hinke, I, 470.

ENGELBRECHT, MARIA GOTTLIEBIN (1)—Nordheim

B. 6-6-1680, daughter of PETER ENGELBRECHT.

ENGLERT, HANS GEORG (1)—Nordheim

B. 3-11-1670, son of JACOB ENGLERT. // Three listed in Hinke: JOHANN GEOERG ENGLERT, *Duke of Wirtenberg*, October 16, 1751, Hinke, I, 476; JOHANN GEORG ENGLERT, *Forest*, October 10, 1752, Hinke, I, 494; HANS JUERG ENGLERT, *Phoenix*, November 2, 1752, Hinke, I, 503. 3PA, 19, 85: GEORGE ENGLER, Williams Tp., Northampton Co., Pa., 1785.

ENGLERT, JOHANN CHRISTOPH (1)—Nordheim

B. 4-13-1701, son of HANS JACOB ENGLERT. // HANS CHRISTOPH ENGLERTH, *Two Brothers*, August 28, 1750, Hinke, I, 438. 3PA, 15, 644: CHRISTOPHER ENGLER, Mulberry Ward (West Part), City of Philadelphia, Pa., 1781.

EPPLE, JOHANN MARTIN (2)—Rutesheim (1751)

B. 12-27-1729. "This man, with others from this place, departed for Pennsylvania, May 24, 1751." Ludwigsburg Protocol, 4-16-1751, *venia emigrandi*. // MARTIN EBBLY, *Duke of Wirtenberg*, October 16, 1751, Hinke, I, 475. 3PA, 18, 126, MARTIN EBLE, weaver, Greenwich Tp., Berks Co., Pa., 1768.

ERNST, JOHN MICHAEL (2)—Gündelbach

B. 1741. // 3PA, 13, 396: MICHAEL EARNST, Springfield Tp., Bucks Co., Pa., 1783. 3PA, 19, 35: MICHEL ERNST, farmer, Lower Saucon Tp., Northampton Co., Pa., 1772. The will of MICHAEL ERNST, of Lower Saucon Tp., Northampton Co., Pa., weaver, is dated June 21, 1792, probated December 21, 1792, *Northampton County Will Abstracts*, No. 561, GSP.

EYLER, PHILIPP (1-2)—Oberboihingen

Catholic stockingweaver [*katholischer Strumpfweber*]. Wf: ROSINA. Ch: (1) Johann Michael, b. 6-7-1744; (2) Anna Christina, b. 8-13-1748. To "Pennsylvania." // PHILIPP EULER, *Anderson*, September 27, 1752, Hinke, I, 488.

# F

FACKH, PHILIPP JACOB (2)—Markgröningen (see Stammheim (Calw) (1754)

Miller's son [*Müllersohn*] from Markgröningen. Wf: ANNA MARGARETHA (LOSER). Ch: (1) daughter, b. 1737; (2) daughter, b. 1741. Not in Burial Register. Ludwigsburg Protocol, MATTHES FACKH, *venia emigrandi* 4-5-1754.

FAUSER, ANNA (1)—Bodelshausen (1766)

B. 3-17-1731, daughter of CUNRAD FAUSER and wf ANNA, *née* EBERHARD. Ch: (1) Catharina, b. (illeg.), 1-31-1762. To America, June 3, 1766.

FAUSER, HANS JERG (2)—Jettenburg (1752)

Baker [*Beck*]. Wf (1st): ANNA MARIA (d. 1740). Ch: (1) Margaretha, b. 2-6-1734; (2) Hans Jerg, b. 6-28-1737. Wf (2d): ELISABETHA (GRAUER) of Imenhausen. Ch: two. Ludwigsburg Protocol, 3-28-1752, children of first marriage allowed to go to Carolina. // Cf. *Philadelphische Correspondenz*, May 26, 1789, quoted in Hocker, 196. "JOHANN FAUSSER, smith, with GEORG ADAM SCHNEIDER, North Wales." *Ibid.*, November 26, 1790, quoted in Hocker, 198, "JOHANNES FAUSSER, Third St. Phila., born in Bodelhausen, is going to Germany."

FEILER, GOTTFRIED (2)—Oeschelbronn (now Baden) (1753)

Baker [*Bäcker*]. Wf: REGINA (FAHS). Married 1744. Ch: five. Ludwigsburg Protocol, 3-23-1753, to "Pennsylvania."

FELBER, CATHARINA (1)—Schlaitdorf

Single. Ch: (1) Johann Jacob. b. (illeg.), 12-24-1751, "died in Pennsylvania with the mother."

FIDLER, MELCHIOR (1)—Lomersheim

Wf: ANNA. Ch: (1) Johann Jacob, b. 2-4-1749; (2) Johann Martin, b. 11-9-1752. To "Pennsylvania." // 3PA, 12, 138: JACOB FIDDLER, freeman, Radnor Tp., Chester Co., Pa., 1779. 3PA, 21, 613: JACOB FIDLER (single), with PHILIP FIDLER, Tyrone Tp., York Co., Pa., 1782.

FIMPEL, JOHANNES (1)—Oberboihingen

Farrier's son [*Hufschmiedssohn*]. Wf: AGNES. Ch: (1) Jerg, b. 2-21-1744; (2) Johann Michael, b. 8-26-1747; (3) Maria Agnes, b. 3-2-1750. To "Pennsylvania." // JOHANNES FIMPEL, with HANS JERG FIMPEL, *Phoenix*, November 2, 1752, Hinke, I, 502. Cf. *Staatsbote*, Philadelphia, August 11, 1772, quoted in Hocker, 124, "JACOB FIMPEL, Merion Tp., wife MARGRETH." 3PA, 14, 101: JOHN FIMPLE, Lower Merion Tp., Philadelphia Co., Pa., 1769. 3PA, 15, 435: JOHN FIMPLE, with GEORGE FIMPLE, Lower Merion Tp., Philadelphia Co., Pa., 1780.

FISCHER, HANS JERG (2)—Neckartailfingen (1749)

B. 1702, son of LUDWIG FISCHER. Wf: CHRISTINA CATHARINA (FUCHS) of Marbach. Ch: (1) Johannes, b. 11-3-1735; (2) Maria Catharina, b. 3-18-1738. The father: "Went to Pennsylvania, April 30, 1749; he was much given to stealing" [*30. April, 1749, nach Pens.; er war dem Stehlen sehr ergeben*]. // HANS JERG FISCHER, *Leslie,* October 7, 1749, Hinke, I, 420; and others.

FISCHER, MARIA AGNES (2)—Neckartailfingen (1752)

B. 2-1-1724, illegitimate daughter of JULIANA FISCHER; niece of HANS JERG FISCHER (q.v.). "To Pennsylvania, 1752."

FISSLER, (HANS) JACOB (1)—Lossburg

Schoolmaster [*Schulmeister*]. Wf: EVA. Ch: (1) Dorothea, b. 11-7-1746; (2) Johannes, b. 3-10-1752. Ludwigsburg Protocol, 1752. To "Pennsylvania." // JOH. JACOB FISSLER, with JOHANN MICHAEL FISSLER and JOHANN GEORG FISSLER, *Duke of Wirtenberg,* October 20, 1752, Hinke, I, 497. 3PA, 18, 647: JACOB FESLER, with ALBRIGHT FESLER, Pine Grove Tp., Berks Co., Pa., 1784.

FLACH, LUDWIG (1)—Gärtringen

Weaver [*Weber*]. B. 4-20-1718. Wf: DOROTHEA, widow of a shoemaker [*Schuhmacher*] in Maichingen. Ch: (1) Johann Georg, b. 7--7-1742; (2) Maria Catharina, b. 12-16-1746. "This family immigrated to America." // LUDWIG FLACH, *Lydia,* October 19, 1749, Hinke, I, 421. Several LUDWIG FLUCKS listed in PA, including LUDWIG FLUCK, weaver, Reading, Berks Co., Pa., 1784, 3PA, 18, 652. 3PA, 15, 621: GEORGE FLACK, Mulberry Ward (East Part), City of Philadelphia, Pa., 1781.

FLEISCHMANN, JOHANN CHRISTOPH (2)—Möckmühl 1753)

Son of the late farmer [*Bauer*] JOHANNES FLEISCHMANN. Wf: MARIA CLARA (MEHLHAEFIN), widow of HEINRICH MEHLHAFEN. Married 7-13-1751. Ludwigsburg Protocol 5-11-1753 to "Pennsylvania."

FLENSBACH (PFLENSPACH), MELCHIOR LEONHARD (2)—Lauffen am Neckar (1753)

Of Grossgartach. Wf: SOPHIA CATHARINA (REMBOLD), b. 1718. Ch: (1) Johann Adam, b. 1741; (2) Georg Martin, b. 1742; (3) Christoph Ludwig, b. 1745; (4) Sophia Catharina, b. 1747: (5) Rosmaria, b. 1750; (6) Regina Margaretha, b. 1-16-1753. Ludwigsburg Protocol, 3-9-1753, to "Pennsylvania." // MELCHIOR FLINTSHBACK (FLINSPACH), age 24, with HANS PHILIP FLINSBACK (JOHANN PHILIPP FLINSPACH), age 22, *Brothers,* September 26, 1753, Hinke, I, 551. 3PA, 21, 342: MARTIN FLINSHBACH, with ADAM FLINSHBACH, York Tp., York Co., Pa., 1781. 3PA, 26, 432: FREDERICK and ADAM FLINCHBOUGH, 400 acres, Westmoreland Co., Pa., survey May 8, 1794.

FOEHL, ANDREAS (1-2)—Steinenberg (1749)

Of Oberschlechtbach. B. 4-1-1730. To "America," 1749. // ANDREAS FOEHL, *Patience,* September 19, 1749, Hinke, I, 409. Sower's newspaper, August 16, 1750, quoted in Hocker, 20: "JOSEPH STEINMAN, Conestoga Tp., advertises that his German servant, ANDREAS FEHL, 19 years old, ran away." 3PA, 17, 541: ANDREW FEHL, Conestoga Tp., Lancaster Co., Pa., 1779. The will of ANDREW FOEHL, of Conestoga Tp., Lancaster Co., Pa., dated December 16, 1794, probated March 21, 1795, mentions wife ANNA FOEHL and children GEORGE, JACOB, FREDERICK; executors: wife ANNA and HENRY DIETRICH, *Lancaster County Will Abstracts*, I, 302, GSP.

FOEHR (FEER), JOHANNES (2)—Simmozheim (1751)

Linenweaver [*Leineweber*]. Wf: ANNA DOROTHEA. Ch: (1) Jacob Cunrad, b. 5-31-1743; (2) Catharina Dorothea, b. 5-26-1745. No children listed after 1751. Ludwigsburg Protocol, 4-6-1751, to "Pennsylvania." // JOHANNES FEHR, *Rawley*, October 23, 1753, Hinke, I, 500; a fellow-passenger was JOHN GEORGE BAGER, Lutheran minister. 3PA, 26, 261: JOHN FEHR, 136.15 acres, Berks Co., Pa., survey January 2, 1771.

FREY, MICHAEL (1)—Dornhan

Wf: CATHARINE. Ch: (1) Elisabetha, b. 9-23-1732. // MICHAEL FREY, with JOHANN MARTIN FREY and JACOB FRY, Brig *Betsey*, December 4, 1771, Hinke, I, 738.

FRIDLIN (FRIDLE), HANS JERG (2)—Möckmühl (1751)

B. 3-16-1717, son of the shoemaker [*Schuhmacher*] JOHANN GEORG FRIDLIN and wife MARIA URSULA. Ludwigsburg Protocol, 1-22-1751, "FRIDLE and associates [*Consorten*], to Pennsylvania." // 3PA, 17, 567: GEORGE FRIDLY, with BARNED FRIDLY, Paxton Tp., Lancaster Co., Pa., 1779. 3PA, 20, 707: GEORGE FRIDLEY, with CONRAD FRIDLEY, East Pennsboro Tp., Cumberland Co., Pa., 1785.

FRIED, MARGARETHA (1)—Plattenhardt (1752)

*Née* LOEFFLER, widow of JACOB FRIED, tailor [*Schneider*]. Ch: (1) Maria Catharina, b: 6-27-1745 (2) Anna, b. 6-19-1746; (3) Johann Georg, b. 11-13-1749; (4) Margaretha, b. 6-27-1751. To "Pennsylvania," 1752. //3PA, 13, 81: WIDOW FREEDS, Richland Tp., Bucks Co., Pa., 1779. 3PA, 14, 589: WIDOW FRIED, Franconia Tp., Philadelphia Co., Pa., 1779.

FRITZ, CASPAR (1)—Beihingen, Oberamt Ludwigsburg (1744)

Of the court [*des Gerichts*]. Wf: ANNA CATHARINA. Ch: (1) Jacob, b. 9-6-1727. To "Pennsylvania", May 4, 1744.

FRITZ, JOHANNES (2)—Beihingen, Oberamt Ludwigsburg

"In Pennsylvania." // Two listed in Hinke: JOHANNES FRITZ, *Edinburgh*, September 15, 1749, Hinke, I, 404; JOHAN FREITZSCH (JOHANNES FRITZ), *Adventure*, September 25, 1754, Hinke, I, 601-2. Cf. also the *Staatsbote*, Philadelphia, September 20, 1774, quoted in Hocker, 144: "JOHANNES FRITZ, landlord of the Green Tree Inn, Race street, Phila."; also *ibid.*, November 24, 1775, quoted in Hocker, 158: "SIMON KLAS, Lower Merion Tp., advertises that his German servant, PHILIP KOLB, ran away. He is 18-19 years old, and he left with JOHANNES FRITZ.".

FROMM, JERG ULRICH (1)—Oberboihingen

Weaver [*Weber*]. Wf: BARBARA. Ch: (1) Georg David, b. 11-8-1743. To "Pennsylvania." // 3PA, 17, 319: ULRICK FROM, Middle Town, Lancaster Co., Pa., 1772.

FUNCK, BENEDICT (2)—Gebersheim (1751)

Wf: JOHANNA DOROTHEA. "Went to Pennsylvania, May 25, 1751". //BENEDICK FUNCK, *Duke of Wirtenberg,* October 16, 1751, Hinke, I, 477. 3PA, 21, 142: BENEDICK FUNK, York Tp., York Co., Pa., 1779; 3PA, 21, 329: BENEDICK FUNCK, with JACOB FUNCK, York Town, York Co., Pa., 1781.

# G

GAJER, JOHANN CASPAR (1)—Schlaitdorf

Prefect [*Praefectus oder Praetor loci*]. Wf: ANNA MARIA née WALTHER. Ch: (1) Regina Barbara, b. 10-18-1741; (2) Christina Catharina, b. 12-27-1743; (3) Anna Magdalena, b. 6-13-1747. // Two listed in Hinke: JOH. CASPER GEYER (GAYER), heading the list, with JOH. JACOB GEYER, *Richard and Mary,* September 17, 1753, Hinke, I, 531-2, with HANS JACOB ADAM (of Schlaitdorf). 3PA, 24, 679: CASPER GEYER, 301-80 acres, Cumberland Co., Pa., survey August 4, 1770. 3PA, 26, 435: CASPER GEYER, 253 acres, Westmoreland Co., Pa., survey December 3, 1785. 3PA, 22, 476: GASPER GEYER, Rostraver Tp., Westmoreland Co., Pa., 1786. 3PA, 14, 193: CASPER GEYER, stonecutter, North Ward, City of Philadelphia, Pa., 1769.

GALGENMEYER, SIMON (2)—Kirchheim unter Teck (1752)

Stockingknitter [*Strumpfstricker*]. Wf: SABINA CATHARINA. Not listed in Church Register after Pentecost Communion of 1752. Ludwigsburg Protocol, 5-16-1752, to "America."

GALLER, HANS CONRAD (1)—Nordheim

B. 3-21-1715, son of SAMUEL GALLER.

GAMERDINGER, GOTTLIEB (1)—Unterjesingen

Wf: [?]. Ch: (1) Maria Magdalena, b. 4-22-1753, to "Pennsylvania."

GANN, HANS JERG (1)—Ostelshein

Wf: ANNA CATHARINA. Ch: (1) Anna Maria, b. 5-25-1728. To "New England." // Others listed in Hinke.

GAUTIER, JAQUES (2)—Grossvillars (1753)

Wf: JEANNE SUSANNE (COCHET). Ch: (1) Marie Susanne, b. 10-12-1743; (2) Marguerite, b. 8-17-1746; (3) Catherine Rachel, b. 1-15-1748; (4) Isaac, b. 3-14-1751. From the Waldensian Church Register for Gross- and Kleinvillars, including Knittlingen and Diefenbach. Ludwigsburg Protocol, 4-27-1753, to "New England." // JACOB GOODIER JAQUE GOUTIER), age 27, with PETER GOODIER (PIERRE GAUTIER), age 31, *Patience,* September 15 [17], 1753, Hinke, I, 526, 527, 528.

GEJER, JOHANN CASPAR (1)—Schlaitdorf (1754)

Farrier and forest-ranger, formerly groom [*Hufschmied u. Waldschütz, vormals Reitknecht*]. Wf: ANNA BARBARA, née KIENZLEIN (KIENZLERIN) of Hengstätt. Ch: (1) Anna Barbara, b. 7-17-1741; (2) Johann Caspar, b. 9-11-1742; (3) Anna Maria, b. 2-20-1744; (4) Christina, b. 5-4-1746; (5) Andreas, b. 11-30-1747; (6) Johannes, b. 2-10-1750. According to a reference in the Marriage Register, "this couple left 1754 for Pennslyvania, with six children." // CASPER GEYER (HANS CASPER

GEYER), *Richard and Mary*, September 30, 1754, Hinke, I, 604, 606, with JACOB ADAM of Schlaitdorf. For possibilities as to his residence in Pennsylvania, cf. notes to JOHANN CASPER GAJER, *supra*.

GENDER (?), GOTTLIEBIN (1)—Nordheim.

B. 6-16-1712, daughter of CHRISTOPH GANDER.

GENTNER, AUGUSTINUS (1)—Grötzingen (1749)

Went to "Pennsylvania", May 1, 1749, with wife and others from the same village. // AUGUSTINUS GINTNER, *Albany*, September 2, 1749, Hinke, I, 395.

GENTNER, JOHANNES (1)—Grötzingen (1748)

Wife: MARIA AGNES. Ch: (1) Johannes, b. 12-7-1740, "to Pennsylvania, 1749 (?)." Went to Pennsylvania, May 15, 1748, after private communion, along with MICHAEL MUELLER (q.v.), JACOB MUELLER (q.v.), MARGARETHA (q.v.) and ANNA MARIA HOFSAESS (q.v.), and MARGARETHA MUELLER (q.v.), of Grötzingen. // JOHANNES HINKNER (GINTNER), age 30, with JOHAN JACOB and MICHAEL MUELLER of Grötzingen, *Patience*, September 16, 1748, Hinke, I, 383-6.

GERNGROSS, JOHANN (2)—Lauffen am Neckar

Vinedresser [*Weingärtner*]. B. 1700. Wf: MARIA BARBARA (NEUBERTH) of Beilstein. Ch: (1) Georg Heinrich, b. 1737: (2) Sophia Catharina, b. 1738; (3) Christiane Dorothea, b. 1740; (4) Johann Ludwig, b. 1742. "Went to the New World."

GEYGER (GEIGER), JACOB (1)—Beihingen, Oberamt Ludwigsburg (1744)

B. 10-16-1724, son of JACOB and AGNESA GEYER. "To Pennsylvana [or] South Carolina." "To Pennsylvania, May 4, 1744." // JACOB GEIGER, *Duke of Bedford*, September 14, 1751, Hinke, I, 460; others earlier and later. 3PA, 16, 269: JACOB GIGER, Plymouth Tp., Philadelphia Co., Pa., 1782.

GEYGER (GEIGER), JOHANN MICHAEL (1)—Beihingen, Oberamt Ludwigsburg (1744)

B. 3-11-1723, son of JACOB and AGNESA GEYGER. "To Pennsylvania [or] South Carolina." "To Pennsylvania May 4, 1744." // JOHANN MICHAEL GEIGER, Snow *Louisa*, November 8, 1752, Hinke, I, 506. 3PA, 18, 324: MICHAEL GICKER, single freeman, Bern Tp., Berks Co., Pa., 1780. 3PA, 25, 147: MICHAEL GEIGER, 100 acres, Northumberland Co., Pa., survey July 30, 1773. 3PA, 19, 475: MICHAEL GEIGER, with CHRISTIAN GEIGER, Augusta Tp., Northumberland Co., Pa., 1781.

GLOCKH, HANS CASPAR (1)—Beihingen, Oberamt Ludwigsburg (1744)

B. 7-17-1721. "To Pennsylvania, May 4, 1744." // *Staatsbote*, Philadelphia, April 19, 1774, quoted in Hocker, 140, "JOHANN CASPAR KLOCK, behind Carolina."

GOEHRING, JOHANN JACOB (1)—Unterjesingen

Smith [*Schmied*]. Wf: MAGDALENA. Ch: (1) Johann Jacob, b. 7-29-1750; (2) Gottlieb Friedrich, b. 7-25-1753. // Others listed in Hinke.

GOETZ, HANS (JOHANN) MICH(A)EL (1) — Beihingen, Oberamt Ludwigsburg (1744)

Vinedresser [*Weingärtner*]. Wf: ANNA. Ch: (1) Johann Georg, b. 2-5-1729; (2) Johann Heinrich, b. 8-7-1730; (3) Anna Barbara, b. 2-5-1732; (4) Johannes, b. 4-22-1735; (5) Johann Michael, b. 12-[?]-1738. "To Pennsylvania, May 4, 1744." // JOHANN MICHAEL GOETZ, *Juno*, January 13, 1767, Hinke, I, 713. 3PA, 24, 680: GEORGE GOETZ, 95.65 acres, Cumberland Co., Pa., survey April 29, 1772; several others listed in PA.

GOETZ, ANNA (2)—Beihingen, Oberamt Ludwigsburg (1744)

Widow, "Went to Pennsylvania in May, 1744," accompanying her sons.

GOTTSCHALL, AGATHA (1)—Döffingen (1750)

B. 5-25-1736, daughter of the linenweaver [*Leineweber*] GOTTSCHALL. To America with her brother-in-law, ANDREAS BETTINGER (q.v.)

GOTTSCHALL, HEINRICH (1)—Döffingen (1750)

B. 11-2-1742, son of the linenweaver [*Leineweber*] GOTTSCHALL. To America with his brother-in-law, ANDREAS BETTINGER (q.v.).

GOTZGER, CHRISTIAN (1)—Grötzingen (1754)

Wf: ANNA BARBARA. Ch: (1) Anna Barbara, b. 7-29-1731; (2) Anna Maria, b. 10-31-1733. To "Pennsylvania."

GRAEBER, HIERONYMUS (2)—Onstmettingen (1747)

Wf: ANNA MARIA. Ch: (1) Anna Barbara, b. 11-16-1743. "Went to New England." // HIERONIMUS GREBER, heading the list, *Restauration*, October 9, 1747, Hinke, I, 465.

GRAF, CATHARINA (1)—Beihingen, Oberamt Ludwigsburg (1744)

B. 12-3-1716. "To Pennsylvania, May 4, 1744."

GRATZ, JOHANN JACOB (2)—Magstadt (1749)

Tailor [*sartor*]. Wf: ANNA MARIA. Ch: (1) Johann David, b. 1-10-1743; (2) Maria Catharina, b. 3-1-1744; (3) Johann Georg, b. 11-16-1746; (4) Rosina Dorothea, b. 6-23-1748. According to Gerber, this family appears to have come to Mägstadt from elsewhere, and disappeared again from the Church Register after 1749. Ludwigsburg Protocol, 4-15-1749, to "Pennsylvania." // JACOB GRATZE, *Phoenix*, September 15, 1749, Hinke, I, 406. 3PA, 19, 5: JACOB GROTZ, SR., carpenter, with ANDREW GROTZ, carpenter, and JACOB GROTZ, JR., carpenter, Easton, Northampton Co., Pa., 1772.

GRAUER, JOHANNES (1)—Grötzingen (1749)

Wf: ANNA MARIA. Ch: (1) Johannes, b. 4-2-1739; (2) Christian, b. 8-13-1740; (3) Joseph David b. 1-1-1743; (4) Hans Jerg, b. 12-23-1743; (5) Margaretha, b. 8-18-1745. To "Pennsylvania, May 1, 1749." // JOHANNES GRAUER, *Albany*, September 2, 1749, Hinke, I, 395, with JOHANNES NIBLING of Grötzingen.

GRETZING, HANS JERG (1-2)—Ofterdingen (1743)

Clothmaker [*Zeugmacher*]. Wf: BARBARA, née HALDENWANG. Ch: (1) Anna Maria, b. 8-12-1735; "this child was taken by its father to

Carolina, May 9 1743." // HANCE YARAH CREATSENER (HANS JERG GRETZINGER, *Rosannah*, September 26, 1743, Hinke, I, 343, 345.

GROSS, HEINRICH, JR. (2)—Mähringen (1752)

Wf: APOLLONIA.. Ch: (1) Anna, b. 12-17-1740; (2) Johann Jacob, b. 12-8-1747. Ludwigsburg Protocol, 5-3-1752, to "Pennsylvania." // HENRY GROSS, with JUNG HEINRICH GROSS and the Baders, (from Filial Jettenburg), *Forest*, October 10, 1752, Hinke, I, 495.

GROZ, JOHANN MARTIN (1)—Ebingen

Cobbler [*Schuster*]. Wf: ANNA MARIA, *née* KEPPLER. Ch: (1) Johann Georg, b. 1-18-1737. To "Pennsylvania."

GRUBER, (SYLVESTER) FRIEDRICH (2)—Beilstein (1753)

Cooper [*Küfer*]. Wf (1st): EVA SCHRAMM (d. 1739). Ch: (1) Johanna Gottliebin, b. 7-26-1735. Wf (2d): MARGARETHA DOROTHEA STAUD. Ch: (2) Johanna Friederica, b. 6-25-1741; (3) Margaretha Dorothea, b. 4-3-1744; (4) Catharina Christian, b. 4-12-1746; (5) Rosina, b. 2-15-1748. The family disappears from the Church Register after 1753. Ludwigsburg Protocol, 4-24-1753, to "Pennsylvania." // FREDERICK GRUBER, *Beulah*, September 10, 1753, Hinke, I, 513. 3PA, 17, 15: SILVESTER GRUBER, Elizabeth Tp., Lancaster Co., Pa., 1771.

GRUENDELMAYER, JACOB (2)—Neckartenzlingen (1766)

No information about his family, if any. According to Gerber, he was "always peaceable and loving, and a good and industrious worker. Is worth 200 Gulden". *"Jederzeit friedlich und liebreich, auch fleissig und arbeitsam. 200 Gulden."*

GRUENDLER, PHILIPP JACOB (1)—Ostelsheim

Wf: MARIA ELISABETHA. Ch: (1) Anna Magdalena, b. 10-13-1735; (2) Maria Agnes, b. 10-19-1740; (3) Dorothea, b. 11-18-1742; (4) Christina Catharina, b. 11-9-1747. All the children: "with parents," to New England. // PHILIP JACOB GRINLER (PHILIPP JACOB GRINDLER), age 50, *Barclay*, September 14, 1754, Hinke, I, 596, 598.

GUTEKUNST, HANS JERG (2)—Nagold (1750)

Shoemaker [*Schumacher*]. Son of the farmer [*Bauer*] MICHAEL GUTEKUNST in Niefern. Wf (1st): MAGDALENA (SCHUH). Ch: (1) Philipp Jacob, b. 2-18-1730; (2) Barbara, b. 1-26-1731; (3) Paul, b. 5-8-1733. Wf (2d): BARBARA (BRAUN). Married 11-5-1749. Ludwigsburg Protocol, 5-19-1750, to "Pennslyvania." // HANS JERG GUTEKUNST, *Osgood*, September 29, 1750, Hinke, I, 446; a fellow-passenger was Gottlieb Mittelberger. 3PA, 26, 80-82: GEORGE GUTTEKUNTS, 20, 25, and 6 acres, Northampton Co., Pa., survey August 9, 1753 and April 28, 1775.

GUTH, JOHANN JACOB (1)—Schopfloch, Oberamt Freudenstadt

Wf: ELISABETHA. Ch: (1) Adam, b. 8-13-1748. To "Pennsylvania," *ca.* 1750. // Several in Hinke, including JACOB GUTH, *Nancy*, September 16, 1751, Hinke, I, 462; and JACOB GUTH, with JOHAN MICHAEL and JOHAN GEORG GUTH, *Duke of Wirtenburg*, October 20, 1752, Hinke, I, 497.

GUTTBROD, JOERG PETER (1)—Nordheim

B. 4-15-1724, son of LUDWIG and BARBARA GUTTBROD.

GUTTBROD, JOHANNES (1)—Nordheim

B. 11-28-1701.

GUTTBROD, JOHANN LUDWIG (1)—Nordheim

B. 4-11-1698. // LUDWIG GOODBROD, *Samuel,* August 16, 1731, Hinke, I, 39-41; with him is BARBARY GOODBROD, over 16; and two children, GEORGE GOODBROD, and GEORGE GOODBROAD. Cf. 3PA, 24, 413, LUCAS GOODBREAD, 200 acres, Lancaster Co., Pa., survey January 15, 1736. 3PA, 24, 76; LUDOWYK GOODBREAD, 50 acres, Chester Co., Pa., survey February 3, 1738, Sower's newspaper, May 22, 1761, quoted in Hocker, 94: "LUDWIG GUTBROD, Codorus, York County; wife, ELISABETH."

GUTTBROD, PHILIPPUS (1)—Nordheim

B. 11-23-1726, son of LUDWIG and BARBARA GUTTBROD.

## H

HAAGA, HANS MARTIN (1)—Unterjesingen

Wf: CATHARINA. Ch: (1) Dorothea, b. 6-7-1745; (2) Magdalena, b. 4-17-1748; (3) Anna Maria, b. 7-1-1752. To "Pennsylvania."

HAASS, HANS JERG (1)—Alpirsbach

B. 5-5-1725, son of BARTHOLOMAEUS HAASS, day laborer [*Tagelöhner*], and wf. CHRISTINA. To the "New World." // Several listed in Hinke, 1749, 1752, 1753, and 1764. Cf. also *Philadelphische Correspondenz,* October 7, 1783, quoted in Hocker, 177, stating that FRIEDERICH DOERSCH and GEORG HAAS operate the post wagon between Phladelphia and Lancaster.

HABERER, JACOB FRIEDRICH (1)—Rötenberg

Joiner [*Schreiner*]. Wf: ANNA BARBARA. Ch: (1) Anna Maria, b. 10-8-1730; (2) Philipp, b. 4-6-1736, "went with his parents to America."

HAEBERLE, (SIMON?) (2)—Maichingen (1752)

Weaver and Ranger [*Weber u. Feldschütz*]. Ludwigsburg Protocol, 4-12-1752, *venia emigrandi.* // Others listed in Hinke.

HAGENLOCHER, JOSEPH BERNHARD (1)—Weil im Schönbuch (1754)

Cobbler [*sutor*]. Wf: MARIA CATHARINA née ROTENBACH. Ch: (1) Johann Georg, b. 1-30-1742; (2) Sibylla, b. 10-30-1743; (3) Margaretha, b. 3-1-1746; (4) Johann Stephen, b. 12-11-1748; (5) Ann Maria, b. 1-12-1753. Ludwigsburg Protocol, 1754.

HAHN, GEORG PHILIPP (1)—Nordheim

B. 4-16-1723, son of LUDWIG and ANNA BARBARA HAHN. // 3PA, 14, 594: PHILIP HAHN, Frankford and New Hanover Tps., Philadelphia Co., 1779; *ibid.,* 16, 8: New Hanover Tp., farmer, 1781. 3PA, 25, 166: PHILIP HAHN, 300 acres, Northumberland Co., Pa., survey November 28, 1774. Sower's newspaper, April 16, 1749, quoted in Hocker, 13: PHILIP HAHN, Falckner Swamp. *Staatsbote,* Phialdelphia, October 29,

1776, quoted in Hocker, 164: "PHILIP HAHN, New Hanover Tp., ad vertises that his German servant, PHILIP JUNG, ran away. He is middle aged and was born in the Palatinate."

## HAHN, SABINA (2)—Weissach (1751)

B. 4-26-1725, daughter of ISAAC and SABINA HAHN. Not in Marriage Record. Entire family missing from Communicant Register in 1751. Ludwigsburg Protocol, 4-20-1751, to "Nova Scotia" [*Neu Schottland*].

## HAIGESS, JERG (1)—Dürrwangen

Brother of Valentin Haigess, *supra*. B. 2-11-1727. "Said to live in the New World and have a wife and children." // JERG HEIGIS, with VALLENTIN HEYGIS, *Osgood*, September 29, 1750, Hinke, I, 446. 3PA, 21, 128: GEORGE HICKES, Huntington Tp., York Co., Pa., 1779. The following interesting *Taufschein*, framed, is part of the Pennsylvania German exhibit at the Phialdelphia Art Museum: "*Diese beyden Ehegatten als Georg Heigis und seine Ehe Frau Margaretha ist eine tochter zur Welt gebohren als Sabina ist gebohren im Jahr Christi* 1776 *den* 31. *July am* [—] *Uhr* [—] *im Zeichen d* [—] *Getauft durch Pfarrer* [*Lucas*] *Rauss. Taufzeugen Johannes Huber und seine Ehe Frau Gebohren im Staat Pensilvanien—Yorck Caunty in Monachen* [*Monoghan*] *Taunschip. Gott alleine die Ehre.*"

## HAIGESS, VALENTIN (1)—Dürrwangen (1750)

B. 3-21-1704. Wf: ANNA, *née* LUIPPOLD, b. 11-9-1705. Ch: (1) Johann Georg, b. 11-19-1736; (2) Anna Maria, b. 6-1-1740; (3) Johannes, b. 3-1-1748. "With wife and three children to the New World, 1750." //VALENTIN HEYGIS, with JERG HEIGIS, *Osgood*, September 29, 1750, Hinke, I, 446.

## HAILER, GEORG FRIEDRICH (1)—Bebenhausen

B. 8-28-1735, son of JOHANN GEORG HAILER, caterer [*Speissmeister*], and wife MARIA BARBARA. "Died at 74 as surgeon in Philadelphia, 24 Arch Street." // 3PA, 14, 523: FREDERICK HEILER, High Street Ward, City of Philadelphia, Pa., 1779. 3PA, 25, 164: FREDERICK HAILER, 300 acres, Northumberland Co., Pa., survey November 24, 1773; according to the PA, a FREDERICK HAILER later registered 300 acres in Northampton Co., Pa., 1786; 400 acres in Washington Co., Pa., 1784; and 800 acres in Luzerne Co., Pa., in 1792. Cf. *Philadelphische Correspondenz,* June 19, 1787, quoted in Hocker, 190: "DAVID HAILER, surgeon, Appletree alley, between Fourth and Fifth streets, near the old Lutheran Church, Philadelphia."

## HAILMANN, JOHANNES (1)—Nordheim (*ca.* 1733)

The following interesting reference in the Marriage Register relates how a Nordheimer, after twenty years' residence in Pennsylvania, gets a wife in the old home town: May 15, 1753, "JOHANNES HAILMANN, naturalized resident of 'Wiesentaunschöpp', near Philadelphia in Pennsylvania, a region belonging in America, married son of the late JOHANNES HAILMANN, former citizen here, who went to the above mentioned Pennsylvania with his family about twenty years ago [married] MARIA BARBARA, orphaned daughter of JOHANN MARTIN PLIENINGER, late citizen and vinedresser here." [*Johannes Hailmann, bürgerlicher nnwohner zu Wiesentaunschöpp, nacher Philadelphia in Pensylvanien, einer Landschaft in America gehörig, weyland Johannes Hailmanns ehemaligen Burgers allhier, so aber vor ohngefähr* 20 *Jahren mit seiner Familie in gedachtes Pensylv. gezogen, hinderlassener ehlicher Sohn mit Maria Barbara, Joh. Martin Plieningers sel., gewesenen Bürgers u. Weingärtners allhier, hinterbliebener ehelicher Tochter.*]. // JOHANNES HEYLMAN (HEILMANN), age 16, with MARTIEN HEYLMAN (MARTHIN HEILMANN), with BARNARD (BERNARD) WALTER of Nordheim, age 23, *Loyal Judith*, September 25, 1732, Hinke, I, 88, 90; list headed by Johannes Christian Schultz, Lutheran minister.

## HAISCH, HANS JERG (2)—Steinenbronn (1749)

Smith [*Schmied*]. B. 2-6-1718. Wf: CATHARINE HANSELMANN, b. 11-15-1721. Married 11-5-1743. "Went to America, 1749." // HANNS JERCH HAISCH, *Chesterfield*, September 2, 1749, Hinke, I, 394; with the Hanselmanns. 3PA, 17, 53: GEORGE HEISH, Conestoga Tp., Lancaster Co., Pa., 1771.

## HAIST, JOHANNA (1)—Göttelfingen

Daughter of the late JOHANN GEORGE HAIST, day laborer [*Taglöhner*], at Besenfeld. Ch: (1) Elisabetha, b. (illeg.) 11-7-1743. "This mother went to the New World with her daughter."

## HAMMER, JOHANN MELCHIOR, JR. (2)—Kuppingen (1751)

Baker [*Bäcker*] in Oberjesingen. B. 3-21-1716, son of the baker "*alt* MELCHIOR HAMMER" there. Wf: ELISABETHA (HAEMMERLIN), farmer's daughter [*Bauerntochter*] from Haslach. Ch: (1) Johann Melchior, b. 7-7-1739; (2) Balthass, b. 11-28-1740; (3) Hans Michael, b. 9-11-1742; (4) Maria Elisabetha, b. 2-16-1744; (5) Johann Caspar, b. 1-6-1746; (6) Maria Agnes, b. 11-15-1747. No members of this family in Baptismal or Confirmand Registers after 1751. Ludwigsburg Protocol, 4-6-1751, to "Pennsylvania." // MELCHER HAMMER, *Nancy*, September 16, 1751, Hinke, I, 463. Cf. Sower's newspaper, March 4, 1758, quoted in Hocker, 71, "JOHANN HAMMER, maltmaker, Cresheim, Germantown, Philadelphia." 3PA, 21, 69: BALTIS HAMMER, Menallen Tp., York Co., Pa., 1779. 3PA, 20, 236: CASPER HAMMER, West Pennsboro Tp., Cumberland Co., Pa., 1779. 3PA, 21, 607: CASPER HAMMER, Reading Tp., York Co., Pa., 1782. 3PA, 21, 587: BALSER HAMMER and CHRISTIAN HAMMER, Dover Tp., York Co., Pa., 1782.

## HANSELMANN, ANNA BARBARA (2)—Steinenbronn

B. 1717, orphan of the day laborer and cowherd [*Tägelohner u. Kuhhirt*] JACOB HANSELMANN, commonly called "HOHLEN". "Went to America", *ca.* 1754-1756.

## HANSELMANN, CATHARINA (2)—Steinenbronn

B. 1720, orphan of the day laborer and cowherd [*Tagelöhner u. Kuhhirt*] JACOB HANSELMANN, commonly called "HOHLEN." "Went to America," *ca.* 1754-1756.

## HANSELMANN, CHRISTINA (2)—Steinenbronn

B. 6-25-1723, orphan of the day laborer and cowherd [*Tagelöhner u. Kuhhirt*] JACOB HANSELMANN, commonly called "HOHLEN." "Went to America," *ca.* 1754-1756.

HANSELMANN, HANS JERG (2)—Steinenbronn (1749)

B. 10-4-1724, son of the carpenter [*Zimmermann*] JERG HANSELMANN, commonly called "MEILISJERG," and his first wf BARBARA (DAST). // HANS JERG HANSELMANN, *Chesterfield,* September 2, 1749, Hinke, I, 394. 3PA, 18, 122: GEORGE HANSELMAN, Douglass Tp., Berks Co., Pa., 1768. 3PA, 19, 117: GEORGE HANSELMAN, Lynn Tp., Northampton Co., Pa., 1785. 3PA, 19, 338: ANDREW and GEORGE HEINTZELMAN, Lynn Tp., Northampton Co., Pa., 1788.

HAUG, GEORG FRIEDRICH (2)—Beutelsbach (1750)

Vinedresser [*Weingärtner*]. B. 11-12-1711. Wf: ANNA SARA née NEGLE, b. 1715. Ch: (1) Catharina Magdalena, b. 1-26-1744; (2) Johann Friedrich, b. 11-16-1745; (3) Johann Georg, b. 11-16-1748. "To Pennsylvania, 5-4-1750," with wife and children. // GEORG FRIEDRICH HAUG, *Patience,* August 11, 1750, Hinke, I, 427.

HAUSCH, JOHANNES (1-2)—Reudern (1750)

Farrier [*Hufschmied*]. Wf (1st): AGATHA (MUELLER). Ch: (1) Hans Adam, b. 8-13-1730; (2) Maria Barbara, b. 12-13-1735; (3) Catharina, b. 11-2-1738, "went to Pennsylvania, 1750." No children of the second marriage listed in Baptismal Register. Because they were minors, these children were not permitted to take their property along; in 1751 they sent an attorney from Philadelphia to secure their property. Gerber is uncertain whether the father emigrated. See also the ducal letter of 1749 in our Introduction.

HAUSSMANN, DAVID (1)—Oberboihingen (1751)

Wf: ELISABETHA. Ch: (1) Johann Michael, b. 6-13-1745; (2) Margaretha, b. 11-13-1748. "Went 1751" to "Pennsylvania." // DAVID HAUSMANN, *Anderson,* September 27, 1752, Hinke, I, 488, with PHILIPP EULER of Oberboihingen. 3PA, 22, 625: MICHAEL HOUSEMAN, German Tp., Fayette Co., Pa., 1786.

HAUSSMANN, JOHANNES (1-2)—Reudern

Wf: MARGARETHA. Ch: (1) Johann Georg, b. 2-7-1748, "emigrated with his parents." To "Pennsylvania," ca. 1750. // JOHANNES HAUSMAN, with JOSEPH and PAULUS HAUSMAN and immediately following HANS JERG BOESMER of Reudern and JOHANN CHRISTOPH BESMER, Snow *Good Intent,* November 9, 1749, Hinke, I, 426. 3PA, 15, 264: JOHN HOUSEMAN, with JACOB HOUSEMAN, Southwark, City of Philadelphia, Pa., 1780. 3PA, 19, 326: JOHN HAUSMAN, "taylor," with JACOB HAUSMAN and FREDERICK HAUSMAN, Heidelberg Tp., Northampton Co., Pa., 1788.

HAUSSMANN, JACOB (2)—Reudern

See the ducal letter of 1749 in our Introduction.

HAYD, REGINA (2)—Grötzingen

Mentioned in the Nürtingen Documents as an orphan, 16 years old; missing in the Grötzingen Baptismal Register

HEER, ANNA (2)—Laufen/Eyach (1750)

B. 2-13-1713, daughter of LUDWIG and CATHARINE HEER. // Cf. Schultze, 25: "JACOB HERR, 1718-83, born at Laufen, Würtemberg, joined the [Moravian] Church at Herrnhaag and came to America in 1753; worker in the "Economy" for thirty years, lastly at the oil mill. Unmarried."

HEINTZELMANN, SIMON (1)—Lossburg

Wf: ANNA MARIA. Ch: (1) Catharina, b. 2-23-1746; (2) Anna Maria, b. 3-26-1748; (3) Lucia, b. 12-28-1749. To "Pennsylvania." // Others listed in Hinke and PA.

HEMMINGER, GEORG FRIEDRICH (2)—Neckartenzlingen (1753)

Son of the farmer [*Bauer*] CUNRAD HEMMINGER. Wf: ANNA MAGDALENA (SCHLOTTERBECK[ER] of Mittelstadt. Ch: (1) Agatha, b. 12-5-1745. Ludwigsburg Protocol, 4-6-1753, to "Pennsylvania." // JURG FRED'K HEMMINGER (GEORG FRIEDERICH HEMMINGER), *Richard and Mary*, September 17, 1753, Hinke, I, 532-533.

HEMMINGER, JOHANNES, JR. (2)—Neckartenzlingen (1749)

Farmer [*Bauer*]. Wf: MARGARETHA. Ch: (1) Johannes, b. 2-15-1728; (2) Georg Friedrich, b. 10-4-1731; (3) Sophia, b. 12-19-1742; (4) Andreas, b. 11-30-1747. // Cf. JOHANNES HEININGER and JACOB HEININGER, with HANS JERG KUNTZELMAN and MATHEAS PLENNINGER, both of Neckartenzlingen. Snow *Good Intent*, November 9, 1749, Hinke, I, 426. // 3 PA, *18*, 690: JOHN HEMMINGER, single, freeman, Brecknock Tp., Berks Co., Pa. 1784.

HENSINGER, HANS (2)—Dürrmenz (1753)

Wf (1st): DOROTHEA. Ch: (1) Dorothea, b. 12-25-1723.
Wf (2d): BARBARA. Ch: (2) Andreas, b. 4-21-1735. Ludwigsburg Protocol 3-23-1753, to "Pennsylvania." // JOHANNES HENSINGER (HANS HENSINGER, HENTZINGER), age 26, *Patience*, September 15, [17], 1753, Hinke, I, 526.

HENTZ, MICHAEL (2)—Machtolsheim

Farmer's son [*Bauernsohn*] from Gervelfingen. Wf: ANNA BARBARA (OERTLER), weaver's daughter [*Weberstochter*] from Bermaringen. Married 4-23-1753, with the foreknowledge of the Lord Dean, on the day after the marriage of their fellow-villager ANDREAS DOMINICK (q.v.). Of them the pastor wrote, "these people likewise made the resolution to go at once to the New World with others. Because there was no longer time for their banns to be proclaimed in the territory of Ulm, marriage was denied them. They came therefore to me, and asked me, in tears, to marry them." // Several in Hinke, earlier and later. 3PA, 21, 184: MICHAEL HENTZ, Manchester Tp., York Co., Pa., 1780.

HEPDING, HANS JACOB (1)—Rötenberg

Potter [*Hafner*]. Wf: JOHANNA *née* BENZ. Ch: (1) Christian, b. 3-30-1728. // CHRISTIAN HEBTING, *Duke of Wirtenburg*, October 20, 1752, Hinke, I, 498, immediately following Matthias Wesner of Rötenberg. 3PA, *17*, 549: CHRISTIAN HEPTING, Lebanon Tp., Lancaster Co., Pa., 1779. For the name, cf. also WIDOW HEFTIN, Cocalico Tp., Lancaster Co., Pa., 1782, in 3PA, 17, 869.

HEPDING, JOHANN ADAM (1)—Rötenberg (1749)

Day laborer [*Tagelöhner*]. Wf: CHRISTINA BARBARA *née* OSIANDER. Ch: (1) Catharina, b. 9-13-1739; (2) Johann Jacob, b. 4-28-1745; (3) Matthias, b. 5-29-1748. "This man went to Pennsylvania 1749, with wife and children."

HEPDING, JOHANN ADAM (1)—Rötenberg

B. 10-5-1730, son of JACOB HEPDING, day laborer [*Tagelöhner*], and wf. BARBARA *née* HABERER.

HERMANN, JACOB (2)—Scharnhausen

"In the poorhouse," at Scharnhausen. Emigrated, though Gerber is uncertain whether destination was America. // Many listed in Hinke.

HERMANN, JOHANNES (1)—Grötzingen

Wf: BARBARA. Ch: (1) Hans Jerg, b. 11-22-1741. "In Philadelphia."

HERMANN, JOHANNES (1)—Grötzingen (1747)

With wife. Ch: (1) Anna Maria; (2) Agnes Barbara. May 9, 1747, departed for Pennsylvania after taking private communion in the church; emigrating from Grötzingen with them were HANS JERG WALCKER (q.v.), ANNA CATHARINA SCHINDELBERGER (q.v.), ANNA CATHARINA WERNER (q.v.), CATHARINA MAYER (q.v.), and MICHAEL MAYER (q.v.). // Many listed in Hinke, including two in 1747; JOHANNES HERMANN, with MICHEL MEYER, *Restauration*, October 9, 1747, Hinke, I, 366; and JOHANNES HERMANN, with JOHANN FILB and GERG HERMAN(N), *Two Brothers*, October 13, 1747, Hinke, I, 367.

HERMANN, MICHAEL (1)—Oeschelbronn, Oberamt Herrenberg (p. 1746)

Cooper [*Kieffer*]. B. 4-4-1689. Wf: URSULA, *née* BUEHLER, of Bondorf. Ch: (1) Michael (q.v.), b. 12-1-1716. "Both (father and mother) went to America after 1746." Ludwigsburg Protocol, 1753, father and son.

HERMANN, MICHAEL, JR. (1)—Oeschelbronn, Oberamt Herrenberg (1753)

Cooper [*Küfer*]. B. 12-1-1716, son of MICHAEL and URSULA (BUEHLER) HERMANN. Wf: EVA CHRISTINE WALZ, schoolmaster's daughter [*Schulmeisterstochter*], b. 3-17-1717. Ch: (1) Michael, b. 8-11-1742; (2) Hans Jacob, b. 12-23-1743. "Went to America,"presumably with their children. Ludwigsburg Protocol, 1753, father and son. // JOHAN MICH'L HERMAN, *Richard and Mary*, September 30, 1754, Hinke, I, 605.

HERRMANN, JOHANN GEORG (1)—Grünwettersbach (1751)

Day laborer [*Tagelöhner*]. B. 5-30-1718, son of PHILIPP JACOB and ELISABETHA CATHARINA HERMANN. Wf: CHRISTINA *née* HAUG. Ch: (1) Elisabetha, b. 1-18-1745; (2) Philipp Jacob, b. 9-6-1747. Baptismal Certificate made for them, May 14, 1751, for "Pennsylvania." // JOHANN GEORG HERMAN, with HENRY HERMAN, *Phoenix*, August 28, 1750, Hinke, I, 440; others earlier and later.

HERRMANN, PHILIPP JACOB (1)—Grünwettersbach (1744)

Farmhand [*Bauersmann*]. Wf: SYBILLA CATHARINE *née* KULLIN. Ch: (1) Maria Magdalena, b. 3-2-1741, "went to Pennsylvania with her parents in 1744, and is said to have died on the way." // Many listed in Hinke, of which the nearest in time is JACOB HERMANN, *Edinburgh*, September 5, 1748, Hinke I, 372; others earlier and later.

HERWICK, JACOB, JR. (2)—Gerlingen (1750)

Ludwigsburg Protocol, 4-7-1750, and 4-30-1750, urgently demanded "traveling expenses [*Reisegeld*] for his three stepchildren, who wanted to go with him to Pennsylvania; however, despite this reference, Herwick appears after 1750 in the Church Register. // Others listed in Hinke. 3PA, *13*, 24: JACOB HERWICK and JACOB HERWICK, JR., Millford Tp., Bucks Co., Pa., 1779. 3PA, 20, 134-5. JACOB HERWICK, clockmaker, and ANTHONY HERWICK, baker, Carlisle, Cumberland Co., Pa., 1779. 3PA, *20*, 598: JACOB HERWICK, Lurgan Tp., Cumberland Co., Pa., 1782. Cf. also the will of JOHN HERWICK, of Bucks Co., Pa., dated 1753, probated 1761, mentioning son JACOB; Bucks County Will Book *M*, 164.

HESS, JOHANN MICHAEL (1)—Grötzingen

Wf: BARBARA. Ch: (1) Michael, b. 9-10-1741. "In Philadelphia." // Many by this name in PA.

HETZEL, CHRISTIAN (1)—Bodelshausen (1766)

Wf (1st): MAGDALENA. Ch: (1) Johann Bernhard, b. 9-25-1759; (2) Agnes, b. 11-6-1760. Wf (2d): ANNA BARBARA *née* SCHLOT[TE]RER, baker's daughter [*Beckstochter*], b. 7-25-1734. Ch: (3) Anna Barbara, b. 5-17-1765. "To America, June 3, 1766." // 3PA, *14*, 583: CHRISTIAN HETZEL, Douglass Tp., Philadelphia Co., Pa., 1779. 3PA, *16*, 164: CHRISTIAN HETZEL, Frederick Tp., Philadelphia Co., Pa., 1782.

HEUSSLER, CHRISTIAN (2)—Niederhofen (1750)

Son of PETER HEUSSLER. Wf: EVA ELISABETHA. Ch: (1) Maria Elisabetha, b. 11-5-1728, married 4-21-1750, HANS GEORG KNOEDLER (q.v.); (2) Margaretha, b. 7-9-1730; (3) Eberhardina, b. 7-6-1734; (4) Christian, b. 5-15-1738; (5) Christina, b. 11-4-1745; (6) four or five others, died young. Ludwigsburg Protocol, 5-22-1750, to "America." According to further researches by Pastor Schnabel of Niederhofen, CHRISTIAN HEUSSLER came as a child to Niederhofen, with parents and sister, lost his father early and married out of the village. From the beginning of the Communicant Register in 1732 until Pentecost of 1750 he, with his wife, and partly also with his children, was regularly communicant three times yearly; then the family disappears from the Church Register. // CHRISTIAN HEUSLER, with HANS JERG GNOEDLER, *Osgood*, September 29, 1750, Hinke, I, 446; a fellow-passenger was Gottlieb Mittelberger. 3PA, *18*, 315; CHRISTIAN HEISLER, Albany Tp., Berks Co., Pa., 1780. *Philadelphische Correspondenz*, July 3, 1799, quoted in Hocker, 211: "CHRISTOPH HEISZLER, butcher, five miles from Reading, fell from his horse on June 21 and was killed."

HEYLMANN, HANS MICHAEL (1)—Nordheim

B. 2-27-1716, son of Johannes Heylmann.

HEYLMANN, JOHANNES (1)—Nordheim

B. 3-3-1688, son of HANS MARTIN HEYLMANN. // JOHANNES HEILLMANN, *Patience*, September 19, 1749, Hinke, I, 409.

HIEBER, GEORGE MICHAEL (1)—Rommelshausen (1769)

B. 2-13-1741. "Went to America as journeyman tailor, 1769." // MICHAEL HIEBER, *Minerva*, December 12, 1768, Hinke, I, 722. Cf. also 3PA, *19*, 89: GEORGE HIEBHER, Lower Saucon Tp., Northampton Co., Pa., 1785.

HILDENBRAND, ANDREAS (1)—Nordheim

B. 11-27-1710, son of ANDREAS and DOROTHEA HILDENBRAND. Wf: ANNA MAGDALENA *née* WAGNER. Ch: (1) Catharina, b. 4-6-1746. // ANDREAS HILDENBRANDT, *Phoenix*, September 25, 1751, Hinke, I, 470.

HINDERMANN, MARTIN (2)—Hirschlanden (1753)

Vinedresser [*Weingärtner*]. B. 8-16-1700, son of the farmer [*Bauer*] JOHANN GEORG HINDERMANN. Wf: (1st): ANNA BARBARA (KRAEMER), daughter of the justiciary [*Gerichtsverwalter*], d. 1750. Ch: (1) Anna Catharina, b. 11-27-1725, wf. of JOHANN GEORG SANTER (q.v.); (2) Johann Georg, did not emigrate; (3) Maria Barbara, did not emigrate, had a child 5-26-1755, by which is mentioned that she is the married daughter of MARTIN HINDERMANN, left here when he went to Pennsylvania in 1753. Wf (2d): CHRISTINA. Ch: (4) died. Ludwigsburg Protocol, 5-4-1753, HINDERMANN and SANTER, to "Pennsylvania." // HINDERMANN may have died at sea, since he is not listed with SANTER in Hinke.

HIRSCH, MARTIN (1)—Täbingen (1749)

B. 8-16-1715. To "New England", April 16, 1749. // MARTIN HIRSCH, CHRISTIAN, September 13, 1749, Hinke, I, 400. 3PA, *19*, 20: MARTIN HARSH, laborer, Allen Tp., Northampton Co., Pa., 1772.

HOCH, HANS (JOHANN) JERG (GEORG) (1)—Weil im Schönbuch

Weaver, also farmer [*Weber, auch Bauer*] at Breitenstein. Wf: CHRISTINA (LOEFFLER). Ch: (1) Johann Martin, b. 6-28-1743; (2) Maria Magdalena, b. 6-5-1749; (3) Johannes, b. 5-10-1751; (4) Christina, b. 1-12-1754. // Several listed in Hinke. 3PA, *17*, 480: MARTAIN HOE, GEORGE HOE and GEORGE HOAK, Cocalico Tp., Lancaster Co., Pa., 1773; other George Hochs and Highs in PA.

HOEFELBAUER, JOERG BALTHAS (1)—Nordheim

B. 9-27-1724, son of HANS JACOB and CATHARINA HOEFELBAUER. // YERICK BALTUS HEIFELBOWER (GEORG BALTHAS HOEFFELBAUER), age 24, *Patience*, September 16, 1748, Hinke, I, 383, with PHILIPP HOEFFELBAUER.

HOEFELBAUER, PHILIPP JACOB (1)—Nordheim (1748)

Carpenter [*Zimmermann*]. B. 9-23-1718, son of HANS JACOB and CATHARINA HOEFELBAUER. Brother of JOERG BALTHAS HOEFELBAUER q.v.) Wf: [ ? ] (WEBER). Ludwigsburg Protocol, 1748. // PHILIP HEFELBOWER (PHILIPP HOEFFELBAUER), age 30, *Patience*, September 16, 1748, Hinke, I, 383, with GEORGE BALTHAS HOEFFELBAUER. PHILIP and BARBARA HEFELBAUER, daughter CHRISTINA, born November 10, 1748, baptized December 1, 1748, sponsor PHILIP MUNZER': wife. *Records of the Augustus Lutheran Church, Trappe, Pa.*, 57, GSP.

HOERLIN (HAERLIN) JOHANNES (2)—Schönaich (1751)

Listed in Communicant Register, later disappearing without indicating destination. Ludwigsburg Protocol, 6-18-1751, [—] HAERLIN. // JOHANNES HELEREN (HERLEIN), age 30, *Brothers*, September 26, 1753, Hinke, I, 551, 553. 3PA, *12*, 172: JNO. HARLIN, Pikeland Tp., Chester Co., Pa., 1779, which may, however, be the English Quaker family of Harlan.

HOEROLD, GEORG CHRISTOPH (1) — Steinheim an der Murr.

Vinedresser [*vinitor*]. Wf: MARIA CHRISTINA. Ch: (1) Maria Margaretha, b. 7-28-1721; (2) Georg Christoff, b. 10-22-1723; (3) Anna Maria, b. 3-22-1726; (4) Johann Georg, b. 8-18-1728; (5) Regina Catharina, b. 6-19-1734. All children: "with parents to the New World." // CHRISTAF HERALDE (GEORG CHRISTOPH HEROLDT), with JOHAN EARAH HERALD, *Rosannah*, September 26, 1743, Hinke, I, 343, 345. 3PA, *18*, 21: CHRISTOPHER HEROLD, Bethel Tp., Berks Co., Pa., 1767. 3PA, *18*, 49: GEORGE HEROLD, Heidelberg Tp., Berks Co., Pa., 1767. 3PA, *24*, 436: GEORGE HEROLD, 100 acres, Lancaster Co., Pa., survey August 16, 1751. 3PA, *25* 165ff: GEORGE HERROLD, land in Northumberland Co., Pa., surveyed 1772, 1774. 3PA, *19*, 451: GEORGE HEROLD, Penns Tp., Northumberland Co., Pa., 1781. 3PA, *22*, 404: CHRISTOPHER HARDLD, SR. and JR., PETER HAROLD and JOHN HAROLD, Hempfield Tp., Westmoreland Co., Pa., 1783.

According to the researches of Dr. Charles A. Fisher of Selinsgrove, Pa., historian of the Herrold Family (see THE SNYDER COUNTY PIONEERS, [Selinsgrove, Pennsylvania, 1938] pp. 39-40), GEORGE CHRISTOPHER HERROLD, was born 1688, and settled, with wife MARIA CATHARINA, and sons, in Heidelberg Township, then Lancaster County, Pa., near Stouchburg, in the present county of Berks, where he died *ca.* October 27, 1749, and is buried in the old Tulpehocken Lutheran Cemetery near Stouchsburg. The eldest son, GEORGE CHRISTOPHER HERROLD, JR., moved to the present Bethel Tp., Berks County, shortly after 1750, where he resided until 1770-1771, when he removed to Hempfield Township, Westmoreland County, where he died in 1787. JOHN GEORGE HERROLD moved to what is now Snyder County, where he was assessed as a resident of Penn Township as early as 1771; he died in Union Township, Snyder County, in 1803.

HOESS, JOHANN MARTIN (1)—Grötzingen (1754)

Weaver [*Weber*]. Wf: ANNA BARBARA. Ch: (1) Johann Georg, b. 12-5-1749; (2) Anna Catharina, b. 1-27-1751. To "Pennsylvania." // Cf. JOHANN MARTIN HESS, *Chance*, August 8, 1764, Hinke, I, 688.

HOERZ, HANS GEORG (1)......Plattenhardt

Journeyman mason [*Maurergeselle*]. Wf: ANNA. Ch: (1) Agnes, b. 3-27-1752.

HOFELIN, JOHANN PETER (1)—Stainheim am Albach

Lawyer [*Anwalt*]. Wf: ANNA CATHARINA *née* STAUDENMAYER. Ch: (1) Johann Jacob, b. 2-6-1739. To "America." // Cf. JOHANN JACOB HOFELEN, *Polly*, August 24, 1765, Hinke, I, 704.

HOFFSAESS, ANNA MARIA (1)—Grötzingen (1748)

Left for Pennsylvania, May 15, 1748, after private communion, along with JOHANNES GENTNER (q.v.), MICHAEL MUELLER (q.v.), JACOB MUELLER (q.v.), and MARGARETHA MUELLER (q.v.).

HOFFSAESS, MARGARETHA (1)—Grötzingen (1748)

Left for Pennsylvania, May 15, 1748, after private communion, along with JOHANNES GENTNER (q.v.), MICHAEL MUELLER (q.v.), JACOB MUELLER (q.v.), and MARGARETHA MUELLER (q.v.). // Sower's newspaper, January 16, 1750, quoted in Hocker, 17: "MARGRETHA HOFFSESSIN, who recently arrived in this country and is now at Oley with ANTONI JAEGER, seeks her daughter, MARIA HOFFSESSIN."

## HOFSAESS, HANS JERG (1)—Grötzingen (1749)

To "Pennsylvania," May 1, *1749*, with wife. // 3PA, *14*, 356: GEORGE HOFFSESS, Lower Merion Tp., Philadelphia Co., Pa., 1774.

## HOL(T)ZHAEUSER (HOLTZHAUSER), JOHANN MARTIN (1)—Merklingen

Mason [*Maurer*]. Wf: CATHARINA DOROTHEA *née* RAETZLER (RETZLER.) Ch: (1) Juliana Elisabetha, b. 7-12-1745; (2) Johann Martin, b. 1-7-1747; (3) Johann Christoph, b. 1-31-1749. Emigrated in the early 1750's. // MARTIN HOLTZHAEUSSER, *Richard and Mary*, September 26, 1752, Hinke, I, 488. 3PA, *26*, 92: CHRISTOPHER HOLSHISER, 800 acres, Northampton Co., Pa., survey January 13, 1786.

## HOOCK, CATHARINA DOROTHEA (1)—Merklingen

B. 6-20-1730, daughter of JACOB HOOCK, tailor [*Schneider*] and wife ANNA MARIA *née* SCHINDLER.

## HOPPACHER, ADAM (2)—Grosssachsenheim (1753)

"Beadle" [*Bettelvogt*]. B. 3-23-1700. Wf: ANNA BARBARA (MERKLIN), b. 11-6-1698. Married, 11-24-1723, after previously undergoing legal punishment for fornication. Ch: (1) Hans Michael, b. 1-10-1726; (2) Adam Friedrich, b. 3-24-*1741;* (3) three other children, and the wife, died before emigration. Ludwigsburg Protocol, 5-15-1753, asks for permission to go to "Pennsylvania" as well as for the transfer of his property. // ADAM HOBACH (HOPPACHER), with JOHANN MICHAEL HOBBACHER, *Windsor*, September 26, 1753, Hinke, I, 556-7. Others in PA: Hoffacher, Hofecker, Hobacker, Hapicker, Habecker, Habacker. Perhaps the sons can be identified with 3PA, *14*, 741: MICHAEL HOFFACRE, Whitpain Tp., Philadelphia Co., Pa., 1779; 3PA, *21*, 22: MICHAEL HOFFACHER, Manheim Tp., York Co., Pa., 1779; and 3PA, *14*, 596: FREDERICK HABACKER, Germantown, Philadelphia Co., Pa., 1779.

## HOPFF, JOHANNES (2)—Weissach (1751)

Cooper [*Küfer*]. Son of CHRISTOPH HOPFF in Eltingen. Wf: MARGARETHA WENDEL, daughter of the late SAMUEL WENDEL, farmer [*rusticus*]. Married 10-19-1745. Not in Communicant Register 1751. Ludwigsburg Protocol, 4-16-1751, *venia emigrandi* only. // JOHANNES HOPFF, *Nancy*, September 16, 1751, Hinke, I, 462; more probably JOHANNES HOPF, with JOHAN CASPAR HOPF, also JOH. DUETT of Weissach, *Eastern Branch*, October 3, 1753, Hinke, I, 585-6. 3PA, *26*, 270 and 272: JOHN HOPFF, two tracts of land, Berks Co., Pa., survey 1759 and 1776. 3PA, *18*, 420, JNO. HOPH, Tulpehocken Tp., Berks Co., Pa., 1780. MARGARET HOPF, of Reading, Berks Co., Pa., March 30, 1773, administration of estate to JOHN HOPF, only brother and next of kin, *Berks County Will Abstracts*, I, 176, GSP. JOHANNES HOPFF, witness to will of JOHN GEORGE GRUCKER, of Tulpehocken, dated and probated 1775, *Ibid.*, I, 201, GSP.

## HORLACHER, JOHANN DAVID (1)—Aich

B. 2-1-1733, son of "Mr." [*Herr*] JOHANNES HORLACHER, schoolmaster [*Schulmeister*] and wf ELISABETHA. "Died in Pennsylvania." // JOHAN DAVID HORLACHER, *Anderson*, September 27, 1752, Hinke, I, 489. Others listed in PA.

HOSS, JOHANN (1)—Neuffen

Tailor [*Schneider*]. Wf: AGNES CATHARINA. Ch: (1) Maria Jacobina, b. 3-20-1750. // JOHANNES HUSS, *Forest*, October 10, 1752, Hinke, I, 495. 3PA, *11*, 34: JOHANNES HUSS, inmate, West Nottingham Tp., Chester Co., Pa., 1765. 3PA, *17*, 109: JNO. HUSE, Lampeter Tp., Lancaster Co., Pa., 1771. 3PA, *21*, 60: JOHN HOSS, Dover Tp., York Co., Pa., 1779.

HUEBER, ABRAHAM (1)—Täbingen (1749)

Schoolmaster's son [*Schulmeisterssohn*]. B. 1-20-1711. Wf: CHRISTINA, *née* SPRINGER, glazier's daughter [*Glaserstocher*] of Ostdorf. Ch: (1) Abraham, b. 9-4-1744. To "New England", April 15, 1749. Wife died in New England in the same year. // Many listed in PA.

HUEBER, JOHANN (1)—Eberstadt

Smith's apprentice [*Schmiedknecht*]. Father of an illegitimate child, b. 11-11-1749. (Evidently from Gellmersbach.) "Went to America." [*obiit (abiit?) in Americam*].

HUEBER, JOHANN JACOB (1)—Magstadt

B. 4-26-1731. "Went to Pennsylvania."
// JACOB HUEBER, *Phoenix*, September 15, 1749, Hinke, I, 406.

HUERN, JOHANN GEORG (2)—Grossaspach (1753?)

Wf: ANNA MARIA. Ch: Anna Maria, b. 6-5-1749; (2) Catharina, b. 6-14-1750. No further entries. Ludwigsburg Protocol, 5-8-1753, [—] Hürn, to take his marital possessions along to New England. // GEORG HORN, *Neptune*, September 24, 1753, Hnke, I, 541; others earlier and later. Several Herns listed in PA.

HUMMEL, JOHANNES (1)—Ebingen

Joiner [*Schreiner*]. Wf: ANNA BARBARA, *née* BINDER. Ch: (1) Anna Barbara, b. 11-19-1740. To "Pennsylvania." // Two listed in Hinke: JOHANNES HUMMEL, *Ann Galley*, September 27, 1746, Hinke, I, 360; and JOHANNIS HUMMEL, *Ann*, September 28, 1749, Hinke, I, 417, along with Hans Rudolf Kittweiler, Reformed preacher. 3PA, *18*, 239: JOHN HUMMEL, laborer, with ANDREW HUMMEL, laborer, and MARTINE HUMMEL, Greenwich Tp., Berks Co., Pa., 1779. 3PA, *26*, 273: JOHN HUMMEL, several tracts of land in Berks Co., Pa., survey 1785 and 1786.

# I

ISCHLER, LUDWIG (2)—Niederhofen (1765)

Son of FRIEDRICH ISCHLER at Mühlbach. Wf: APOLLONIA HOLL of Riechen. Married 5-13-1765. "Left for America immediately after marriage." // LUDWIG ISCHLER, *Myrtilla*, September 21, 1765, Hinke, I, 708. 3PA, *17*, 414: LODWICK ESHLER, (sp. Ishler, 1779, p. 549) Lebanon Tp., Lancaster Co., Pa., 1773.

# J

## JAECKLE, CHRISTOPH (1)—Grötzingen (1749)

Barber [*Barbierer*]. To "Pennsylvania," May 1, 1749, with others from Grötzingen. // 3PA, *14,* 60: CHRISTOPHER YEAKLE, Upper Hanover Tp., Philadelphia Co., Pa., 1769. 3PA, *15,* 548: CHRISTOPHER YEAKLE'S estate, Springfield Tp., Philadelphia Co., Pa., 1780.

## JENSEL, FRIEDRICH (1)—Lomersheim

Wf: ANNA. Ch: (1) Regina, b. 10-28-1742; (2) Maria Catharina, b. 8-30-1744; (3) Johann Martin, b. 11-11-1746. To "Pennsylvania." Arrived in Philadelphia, September 17, 1753.

// FRED'K GINSEL (FRIEDERICH JENSEL), age 28, *Patience,* September 15 [17], 1753, Hinke, I, 526, 528. 3PA, *17,* 143: FRED'K YENSEL, Lebanon Tp., Lancaster Co., Pa., 1771. 3PA, *17,* 796: FREDERICK JENSEL, with MARTIN JENSEL, Lebanon Tp., Lancaster Co., Pa., 1782.

## JENSEL, MICHAEL (1)—Lomersheim

Farmer [*Bauer*]. Wf: BARBARA. Ch: (1) Maria Barbara, b. 11-21-1748. To "Pennsylvania." // MICHAEL JENSEL, *Nancy,* August 31, 1750, Hinke, I, 442. 3PA, *17,* 194: MICHAEL YENSEL, Upper Paxton Tp., Lancaster Co., Pa., 1772.

## JETTER, JOHANN (2)—Lauffen/Eyach (1748)

Wf: CATHARINA. Ch: (1) Christoph, b. 8-23-1743; (2) Andreas, b. 4-4-1746. To "Pennsylvania," 1748. // Two Johannes Yetters listed in Hinke, one 1747 (I, 365), the other 1753 (I, 551-2). Many JOHN YETTERS listed in PA.

## JOOS, JOHANN MELCHER (1)—Steinheim an der Murr (1749)

B. 12-19-1727, son of AEGIDIUS JOOS, vinedresser [*Vinitor*], and wf. (ANNA) MARIA.

## JOOS, SAMUEL (1)—Steinheim an der Murr (1749)

B. 2-12-1725, son of AEGIDIUS JOOS, vinedresser [*Vinitor*], and wf. (ANNA) MARIA. To "America," 1749.

## JUNG, MICHAEL (2)—Neckartenzlingen (1749)

Cowherd and shepherd [*Kuhhirt u. Schäfer*]. Wf: CATHARINA. Ch: died. // Rupp 144: MICHAEL JUNG, given as HUG in Hinke, I, 426, Snow *Good Intent,* November 9, 1749, with CONZELMAN, PLIENINGER and REINOEHL, all of Neckartenzlingen. If not this, perhaps MICHAEL JUNGE, with JOHANN DAVID and PETER JUNGE, *Patience,* August 11, 1750, Hinke, I, 426; others listed earlier and later. Many listed in PA.

## JUENGLING, [JACOB ?] (2)—Rutesheim (1751)

Ludwigsburg Protocol, 4-30-1751, mentions two children of ESAIAS JUENGLING. These are not indicated in the Church Register, but // JACOB JUENGLING arrived on the *Duke of Wirtenberg,* October 16, 1751, with MARTIN EBBLY of Rutesheim, Hinke, I, 476.

# K

## KAERCHER, ELISABETHA (2)—Rutesheim (1752)

B. 3-29-1723. "Said to have emigrated to the New World or America and died there." Ludwigsburg Protocol, 4-4-1752, *venia emigrandi.* // Others listed in Hinke.

## KAITER, MICHAEL (1)—Pfaffenhofen (1753)

Wf: CATHARINA BARBARA. "Went to America, 1753" [*1753 Amer. petiit*] // MICHEL LUDWIG KEYDER (MICHEL LUDWIG KEITTER), *Eastern Branch,* October 3, 1753, Hinke, I, 585-6. Others listed in PA.

## KARG, JOSEPH (1)—Grünwettersbach

Mason [*Maurer*]. Wf: MARGARETHA. Ch: (1) Georg Jacob, b. 11-18-1735; (2) Georg Adam, b. 9-20-1737; (3) Johann Andreas, b. 3-2-1744. All: "Baptismal Certificate prepared May 17, 1751, for Pennsylvania." // JOSEPH KARG, with JACOB KARG, *Duke of Wirtenberg,* October 16, 1751, Hinke, I, 477. 3PA, *17,* 126: JNO. and JACOB KARG, Warwick Tp., Lancaster Co., Pa., 1771. 3PA, 21, 789: *Andrew Karg,* Manheim Tp., York Co., Pa., 1783.

## KATZ, MARTIN (1)—Renfrizhausen (1762)

Wf: BARBARA *née* ROMMANN. Ch: (1) Johann Jacob, b. 1-17-1748. "These people went to Pennsylvania in 1762."
// Others listed in Hinke and PA.

## KAYSER, JOHANN ULRICH (2)—Bolheim (1752)

Day laborer [*Tagelöhner*] from Niederstotzingen. Wf: ANNA CATHARINA (FRECH). Ch: (1) Elisabetha, b. 2-7-1742. (2) Anna Catharina, b. 12-14-1745; (3) Anna Margaretha, b. 4-12-1747; (4) Anna Maria, b. 5-14-1748; (5) Maria, b. 12-5-1750. Name no longer found in the village. Ludwigsburg Protocol, 5-9-1752, to the "West Indies" [*West Indien*]. // Other ULRICH KEYSERS listed in Hinke, one 1731, another 1771. 3PA, *17,* 507: ULRICH KEYSER, inmate, Warwick Tp., Lancaster Co., Pa., 1779. 3PA, 17, 789: ULRICH KISER, Manheim Town, Lancaster Co., Pa., 1782.

## KECK, ANNA BARBARA (1)—Oberiflingen

B. 2-17-1726, daughter of ANDREAS KECK. To the "New World." // 3PA, *19,* 109: JOHN and ANDREW KECK, Salisbury Tp., Northampton Co., Pa., 1785.

## KEMMLER, ANNA MARIA (1)—Mähringen (1754)

Probably b. 6-26-1740, daughter of HANS JERG and CATHARINA KEMMLER. Ludwigsburg Protocol, 4-30-1754, *venia emigrandi.* // Others listed in Hinke.

## KERN, GEORG ADAM (2)—Siglingen (1752)

Ludwigsburg Protocol, 4-21-1752, to "Pennsylvania." Emigrated with wife. // GEORG ADAM KERN, *Rawley,* October 23, 1752, Hinke, I, 500, with FREDERICK KERN and John George Bager, Lutheran pastor. 3PA, *13,* 78: ADAM KERN, and PETER KERN's estate, Rockhill Tp., Bucks Co., Pa., 1779.

KERN, MATTHIAS (2)—Siglingen (1752)

Ch: (1) Georg; (2) Friedrich; (3) Michel. Ludwigsburg Protocol, 4-21-1752, to "Pennsylvania." Emigrated with wife. // MATH'S KERN, with JACOB KERN, *Edinburgh*, September 30, 1754, Hinke, I, 614; two others, 1747, and 1751. According to Dr. Charles A. Fisher's *The Snyder County Pioneers*, pp. 46-47, MATTHIAS KERN, Sr. and Jr., removed from Upper Milford Tp., Northampton Co., Pa., to what is now Snyder Co., Pa., *ca.* 1789. MATHIAS KERN is assessed in Penn Tp., Northumberland (now Snyder) Co., Pa., in 1790. 3PA, *14*, 49: MATTHIAS KERN, Frederick Tp., Philadelphia Co., Pa., 1769. 3PA, *19*, 9: MATHIAS KERN, farmer, Upper Milford Tp., Northampton Co., Pa., 1772. 3PA, *22*, 446: MATTHIAS and WILLIAM KERN, Donegal Tp., Westmoreland Co., Pa., 1783.

KICHERER, HANS JERG (1)—Unterlenningen

Wf: ELISABETHA CATHARINA. Ch: (1) Hans Jerg, b. 12-11-1729, went with his parents to the New Land." // Others listed in Hinke.

KIELMANN, PHILIPP (2)—Steinenbronn (1754)

B. 6-8-1715. Wf: ANNA MARIA *née* MAYER, b. 3-9-1715. Ch: (1) Jacob Friedrich, b. 4-7-1747; (2) Christina, b. 6-15-1748; (3) Johannes, b. 11-21-1749. "Went to America 1754 with wife and children."
// Several Philip Coleman's in PA.

KIEMLIN, JOHANNES (1) — Bechingen, Oberamt Ludwigsburg (1763)

B. 7-12-1747, son of JOHANN JACOB, tailor [*Schneider*], and wf. MARGARETHA *née* FRIZ. "To Pennsylvania to his father's brother's, 1763." // 3PA, *24*, 241: JOHN KEEMELE, 100 acres, Luzerne County, Pa., survey Aug. 17, 1793.

KIENLE, JACOB (1)—Döffingen (1750)

Toolmaker [*Zeugmacher*]. B. 4-16-1718. "To Pennsylvania with wife and children (?) 1750. Died there before 1765 without heirs."
// Others in Hinke.

KIENLE, MICHAEL (1)—Döffingen (1750)

Brother of JACOB, *supra*. B. 5-3-1708. Wf: CATHARINA *née* ROHRER. Ch: (1) Anna Margaretha, b. 8-25-1737; (2) Maria Catharina, b. 11-16-1738; (3) Anna Maria, b. 8-30-1740; (4) Johannes, b. 11-2-1743; (5) Sabina, b. 2-16-1746. "Left with [his brother]." // Others in Hinke. 3PA, *18*, 219: JOHN CENLY, "taylor," Exeter Tp., Berks Co., Pa., 1779. 3PA, *26*, 253: JOHN CINLEY, 50 acres, Berks Co., Pa., survey, April 29, 1788.

KIMMICH, JOHANNES (2)—Altdorf (Nürtingen) (1754)

B. 6-6-1717, son of CASPAR KIMMICH. Wf: ANNA MARIA (KUEHNER), weaver's daughter [*Weberstochter*], b. 7-20-1716. Ch: (1) Jacob, b. 12-9-1748. "To Pennsylvania 1754."

KIMMICH, MATTHIAS (MATTHAEUS) (2)—Altdorf (Nürtingen) (1754)

B. 8-30-1696, son of CASPAR KIMMICH. Wf: ANNA CATHARINA *née* (THUMM), b. 2-23-1706. Ch: (1) Matthäus, b. 3-20-1730; (2) Anna,

b. 9-23-1732; (3) Hans Jerg, b. 2-4-1735; (4) Anna Catharina, b. 3-27-1738; (5) Johann Martin, b. 3-13-1741; (6) Anna Maria, b. 6-9-1744. "To Pennsylvania 1754."

KINCKHELE (KUENKELE), DANIEL (2)—Grötzingen (1746)

Son of the late baker [*Bäcker*] CASPAR KINCKHELE. Left Friday, March 25, 1746. Brother-in-law of HANS JERG DANNENHAUER (q.v.). According to a report on the emigrants of 1746, forwarded March 27, 1746, by Mayor MATTHESS DAMMEL of Grötzingen to the authorities at Nürtingen, "The said DANNENHOWER and his brother-in-law DANIEL KINCKHELE for these reasons remained here longer, because they, on account of their poverty, appealed for and solicited traveling expenses from some good-hearted people." For complete text, see Introduction.

KIRCHNER, AGNES CATHARINA (2)—Neuffen (1752)

B. 8-17-1738. Daughter of the vinedresser [*Weingärtner*] JOHANNES KIRCHNER and wf. AGNES CATHARINA. "Confirmed, by dispensation of the Consistory, on account of her intended journey to Pennsylvania with her parents." Came to America with parents and CHRISTOPH HEINRICH PLETZGER (q.v.). *Ludwigsburg Protocol*, 4-11-1752, Pletzger and associates, *venia emigrandi.*

KIRCHNER, JOHANNES (2)—Neuffen (1752)

Vinedresser [*Weingärtner*]. Wf: AGNES CATHARINA. Ch: (1) Agnes Catharina (q.v.), b. 8-17-1738. "To Pennsylvania 1752, with daughter, in the company of CHRISTOPH HENRICH PLETZGER (q.v.), *Ludwigsburg Protocol*, 4-11-1752, Pletzger and associates, *venia emigrandi.* // One in Hinke, earlier; others in PA.

KITTEL, HANS JERG (1)—Unterjesingen (1754)

Smith [*Schmied*]. Wf: BARBARA. Ch: (1) Rosina Magdalena, b. 12-8-1745; (2) Maria Barbara, b. 4-2-1749. *Ludwigsburg Protocol*, 1754. "To Pennsylvania." // 3PA, *16*, 70: GEORGE KITTLE, laborer, Northern Liberties (West Part), Philadelphia Co., Pa., 1781.

KLAIS, JOHANN (1)—Schopfloch (Oberamt Freudenstadt)

Wf: CATHARINA. Ch: (1) Friedrich, b. 3-22-1751. "To Pennsylvania," *ca.* 1750 ff.

KLEIN, JOHANN JACOB (1)—Schlaitdorf

Butcher [*Metzger*]. Wf: ANNA MARIA, *née* RUCKABER. Ch: (1) Johann Jacob, b. 11-5-1755. "Died in Pennsylvania," // Several in Hinke; several in PA.

KLEIN, MICHAEL (1)—Schlaitdorf

Farmer [*Bauer*]. Wf: GERTRUDIS. Ch: (1) Regina Barbara, b. 12-3-1746. // Several others listed in Hinke; perhaps MICHAEL KLEIN, immediately following JOHANNES SPEYER of Schlaitdorf, *Peggy*, October 16, 1754, Hinke, I, 637, 639.

KLETT, HANS JACOB (2)—Dusslingen (see Mähringen) (1751)

*Ludwigsburg Protocol*, 5-4-1751, to "America." // HANS JACOB KLETT, heading list, with HANS LUDWIG NONNENMACHER (q.v.) of Mähringen, *Nancy*, September 16, 1751, Hinke, I, 462.

KLINCK, JOHANN JACOB (1)—Plattenhardt (1754)

Carpenter [*Zimmermann*]. Wf: MARGARETHA, *née* FICHTER, of Plieningen. Ch: (1) Johann Michael, b. 8-15-1748; (2) Johann Friedrich, b. 2-18-1752; (3) Georg Ludwig, b. 5-25-1754. *Ludwigsburg Protocol*, 1754, asks for permission to use children's property for traveling expenses. "To Pennsylvania!" // Cf. MICHAEL KLINK, *Nancy*, September 14, 1754, Hinke, I, 591.

KLINGELE, MARGARETHA (2)—Laufen/Eyach (1750)

B. 6-19-1718, daughter of CHRISTOPH KLINGELE and wf. LUCIA. "To Pennsylvania 1750."

KLINGENMAYER, (KLINGENMEYR), CONRAD (CUNRAD) (1)—Höfingen (1751)

Wf. (2nd), ANNA MARIA. Ch: (1) Conrad, 10-17-1737, "went to America with his parents." *Ludwigsburg Protocol*, 1751. "To America." // CONRAD KLINGEMEYER, *Duke of Wirtenberg*, October 16, 1751, Hinke, I, 476.

KLINGENMAYR, JOHANN GEORG (1)—Höfingen

B. 10-2-1727, son of CONRAD KLINGENMEYER, *supra*, by his first wife. "Württemberg soldier, deserted 1753. Probably followed his parents to the New World."

KLOEPFER, JERG ADAM (2)—Ossweil (1752)

Son of the late vinedresser [*Weingärtner*] JERG ADAM KLOEPFER at Metterzimmern. Wf: JACOBINA (DANZER), mason's daughter [*Maurerstochter*]. Ch: (1) Maria Catharina, b. 12-27-1744; (2) Christina, b. 10-7-1749; (3) others, died early. "Left for Pennsylvania with wife and children, May 22, [1752]." *Ludwigsburg Protocol*, 4-21-1752, to "Pennsylvania. // Others in Hinke; others in PA.

KLOTZ, JOHANN JACOB (2)—Simmozheim (1749)

Carpenter [*Zimmermann*]. Wf (2d) MARTHA (FEISSLER), cartwright's daughter [*Wagnerstochter*]. Ch: (1) Johann Jacob, b. 9-13-1726; (2) Ursula, b. 8-27-1732; (3) Johann Leonhard, b. 3-31-1734. *Ludwigsburg Protocol*, 4-17-1749, permission to emigrate, without specifying destination. // JACOB KLOTZ, with JACOB KLOTZ, sick, and HANS LEONHARDT KLOTZ, *Chesterfield*, September 2, 1749, Hinke, I, 393. Estate of PHILIP JACOB TRAUTMAN, Rockland Tp., Berks Co., Pa., March 20, 1793, administration to MARIA, the widow, and JACOB KLOZ, brother-in-law, *Berks County Will Abstracts*, I, 504. 3PA, 18, 56: JACOB KLOTZ and MARTIN KLOTZ, weaver, Western District Tp., Berks Co., Pa., 1767. 3PA, 18, 11: LEONARD KLOTZ, Rockland Tp., Berks Co., Pa., 1767. 3PA, 25, 728: JACOB KLOTZ, 400 acres, Huntingdon Co., Pa., survey June 17, 1793.

KLOTZBUECHER, DOROTHEA (2)—Gündelbach

B. 1729.

KNAUS, JOHANN JACOB (1)—Dornhan

Butcher [*Metzger*]. Wf: ANNA MARIA. Ch: (1) Georg Jacob, b. 9-9-1733; (2) Johann Georg, b. 4-2-1736. To "Pennsylvania." // 3PA, *19*, 98: JACOB KNOWS, with Baltzer, Michael, and Abraham Knows, Upper Milford Tp., Northampton Co., Pa., 1785. 3PA, *19*, 109: JACOB, JOHN, and HENRY KNOWS, Salisbury Tp., Northampton Co., Pa. 1785. 3PA, *19*, 127 and 132, GEORGE KNOWS, Whitehall and Lowhill Tps., Northampton Co., Pa., 1785.

## KNITTEL, JOSEPH (2)—Oberesslingen (1753)

Farmer on the manor [*Hofbauer*]. Wf: REGINA MAGDALENA (FUEGLIN). Ch: (1) Johann Georg, b. 10-9-1740. *Ludwigsburg Protocol*, 5-18-1753, to "Pennsylvania." // JOSEPH NEEDLE (KNITTEL), age 40, *Patience*, September 15 [17], 1753, Hinke, I, 526, 528. 3PA, *14*, 96: JOSEPH KNITTLE, Germantown Tp., Philadelphia Co., Pa., 1769. 3PA, *15*, 175: JOSEPH KNITTLE, Worcester Tp., Philadelphia Co., 1779. Several George Knittles in PA.

## KNOBLOCH, HANS ADAM (1)—Kusterdingen

Night-watchman [*Nachtschütz*]. Wf: ANNA MARIA *née* KAYSER. Ch: (1) Johann Martin, b. 6-18-1752. "Went to what is commonly called the New World with his parents." // Two in Hinke: ADAM KNOBELICK (KNOBELICH, NOBLIG), *Richard and Mary*, September 30, 1754, Hinke, I, 605; and ADAM KNOBLAUCH, *Sally*, October 5, 1767, Hinke, I, 714. JOHANN MARTIN KNOBLOCH, *Richmond*, October 20, 1764, Hinke, I, 695. 3PA, 14, 215: ADAM KNOBLOCK, Mulberry Ward, City of Philadelphia, Pa., 1769. 3PA, 14, 695: MARTIN KNOBLAUCH, Roxborough Tp., Philadelphia Co., Pa, 1779.

## KNODEL, JOHANN FRIEDRICH (1)—Grünwettersbach (1752)

Day laborer [*Tagelöhner*]. B. 9-13-1714, son of the village mayor [Schultheiss] in Mutschelbach. Wf: [——] *née* SCHLEGLIN. Ch: six. Baptismal certificates [Taufscheine] made for him, his wife, and six children, May 2, 1752, "since he has left." Note that on the same day certificates were made for Margaretha Magdalena Bodamer (q.v.), who was leaving for Pennsylvania. Knodel's destination not stated. // The will of ADAM SCHLEGEL, of Reading, Berks Co., Pa., dated December 19, 1785, and probated June 1, 1786, mentions "Margaret, wife of Frederick Knodel," of Carolina, *Berks County Will Abstracts*, I, 372. For further relationships from this will, cf. *infra*, JOHANN CHRISTOPH SCHLEGEL.

## KNOEDLER, HANS GEORG (2)—Niederhofen (1750)

Baker [*Beck*]. Wf: MARIA ELISABETHA, *née* HEUSSLER, b. 11-5-1728, daughter of CHRISTIAN HEUSSLER (q.v.) and wf. E-A ELISABETHA. Married 4-21-1750. "Went to the New World." *Ludwigsburg Protocol*, 5-22-1750, HEUSSLER to "America." // HANS JERG GNOEDLER, with ANDREAS KNOEDLER and CHRISTIAN HEUSLER, *Osgood*, September 29, 1750, Hinke, I, 446; a fellow-passenger was Gottlieb Mittelberger. 3PA, 26, 107: HANS YERICK KNEIDLER, 25 acres, Northampton Co., Pa., survey October 11, 1756. 3PA, 19, 57: GEORGE KNEDLER, farmer, Lowhill Tp., Northampton Co., Pa., 1772. HANS JURG KNOEDELER and wf. MARIA ELISABETHA, son ANDREAS KNOEDELER, baptized at home (Schmaltzgass) 14 days old, February 5, 1759, *Pastoral Record of the Reverend Daniel Schumacher*, 1754-1774, 63, GSP. Estate of GEORGE KNEDLER of Alsace Tp., Berks Co., Pa., May 1, 1771, administration to CATHARINE KNEEDLER, the widow, *Berks County Will Abstracts*, I, 155, GSP.

## KNOLL, MARGARETHA (1)—Wolfschlugen

Ch: (1) Margaretha, b. (illeg.) 11-24-1744, who "went with her mother to Pennsylvania."

## KNOLL, GEORGE LUDWIG (1)—Neuffen

Butcher [*Metzger*]. Wf: URSULA BARBARA. Ch: (1) Eva Barbara, b. 9-11-1749; (2) Georg Ludwig, b. 12-5-1750. // LUDWIG KNOLL, *Neptune,* September 24, 1751, Hinke I, 468. 3PA, *16,* 127: LUDWICK KNOLL, Lower Merion Tp., Philadelphia Co., Pa., 1782. The will of LUDWICK KNOLL of Lower Merion Tp., Philadelphia Co., Pa., dated Dec. 5, 1763, probated Jany. 17, 1764, Will Book N, p. 91, mentions Wf: URSILA BARBARAH; Children: Jacob, Annah May, Eve, Ludwick, and Catharine. Executors: Ursila Barbara and Jacob Knoll. Witnesses: George Colss, John Fimple, D. Dewelyn.

## KOENIG, JACOB (2)—Laufen/Eyach (1750)

B. 10-14-1728, son of HANS and ANNA MARIA KOENIG. "To Pennsylvania 1750." // Probably JACOB KEANIGH, with JOHANNIS WOLFER and HANS MARTIN WOLFFER of Laufen/Eyach, *Osgood,* September 29, 1750, Hinke, I, 445-6; a fellow-passenger was Gottlieb Mittelberger. However, a JACOB KOENIG, with MATHEUS KOENIG, arrived October 7, 1751, on the *Janet,* Hinke, I, 474; a fellow-passenger was Jacob Weimer, Reformed minister. 3PA, 18, 40: JACOB KOENIG, shoemaker, Maxatawny Tp., Berks Co., Pa., 1767. 3PA, 18, 459: JACOB KOENIG, s. m., 912 acres, Brunswick Tp., Berks Co., Pa., 1781.

## KOENIG, JOHANN LUDWIG (2)—Laufen/Eyach (1749)

B. 12-9-1730, son of MARTIN and SALOME (SCHERLER) KOENIG. "To Pennsylvania, 1748-1750." // LUDWIG KOENIG (two by this name), *Chesterfield,* September 2, 1749, Hinke, I, 394.

## KOERBER, JOHANN DAVID (2)—Bietigheim (1754)

B. 3-22-1738, son of the farmer [*Bauer*] JOHANN DAVID KOERBER (died 1756). No further entries. *Ludwigsburg Protocol,* 4-9-1754, to "Pennsylvania." // Others in Hinke and PA.

## KOESTLIN, ANDREAS (1)—Wurmberg

Wf: MARIA AGATHA. Ch: (1) Anna Catharina, b. 10-21-1726; (2) Johann Georg, b. 3-29-1732; (3) Anna Maria, b. 7-9-1735. All three children "died on the way across the ocean."

## KOHLER, JOHANNES (2)—Kuppingen (1751)

Tailor [*Schneider*]. B. 6-16-1719, son of the farmer [*Bauer*] VEIT KOHLER. Wf: MARIA AGATHA *née* HAMMER, b. 1-11-1720, daughter of MELCHIOR HAMMER, SR., baker [*Bäcker*], of Oberjesingen, and sister of Johann Melchior Hammer (q.v.) Ch: After 3 died, (1) Maria Margaretha, b. 12-16-1744; (2) Anna Maria, b. 2-19-1747; (3) Veit, b. 12-8-1748; (4) Johannes, b. 1-27-1751. *Ludwigsburg Protocol,* 4-16-1751, venia emigrandi. No members of either family (Hammer or Kohler) in Baptismal or Confirmand Register after 1751. // JOHANNES KOHLER, with MELCHER HAMMER, *Nancy,* September 16, 1751, Hinke, I, 463. 3PA, 18, 671: JOHN KOHLER, Richmond Tp., Berks Co., Pa., 1784. 3PA, 21, 709: JOHN KOHLER, with BALTZER and JACOB KOHLER, Shrewsbury Tp., York Co., Pa.

## KOSER, LEONHARDT (1)—Steinenberg (1709)

Set out Aug. 19, 1709, with wife and three children, along with Caspar Auperle and family, from their home in Michelau, "for the faraway island of Pennsylvania." Got no farther than Koblenz, from whence

Auperle returned to Württemberg, while Koser remained at Neuenstadt on the Linden. For full account of their unsuccessful emigration, cf. CASPAR AUPERLE, *supra.*

## KOTZ, CHRISTOPH (1)—Hülben (1751)

Journeyman weaver and non-citizen [*Webergeselle u. Beisitzer*] of Münsingen. Wf: ELISABETHA *née* SPOHN. "Both admonished in the previous year for bad conduct." Ch: (1) Maria Barbara, b. 4-19-1748, who "is in the New World." // CHRISTOPH COTZ, *Neptune,* September 24, 1751, Hinke, I, 468, with the other emigrants who left Hülben in 1751.

## KRAEMER, HANS JERG (2)—Malmsheim (1754)

B. 4-21-1701, son of the shoemaker [*Schuhmacher*] JOHANNES KRAEMER. Wf: ANNA BARBARA. Ch: (1) Johannes, b. 9-26-1728; (2) Christian, b. 9-8-1732; (3) Johannes Conrad, b. 12-18-1741; (4) Elisabetha Barbara, b. 3-17-1745. Gerber writes that the elder son, Johannes, disappears in 1753 from the Communicant Register and is found neither in the Marriage nor the Burial Register. For the rest there is the following entry in the Communicant Register for 1754: "JOH. G. KRAEMER, communicant at Easter; children: CHRISTINA, communicant on Palm Sunday; JOHANN CONRAD, catechumen; ELISABETHA BABRARA, catechumen." All "bade farewell to their Fatherland, May 16, 1754, seeking Pennsylvania." [*d. 16 Maji Patriae valedixerunt, Pennsylvaniam, petierunt.*] *Ludwigsburg Protocol,* 3-22-1754, to "America." // Two listed in Hinke: CHRISTIAN KRAEMER, *Richard and Mary,* September 30, 1754, Hinke, I, 605; and CHRISTIAN KRAEMER, *John and Elizabeth,* November 7, 1754, Hinke, I, 666, 668.

## KRAEUTLER, GEORG MARTIN (1)—Grünwettersbach (1753)

B. 1-2-1735, son of JACOB KRAEUTLER, JR. [*Jung Jacob*] and wf. CATHARINA of Mutschelbach. "Baptismal certificate sent after him to Pennsylvania." // YERRICK KREYTLER (GEORG MARTIN KREIDLER), age 22, *Patience,* September 15 [17], 1753, Hinke, I, 526, 528. 3PA, 19, 25: GEORGE KREIDLER, farmer, Bethlehem Tp., Northampton Co., Pa., 1772.

## KRAFFT, MARTIN (1)—Höfingen

Tailor [*sutor*]. Wf: MARIA MAGDALENA. Ch: (1) Anna Catharina, b. 9-27-1744. "Went to America." // 3PA, 26, 278: MARTIN KRAFT, [Lot] 381 in Reading, Berks Co., Pa., survey October 8, 1753. 3PA, 18, 6: MARTIN KRAFT, with CONRAD KRAFT, Reading Town, Berks Co., Pa., 1767. The will of MARTIN KRAFFT, Reading, Berks Co., Pa., dated June 23, 1777, probated September 10, 1777, makes bequests to Holy Trinity Church, Reading, and mentions wife MARIA MAGDALENA and son CONRAD; letters to Maria Magdalena Krafft, the widow, *Berks County Will Abstracts,* I, 231, GSP.

## KRAFT, CHRISTOPH (1)—Schopfloch (Oberamt Freudenstadt)

Wf: BARBARA. Ch: (1) Catharina, b. 3-6-1744; (2) Christian, b. 11-8-1750. "To Pennsylvania," ca. 1750.

## KRAUSS, DAVID (2)—Sielmingen (1754)

*Ludwigsburg Protocol,* 4-3-1754, *venia emigrandi.* // JOH. DAVID KRAUSS, with the Ruesses (q.v.) of Sielmingen, *Bannister,* October 21, 1754, Hinke, I, 647.

## KRAUS(S), HANS JOERG (1)—Plüderhausen

Vinedresser [*Weingärtner*]. Wf: (ANNA) MARGARETHA *née* ZELLER. Ch: (1) Hans Jörg, b. 1-2-1731; (2) Johann Jacob, b. 11-25-1732; (3) Maria Barbara, b. 12-2-1734; (4) Johann Friedrich, b. 6-2-1737; (5) Christine, b. 6-27-1744; (6) Matthäus, b. 6-18-1746. All children "went with parents to America." // JOH. GEORG KRAUSS, with JACOB KRAUSS, *Dragon,* September 26, 1749, Hinke, I, 414; three HANS GEORG KRAUSSES emigrated 1754, according to Hinke.

## KRAUT, CHRISTIAN (1)—Neuffen

Shoemaker [*Schuhmacher*]. Wf: DOROTHEA. Wf: (1) Matthias, b. 2-24-1749. // Others in Hinke.

## KREIDLER (KRAEUTLER), JOHANN GEORG (1)—Grünwettersbach (1751)

Farmhand [*Bauersmann*]. B. 1-30-1716, son of JOHANN JACOB and ANNA ELISABETHA KREIDLER. Wf: (1) SIBYLLA, *née* FUCHS. Ch: (1) Johann Georg, b. 11-27-1739; (2) Johann Friedrich, b. 4-21-1743. By the names of father and children: "Baptismal Certificate prepared, May 17, 1751, for Pennsylvania." // JERG KREIDLER, *Shirley,* with Georg Conrad Schweikart of Grünwettersbach, September 5, 1751, Hinke I, 454.

## KRIMMEL, DOROTHEA CHRISTINA (1)—Ebingen

Daughter of JOHANN ANDREAS KRIMMEL, barber [*Tonsor*]. Ch: (1) Anna Barbara, b. (illeg.), 6-7-1735. To "Pennsylvania." // Others in Hinke. Note that JOHANN LUDWIG KRIMMEL (1786-1821), early Philadelphia artist, was a native of Ebingen [Kapff, *Schwaben in Amerika,* 47].

## KROLL, HANS JERG (1)—Beihingen, Oberamt Ludwigsburg (1743)

Wf: MARGARETHA. Ch: (1) Maria Rosina, b. 12-31-1731. "To Pennsylvania 1743."

## KUEBLER, JACOB (2)—Magstadt (1749)

Farmer [*Bauer*]. Wf: ANNA CATHARINA. Ch: (1) Johann Jacob, b. 7-23-1740; (2) Rosina, b. 5-29-1744; (3) Gottlieb, b. 12-8-1747. According to Gerber, the Küblers appear to have come to Magstadt from elsewhere and disappear again from the Church Register after 1749. *Ludwigsburg Protocol,* 4-15-1749, to "Pennsylvania." // 3PA, 14, 96: JOHN KIBLER and JACOB KIBLER, Germantown Tp., Philadelphia Co., Pa., 1769. 3PA, 17, 503: JACOB KIBLER, Warwick Tp., Lancaster Co., Pa., 1779.

## KUEFER, GEORG FRIEDRICH (1)—Nordheim

B. 2-2-1715, son of HANS JOERG KUEFER. // 3PA, 24, 27: FREDERICK KIEFFER, 50 acres, Philadelphia Co., Pa., survey September 1, 1746. 3PA, 21, 105: FREDERICK KEEFER, Germany Tp., York Co., Pa., 1779. 3PA, 25, 557: FREDERICK KEAFER, 400 acres, Bedford Co., Pa., survey October 23, 1795.

## KUEFER, HANS JERG (1)—Nordheim

B. 7-1-1721, son of HANS JOERG KUEFER, and brother of GEORG FRIEDRICH KUEFER, *supra.* // Two in Hinke: JERG KIEFFER, Brigantine *Mary,* August 25, 1742, Hinke, I, 322; and JOHN GEORGE KUEFFER, *St. Andrew,* September 23, 1752. *Philadelphische Correspondenz,* November 4, 1788, quoted in Hocker, 195: "JOHANN CHRISTIAN GROTIAN, schoolmaster of St. Michael's and Zion Lutheran Church, Philadelphia, proposes to open a German night school in the school house. His residence is with GEORG KUEFER, Race and Fifth Streets."

## KUEMMERLE (KUEMMERLIN), JOHANN JACOB (2) Neckartenzlingen (1753)

Wf: MARGARETHA (HEINTZELMANN) of Möglingen. Ch: (1) Anna Margaretha, b. 12-27-1742; (2) Johann Jacob, b. 12-6-1744. // HANS JACOB KUEMMERLIE, *Richard and Mary,* September 17, 1753, Hinke, I, 534. JACOB KIMBERLING (KEMERLING, KEMMERLY, KEMPERLIN): several in PA, including Brecknock and Brunswick Tps., Berks County; Windsor Tp., York County; and Earl and Londonderry Tps., Lancaster County.

## KUEMMERLIN, HANS (JOHANN) MARTIN (1)—Schlaitdorf (1751)

Baker [*Beck*]. Wf: ANNA MARIA. Ch: (1) Anna Maria, b. 3-14-1738, "to the New World;" (2) Matthäus Jacob, b. 9-22-1741; (3) Christianus, b. 5-26-1749. *Ludwigsburg Protocol,* 1751; arrival at Philadelphia, 9-16-1751. // HANS MARTIN KIMMERLIN, with JOHANNES KIMMERLEN, *Nancy,* September 16, 1751, Hinke, I, 463. Sower's newspaper, February 29, 1760, quoted in Hocker, 87: "MARTIN KUEMMERLING, Bethel Township, Lancaster County." 3PA, 21, 214: CHRISTIAN KEMMERLY, Manheim Tp., York Co., Pa., 1780.

## KUEMMERLIN, JOHANNES (HANS) (1)—Schlaitdorf (1751)

Farmer [*Bauer*]. Wf: EVA *née* ENZLIN. Ch: (1) Johann Michael, b. 4-8-1743; (2) Anna, b. 7-25-1746; (3) Johann Georg, b. 2-1-1748; (4) Anna Maria, b. 7-13-1749; (5) Johann Jacob, b. 5-30-1751. Arrival at Philadelphia, 9-16-1751. // JOHANNES KIMMERLEN, with HANS MARTIN KIMMERLIN, *Nancy,* September 16, 1751, Hinke, I, 463. 3PA, 24, 453: JOHN KIMERLINE, tract in Lancaster Co., Pa., survey March 24, 1759. 3PA, 14, 115: JOHN KIMERLEY, skinner, Northern Liberties (East Part), Philadelphia Co., Pa., 1769. 3PA, 18, 228: JOHN KEMPERLIN, Hereford Tp., Berks Co., Pa., 1779. 3PA, 17, 550: GEORGE KIMMERLING, Lebanon Tp., Lancaster Co., Pa., 1779. *Staatsbote,* Philadelphia, December 19, 1769, quoted in Hocker, 106-7: "MICHAEL KUEMMERLY, Tyrone Township, York County, seeks his brother, HANS KUEMMERLY, born in Schleydorf, Württemberg, who came to America fifteen years ago. Their father died on the voyage and their mother soon after arriving at Philadelphia. Address, care of William Walker, storekeeper, in Tyrone Township."

## KUEMMLER, HANS JACOB (1)—Neuhausen *ob Eck*

Wf: ROSINA. Ch: (1) Ursula, b. 12-7-1736. "These people went to America." // JACOB CIMBLER (HANS JACOB KEMMLER), *Rosannah,* September 26, 1743, Hinke, I, 344-5. 3PA, 18, 36: JACOB KIMLER, Oley Tp., Berks Co., Pa. 1767.

## KUGLER, JOHANNES (1)—Rötenberg

B. 8-26-1728, at Altenberg. // JOHANNES KUGHLER, *Duke of Wirtenburg*, October 20, 1752, Hinke, I, 498. 3PA, 14, 416: JOHN and PAUL COOGLER, Providence Tp., Philadelphia Co., Pa., 1774. 3PA, 13, 9: J/HN COOGLAR, Solesbury Tp., Bucks Co., Pa., 1779. 3PA, 24, 241: JOHN and PAUL KUGLAR, tracts in Luzerne Co., Pa., survey 1793-4.

## KUHN, FRANZ (2)—Aich (1764)

Cooper [*Küfer*]. Wf: MARIA ELISABETHA (HORLACHER). Ch: two boys and a girl [*2 Büblen u. 1 Mägdlen*], of 4, 2½, and ½ years. *Ludwigsburg Protocol*, 5-2-1764, to "Pennsylvania." According to Gerber, "The certificate of good conduct describes man and wife as especially God-fearing, pious, obedient, upright, honest, and honorable [*besonders Gottesfürchtig, fromm, gehorsam, aufrecht, redlich, ehrlich*], and says at the same time that as far as their feudal relationship is concerned, they are 'entirely free, secure, and unencumbered' [*gantz frey, sicher, ledig und loss*]. According to another report, he had not been a bad manager, but Aich was not the right place for his trade, and his property, after subtraction of debts, amounted to only 40 Gulden. So not even the Duke himself succeeded, in the audience which he requested with him, in dissuading him from emigration, and on October 20, [1764], despite his meagre means, he landed in Philadelphia." // FRANTZ KUHN, *Richmond*, October 20, 1764, Hinke, I, 695. 3PA, 21, 673: FRANCIS KOONS, York Tp., York Co., Pa., 1783. 3PA, 25, 481: FRANCIS COON, 69 acres, Bedford Co., Pa., survey March 18, 1790.

## KUHN, JOHANNES (1)—Schlaitdorf (1753)

Farmer [*Bauer*]. Wf: ANNA BARBARA, *née* ADAM. Ch: (1) Anna Barbara, b. 10-10-1742; (2) Johann Jacob, b. 10-22-1744; (3) Euphrosina, b. 10-16-1746; (4) Anna Catharina, b. 9-28-1749. None of the children appear in the Burial Register. In the Marriage Register: "JOHANNES KUHN, farmer, and ANNA BARBARA, daughter of HANS JACOB ADAM (q.v.), the village watchman, went to Pennsylvania 1753 with her old father and three children." // JOHANNES KUOHN, with HANS JACOB ADAM, *Richard and Mary*, September 17, 1753, Hinke, I, 533. Sower's newspaper, August 11, 1760, quoted in Hocker, 90: "JOHANNES KUHN and BARBARA KUHNIN, New York, opposite the High School, seek information about their daughter, ANNA MARIA, whom they have not seen for thirteen years."

## KULLE(N), DAVID (1)—Hülben (1751)

Farmer [*Bauer*]. Wf: MARIA *née* MUFF. Ch: (1) Maria Barbara, b. 12-16-1731; (2) Agnes Barbara, b. 11-21-1737; (3) Johann Ulrich, b. 6-10-1741; (4) Ursula Barbara, b. 6-5-1743; (5) Christina, b. 3-20-1748. Father "is in the New World." // DAVID KULLING, *Neptune*, September 24, 1751, Hinke, I, 469, with other families from Hülben. Others in PA.

## KUMPF, CHRISTOPH (2)—Gündelbach (1785)

B. 1736. Emigrated 1785, with wife and niece GOTTLIEBIN SCHAEFER (q.v.) Others in PA.

## KURFESS, JACOB (1)—Plattenhardt

Farmer [*Bauer*]. Wf: ANNA MARIA *née* HEINTZMANN. Ch: (1) Emma Catharina, b. 9-11-1737; (2) Hans Jörg, b. 10-16-1738; (3) Anna Maria, b. 2-25-1740; (4) Johannes, b. 2-9-1743; (5) Jacob, b. 9-21-1746; (6) Michael, b. 11-15-1750. To "Pennsylvania."

KURFESS, JOERG (1)—Plattenhardt

Baker [*Beck*]. Wf: MARIA, *née* ROTH. Ch: (1) Anna Maria Elisabetha, b. 6-26-1741; (2) Johannes, b. 3-18-1743; (3) Georg, b. 6-10-1748; (4) Gottlieb, b. 3-30-1751. To "Pennsylvania."

KUR(T)Z, JOHANNES (1)—Grötzingen (1752)

Mason [*Maurer*]. Wf (2d): MARGARETHA. Ch: (1) Maria Agnes, b. 6-4-1741; (2) Christianus, b. 2-1-1746; (3) Johann Jacob, b. 6-12-1751. Left for Pennsylvania, May 6, 1752, with his wife and *six* children, in company with Jacob Raisser (q.v.), Hans Jerg Reichenecker (q.v.), Daniel Reiter (q.v.), and Johannes Rist (q.v.). // JOHANNES KURTZ, *Anderson*, September 27, 1752, Hinke, I, 489.

KURZ, CHRISTOPH (2)—Oberboihingen (p. 1751)

Probably cobbler apprentice [*Schukknecht*]. Not in the Communicant Register after Advent 1751. Mentioned in the Nürtingen Documents. // Probably CHRISTOPH KURTZ, Snow *Louisa*, November 8, 1752, Hinke, I, 506; a JOHANN CHRISTOPHEL KURTZ came 1765.

KURZ, DANIEL (1)—Steinenberg

B. 2-12-1725, at Miedelsbach. "To America, 1745." // DANIEL KURTZ, *Patience*, with ANDREAS FOEHL of Steinenberg, September 19, 1749, Hinke, I, 409.

# L

LAEMLER, JOHANN GOTTLIEB (1)—Rommelshausen

B. 2-4-1744, son of HANS JERG LAEMLER and wf. ESTHER, *née* CHUR. "Went to America, where he is said have died."

LANDAUER, JOHANNES (1)—Ebingen

Needle and pinmaker [*Nadler*]. Wf: URSULA CATHARINA, *née* SCHOTT. Ch: (1) Eberhardina, b. 1-30-1741; (2) Catharina Maria, b. 7-5-1742. To "Pennsylvania."

LANDENBERGER, JOHANN JACOB (1)—Ebingen

Baker [*Beck*]. Wf: ANNA MARIA, *née* GROZ. Ch: (1) Johannes, b. 8-29-1740. To "Pennsylvania." A "Newlander," according to Gerber's description of him as "LANDENBERGER of Ebingen, who made several trips between Germany and America." It was he who in 1749, by bringing back favorable letters from two emigrants who had left Laufen/Eyach in 1746, precipitated the large Laufen emigration of 1750. Cf. *supra*, HANS BALTHASS BITZER of Laufen/Eyach, for fuller account. 3PA, 15, 492: JACOB LANDENBERGER, laborer, Northern Liberties (West Part), Philadelphia Co., Pa., 1780.

LANG, CHRISTOPH (2)—Onstmettingen

Tailor [*Schneider*]. Wf: URSULA. Ch: (1) Catharina, b. 1-10-1741. According to records kept by Pastor Johann Georg Stählen, 1746-1756, this family "went to New England." *Ludwigsburg Protocol*, 5-3-1752, mentions emigrants from Onstmettingen to Pennsylvania, without giving names. // (JOHANN) CHRISTOPHEL LANG, *Friendship*, October 21, 1754, Hinke, I, 642-3; or JOHANN CHRISTOPH LANG, Snow *Good Intent*, October 23, 1754, Hinke, I, 655, 657. According to PA, various CHRIST-

OPHER LANGS were resident in East Hanover Tp., Lancaster Co., Pa., 1771; Penns Tp., Northumberland Co., Pa., 1781; Caernarvon Tp., Berks Co., Pa., 1784; and Buffalo Tp., Northumberland Co., Pa., 1786.

## LANG, JOHANN JACOB (2)—Maichingen (1752)

Wf: MARIA ELISABETHA. Ch: (1) Maria Elisabetha, b. 10-14-1744; (2) Elisabetha, b. 2-21-1746; (3) Anna Maria, b. 8-4-1748. *Ludwigsburg Protocol*, 4-12-1752, JOHANN GEORG SCHNEIDER of Maichingen, and [——] LANG, *venia emigrandi*. // JOHANN JACOB LANG, with JACOB LANG, *President*, and JOHANN GEORG SCHNEIDER of Maichingen, who heads the list, September 27, 1752, Hinke, I, 490. Many listed in PA.

## LANG, JOHANN MARTIN (2)—Renningen (1751)

Shoemaker [*Schuhmacher*]. Wf: AGNES. Ch: (1) Jacob Friedrich, b. 9-7-1741; (2) Philipp Leoboldus, b. 11-16-1746; (3) Johann Jacob, b. 7-4-1749. No further children listed. *Ludwigsburg Protocol*, 4-6-1751, "Lang and associates" to "Pennsylvania." // Probably JOHANN MARTIN LANG, *Nancy*, September 16, 1751, Hinke, I, 462; though others came 1752 and 1769. Several listed in PA.

## LAUB, BALTHASAR (2)—Weilheim unter Teck (1751)

Tailor [*Schneider*]. Wf: MARIA BARBARA, *née* MOESSNER, daughter of the tailor [*sartor*] MICHAEL MOESSNER. Ch: (1) Johann Michael, b. 7-21-1733; (2) Catharina Dorothea, b. 6-24-1734; (3) Anna Barbara, b. 4-7-1739; (4) Johannes, b. 3-14-1741; (5) Anna Elisabetha, b. 2-12-1744; (6) Anna Maria, b. 4-24-1749. Acording to the *Liber Notarius*, Laub "went with wife and children to Pennsylvania in 1753." The two references in the *Ludwigsburg Protocol* (4-30-1751, BALTHASAR LAUB, to "Pennsylvania"; and 5-8-1753, LAUB, to "Pennsylvania), when collated with the shiplists, seem to indicate that the father went on ahead in 1751, and at least the son JOHANN MICHAEL, and perhaps the rest of the family, did not follow until 1753. // BALTES LAUB, *Neptune*, September 24, 1751, Hinke, I, 469. 3PA, 18, 240: BALTASER LAUB, with MICH'L LAUB, s. m., Greenwich Tp., Berks Co., Pa., 1779.

## LAUB, JOHANN MICHAEL (2)—Weilheim unter Teck (1753)

B. 7-21-1733, son of BALTHASAR and MARIA BARBARA (MOESSNER) LAUB, q.v. // JOHANNES MICH'L LAUP (MICHEL LAUB), age 20, with JOHANNES LAUB, age 18, September 28, 1753, Hinke, I, 560-1.

## LAUB, MICHAEL (1)—Grötzingen (1749)

Carpenter [*Zimmermann*]. Wf: ANNA. Ch: (1) Matthäus, b. 2-26-1737; (2) Elisabetha, b. 9-7-1738; (3) Johannes, b. 10-26-1740; (4) Dorothea, b. 5-6-1744; (5) Barbara, b. 5-25-1745. One in 1739. To "Pennsylvania," May 1, 1749, with wife and six children, along with others from the same village; see JOHANN MICHAEL PFRANG, MATTHAEUS PFRANG, SR., ELISABETHA NEIBLING, JOHANNES GRAUER, AUGUSTINUS GENTNER, HANS JERG HOFSAESS, JOHANNES NIEBLING, CHRISTOPH JAECKLE, and CONRAD RAISCH. // 3PA, 18, 30: MICH'L and JOHN LAUB, Cumru Tp., Berks Co., Pa., 1767. 3PA, 18, 240: MICH'L LAUB, s. m., and BALTHASER LAUB, Greenwich Tp., Berks Co., Pa., 1779. // The will of MICHAEL LAUB, of Cumru Tp., Berks Co., Pa., dated May 28, 1785, probated December 14, 1786, mentions son MATHIAS, and daughters ELIZABETH and ANNA MARIA; Executors: son JOHN and wife

ANNA; Letters to JOHN, the wife being deceased; witness: JACOB FREITCH and MICHAEL SCHLAUCH, *Berks County Will Abstracts,* I, 578, GSP.

## LAUFFER, (JOHANN) CONRAD (2)—Eberstadt (1749)

In the Communicant Register, under the classification "Unmarried Sons and Servants" [*Coelibes filii et servi*] at Filial Lennach-Buchhorn, is the following entry, scribbled in at the bottom: "From Dörtzbach, MOLITOR, going to Pennsylvania with CONRAD LAUFFER and others." The Baptismal Register, three weeks previously, lists a child of Lauffer's. // The will of CONRAD LAWFER, of Lancaster Borough, Lancaster Co., Pa., dated April 29, 1751, probated May 2, 1753, names brothers and sisters, JOHN, ELIZABETH, URSULA, MICHAEL, CHRISTIAN, and MARX; executrix: wf. CATHARINE ELISABETH LAWFER, *Lancaster County Will Abstracts,* II, 594-5, GSP. See also Joseph A. Lauffer, et al., *The Lauffer History. A Genealogical Chart of the Descendants of Christian Lauffer, the Pioneer, with a few Biographical Sketches* (Jeannette, Pa.: The Westmoreland Journal, 1906), 6. which lists as brothers and sisters: JOHN GEORGE, ELIZABETH, ORSULA, JOHN MICHAEL, JOHN, and CHRISTIAN MARX LAUFFER.

## LEDERER, PHILIPPUS (1)—Rommelshausen

B. 4-16-1744. "Died as a confectioner in the West Indies." // Others listed in PA.

## LEICHT, HANS JERG (2)—Oeschelbronn (now Baden) (1753)

Cartwright [*Wagner*]. Wf: ANNA (ZOLLER). Married 1741. Ch: four, the last one born 1752. *Ludwigsburg Protocol,* 5-4-1753, to "Pennsylvania." Brother of BARBARA (LEICHD), wf. of HANS JERG STOERER (q.v.).

## LENGENFELDER (LINGENFELDER), PANCRATIUS (2) —Sillenbuch (1754)

Convert [*Proselyt*] i.e., from Roman Catholicism. Baker [*Beck*] from the Diocese of Bamberg or Würtzburg [*aus dem Bambergschen oder Würzburgschen*]. Wf (2d): CATHARINA [——], of Oberkochen. Ch: (1) Johannes, b. 6-8-1746; (2) Johann Michael, b. 8-30-1748; (3) a daughetr, d. 1751. In the following twenty years the name appears neither in the Baptismal, Marriage, nor Burial Register. *Ludwigsburg Protocol,* 3-12-1754, to "Pennsylvania." // Others in Hinke.

## LENZ, CHRISTIAN (2)—Beutelsbach (1746)

Mason [*Maurer*]. B. 1-4-1699. Wf: ANNA MARIA, *née* WIDENMAYER, b. 4-16-1702. Ch: (1) Christian, b. 1-16-1728; (2) Johann Jacob, b. 10-15-1729; (3) Maria Barbara, b. 1-27-1736; (4) Anna Maria, b. 10-27-1738. "Went to Pennsylvania, 3-25-1746, on account of an aggravated case of syphilis, taking leave neither from his father nor his pastor. Was a restless fellow here. Died before he got to Pennsylvania." [*"Ist aus besonderer Lustseuche d. 25-3-1746 nach Pens. gezogen; hat weder von s. Vater noch von s. Pfarrer Abschied genommen. War ein unruhiger Kopf allhier. Ist, ehe er in Pens. kommen,* †."] // CHRISTIAN LENTZ, with JOHN JACOB and CHRISTOPH LENTZ, and PHILLIP ZIEGLER of Grötzingen, *Ann Galley,* September 27, 1746, Hinke, I, 360. Cf. also, HENRY LENZ, with wife and four children, age 43, from Beutelspach, farmer, 5½ feet tall, dark brown hair, landed at Philadelphia September 19, 1804, from the ship *Margaret;* Hinke, III, 154. Several listed in PA.

LENZ, CHRISTOPH (2)—Beutelsbach (1746)

Mason and stonecutter [*Maurer u. Steinhauer*]. B. 12-14-1696. "Went to Pennsylvania, 3-25-1746, on account of discontent, and, before he got there, died." ["*ist aus Missvergnügen d. 25-3-1746 in Pens. gez. und, ehe er hineingekommen,* †."] Whether emigrated with his wife and four children, is questionable. // CHRISTOPH LENTZ, with JOHN JACOB and CHRISTIAN LENTZ, *Ann Galley,* September 27, 1746, Hinke, I, 360. Several listed in PA.

LENZ, JOHANN JACOB (2)—Beutelsbach (1769)

Vinedresser [*Weingärtner*]. B. 1-7-1727. Wf: ANNA MARIA, *née* LOEFFLER, b. 5-17-1735, "went to America, autumn of 1769," probably with two or three children. The father "went to the New World in the Spring of 1769." // JOHANN JACOB LENTZ, *Minerva,* October 13, 1769, Hinke, I, 726. Several listed in PA.

LETSCH, CHRISTOPH (2)—Neckartenzlingen (1749)

Stockingweaver [*Strumpfweber*]. Son of the late tailor [*Schneider*] JOHANN MICHAEL LETSCH at *Hausen an der Lauchert.* Wf: ANNA MARIA, widow of the town-shepherd [*Fleckenschäfer*] HESS. Ch: (1) Johann Georg, b. 4-12-1735. // Perhaps CHRISTOPF ETSCH, *Leslie,* October 7, 1749, Hinke, I, 419.

LEUCHT, SIMON (2)—Gündelbach

B. 1750. "Died on the way across the ocean."

LEYHR, ANNA MAGDALENA (2)—Apfelstetten

B. 10-6-1735, daughter of GEORGE and MAGDALENA LEYHR. Stepdaughter of JOHANN JACOB TRENTZ (q.v.) of Apfelstetten.

LEYHR, JOHANN GEORG (2)—Apfelstetten (1749)

B. 3-3-1733, son of GEORG and MAGDALENA LEYHR. Stepson of JOHANN JACOB TRENTZ (q.v.) of Apfelstetten. Nothing in the Burial Register after 1749. *Ludwigsburg Protocol,* 4-24-1749, [JOH. JACOB TRENTZ to] "take stepchildren's property along to America." // Perhaps JOHANN GEORG LEYSS, *Phoenix,* August 28, 1750, Hinke, I, 439.

LINSENMEYER, JOHANNES (1)—Ohmden

B. 9-24-1738, son of JOHANNES and CATHARINA LINSENMEYER. "Went to the New World and died."

LIPS, JOHANN FRIEDRICH (1)—Marschalkenzimmern and Betzweiler (see Dornhan) (1751)

Servant [*Knecht*] at Betzweiler. Son of JOHANN GEORGE LIPS, day laborer [*Tagelöhner*], and wife URSULA, of Marschalkenzimmern. Wf: CHRISTINA, *née* WEYDENBACH, daughter of Andreas Weydenbach, schoolmaster [*Schulmeister*]. Married 7-11-1751, along with JERG JAKOB WALTER (q.v.) and ROSINA SECKINGER. "Because these two couples were to go to America the following day, they were previously married at Betzweiler, after catechetical instruction [*Kinderlehre*]."

## LIPS, JOHANN GEORG (1)—Marschalkenzimmern (1751)

Born 3-21-1725, son of JOHANN GEORGE LIPS, day laborer [*Tagelöhner*] and wf. URSULA. Brother of Johann Friedrich Lips (q.v.). Married out of the village. To America with Anna Raigel (q.v.) and others, who, the pastor wrote, "left the country on foot, July 12, 1751, with some other young people. Their intention was to immigrate to New Georgia [*Neu Georgien*] in America. But after that we never heard the least bit of news from them."

## LOELL (LOEHL) (2)—Neckartenzlingen (1749)

Given ducal permission to emigrate, with his daughter; see ducal letter of 1749, in Introduction.

## LUDWIG, ANNA MARGARETHA (1)—Grünwettersbach (1752)

Ch: (1) Maria Christina, b. (illeg.) 9-17-1749. This child "went away to America in 1752 with her frivolous mother" ["*kam 1752 fort in Amer. m. ihrer leichtfertigen Mutter.*"]

## LUDWIG, LORENTZ (1)—Grünwettersbach (1751)

B. 10-2-1713, son of JOHANN JACOB and ANNA MARIA LUDWIG. "Baptismal Certificate to Pennsylvania, May 12, [1751]." // LORENTZ LUDEWIG, *Shirley*, September 5, 1751, Hinke, I, 454, with GEORG CONRAD SCHWEIKART of Grünwettersbach. 3PA, 17, 578: LORENTZ LUDWICK, Cocalico Tp., Lancaster Co., Pa., 1779.

## LUIPPOLD, AGNES (1)—Dürrwangen (1750)

B. 1-27-1720. "Went to Pennsylvania, 1750."

## LUTZ, MATTHAEUS (1)—Grötzingen (1754)

Wf: CATHARINA. Ch: (1) Johannes, 8-18-1751. "To Pennsylvania, 1754." // MATTHEIS LUTZ, *Neptune*, September 23, 1751, Hinke, I, 467, with Johann Egidius Hecker, Reformed preacher. 3PA, 15, 680: JOHN LOOTS, next to GEORGE GENTNER (a Grötzingen name), Northern Liberties (East Part), City of Philadelphia, Pa., 1781.

# M

## MACHLEYD, DANIEL (2)—Poppenweiler (1752)

Two by this name in the same year. [I] Son of ANDREAS MACHLEYD. B. 4-14-1709. Wf: EUPHROSINA (BEURER). Ch: (1) Anna Catharina, b. 1735; (2) Euphrosina, b. 1737; (3) Anna Margaretha, b. 1738; (4) Daniel, b. 1742; (5) Anna Christina, b. 1744; (6) Wilhelm, b. 1745; (7) Adam Friedrich, b. 1747; (8) Jacob, b. 1750; (9) Anna, b. 5-5-1751. This family not in the Communicant or Burial Registers after 1752. *Ludwigsburg Protocol*, 5-2-1752, Daniel Machleyd and associates, to Pennsylvania." // DANIEL MACHLEIT, *Rawley*, October 23, 1752, Hinke, I, 500; list headed by John George Bager, Lutheran pastor. [II] Son of CHRISTOPH MACHLEYD. B. 10-13-1731.

## MACK, GEORG (2)—Asch (1752)

Journeyman weaver [*Webergeselle*]. Son of the Justiciary and weaver [*Gerichtsverwalter u. Weber*] JOHANN HEINRICH MACK at Laichingen. Wf: ANNA MARIA HAIL, daughter of the shoemaker [*Schuhmacher*]

JOHANNES HAIL. Ch: (1) Johann Heinrich, b. 8-24-1745; (2) last child, b. 1749; died young. *Ludwigsburg Protocol,* 4-21-1752, to "Pennsylvania." // HANS JORG MOCK, *Rawley,* October 23, 1752, Hinke, I, 500; list headed by JOHN GEORGE BAGER, Luth. pastor. Many listed in PA.

## MACK, JOHANNES (2)—Neckartenzlingen (1766)

Baker [*Beck*]. Wf: (ANNA) JUDITH VEIZHANS. Ch: (1) Anna Barbara, b. 3-14-1760; (2) Elisabetha Margaretha, b. 3-17-1762. "Went away" [*"weggezogen"*]. Gerber writes that "he had always been somewhat frivolous, had not liked to work, but tried in vain to get rich by other schemes, but, in spite of everything, was worth 300 Gulden." [*"Er war jederzeit etwas leichtsinnig gewesen, hatte nicht gern gearbeitet, sondern durch andere 'Commercien' vergeblich reich zu werden gesucht, besass aber immerhin 300 Gulden. Im Uebrigen friedlich und dienstfertig gegen Jedermann."*] "Otherwise [he was] peaceable and obliging toward everyone." // The will of JOHN MACK, of Reading, Berks Co., Pa., dated April 15, 1782, and probated October 2, 1784, mentions wf JUDITH, and sons GEORGE, THEOBALD, PHILIP, GODLIEP, and JACOB; Witnesses: JOHN STROHECKER and JOHN SHOEMAKER, *Berks County Will Abstracts,* I, 333-4, GSP.

## MADER, ELISABETHA (1)—Plüderhausen

B. 1-6-1738, daughter of HANS JOERG MADER, vinedresser [*Weingärtner*] and wf ANNA MARIA, *née* MUELLER. According to records kept by Pastor Johann Melchior Kapff, who was in charge of the parish 1725-1770, she "married outside Württemberg." "Went to New England." // Cf. JOERG MADER, with VALTIN MATTER, September 16, 1751, Hinke, I, 464.

## MAEULE, MATTHIAS FRIEDRICH (1)—Rommelshausen

Married, in Fellbach, to CATHARINA BARBARA OF[F], b. 1-14-1756, daughter of JACOB OF(F), tailor [*Schneider*] and wf MARIA, *née* OESCHLER. "From there she went with her husband to Phila." // This family landed at Philadelphia, September 5, 1805, from the ship *Verny* [Hinke, III, 171]: MATTHIS FRIEDERICH MAILLE, of Feldbach, age 47 years; wf CATHARINA BARBARA, age 50. Ch: (1) Catharina Barbara, age 25; (2) Mathias Friederich, age 22; (3) Johannes, age 21; (4) Friederika, age 19; (5) Walburga, age 15. Listed with them are MARIA MAGDELINA [——], of Feldbach, age 12 [a daughter?], and FRIEDRICH HAUSER, of Feldbach, age 31.

## MAIER, JOHANN JACOB (1)—Sondelfingen

Wf: ANNA MARIA. Ch: (1) Jacob, b. 10-23-1740; (2) Anna Maria, b. 10-16-1747, to "New England." All: "Went to the English colonies."

## MAJER, ELISABETHA (2)—Neuffen (1749)

B. 12-22-1735, daughter of JOSEPH and BARBARA MAJER. Went to America with GEORG LUDWIG ULMER (q.v.) of Neuffen, after hurried confirmation and *special* communion in the sacristy, April 3, 1749. The pastor added the following blessing to their record: "The Lord accompany both with the Holy Spirit, to America, their intended country, on which account this dispensation is granted." [*"Der Herr begleite auch diese beide mit dem werten heiligen Geiste in die von ihnen intendirten amerikanischen Lande, weshalb obige Dispensation erteilt ist"*].

## MAJER, JOHANN MARTIN (1)—Bodelshausen (1772)

Shoemaker [*Schuhmacher*]. Wf: DOROTHEA (GUTBROD). Ch: (1) Anna Maria, b. 5-4-1760; (2) Anna, b. 9-14-1761; (3) Daniel, b. 6-1-1769. "To America, May 14, 1772." // HANS MARTIN MEYER, *Crawford*, October 16, 1772, Hinke I, 741.

## MANN, JOHANNES (1)—Beihingen, Oberamt Ludwigsburg (1744)

Wf: MARGARETHA. Ch: (1) Johann Michael, b. 3-21-1730. "To Pennsylvania, May 4, 1744." Many listed in PA.

## MANN, JOHANN JACOB (2)—Laufen am Neckar (1753)

Shoemaker [*Schuhmacher*]. B. 1707. Wf: CHRISTINA CATHARINA (MENOLD), b. 1709. Ch: (1) Catharina Dorothea, b. 1737; (2) Christina, b. 1742; (3) Maria Barbara, b. 1751. "Went to the New World." // JACOB MANN, age 41, with JACOB MANN, age 31, HANS GEORG MANN, (two), and JOHANNES MANN, also with MELCHER MINOLT, age 22, *Brothers*, September 26, 1753, Hinke, I, 551, 553. 3PA, 22, 100: JACOB and AND'W MANN, Bethel Tp., Bedford Co., Pa., 1775. 3PA, 25, 570, 573, 581, 583: JACOB MANN, several tracts of land in Bedford Co., Pa., survey 1783, 1785, and 1794. 3PA, 26, 130: JACOB MAN, 280 acres, Northampton Co., Pa., survey April 18, 1785.

## MASER, JACOB (1)—Rötenberg

Day laborer [*Tagelöhner*]. Wf: MAGDALENA. Ch: (1) Gallus, b. 10-21-1732; (2) Matthäus, b. 9-22-1736. // Several JACOB MOSERS listed in Hinke, 1747, 1754, and 1772. 3PA, 18, 37: MATHIAS MASER, carpenter, Oley Tp., Berks Co., Pa., 1767.

## MASER, MAGDALENA (1)—Rötenberg

Ch: (1) Magdalena, b. (illeg.) 6-7-1750, "went to Pennsylvania with her mother."

## MASSER, CHRISTIAN (1)—Schlaitdorf

Smith [*Schmied*]. Wf: ANNA MARIA, *née* BRODBECK. Ch: (1) Anna Maria, b. 1-7-1743. // CHRISTIAN MOSSER, *Muscliffe Galley*, December 22, 1744, Hinke, I, 359. 3PA, 21, 57: CHRISTIAN MOSSER, with MICHAEL MOSSER, Hellam Tp., York Co., Pa., 1779.

## MASSER, JACOB (1)—Lossburg

Wf: ANNA MARIA. Ch: (1) Catharina, b. 9-26-1748. To "Pennsylvania." // Several JACOB MOSERS listed in Hinke, 1747, 1754, and 1772.

## MAUL, HANS (2)—Emmingen (see Unterjettingen) (1751)

Farmhand at the Miller's at Emmingen [*Bauernknecht beim Müller zu Emmingen*]. Son of the day laborer [*Tagelöhner*] JACOB MAUL at Buttenhard bei Lahr, *Reformed* [*reformirter Religion*]. Wf. [at least intended] ANNA MARIA (SCHNAUFER), butcher's daughter [*Metzgertochter*]. Bans proclaimed once [*prima vice proclamirt*], 5-2-1751. "Are going to America" ["*emigrant in Americano*"]. // J. JACOB MAUL, *Brothers*, September 16, 1751, Hinke, I, 464. Cf. also HANS MICHAEL SCHNAUFFER, *Nancy*, September 16, 1751, Hinke, I, 462.

## MAUL, JOHANN GEORG (1)—Dagersheim

B. 2-9-1727, son of JOHANN GEORG MAUL, shoemaker [*Schuhmacher*] and wf ANNA BARBARA, *née* HOEGER. To the "New Land." // JOHN GEORGE MAUL, *Halifax*, October 20, 1754, Hinke I, 653. 3PA, 21, 8: GEORGE MAUL, blacksmith, York, York Co., Pa., 1779.

## MAURER, JOHANNES (1)—Ebingen

Stocking weaver [*Strumpfweber*]. Wf: MARIA AGNES, *née* BECK. Ch: (1) Susanna Catharina, b. 6-30-1742. To "Pennsylvania." // JOHANNES MAURER, *Chesterfield*, September 2, 1749, Hinke, I, 393. Sower's newspaper, August 19, 1758, quoted in Hocker, 75: "JOHANNES MAURER, Great Swamp, Bucks County, near MICHEL HORLACHER." Many listed in PA.

## MAUSER, HANS MICHAEL (2)—Oeschingen (1751)

B. 6-11-1707, son of CASPAR MAUSER. Wf: AGATHA, *née* GOMMINGER, daughter of HANS JERG GOMMINGER at Ofterdingen. Ch: (1) Johannes, b. 3-11-1735; (2) Agnes, b. 6-9-1737; (3) Johann Friedrich, b. 9-26-1740, at Charlottenhof; (4) Johann Jacob, b. 4-12-1743, at Charlottenhof; (5) Anna Maria, b. 1-2-1746; (6) Nicolaus, b. 5-28-1749. "This Hans Michael Mauser and his wife Agatha, along with his two children Johannes and Agnes, because they want to go to the New World, have all four (even Agnes, because she has been confirmed) received Holy Communion publicly in the church after the Vesper reading, on May 2, 1751." [*Dieser Hans Michael Mauser und sein Weib Agatha, sambt seinen 2 Kindern Johannes und Agnes, weilen sie wollen in die Neu-Welt ziehen, so haben sie alle 4, auch die Agnes, weil sie eine Confirmata war, das h. Nachtmahl in der Kirche öffentlich nach der Vesper Lection empfangen den 2. Mai, 1751."*] // MICHEL MAUSER, with JOHANNES MAUSER, *Nancy*, September 16, 1751, Hinke, I, 463. 3PA, 26, 124: MICHAEL MAUSER, 25 acres, Northampton Co., Pa., survey July 27, 1752. 3PA, 18, 40: JOHN MAUSER, Maxatawny Tp., Berks Co., Pa., 1767. 3PA, 18, 58: FRED'K MAUSER, Greenwich Tp., Berks Co., Pa., 1767. 3PA, 18, 382: JACOB MAUSER, with NICH'S MOISER, Maxatawny Tp., Berks Co., Pa., 1780. 3PA, 18, 250: NICH'S MOUSER, with JACOB MOUSER, "taylor", Maxatawny Tp., Berks Co., Pa., 1779.

## MAUTHE, BALTHAS (2)—Onstmettingen (1752)

SALOMON PETER'S son [*saltpeter maker*]. Wf: ANNA BARBARA (LANG). Ch: (1) Catharina, b. 6-3-1750. According to records of Pastor Johann Georg Stählen, 1746-1756, this family "went to New England." *Ludwigsburg Protocol*, 5-3-1752, mentions immigrants to Pennsylvania from Onstmettingen, without giving names. // Two listed in Hinke, 1752: BALTHAS MAUTE, *Ann Galley*, September 23, 1752, Hinke, I, 486; and BALTHAS MAUTE, *Forest*, October 10, 1752, Hinke, I, 494. For the family name MAUTE, see also JOHANNES WEIS(S)MANN, of Ebingen.

## MAUTTE, MATTHAEUS (2)—Laufen/Eyach

Went to Pennsylvania in 1746, with HANS BALTHASS BITZER (q.v.) of Laufen/Eyach. In the summer of 1749, LANDENBERGER (q.v.) of Ebingen, who made frequent trips between Germany and America, brought back favorable letters from both. According to a report made 1749 by Mayor Venninger of Laufen, preserved at Ludwigsburg, the letters are said to have "made such an impression among different families, that they even now appear to be intent on leaving next Spring." This resulted in the large Laufen emigration of 1750. //

MATTHEIS MAUT, *Restauration,* October 9, 1747, Hinke, I, 366. 3PA, 18, 27: MATHIAS MAUTY, Alsace Tp., Berks Co., Pa., 1767.

## MAUZ, (GEORG) FRIEDRICH (2)—Neckartenzlingen (1749)

Butcher [*Metzger*]. Son of JACOB MAUZ at Riederich. Wf: ANNA CATHARINA, widow of JOHANNES GREINER, married 1736.

## MAYER, ANNA (2)—Nehren (1753)

B. 6-8-1725, daughter of JOHANN JACOB MAYER, deceased, and his widow MARIA BARBARA, *née* KEGEL (q.v.). Ch: (1) Johannes, b. (illeg.) 3-13-1751; father, HANS MAYER, journeyman cartwright [*Wagnergeselle*] at Bodelhausen. "Went with him and son to Pennsylvania," May 9, 1753. *Ludwigsburg Protocol,* 4-3-1753, to "Pennsylvania."

## MAYER, FRIEDRICH (1)—Weil im Schönbuch (1754)

Weaver [*Weber*]. Wf: MARIA AGNES. Ch: (1) Johannes, b. 12-30-1744. *Ludwigsburg Protocol,* 1754. // JACOB FREDRICK MEYER, with JOHANN VALLENTIN MEIER, *Peggy,* October 16, 1754, Hinke, I, 636, 638; others before and after.

## MAYER, HANS (2)—Bodelshausen (see Nehren) (1753)

Journeyman cartwright [*Wagnergeselle*] at Bodelshausen. Father of an illegitimate son, Johannes, b. 3-13-1751, to ANNA MAYER (q.v.), daughter of JOHANN JACOB MAYER, deceased, and his widow MARIA BARBARA, *née* KEGEL (q.v.). Went to Pennsylvania with ANNA MAYER and son, May 9, 1753. *Ludwigsburg Protocol,* 4-3-1753, to "Pennsylvania." // Several Johannes Mayers listed in Hinke, one in 1753: JOHANNES MYER (MAYER), age 37, with JOHANNIS MARTIN MYER, age 18, *Halifax,* September 28, 1753, Hinke, I, 560-1.

## MAYER, JOHANN JACOB (1)—Kleinengstingen (1749)

B. 9-24-1709. Wf: ANNA MARGARETHA, *née* SCHUMACHER, daughter of ANDREAS SCHUMACHER and wf. ANNA MARIA, *née* MUELLER. Ch: (1) Andreas, b. 1-16-1730; (2) Anna Barbara, b. 7-10-1732; (3) Waldburga, b. 2-25-1734; (4) Johann Georg, b. 6-13-1736; (5) Johann Jacob, b. 9-13-1740; (6) Eva Maria, b. 1-8-1746. "To Pennsylvania 1749." // JACOB MEYER, with JOHANN NICKKLAS MAYER, *Leslie,* October 7, 1749, Hinke, I, 420. Cf. also JOHANN ANDREAS MAYER, (two) with JOHANN GEORGE MAYER, *Duke of Wirtenberg,* October 16, 1751, Hinke, I, 475.

## MAYER, MARGARETHA (2)—Steinenbronn (1754)

B. 8-3-1728, daughter of the late farmer [*Bauer*] HANS JERG MAYER and wf BARBARA (HERTFELDER). "Went to America 1754."

## MAYER, MARIA BARBARA (1)—Dornhan

B. 4-20-1723, daughter of HANS MARTIN and ANNA MAYER.

## MAYER, MARIA BARBARA (2)—Nehren (1753)

*Née* KEGEL. Widow of JOHANN JACOB MAYER (†1746) married 1719, widowed 1746. Ch: (1) Anna, b. 6-8-1725 (q.v.); (2) Agnes Catharina, b. 6-14[Baptismal Register 12]-1727; (3) Agnes Maria, b. 6-18-1735. "Went to Pennsylvania, May 9, 1753." *Ludwigsburg Protocol,* 4-3-1753, to "Pennsylvania."

MAYER, MATTHAEUS (2)—Neckartenzlingen (1752)

Weaver [*Weber*]. Wf: MARIA BARBARA. Ch: (1) Maria Catharina, b. 5-31-1746; (2) Johannes, b. 5-20-1749. *Ludwigsburg Protocol,* 5-16-1752. Gerber: "A tailor and grave digger [*Schneider u. Totengräber*] of the same name remained." // JOHANN MATTHEUS MAYER, *Beulah,* September 10, 1753, Hinke, I, 513, 515. 3PA, 11, 616: MATHIAS MIRE, freeman, East Nantmeal Tp., Chester Co., Pa., 1769. 3PA, 18, 655: MATH'W MAYER ESTATE, with MELCHOR MAYER and PETER MAYER, Reading, Berks Co., Pa., 1784.

MAYER, MICHAEL (1)—Grötzingen (1747)

Wf: ANNA MARIA. Ch: Johann Georg, 7-21-1740, "in Philadelphia 1749" (sic); (2) Michael, b. 3-7-1743. After the other emigrants of May 9, 1747, who had private communion the day they left, the pastor names "Michael Mayer and wife, besides one child, [who] went away too, but took communion previously." [*"Michael Mayer et uxor, sammt 1 Kind sind auch weggezogen, aber vorher communicirt worden."*] // Two in Hinke, 1747: MICHEL MEYER, with PHILIPP JACOB MAYER, *Restauration,* October 9, 1747, Hinke, I, 366, and MICHAEL MEYER, *Lydia,* September 24, 1747, Hinke, I, 364.

MAYR, GEORG BALTHASAR (1)—Wurmberg

B. 4-11-1730, son of CHRISTOF and URSULA MAYR. "Is now in Philadelphia in New England in America." [*ist i[e]tzt in Philadelphia in Neu-Engelland in Amer."*]! // BALTAS MAYER, *Chesterfield,* September 2, 1749, Hinke, I, 394. 3PA, 22, 488: BALTZER MYERS, with MARTHA MYERS, JAMES MYERS, ELY MYERS, JACOB MYERS, LEWIS MYERS (single), and CHRIST'N MYERS (single), Pitt Tp., Westmoreland Co., Pa., 1786. 3PA, 26, 472: BALTZER MEYERS, 275 acres, Westmoreland Co., Pa., survey February 26, 1787.

MEERWALD, ANNA MARGARETHA (1)—Nordheim

B. 11-2-1696, daughter of BERNHARD MEERWALD.

MENOLD, GEORG MELCHIOR (2)—Lauffen am Neckar (1753)

Vinedresser [*Vinitor*]. B. 1703. Wf: MARIA BARBARA (DOERRER), b. 1705. Ch: (1) Georg Melchior, b. 1730; (2) Catharina Barbara, b. 1732; (3) Regina Catharina, b. 1735; (4) Johann Michael, b. 1737; (5) Johann Martin, b. 1739; (6) Maria Elisabetha, b. 1741. "Went to the New World." *Ludwigsburg Protocol,* 4-24-1753, *"Minaldin"* to "Pennsylvania." // MELCHIOR FINHOLD (MELCHER MINOLT), age 22, *Brothers,* September 26, 1753, Hinke, I, 551-2.

MERCKLE (MERCKLIN), JOHANN MICHAEL, (?) JR.—Hoheneck (1752)

B. 11-7-1719, son of Judge [*Richter*] JOHANN MICHAEL MERCKLE. Wf: MARGARETHA. Ch: (1) Dorothea, b. 2-26-1744; (2) Anna Maria, b. 12-9-1746, "went to America"; (3) Johann Michael, b. 3-19-1748; (4) Barbara, b. 8-19-1752, "went away" [*"weggezogen"*]. // 3PA, 26, 298: MICH'L MARKLE and JOHN SCHNEIDER, 150 acres, Berks Co., Pa., March 13, 1794.

## MER(T)Z, ANNA MARGARETHA (1)—Pfaffenhofen (1743)

Widow of the carpenter [*Zimmermann*] MICHAEL MERTZ from Truchtelfingen (d. 11-22-1737). Ch: (1) Anna Margaretha, b. 10-15-1713; (2) Maria Juditha, b. 9-21-1726. Disappears from the Church Register, 1743. *Ludwigsburg Protocol,* 1743, to "Pennsylvania." In the Baptismal Register other children are listed, but without reference to their emigration. // 3PA, 18, 34: MARGARET MERTZ, with PETER and JACOB MERTZ, Longswamp Tp., Berks Co., Pa., 1767.

## METZ, JOHANN JACOB (2)—Weilheim, Tübingen

Farmer [*Bauer*]. Emigrated, but destination is not specified. // Several in Hinke. 3PA, 17, 261: JACOB METZ, with LUD'W METZ, Rapho Tp., Lancaster Co., Pa., 1772. 3PA, 25, 255: JACOB METZ, 400 acres, Northumberland Co., Pa., survey March 15, 1794.

## METZGER, JOHANN JACOB (2)—Steinenbronn (1749)

B. 2-2-1715. Wf: BARBARA (DAST), b. 5-27-1722. Ch: (1) Jacob, 1-10-1747. "Went to America, 1749." // JACOB METZGER, with HANS JERCH HAISCH and HANS JERG HANSELMANN, both of Steinenbronn, *Chesterfield,* September 2, 1749, Hinke, I, 394. 3PA, 17, 9: JACOB METZGER, with GEORGE METZGER and JONAS MATZGER, Lancaster Borough, Lancaster, Pa., 1771. 3PA, 19, 458: JACOB METZGER, Buffalo Tp., Northumberland Co., Pa., 1781.

## MEYER, CATHARINA (1)—Grötzingen (1747)

Single. To Pennsylvania, May 9, 1747, after private communion in the church, with Johannes Hermann (q.v.), Hans Jerg Walcker (q.v.), Anna Catharina Schindelberger (q.v.), Anna Catharina Werner (q.v.), and Michael Mayer (q.v.).

## MEYER, JOHANNES (2)—Ofterdingen (1752)

Son of the late weaver [*Weber*] MARTIN MEYER. Wf: AGNES, *née* GRETZING, daughter of SEBASTIAN GRETZING. Married 5-13-1752. Ch: (1) Johannes, b. 5-6-1752. "Because the wife was in the eighth day of confinement, these people, with magisterial permission, were married in the schoolroom, and left the following day with their son Johannes for Pennsylvania." [*Diese wurden, weil sponsa eine 8tägige Kindbetterin, auf Oberamtl. Erlaubnuss in der Schulstube copulirt, zogen des andern Tags darauf mit ihrem K. Johannes von hier in Pennsylvanien."*] // Three JOHANNES MEYERS listed in Hinke, 1752: I, 483-; I, 495; and I, 506.

## M(O)EHLER, JOHANN MARTIN (2)—Möckmühl (1754)

Son of the late vine-dresser [*Weingärtner*] MARTIN M(O)EHLER. Wf: ELISABETHA HAYN, hatter's daughter [*Hutmacherstochter*]. Married 2-8-1747. *Ludwigsburg Protocol,* 5-31-1754, to "Pennsylvania." // Cf. MARTEN MOELLER, *Sally,* November 10, 1767, Hinke, I, 720. 3PA, 17, 267: MARTIN MOHLER, Cocalico Tp., Lancaster Co., Pa., 1772.

## MOESSNER, HANS JACOB (1)—Lossburg

Wf: ELISABETHA. Ch: (1) Mattheus, b. 1-23-1746. To "Pennsylvania." // 3PA, 20, 370: JACOB MESNER, West Pennsboro Tp., Cumberland Co., Pa., 1780.

## MOHR, JACOB (1)—Dagersheim

Day laborer [Tagelöhner]. Wf: ANNA BARBARA, *née* HORBER. Ch: (1) Johanna, b. 12-27-1743. To "New America" [*Neu Amerika*]. // Several in Hinke: 1749, 1754, and 1765. Sower's newspaper, June 16, 1755, quoted in Hocker, 51: "JACOB MOHR, Salisbury Township, Northampton County, advertises that a servant, GEORG GOETZ, 31 years old, ran away, taking with him his wife, 45 years old." Many listed in PA.

## MOLITOR, [ —— ] (2)—Eberstadt (1749)

In the Communicant Register, under the classification "Unmarried Sons and Servants" [*Coelibes filii et servi*] at Filial Lennach-Buchhorn, is the following entry, scribbled in at the bottom: "From Dörtzbach, MOLITOR, going to Pennsylvania with CONRAD LAUFFER (q.v.) and others." // Cf. ADAM MOLITOR, *Minerva,* September 17, 1771, Hinke, I, 734. 3PA, 14, 420: ADAM MULLIDORE, Passyunk Tp., Philadelphia Co., Pa., 1774. 3PA, 14, 396: GEORGE MULADORE, Northern Liberties (East Part), Philadelphia County, Pa., 1774.

## MOOG, JOHANNES (2)—Niederhofen (1750?)

B. 11-28-1706, son of FELIX MOOG at Mentzisheim. Wf: ROSINA, *née* BRICKER, daughter of ABRAHAM BRICKER. Married 5-2-1732. "Went to Pennsylvania." // HANS MOOGH, age 38, *Jamaica Galley,* February 7, 1739, Hinke, I, 252-3. 3PA, 14, 687: HENRY and JOHN MAAG, Passyunk Tp., Philadelphia Co., Pa., 1779. 3PA, 14, 26: JOHN MAAK, Marlborough Tp., Philadelphia Co., Pa., 1769. 3PA, 15, 215: JOHN MAAG, Dock Ward (South Part), City of Philadelphia, Pa., 1780.

## MOREL, MATTHIEU (2)—Dürrmenz (1751)

Wf (1st): MARIE (ROCHON). Ch: (1) Jean Pierre, b. 3-4-1742, at Pinache. Wf (2d): JEANNE MARIE (OZIAS). Ch: (2) Marie Madeleine, b. 10-29-1746, at Pinache; (3) Lucresse, b. 4-29-1749. From the German and Waldensien Church Register for Dürrmenz-Schönenberg. *Ludwigsburg Protocol,* 4-23-1751, "Morell and associates, all naturalized Waldenses, to the New World." // MATTHIEU MORET, *Patience,* September 9, 1751, Hinke, I, 455, with EBERHART CHAPELLE and others.

## MUCKENBERGER, MARIA BARBARA (2)—Mockmühl (1751)

*Ludwigsburg Protocol,* 1-22-1751, to "Pennsylvania."

## MUEH, JOHANNES (1)—Hausen an der Lauchert (1752)

Cartwright [*Wagner*]. Wf: ANNA. Ch: (1) Peter Christian, b. 2-22-1738; (2) Christina, b. 12-25-1741; (3) Agatha, b. 10-13-1748. All three children: "emigrated with parents." Son "went to the New World with his parents in the Spring of 1752." // Cf. PETER MUEH, *Edinburgh,* September 19, 1752, Hinke, I, 480. 3PA, 17, 56: JOHN MEEH, Upper Paxton Tp., Lancaster Co., Pa., 1771.

## MUEHLEISEN, HANS JERG (1)—Grötzingen

Wf: CATHARINA. Ch: (1) Johann Michael, b. 5-4-1743. To "Pennsylvania." // Others (Mihleisen, Milliron) listed in PA.

## MUENSINGER, JOHANN JACOB (1)—Eltingen

Evidently went to the "New World," but came back [*aber wiederkommen*].

## MUELLER, CATHARINA (2)—Reudern (1752)

Single sister of JACOB MUELLER (q.v.) of Reudern. Mentioned in the *Nürtingen Documents. Ludwigsburg Protocol,* 5-2-1752, evidently included under Ludwig Pfeiffer and associates.

## MUELLER, CHRISTIANUS (1)—Nordheim

B. 12-19-1723, son of JOHANN JACOB MUELLER and MARIA ELISABETHA MUELLER. // Several listed in Hinke.

## MUELLER, JACOB (1)—Grötzingen (1748)

Single son of HANS MUELLER. Left for Pennsylvania, May 15, 1748, after private communion, along with JOHANNES GENTNER (q.v.), MICHAEL MUELLER (q.v.), MARGARETHA (q.v.) and ANNA MARIA HOFFSAESS (q.v.) and MARGARETHA MUELLER (q.v.). // JOHAN JACOB MILLER, age 21, with JACOB MILLER, age 23, MICHAEL MILLER, age 24, other Millers, and JOHANNES GINTNER, *Patience,* September 16, 1748, Hinke, I, 383, 385-6.

## MUELLER, JACOB (2)—Reudern (1752)

Shoemaker [*Schuhmacher*]. Wf: ANNA MARIA (MUELLER). Ch: (1) Johann Georg, b. 2-24-1750. "Is in Pennsylvania." Brother of CATHARINA MUELLER (q.v.) of Reudern. From the *Nürtingen Documents. Ludwigsburg Protocol,* 5-2-1752, evidently included under LUDWIG PFEIFFER and associates. // Four Jacob Müller's in Hinke, 1752.

## MUELLER, JOHANNES (1-2)—Oberboihingen

Cartwright's son [*Wagnerssohn*]. Wf: ROSINA. Ch: (1) Jerk, b. 8-22-1742. To "Pennsylvania." According to the Nürtingen Documents, he was a "fisherman and debtor" [*Fischer u. Obaeratus*], and did not leave until after selling his property to pay his debts.

## MUELLER, JOHANNES (2)—Sondelfingen (see Sielmingen) (1754?)

Baker [*Beck*] in Sondelfingen. Wf: (ANNA) MARIA (ARNOLD), b. 9-23-1731, daughter of MICHAEL ARNOLD of Harthausen. Married 1751. From the old Family Register: "CATHARINA, ANNA MARIA, and BARBARA ARNOLD, immigrated to Pennsylvania." The wife was a sister to ANNA CATHARINA (ARNOLD), wife of JOHANN GEORG STAEBLER (q.v.), and of BARBARA (ARNOLD), wife of GEORGE BAYHA, JR. (q.v.)

## MUELLER, JOHANN HEINRICH (2)—Gündelbach

B. 1764. // JOHANNES HEINERICH MULLER, Brig *Dispatch,* October 31, 1786, Hinke, III, 20; also other late emigrants by this name. The will of HENRY MILLER, heretofore citizen and printer of Philadelphia, now of Bethlehem, recorded in Will Book, I, p. 297, Easton, Northampton Co., dated Sept. 27, 1781, probated April 30, 1782, mentions various Moravian ministers, then "Nephew JOHANN HENRICK MULLER, schoolmaster and land surveyor at Gundelbach, Maulbrunnen Amts, in the Dukedom of Würtemberg." For a brief biography of the well-known Pennsylvania printer, Heinrich Miller (1702-1782), a native of Rhoden in Waldeck, see Oswald Seidensticker, *The First Century of German Printing in America, 1728-1830* (Philadelphia: Schaefer & Koradi, 1893), 54.

MUELLER, MARGARETHA (1)—Grötzingen (1748)

Single. Left for Pennsylvania, May 15, 1748, after private communion, along with JOHANNES GENTNER (q.v.), MICHAEL MUELLER (q.v.), JACOB MUELLER (q.v.), MARGARETHA (q.v.) and ANNA MARIA HOFFSAESS (q.v.)

MUELLER, MATTHAEUS (2)—Grötzingen

Though mentioned in the Nürtingen Documents, he seems not to have emigrated.

MUELLER, MICHAEL (1)—Grötzingen (1748)

Single, mason's apprentice [*Maurergeselle*]. Left for "Pennsylvania," May 15, 1748, after private communion, along with JOHANNES GENTNER (q.v.), JACOB MUELLER (q.v.), MARGARETHA (q.v.) and ANNA MARIA HOFSAESS (q.v.), and MARGARETHA MUELLER (q.v.). // MICHAEL MILLER, age 24, with JOHAN JACOB MILLER, age 21, JACOB MILLER, age 23, other MILLERS, and JOHANNES GINTNER, *Patience*, September 16, 1748, Hinke, I, 383, 385-6.

MUGLER, BARBARA (1)—Lomersheim

Ch: (1) JOHANN GEORG, b. (illeg.) 3-14-1750. To the "New Land," i.e. Pennsylvania. // Others in Hinke.

MUNZ, ANNA MARIA (1)—Steinenberg

B. 8-8-1729. "Died in America." From records kept 1766-1816, by Abraham Gottlieb Majer.

MUNZ, JOHANN CHRISTIAN (1)—Steinenberg

B. 2-11-1726. To "America." From records kept 1766-1816, by Abraham Gottlieb Majer.

MUTSCHLER, ANNA (1)—Dornhan (1754?)

B. 9-4-1733, daughter of JOHANN JACOB and MARIA MUTSCHLER. Ludwisburg Protocol, 1754(?). // Others in Hinke.

# N

NAEGELE, HANS GEORG (1)—Steinenberg

B. 11-2-1721, son of CHRISTOPH and MARGARETHA NAEGELE. To America, 1744. // 3PA, 17, 108: GEORGE NEGLEY, Lampeter Tp., Lancaster Co., Pa., 1771. 3PA, 24, 599: GEORGE NEAGLEY, tracts in Dauphin Co., Pa., survey August 28, 1786.

NAGEL, CHRISTIAN (1)—Döffingen (1751)

Tailor [*Schneider*]. B. 12-7-1693. Wf (1st): DOROTHEA *née* GECKLIN, b. 12-16-1688, d. 1739; Ch: (1) Christine, b. 7-2-1723, "died enroute to America"; (2) Gottlieb, b. 11-25-1726, "followed his brother to America." Wf. (2d): ANNA, *née* GOTTSCHALL, b. 11-29-1713; Ch: (3) Anna Maria, b. 2-13-1741; "to America." (4) Christian, b. 1-5-1747; "to America." (5) Maria Agnes, b. 10-23-1749; "to America." Nagel and his second wife and the above named children "went to Pennsylvania in 1751. He died there after 1½ years." [*1751 n. Pens. Er starb dort nach 1½ Jahren.*"] From the Baptismal Register and the Family Register

(1808). // CHRISTIAN NAGEL, with ANDREAS BITINGER of Döffingen, *Nancy,* September 16, 1751, Hinke, I, 463. GOTTLIEB NAGEL, age 26, *Barclay,* September 14, 1754, Hinke, I, 596, 598. Several listed in PA.

NAGEL, HANS JERG (2)—Beutelsbach (1750)

Ludwigsburg Protocol, 3-23-1750, to "Pennsylvania." // HANS JERG NAGEL, *Patience,* August 11, 1750, Hinke, I, 427. Several listed in PA.

NAGEL, JOHANN (2)—Beutelsbach

B. 3-26-1726, son of JOHANN NAGEL. // JOHANN NAGEL, *Nord America,* October 10, 1787, Hinke, III, 24; others later.

NEHER, HANS MARTIN (1)—Dürrwangen (1750)

B. 10-5-1713. Wf: URSULA *née* JETTER of Heselwangen. Ch: (1) Anna Maria, b. 8-26-1737; (2) Hans Martin, b. 5-15-1739; (3) Agnes, 6-1-1744; (4) Hans Jerg, b. 9-21-1746. "Went to Pennsylvania in 1750, with family of four children." // JOHAN MARTIN NEHER, *Osgood,* September 29, 1750, Hinke, I, 445. 3PA, 17, 887: MARTIN NEHER, Earl Tp., Lancaster Co., Pa., 1782. The will of MARTIN NEHER, of Earl Tp., Lancaster Co., Pa., dated February 19, 1793, probated April 18, 1797, mentions wife URSULA and children MARTIN, MARY, AGNES, CATHARINE, and CHRISTINA; Executors: MARTIN NEHER and ANDREW HERTER, *Lancaster County Will Abstracts,* II, 781, GSP.

NEIPP, JOHANNES (1-2)—Hirschlanden (1754)

Shepherd [*Schäfer*]. Wf: AGATHA. Ch: (1) Barbara, b. 12-31-1746, "went to Pennsylvania with her father" [1754]. // JOHANNES NEIPP, heading the list, *Henrietta,* October 22, 1754, Hinke, I, 648, 650. 3PA, 17, 668: JOHN NEIB, Heidelberg Tp., Lancaster Co., Pa., 1779.

NEPS, FRIEDRICH (1)—Schlaitdorf

Cowherd [*Kuhhirt*]. Wf: BARBARA (MEYER). Ch: (1) Dorothea, b. 1-13-1738, "to the New World"; (2) Christianus, b. 4-1-1741; (3) Justina, b. 4-3-1743; (4) Christina, b. 5-4-1745.

NESTEL, (JOHANN) MARTIN (1)—Weil im Schönbuch (1751)

Baker [*Beck*]. Wf: ANNA MARIA; *née* SEEL. Ch: (1) Johann Gottlieb, b. 11-4-1743, "to the New World"; (2) Jacob Ulrich, b. 2-21-1750, to "America." Ludwigsburg Protocol, 1751. // *Staatsbote,* Philadelphia, May 31, 1774, quoted in Hocker, 142: "MARTIN NESTELL, Stone Arabia, Tryon County, Province of New York, advertises that his servant, ADAM KUHN, 40 years old, ran away."

NESTEL, JOHANN MICH(A)EL (1)—Weil im Schönbuch

Smith [*Schmied*]. Wf: ANNA DOROTHEA *née* KRAFFT. Ch: (1) Anna Margaretha, b. 1-14-1746; (2) Johann Michael, b. 1-15-1748; (3) Anna Maria, b. 7-23-1750; (4) Christina, b. 4-3-1753.

NEUFFER, JOHANN MICHAEL (2)—Kemnat

Weaver [*Weber*]. Wf: MARGARETHA (GEHRUNG), weaver's daughter [*Weberstochter*]. Ch: (1) Johann Michael, b. 1746; (2) Johann David, b. 1748; (3) Georg, b. 1751; (4) Philipp Jacob, b. 1753. "Went to America." Ludwigsburg Protocol, *venia emigrandi* only. // 3PA, 18, 316: JACOB NEUFERT, Albany Tp., Berks Co., Pa., 1780.

NIEBLING, ELISABETHA (1)—Grötzingen (1749)

Widow. "Emigrated May 1, 1749," with JOHANN MICHAEL PFRANG, MATTHAEUS PFRANG, SR., MICHEL LAUB, JOHANNES GRAUER, AUGUSTINUS GENTNER, HANS JERG HOFSAESS, CHRISTOPH JAECKLE, and CONRAD RAISCH, all (q.v.).

NIEBLING, JOHANNES (1)—Grötzingen (1749)

"Emigrated with wife, May 1, 1749," along with JOHANN MICHAEL PFRANG, MATTHAEUS PFRANG, SR., MICHEL LAUB, JOHANNES GRAUER, AUGUSTINUS GENTNER, HANS JERG HOFSAESS, CHRISTOPH JAECKLE, and CONRAD RAISCH, all (q.v.). // JOHANNES NIBLING, Albany, with JOHANNES GRAUER of Grötzingen, September 2, 1749, Hinke, I, 395.

NILL, JOHANN CASPAR (1)—Bodelshausen (1753)

Wf: ANNA. Ch: (1) Anna Maria, b. 7-8-1745; (2) Agnes, b. 11-1-1748. "Went to America," or "Pennsylvania." Ludwigsburg Protocol, 1753. // JOHAN CASPER NILL, age 33, *Peggy*, September 24, 1753, Hinke, I, 545. 3PA, 16, 98: CASPER NELL, Germantown, Philadelphia Co., Pa., 1782.

NONNENMACHER, HANS LUDWIG (2)—Mähringen (1751)

Wf: ANNA MARIA.. Ch: (1) Heinrich, b. 4-22-1745; (2) Johann Adam, b. 11-17-1747; (3) Anna Margaretha, b. 3-22-1750. Ludwigsburg Protocol, 4-27-1751, [——] Nonnenmacher to "Pennsylvania." // JOHAN LUDWIG NONNENMACHER, *Nancy*, September 16, 1751, Hinke, I, 462. Cf. *Staatsbote*, Philadelphia, June 1, 1773, quoted in Hocker, 130: "JACOB NONNENMACHER, Goshenhoppen." 3PA, 14, 95: LODWICK NONNAMAKER, near GEORGE SNEERING and CHRISTOPHER YEAKLE, Germantown Tp., Philadelphia Co., Pa., 1769. 3PA, 26, 300: LUDWICK NUNUMACHER, 50 acres, Berks Co., survey November 30, 1772. 3PA, 18, 322: LUDWIG NONEMAKER, Bern Tp., Berks Co., Pa., 1780. 3PA, 13, 174: HENRY and ADAM NUNNEMAKER, Rockhill Tp., Bucks Co., Pa., 1781. 3PA, 19, 218: HENRY NUNEMACHER, Northampton Town, Northampton Co., Pa., 1786.

NUFFER, CHRISTOPH (1)—Neuffen

Wf: CHRISTINA. Ch: (1) Eleanora Catharina, b. 10-12-1750. // CHRISTIAN NEUFFER, *Phoenix*, September 25, 1751, Hinke, I, 471. Cf. *Philadelphische Correspondenz*, June 3, 1783, quoted in Hocker, 175: "CHRISTIANA NUFFERIN, from Rothenburg, on the Necker, who came to America about thirty-four years ago and lived at Allentown, seeks her son CHRISTIAN and her three daughters, CHRISTIANA, CATHARINA and VERONICA." 3PA, II, 403: CHRISTOPHER NUFER, laborer, Thornbury Tp., Chester Co., Pa., 1768.

## O

OCKER, JOHANN MICHAEL (2)—Rudersberg (1749)

Smith and Judge [*Schmied u. Richter*]. Widower. Wf (2d): BARBARA BENZER. Ch: (1) Christina Margaretha, b. 4-11-1737; (2) Anna, b. 9-10-1738; (3) Christina Sara, b. 8-25-1740; (4) Elisabetha, b. 4-7-1743; (5) died early; (6) died early; (7) Johann Michael, b. 2-26-1747. No later children listed. Ludwigsburg Protocol, 4-24-1749, to "Pennsylvania," with wife and five children. On same ship with ANDREAS FOEHL, from neighboring Steinenberg. // MICHAL OKHER, *Patience*, September 19, 1749, Hinke, I, 409. Cf. will of JOHN MICHAEL OCKERS, of Northampton Co., Pa., dated January 27, 1755, probated May 13, 1760, mentioning wife and son NICHOLAS and other children; witness: NICHOLAS MAYER and NICHOLAS FISHER; unrecorded.

## OEFFINGER, GEORG HEINRICH (1)—Wurmberg

Ropemaker and cowherd [*Seiler bezw. Kuhhirt*]. Wf: AGNES. Ch: (1) Johann Melchior, b. 9-23-1739, "emigrated with parents"; (2) Regina, b. 3-7-1745, "emigrated with parents." To "Pennsylvania." // 3PA, 11, 112: HENRY EFFINGER, with HENRY EFFINGER, freeman, Springfield Tp., Chester Co., Pa., 1779. 3PA, 11, 199: MALACI EFFINGER, freeman, Ridley Tp., Chester Co., Pa., 1766. 3PA, 11, 528: MALCHIA EFINGER, freeman, Marple Tp., Chester Co., Pa., 1769.

## OEHRLE, HANS JACOB (2)—Laufen/Eyach (1750)

Carpenter [*Zimmermann*]. B. 10-19-1720, son of the carpenter PHILIPP OEHRLE, and wf MARGARETHA. Wf: CHRISTINA. Ch: (1) Lucia, b. 8-11-1746; (2) Johannes, b. 1-26-1750. "Went to Pennsylvania, 1750." // JOHANNES OHRLE, *Brothers*, August 24, 1750, Hinke, I, 436. 3PA, 17, 87: JACOB EARLY, Donegal Tp., Lancaster Co., Pa., 1771. The will of JACOB EARLY, of Donegal Tp., Lancaster Co., Pa., dated April 27, 1777, probated May 5, 1777, mentions wife CHRISTIANA, children JOHN, JACOB, LUTEY, AGNESS, and EVE; executors: NICHOLAS RIDSAKER and JOHN WILAND, *Lancaster County Will Abstracts*, I, 242, GSP.

## OLPP, HANS BERNHARD (1)—Merklingen

Shoemaker [*Schuhmacher*]. Wf: CATHARINA, *née* REIS. Ch: (1) Catharina Christina, b. 6-7-1749. // BERNHART ALLPP, *President*, September 27, 1752, Hinke, I, 490. 3PA, 24, 739: BARNARD OLPH, 300 acres, Cumberland Co., Pa., survey May 31, 1762.

## OSTER, CHRISTOPH (2)—Aich (1749)

Granted ducal permission to emigrate in 1749; see the ducal letter of that year quoted in our Introduction.

## OSSWALD, JACOB FRIEDRICH (2)—Ossweil (1752)

Huntsman [*Jäger*]. B. 8-21-1713, son of the tax collector [*Steuerbürgermeister*] JOHANN MARTIN OSSWALD, and wf CHRISTINA (KINDLER). Wf: ANNA MARIA (REBSTOCK), the cloister cooper's daughter [*Klosterküferstochter*] at Offenhausen, b. 10-7-1709. Ch: (1) Friederica Barbara, b. 11-2-1740, at Steinhülben; (2) Johann Jacob, b. 12-29-1747. "Went with wife and child to Nova Scotia [*NeuSchottland*], April 28, 1752." Ludwigsburg Protocol, 4-11-1752, *venia emigrandi* only. // Cf. FRIEDERICH OSSWALD, age 27, *Patience*, September 15 [17], 1753, Hinke, I, 527, 529. 3PA, 24, 739: JACOB OSWALT, 100 acres, Cumberland Co., Pa., survey June 8, 1762. 3PA, 24, 740: JACOB OSWALD, 100 acres, Cumberland Co., Pa., survey April 3, 1765. 3PA, 18, 9: JACOB OSWALD, single, Reading Town, Berks Co., Pa., 1767. 3PA, 19, 240: DANIEL and JACOB OSWALD, Lynn Tp., Northampton Co., Pa., 1786.

## OZIAS, ELISABETHA (2)—Dürrmenz (1753)

*Née* MARNEVAL. Ch: born after 1725. Ludwigsburg Protocol, 3-30-1753, to "Pennsylvania." From the German and Waldensian Church Registers for Dürrmenz-Schönenberg. // Cf. *Philadelphische Correspondenz*, August 19, 1794, quoted in Hocker, 206: "GEORG OZEAS, Water street, third house below South, Philadelphia, advertises that his German servant, Johann Georg Jaeger, ran away. He is a baker, 19 years old." Others listed in PA.

# P

## PARIS, ISAAC (2)—Knittlingen (Grossvillars Parish) (1751)

Wf (1st): JEANNE MARIE (TRENCHANT), death not recorded. Ch: (1) Isaac Barthelemi, b. 2-24-1741. Wf (2d): RACHEL (COCHET). Ch: (2) Pierre, b. 7-11-1744; (3) Jean Martin, b. 4-1-1746; (4) Daniel, b. 3-10-1747; (5) Anne Marie Rachel, b. 1-22-1749. From the Waldensian Church Register for Gross- and Kleinvillars, including Knittlingen and Diefenbach. Ludwigsburg Protocol, 3-12-1751, "Barri," permission to go to "Pennsylvania," and to take his son Isaac's property with him. // ISA PARIS, *Shirley,* September 5, 1751, Hinke, I, 454. Note, however, PIERRE and ISAAC PARIS, *Brotherhood,* November 3, 1750, Hinke, I, 447. *Staatsbote,* Philadelphia, June 15, 1773, quoted in Hocker, 131: "SIMON PETER BAIDEMAN, cooper, with ISAAC PARIS, Stone Arabia, on the Mohawk River, in the Province of New York, seeks information about his brother, JOHANN HENRICH, a cooper and beer brewer, born in Rhine Graffschaft Daun, who came to America and was apprenticed with —— FRICK, brewer, in Lancaster. Address, PETER PARIS, merchant, Phila——, or his brother, ISAAC PARIS, Stone Arabia."

## PEIROT, JAQUES (2)—Diefenbach (Grossvillars Parish) (1752)

Wf: LOUISE (CHANNET). Ch: (1) Michel, b. 12-7-1740; (2) Jean Pierre, b. 4-24-1743; (3) Susanne Catherine, b. 11-30-1745; (4) Jean Charles, b. 6-9-1749. From the Waldensian Church Register for Gross- and Kleinvillars, including Knittlingen and Diefenbach. Ludwigsburg Protocol, 4-21-1752, "to Pennsylvania." // JAQUE PEIROT, *Nancy,* September 27, 1752, Hinke, I, 491.

## PFAEFLE, JOHANNES (1)—Merklingen

Farmer [*Bauer*]. Wf: MARGARETHA. Ch: (1) Eva, b. 12-12-1748.

## PFAFF, HANS PHILIPP ADAM (1)—Steinheim an der Murr (1752)

Schoolmaster [*Schulmeister*]. Wf: [FRAU!] SOPHIA CATHARINA. Ch: (1) Friderica Magdalena, b. 3-25-1745, "emigrated with her parents to the New World, 1752."

## PFEIFFER, LUDWIG (2)—Reudern (1752)

Day laborer [*Tagelöhner*]. Wf: MARGARETHA, *née* KURZ, daughter of SIXT KURZ. Married 4-29-1749. Ch: (1) Stillborn son, b. 1751. No later children in the Baptismal Register. Mentioned in the Nürtingen Documents, 1752. Ludwigsburg Protocol, 5-2-1752, LUDWIG PFEIFFER and companions. // 3PA, 18, 84: LUDWIG PFEIFFER, farmer, Bern Tp., Berks Co., Pa., 1767.

## PFINGSTAG, CHRISTIANUS (1-2)—Altenriet

Gravedigger [*Totengräber*]. Wf: ANNA, *née* EBERWEIN. Ch: (1) Rosina, b. 9-18-1748. To "Pennsylvania." Disappears from Church Register, 1748. // CHRISTIANUS PFINGSTAG, Snow *Good Intent,* November 9, 1749, Hinke, I, 426.

PFINGSTAG, JOHANN MICHAEL (2)—Wiernsheim

Wf: ROSINA. Ch: (1) Maria Agnes, b. 4-5-1734, "went with her parents to Pennsylvania." // MICH'L PHINSTAAG (MICHAEL PFINGSTAG), age 32, *Samuel,* August 30, 1737, Hinke, I, 169-170.

PFINGSTAG, MARTIN (1)—Schlaitdorf

Wf: REGINA JUDITH. Ch: (1) Anna Maria, b. 5-19-1740. // MARTIN PFINGSTAG, *Restauration,* October 9, 1747, Hinke, I, 365.

PFITZ, MICHAEL (1)—Grötzingen (1754)

Weaver [*Weber*]. Wf: (ANNA) BARBARA. Ch: (1) Margaretha, b. 1-18-1742; (2) Michael, b. 1-24-1745; (3) Jacob, b. 2-7-1751. To "Pennsylvania." // 3PA, 25, 144: JACOB FITZ, 400 acres, Northumberland Co., Pa., survey March 15, 1794.

PFRANG, MATTHAEUS, SR. (1)—Grötzingen (1749)

"ALT MATTHAEUS PFRANG." Left May 1, 1749, with Johann Michael Pfrang, Michel Laub, Johannes Grauer, Augustinus Gentner, Hans Jerg Hofsäss, Christoph Jäckle, and Conrad Raisch, all (q.v.).

PFRANG, JOHANN MICHAEL (1)—Grötzingen (1749)

Wf: ANNA MARIA. Ch: (1) Anna Maria, b. 1-22-1734; (2) Maria Agnes, b. 1-14-1740; (3) Eva, b. 10-27-1742; (4) Anna, b. 1-29-1748. Left May 1, 1749, with others from the same village (cf. *supra,* MATTHAEUS PFRANG, SR.). The record of emigration in the Church Register states, "Johann Michael Pfrang and wife and three children," adding the further remark, however, that the father "returned with happiness and blessing on March 5, 1754." [*ist den 5. Märtz 1754 m. Glück u. Segen wiederkommen*]. // MICHAEL PFRANG, *Chesterfield,* September 2, 1749, Hinke, I, 394.

PLATZ, JOHANN JACOB (2)—Emmingen (1751)

Day laborer [*Tagelöhner*]. B. 1705, son of JOHANN JACOB PLATZ at Hochdorf. Wf: CHRISTINA, *née* RENTZ, daughter of JACOB RENTZ, b. 1710. Ch: (1) Maria Barbara, b. 11-11-1734; (2) Christina, b. 4-6-1737; (3) Anna Maria, b. 3-9 [Baptismal Register *27*]-1739; (4) Johann Jacob; (5) Johanna; (6) Christoph (neither in Baptismal nor Burial Register); (7) Maria Magdalena, b. 4-23-1747; (8) Martin, b. 11-12-1749. "Went to the New World with wife and all his children." Ludwigsburg Protocol, 3-21-1751, Platz and associates, to "Pennsylvania."

PLETZGER (BLETZGER), CHRISTOPH HEINRICH (2)—Neuffen (1752)

B. 4-22-1740, son of JOHANN GEORG PLETZGER and wf MAGDALENA CATHARINA, b. 4-22-1740. Confirmed, along with AGNES CATHARINA KIRCHNER (q.v.) of Neuffen, with dispensation of the consistory "on account of their intended journey with their parents to Pennsylvania" ["*wegen ihrer vorhabenden Reise mit ihren Eltern nach Pens.*"] Ludwigsburg Protocol, 4-11-1752, Pletzger and associates, *venia emigrandi.*

PLETZGER (BLETZGER), JOHANN GEORG (2)—Neuffen (1752)

Wf: MAGDALENA CATHARINA. Ch: (1) Christoph Heinrich (q.v.). Ludwigsburg Protocol, 4-11-1752, Pletzger and associates, *venia emigrandi.*

PLIENINGER (BLIENINGER), MATTHAEUS (2)—Neckartenzlingen (1749)

Miller's apprentice [*Müllerknecht*] of Urach. Wf: CATHARINA (HOHLSCHEIT). Married 10-7-1748. // MATHEAS PLENNINGER, Snow *Good Intent*, November 9, 1749, Hinke, I, 426.

PREISS, JOHANNES (1)—Grünwettersbach (1753)

Farmhand [*Bauersmann*]. B. 7-13-1729, son of HANS JOERG and MARIA MARGARETHA PREISS. Wf: MARIA CATHARINA, *née* KRAEUTLER), married 10-12-1732. Ch: (1) Elisabetha Barbara, b. 2-15-1753. "Baptismal certificate made May 22, [1753], for Pennsylvania." // JOHANNES PRICE (PREYSS), age 30, with YERRICK KREYTLER (GEORG MARTIN KREIDLER), age 22, *Patience*, September 15 [17], 1753, Hinke, I, 526, 528. Many listed in PA.

PREISS, JOHANNES (1)—Grünwettersbach (1753)

Discharged Sardianian soldier and non-citizen [*abgedankter Sardin, Soldat u. Beisitzer*], formerly citizen here [*vorhin Bürger allhier*]. Wf: BARBARA, *née* HERMANN. Ch: (1) Salome, b. 5-10-1748, "emigrated with parents to Pennsylvania, 1753." // JOHANNES PREYSS, age 33, *Louisa*, October 3, 1753, Hinke, I, 581, 584. Many listed in PA.

PRINTZIGHOFER (BRENZIGHOFER), HANS GEORG (JERG) (2)—Sersheim (1752)

Cartwright [*Wagner*]. B. 1698. Wf: ANNA MARIA (RIEGER). Married 7-9-1737. Ludwigsburg Protocol, 4-12-1752, Hans Jerg Brenzighofer and associates, *venia emigrandi*. // Cf. CASPAR BRINTZIGHOFER, *President*, September 27, 1752, Hinke, I, 490, with MELCHER BELZHUBER, of neighboring Metterzimmern. Cf. also CHRISTOPHER PRINCEKOFFER, September 5, 1803, Hinke, III, 126.

PULMER, JOHANNES (2)—Emmingen

B. 7-1-1742, son of MARTIN PULMER, linen weaver [*Leineweber*], and wf CATHARINA, *née* MAJER, at Oberjettingen,, b. 1-14-1720. "Went to the New World with his mother and stepfather [GEORGE RENTZ (q.v.) of Emmingen]."

# R

RAAF, MICHAEL (2)—Iselshausen (1751)

Clothmaker [*Zeugmacher*]. B. 6-6-1701. Wf: MARGARETHA (BAUMANN). Ch: (1) Johann Georg, b. 1-23-1738, died; (2) Johannes, b. 1-18-1741; (3) Andreas, b. 10-17-1744; (4) Maria Barbara, b. 10-21-1746. Gerber writes that "in the following fourteen years, Michel Raaf does not appear in the Baptismal Register either as father or sponsor." Ludwigsburg Protocol, 3-12-1751, to "Pennsylvania."

RAIGEL, ANNA (1)—Marschalkenzimmerm (1751)

B. 12-11-1725, orphaned [*hintergelassene*] daughter of MELCHIOR RAIGEL, tilemaker [*Ziegler*], and wf BARBARA. Married elsewhere, and "left the country on foot, July 12, 1751, with some other young people. Their intention was to immigrate to New Georgia [*Neu Georgien*] in America. But after that we never heard the least bit of news from them." In the same party were JOHANN FRIEDRICH LIPS (q.v.) of Betzweiler, and his brother JOHANN GEORG LIPS (q.v.) of Marschalkenzimmern.

## RAISCH, CONRAD (CUNRAD) (1)—Grötzingen (1749)

Mason [*Maurer*] . Wf: CHRISTINA. Ch: (1) Maria Agnes, b. 12-[?]-1739; (2) Catharina, b. 2-20-1741; (3) Jacob, b. 12-4-1742; (4) Christina, b. 4-9-1747; (5) Georg, b. 4-23-1749. Left for Pennsylvania, May 1, 1749, with wife and four children, in a party of thirty-six persons from the same village. // JOHAN CONRAD RAISCH, *Nancy*, August 31, 1750, Hinke, I, 442. 3PA, 18, 359: JACOB REISH, Greenwich Tp., Berks Co., Pa., 1780. 3PA, 24, 515: JACOB REISH, 100 acres, Lancaster Co., Pa., survey November 3, 1773.

## RAISCH, MICHAEL (1)—Wolfschlugen

B. 10-1-1729, son of MICHEL RAISCH, weaver [*Weber*], and wf MARIA AGNES. To "America." // JOHAN MICHEL RAISCH, *Neptune*, September 23, 1751, Hinke, I, 467.

## RAISSER, JACOB (1)—Grötzingen (1752)

Wf: ANNA MARIA. Left for Pennsylvania, May 6, 1752, with wife and six children, who Gerber thinks were born elsewhere. With them went JOHANNES KURTZ (q.v.), HANS JERG REICHENECKER (q.v.), DANIEL REITER (q.v.), JOHANNES RIST (q.v.), making a party of twenty-six in all. // JACOB REISER, with DANIEL REUTTER of Grötzingen, *Anderson*, September 27, 1752, Hinke, I, 488-9; a fellow-passenger was JACOB FRIEDRICH SCHERTLEIN, Lutheran pastor. 3PA, 14, 210: JACOB RISER, tinman, Mulberry Ward, City of Philadelphia, Pa., 1769. 3PA, 15, 344: JACOB REISSER, grocer, Mulberry Ward (East Part), City of Philadelphia, Pa., 1780.

## RAU, JOHANN JACOB (1)—Grünwettersbach (1752)

Shoemaker [*Schuhmacher*]. Wf: SYBILLA, *née* LUTZ. Ch: (1) Catharina Barbara, b. 3-10-1750. "To Pennsylvania, 1752, with his parents, who left secretly." [*1752 m. s. heiml. durchgegangenen Eltern in Pens.*] // JOHANN JACOB RAU, *Ann Galley*, September 23, 1752, Hinke, I, 486. Sower's newspaper, August 1, 1754, quoted in Hocker, 44: "JACOB RAUW, Allemangel, Hill Township." Many listed in PA.

## REHFUSS, HANS JACOB (1)—Lossburg (1751)

Wf: CATHARINA. Ch: (1) Anna Maria, b. 9-27-1746; (2) Johann Georg, b. 12-15-1747; (3) Christina, b. 7-19-1750. Ludwigsburg Protocol, 1751. To "Pennsylvania."

## REICHENECKER, HANS JERG (1)—Grötzingen (1752)

Wf: CATHARINA. "With wife and two children," who, according to Gerber, were born elsewhere, left Grötzingen May 6, 1752, in a party of twenty-six villagers, along with JOHANNES KURTZ (q.v.), JACOB RAISSER (q.v.), DANIEL REITER (q.v.) and JOHANNES RIST (q.v.).

## REINOEHL, GEORG HEINRICH (2)—Neidlingen (see Neckartenzlingen) (1749)

Wf: EVA CATHARINA (GRUENZWEIG), schoolmaster's daughter [*Schulmeisterstochter*]. Married in Neidlingen. // GEORG HEINRICH REINOEHL, with HANS JERG KUNTZELMAN and MATHEAS PLENNINGER of Neckartenzlingen, Snow *Good Intent*, November 9, 1749, Hinke, I, 426.

Sower's newspaper, March 1, 1751, quoted in Hocker, 25: "GEORG HEINRICH STEINOEHL [REINOEHL], from Württemberg, a smith in Conestoga (Lancaster County), with Christian Weber, near Jacob Beyerle's mill, inquires for his brother-in-law, GOTTFRIED [GRUENZWEIG], a woolcomber" 3PA, 17, 141: HENRY REINOLE, Lebanon Tp., Lancaster Co., Pa., 1771. 3PA, 17, 798-9: HENRY REINEHL, SR., with GEORGE, HENRY and CONRAD REINEHL, Lebanon Tp., Lancaster Co., Pa., 1782.

## REISSER, ANNA MARIA (1)—Dornhan

B. 2-15-1725, daughter of HANS JACOB and ANNA MARIA REISSER.

## REITER (REUTER) DANIEL (1)—Grötzingen (1752)

Carpenter [*Zimmermann*]. Wf: ANNA. Ch: (1) Catharina, b. 3-12-1749; (2) Anna Maria, b. 11-17-1750. Left Grötzingen May 6, 1752, for Pennsylvania, with wife and two children, in a company of twenty-six villagers, including JOHANNES KURTZ (q.v.), JACOB RAISSER (q.v.), HANS JERG REICHENECKER (q.v.), and JOHANNES RIST (q.v.). // DANIEL REUTTER, *Anderson*, September 27, 1752, Hinke, I, 488. 3PA, 21, 622: DANIEL REIDER, with LAWRENCE REIDER, Windsor Tp., York Co., Pa., 1782.

## REMP(P), ANDREAS (1)—Oeschelbronn, Oberamt Herrenberg (1754)

Tailor [*Schneider*]. B. 10-10-1714. Wf: ANNA, daughter of the mason [*Maurer*] MICHEL EITELBUSS. Ch: (1) Jacob, b. 4-4-1735; (2) Michel, b. 9-8-1736; (3) Johannes, b. 3-2-1741; (4) Johann Martin, b. 5-24-1742; (5) Andreas, b. 1-26-1748; (6) Gottlieb, b. 11-3-1749. "Went with wife and children to America after 1753." Ludwigsburg Protocol, 1754. // 3PA, 18, 339: JACOB REMP, cordwainer, Cumru Tp., Berks Co., Pa., 1780.

## RENTSCHLER, MICHAEL (2)—Stammheim (Calw) (1754)

B. 10-18-1722, son of Michael Rentschler. Ludwigsburg Protocol, 4-5-1754, *venia emigrandi*. // MICH'L RENSHLAR (MICHAEL RENTSCHLER), age 34, with MATHIAS RENSHLAR, age 27, *Barclay*, September 14, 1754, Hinke, I, 595-6, 598. 3PA, 26, 306: MICH'L RENSHLER, 25 acres, Berks Co., Pa., survey November 4, 1755. Sower's newspaper, September 17, 1757, quoted in Hocker, 67: "MICHAEL RENTZLER, Bern Township" (Berks County). 3PA, 18, 203: MICH'L RENSHLER, with GEORGE RENSHLER (single freeman), Bern Tp., Berks Co., Pa., 1779. Estate of MICHAEL RENSLER, of Bern Tp., Berks Co., Pa., March 20, 1797, administration to GEORGE RENSHLER, eldest son, *Berks County Will Abstracts*, I, 585, GSP. A daughter of Michael Rentschler married JOHANNES DUNKELBERGER (1745-1818) of Little Mahanoy Valley, Northumberland Co., Pa., and was the ancestor of Dr. Gustav Dunkelberger, former Dean of the Chicago Musical College. Another descendant of Michael Rentschler through the Dunkelberger line is Dr. Albert F. Buffington, Professor of German at the Pennsylvania State College.

## RENTZ, GEORG (2)—Emmingen (1751)

Weaver [*Weber*]. B. 3-15-1720, son of the clothmaker [*Tuchmacher*] MICHAEL RENTZ at Ebhausen. Wf: CATHARINA MAJER, daughter of SIMON MAJER at Oberjettingen, b. 1-14-1720. Ch: (1) Johann Georg, b. 3-25-1745; (2) Anna Catharina, b. 11-2-1746; (3) Simon, b. 1-9-1749. "Went to the New World with wife and children." Ludwigsburg Protocol, 3-12-1751, "to take inherited property to Pennsylvania." Accompanying them was JOHANNES PULMER (q.v.), son of Catharina (Majer) Rentz's first marriage, to MARTIN PULMER. // Sower's newspaper, April 16, 1757, quoted in Hocker, 63: "JOHANNES RENTZ, baker and innkeeper, Ebenezer, South Carolina (Georgia?) is informed his brother, JOHANN GEORG RENTZ, from Weihl, in Schoenbuch, arrived in Pennsylvania five years ago and seeks information about Johannes."

REUTTER, MATTHAEUS (1)—Grünwettersbach (1751)

Mason [*Maurer*]. Wf: ANNA BARBARA, *née* MAEURLIN. Ch: (1) Maria Catharina, b. 9-7-1728; (2) Anna Catharina, b. 7-23-1732; (3) Anna Barbara, b. 2-12-1736; (4) Clara Sybilla, b. 9-22-1747. "Baptismal certificate made May 14, [1751], for Pennsylvania." // MATTHEUS REUTTER, *Shirley*, September 5, 1751, Hinke, I, 453.

RHEINTALER, (JOHANN) GEORG (2)—Simmozheim (1751)

Day laborer [Tagelöhner]. Wf: MARIA BARBARA. Ch: (1) Georg Immanuel, b. 1742; (2) Stillborn child, b. 1750. No children born after 1751. Ludwigsburg Protocol, 4-6-1751. [——] REINTHALERE to "Pennsylvania." // HANS JERG REINTHALER, *Nancy*, September 16, 1751, Hinke, I, 462. 3PA, 11, 189: GEORGE RIDDOLLER, farmer, Radnor Tp., Chester Co., Pa., 1766.

RICHARDON, JEAN (2)—Pinache (1753)

Wf: CAT. (JOURDAN). Ch: (1) Jean Pierre, b. 5-22-1735; (2-4) three ch., died young; (5) Catherine, b. 7-14-1744; (6) Matthieu, b. 7-8-1748; (7) Etienne, b. 10-10-1751. Ludwigsburg Protocol, 4-24-1753, "Rigarton," to "Pennsylvania." // JOHN (JEAN) RICHARDON, age 25, *Patience*, September 15 [17], 1753, Hinke, I, 526-7.

RIEBER, GEORG PHILIPP (1)—Ebingen

Butcher [*Metzger*]. Wf: MARGARETHA, *née* BECK. Ch: (1) Eva Barbara, b. 6-21-1742. To "Penna." // JERG PHILIPP RIEBER, *Fane*, October 17, 1749, Hinke, I, 425.

RIECKER, JOHANN JACOB (1)—Bodelhausen

Miller [*Müller*]. Wf: ANNA MARIA. Ch: (1) Georg, b. 7-17-1745. "Went to America." // JACOB RIGER, *Phoenix*, September 25, 1751, Hinke, I, 470. Several listed in PA, under spellings Rieger, Reigher, Reiger. Cf. also 3PA, 22, 107. GEORGE REEKER, renter, Barree Tp., Bedford Co., Pa., 1775.

RIST, JOHANNES (1)—Grötzingen (1752)

Emigrated with his wife, leaving Grötzingen May 6, 1752, in a party of twenty-six villagers, along with HANS JERG REICHENECKER (q.v.), JOHANNES KURTZ (q.v.), JACOB RAISSER (q.v.), and DANIEL REITER q.v. // Cf. J. GEORGE REEST, with JACOB REISER, JOHANNES KURTZ, and DANIEL REUTTER, all possibly from Grötzingen, *Anderson*, September 27, 1752, Hinke, I, 488-9. Sower's newspaper, April 13, 1759, quoted in Hocker, 80: "JOHANNES RIEST, Germantown, advertises that his apprentice, CHRISTIAN MAYER, 14 years old, ran away." 3PA, 17, 127: JNO. RIST, with ABRAHAM and CHRISTIAN RIST, Warwick Tp., Lancaster Co., Pa., 1771. 3PA, 21, 288: JOHN RIST, Hellam Tp., York Co., Pa., 1780.

ROECKER (REKER), HANS MARTIN (1)—Bodelhausen (1766)

Weaver [*Weber*]. B. 12-1-1738, son of HANS MARTIN ROECKER, weaver. Wf: ANNA MARIA (SCHAU[W]ECKER, b. 6-11-1736, daughter of BERNHARD and MARGARETHA SCHAUECKER. Ch: (1) Georg, b. 3-6-1765. They also had a son, JOHANN MARTIN, b. 3-7-1760, before their marriage, when the father was a soldier. Wife was sister of MARGARETHA SCHAUECKER (q.v.). "Left for America, June 3, 1766."

ROECKER, CATHARINA (1)—Kleinengstingen (1749)

B. 1-8-1723, daughter of BERNHARD ROECKER, and wf ANNA MARIA, *née* OBERACKER. "To Pennsylvania, 1749."

ROECKER, JOHANN GEORG (1)—Kleinengstingen (1749)

B. 7-1-1726, son of BERNHARD ROECKER and wf ANNA MARIA, *née* OBERACKER.. "To Pennsylvania, 1749."

ROECKER, MICHAEL (1)—Kleinengstingen (1749)

B. 2-18-1715, son of BERNHARD ROECKER and wf ANNA MARIA, *née* OBERACKER. Wf: BARBARA, *née* RAUSCHER. Ch: (1) Anna Barbara, b. 4-2-1742; (2) Johann Bernhard, b. 7-29-1746. // 3PA, 24, 511: MICHAEL REKER, 50 acres. Lancaster Co., Pa., survey January 30, 1750.

ROESSLER, MICHAEL (2)—Dürrmenz (1753)

Farmer [*Bauer*]. Wf: MARIA BARBARA. Ch.: (1) Rosina Barbara, b. 1-3-1748; (2) Maria Agnes, b. 3-5-1751; (3) Johann Christoph, b. 6-15-1753 [!]. From the German and Waldensian (i.e., Huguenot) Church Registers for Dürrmenz-Schönenberg. Ludwigsburg Protocol, 3-30-1753, to "Pennsylvania." // MICHAEL RESSEL (ROESZLER, ROESSLER), age 20, *Patience*, September 15 [17], 1753, Hinke, I, 526, 527, 529. Others listed in PA.

ROMANN, ANDREAS (2)—Dürrmenz (1750)

Smith's apprentice [*Schmiedknecht*] of Glatten. Wf: MARIA BARBARA, *née* BAPP, daughter of MATTHEIS and DOROTHEA BAPP, b. 11-4-1717. Ch: (1) Johann Jacob, b. 7-24-1742; (2) Elisabetha, b. 2-15-1745; (3) Johann Friedrich, b. 6-15-1746; (4) Susanna Margaretha, b. 3-11-1748; (5) Maria Barbara, b. 8-20-1749. From the German and Waldensian Church Registers for Dürrmenz-Schönenberg. Wife was a sister of MARIA MARGARETHA BAPP (q.v.). Ludwigsburg Protocol, 4-30-1750, MARIA BARBARA ROMANN and MARGARETHA BAPP ask for manumission, and for permission to go to Pennsylvania.

ROMINGER, CHRISTINA (2)—Laufen/Eyach (1750)

B. 2-14-1732, daughter of PHILIPP and AGNES ROMINGER. "To Pennsylvania, 1750." // See Kapff, *Schwaben in Amerika* (Stuttgart, 1893), 42, for life of DR. KARL ROMINGER, German-American geologist, born 1820 at Ebingen, Württemberg.

ROMMEL, CHRISTOPH (2)—Neckartenzlingen (1749)

His son, not named, was given ducal permission to emigrate, in 1749; see the ducal letter of that year in our Introduction.

## ROTH, BALTHAS (1)—Pfaffenhofen (1752)

Wf: MARIA CATHARINA. Ch: (1) Jerg Friedrich; (2) Maria Catharina. Disappear from Church Register in 1752. Ludwigsburg Protocol, 1752, to "Pennsylvania."

## ROTH, CHRISTIAN (1)—Gärtringen

Tailor [*Schneider*]. B. 12-25-1708. Wf: BARBARA. Ch: (1) Margaretha Barbara, b. 4-14-1733; (2) Johann Georg, b. 4-9-1735; (3) Johann Michael, b. 12-8-1739. "Went to America." In the detailed Family Register for Gärtringen Parish, made in 1799, this family is said to have "immigrated to America." // Several in Hinke, all after 1753. Several listed in PA.

## ROTH, GOTTLIEB (1)—Grünwettersbach (1751)

Farmhand [*Bauersmann*]. Wf: ANNA MARIA, *née* HOERMANN. Ch: (1) Catharina, b. 11-28-1747, "to Pennsylvania with her parents, May 14, 1751." // 3PA, 25, 285: GODLEIB ROTH, 150 acres, Northumberland Co., Pa., survey January 10, 1786. 3PA, 19, 739: GOTTLIEB ROTH, Penns Tp., Northumberland Co., Pa., 1787.

## ROTHENBURGER, JOHANNES (1)—Pfaffenhofen (1754)

Crossed out of Church Register in 1754. Ludwigsburg Protocol, 1754, *venia emigrandi*, 10-22-1754, landed at Philadelphia. // JOHAN ROTEBURGER (JOHANNES ROTHENBURGER), *Henrietta*, October 22, 1754, Hinke, I, 649-650.

## RO(U)CHON, PHILIPPE (2)—Pinache (1754)

B. 6-3-1728, son of PIERRE (q.v.) and CATHERINE (GAYDE) RO(U)CHON. Wf: MARIE (TALMON). Ch: (1) Marie, b. 6-25-1752. They left home after the death of his mother in 1754. // PHILIP ROSCHON (PHILIPPE ROUCHON), *Bannister*, October 21, 1754, Hinke, I, 646-647. Sower's newspaper, May 29, 1757, quoted in Hocker, 64: "PHILIP ROSCHAN, Oley Hills, on Beaver Creek" (Berks County). 3PA, 14, 42: PHILIP ROSHONG, Frankford and New Hanover Tps., Phila. Co., 1769. 3PA, 15, 444: PHILIP ROSHONG, with PETER ROSHONG (single), Limerick Tp., Philadelphia Co., Pa., 1780.

## RO(U)CHON, PIERRE (2)—Pinache

Died in Piemont, 10-9-1747. Wf: CATHERINE (GAYDE), d. at Pinache, 4-28-1754. Ch: after several died young, (1) Jean Jaques, b. 12-10-1724; (2) Catherine, b. 9-1-1725 [!]; (3) Philippe (q.v.), b. 6-3-1728; (4) Henri, b. 9-23-1730 or 10-1-1730; (5) Pierre, b. 12-14-1732. // PETER ROSHON (PIERRE ROUCHON), age 22, with HENDRICK ROSHON (HENRI ROUCHON), age 20, *Patience*, September 15 [17], 1753, Hinke, I, 526-7. 3PA, 14, 131: HENRY ROSHAN, Northern Liberties (West Part), Philadelphia Co., Pa., 1769. 3PA, 14, 49: PETER ROSHONG, Frederick Tp., Philadelphia Co., Pa., 1769.

## RUEHLE, JOHANN MICHAEL (2)—Stammheim (Calw) (1751)

Miller's son [*Müllersohn*]. Wf: CHRISTINA (ROECKER), non-citizen's daughter [*Beisitzerstochter*] of Gruorn. Married 1744. Neither is in the Burial Register. Ludwigsburg Protocol, 4-30-1751, to "Pennsylvania." // JOHAN MICHAEL RUEHLE, *Nancy*, September 16, 1751, Hinke, I, 462. *Staatsbote*, Philadelphia, March 22, 1776, quoted in Hocker, 160:

"Johann Friedrich Kuecherer, Raccoon Creek, Gloucester County, N. J., twenty miles from Philadelphia, seeks two brothers, GEORG FRIEDRICH RIEHLE, who has been in America *twenty* years, and JOHANN MICHAEL RIEHLE, a flour miller, who has been in America *four* years."

RUESS, HANS GEORG (2)—Sielmingen (1754)

B. 10-8-1735, son of LUCAS RUESS. Followed his brother, JOHANN JACOB RUESS (RUOS) (q.v.), to America. // HANS GEORG RUST (RUOSS), with HANS JACOB RUST (RUOS), *Bannister,* October 21, 1754, Hinke, I, 646-7.

RUESS (RUOS), JOHANN JACOB (2)—Sielmingen (1754)

Son of LUCAS RUESS. Wf: CATHARINA, *née* BAYHA, b. 12-1-1732, daughter of GEORG BAYHA (q.v.) and his second wf ANNA MARIA (SCHWEITZER). Married 1751. // HANS JACOB RUST (RUOS), with HANS GEORG RUST (RUOSS), *Bannister,* October 21, 1754, Hinke I, 646-7. 3PA, 13, 423: JACOB RUSS, Lower Milford Tp., Bucks Co., Pa., 1784. 3PA, 13, 553: JACOB RUFFE, SR., with HENRY RUSE, JACOB RUSE, JR., and GEORGE RUSE, Nockamixon Tp., Bucks Co., Pa., 1785.

RUPP, CHRISTOPH (1)—Plüderhausen

Shoemaker [*Schuhmacher*]. Wf: (ANNA) MARGARETHA. Ch: (1) Anna Catharina, b. 7-8-1732; (2) Anna Maria, b. 12-26-34; (3) Christoph, b. 11-16-1737. The records kept by Pastor Johann Melchior Kapff, 1725-1770, make it clear that all the children "went with their parents to Pennsylvania" (or "America").

RUSS, JOHANN JACOB (1)—Plüderhausen

Tailor [*Sartor*]. Wf: ANNA BARBARA, *née* WOEHRLE. Ch: (1) Johannes, b. 9-27-1740. // For PA, cf. *supra,* JOHAN JACOB RUESS.

## S

SALOMON, EBERHARD (2)—Gündelbach (p. 1758)

B. 1715. Emigrated after 1758 with wife and daughter. // Cf. EVERHARD SOLOMON (EBERHART SALLOMON), age 27, *Brothers,* September 26, 1753, Hinke, I, 551, 554; a fellow-passenger was PETER EYSENBREIT of Gündelbach.

SAL(T)ZER, CHRISTOPH (1)—Eningen u. A. (1749)

Dealer in lace [*Spitzenhändler*]. B. 5-11-1719, son of JOHANNES and MARIA BARBARA SAL(T)ZER. Wf: ANNA MARIA, *née* WOLFFART. Married 1741. Ch: (1) Johann Georg, b. 1-9-1747. (2) Zacharias, b. 8-4-1748; and others. "This Christoph Saltzer went to America in 1749, with his entire household."

SAUTER, JOHANN GEORG (2)—Schöckingen (see Hirschlanden) (1753)

Fancy baker [*Haus u. Weissbeck*] of Schöckingen. Wf: ANNA CATHARINA, *née* HINDERMANN, b. 11-27-1725, daughter of MARTIN HINDERMANN (q.v.) and wf ANNA BARBARA, *née* KRAEMER. Ch: (1) Johann Jacob, b. 9-19-1747. No further entry. Ludwigsburg Protocol, 5-4-1753, Hindermann and Sauter, to "Pennsylvania." // JOHAN JERICK SAUTER (JOHANN GEORG SAUTTER), age 32, *Peggy,* September 24, 1753, Hinke, I, 546, 548. For residence in Pennsylvania. cf. notes to GEORG SAUTTER, *infra.*

## SAUTTER, CONRAD (2)—Onstmettingen

Wf: ANNA. Ch: (1) Johannes, b. 5-17-1740. According to records kept by Pastor Johann Georg Stählen, 1746-1756, this family "went to New England." Ludwigsburg Protocol, 5-3-1752, mentions Onstmettingen immigrants to Pennsylvania, without giving names.

## SAUTTER, GEORG (1)—Dürrwangen

B. 3-31-1727, brother of Johannes Sautter (q.v.). "Went to Pennsylvania and died." // JOHAN JERICK SAUTER (JOHANN GEORG SAUTTER), age 32, *Peggy*, September 24, 1753, Hinke I, 546, 548; cf. also GEORG SAUTER, *Britannia*, September 26, 1764, Hinke, I, 692. 3PA, 18, 649: GEO. SOUDER, Pine Grove Tp., Berks Co., Pa., 1784. 3PA, 26, 317 and 319: GEORGE SAUTER, tracts in Berks Co., Pa., 1785 and 1792.

## SAUTTER, JOHANNES (HANS)—Dürrwangen (1749)

B. 4-7-1721, brother of GEORG SAUTTER (q.v.). Wf: ANNA MARIA. Ch: (1) Hans Martin, b. 7-20-1748. "Went to Pennsylvania, 4-28-1749." // JOHANNES SAUTER, *Dragon*, October 17, 1749, Hinke, I, 423. Sower's newspaper, October 29, 1757, quoted in Hocker, 68: "JOHANNES SAUTER, Coventry Township, Chester County."

*Staatsbote*, Philadelphia, July 13, 1773, quoted in Hocker, 132: "JOHANNES SAUTER conducts a dry goods store on Second Street, Philadelphia, above Vine street, near the German auction house, in the house where Nicolaus Schreiner formerly lived."

*Staatsbote*, Philadelphia, December 27, 1774, quoted in Hocker, 147: 3PA, 18, 452: JOHN SAUTER, Bern Tp., Berks Co., Pa., and elsewhere. "JOHANNES SAUTER, Second street, Philadelphia, is going to Germany and to Zurich to obtain an inheritance from his father."

## SAUTTER, MARTIN (2)—Bergfelden

Cobbler [*Schuster*]. Wf: CATHARINE (SCHATZ) of Rotenzimmern. Ch: (1) Martin, b. [ ? ]; (2) Anna, b. 12-5-1738. Came with their two children from Täbingen to Bergfelden, and were regularly communicants from Pentecost 1741 (from 1744, with son) until Good Friday 1749, after which they disappear from the Church Registers. Evidently went to "New England," whither others from Täbingen were going at the time.

## SCHAD, JOHANN GEORG (2)—Gönningen (1748)

Weaver [*Weber*]. Wf: MARTHA. Ch: (1) Anna Barbara, b. 7-31-1738. "In the New World." // YERRICK SHADE (JOHANN GEORG SCHAD), age 27, *Patience and Margaret*, October 25, 1748, Hinke, I, 387-8. Several George Shades listed in PA.

## SCHAEFER, AGNES (1)—Wolfschlugen

B. 5-18-1730, daughter of JOHANNES and MARGARETHA SCHAEFER. "To America with Michael Raisch" (q.v.), of Wolfschlugen.

## SCHAEFER, GOTTLIEBIN (2)—Gündelbach (1785)

Niece of Christoph Kumpf (q.v.) of Gündelbach, wtih whom she emigrated, 1785.

## SCHAEFER, MARIA AGNES (1)—Eltingen

B. 8-18-1731, daughter of JACOB and MARGARETHA SCHAEFER. "Went to the New World."

SCHAEFFER, DOROTHEA (1)—Ostelsheim (1754)

B. 2-4-1723. Ch: (1) Johann Georg, b. (illeg.). To "New England," 1754, with her son.

SCHAEFFER, HANS MARTIN (1), JR.—Sondelfingen

Wf: MARIA ROSINA. Ch: (1) Johann Jacob, b. 10-3-1742. "Went to New England." // Several in Hinke, 1749, 1750, and 1754. Several listed in PA.

SCHAHL, ANNA MARIA (1)—Steinenberg

B. 10-5-1725, daughter of MICHEL and CATHARINA SCHAHL. Records kept by Abraham Gottlieb Majer, of Steinenberg, in 1766-1816, indicate that she went to "America."

SCHAHL, HANS GEORG (1)—Steinenberg

B. 3-30-1723, son of HANS JACOB and ANNA MARIA SCHAHL. Records kept by Abraham Gottlieb Majer, of Steinenberg, in 1766-1816, indicate that he went to "America." // GEORG SCHOELL, *Neptune,* September 24, 1751, Hinke, I, 469.

SCHANTZ, BLASIG (1)—Lossburg

Wf: CHRISTINA. Ch: (1) Johann Michael, b. 11-24-1746. To "Pennsylvania."

SCHATZ, DAVID (1)—Neuhausen ob Eck

Miner [*Erzgraber*]. Wf: ELISABETHA, *née* REUCHLIN. Ch: (1) Johann Jacob, b. 6-6-1737, "went to America." // DAVID SCHATS (SCHATZ), *Rosannah,* September 26, 1743, Hinke, I, 344-5.

SCHAUECKER, MARGARETHA (1)—Bodelshausen (1766)

B. 3-25-1741, daughter of BERNHARD and MARGARETHA SCHAUECKER. Sister of ANNA MARIA (SCHAU[W]ECKER) ROECKER, wf of HANS MARTIN ROECKER (q.v.). "Left for America, June 3, 1766."

SCHAUEKER, HANS CONRAD (2)—Bodelshausen (1749)

B. 9-19-1720, son of BERNHARD and MARGARETHA SCHAUEKER. Brother of ANNA MARIA (SCHAU[W]ECKER) ROECKER, wife of HANS MARTIN ROECKER (q.v.). // HANS CUNRAD SCHAUWECKER, with MARTIN SCHAUWECKER and the Speidels and Schlotterers of Bodelshausen, *Chesterfield,* September 2, 1749, Hinke, I, 393. 3PA, 15, 403: CONRAD SHAWAKER, with JACOB and JOHN SHAWAKER, Germantown, Philadelphia Co., Pa., 1780.

SCHAUEKER, MARTIN (2)—Bodelshausen (1749)

B. 4-6-1727, son of BERNHARD and MARGARETHA SCHAUEKER. Brother of ANNA MARIA (SCHAU[W]ECKER) ROECKER, wife of HANS MARTIN ROECKER (q.v.). // MARTIN SCHAUWECKER, with HANS CUNRAD SCHAUWECKER and the Speidels and Schlotterers of Bodelshausen, *Chesterfield,* September 2, 1749, Hinke, I, 393.

SCHAUTT, JOHANNES (2)—Onstmettingen

Wf: BARBARA. Ch: (1) Johannes, b. 8-1-1740; (2) Claudius, b. 5-8-1743; (3) Jacob, b. 7-26-1745. According to records kept by Pastor Johann Georg Stählen, 1746-1756, this family "went to New England." Ludwigsburg Protocol, 5-3-1752, mentions emigrants from Onstmettingen to Pennsylvania, without giving names. // 3PA, 26, 169: JOHN SHOUT ET AL., land in Northampton Co., Pa., survey March 8, 1769.

## SCHECKELER, PHILIPP (1)—Rommelshausen

B. 12-16-1741, son of PHILIPP SCHECKELER, vinedresser [*Weingärtner*] and wf CATHARINA, *née* LEDERER. To "America." // PHILIPP SCHECKLER, with MICHAEL HIEBER of Rommelshausen, *Minerva*, October 10, 1768, Hinke, I, 722.

## SCHE(E)R (SCHEHR), JOHANN MICHAEL (2)—Markgröningen (1752)

B. 6-4-1703. Son of THOMAS SCHEER. Wf: MARGARETHA (MATTHEIS). Ch: (1) Christina, b. 9-27-1729; (2) Daniel, b. 4-9-1732; (3) Maria Jacobina, b. 8-22-1736; (4) Margaretha, b. 5-29-1738; (5) Barbara, b. 5-13-1740; (6) Johann Bernhard, b. 2-28-1742; (7) Elisabetha, b. 12-13-1743; (8) Georg Friedrich, b. 1-29-1746; (9) Georg Adam, b. 6-5-1749; (10) Johann Michael, b. 9-27-1751. No record of father in Burial Register; children disappear from records 1752-1759. Ludwigsburg Protocol, 4-21-1752, to "Pennsylvania."

## SCHEIBLE, ANNA URSULA (1)—Lomersheim

B. 3-31-1728, daughter of JACOB and AGNES SCHEIBLE. To "Pennsylvania."

## SCHEIBLE, JOHANN MICHAEL (1)—Lomersheim

Joiner [*Schreiner*]. Wf: ANNA BARBARA. Ch: (1) Maria Margaretha, b. 7-[ ? ]-1739; (2) Maria Barbara, b. 10-27-1742. Ludwigsburg Protocol, 1753, Philadelphia, September 17, 1753. To "Pennsylvania." // MICHAEL SCHIBLEY (SCHEIBLE), age 29, *Patience*, September 15 [17], 1753, Hinke, I, 526, 528.

The will of MICHAEL SCHEIBLE, of Upper Milford Tp., Northampton Co., Pa., dated June 12, 1770, probated August 1, 1770, mentions wife BARBARA, children MARTIN and MARGARET, and deceased daughter BARBARA's children ELISABETH and GEORGE; executors: son MARTIN, and BERNHART WENSCH; witnesses: SEBASTIAN TRUCKENMILLER, JACOB HOLTZHAUSER, and RUDOLPH WEISS, *Northampton County Will Abstracts*, No. 149, GSP.

## SCHERTLE, JOHANNES (1)—Dagersheim

Carpenter [*Zimmermann*]. Wf: BARBARA, née SCHWAB. Ch: (1) Georg Friedrich, b. 11-17-1735. To the "New Land." // JOHANNES SCHAERTHLE, *President*, September 27, 1752, Hinke, I, 490. 3PA, 17, 463: JOHN SHERTLE, Lancaster Borough, Lancaster Co., Pa., 1773. 3PA, 18, 323: JNO. SHERTLE, with JACOB SHERTLE, blacksmith, Bern Tp., Berks Co., Pa., 1780. According to information sent the editor by the staff of the Historical Society of York County, the son was a member of Strayer's Lutheran Church in York Co., Pa.: "GEORG FRIEDRICH SCHAERTEL, born 10 November, 1736, in Tagersheim in the duchy of Württemberg, son of JOHANNES and BARBARA; they came to America in 1752."

## SCHEURER, CUNRAD (2)—Gönningen

Shepherd [*Hirth*]. Wf: MARGARETHA. Ch: (1) Johann Michael, b. 8-5-1736; (2) Johann Cunrad, b. 10-5-1741; (3) Matthäus, b. 9-21-1748. All three children "in the New World." Ludwigsburg Protocol, 2-11-1752, MATTHAEUS SCHEURER, to South Carolina. Perhaps this family went there also. // Others listed in PA.

SCHIENLE, AGNES BARBARA (2)—Steinenbronn (1754?)

B. 12-18-1729, daughter of the late baker and justiciary [*Beck u. Gerichtsverwalter*] FRIEDRICH SCHIENLE and wf MARIA CATHARINA (LIEB) of Neuenhaus. "Went to America," evidently without her mother, ca. 1754, since they are no longer listed in the Membership Register in 1755.

SCHIENLE, FRIEDRICH (2)—Steinenbronn (1754?)

B. 10-14-1732, son of the late baker and justiciary [*Beck u. Gerichtsverwalter*] FRIEDRICH SCHIENLE and wf MARIA CATHARINA (LIEB) of Neuenhaus. "Went to America," evidently without his mother, ca. 1754, since they are no longer listed in the Membership Register in 1755.

SCHILLINGER, JOHANN MARTIN (2)—Gündelbach

B. 1728. // MARTIN SCHILLINGER, *President*, September 27, 1752, Hinke, I, 490. Others listed in PA.

SCHINDELBERGER, ANNA CATHARINA (1)—Grötzingen (1747)

Single. Left for Pennsylvania, May 9, 1747, after private communion in the church, along with JOHANNES HERMANN (q.v.), HANS JERG WALCKER (q.v.), ANNA CATHARINA WERNER (q.v.), CATHARINA MAYER (q.v.), and MICHAEL MAYER (q.v.).

SCHLAISS, ULRICH (1)—Söhnstetten

Wf: ANNA. Ch: (1) Hans Conrad, b. 1-8-1739; (2) Anna Catharina, b. 9-22-1742. Children "with parents to Carolina." According to Gerber, the parents had a bad reputation [*letztere Eltern kein gutes Vorleben*].

SCHLECHT, DANIEL (1)—Plattenhardt

Shoemaker [*Schuhmacher*]. Wf: ANNA, *née* WOLLENBEHR. Ch: (1) Hans Jörg, b. 11-29-1738; (2) Jörg Friedrich, b. 2-25-1743; (3) Daniel, b. 8-21-1745; (4) Anna Barbara, b. 4-9-1751; (5) Johann Jacob, b. 4-22-1754. To "Pennsylvania." // 3PA, 19, 383: JACOB SLECHT, Plainfield Tp., Northampton Co., Pa., 1788.

SCHLEGEL, ANNA BARBARA (1)—Grünwettersbach (1744)

Went to Pennsylvania in 1744, with her sister ANNA ROSINA SCHLEGEL (q.v.)

SCHLEGEL, ANNA ROSINA (1)—Grünwettersbach (1744)

B. 1-19-1720, at Mutschelbach, daughter of ADAM and ANNA MAGDALENA SCHLEGEL. "Went, married, to Pennsylvania, in company with her little sister ANNA BARBARA, Pentecost, 1744." [*1744 am Pfingsttag als geheyrathet m. ihrer kleinen Schwester A. Barb. in Pens. gez.*] // The will of ADAM SCHLEGEL, of Reading, Berks Co., Pa., dated December 19, 1785, probated June 1, 1786, mentions a sister ROSINA SCHNEIDER, of Carolina. For other brothers and sisters, cf. *infra*, JOHANN CHRISTOPH SCHLEGEL.

SCHLEGEL, JOHANN CHRISTOPH (1)—Grünwettersbach (1751)

B. 1-31-1733, at Mutschelbach, son of ADAM and ANNA MAGDALENA SCHLEGEL. May 21, 1751, a baptismal certificate was made for him, for "Pennsylvania." // CHRISTOPH SHLEGEL, with GEORGE ADAM SCHLEGEL,

*Duke of Wirtenberg,* October 16, 1751, Hinke, I, 475. The will of ADAM SCHLEGEL, of Reading, Berks Co., Pa., dated December 19, 1785, probated June 1, 1786, mentions a dwelling in Reading and a plantation in Cumru Township; makes bequests to the Evangelical Lutheran Church and the Lutheran School in Reading; names wf CHRISTINA, brothers CHRISTOPHER SCHLEGEL, in Carolina, and PHILIP SCHLEGEL of London; sisters ROSINA, wife of [——] SCHNEIDER, of Carolina, and MARGARET, wf of FREDERICK KNODEL (q.v.), of Carolina; executors: wf CHRISTINA and friend FREDERICK HELLER; witness: KRAFFT HEINNER and DANIEL HEISTER, *Berks County Will Abstracts,* I, 372, GSP.

## SCHLEPPE, ALBRECHT (1)—Bebenhausen (see Hülben) (1751)

Of Bebenhausen. Wf: ANNA MARIA, *née* SCHILL. Ch: (1) Johannes, b. 1-24-1749; (2) Maria Magdalena, b. 2-15-1750. "Emigrated" [*demigrarunt*]. // ALBRECHT SHLEPPY, *Neptune,* September 24, 1751, Hinke, I, 469, with other families from Hülben. Others listed in PA.

## SCHLOTTERER, ANNA MARIA (1)—Bodelshausen (1766)

B. (illeg.) 10-8-1757. "Went to America, June 3, 1766."

## SCHLOTTERER, HANS CUNRAD (2)—Bodelshausen (1749)

B. 8-23-1726, son of MATTHEIS and ANNA BARBARA SCHLOTTERER. // JOHANN CONRADT SCHLOTTERER, with MATHIES, MARTIN, and JACOB SCHLOTTERER, *Chesterfield,* September 2, 1749, Hinke, I, 393-4.

## SCHLOTTERER, JACOB (2)—Bodelshausen (1749)

B. 7-25-1732, son of JACOB and ANNA BARBARA SCHLOTTERER, and brother of MARTIN SCHLOTTERER (q.v.). // JACOB SCHLOTTERER, with MARTIN, MATHIES, and JOHANN CONRADT SCHLOTTERER, *Chesterfield,* September 2, 1749, Hinke, I, 393-4.

## SCHLOTTERER, JACOB (2)—Bodelshausen (1749)

B. 4-28-1726, son of JACOB and URSULA SCHLOTTERER.

## SCHLOTTERER, MARTIN (2)—Bodelshausen (1749)

B. 4-15-1752, son of JACOB and ANNA BARBARA SCHLOTTERER, and brother of JACOB SCHLOTTERER (q.v.). // MARTIN SCHLOTTERER, with JACOB, MATHIES, and JOHANN CONRADT SCHLOTTERER, *Chesterfield,* September 2, 1749, Hinke, I, 393-4.

## SCHLOTTERER, MATTHEIS (2)—Bodelshausen (1749)

B. 12-25-1722, son of MICHAEL and AGNES SCHLOTTERER. // MATHIES SCHLOTTERER, with JOHANN CONRADT, MARTIN, and JACOB SCHLOTTERER, *Chesterfield,* September 2, 1749, Hinke, I, 393-4.

## SCHMID, JOHANNES (1-2)—Oberboihingen

Cooper [*Küfer*]. Wf: MARGARETHA. Ch: (1) Barbara, b. 7-10-1744; (2) Johann Ulrich, b. 9-17-1747. Was bankrupt. "Went to Pennsylvania.' // Perhaps JOHANNIS SCHMID (SCHMIT) (two), with JOHANNES FIMPEL and JOSEPH SOMMER, both of Oberboihingen, *Phoenix,* November 2, 1752, Hinke, I, 501.

## SCHMID, MARTIN (2)—Neckartenzlingen (1752)

Farmhand [*Bauernknecht*]. Wf: ANNA MARIA, *née* WEBER, daughter of MARTIN WEBER (q.v.) of Schlaitdorf. Married in the Spring of 1752. Ludwigsburg Protocol, 4-14-1752, to "Pennsylvania." // MARTIN SMITH (SCHMIDT), *Richard and Mary*, September 30, 1754, Hinke I, 605-6.

## SCHMID, PHILIPP KARL (1)—Oberboihingen

Farmer [*Bauer*]. Wf: ANNA. Ch: (1) Matthäus, b. 10-4-1742; (2) Anna, b. 8-27-1747. // Perhaps CARLE SCHMID, with JOHANNES FIMPEL and JOSEPH SOMMER, and perhaps JOHANNIS SCHMID, all of Oberboihingen, *Phoenix*, November 2, 1752, Hinke, I, 503.

## SCHNAIDT, GEORG (1)—Unterjesingen (1752)

Wf: MARIA. Ch: (1) Anna, b. 7-26-1742, "went to Pennsylvania with her mother." Ludwigsburg Protocol, 1752. Father died previously. // Others listed in PA.

## SCHNECK(E), ALBERT (2)—Aurich (1752)

Tailor [*Sartor*], surviving son of the cartwright J. J. Schneck [*filius... superstes des Wagners J. J. Schneckii*]. Wf: JUDITH, *née* SCHEFFER, daughter of the late weaver [*Weber*] FRIEDRICH SCHEFFER in Serres. Married 1751. Ludwigsburg Protocol, 5-4-1752, ALBRECHT SCHNECK, to "Pennsylvania." // ALBERT SCHNECK, *Phoenix*, September 25, 1751, Hinke, I, 470.

## SCHNEIDER, JOHANN GEORG (2)—Maichingen (1752)

Apparently unmarried. Ludwigsburg Protocol, 4-12-1752, *venia emigrandi*. // Perhaps JOHANN GEORG SCHNEIDER, with JOHANN JACOB LANG of Maichingen, *President*, September 27, 1752, Hinke, I, 490.

## SCHNEIDER, MARGARETHA (2)—Rutesheim (1751)

B. 10-25-1724. "Went to Penna., May 24, 1751." Ludwigsburg Protocol, 4-30-1751, *venia emigrandi* only.

## SCHNEPF, FRIEDRICH (2)—Stammheim, Ludwigsburg (1753)

Wf: MAGDALENA (PFISTERER) of Zuffenhausen. Ch: (1) Elisabetha Dorothea, b. 10-26-1751. With the birth of this daughter, this family disappears from the Church Register. Ludwigsburg Protocol, 4-24-1753, to "Pennsylvania."

## SCHNEPF, JOHANN GEORG (2)—Merklingen (see Gechingen) (1752)

Tailor [*Schneider*] of Merklingen. Son of the baker [*Bäcker*] JACOB SCHNEPF there. Wf: MARGARETHA, *née* DREHER, daughter of the baker JOHANN JERG DREHER. Married 7-6-1734. Ch: several. After 1750, this family disappears from the Church Register. Ludwigsburg Protocol, 4-18-1752, to [New] "England." // Two listed in Hinke after 1752: HANS JERG SCHNEPP, *Chance*, September 23, 1766, Hinke, I, 709; and JOHANN GEORG SCHNEPP, *Minerva*, October 1, 1770, Hinke, I, 729. 3PA, 18, 15: GEO. SNEP, laborer, Colebrookdale Tp., Berks Co., Pa., 1767.

SCHNETZER, JOHANN WOLFGANG (2)—Heimhausen (see Lauffen am Neckar)

Of Heimhausen. Wf (1st): ELISABETHA (KRAFFT). Ch: (1) Catharina Margaretha, b. 1737; (2) Maria Magdalena, b. 1739. Wf (2d): ANNA (METZGER). Ch: (3) Johanna Rosina, b. 1744; (4) Maria Elisabetha, b. 1746. "Went to the New World."

SCHNOERRING (SCHNIRING), (HANS) JERG (1-2) Grötzingen (1746)

Weaver [*Weber*]. Wf: CATHARINA. Ch: (1) Agnes, b. 3-31-1744. Left for Pennsylvania, March 23, 1746, according to a report of the mayor of Grötzingen; see *Introduction*. // GEORGE SCHNEERING, *Ann Galley*, September 27, 1746, Hinke, I, 360.

SCHOENBEIN (SCHIENBEIN), PETER (2)—Möckmühl (1751)

Linenweaver [*Leineweber*]. Wf: ANNA MARIA (BAEURLIN). Ch: (1) Susanna Elisabetha, b. 4-1-1746. Ludwigsburg Protocol, 1-22-1751, to "Pennsylvania."

SCHOENECK, HANS JERG (1)—Pfaffenhofen (1753)

Shoemaker [*Schumacher*]. Wf: SOFIA AGATHA. Ch: (1) Johann Michael, b. 3-20-1735; (2) Anna Barbara, b. 8-24-1736; (3) Georg Friedrich, b. 5-31-1742. "Went to America, 1753." [*1753 Amer. petiit.*] No information as to emigration of Anna Barbara and Georg Friedrich. // HANS MICHAEL SCHENICK (JOHANN MICHEL SCHOENECKH), *Eastern Branch*, October 3, 1753, Hinke, I, 585-6.

SCHOLL, HANS JACOB (1)—Wurmberg

Wf: ELISABETHA. Ch: (1) Agnes Barbara, b. 8-21-1730, "went with her mother to New England." // Several listed in Hinke, including JACOB SCHELL (SCHOLL), *Neptune*, September 24, 1753, Hinke, I, 540, 542, and JACOB SCHOLL, *Betsy*, October 26, 1768, Hinke, I, 725.

SCHRADE, GEORG FRIEDRICH (1)—Neuffen

Shoemaker [*Schuhmacher*]. Wf: DOROTHEA. Ch: (1) Elisabetha Dorothea, b. 5-28-1749. // FRIDRICH SCHRADE, Snow *Louisa*, November 8, 1752, Hinke, I, 507.

SCHRADE (SCHRADIN), JOHANN CHRISTOPH EHRENREICH (2)—Gächingen (1752)

Mason [*Maurer*]. Son of the farmer [*Bauer*] HANS MARTIN SCHRADE (SCHRADIN). Wf: ANNA MARGARETHA, *née* SOENNE, daughter of the shepherd [*Schäfer*] JOHANN JACOB SOENNE, on the ridge [*auf dem Fürst*] near Mössingen. Married 2-5-1750. Ch: (1) Maria Agnes, b. 2-2-1752. "Went to South Carolina or Pennsylvania." Ludwigsburg Protocol, 3-14-1752, *venia emigrandi* only.

SCHUB, ELISABETHA (1)—Nordheim

B. 1-21-1728, daughter of JACOB and ANNA EVA SCHUB.

SCHUETTELBAUER, JOHANN GEORG (1)—Tamm.

Mason [*Maurer*]. Wf: EVA. Ch: (1) Johann Andreas, b. 9-12-1738. To "America."

SCHULER, HANS (JOHANNES) (1)—Dürrwangen (1754)

B. 12-13-1699. Wf: SYBILLA. Ch: (1) Hans Ludwig, b. 2-15-1728; (2) Christian, b. 9-30-1730; (3) Anna Maria, b. 4-19-1733; (4) Agnes, b. 9-20-1735; (5) Andreas, b. 11-30-1740; (6) Martin, b. 8-9-1745. "Went to Pennsylvania with family of six children in 1754. One child died on the passage over." // HANS SCHOULER (SCHUHLER), *Peggy,* October 16, 1754, Hinke, I, 637, 639. Several listed in PA.

SCHUMACHER, ADAM (1)—Nordheim

Wf: MARIA CHRISTINA. Ch: (1) Jerg Adam, b. 11-28-1720; (2) Johann Michael, b. 12-15-1723; (3) Johann Balthas, b. 1-1-1730. // JOHAN ATAM (ADAM) SCHUMACHER, *Aurora,* October 8, 1744, Hinke, I, 353-4. Several listed in PA.

SCHUMACHER, ALBRECHT (1)—Alpirsbach

B. 12-28-1729, son of HANS JACOB SCHUMACHER, *potter* [*Häfner*] and wf MARIA ELISABETHA, *née* SCHLEEHAUF. "Emigrated to America, 1751." // Cf. ALBRECHT SCHUHMACHER, *Hero,* October 27, 1764, Hinke, I, 698.

SCHUMACHER, HANS JACOB (1)—Grötzingen (1754)

Wf: ANNA. Ch: (1) Anna Barbara, b. 1-11-1726; (2) Helena, b. 1-12-1728. Helena had a son JACOB, b. (illeg.) 4-11-1750. // Several listed in Hinke, none 1754.

SCHUMACHER, HANS JACOB (1)—Täbingen (1749)

B. 3-28-1706. Wf: ANNA MARIA. Ch: (1) Anna Catharina, b. 1-7-1733; (2) Conrad, b. 10-14-1737; (3) Elisabetha, b. 7-28-1747. To "New England," April 16, 1749, "with wife and four children." // HANS JACOB SHOEMAKER, *Lydia,* October 19[9], 1749, Hinke, I, 421.

SCHUPP, FRIEDRICH (2)—Neckartenzlingen (1752)

Baker and former lance Corporal [*Beck u. gewesener Gefreiter*]. Wf: MARGARETHA (WETZEL). Married 1749. Ludwigsburg Protocol, 5-16-1752, to "America." // Several listed in PA.

SCHUSTER, JOHANNES (2)—Lomersheim (1754)

B. 6-13-1688, son of Martin Schuster. Wf: ELISABETHA ZANDEL, carpenter's daughter [*Zimmermannstochter*] of Wiernsheim. Ch: (1) Maria Barbara, b. 10-13-1717; (2) Hans Jerg, b. 10-19-1722. Ludwigsburg Protocol, 4-5-1754, *venia emigrandi.* // Evidently JOHN SCHUSTER, immediately following JOSEPH BOGER of Lomersheim, *Peggy,* October 16, 1754, Hinke, I, 637, though another arrived later in the same year. 3PA, 14, 605: JOHN SHUSTER, with ANDREW SHUSTER, Germantown, Philadelphia Co., Pa., 1779.

SCHWARZ, JOHANNES (2)—Weilheim unter Teck (1753)

B. 3-30-1730. "Went away to Pennsylvania in 1753, with other single persons." Ludwigsburg Protocol, 5-8-1753. // JOHANNES SCHWARTZ, age 21, with MICHEL LAUB of Weilheim unter Teck, *Halifax,* September 28, 1753, Hinke, I, 560-1.

SCHMEGLER, JOHANN FRIEDRICH (2)—Beutelsbach (1798)

B. 1-16-1749. Ch: (1) Christian Friedrich, b. 3-6-1784. To "America" in 1798, with son.

SCHWEICKART, GEORG CONRAD (1)—Grünwettersbach (1751)

Day laborer [*Tagelöhner*]. [B.?] at Mutschelbach. Wf: JUSTINA CATHARINA, *née* BODAMER (BODEMER), b. 10-9-1712, daughter of PHILIPP and BARBARA BODAMER (BODEMER). Ch: (1) Eva, b. 2-9-1750; "went with her parents to Pennsylvania." // GEORG CONRAD SCHWEICHERT, with JACOB SCHWEICKERT and HANS SAMUEL SHWEYART, *Shirley*, September 5, 1751, Hinke, I, 454.

SCHWEIKERT, JOHANN BALTHAS (1)—Nordheim (1748)

Wf: ANNA MARGARETHA. Ch: (1) Johannes, b. 3-18-1745; (2) Johann Michael, b. 3-23-1747; (3) Johann Philipp, b. 1-26-1749. Ludwigsburg Protocol, 1748. // Several John Schweikerts in PA.

SCHWEIKHARDT, SEBASTIAN (1)—Bodelshausen (1772)

Joiner [*Schreiner*]. Wf: AGNES MARIA, *née* KELLER, joiner's daughter, b. 12-22-1743. Ch: (1) Agnes Maria, b. 11-26-1761; (2) Felix, b. 7-10-1765; (3) Anna Margaretha, b. 3-12-1769; (4) Anna Barbara, b. 11-18-1770. Left for America, May 14, 1772, with others from the same village. // Cf. JOHAN CHRISTOPH SCHWEIGERTS, *Catharine*, April 30, 1773, Hinke, I, 746. The will of SEBASTIAN SWEIGART of Martic Tp., Lancaster Co., Pa., dated March 16, 1808, probated August 1, 1808, mentions wife Maria and children Maria, Felix, Margaret, Barbara, John, Hannah, wf of Adam Barget, Henry, and George; executors: wf Maria, and Felix Sweigart, *Lancaster County Will Abstracts*, II, 1007, GSP. For the German text of the Family Record of the Schweikhardts, prepared by Pastor Luz of Bodelshausen, see the facsimile reproduced elsewhere in this paper; for a translation, see our Introduction. For this document, kindly supplied the editor by a descendant, Mrs. M. Luther Heisey of Lancaster, Pennsylvania, can be added the death records of Sebastian Schweikert and his wife, also written on the above-mentioned document: (1) "SEBASTIAN SCHWEIKART died the 19th day of March in the year of Our Lord 1808; his age was 71 years, 4 months and 4 days." (2) "AGNES MARIA blessedly fell asleep in Jesus the 25th day of April in the year of Our Lord 1812; her age was 68 years, 4 months and 3 days."

SCHWEITZER, JOHANNES (2)—Weilheim unter Teck (1750)

"1st dragon, then hussar" [*zuerst Dragoner, dann Husar*]. B. 6-24-1723. Wf: ANNA CATHARINA (BLESSING). Married 7-12-1746; no children. "Went to Pennsylvania, May 4, 1750, with almost 800 florins." // Somer's newspaper, February 2, 1759, quoted in Hocker, 78: "JOHANNES SCHWEITZER, Germantown, soldier in Captain Diefe's (Davis?) company, offers a reward for the capture of a runaway soldier."

SCHWENKEL, (HANS) ULRICH (1)—Hülben (1751)

Wf: BARBARA, *née* SCHELL. Ch: (1) Hieronymus, b. 4-11-1741, "is in Pennsylvania." // UHLLERICH SCHWENCKEL, *Neptune*, September 24, 1751, Hinke, I, 469, with other families from Hülben. 3PA, 18, 34: URICH SCHWENKLE, Longswamp Tp., Berks Co., Pa., 1767. 3PA, 26, 179: ULRICH HANS SWINGLE, 50 acres, Northampton Co., survey August 4, 1792.

SECKINGER, MATTHIAS (1)—Rötenberg (1749)

Cooper [*Kübler*]. Wf: ANNA CATHARINA. Ch: (1) Christian, b. 5-13-1741, "went to Pennsylvania, 1749." (2) Maria Catharina, b. 8-13-1742; (3) Anna, b. 12-25-1747.

SEEGER, JOHANN GEORG (1)—Schopfloch, Oberamt Freudenstadt

Wf: [ ? ]. Ch: (1) Johann Georg, b. 6-6-1743. To "Pennsylvania," ca. 1750. // 3PA, 14, 89: GEORGE SAGER, Germantown Tp., Philadelphia Co., Pa., 1769. 3PA, 24, 763: GEORGE SEAGER, 163.19 acres, Cumberland Co., Pa., survey January 17, 1774.

SEIDELMAIER, HANS JERG (1)—Altenriet (1754)

Wf: MARGARETHA. Ch: (1) Johannes, b. 4-2-1739. To "Pennsylvania," 1754.

SIGLER, CATHARINA BARBARA (1)—Nordheim

B. 3-22-1699, daughter of HANS BERNHARD SIGLER.

SIGLIN, JOHANNES (2)—Neckartenzlingen (1753)

In the Baptismal Register, called "butcher, landlord at the Stag Inn, judge, senator" [*Metzger, Hirschwirt, Judex, Senator*], in the Nürtingen documents, called "farmer" [*Bauer*]. Wf: ANNA. Ch: (1) Johannes, b. 4-4-1740; (2) Johann Georg, b. 3-30-1741; (3) Johann Jacob Heinrich, b. 10-26-1747, "in Pennsylvania"; (4) Anna, b. 3-30-1749, "in Pennsylvania"; (5) Anna Justina, b. 1-10-1752, "went to the New World." Ludwigsburg Protocol, 4-10-1753, to "Pennsylvania." // JOHANS ZIEGLIN (JOHANNES SIGLIN), *Richard and Mary*, September 17, 1753, Hinke, I, 531-2. 3PA, 19, 123: JOHN SIEGLIN, Heldelberg Tp., Northampton Co., Pa., 1785. 3PA, 19, 76: JOHN SIGLING, Chestnuthill Tp., Northampton Co., Pa., 1772; 3PA, 26, 175: HENRY SIGLIN, 100 acres, Northampton Co., Pa., survey September 6, 1786. 3PA, 19, 264: HENRY SIGLIN, Chestnuthill Tp., Northampton Co., Pa., 1786.

SIGLIN, JOHANN JACOB (2)—Beutelsbach (1746)

B. 5-15-1722. "Went to Pennsylvania, 3-26-1746." // JACOB ZIEGLY, with JOHANNES SIGLE, *Ann Galley*, September 27, 1746, Hinke, I, 360. 3PA, 17, 800: JACOB SIGLY, Lebanon Tp, Lancaster Co., Pa., 1782.

SIGLIN, JOHANNES (2)—Beutelsbach (1746)

B. 3-6-1725. "Went to Pennsylvania, 3-26-1746." // JOHANNES SIGLE, with JACOB ZIEGLY, *Ann Galley*, September 27, 1746, Hinke, I, 360.

SIMON, LORENTZ (1)—Neckarhausen (1753)

Farmer [*Bauer*]. Wf: ANNA MARIA. Ch: (1) Johannes, b. 1-11-1739, "went with his mother to Pennsylvania in 1753." (2) Maria Elisabetha, b. 3-30-1741, "went to Pennsylvania in 1753." // Cf. LORANCE (LORENTZ) SIMON, age 30, with CHRISTIAN SIMON, age 60, *Princess Augusta*, September 16, 1736, Hinke, I, 162, 166. Cf. the will of LAURENCE SIMON, of Heidelberg Tp., Northampton Co., Pa., dated January 2, 1757, probated June 5, 1758, mentioning wf Barbara; children Laurence, Catharina, wf of Christian Zimmerman, Elisabeth Margaret, Elisabeth, wf of Peter Sholl, Elisabeth Catharine, wf of William Bricius, and Margaret Barbara; executors: George Rex and Jno. Lenard Fuhr; witness: George Rex, Jacob Bender, Philip Feedler, and Jno. Dietrich Baldauff, *Northampton County Will Abstracts*, No. 27, GSP.

SING, JOHANN GEORG (2)—Beutelsbach (1750)

Perhaps butcher [*Metzger*]. B. 2-16-1720. Wf: CATHARINA, *née* HARTMANN, b. 1724. Ch: (1) Johann Georg, b. 9-18-1749. Ludwigsburg Protocol, 2-27-1750, Sing and associates, to "Pennsylvania." "Went to Pennsylvania, 5-4-1750," with wife and family. // HANS JERG SING, *Patience,* August 11, 1750, Hinke, I, 427. 3PA, 11, 203: GEO. SING, freeman, Chester, Chester Co., Pa., 1766. 3PA, 14, 86: GEORGE SING, Springfield Tp., Philadelphia Co., Pa., 1769.

SIRGER (SIEGER?), JOHAN GEORG (1)—Lomersheim

Wf: MARGARETHA. Ch: (1) Christian, b. 1-3-1748. To "Pennsylvania." // JOHANN GEORG SIEGER, with MICHAEL JENSEL and JOHANNES VOLLMER, both of Lomersheim, *Nancy,* August 31, 1750, Hinke, I, 442; a fellow-passenger was "Baron" Henderick Willem Stiegel.

SIRGER (SIEGER?), JOHANNES (1)—Lomersheim

Non-citizen [*Beisitzer*]. Wf: CATHARINA. Ch: (1) Johann Daniel, b. 11-9-1749; (2) Clara Sabina, b. 1-18-1752. // JOHANNES SI(E)GER, age 29, with FRIEDRICH JENSEL of Lomersheim, *Patience,* September 15 [17], 1753, Hinke, I. 526, 528. 3PA, 19, 115: JOHN SIEGER, Weisenberg Tp., Northampton Co., Pa., 1785.

SOMMER, JOSEPH (1-2)—Oberboihingen (1752)

Wf: WALBURGA, *née* HAUSSMANN. Ch: (1) Catharina, b. 1-13-1731; (2) Elisabetha, b. 1-21-1736; (3) Georg Philipp, b. 12-9-1740; (4) Maria Magdalena, b. 8-28-1743. To "Pennsylvania." Ludwigsburg Protocol, 1752. According to the Nürtingen Documents, he had "shortly before this, been sentenced to four weeks imprisonment in the Ludwigsburg House of Correction, for his prodigally dissolute conduct [*wegen seines 'verthunerischen' liederlichen Lebenswandels*]. Punishment dispensed with on account of his immigration to Pennsylvania." // JOSEPH SOMMER, *Phoenix,* November 2, 1752, Hinke, I, 503. *Philadelphische Correspondenz,* September 30, 1788, quoted in Hocker, 194: "Letters for JOSEPH or PHILIP SOMMER, from Ober-Boyhingen."

SPAETH, ANDREAS (1)—Dornhan

Joiner [*Schreiner*]. Wf: ANNA CATHARINA. Ch: (1) Anna Catharina, b. 9-8-1736, is "in America."

SPAETH, ELISABETHA (2)—Gündelbach (p. 1763)

Widow. Emigrated after 1763, with two daughters.

SPAETH, PHILIPP SAMUEL (2)—Gündelbach)

B. 1720. Emigrated with wife and two sons. // 3PA, 18, 31: PHILIP SPATH, Cumru Tp., Berks Co., Pa., 1767.

SPAHN, ANNA CATHARINA DOROTHEA (1)—Nordheim

B. 2-24-1701, daughter of HANS MARTIN SPAHN.

SPAHN, EVA (1)—Nordheim

B. 12-3-1698, daughter of HANS MARTIN SPAHN. Sister of Anna Catharina Dorothea Spahn (q.v.).

SPEIDEL, HANS (1)—Bodelshausen (1753)

Weaver [*Weber*]. Wf: CHRISTINA. Ch: (1) Christina, b. 11-22-1734. "Went to Pennsylvania, May 10, 1753."

## SPEIDEL, HANS JERG (2)—Bodelshausen (1749)

B. 10-22-1719, son of HANS and ANNA BARBARA SPEIDEL. HANS JORG SPEIDEL, with MAXIMILIANUS SPEIDEL, *Chesterfield,* September 2, 1749, Hinke, I, 393; a JOHAN GEORG SPEIDEL arrived in 1750.

## SPEIDEL, MAXIMILIAN (2)—Ofterdingen (1749)

B. 4-30-1730, son of JACOB and ANNA (LUTZ) SPEIDEL. "Died in the East Indies in 1763" [† *in Ostinden 1763*]; probably West Indies [America] is meant. // MAXIMILIANUS SPEIDEL, with JOSEPH SPEIDEL and HANS JORG SPEIDEL, *Chesterfield,* also with the SCHAUWECKERS and SCHLOTTERERS from neighboring Bodelshausen, September 2, 1749, Hinke, I, 393.

## SPENGLER, (JOHANN) BALTHASAR (2)—Nackartenzlingen (1752)

Butcher [*Metzger*]. Son of the baker and justiciary, later Burgomaster Spengler of Jux (Spiegelberg) [*Sohn des Becks u. Gerichtsverwalters, späteren Bürgermeisters Spengler von Jux (Spiegelberg)*]. Wf (1st): (ANNA) ROSINA (STOTZ). Ch: (1) Johann Jacob, b. 10-2-1736. Wf (2d): ROSINA, *née* MOESSNER, cobbler's daughter [*Schusterstocher*]. Ch: (2) Christoph Heinrich, b. 11-22-1747; (3) Catharina Barbara, b. 6-29-1750. Ludwigsburg Protocol, 4-14-1752, to "Pennsylvania." According to a certificate of good conduct dated March, 1752, sent Gerber by Pastor Zink of Marbach, Spengler's wife and the three above-named children emigrated with him. Descendants in New York.

## SPEYER, JOHANN (1)—Schlaitdorf

Councilor and baker [*des Raths u. Beck*]. Wf: BARBARA, *née* LUETTICH. Ch: (1) Matthäus, b. 4-29-1743; (2) Johannes, b. 10-13-1751. // JOHN (JOHANNES) SPEYER, with MICHEL KLEIN of Schlaitdorf, *Peggy,* October 16, 1754, Hinke, I, 637, 639.

## SPEYR, MATTHAEUS (1)—Schlaitdorf

Baker [*Beck*]. Wf: ANNA CATHARINA. Ch: (1) Anna Catharina, b. 3-9-1730, "went with parents to Pennsylvania"; (2) Johann Caspar, b. 9-15-1733, "died in Pennsylvania in 1742."

## SPO(H)N, JOHANN MATTHIAS (2)—Laufen/Eyach (1750)

Wf: LUCIA. Ch: (1) Anna Maria, b. 11-1-1743; (2) Martin, b. 9-18-1746. "Went to Pennsylvania, 1750." // HANS MOTIS SPOHN, with CHRISTIAN STOTZ of Laufen, *Osgood,* September 29, 1750, Hinke, I, 446; a fellow-passenger was Gottlieb Mittelberger.

This family became Moravians and from materials appearing in Schultze, 22, 68, 91-2, and in Kluge, 107, it appears that MATTHEW SPOHN, born March 1, 1711, married LUCIA BIEZER in 1730, and on coming to America, lived at Bethlehem, Nazareth, and Christianspring; he died at Nazareth, July 16, 1781, and is buried in the Moravian Graveyard there. The wife, LUCIA (BIEZER) SPOHN, was born in 1714 and died in 1788. Of their children, (1) ANNA MARIA (1743-1810) married CHRISTIAN HORNIG (1733-1812), a native of Wenigmonden, Silesia, a shoemaker, gardener, and forester; and (2) JOHN MARTIN died at Bethlehem in 1758.

SPRECHER (SPRAECHER), JOHANN CHRISTOPH (2)—Grossgartach (1751)

Ludwigsburg Protocol, 5-3-1751, describes him as blacksmith's apprentice from Pennsylvania [*Schmiedknecht aus Pens.*] // Perhaps JOHN CHRISTOPHER SPRECHER (JOHANN CHRISTOPH SPEICHER), age 25, *Patience*, September 16, 1748, Hinke, I, 384, 386.

SPRECHER, JOHANN GEORG (2)—Grossgartach

Farrier [*Hufschmied*]. Widower [*Wittwer*]. Wf: (dec.) CATHARINA BARBARA (EBERHARD) of Kochendorf. Ch: (1) Maria Elisabetha, b. 12-27-1736; (2) Maria Margaretha, b. 2-19-1746. Not in the Burial Register up to 1808. // HANS JORG SPRECHER, with JACOB SPRECHER, *Janet*, October 7, 1751, Hinke, I, 474-5. 3PA, 17, 142: GEO. SPRECKER, with JACOB SPRECHER, Lebanon Tp., Lancaster Co., Pa., 1771.

STAEBLER, JOHANN GEORG (2)—Rohr (see Sielmingen) (1754?)

Of Rohr. Wf: ANNA CATHARINA (ARNOLD), b. 7-19-1730, daughter of Michael Arnold, of Harthausen. Married 1752. To "Pennsylvania." Wife was a sister of MARIA (ARNOLD) MUELLER, wf of JOHANNES MUELLER (q.v.); and of BARBARA (ARNOLD) BAYHA, wf of GEORG BAYHA, JR. (q.v.). According to the old Family Register: "CATHARINA, ANNA MARIA, and BARBARA ARNOLD emigrated to Pennsylvania."

STAHL, MARGARETHA (2)—Magstadt (1752)

*Née* WIDMAIER. Deserted wf of of the cooper [*Küfer*] JOHANN JACOB STAHL. Married 11-21-1724. Ludwigsburg Protocol, 4-7-1752, to "Pennsylvania." // Several JACOB STAHLS listed in Hinke.

STAIGER, CATHARINA (1)—Bodelshausen (1772)

B. 1-29-1737, daughter of HANS STAIGER, cartwright [*Wagner*]. "Left for America, May 14, 1772," with others from the same village.

STAUCH, ANDREAS (2)—Münklingen (1754)

Ludwigsburg Protocol, 4-5-1754, with "ALT MICHAEL STAUCH" (q.v.), *venia emigrandi.* // ANDREAS STOW (STAUCH), age 30, with JOHANN JACOB STAUCH, age 18, NICH'LS STOW (MICHAEL STAUCH), age 18, MICHEL STAUCH, age 40, and HANS YERR'K STOWK (HANS GERG STAUCH), *Barclay*, September 14, 1754, Hinke, I, 596-8. 3PA, 21, 64: ANDREW STAUCH, single, with GEORGE and FREDERICK STOUCH, Dover Tp., York Co., Pa., 1779.

STAUCH, GOTTFRIED (2)—Gebersheim (1752)

Workman [*Schaffknecht*]. Listed in Church Register until the nineteenth Sunday after Trinity, 1751, then disappears. Ludwigsburg Protocol, 4-21-1752, to "Pennsylvania." // GODFRIED STOUGH, *President*, September 27, 1752, Hinke, I, 490.

STAUCH, HANS JACOB (2)—Möttlingen (1749)

B. 10-9-1720, son of the weaver [*Weber*] LORENTZ STAUCH. Wf: SOPHIA [ ? ] of Simmozheim. Ch: (1) Lorentz, b. 11-16-1747. Ludwigsburg Protocol, 5-8-1749, to "Pennsylvania." // JACOB STAUCH, with HANS JERG STAUCH, *Phoenix*, September 15, 1749, Hinke, I, 407. Several JACOB STAUCHS listed in PA, in Lancaster, Berks, York, Northampton, and Northumberland Counties.

STAUCH, HANS JERG (2)—Möttlingen (1754)

B. 9-30-1727, son of the weaver [*Weber*] LORENTZ STAUCH. Brother of HANS JACOB STAUCH (q.v.). Wf: EVA MARGARETHA (HELDMAYER). Married 5-17-1754, with dispensation from banns, after which "they went to Pennsylvania, 5-21-1754." // HANS YERR'K STOWK (HANS GERG STAUCH), age 37, with ANDREAS, JOHANN JACOB, NICH'LS (MICHAEL), and MICHEL STAUCH, *Barclay*, September 14, 1754, Hinke, I, 596-8. 3PA, 18, 78: GEORGE STAUCH, Tulpehocken Tp., Berks Co., Pa., 1767. 3PA, 21, 460-1: GEORGE STOUCK, with GODFRIED STOUCH, ANDREW STOUCH and JACOB STAUCH (single), Dover Tp., York Co., Pa., 1781.

STAUCH, JOHANN JACOB (2)—Münklingen

B. 1735. To "Pennsylvania." // JOHN JACOB STOW (JOHANN JACOB STAUCH), age 18, with ANDREAS, NICH'LS (MICHAEL, HANS GERG, and MICHEL STAUCH, *Barclay*, September 14, 1754, Hinke, I, 596-8. Several JACOB STAUCHS listed in PA, in Lancaster, Berks, York, Northampton, and Northumberland Counties.

STAUCH, JOHANN MICHAEL (2)—Münklingen

Wf: AGNES. Ch: Maria Catharina, b. 1740. // NICH'LS STOW (MICHAEL STAUCH), age 18, MICH'L STOW (MICHEL STAUCH), age 40, with ANDREAS, JOHANN JACOB, and HANS GERG STAUCH, *Barclay*, September 14, 1754, Hinke, I, 596-8. 3PA, 18, 54: MICHAEL STAUCH, Eastern District Tp., Berks Co., Pa., 1767.

STAUCH, LORENTZ (2)—Möttlingen (1754)

Weaver [*Weber*]. Wf: CATHARINA [ ? ] (SIMMOZHEIM). Married 9-29-1718. Ch: two besides HANS JERG (q.v.) and JACOB (q.v.) Ludwigsburg Protocol, 3-5-1754, LORENTZ and HANS JERG STAUCH, with wives, to "Pennsylvania."

STAUCH, MARIA ELISABETHA (2)—Münklingen

B. 1730, daughter of JOSEPH STAUCH. "Went to Pennsylvania." // Cf. JOSEPH STAUCH, *Betsy*, October 13, 1766, Hinke, I, 710.

STAUCH, MICHAEL, SR. (2)—Münklingen (1754)

"ALT MICHAEL STAUCH." Ludwigsburg Protocol, 4-5-1754, ANDREAS STAUCH and "ALT MICHAEL STAUCH," *venia emigrandi*. // MICH'L STOW (MICHAEL STAUCH), age 18, and ANDREAS, JOHANN JACOB, and HANS GERG STAUCH, *Barclay*, September 14, 1754, Hinke, I, 596-8. 3PA, 18, 54: MICHAEL STAUCH, Eastern District Tp., Berks Co., Pa., 1767.

STEB, HANS BERNHARD (1)—Bodelshausen (1772)

B. 10-14-1737, son of HANS MARTIN, *tailor* [*Sartor*] and wf ANNA, *née* MAJER. "Went to America, May 14, 1772," with others from same village.

STECK, JOHANN GEORG, JR. (2)—Steinenbronn (1754)

Widower [*Viduus*]. Weaver [*Weber*]. B. 5-27-1716. Wf: ANNA of Feuerbach, b. 10-1-1710; died January, 1754, from a wound received from her husband. [Gerber: "*Frau † Jan. 54 an casu von ihrem Mann empfangener Wunde.*"] Ch: (1) Barbara, b. 2-26-1734; (2) Johann Michael, b. 4-29-1740; (3) Christina, b. 3-9-1749. "Went to the new world with his children, 1754."

## STECK, FRIEDRICH (2)—Steinenbronn (1754)

Widower [*Viduus*]. Weaver [*Weber*]. B. 5-27-1716. Wf: ANNA MARIA (KAPFMAYER), died after childbirth, May, 1753. Ch: (1) Anna Margaretha, b. 10-3-1741; (2) Anna Maria, b. 8-5-1743, at Treptow in Pomerania (!); (3) Friedrich, b. 10-18-1746; (4) Johann Georg, b. 4-2-1750. "Left the country for the New World with his children in 1754." // 3PA, 14, 75: FREDERICK STECK, Providence Tp., Philadelphia Co., Pa., 1769.

## STEEB, ELIAS (2)—Bodelshausen (1749)

B. 10-31-1721, son of HANS CUNRAD and URSULA STEEB. // ELIAS STEEB, with MICHAEL STEB and the SPEIDELS of Bodelshausen, *Chesterfield*, September 2, 1749, Hinke, I, 393-4.

## STEEB, MICHAEL (2)—Bodelshausen (1749)

B. 1-[ ? ]-1730, son of HANS CUNRAD and URSULA STEEB. // MICHAEL STEB, with ELIAS STEEB and the SPEIDELS of Bodelshausen, *Chesterfield*, September 2, 1749, Hinke, I, 393-4. 3PA, 18, 261: MICH'L STEEP, Richmond Tp., Berks Co., Pa., 1779.

## STEHLE, BALTHASAR (2)—Isingen (see Erzingen) (1749)

Of Isingen. Wf: ANNA (WEZEL). Married 4-23-1749. "Went to Pennsylvania, 4-26-1749." // 3PA, 19, 141: BALTZER STEALY, Moore Tp., Northampton Co., Pa., 1785.

## STEIGER, CONRAD (1)—Bodelshausen

Cartwright [*Wagner*]. Wf: ANNA MARIA. Ch: (1) Agnes, b. 12-22-1743; (2) Catharina, b. 8-13-1746; (3) Anna Maria, b. 4-20-1749. "Went to America," or "Pennsylvania." // CONRAD and HANS CONRAD STAIGER, *Nancy*, September 16, 1751, Hinke, I, 463. 3PA, 14, 115: CONRAD STEIGER, Northern Liberties (East Part), Philadelphia Co., Pa., 1769.

## STEINLER (STEINLIN), URSULA (2)—Stammheim (Calw) (1751)

B. 3-8-1728, daughter of the late Mayor [*Schultheiss*] KOEMPF, widow of the mason [*Maurer*] STEINLIN. Ch: (1) Anna Catharina, b. (illeg.) 1-8-1750. "Afterwards went to America with [Melchior] Stock" (q.v.), to whom she was promised in marriage. The marriage could not take place in Stammheim on account of Stock's earlier marital difficulties. For the complete story, see Stock. Ludwigsburg Protocol, 4-30-1751, to "Pennsylvania."

## STERN, ANNA CATHARINA (2)—Altdorf, Nürtingen (1754)

B. 10-10-1745, daughter of JACOB STERN. "Went to Pennsylvania, 1754."

## STIEFF, GEORG FRIEDRICH (1)—Schlaitdorf (1753)

Cobbler [*Schuster*]. Wf: CATHARINA, *née* HAUBENSACKER. Ch: (1) Regina, b. 10-7-1744; (2) Georg Friedrich, b. [?]-23-1746; (3) Anna Maria, b. 12-9-1747; (4) Jacob Friedrich, b. 5-5-1749; (5) Maria Catharina, b. 8-22-1751. Ludwigsburg Protocol, 1753. // JURG FRED'K STHIEFF (GERG FRI[E]DRICH STIEF), *Richard and Mary*, September 17, 1753, Hinke, I, 531, 533-4. 3PA, 18, 7: FRED'K STEEF, shoemaker, Reading Town, Berks Co., Pa., 1767.

STOCK, JOHANN MELCHIOR (2)—Neuffen (see Stammheim [Calw]) (1751)

Journeyman mason [*Maurergesell*] of Neuffen. B. 12-2-1725. Promised in marriage to URSULA (KOEMPF) STEINLER (STEINLIN) (q.v.), daughter of the late Mayor [SCHULTHEISS] KOEMPF, and widow of the Mason STEINLIN.

According to the many and voluminous entries in regard to Stock in the Records of the Lutheran State-Church Convocation, the story of Stock and Steinlin is as follows: When marriage was denied him in Neuffen, Stock came to Stammheim in February, 1749, where as a journeyman of her late husband's trade, he approached the young Widow Steinlin, who was not yet twenty-one, and soon made her an offer of marriage. In the beginning of March, three "fellows" [*Buben*], who would have liked to drive the "outsider" [*fremden Kerl*] out of the village, got together, and two of them climbed a ladder one night, to surprise Stock in his mistress' chamber. Although they did not find him there, he was in the house and, flourishing a knife, drove them away. Thus they were unsuccessful in their complaints against him. The mistress defended her reception and housing of the journeyman, by calling it the general "custom of the trade" [*Handwercks-Gebrauch*]. On St. George's day (April 23), in the presence of her brothers, they were engaged to be married, and, without waiting for actual marriage, which in their case had its difficulties, had a child in January.

Since the pastor could not accomplish their separation, he asked his superiors to support him in his desire to help Stock to receive naturalization and formal marriage, "because," as he wrote, "Stock well understands his trade of mason" [*weil der Stock sein Maurer-Handwerck wol vertehet* . A request for information in Neuffen disclosed that several years previously Stock had eloped with a serving-maid [*Dienstmagd*] from Reutlingen and had enlisted in Switzerland for service in Gorckum (Gorinchem) in Holland, where, according to his account, she was married to him and died. Thereupon he deserted to return home and wanted to get married again. At the protest of the relatives of the deceased, the authorities demanded that he produce a certificate of marriage and death from Holland, but to this no answer arrived from either his regiment or the local magistrate. So Stock was denied citizenship at Stammheim, and went with his betrothed to America. // 3PA, 24, 760: MELCHIOR STOCK, 120 acres, Cumberland Co., Pa., survey October 30, 1765. 3PA, 25, 295, 298, and 301: MELCHIOR STOCK, tracts in Northumberland County, Pa., survey 1772-3 and 1776. 3PA, 19, 415: MELCHIOR STOCK, Penns Tp., Northumberland Co., Pa., 1778-1780.

The will of MELCHIOR STOCK, SR., of Penns Tp., Northumberland Co., Pa., dated December 25, 1797, and probated May 5, 1798, mentions wf ANN MARY; sons MELCHIOR, GEORGE, MICHAEL, and heirs of son PETER; executors, son MELCHIOR and DANIEL RUSH; witness: JONAS HUMPSHAUSER, and FRED'K FREEN, "Northumberland County Will Abstracts," in *Publications of the Genealogical Society of Pennsylvania*, XIV, 157.

For this Stock family, see also Fisher, *Snyder County Pioneers*, 89-90.

STOEHR, CONRAD (1)—Schopfloch, Oberamt Freudenstadt

Wf: JOHANNA. Ch: ROSINA, b. 4-25-1744. To "Pennsylvania," ca. 1750. // CONRADT STOEHR, *Duke of Wirtenberg*, October 16, 1751, Hinke, I, 477. Others listed in PA.

STOER(R)ER (STOEHRER), HANS JERG (2)—Oeschelbronn (now Baden) (1752)

Tailor [*Schneider*]. Wf: BARBARA (LEICHT), "who served several years in Strassburg" [*so unterschiedl. Jahr in Strassburg gedient*]. Married 1741. Ch: three. Ludwigsburg Protocol, 4-22-1752, to "Carolina."

STOTZ, CHR(ISTIAN) (2)—Laufen/Eyach (1750)

Wf: ANNA. Ch: (1) Ludwig, b. 5-13-1745; (2) Samuel, b. 11-28-1746. // CHRISTIAN STOTZ, with HANS BALTES OTZ, and PETTER and LUDWIG STOTZ, *Osgood,* September 29, 1750, Hinke, I, 445-6; a fellow passenger was Gottlieb Mittelberger.

STOTZ, HANS BALTHASS (2)—Laufen/Eyach (1750)

B. 4-21-1713, son of PETER and MAGDALENA STOTZ. Wf: MARGARETHA. Ch: (1) Anna Maria, b. 2-22-1740; (2) Lucia, b. 4-20-1743; (3) Christoph, b. 3-2-1748; (4) Johann Martin, b. 4-26-1749. "To Pennsylvania, 1750." // HANS BALTES OTZ, with CHRISTIAN, PETTER, and LUDWIG STOTZ, *Osgood,* September 29, 1750, Hinke, I, 445-6; a fellow-passenger was Gottlieb Mittelberger.

STOTZ, HANS PETER (2)—Laufen/Eyach (1750)

B. 5-23-1729, son of CHRISTIAN and LUCIA STOTZ. // PETTER STOTZ, with CHRISTIAN and LUDWIG STOTZ and HANS BALTES OTZ, *Osgood,* September 29, 1750, Hinke, I, 445-6; a fellow-passenger was Gottlieb Mittelberger.

STOTZ, LUDWIG (2)—Laufen/Eyach (1750)

B. 8-2-1710, son of PETER and MAGDALENA STOTZ. Wf: CATHARINA. Ch: (1) Anna Maria, b. 8-11-1739; (2) Magdalena, b. 11-21-1744; (3) Johann Jacob, b. 10-20-1748. // LUDWIG STOTZ, with PETTER STOTZ and HANS BALTES OTZ, *Osgood,* September 29, 1750, Hinke, I, 445.

This family joined the Moravian Church, and records of them can be found in Schultze, 9, 13, 61, 68. The father, LUDWIG STOTZ (1710-1782), from Lauffen, Württemberg, was a weaver and farmer. His wife, CATHARINE (WOLFER) STOTZ (1716-1786) was likewise a native of Lauffen. According to Kluge, 119, the son JOHN JACOB STOTZ died unmarried, at Nazareth, January 15, 1800; the date of his birth as given in the Moravian records is October 19, 1748.

The will of LUDWIG STUTZ, of Bethlehem, Northampton Co., Pa., dated August 11, 1782, mentions wf CATHERINE; children PETER, JACOB, JOHN, JOSEPH, and MAGDALENA Demuth; executors: wf CATHARINA and CHRISTIAN HORNING; witness: JOHN HASSE, FRAN THOKAS, *Northampton County Will Abstracts,* No. 328, GSP.

STRAUB, JOHANN GEORG (1)—Neuffen

Wf: ANNA CATHARINA. Ch: (1) Johann Georg, b. 8-5-1749. // JERG STRAUB, *Two Brothers,* September 21, 1751, Hinke, I, 446.

STUBER, GEORG FRIEDRICH (2)—Lauffen am Neckar (1754)

Surgeon [*Chirurg*]. Formerly of Vaihingen (Enz). B. 1709. Married four times. Wf (4th): REGINA CATH. (DEMMLER). Ch: (1) Chr(istian) Friedrich, b. 1735 (of first marriage); (2) Heinrich Jeremias Friedrich, b. 1739 (of third marriage); (3) Maria Jacobina, b. 1750 (of fourth marriage); (4) Sigmund Friedrich, b. 1751 (of fourth marriage). Ludwigsburg Protocol, 3-12-1754, to "Pennsylvania." "Went to Philadelphia in 1754." // GEO. FRED'K STUGER (GEORG FRIEDRICH STUBER), with FRED'K STUGER, JR. (under age), *Henrietta,* October 22, 1754, Hinke, I, 649-650. 3PA, 14, 182: FREDERICK STUBER, South Ward, City of Philadelphia, Pa., 1769. 3PA, 15, 235: FREDERICK STUBER, Dock Ward (North Part), City of Philadelphia, Pa., 1780. Cf. also 3PA, 19, 110: FRIEDRICH STUBER, Salisbury Tp., Northampton Co., Pa., 1785. *Staatsbote,* Philadelphia, September 17, 1771, quoted in Hocker, 115: "HENRICH STUBER, drug store, Lancaster, sign of the golden mortar and pestle, Queen street, several houses from GEORGE Ross and near the court house."

STUCKI, JOHANN GEORG (1)—Beihingen, Oberamt Ludwigsburg (1743)

Wf [?]. Ch: (1) Anna Maria, b. 5-19-1743. "Went to America two days after the baptism of Anna Maria, but his wife went with their children to Murr." // HANS JERG STUCKI, *Robert and Alice,* September 30, 1743, Hinke, I, 347.

STUMPP, GOTTLIEB (1)—Schlaitdorf

Wf: BARBARA. Ch: (1) Johann Georg, b. 1-6-1741. // 3PA, 18, 275: GODLIEB STUMP, "joyner," Reading, Berks Co., Pa., 1779.

STUMPP, HANS MICHAEL (1)—Schlaitdorf

Cobbler [*Schuster*]. Wf: MARIA CATHARINA. Ch: (1) Maria Catharina, b. 10-22-1741. // Hs. MICHAEL STUMPF, *Phoenix,* September 30, 1743, Hinke, I, 346; a MICHEL STUMPF arrived also in 1773. 3PA, 24, 533: MICHAEL STUMP, 75 acres, Lancaster Co., Pa., survey November 15, 1750. 3PA, 17, 669: MICH'L STUMP, JR., with LEONARD STUMP, Heidelberg Tp., Lancaster Co., Pa., 1779. 3PA, 18, 8: MICH'L STUMP, painter, Reading Town, Berks Co., Pa., 1767.

SULGER, HANS JERG (2)—Gomaringen (see Mähringen) (1752)

Ludwigsburg Protocol, 4-27-1752, *venia emigrandi.* // HANS JERG SULGER, *Forest,* October 10, 1752, Hinke, I, 495. Others listed in PA.

# T

TALMON, PIERRE (2)—Pinache (1754)

Identity uncertain on account of frequency of name. If from Pinoche, his wife was CATHARINA MUELLER; his Ch: (1) Magdalena; (2) Catharina; (3) Jeanne; (4) Frederic. These children born 1741-1751. // PIERE TOLMAN, lame, with JACOB TOLMAN (JAQUES TALMON), *Bannister,* October 21, 1754, Hinke, I, 646-8. 3PA, 19, 709: PETER TALLMAN (single), Muncy Tp., Northumberland Co., Pa., 1786.

TEUFFEL, GEORG (2)—Unterjettingen (1751)

B. 5-29-1712, sixth child of HANS TEUFFEL. Is not in Marriage or Baptismal Register. Ludwigsburg Protocol, 4-6-1751, to "Pennsylvania." // GEORG TEUFELL, with LUDWIG TEUFFEL, *Phoenix,* September 25, 1751, Hinke, I, 470-1.

## THUMM, JACOB (1)—Neckarhausen (1754)

Weaver [*Weber*]. Ch: (1) Johann Georg, b. 12-5-1746; (2) Andreas, b. 12-14-1747. "Went to Pennsylvania, 1754." // JACOB DOM (THUM), with HANS GEORGE DOM (GEORG THUM [?]), *Peggy*, October 16, 1754, Hinke, I, 637, 639. 3PA, 26, 256: JACOB DUM, 30 acres, Berks Co., Pa., survey January 25, 1787. 3PA, 25, 647: JACOB TOM, 400 acres, Bedford Co., Pa., survey February 5, 1794. 3PA, 14, 439: GEORGE THUMB, Southwark, Philadelphia Co., Pa., 1774. 3PA, 20, 732: ANDREW DUM, Middleton Tp., Cumberland Co., Pa., 1785.

## TIERS, DANIEL (2)—Dürrmenz (1751)

Wf: MARIE (CONTE). Ch: (1) Matthieu, b. 5-28-1744, at Kleinvillars; (2) Madeleine, b. 4-21-1747; (3) Jean Daniel, b. 9-30-1749. From the German and Waldensian Church Registers for Dürrmenz-Schönenberg. Ludwigsburg Protocol, 5-21-1751, "THIER", to the "New World." // DANIEL TIEN, with STEPHAN DEER *and* JEAN HENRI TIEN, and others from Dürrmenz, *Patience*, September 9, 1751, Hinke, I, 455. 3PA, 13, 414: DANIEL TEER, Milford Tp., Bucks Co., Pa., 1783.

## TIERS, JEAN HENRI (2)—Dürrmenz (1751)

Wf: CATHERINE (CHAPELLE). Ch: (1) Daniel, b. 6-6-1742; (2) Catherine, b. 5-3-1748. From the German and Waldensian Church Registers for Dürrmenz-Schönenberg. // JEAN HENRI TIEN, with DANIEL TIEN, STEPHAN DEER, EBERHART CHAPPELLE and MATTHIEU MORET, *Patience*, September 9, 1751, Hinke, I, 455.

## TREUTZ, JOHANN JACOB (2)—Apfelstetten (1749)

Son of JOHANN JACOB TREUTZ, in Bitz. Wf: MAGDALENA, widow of GEORG LEYHR. Ch: (1) Johann Martin, b. 1738; (2) Johannes, b. 3-7-1740; (3) Johann Jacob, b. 3-1-1743; (4) Johann Martin, b. 12-20-1746. No record in the Burial Register after 1749. To America with his stepchildren, the children of wife's first husband, e.g., (1) Johann Georg Leyhr (q.v.), and (2) Anna Magdalena Leyhr (q.v.). Ludwigsburg Protocol, 4-24-1749, permission to take stepchildren's property to Pennsylvania.

## TUERINGER (TIRINGEN), JOHANN CHRISTOPH (2)—Neuffen (1752)

Sergeant [*Corporal*]. Mentioned in Church Register in 1751 only. Ludwigsburg Protocol, 4-7-1752, [—] Türinger, to "Pennsylvania." // Others listed in Hinke. Two listed in PA, including STOPHEL DERINGER, hatter, Lancaster Borough, Lancaster County, Pa., 1782, in 3PA, 17, 755; and CHRISTOPHER DERINGER, Mahoning Tp., Northumberland Co., Pa., 1783-4, in 3PA, 19, 563.

# U

## UEBEL, JOHANN FRIEDRICH (2)—Siglingen (1752)

With wife. Ludwigsburg Protocol, 4-21-1752, to "Pennsylvania." // JOHAN UBEL (JOHANN FRIEDERICH UEBEL), age 30, *Peggy*, September 24 [25], 1753, Hinke, I, 546, 548. Cf. 3PA, 11, 444: FRED'K EVIL (single), Coventry Tp., Chester Co., Pa., 1768; also 3PA, 18, 43: FREDRICK EVIL, Exeter Tp., Berks Co., Pa., 1767. Estate of FREDERICK UBEL, of Exeter Tp., Berks Co., Pa., April 22, 1777, administration to MICHAEL DIEBER, next of kin, *Berks County Will Abtracts*, I, 223, GSP.

ULMER, GEORG LUDWIG (2)—Neuffen (1749)

B. 7-8-1736, son of GEORG WERNER ULMER and wf URSULA. Went to America in company with ELISABETHA MAJER (q.v.) of Neuffen, after hurried confirmation and special communion in the sacristy, April 3, 1749. The pastor added the following blessing to their record: "The Lord accompany both with the Holy Spirit, to America, their intended country, on which account this dispensation is granted." [*Der Herr begleite auch diese beide mit dem werten heiligen Geiste in die von ihnen intendirten amerikanischen Lande, weshalb obige Dispensation erteilt ist*].

UNTERKOFLER, FLORIAN (2)—Beihingen, Oberamt Ludwigsburg.

According to records dated 1752-1757: "is in Pennsylvania." // Others listed in Hinke, also in PA.

## V

VEITH, MICHAEL (2)—Gebersheim (1751)

Son of JACOB VEITH. "Went to Pennsylvania, 1751." Ludwigsburg Protocol, 5-3-1751, to "Pennsylvania." // Others listed in Hinke. 3PA, 17, 292: MICH'L FEIT, Lancaster Borough, Lancaster Co., Pa., 1772.

VELTEN, JACOB (1)—Pfäffingen (1752)

B. 7-15-1711; butcher's son [*Metzgerssohn*]. "Went to Pennsylvania, May 11, 1752." // Others listed in Hinke, also in PA.

VELTEN, MAGDALENA (1)—Pfäffingen (1752)

Sister of JACOB VELTEN (q.v.). "Went to Pennsylvania, May 11, 1752," but "returned."

VELTEN, JACOB (1)—Unterjesingen

Wf: MARIA AGNES. Ch: (1) Josef, b. 9-20-1745. To "Pennsylvania."

VOEGELE, ANNA MARIA (1)—Oeschelbronn, Oberamt Herrenberg (1755-7)

B. 7-29-1734. "To Philadelphia, 1755-1757." // Others listed in Hinke.

VOEHR, SIMON (1)—Schopfloch, Oberamt Freudenstadt

Wf: MARGARETHA. Ch: (1) Carl, b. 6-24-1748; (2) Johann Michael, b. 3-22-1750.

VOETH, HANS JERG (1)—Kusterdingen

Wf: ANNA MARIA, *née Zeeb*. Ch: (1) Hans Stephan, b. 2-12-1760, "Philadelphia"; (2) Anna Maria, b. 2-28-1761, "Philadelphia." The words "Philadelphia,"added by the pastor who served Kusterdingen in 1762-1776. // Others listed in Hinke. 3PA, 17, 78: GEORGE FEIGHT, Martick Tp., Lancaster Co., Pa., 1771.

VOGEL, JOHANN MICHEL (1)—Beihingen, Oberamt Ludwigsburg (1744)

Day laborer [*Tagelöhner*]. Wf: MARIA MARGARETHA. Ch: (1) Johann Peter, b. 4-1-1732, "went to Pennsylvania with his parents." "Went to Pennsylvania, May 4, 1744." // Cf. MICHA(E)L VOGEL, *Eastern Branch,* October 3, 1753, Hinke, I, 586-7.

VOGELMANN, MELCHIOR (2)—Mockmühl (1749)

Farmer [*Bauer*]. B. 11-25-1709, fifth child of the justiciary [*Gerichtsverwalter*] HANS THOMAS VOGELMANN and wf. ANNA WALBPURGIS (KUEHNER) at Widdern. Wf (1st): Catharina Elisabetha (Hettenbach. Ch: (1) Johann Melchior, b. 10-2-1741; (2) Johann Philipp, b. 10-26-1744. Wf (2d): MARIA BARBARA (GRAMLICH). Ch: (3) Georg Friedrich, b. 11-18-1746. Ludwigsburg Protocol, 4-11-1749, (to take along to Pennsylvania) the maternal inheritance of the two children of his first marriage. Sends SPRECHER of Grossgartach as his attorney in 1751. // MELLICHER VOGELMANN, JACOB, October 2, 1749, Hinke, I, 418. The will of MELCHIOR VOGELMANN, of Macungie Tp., Northampton Co., Pa., dated December 3, 1785, probated September 22, 1789, mentions wf MARY BARBARA, and two children yet living: MELCHIOR, and MARY BARBARA, who married JOHN WUERTZ; executor, Michael Shaffer of Macungie; witnesses: Fred'k Limbach, Geo. Reiss, and Christian Fisher, *Northampton County Will Abstracts*, No. 467, GSP. 3PA, 19, 43: MELCHER FOGELMAN, farmer, Macungie Tp., Northampton Co., Pa., 1772.

VOLLMAR, JOHANNES (1)—Lomersheim

Farmer [*Bauer*]. Wf: CATHARINA. Ch: (1) Johann Michael, b. 1-5-1737, "to the New Land"; (2) Margaretha, b. 2-1-1743. To "Pennsylvania." // JOHANNES VOLLMER, heading list, with MICHAEL JENSEL of Lomersheim, *Nancy,* August 31, 1750, Hinke, I, 442; a fellow passenger was "Baron" Henderick Willem Stiegel; another JOHANNES VOLLMER arrived in 1770. 3PA, 13, 30: JOHN and JACOB FULLMER, Springfield Tp., Bucks Co., Pa., 1779; cf. also 3PA, 19, 362: JOHN FULLMER, saddler, Bethlehem Tp., Northampton Co., Pa., 1788. 3PA, 18, 458: MICH'L FULLMER, Brunswick Tp., Berks Co., Pa., 1781.

VYL, ANNA MARIA (1-2)—Schlaitdorf (1754)

B. 4-26-1723, daughter of MICHAEL and ANNA MARIA VYL. "Went to Pennsylvania, 1754."

# W

WACKER, MICHAEL (1)—Weil im Schönbuch (1751)

Former soldier [*gewesener Soldat*]. Wf: BARBARA. Ch: (1) Maria Barbara, b. 11-11-1746. Ludwigsburg Protocol, 1751. // MICHEL WACKER, with GEOERG WACKER, *Edinburgh,* September 15, 1749, Hinke, I, 403. Others listed in PA.

WAEGELIN, GEORG LUDWIG (1)—Mägerkingen

Carpenter [*Zimmermann*]. Wf: CATHARINA, *née* RUCKWID. Ch: (1) Anna Barbara, b. 11-21-1762. According to records kept by Pastor Hauff, who served Mägerkingen, 1770-1809, the daughter "went with her parents to Carolina in America." // Others listed in PA.

WAESTER (WESTER), JOHANN GEORG (2)—Rottenacker (1751)

Son of the baker [*Bäcker*] MATTHAEUS WAESTER, at Hirrweiler. Wf: CATHARINA (GROEZINGER), daughter of the tailor [*Schneider*] STEPHAN GROEZINGER. Married 11-20-1750. "Went to Pennsylvania also." Ludwigsburg Protocol, 4-6-1751, Wäster and associates, to "Pennsylvania." // Others listed in Hinke.

WAGNER, JOHANN JACOB (2)—Onstmettingen (1750)

Tailor [*Schneider*]. Wf: ANNA (HAEGIN). Ch: (1) Anna Catharina, b. 6-1-1747. According to records kept by Pastor Johann Georg Stählen, 1746-1756, this family "went to New England." Ludwigsburg Protocol, 5-3-1752, mentions emigrants from Onstmettingen to Pennsylvania, without giving names. // Perhaps JOH. JACOB WAGENER, with ENGELHART WAGNER, Brothers, August 24, 1750, Hinke, I, 437.

WAGNER, VALERIUS (2)—Gerlingen (1754)

The Communicant Register, Easter, 1754, lists him as "going to America" [*geht nach America*]. Ludwigsburg Protocol, 4-2-1754, *venia emigrandi* only.

WAHLISSER, MICHAEL (2)—Sontheim (1751)

Cooper [*Küfer*]. Wf: ELISABETH (RENNER), mercenary soldier's daughter [*Söldnerstochter*] from Memmingen. Ch: (1) Joh. Georg, b. 6-28-1747, "emigrated" [*emigravit*]; (2) Johann Michael, b. 5-16-1750. Ludwigsburg Protocol, 6-11-1751, WALLISER with wife and child, to "America." // Others listed in Hinke. 3PA, 18, 193: MICH'L WALLISER, Cumru Tp., Berks Co., Pa., 1779; cf. also 3PA, 21, 361: MICHAEL WALISER, Windsor Tp., York Co., Pa., 1781.

WALCKER, HANS JERG (1)—Grötzingen (1747)

Single, mason's apprentice [*Maurergesell*]. Left for Pennsylvania, May 9, 1747, after private communion in the church, along with JOHANNES HERMANN (q.v.), ANNA CATHARINA SCHINDELBERGER (q.v.), ANNA CATHARINA WERNER (q.v.), CATHARINA MAYER (q.v.), and MICHAEL MAYER (q.v.) // GORG WALKER, *Edinburgh*, September 16, 1751, Hinke, I, 462.

WALCKER, JOHANNES (1)—Grötzingen (1754)

Weaver [*Weber*]. Wf: BARBARA. Ch: (1) Jacob, b. 3-4-1750; (2) Matthäus, b. 9-12-1753. "Went to Pennsylvania, 1754." // JOHN WALKER (JOHANNES WALCKHER), *Peggy*, October 16, 1754, Hinke, I, 637, 639. Many listed in PA.

WALTER, ANNA MARIA (1)—Dornhan

B. 3-17-1729, daughter of the baker [*Beck*] MATTHEIS WALTER. "Is in Pennsylvania."

WALTER, JERG JAKOB (1)—Dornhan (1751)

Servant [*Knecht*]. B. 11-9-1722, son of the baker [*Beck*] MATTHEIS WALTER. Wf: ROSINA, *née* SECKINGER, daughter of JACOB SECKINGER, cobbler [*Schuster*]. Married 7-11-1751, with JOHANN FRIEDRICH LIPS (q.v.), and wife, with whom they went to America. Of both couples the pastor wrote, "Because these two couples were going to America the following day, they were previously married at Betzweiler, after instruction" [*weil diese 2 Ehepaare folgenden Tages in Americam zogen, so wurden sie vorher zu Betzweiler nach der Kindertaufe zusammengegeben*]. // Two listed in 1751: JACOB WALDER, with MATTHAEUS WALTER, *Phoenix*, September 25, 1751, Hinke, I, 471; and JACOB ....WALTER, a fellow-passenger of Jacob Weimer, Reformed minister, *Janet*, October 7, 1751; another arrived in 1752.

WALTER, JOHANNES (2)—Beihingen, Oberamt Ludwigsburg (1744)

"Went to South Carolina, May 4, 1744." // Others listed in Hinke.

WALTER, MAGDALENA (1)—Dornhan

B. 10-30-1731, daughter of the baker [*Beck*] MATTHEIS WALTER. "Is in Pennsylvania."

WALTHER, BERNHARD (1)—Nordheim

B. 2-17-1721, son of BERNHARD WALTHER. // BARNARD (BERNARD) WALTER, age 58, with CONRAD WALTHER, *Loyal Judith*, September 25, 1732, Hinke, I, 88-90; list headed by Johannes Christian Schultz, Lutheran pastor. 3PA, 19, 66: BERNHART WALTER, farmer, Forks Tp., Northampton Co., Pa., 1772. The will of BEARNAT WALTER, of Forks Tp., Northampton Co., Pa., dated and probated June 2, 1780, mentions wf EVE and children, *Northampton County Will Abstracts*, No. 301, GSP.

WALTHER, HANS CONRAD (1)—Nordheim

B. 3-9-1714, son of BERNHARD WALTHER, and brother of BERNHARD WALTHER (q.v.). // CONRAD WALTHER, with BERNARD WALTER, *Loyal Judith*, September 25, 1732, Hinke, I, 88-90; list headed by Johannes Christian Schultz, Lutheran pastor. 3PA, 15, 626: CONRAD WALTER, Mulberry Ward (East Part), City of Philadelphia, Pa., 1781; cf. also 3PA, 22, 50: CONRAD WALTER, Tyrone Tp., Bedford Co., Pa., 1773; others in Westmoreland Co., Pa., 1783, and Fayette Co., Pa., in 1785.

WALTZ, HANS JERG (1)—Pfäffingen (1752)

"Went to Pennsylvania, May 11, 1752," but "returned May 20." // Cf. 3PA, 25, 660: GEORGE WALTS, 200 acres, Bedford Co., Pa., survey June 5, 1792.

WALTZ, HANS MICHAEL (1)—Nordheim

B. 1-27-1712, son of HANS MICHAEL WALTZ. // MICHAEL WALTZ, *Two Brothers*, August 28, 1750, Hinke, I, 438. 3PA, 14, 454: MICHAEL WALTZ, Upper Merion Tp., Philadelphia Co., Pa., 1774; cf. also 3PA, 18, 726: MICH'L WALTZ, Cumru Tp., Berks Co., Pa., 1785.

WALTZ, MARGARETHA (1)—Pfäffingen (1752)

"Went to Pennsylvania, May 11, 1752," but "returned May 20."

WALZ, ANNA DOROTHEA (1)—Nordheim

B. 6-11-1681, daughter of HANS CONRAD WALTZ.

WARTH, PHILIPP FRIEDRICH (1)—Pfaffenhofen (1753)

Wf: MARIA MARGARETHA. "America welcomed them in 1753" [*1753 Amer. se recepit*]. // PHILIPS FREDRICK WARTH (PHILIPP FRIDRICH WARTH), age 27, *Louisa*, October 3, 1753, Hinke, I, 582-3. Others listed in PA.

## WE(E)BER, HANS MARTIN (1-2)—Schlaitdorf

Farmer [*Bauer*]. Wf: ANNA MARIA, *née* GAJER. Ch: (1) Hans Martin, b. 3-16-1739; (2) Anna Barbara, b. 12-14-1744; (3) Anna Magdalena, b. 5-11-1746; (4) Anna, b. 8-25-1748. // Several listed in Hinke, 1749, 1750 (two), 1765, 1773. Several also listed in PA.

## WEEBER, JONAS (2)—Nussdorf (1753)

Son of HANS JACOB WEBER in Eberdingen. Wf: ANNA MARGARETHA ELB. Ch: (1) Maria Catharina, b. 10-7-1727; (2) Johann Martin, b. 4-4-1729; (3) Johann Conrad, b. 6-9-1731; (4) Anna Maria, b. 5-22-1733; (5) Elisabetha, b. 1-9-1737; (6) Hans Jerg, b. 11-8-1738. None of these listed in the Burial Register (1727-1770), or in the Family Register (1766). Ludwigsburg Protocol, 4-27-1753, to "New England." // Many listed in PA.

## WEEBER, JONAS (2)—Nussdorf (1753)

Wf: MARIA CATHARINA (MAUCH). Ch: (1) Melchior, b. 4-29-1736; (2) Jonas, b. 11-9-1743; (3) others, died young. None of these, except (3), listed in the Burial Register (1727-1770), or in the Family Register (1766). Ludwigsburg Protocol, 4-27-1753, to "New England". // Many listed in PA.

## WEGER, JOHANN JACOB (2)—Hoheneck (1753)

Wf: MARIA MAGDALENA. Ch: ANNA BARBARA, b. 9-11-1750. Ludwigsburg Protocol, 4-6-1753, to "Neu York." // Others listed in Hinke; also in PA.

## WEH, ANNA CATHARINA (2)—Gebersheim (1751)

Daughter of the judge [*Richter*] GEORG WEH and wf URSULA. Communicant 1743-1750, then "went to Pennsylvania."

## WEH, JOHANN ANDREAS (2)—Gebersheim (1752)

Wf: CATHARINA. Ch: (1) Catharina, b. 9-25-1737; (2) Anna Maria, b. 8-14-1739; (3) Margaretha, b. 7-26-1743; (4) Georg Michael, b. 8-26-1745; (5) Johann Conrad, b. 10-14-1747; (6) Johann Andreas, b. 5-24-1750. "Went to Pennsylvania with his wife, May 12, 1752." Ludwigsburg Protocol, 4-21-1752, to "Pennsylvania." Emigration of children uncertain; CATHARINA, at least, stayed, for she attended communion on the eighth and twenty-second Sunday after Trinity, 1752. // ANDRAS WEG, *Anderson*, September 27, 1752, Hinke, I, 489; a fellow passenger was Jacob Friderich Schertlein, Lutheran pastor.

## WEIGOLD, HANS JACOB (1)—Altenberg (see Rötenberg)

Day laborer [*Tagelöhner*] of Altenberg. Wf: LUCIA. Ch: (1) Johannes, b. 7-5-1728; (2) Andreas, b. 2-16-1730. // JOHANNIS WIGOLD, with the WESNERS and HEBTINGS of Rötenberg, *Duke of Wirtenburg*, October 20, 1752, Hinke, I, 498.

## WEISS, JOHANNES (1)—Gechingen

Judge [*Richter*]. Wf: ESTHER. Ch: (1) Anna Magdalena, b. 3-25-1749, to the "New World." Parents emigrated with her, since they are not listed in the Burial Register. // JOHANNES WEISS, *Lydia*, October 19[9], 1749, Hinke, I, 422; others in 1754, 1764, and 1767.

## WEISS, MATTHAEUS (1)—Grötzingen

Nailsmith [*Nagelschmied*]. Wf: CHRISTINA HEINRICA (HENRIETTA). Ch: (1) Christina Heinrica, b. 1-2-1742, is "in Pennsylvania." (2) Johann Christoph, b. 12-25-1746, "went away" [*weggezogen*]. // According to a ducal letter of permission to emigrate, preserved among the Nürtingen Documents and dated 1749, "Matthes Weissen Wittib" was listed among the intended emigrants from Grötzingen; see the ducal letter of 1749, quoted in our Introduction Several listed in Hinke: cf. MATHEAS WEISE, with HANS JACOB WEYSE and JACOB WEISS, SR., *Saint Andrew,* September 9, 1749, Hinke, I, 397; also MATHEIS WEISS, *Christian,* September 13, 1749, Hinke, I, 400; also MATHIAS WEYS (WEISS), with JOH. MICH'L WEYS, *Neptune,* October 7, 1785, Hinke, I, 677-9. 3PA, 18, 245: MATHEAS and JACOB WEISS, Longswamp Tp., Berks Co., Pa., 1779; Cf. also 3PA, 19, 137: MATHIAS WEISS, fulling mill, Bethlehem Tp., Northampton Co., Pa., 1785.

## WEIS(S)MANN, JOHANNES (1-2)—Ebingen (1751)

Nailsmith [*Nagelschmied*]. Married, 1738, to ANNA MARIA, *née* LETSCH, widow of nailsmith JOHANNES MAUTE (d. 1736), by whom she had the following five children: (1) Maria Magdalena, b. 8-23-1724; (2) Rosina, b. 2-4-1726; (3) Maria Margaretha, b. 6-27-1729; (4) Johann David, b. 1-8-1731; (5) Regina, b. 3-10-1733. The children of JOHANNES and ANNA MARIA (LETSCH) WEIS(S)MANN were: (1) Georg Philipp, b. 5-7-1739; (2) Christina, b. 12-25-1740; (3) Catharina Barbara, b. 11-6-1742, d. 1743. Ludwigsburg Protocol, 2-19-1751, JOHANNES WEISSMANN'S wife, with seven children, to "Philadelphia." // 3PA, 14, 540: PHILIP WEISSMAN, Mulberry Ward (East Part), City of Philadelphia, Pa., 1779.

## WEIS(S)MANN, JOHANNES (1-2)—Ebingen

Nailsmith [*Nagelschmied*]. Wf: ANNA BARBARA, *née* WAGNER. Ch: (1) Christine, b. 12-25-1740. To "Pennsylvania." // JOHANNES WEISSMAN, *Restauration,* October 9, 1747, Hinke, I, 366. Several listed in PA.

## WELSCH, CHRISTIANUS (1)—Hesslach (see Schlaitdorf)

Of Hesslach. Wf: MARIA AGNES, *née* KUEMMERLIN. Ch: (1) Christian, b. 9-1-1748; (2) Johannes, b. 12-4-1749. // Others listed in PA.

## WENNAGEL, JACOB (1)—Schopfloch, Oberamt Freudenstadt

Wf: EVA. Ch: (1) Johann Adam, b. 10-12-1748. To "Pennsylvania." // Others listed in PA.

## WERNER, ANNA CATHARINA (1)—Grötzingen (1747)

Single. Ch: (1) Maria Agnes, b. (illeg.) 5-12-1744. Left for Pennsylvania, May 9, 1747, after private communion in the church, along with JOHANNES HERMANN (q.v.), HANS JERG WALCKER (q.v.), ANNA CATHARINA SCHINDELBERGER (q.v.), CATHARINA MAYER (q.v.), and MICHAEL MAYER (q.v.)

## WERNER, JOHANN CONRAD (2)—Beutelsbach (1746)

B. 2-29-1704. "On 3-26-1746, without the knowledge of his pastor, he was sent by his wife and brothers and sisters to Pennsylvania with the Lentzes; soon died there." [*ist d. 26-3-1746 inscio pastore von seinem Weib und Geschwistrigten mit den Lentzen in Pens. geschickt worden; bald daselbst* †]. // 3PA, 14, 604: CONRAD WERNER, Germantown, Philadelphia Co., Pa., 1779.

## WERNER, JOHANN FRIEDRICH (2)—Unterjesingen (1753)

B. 11-16-1726, son of the linenweaver [*Leineweber*] HANS JACOB WERNER. Ludwigsburg Protocol, 3-23-1753, to "America." // FREDERICK VERNER (JOHANN FRIDERICH WERNER), *Patience*, September 15, [17], 1753, Hinke, I, 526, 528, 530. 3PA, 13, 399: FREDERICK WERNER, Springfield Tp., Bucks Co., Pa., 1783. 3PA, 24, 176: FREDERICK WERNER, 23 acres, Bucks Co., Pa., survey January 16, 1786. Cf. also 3PA, 18, 373: FRED'K WERNER (single freeman), Hereford Tp., Berks Co., Pa., 1780.

## WESSNER, (HANS) JACOB (1)—Lossburg

Wf: ELISABETHA. Ch: (1) Hans Jerg, b. 7-6-1748; (2) Martin, b. 1-6-1751. To "Pennsylvania." // JACOB WESSENER, with ANDEREAS WESENER (?) and MATHES WESNER, *Duke of Wirtenburg*, October 20, 1752. Hinke, I, 498. 3PA, 13, 72: JACOB WISNER, Plumstead Tp., Bucks Co., 1779. 3PA, 18, 38: JACOB WESNER, Oley Tp., Berks Co., Pa., 1767. 3PA, 18, 173: JACOB WESNER, laborer, with MARTIN WESNER, mason, Oley Tp., Berks Co., Pa., 1768.

## WEZEL, MARTIN, JR. (1)—Erzingen

Wf: CATHARINA. Ch: (1) Catharina, b. 6-9-1742. "Went to America with mother." // 3PA, 18, 38: MARTIN WETZEL, Oley Tp., Berks Co., Pa., 1767.

## WEYH, ANNA (1)—Täbingen (1749)

B. 3-1-1721, tenth child of the Catholic HANS WEYH and wf MARGARETHA (OTT), of scandalous conduct [*anstössigen Lebenswandel*]. May 23, 1749, to "New England."

## WEYH, CHRISTIAN (1)—Täbingen (1749)

B. 5-28-1725, twelfth child of the Catholic HANS WEYH and wf MARGARETHA (OTT), of scandalous conduct [*anstössigen Lebenswandel*]. To the "New World." Some of the mothers and sisters, who remained behind, are listed in the Marriage Register.

## WIDENMAJER (WIDMAJER), HANS (JOHANN) JERG (GEORG) (1)—Nordheim (1751)

B. 3-11-1705. Wf: EVA CATHARINA. Ch: (1) Georg Balthas, b. 4-16-1731; (2) Hans Philipp, b. 12-24-1732; (3) Johann Christoph, b. 2-20-1738; (4) Christina Magdalena, b. 5-9-1742; (5) Johann Gottfried, b. 5-5-1744; (6) Eva Catharina, b. 1-2-1746. Ludwigsburg Protocol, 1751. // Cf. JOHANN GEORG WEYDENMEYER, with URBAN WEIDENMEIER, EBERHARDT WEYDENMYER, and MELCHIOR WEYDENMEYER, *Hero*, October 27, 1764, Hinke, I, 697-8. 3PA, 13, 175: GEO. WIDMIRE, Rockhill Tp., Bucks Co., Pa., 1781. 3PA, 15, 553: GEORGE WEITMYAR, Upper Salford Tp., Philadelphia Co., Pa., 1780.

## WIDMEYR (WIDMAJR), MARTIN (1)—Höfingen (1751)

Wf (1st): MARGARETHA. Wf (2d): MAGDALENA. Ch: (1) Martin, b. 7-5-1732; (2) Anna Maria, b. 10-18-1734; (3) Christoph, b. 1-3-1737; (4) Johann Cunrad, b. 9-28-1744; (5) Margaretha, b. 12-6-1748. By all, "Went to America [*Am. prof.*]; by MARGARETHA the further note is added, "with parents" [*cum parentibus*]. Ludwigsburg Protocol, 1751. // 3PA, 18, 131: CONRAD WEITMYER, shoemaker, Hereford Tp., Berks Co., Pa., 1768. 3PA, 19, 101: CONRAD WIDMEYER, Upper Milford Tp., Northampton Co., Pa., 1785.

WINTER, JOHANN GEORG (2)—Rottenacker (1751)

B. 6-17-1735, son of the innkeeper's servant [*Wirtsknecht*] JACOB WINTER. No other reference to this name in the Baptismal or the Marriage Register. Ludwigsburg Protocol, 4-27-1751, to "Pennsylvania." // HANS JERG WINTTER, with JOHANNES WINTTER, *Duke of Wirtenberg*, October 16, 1751, Hinke, I, 476; c. also JOH. JURG WINTTER, *Two Brothers*, September 28, 1753, Hinke, I, 564. 3PA, 18, 291: GEO. WINTER (single freeman), with CHRISTOPHER and FRED'K WINTER, Tulpehocken Tp., Berks Co., Pa., 1779. 3PA, 18, 704: GEO. WINDER, non-resident, Alsace Tp., Berks Co., Pa., 1785.

WIRSUMB, JOHANN JACOB (1)—Schlaitdorf

Stonecutter [*Steinhauer*]. Wf: DOROTHEA. Ch: (1) Johann Jacob, b. 7-16-1740. // Cf. JOHN WINSCHUM (JOHANNES WIRSUM, WERSUM), *Peggy*, October 16, 1754, Hinke, I, 637, 639, 641.

WOELFLIN, JOHANN CONRAD (2)—Beutelsbach (1750)

B. 1-29-1729, at Besigheim. Ludwigsburg Protocol, 3-6-1750, "to take property along to Pennsylvania. His brother, JOHANN LUDWIG WOELFLIN, remained." // JOH. CONRADT WOELFFLE, *Patience*, August 11, 1750, Hinke, I, 427. 3PA, 17, 37: CONRAD WOLFLY, Middletown, Lancaster Co., Pa., 1771.

WOESSNER, ANDREAS (1)—Rötenberg

Wf: JACOBINA. Ch: (1) Jacob, b. 7-21-1746. To "Pennsylvania." // ANDEREAS WESENER (?), with JACOB WESSENER and MATHES WESNER, *Duke of Wirtenburg*, October 20, 1752, Hinke, I, 498.

WOESSNER, CHRISTIAN (1)—Rötenberg

B. 8-18-1733, at Baach.

WOESSNER, HANS JACOB (1)—Gundelshausen (see Dornhan) (1753)

Of Gundelshausen. Wf. URSULA. Ch: (1) Hans Martin, b. 8,21-1725; (2) Johannes, b. 12-12-1726; (3) Matthias, b. 2-20-1730; (4) Johann Georg, b. 3-7-1732; (5) Johann Michael, b. 10-18-1734. To "Pennsylvania." Ludwigsburg Protocol, 1753. // JACOB WESSENER, with MATHES WESNER and ANDEREAS WESENER (?), *Duke of Wirtenburg*, October 20, 1752, Hinke, I, 498. Cf. also Hinke, I, 419: MARTIN WOESENER, with JOHANNES WESSENER and JOHANN MICHAEL MESSENER, *Leslie*, October 7, 1749; also Hinke, I, 444: HANS MICHAEL WISNER and JOHAN GEORG WISSNER, *Priscilla*, September 12, 1750. 3PA, 18, 20: JOHN WESNER, Albany Tp., Berks Co., Pa., 1767; cf. also 3PA, 22, 532: JNO. WISNER, Derry Tp., Westmoreland Co., Pa., 1786. Estate of JOHN WISNER of Albany Tp., Berks Co., Pa., June 1, 1795, administration to Mathias, only son, MARIA [the widow] not appearing, *Berks County Will Abstracts*, I, 549, GSP. 3PA, 13, 18: GEO. WISNOR, Wrightstown Tp., Bucks Co., Pa., 1779. 3PA, 18, 173: JACOB WESNER, laborer, with MARTIN WESNER, mason, Oley Tp., Berks Co., Pa., 1768. For references to JACOB, see the notes to (HANS) JACOB WESSNER of Lossburg.

WOESSNER, MARIA CHRISTINA (1)—Rötenberg

B. 10-19-1729, at Baach.

WOESSNER, MATTHIAS (1)—Rötenberg

B. 2-4-1732, at Baach. To "Pennsylvania." // MATHES WESNER, with JACOB WESSENER and ANDEREAS WESENER, *Duke of Wirtenburg*, October 20, 1752, Hinke, I, 498. 3PA, 13, 8: MATTHIAS WISNER, Lower Makefield Tp., Bucks Co., Pa., 1779. 3PA, 18, 699: MATHIAS WESNER, with MATHIAS WESNER (single), Albany Tp., Berks Co., Pa., 1785.

WOLF, ANNA MARIA (1)—Pfäffingen (1752)

"Left for Pennsylvania, May 11, 1752," but "returned on May 20."

WOLF, CONRAD (2)—Steinenbronn (1749)

B. 10-23-1710, son of ELIAS WOLF, miller at the castle mill [*Schlossmühle Müller*]. Wf ANNA MARIA (WANNER), forester's daughter [*Forstknechtstochter*], b. 8-2-1713. Ch: (1) Elias, b. 2-27-1735; (2) Johann Michael, b. 10-26-1736; (3) Johann Friedrich, b. 1741 (not in Burial Register); (4) Anna Margaretha, b. 12-9-1742; (5) Johann Balthasar, b. 1-1-1745; (6) Johann Jonathan, b. 12-29-1747. "Went to America in 1749 with his wife and children." // CONRAD WOLF, *Chesterfield*, September 2, 1749, Hinke, I, 394, with HANS JERCH HAISCH and HANS JERG HANSELMANN, both of Steinenbronn; others later. Many listed in PA.

WOLFF, ZACHARIAS SAMUEL (1)—Steinheim an der Murr (1743)

B. 3-27-1723, son of MICHAEL WOLF, joiner [*Schreiner*] and wf BARBARA. "Went to the New World, November 10, 1743." // SAMUEL WOLFF, with GEORG CHRISTOPH HERALD of Steinheim an der Murr, *Rosannah*, September 26, 1743, Hinke, I, 344.

WOLFER, ANNA (2)—Laufen/Eyach (1750)

B. 10-1-1711, daughter of JOHANN JACOB and ANNA MARIA WOLFER.

WOLFER, CATHARINA (2)—Laufen/Eyach (1750)

B. 10-8-1716, daughter of JOHANN JACOB and ANNA MARIA WOLFER.

WOLFER, JOHANNES (2)—Laufen/Eyach (1750)

B. 5-3-1714, son of JOHANN JACOB and ANNA MARIA WOLFER. Wf: SIBYLLA. Ch: (1) Anna Maria, b. 12-18-1745; (2) Margaretha, b. 11-25-1747; (3) Anna, b. 11-22-1749. Ludwigsburg Protocol, July and September, 1750, two WOLFERS ask for *venia emigrandi*. // JOHANNES WOLFER, with HANS MARTIN WOLFFER and JACOB KEANIGH of Laufen/Eyach, *Osgood*, September 29, 1750, Hinke, I, 445-6; a fellow passenger was Gottlieb Mittelberger.

WOLFER, JOHANN (HANS) MARTIN (2)—Laufen/Eyach (1750)

B. 7-11-1719, son of JOHANN JACOB and ANNA MARIA WOLFER. Wf: CHRISTINA. Ch: (1) Anna Maria, b. 2-14-1742; (2) Jacob, b. 8-12-1745; (3) Lucia, b. 11-22-1746; (4) Christina, b. 8-11-1748; (5) Johann Ulrich, b. 4-10-1750. Ludwigsburg Protocol, July and September, 1750, two WOLFERS ask for *venia emigrandi*. // HANS MARTIN WOLFFER, with JOHANNES WOLFER, and JACOB KEANIGH of Laufen/Eyach, *Osgood*, September 29, 1750, Hinke, I, 445-6; a fellow-passenger was Gottlieb Mittelberger.

WOHLFART, DANIEL (1)—Steinheim an der Murr (1754)

B. 1-27-1736, son of DANIEL WOHLFART, vine dresser [*Vinitor*] and wf CATHARINA. "Went to America, May 30, 1754." // Others listed in Hinke.

WRIBERG, MARIA MAGDALENA (1)—Nordheim

B. 8-17-1701, daughter of HANS MICHAEL WRIBERG.

WUERMLE, JOHANNES (1)—Pfaffenhofen (1753)

Wf: ANNA MARIA. "Went to America, 1753." // JOHANNES WORMLEY (WUERMLE), age 21, *Patience*, September 15 [17], 1753, Hinke, I, 526, 528. 3PA, 26, 307: JACOB RUPLEY and JNO. WORMLEY, 261.10 acres, Berks Co., Pa., survey June 29, 1773. 3PA, 20, 36: JOHN WORMLY, East Pennsboro Tp., Cumberland Co., Pa., 1778. Cf. the town of *Wormleysburg* in East Pennsboro Tp., Cumberland Co., Pa.

WUEST, BERNHARD (1)—Lomersheim

Wf: BARBARA. Ch: (1) Jacob Friedrich, b. 11-5-1748. "Went to the New Land" [Pennsylvania]. // BERNHART WUEST, *Osgood*, September 29, 1750; Hinke, I, 446; a fellow passenger was Gottlieb Mittelberger. Others listed in PA.

WUEST, JERG (JERK) (1)—Lomersheim

Wf: ANNA MARIA. Ch: (1) Anna Elisabetha, b. 9-12-1747, "went to the New Land" [Pennsylvania]; (2) Maria Agnes, b. 10-22-1750. // GEORGE (JERG) WIEST, *Bannister*, October 21, 1754, Hinke, I, 646-7. Others listed in PA.

WURSTER, HANS JACOB (2)—Altenriet (1752)

B. 7-21-1715, son of JACOB and ANNA CATHARINA (FRITZ) WURSTER. Appears neither in the Marriage Register nor the Burial Register. Ludwigsburg Protocol, 5-3-1752, to "Pennsylvania." // Others listed in Hinke.

## Z

ZAHLER, MICHAEL (2)—Sulz bei Nagold (1753)

Shepherd's helper [*Schäferknecht*]. Son of the late shepherd [*Schäfer*] CHRISTIAN ZAHLER and wf ANNA (KIENTZLIN), shepherd's daughter, of Kuppingen. Ch: (1) Maria Elisabetha, b. 4-18-1729; (2) Hans Jacob, b. 7-24-1731; (3) Maria Sara, b. 10-13-1733; (4) Anna, b. 9-23-1735. Family disappears from the Communicant Register, and appears neither in the Burial Register (1754-1773) nor the Family Register of 1774; also, new individuals are listed as the village shepherds. Ludwigsburg Protocol, 4-13-1753, to "Pennsylvania." // HANS JACOB ZALLER, *Crown*, August 30, 1749, Hinke, I, 392.

ZIEGLER, PHILIPP (1-2)—Grötzingen (1746)

Tilemaker [*Ziegler!*]. Wf: BARBARA. Ch: (1) Johannes, b. 5-14-1734; (2) Johann Jacob, b. 2-3-1737; (3) Agatha, b. 11-4-1739, "left here with parents in 1746, for Pennsylvania;" (4) Anna Maria, b. 11-15-1743. According to the report of Mayor MATTHESS DAMMEL of Grötzingen, March 27, 1746, PHILIP ZIEGLER, with wife and *five* children, intended to journey to the "*Indies*" [*Indien*], with other fellow-villagers; for full text, see Introduction. // PHILIP ZIEGLER, with GEORGE SCHNEERING of Grötzingen, *Ann Galley*, September 27, 1746, Hinke, I, 360. Sower's newspaper, February 16, 1750, quoted in Hocker, 17: "PHILIP ZIEGLER, Ridge Valley, Upper Salford." Many listed in PA.

ZIEGLER, ZACHARIAS (1)—Schlaitdorf

Non-citizen [*Beisitzer*]. Wf: ANNA MARIA, *née* VYL. Ch: (1) Nicolaus, b. 12-12-1746.

ZOLL, JACOB FRIEDRICH (2)—Gündelbach

B. 1752. // JACOB ZOLL, *Minerva*, October 10, 1768, Hinke, I, 722. Cf. 3PA, 14, 342: JACOB ZOLL, Germantown, Philadelphia Co., Pa., 1774; also 3PA, 18, 188: JACOB ZOLL, Albany Tp., Berks Co., Pa., 1779; and 3PA, 26, 334: JACOB ZOLL, 400 acres, Berks Co., survey September 5, 1794.

ZWERENZ (ZWERENS), JOHANN(ES) (2)—Neckartenzlingen (1753)

Son of the vinedresser [*Weingärtner*] ZWERENZ at Fellbach. Wf: BARBARA, *née* HEMMINGER, sister of Geo. Friedrich Hemminger (q.v.). Ch: (1) Wilhelm Ludwig Lorenz, b. 6-12-1724; (2) Cunrad, b. 6-6-1728; (3) Barbara, b. 4-25-1730; (4) Regina, b. 2-6-1735; (5) Johannes, b. 12-16-1737; (6) Rosina, b. 2-27-1741. Ludwigsburg Protocol, 4-3-1753, Zwerenz and two associates, to "Pennsylvania."

ZWOERNER (ZWERNER), JOHANN ADAM (1)—Nordheim

Linen weaver [*Leineweber*]. Wf: ELISABETHA MARGARETHA (DEMMLER). Ch: (1) Christina Magdalena, b. 7-15-1752. // JOHAN ADAM ZWIRNER, age 32, *Peggy*, September 24, 1753, Hinke, I, 545. 3PA, 12, 421: ADAM SWERNER, inmate, Pikeland Tp., Chester Co., Pa., 1781.

# PENNSYLVANIA GERMAN PIONEERS from the COUNTY OF WERTHEIM

*By OTTO LANGGUTH*
Historian and Genealogist
Kreuzwertheim-am-Main
Bavaria

Translated and Edited by
DON YODER, Ph.D.
*Muhlenberg College*

# PREFACE TO THE AMERICAN EDITION

If in the old days one boarded a river boat at Mainz and sailed up the Main, he eventually got to the picturesque and historic city of Wertheim, now in Baden, but formerly the capital of the little principality of Löwenstein-Wertheim. On a wooded hill behind the city stand the ruins of the castle of the Counts of Wertheim, which with the town's situation on the water, gives it the nickname *"Klein-Heidelberg."* Here the waters of the Tauber join the Main, after winding through the lovely *Taubergrund*, past the storybook villages of Rothenburg and Tauberbischofsheim. To the south and west of Wertheim lies the *sagenreicher Odenwald*, from the north come cool breezes from the heights of the Spessart. Who is there who will not pardon the exuberance of the Wertheimer poet who wrote, in the dialect of the region:

*Es iss uff der ganzen Erde*
*Nirgends schöner, als in Werthe!*

From this historic little county, in the midst of what is called *Mainfranken*, or *das Badische Frankenland*, there came in the eighteenth century some 250 heads of families to the English colonies in North America, principally to Pennsylvania. Gratified at the reception accorded my American edition of the significant Adolf Gerber Lists of eighteenth-century emigrants from Württemberg, published in the *Yearbook of the Pennsylvania German Folklore Society* for 1945, I am happy to present an American translation and edition of Otto Langguth's *"Auswanderer aus der Grafschaft Wertheim,"* edited in the same fashion as the Gerber Lists.[1] This Langguth List, which appeared in *Familiengeschicht-*

[1]*Otto Langguth*, Kreuzwertheim am-Main, Bavaria, with whom the American editor is carrying on a delightful correspondence, is seventy years of age, and has spent a long and fruitful life directing the *Historischer Verein Alt-Wertheim*, which he helped to found, and editing its *Jahrbücher* (1905-1939) and the *Beiträge zur Heimatkunde* (1932). All of his life he has been interested in the genealogies of the older Wertheim families, and I recommend him to my readers of Wertheimer descent as the best source of further information on their German origins. In addition to his genealogical interests, he has written much in social and industrial history, such as articles on the old trades of ropemaking and pottery making, all of which has an interest to Pennsylvania German scholars.

*liche Blätter* for 1932 and was reprinted in 1935 as part of the *Jahrbuch des Historischen Vereins Alt-Wertheim,* is unfortunately as little available in this country as the privately printed Gerber Lists. And it is a rich source, not only for genealogy, but for social history. It gives us detailed information on some 250 emigrants, mostly heads of families, who, beginning in the late 1740's, applied to the Counts of Löwenstein-Wertheim for manumission from vassalage and permission to emigrate to the New World, due to the hard times that seem to have prevailed generally in southwestern Germany in those years.

Where the Gerber Lists use as their principal source the village parish registers, since the governmental lists of Württemberger emigrants were mostly destroyed by government order in the nineteenth century, the Langguth List is drawn from the official state archives of Wertheim, and represents the petitions for manumission presented to the government by prospective emigrants. The importance of these materials for the social historian is that they afford us, at last, what earlier historians of the eighteenth century emigration did not have — concrete manuscript materials from the local German archives which accent the personal side of this great folk-movement.[2] In these sources, often in the very words of the humble peasant folk who applied for manumission, all phases of that touching story are illustrated. We see in them the hard life our ancestors had in the war-torn Germany of the eighteenth century, saddled with mounting taxes, and burdened with feudal dues which continued to lay the dead hand of the Middle Ages on the laborer's shoulders. We sense the great attraction the "New Land" must have had for our German peasant forebears. Behind the scenes, often under cover of the night, we see at work the despicable "Newlander" or "soulbuyer," who made a racket out of the emigration movement. The interview before the Counts, the request for manumission from vassalage and the payment of the thorny *Nachsteuer* of 20% of the emigrant's fortune, the buying of *Schnitz* and *dürre Zwetschgen*, of Bibles and

[2]The American editor is continuing his search for similar emigration materials and lists in the local German Archives. He has this year unearthed valuable Lists of Emigrants (1) from Hesse, and (2) the Canton of Schaffhausen in Switzerland, which he is to edit for the Folklore Society.

guns and leathern trousers and shoes for the journey — all are vividly portrayed in contemporary documents in this valuable article.

The task of the American editor has been threefold. Firstly, he has carefully translated Dr. Langguth's excellent and detailed historical introduction and his List of eighteenth-century emigrants, to make them available to American researchers. Secondly, he has, he hopes, increased the usefulness of the materials by inserting as Appendices III and IV, new materials discovered on this side of the ocean, relative to Wertheimer emigrants. Thirdly, as in the case of the Gerber Lists, he has collated the individual emigrants' names with the principal Pennsylvania source materials, to identify the date of emigration, and, if possible, the place of settlement in the New World. In many cases a positive identification, in others, only a conjectural identification, was possible.

In his researches, the American editor has attempted to estimate the contributions these people made in the "New Land." Among the emigrants there were all sorts of artisans — weavers, shoemakers, blacksmiths, and others — as well as farmers, all of whom helped to build America. Most of the emigrants settled in Eastern Pennsylvania, which they helped to make blossom as the rose. *Johann Christoph Brettenherd,* a Wertheim gunsmith, settled in Lancaster, where in 1782 he is taxed with a "shop" where doubtless he was making the "Lancaster" or "Kentucky" rifles for which our Pennsylvania German craftsmen were famous. *Lorenz Albert* of Michelrieth, who emigrated in 1754, became a farmer and wagonmaker in the Bermudian Valley of Adams County, Pennsylvania, making the sturdy wagons used to ship freight to Baltimore and Philadelphia in the pioneer days. One of his direct descendants, Miss *Edna Albert,* M.A., formerly Professor of English at Williamsport Dickinson Seminary, has written the lovely children's novel, *Little Pilgrim to Penn's Woods* (New York: Longmans, Green and Company, 1930), which uses as its theme the emigration of the Alberts from Wertheim to the backwoods of Pennsylvania.

Several important church leaders were contributed by little Wertheim to the infant Lutheran Church of Ameirca. For instance, in 1766 a Wertheimer named *Zacharias Endres* emigrated to Philadelphia. When Zacharias Endres' little son was christened in 1775, *Friedrich Ludwig,* Count of Löwenstein-Wertheim, a friend of his father's, asked by letter to stand as sponsor at the christening.[3] That little son was to become perhaps the outstanding American Lutheran of his generation—the Reverend *Christian F. L. Endress,* D.D. (1775-1827). As pastor of Trinity Lutheran Church at Lancaster he was a leader in the movement to Americanize the Lutherans in language; he was head of Franklin College, the joint Lutheran and Reformed institution at Lancaster; and he was one of the leaders in the Lutheran-Reformed union movement in the years following 1817, as well as a leader in the movement to unite the scattered Lutheran synods into a General Synod, in the 1820's.

And there were others — the Fertigs, the Getzelmans, the Etzels, the Scheurichs, the Gerberichs—these are among the many families which Wertheim contributed to the Pennsylvania German stock. There were among the emigrants some of questionable conduct, but these were very much in the minority. The majority of those who came, though heavily indebted in many cases, were honest and upright in life. Proof of all this is the great number of them who were found through my researches to have been communicant members of our Eastern Pennsylvania Lutheran churches. Pennsylvania welcomed them, and they welcomed Pennsylvania. In the words of *Johannes Schlessmann,* who wrote in 1753, in a letter written in simple peasant's German to his relatives back home:

> Ich und meine Kinder und meine Frau danken und loben Gott tausend Mal, dass wir in dem gesunden Land sind, wir denken uns viel besser [zu] ernähren denn im Deutschland, denn dieses ist ein Fry land.

The American editor has left untranslated two sections of

---

[3]William B. Sprague (ed.), *Annals of the American Pulpit,* IX (New York: Robert Carter & Brothers, 1869), 107-110. At the request of Dr. Langguth, the American editor is preparing for the 1948 *Jahrbuch des Historischen Vereins Alt-Wertheim,* an article entitled "*Wertheimer Pfarrer in Amerika,*" to include biographical sketches of (1) *Christian Endress,* (2) *Johann Caspar Dill* (*q.v.* in the List of Emigrants), both Lutheran pastors, and (3) *J. N. Kronmiller* of the Evangelical Association. For a complete account of the Endress Family, see Appendix IV.

Dr. Langguth's original German article. First, it was not thought necessary to translate the data Dr. Langguth has furnished on emigrants from Wertheim to Austria-Hungary, Poland, Russia, and other parts of Europe. These, if they are desired, can be searched out of the German edition. The family names of many of these emigrants are, however, often the same as those who came to America — a fact which establishes our kinship with the emigrants of the ill-fated German Diaspora in Eastern Europe.[4] Secondly, the American editor has omitted the names of the emigrants from Wertheim to America in the nineteenth century. These are of interest chiefly to their descendants, who of course are not Pennsylvania Germans. But they, too, often bore the same family names as our eighteenth-century Pennsylvania German Pioneers.[5] One of the most interesting of these later emi-

[4]The emigrants from Wertheim to Austria-Hungary bore the following family names: *Albert* of Altfeld (1724), *Bishof* of Dertingen (1727), *Bundschuh* of Steinbach (1754, 1774) *Ebert* (1753), *Fender* of Vockenroth (1773), *Fertig* of Grünewörth (1769), *Hintereckert* of Wenkheim (1766), *Knauff* of Wertheim (1794), *Langguth* of Wertheim (1765), *Löhr* of Gickelhof (1765), *Oetzel* of Steinbach (1771), *Meining* of Wenkheim (1772), *Platz* of Wertheim (1760), *Popp* of Bestenheid (1797), *Segner* of Wenkheim (1766), *Rüppel* of Karbach (1806), *Speyer* of Steinbach (1754), *Seitz* of Gickelhof (1771), *Sprenzinger* of Wertheim (1784), *Schmitt* of Oberngløttbach (1777), *Schüssler* of Steinbach (1755, 1779), *Wissmann* (1753). The following emigrated to Poland and Russia from the County of Löwenstein-Wertheim: *Albert* of Höhfeld (1766), *Beck* of Wertheim (1803), *Büttel* of Dietenhan (1766), *Diehm* of Wertheim (1803), *Diehm* of Kreuzwertheim (1806), *Fleischmann* of Wertheim (1796), *Fünkner* of Dietenhan (1766), *Götz* of Wenkheim (1766), *Gresser* of Hafenlohr (1815), *Horn* of Dietenhan (1766), *Lang* of Wertheim (1784), *Lotz* of Kreuzwertheim (1766), *Pflaum* of Höhfeld (1766), *Pfennig* of Kreuzwertheim (1766), *Popp* of Wertheim (1804), *Ross* of Bestenheid (1803). The following settled elsewhere in Europe: *Eirich* of Kembach to France (1764), *Firnhaber* of Wertheim to Lyon (1763), *Frisch* of Wertheim to Holland (1761), *Groetsch* of Wertheim to Amsterdam (1786), *Gross* of Wertheim to Amsterdam (1791), *Horn* of Eichel to England (1761), *Keller* of Wertheim to Holland (1786), *Leineweber* of Wertheim to Amsterdam (1695), *Meyer* of Wertheim to Rotterdam (1761), *Seher* of Wertheim to Holland (1775), *Simmersbach* of Wertheim to Geneva (1776), *Usleber* of Wertheim to Nymwegen (1778). Also omitted are: *Betschler* of Wertheim (1760), Moravian Missionary to India; *Goetz* of Wertheim (*ca.* 1800) to the West Indies; *deHinckeldey* of Wertheim (*ca.* 1800), to the West Indies; *deStädel* of Abstadt (*ca.* 1800) to Batavia; and *Treffz,* of Abstadt (*ca.* 1800), to the Dutch East Indies.

[5]The names of the nineteenth-century Wertheimer emigrants to America are the following: *Adelmann* of Sonderrieth (1832), *Albert* of Urfar (1833), *Bauer* of Freudenberg (1836, 1837), *Baumann* of Sonderrieth (1840), *Beck* of Hasselberg (1840), *Beck* of Nassig (1831), *Bruch* of Bettingen (1833), *Diehm* of Bestenheid (1834), *Diehm* of Hirschlanden (1834),

grants was the Reverend *J. N. Kronmiller* (1817-1896), a native of Nassig, who, coming to America in 1840, joined the Evangelical Association and became one of the most prominent preachers and circuit riders of that denomination in Ohio and Indiana, where he labored among both emigrant Germans of the nineteenth century, and the descendants of the Pennsylvania Germans of Berks, Lehigh, Lancaster and other counties, who had pulled up stakes and transplanted themselves and their language and customs to the Midwest.[6]

In conclusion, the editor desires to express his hearty thanks to his good friend *Edna Albert,* of the staff of the Pennsylvania Archives at Harrisburg, for first directing him to the Langguth List, for the use of the papers of her emigrant ancestor, *Lorenz Albert* of Michelrieth, Löwenstein-Wertheim, and most important of all, for writing that delightful novel, *Little Pilgrim to Penn's Woods,* which first made him "Wertheim-conscious" in his search for the origins of our Pennsylvania German Pioneers. The staffs of the Genealogical Society of Pennsylvania, the Historical Society

---

*Diehm* of Altfeld (1837), *Diehm* of Remlingen (1837), *Diehm* of Kembach (1840), *Dinkel* of Kreuzwertheim (1840), *Ditter* of Urfar (1831), *Dosch* of Nassig (1832), *Eich* of Schollbrunn (1832), *Fertig* of Dietenhan (1840), *Freudenberger* (1833), *Geis* of Oberaltenbuch (1836), *Gerberich* of Altfeld (1837), *Grein* of Mondfeld (1837), *Grein* of Boxtal (1837), *Hoh* of Hasselberg (1837), *Hörner* of Nassig (1840), *Hüblein* of Eichel (1833), *Kempf* of Sonderrieth (1832), *Kettner* of Sonderrieth (1832), *Kettinger* of Freudenberg (1836), *Kern* of Kreuzwertheim (1840), *Klein* of Nassig (1831, 1834), *Klein* of Urfar (1833), *Kohlrieser* of Schollbrunn (1836), *Kronmüller* of Nassig (1834), *Langguth* of Wertheim to Wilkes-Barre, Pennsylvania[!] (1834), *Martin* of Trennfeld (1840), *Merkert* of Steinmark (1836), *Müssig* of Freudenberg (1836, 1837), *Pfenning* of Schollbrunn (1832), *Pfenning* of Kembach (1840), *Rath* of Sonderrieth (1840), *Reiter* of Hasselberg (1832), *Reuter* of Hasselberg (1834), *Ries* of Höhfeld (1834), *Roth* of Schollbrunn (1840), *Seidner* of Hasselberg (1840), *Seitz* of Remlingen (1833), *Solcher* of Nassig (1832), *Sommer* of Kredenbach (1836), *Spatz* of Sonderrieth (1840), *Schlessmann* of Sonderrieth (1840), *Stuber* of Freudenberg (1837), *Väth* of Steinmark (1837), *Weimer* of Sonderrieth (1832), *Weimer* of Kembach (1834), *Weiss* of Nassig (1831, 1834, 1840), *Weiss* of Sonderrieth (1832), *Weiss* of Vockenroth (1831), *Wiesler* of Grünewörth (1832), *Wiessmann* of Schollbrunn (1832, 1840), *Wolpert* of Urfar (1834), *Zöller* of Freudenberg (1836, 1837).

[6]For his life, based in part on a manuscript autobiography, see S. H. Baumgartner, *Historical Data and Life Sketches of the Deceased Ministers of the Indiana Conference of the Evangelical Association, 1835 to 1915,* ed. E. W. Praetorius (Cleveland, Ohio: Publishing House of the Evangelical Association, 1915), pp. 189-194.

of York County, and the Historical Society of the Reformed Church also deserve my thanks, for gracious permission, as always, to use their magnificent collections of transcripts of Pennsylvania church registers. Thanks is due also to my friend and colleague, *Preston A. Barba,* for his constant encouragement of my work as well as painstaking aid on some thorny passages in the translation.

And now, lastly, the deepest thanks of all, to *Otto Langguth,* of Kreuzwertheim, Bavaria, for his kind permission to reprint, in translated form, this article of his which meant months of laborious research in the manuscript archives of his homeland. I have not yet been privileged to meet Dr. Langguth face to face, but from his warm and friendly letters, written in this *Schreckenszeit* in postwar Germany, I picture him as a type of man closely akin in spirit and outlook to our Pennsylvania German people. And so, greetings and thanks from the "New Land" to our friend Otto Langguth in the old homeland of our ancestors.

DON YODER, Ph.D.

Muhlenberg College, 1948

## PREFACE TO THE GERMAN EDITION

The present project was suggested to me by Head Archivist Dr. Haug, of Wertheim, in whose care are placed the rich and well-arranged contents of the Princely Archive of Löwenstein-Wertheim-Rosenberg. In spite of other pressing official duties, Dr. Haug stood at my side for months, constantly ready to help on the text of countless bundles of *Acta*. In short, furnishing many a good hint, he aided me in word and in deed. I have therefore all reason to express to him at this point my warmest thanks.

The *Acta* are kept in the above-mentioned Archive, designated in abbreviated form as "Rosenberg Archive," in the Division *Acta Manumission,* Br. 387 b-s, etc., and are easy to find under the given dates; other archive numbers are given from case to case.*

So far as the texts of the relevant *Acta* in the Princely Archive of Löwenstein-Wertheim-Freudenberg are still at hand, they too were used exhaustively, and are at times denoted as source with the words "Freudenberg Archive"; here too the Government Protocols were employed.

---

*For those of our readers who care to delve further into the Wertheim background, there are two excellent monographs on the Wertheim region, descriptive of its social life, history, and folklore, with photographs of historical monuments and the picturesque villages of the Main and Tauber Valleys. The first of these volumes is Hermann Eric Busse (ed.), *Das Badische Frankenland: Odenwald - Bauland - Taubergrund* (Freiburg im Breisgau: Haus Badische Heimat, 1933), 20. Jahrgang of the *Badische Heimat* series. The second is Friedrich Netz, *Das Tauberland* (Freiburg im Breisgau: Landesverein Badische Heimat, n. d.), No. 37 of the series *Vom Bodensee zum Main.* For some lovely views of Wertheim, see also Mathilde Greim, *"Wertheim am Main," Westermanns Monatshefte,* 62. Jahrg., 124. Bd., 1. Teil (Braunschweig, 1918), pp. 441-449; also Emil Baader, *"Alte Fränkische Städtchen,"* in *Mein Heimatland,* 14. Jahrg. (1927), pp. 146-149. For those interested in the folk-art of the region, see Max Walter, *Die Volkskunst im badischen Frankenlande.* (Karlsruhe: C. F. Müller, 1927), No. 33 of the series *Vom Bodensee zum Main.* The *Jahrbuch des Historischen Vereins Alt-Wertheim* (1905-1939) and the *Beiträge zur Heimatkunde* (1932), both founded and edited by Otto Langguth, are the fullest sources for the history and genealogy of the former County of Löwenstein-Wertheim, and treat all phases of the life of our ancestors there — folklore, customs, dialect, industry, architecture, religion. Unfortunately there is to my knowledge no complete set of the *Jahrbücher* in America, though the New York Public Library has the volumes for 1925, 1927, and 1928; the Library of Congress, that for 1932; and my own personal library, through the courtesy of Dr. Langguth, includes those for 1923 and 1935. Dr. Langguth has prepared two other important genealogical works, which are of importance to any American of Wertheimer descent: (1) his *"Einwanderer in Stadt und Grafschaft Wertheim,"* published in *Familiengeschichtliche Blät-*

The City Archive offered very little material, but it not yet entirely arranged and may perhaps still contain much information in the Guild Reports. If the present work finds interest, then still other offices of the Princely Archive of Löwenstein-Wertheim-Rosenberg can be worked over. Then perhaps also in the contents of the City Archive much can be brought to the light of day.

To the princely governments on both sides as well as to the City Government I express my most humble thanks for permission to use the relevant archives so extensively.

An important source for the family history of the village of Wenkheim, well-known through the knightly family of *Hund von Wenkheim,* is the privately printed *Quellenbüchlein zur Kirchen- & Familiengeschichte des Dorfes Wenkheim,* by Johann Steger, pastor in Dossenheim near Heidelberg (1929). With the help of this book one can draw up the relevant family tree of every Wenkheim family for the time from 1666 to 1871. In the present work, this book is briefly designated with the word "Steger." As a pattern the book can give many suggestions.

Urphar-am-Main, an important locality in the County, is completely written up by Gustav Rommel, Karlsruhe, in the *Jahrbuch des Historischen Vereins Alt-Wertheim* for 1922-1924. In the present work, reference is made to "Rommel" from time to time. Rommel treats all areas of village, church, and family history in unexcelled mastery, and has already drawn the Urphar emigrants into the circle of his researches.*

As far as possible I have retained old expressions and ways of writing, and, where at all desirable, let the emigrants themselves speak to the reader.

OTTO LANGGUTH.

Wertheim-am-Main, October, 1931.

---

*ter,* 32. Jahrgang (Leipzig, 1934), and republishued as Part I of the *Jahrbuch des Historischen Vereins Alt-Wertheim* for 1935; and (2) his genealogical guide, *Die Grafschaft Wertheim* (Leipzig: Verlag Degener & Co., Inh. Oswald Spohr, 1936), Heft 4 of the series *Familiengeschichtlicher Wegweiser durch Stadt und Land,* edited by Dr. Friedrich Wecken. This valuable little booklet of 24 pages contains, among other features, a list of all the extant parish archives for each of the 115 villages of the former County of Löwenstein-Wertheim. To conclude, those seeking more specialized studies on Wertheim, cannot do better than to consult Dr. Friedrich Lautenschlager's monumental *Bibliographie der badischen Geschichte* (Karlsruhe: Badische Historische Kommission, 1933 ff.), which should be in every library specializing in Pennsylvania German studies. — D. Y.

WERTHEIM ON THE MAIN. ON THE HILLSIDE, THE ANCIENT CASTLE AND MODERN PALACE OF THE PRINCE OF LOEWENSTEIN-WERTHEIM

# Pennsylvania German Pioneers from the County of Wertheim

## THE WERTHEIM BACKGROUND

HE County of Wertheim lay between the Dioceses of Würzburg and Mainz — a tiny Protestant state between mighty Catholic powers — and belonged to the Circle of Franconia.

After the line of the old Counts of Wertheim became extinct, the principal part of the County, following an interregnum under a Count of Stolberg-Königstein, finally came into the sole possession of the House of the Counts of Löwenstein, an older branch of the Wittelbachs, the direct descendants of Frederick the Victorious of the Palatinate.

Although Ludwig III, Count of Löwenstein, had already learned to know, to his own sorrow and under the greatest personal sacrifices, the difficulties attendant on a common administration, he willed that his descendants were forever to rule conjointly. So in 1611 his four sons became co-regents of the County of Wertheim and its appendages: the County of Löwenstein near Heilbronn, the Domain of Breuberg in the Odenwald, the County of Virneburg in the Eifel, and still further distant counties and domains in Rochefort, Chassepiere, Cugnon, Montaigu, Neufchateau, Herbimont, etc., in what is now Belgium and Luxemburg, to which at a later time there were added extensive possessions in Bohemia.

Since only two brothers left heirs, two lines of the House were formed, who embittered each other's lives for a long time. The one line was Protestant, the other Catholic; the one let each grown son rule conjointly, the other was practically always devoted to primogeniture; the one became rich, the other relatively poor; the one played a role in politics, the other contented itself with the administration of its own estates, with the cares of personal rule, with the prosecution of century-old proceedings, with the pleasures of the chase, and — at the most — with a journey to the Spa.

With so many antitheses, it could not fail to take place, that each tried to preserve his inherited rights on both sides; two governments had to be watched on these matters. Every trifling event was debated in two Chambers; every petitioner had to present his memorial in duplicate. Naturally there were some offices common to both governments, such as Rentmaster, Master Forester, Coinage Office, and Collector of Customs; but by and large it was an expensive administration for so tiny a land. And there would certainly not be much left for the governments out of the small incomes, if the other possessions had not been early divided between the two dynastic lines.

The Ducal Residence was the capital city of Wertheim, at the confluence of the Main and the Tauber Rivers. After the Castle was destroyed, the Courts lived in various and in part castle-like buildings, until the Catholic line had a large and magnificent palace built for itself by *Johannes Dinzenhofer* at Kleinheubach near Miltenberg, and thereafter resided there most of the time.

In the eighteenth century, which is of most interest to us in the matter of emigrants, the one line of the ruling House had a Catholic Prince as representative, the other not less than five

Protestant Counts as "Co-regents." They were already disunited among themselves, so that one can believe, without pressing the matter further, that under such conditions rulership was really an art!

The County of Wertheim, especially the capital city Wertheim, was exclusively Lutheran, and did not easily permit Catholic emigrants to enter — a Catholic had as hard a time acquiring the right of citizenship as did a member of the Reformed Church. Also, at least in the City, the Jews could not spread unrestricted, for the City had an agreement with the government, that it did not need to put up with more than four families of Jews. Perhaps that is the reason why so many Jews had to emigrate from Wertheim, and meet us everywhere with the family names Wertheim, Wertheimer, Wertheimber, etc. In any case, the Warehouse of Wertheim in Berlin is today better known than the former capital and residence city of Wertheim, whose Jewish congregation belongs to the oldest Jewish settlement in Franconia.

## ECONOMIC MOTIVATION OF THE EMIGRATION

The County lay in the midst of very many military entanglements. Before the Thirty Years War there had been a cruel twenty-year feud with Würzburg, the ancient enemy of Wertheim. Shortly after the Thirty Years War, the troops of the Most Christian King ravaged the lands on the Main and the Neckar; well known is Merian's engraving, which shows French victualling ships being burnt on the Main, in sight of ruins in the city and castle of Wertheim, while imperial troops are seen coming down the hill. But friend and foe were more than all else equally dangerous to the peasants. Each demanded provisions or money, or both, and wrought mischief on the distressed population. And so it went for almost the entire eighteenth century. One continually hears of troop movements which burdened the country.

When one considers the taxes and duties which the subjects had to produce, a long list can be assembled in a moment. Even in the County of Wertheim — especially in the eighteenth century — rulers were not less inventive in the discovery of new possibilities of taxing their subjects, than in other countries. Among the peasants in the country that was still relatively simple. In addition to enforced labor [*Frohnden*], there were gradually introduced grazing fees [*Atzgeld*], hunting fees [*Jagdgeld*], watch fees [*Wachtgeld*], pannage [*Mastgeld*], plowing fees [*Pfluggeld*], dyeing fees [*Waidgeld*], food tax [*Ungeld*], tax on second hay crop [*Ohmgeld*], hand work rendered [*Handlohn*], money paid in lieu of labor with teams [*Spanngeld*], the Prince's personal tax [*Schatoullengeld*], chimney tax [*Schlotzins*], water tax [*Wasserzins*], the so-called hearth tax [*Herdpfennig*], etc., besides the established great and small tithes [*Zehnten*] and ground rents [*Gülten*], assessment [*Schatzung*], the shrovetide fowls [*Sommerhühner*], Martinmas geese [*Martinsgänse*], and so forth. Also the heriot or feudal tribute [*Besthaupt*] was a hard thing. On taxes and burdens, an excellent survey is found in Rommel, page 156ff.

And the peasants paid, as long as they could. One finds, however, many gratifying proofs of the fact that such duties were not inhumanly squeezed out of the people; as a rule, a word at the right time found a good hearing. The locality of Grünewörth, for example, had only two farms in the year 1294, which had to deliver two shrovetide fowls compared with twenty-four at the end of the eighteenth century. If there was in a household a woman in childbed, then the head of the house needed to deliver only the head of the chicken, and could keep the rest—*"Der Herrschaft den Kopf, — dem Bauern das Huhn in den Topf,"* — certainly a fine proof of benevolence on the part of the government.[1]

Then, too, the burdening of the subjects had a certain limit in the example of the neighboring states. What was done there, was usually copied here, not the other way around — and, "it was good to dwell under episcopal rule" *("unter dem Krummstab war gut wohnen")!*

More difficult was the introduction of a new tax in the City of Wertheim itself. Since 1306 the City had the same rights as the Free City of Frankfurt, even though much was lacking in practice. Under the Counts of Stolberg the City had, however,

[1]Fries, *Wertheimer Zeitung*, 1844, No. 29.

attained further privileges as over against the government, which were not to be abolished. For example, the burghers taxed themselves and gave thereof to the government certain portions, which were agreed upon. On this account the burghers could save their skins better than could the peasants.

At any rate we find among the emigrants a very small proportion of burghers and burghers' sons, from which we can safely draw the conclusion that the trades were on a relatively substantial basis. Actually one cannot picture the standard of living modestly enough. The good times before the Thirty Years War, or before the Feud with Würzburg, were long past. Working hours began long before daylight and lasted into the night, if the master thus chose. And yet one could not easily advance himself beyond the others — the guilds saw to it that the trees did not grow up into heaven itself! However, one reads nothing in the *Acta* of direct need, as far as the workmen are concerned. If a person should send his son to Berlin, because there the cooper trade is not yet so overcrowded as it is in Wertheim; or when a crafty purse-maker lets his seven sons all become purse-makers in order to save the apprentice fees, and then wonders why purse-makers aren't needed in Wertheim, one need really attach no significance to that.

If on the other hand one looks somewhat deeper into the conditions in the country, then one finds examples enough, where need cries to high heaven. Two young men from neighboring villages, having served faithfully and honestly as Contingent Soldiers for thirteen years, now feel themselves quite unable "to earn their scanty daily bread for wife and children." In 1753 *Christoph Horn, Sr.,* of Eichel, complains about the bad years he has suffered, and other circumstances, which have consumed his fortune of 500 florins, so that now he must leave everything behind for his creditors. *Georg Schäfer* of Glashofen has left out of his one-time fortune of 6000 florins only 1174 florins in the year 1754; the Mayor of that village was of course of the opinion that he himself was to blame for his losses. A cartwright in Michelrieth has no work because "every farmer now makes his plow himself. It is no preference or desire of mine which drives me out of the country, but poverty and my uneasiness for wife and child." *Johann Michael Dosch* in Nassag has, with five orphaned brothers and sisters, inherited an old dilapidated "half-house" and half of a little barn, in value totaling 50 florins, yet he can find no buyer for them. The widow of small-farmer *Bauer* in Vockenroth had sold her "house" in 1773 for 15 florins; "oppressed by poverty and pursued by much too great misery in these poor and costly times," she wants, with her son, "to seek in foreign lands the daily bread necessary for her destitute and — The Lord have mercy! — her miserable existence."

Another by the name of *Johann Michael Flickert* maintains in 1786 that he has paid the Prince more in hand work than his entire property would have brought in; as a faithful subject he has for twenty-three years "willingly" rendered much in socage money, in assessments and other favors. *Hans Wiessmann* of Schollbrunn complains in 1752 of the fact that the Carthusian Monastery of Grünau has fined him nine florins for eating meat at forbidden times, against which he finds protection in the county government. Others complain of debts to Jews, who seek to take possession of pieces of land they left behind. One *Thomas Diehm* of Kembach complains in 1752 of the exorbitant rents of both Christians and Jews. When Wertheim was under Baden, after the Napoleonic Wars, conditions became still worse. It is impossible, writes *Heinrich Weiss* of Nassig, to live in our impoverished land so miserably burdened with high taxes. That was 1832.

And so since the beginning of the eighteenth century, year after year, thousands have gone into foreign lands, cleared the primeval forest — if they got over alive — and took upon themselves many still greater deprivations of all kinds, even the loss of personal freedom, and are today in their descendants lost to the German people.

### THE PROCESS OF MANUMISSION

Under the oppressive burdens we have not yet named vassalage. This continued a long time in the County, even in the City. Whoever wanted to become a burgher, could not as a rule do so without becoming vassal to the lords of the land. Whoever therefore immigrated into Wertheim, was received into vassalage; whoever emigrated, received manumission, or was manumitted, in return for a certain payment. Only rarely did it happen that someone slipped through, like *Hans Michel Wiesner* of Dietenhan, who was a vassal to the Elector of Mainz, while his wife and his children were vassals of the Counts of Wertheim.

At any rate we are indebted to the so-called Manumission-*Acta* for preserving so much information on our emigrants. There are of course in rare cases original letters; but most of the petitions were drawn up by professional clerks, who often fell into the use of conventional expressions. Yet in spite of this, an atmosphere of reality attaches to the *Acta,* even if one must read between the lines.

In 1754 *Barbara Adelmann* of Höhfeld was so poor that she was not even able to pay for a certificate of manumission. In different cases it happened that freedom from vassalage was graciously granted to the petitioners, as to *Andreas Sell,* Village Mayor of Oberwittbach, who "with trembling hand lays his lines at the feet of the Prince, and wants to go to Pennsylvania, in order no longer to run around as a spectacle for others." A saddler named *Johann Peter Ries* from Wertheim complained in 1753 that he was taking along not a red cent except his good name. The government's decision was short and conclusive: "Where there is nothing left, the Emperor has lost his right; therefore he receives manumission without the usual fee." But less reputable people also at times received manumission without fees, as for instance the *Friedrich* and *Peter Dosch* families in Nassig, 1773, "whom the community would gladly be rid of, since they are a burden to it with their suspicious and scandalous households."

A poor teacher's son by the name of *Platz* had risen to respect in Berlin, but inherited nothing at all from his home country. Despite this he is to pay two florins, since he is now a respected merchant in Berlin, "who would take offense at being classed with the beggars." His Serene Highness considered *Thomas Hörner* of Nassig (1840) an arch poacher, and gladly relaxed the tax for him on account of his emigration — here again one sees the "amiable father of his country," who, although a good Catholic, was memorialized with this very epithet by the Lutheran Superintendent in his Baptismal Register on November 24, 1764. A tenant on the Gickelhof got less gracious treatment: "In order the sooner to free ourselves of this disgraceful wood-thief and his whole tribe, a mere pass shall be given him in place of the Certificate of Manumission."

Servants of the princes and counts enjoyed many mitigations. The son of one *Arnold,* the Prince's butler, appeals to the fact that his father had been for fifty years in the county service, and had endured much therein. He is evidently taken at his word. The prince is informed: "According to the observance of the present Coregency, the dispensations and manumissions in such cases are given *gratis.*" Emigrants to Kleinheubach, the new princely estate, generally received their freedom from vassalage. Whoever was a student became free by virtue of that fact. That was of course no ironbound rule anywhere, but an old custom which was always honored. This privilege resulted from the *Acta* in the case of *Nitzschki* in 1763:

> "There is still a son there, who has been a student; is such a one to be manumitted? Decision: such sons are from time immemorial *ipso facto* free of vassalage, as soon as they enter upon their studies; therefore there is nothing to be demanded from this one either."[2]
>
> Evidently the printer's trade was counted among the learned professions: In 1769 "*Heinrich Valentin Nehr, Jr.,* as a most subservient and faithful servant, requests that by the greatest mercy he and his wife be pronounced forever free. His deceased mother, daughter of *Christoph Hessler,* who was a princely Court Cabinetmaker and Burgher, was by inheritance, through her parents a partaker in local citizenship rights, as well as the vassalage connected with it. His father, as a foreigner licensed by the Coregency as Court and Chancery Printer is, along with his profession and the guild therewith connected, immediately dependent up to the present time, and never became a burgher of Wertheim, and consequently is not a vassal either. While thus I have not indeed inherited, nor can inherit, any citizen rights from my aforesaid father, nevertheless through my mother I am a vassal. The same is true also of my betrothed, *Maria Catharina,* the

---

[2] *Rosenberg Archive,* Br. 387e.

> second eldest and orphaned daughter of the late Mr. *Johann Jacob Bauer,* former Reverence and Officer here, who is subject to vassalage through her parents, therefore have I, etc.

The request was granted without further ado.

Now, however, there were within the County itself different levels of vassalage, again regulated more by custom than by agreement or law. The peasants of Wenkheim, for example, declare in 1753 that they are generally not vassals and therefore receive an attestation of their freedom as follows:

> According to the most subservient announcement made by [ — ] at Wenkheim to the Coregency of the County, seeing that [he] wanted to go to New England and fittingly sought therefore for permission and bestowal of a certificate attesting [his] good conduct, there was found herein no objection to [his] departure. Therefore not only is the requested departure herewith granted, but it is also certified to [his] better success, that the while he was resident at said Wenkheim, he was at all times devoted to an orderly behavior and has observed the duties of a faithful subject.
>
> In Witness Whereof, is here mounted the Great Seal of the Government.
>
> [Signature]

As early as May 19, 1752, the notice appears in a Government Protocol: "Since it has been found that the village of Wenkheim is subject to no vassalage, etc."[3] On October 6, 1775, the Princely Government mentions, in regard to the manumission of the daughter of *Weidner,* the landlord of the Ox Tavern: "This village is subject to a somewhat milder vassalage than the other villages of the County." It is unnecessary, it is pointed out, to go into the provocations of the Village Mayor, suspended at this time, who began a case on this matter in the Imperial Court Council; the oldest tavern accounts show this from year to year. In thousands of cases, the protocol stated, manumission had already been lawful and will also remain lawful. In 1776 the case reached the highest court of the Empire; a year later the judgment went against the village, over which there was almost a riot.

---

[3]*Rosenberg Archive*, Br. 387b, May 19, 1752.

In 1783 it was reported:

> The right and privilege of manumission and the effect of the same on subjects and citizenry in the County of Wertheim cannot be illustrated from the inventory books, because the same are not at hand in the Chamber-Registracy. One should hold to the observance and custom of the usual *status conventiae,* frankly maintained to the present day. So the buying of freedom is considered an *onus reale,* which rests on property.[4]

One sees how very much the idea of "bodily" vassalage itself subsided in official circles. It is property which is of interest, not bodily vassalage. Not that anyone saw anything disgraceful in the concept of vassalage. Quite the contrary — many subjects in their petitions consider themselves "related and attached" to the Prince through vassalage. In their eyes the Lord of the Land is a Patriarch, and the subjects are his larger family. By virtue of this relation they have all kinds of rights, such as protection. The Lord of the Land provides for order, for church and for school. And just as one can, for example, buy the rights of citizenship, so can he also buy his freedom again, if his disposition drives him elsewhere.

In the case of the burghers of the City there was no feudal tribute (heriot) given in connection with vassalage. On February 16, 1768, it was observed by *Hinckeldey:* "In this City, one is not so exacting, because there is no feudal tribute connected with vassalage." But even in the country the emigrant upon being manumitted gave up rights one dares not undervalue. *Nicolaus Schlessmann* of Bestenheid in 1773 paid for his manumission 28 florins, 41 kreuzer. Now he is sorry for his own proposal, which brought him "a lamentable blessing of emigrating from the County." Now he thinks: Remain at home and support thyself honestly! Now he would gladly consider again being allowed to enjoy the refreshing protection of his gracious government and also would make bold to support himself with the work of his hands. He would like therefore to remain a subject, and received the permission to do so — but his 29 florins were gone![5]

---

[4]*Rosenberg Archive,* Br. 387n.
[5]*Rosenberg Archive,* Br. 387i.

As early as 1752 it was made known, that after manumission was achieved, none should be provided with a second chance at citizenship, "so that no dovecote be made of the County."[6] Also in 1768, the petitioner *Hans Jörg Popp* of Grünewörth is given to understand that in case he returns after emigration — as has already often happened with others of his kind — he shall not be permitted to remain, in order not to burden the country with beggars and idlers.[7]

Quite numerous are the cases, where young people escaped under cover of the night, in order to save their manumission fees. One *Jakob Diehm* of Dietenhan is said to have left secretly on account of a woman. One *Johann Samuel Bauernkeller* is, in spite of his poverty, to pay six florins. For his mother, a poor widow, the six florins were too much, and — therefore "this fellow left without manumission." *Andreas Sell,* the above-mentioned Village Mayor of Oberwittbach, was suspected in 1752 of wishing to abscond with his money, leaving his sick wife and his children as a burden on his friends. *Michael Honeck* of Buch-am-Ahorn appears in the records in 1753 as father of an illegitimate child — "the rascal went to New England, but he left behind no means for its support." Gladly they would have made his father pay the eighteen florins fine for the unchastity his son committed, and a compensation of ten Reichstaler *pro defloratione,* and a yearly support of six florins to the child — "but it is found that a father cannot be punished for the sins of his son, and so the only possibility remaining is to seize the son's future inheritance."

What was the actual cost of manumission from vassalage, without which the emigrants could not leave? *Hans Paul Schlessmann* of Nassig was in 1752 given to understand that he had either to pay two florins for a Certificate of Manumission, or to give up the idea of emigrating to New England, at the risk of having his future inheritance confiscated, or seizure as a fugitive vassal. As early as 1754 official circles were considering how they might best extinguish "the frivolous itch of emigration." The best method was perceived at once to be quite a high tax, to be

[6]*Freudenberg Archive, Acta re: Manumission,* May 2, 1752.
[7]*Rosenberg Archive,* Br. 387f.

taken out of the moveable property. Not without justification was the government of the opinion earlier, that a fortune amassed in the country should also be kept there. So from the beginning a fixed supplemental tax [*Nachsteuer*] was levied on the property which was taken away; for the period up to 1752, an amount of 10% was surrendered.[8]

In practice however this rate was many times set at only 5%—so in 1753 *Georg Weiss* of Hasselberg, out of his property of 72 florins and 32 kreuzer, pays three florins and 42 kreuzer for himself, two florins for his wife, and one florin for each of his four children. In the year 1768 the rate for persons who had less than 200 florins was as follows: ten florins for every adult, five florins for a women and two florins for each child, in case they emigrated with their parents.

The rate of 10% of the property was raised as early as 1753 to 20% and applied at once to the emigrants from Wenkheim. Thus they were not at the time vassals, yet had to pay just as much as subjects who were vassals, at least insofar as they had property. Therefore with all their so-called freedom they were not much ahead of the others. In any case they, too, could leave without permission just as little as could the son of a Catholic rector, who received a certificate granting permission to depart, and therewith was turned over to Ottenstein, the domain of the Counts of Bamberg-Springenstein, "with all his present and future property *pleno jure*."[9]

In the year 1772 5% of one's property was taken for manumission, and an additional 20% taken out of the remainder; tax and seal were extra for tax and certification.[10] These two added up to such a great loss of property that in many a person the desire "to turn his back on his Fatherland" passed away! In the nineteenth century, after the County was divided among Baden, Bavaria, etc., a 20% supplemental tax was still levied; however, of a property of 500 florins, one-fourth — in smaller fortunes, one-half — of the tax was to be deducted.

---

[8]*Rosenberg Archive*, Br. 387d, p. 69.
[9]*Rosenberg Archive*, Br. 387, for 1777.
[10]*Rosenberg Archive*, Br. 387 H.

At that time, however, special situations arose which greatly burdened the emigrants. Since 1818 the peasants had refused further to pay the princely burdens of money paid in lieu of statute labor, as well as hunting, watch, and plowing fees. Their case, promoted in common, was not until 1832 decided in favor of the government. Whoever now wanted to emigrate, thus had to pay the fifteen-year total in back taxes. And if in a period of need, anyone took his firewood from the common forest, there were added to this grievous fines. No wonder the *Acta* from this period reveal deplorable conditions! ; And when Prince *Georg* of Löwenstein himself, well known for his humaneness, writes in his own hand under the refusal of a petition:

> Since it is a matter of conscience to give the first blow in any way at all, to the desire for emigration which has already begotten so many sad consequences, the petition is denied, since, following all late reports, those emigrants who take no property to North America, fall a prey to the most nameless misery,

we may take the Prince's word for it that this expresses his innermost convictions.

But there were other cases which defied all customary practices and regulations. For example, there emigrated one *Philipp Friedrich Müller* of Kitzingen, who was poor as Job, but still had an inheritance coming from his grandfather, the old Baker *Nübling*. But *Nübling* is still living,

> almost 80 years old, a rich man, who has turned everything into coin and hires it out on interest, yet no evaluation can be put upon it, since he is very secretive with his fortune and very eccentric, can consequently dispose of his property in various ways, but also easily through chance events lose everything, because he has it all in readiness; consequently one cannot go by his grandson's inheritance in dealing with the question of manumission.

It is clear that the grandson had a claim to freedom, for otherwise his reception into the citizenry of Kitzingen would be made impossible. But he could not pay duty, either, on what he did not yet have.

### THE NEWLANDER AT WORK

The instigation of the emigration came in many cases from professional agents, who promised the people mountains of gold and every freedom, above all free hunting. The dangers of the journey in the overcrowded ships, the deceitful manipulations to which the emigrants were exposed on the way, the possible loss of personal freedom in case the cost of the trip could not be paid in full — all such matters were naturally not mentioned. There are horrible accounts of the fate of such emigrants. For every passenger secured, the agent received a nice sum per head, as a rule one ducat — we can infer from this what profits the agents concerned hoped to derive from their unfortunate victims. The wretched role of the emigration agent or "Newlander" was soon recognized, and where they could be seized, short work was made of them.

In our region in the 1740's a certain *Oberdorf* of Kembach went about, "called *Scheuernhans*"; he was wanted by the Criminal Jurisdiction of Remlingen for trade in redemptioners [*Menschenraub*]. He was to have been tried for his "slave-trading" or "soul-selling," as the contemporary accounts call it. But he escaped from punishment through flight, "established" himself for a time on the Rhine, and finally found reception and protection with one *Freiherr von Rüdt* in Bödigheim, who entrusted him with a gatekeeper's job. He is said to have died there around 1778.[11]

In 1752 a certain *Peter Friedrich Cregut(s)* came to Wertheim claiming to be a Deputy of the English Commissary *Philipp Thomas van Teglingen,* with the request that he be permitted to solicit emigrants. He was asked first to identify himself better; however, he could meanwhile visit the people, "who had made arrangements with *Johann Ickes,* who on that day was sent out of the country, because the agreements were confiscated." His warrant read as follows:

> I, the undersigned, affirm . . . that Mr. *Peter Friedrich Cregut* is named and appointed by me to enlist people for Philadelphia or other localities in America. He is authorized

[11]*Rosenberg Archive,* Br. 387 m, May 3, 1782.

to inform himself among the Newlanders, of the number of people, who will have let themselves be subscribed on my contract, and in all matters to rule as if I were there in person, and at the first opportunity I will forward to him a legal Procuration or Warrant.

Bingen, April 1, 1752

(Signed) P. TH. VAN TEGLINGEN

*Cregut(s)* also received permission to take away those persons who had already made arrangements with *Ickes;* but the better warrant which was demanded apparently never came, and he soon absconded again.[12]

*Johann Philipp Buch,* the son of a boatman of Wertheim, also tried to get rich quickly in this way. He had been in America and knew exactly what lot awaited the poor emigrants. In 1754 an investigation was opened against him due to complaints that he was involved in "slave-trading" or "soul-selling." In the painful inquiry it came out that *Buch* had enlisted many people in the region of Koburg and in the *"Gäu,"* that is, the region around Ochsenfurt, who were then to embark on the Neckar. Presumably he did not dare to go by Wertheim with his victims, for the people could otherwise have traveled better and more cheaply on the Main. With the support of the Würzburg Bailiff *Briel* in Sommerhausen, Buch was arrested by a command of Wertheim soldiers and brought here in chains. From Winterhausen to Würzburg the journey was by water, which cost 30 kreuzer. For the necessary board of the prisoner, eight kreuzer were spent daily, while each soldier could put away ten kreuzer, and the Corporal 20 kreuzer. The entire expedition "into foreign parts," that is, into the Dioceses of Würzburg, cost altogether two florins, 41 kreuzer, exclusive of a rope used to tie the prisoner and including the overnight lodgings for all three days.

*Buch* was described to the Würzburg government as a bad fellow, who had already in the previous year persuaded many subjects through false representations of the exceptional advantages they could enjoy in New England, so that with wife and child they blindly followed their avaricious leader and most of

[12]*Rosenberg Archive,* Br. 417.

them sank into the bitterest grief. This year he had the impudence to try a similar secret solicitation through his accomplices, although from fear of his well-deserved punishment, he himself shunned the County. The Government should early arrest this seducing scoundrel and bring him to punishment, and therewith dispatch justice in the case of such low, pernicious people.

On May 16, his father, a respected shipper and tradesman in Wertheim, petitions for his release. In the petition he says:

> For 14 days my son *Philipp* has been a prisoner in the Jail here. This misfortune weighs deeply on my mind as his father, as also upon his mother and his other friends, especially since the charge is unknown. Until now he has not even once been given a hearing, etc. May he be forgiven his present sin and freed.

In the trial on June 10, *Buch* admits having solicited for Shipman *Hoppe* in Rotterdam in return for gratuities. All in all he has received 100 florins from *Hoppe,* but presumably not from the firm itself but from its agents, who had given him one-half ducat per head for well-to-do people, nothing for the poor ones.

There were letters along with the *Acta,* which some emigrants had written warning against *Buch* as a cheat. Unfortunately these letters, along with the principal *Acta,* many years ago made the journey to the paper mill and are today no longer at hand.

In order to force more out of *Buch,* he was threatened with a stay in the House of Correction, the Prison for Criminals, and with chains. Even execution was hinted at, but nothing worthwhile could be brought from him. Finally the court was of the opinion that he should rather be banished forever from the country and the Circle of Franconia, since he had no means and the costs were considerable, though he was still being supported by his parents. Thus possibly he would forget his free return journey to Pennsylvania! Now he is to be led publicly through the City by armed soldiers, taken to the country's frontier and there he is to swear an oath never more to try to mislead people into emigration; then he is to be exiled from the country. This verdict was carried out — *Buch* was punished with exile from the country, and his inheritance, that of the eldest son, was confiscated, with which his manumission was to be paid. His aged parents left no stone unturned to ward off the worst — execution. In the *Acta* the fact is also mentioned that the parents received a letter from the Firm of *Hoppe*. At any rate *Buch* had his respected parents to thank for his mild and considerate sentence.

*Buch* appears to have given up the return journey to Pennsylvania, for in 1757 mention is again made of him in the *Death Register:*

> On January 15, *Philipp Buch,* a boatman, who was exiled for trading in "slaves" whom he enticed to America, returned in sickness and direst need, however, and after genuine repentance over his sins was given the Communion on his deathbed. And because the guildsmen did not want to carry him out, he was buried in secret.

In the Spring of 1753, *Johann David Kümmich* of Rotterdam asks for permission to solicit emigrants for New England.[13] He was in business for himself and wanted to enlist people, whom the Wertheim boatman *Lösch* would bring to Holland, for New England or Pennsylvania,

> which safe and successful journey across, Your Highness should as soon wish as grant for these poor, honest, needy emigrants, out of the love and clemency inherent in the father of his country. . . So I want to undertake their sure and honest delivery and make a contract with them on the spot for shipping them across the ocean.

His request was also granted, since he wants to enlist only those who have already received their freedom from vassalage. Two days later the Princely Secretary *Rigel* received an order to go to *Kümmich,* the merchant, and to demand his credentials, and to ask him into what provinces he was thinking of conducting the people. Through the Conjoint County Government attention was called to the fact that *Kümmich* had no patent from the Royal Government of Great Britain and perhaps was to be counted among the secret and deceitful agents. *Buch's* son was said to have sold him secretly solicited people for four florins; also it was to be feared that he was still enticing many burghers and subjects

[13] *Rosenberg Archive,* Br. 417.

out of the country. Actually *Rigel* came upon *Kümmich* "in the Golden Chain Tavern" in the company of young *Buch* and one *Wiessmann* and his daughter, from Schollbrunn. In front of the Tavern stood a chaise with a team of three horses, "uncertain whether they were intended for a pleasure trip or for a getaway." *Kümmich's* servant had been seen at *Buch's* house. At any rate, some strongly suspicious indications were present.

*Kümmich* declared that he came from Speyer; and that he is now independently located in Rotterdam. He was requested by his own sub-agent in Heilbronn to come to Wertheim, "so that the emigrants got sight of him." He has no credentials or passes, he said, since such things were never demanded. He still has closed no contracts; he is taking the people wherever they wanted to go — to Pennsylvania, New York, Carolina — whenever they wanted to go. Young *Buch* has made inquiries of him whether he wants to take on the people whom his brother was getting for the Merchant *Hope*. But he claims he had nothing to do with *Buch,* and already has heard that *Buch* is having difficulties with the government. Here the *Acta* become silent; they only add briefly: "*Kümmich* has left here. This protocol is to be placed in the *Acta.*"

*Johann Ernst Kiesecker,* a baker, and son of *Conrad Kiesecker,* a miller of near Steinmark, had "journeyed" to Pennsylvania. For some years he remained there, then presumably got to longing again for his Fatherland and his parental inheritance; but on account of his meager fortune he could find no "opportunity," and then undertook the return journey into the "abovementioned country." And out of pure philanthropy he took others along. So said he.

The Wertheim Government arrested him as an accomplice of *Buch.* An investigation in Steinmark brought nothing damaging to light. In the trial he told the following story:

> Six years ago I went on foot to Worms and there joined a party of emigrants. For five years I have worked with a miller 60 English miles or 15 German hours beyond Philadelphia. Now I want to go on foot to Holland. I have nothing to do with the shipping people.

He has brought over and delivered a letter from America to *Georg Schätzlein,* in Wenkheim, from his son; the contents of this letter are unknown to him. A certain *Gerberich* of Altfeld has likewise returned. He has persuaded no one to emigrate, but always said, it was no better in New England — one must work even harder there. On the contrary, two peasants from Höhfeld testify that in Dertingen, where he was called the "Newlander," *Kiesecker* had been seen in a gold-bordered waistcoat and had drawn much gold out of his purse. To be sure he had not invited any one to emigrate, but pointed to the dangers of the ocean trip— as for the rest, he praised the country. There people throw away sausages and entrails of the cattle, and eat only the flesh. *Sührer* of Höhfeld acknowledges being with him, but was not attracted to him — he looked so bad and stole anything he could get his hands on.

*Kiesecker* wants to take along: (1) his brother *Hans Kiesecker,* of Kredenbach, (2) his brother *Johann Matthäus Kiesecker,* of Kredenbach, and (3) *Caspar Knauer,* of Kredenbach. The following also want to leave with him: *Andreas* or *Hans Knauer* of Altfeld, with 1000 Taler; the two shepherds, *Nicolaus Albert* and *Michael Teuffel* of Altfeld; and the parents of *Gerberich* of Altfeld, a single man who emigrated in 1752.

*Kiesecker* was finally released. His appearance in Dertingen in a gold-bordered waistcoat and with a purse full of gold, was of course typical of the "Newlanders," that is, of people who already had been in the New Land, and were devoting themselves to furnishing "wares" to unscrupulous "slave-dealers" for head money. This method of making money created such bad feeling, that many agents for Emigration Societies were looked at askance far into the nineteenth century.

Through the *Kaiserliche Reichs-Oberpostamts-Zeitung* of Frankfurt,[14] which was also read in the County of Wertheim, a reputable and honest agent tried in vain, in an atmosphere of such general mistrust, to lead the stream of emigration into his province:

---

[14]*Rosenberg Archive,* Br. 417.

> The Royal British Captain *Waldo,* Proprietor of Broad Bay in New England, has come to Frankfurt, is setting up branch offices in Frankfurt, Augsburg, Heilbronn and Speyer, and is seeking emigrants, who can pay their passage in full or half of it. Whoever can pay his passage in full, is to get a deduction.

There follows a warning against unauthorized agents. Chief of the house is Samuel Waldo, colonizing in Broad Bay, where "the most Germans have settled." In Number 47 of the same newspaper, warning is again sounded against people who "bear the same old stamp." *Waldo* has a pass, which is signed by the Duke of Newcastle himself, and a recommendation to His Excellency Mr. *Burrish,* the accredited British Minister at the Imperial Diet at Regensburg, etc.

In his printed *"Description of the Settlement of Foreign Protestants in Massachusetts Bay and Broad Bay,"* Waldo makes known the following: The capital city, Boston, has been in existence for 150 years. Hunting and fishing are free. Every 120 families are to form a community and are permitted to hold the land for their heirs, each having 100 acres or 120 *morgen,* in case they till it for at least seven years. Every man 21 years old counts as an expectant. Every district receives two hundred acres for the church and the preacher, every school likewise two hundred acres. Full political rights are assured, like those the English also have; no military service, but protection in case of war, and the free exercise of all Protestant religions. Every congregation must call a regular preacher; the first two years the preachers receive, besides their passage across, fifteen pounds sterling. Wood for building the church is given free. Farreaching assistance in the sale of the products of the soil is assured, but no persuasion is employed. Those who resolve to go are to examine their own interests, and then complete their journey in the name of God.

Something quite unusual was referred to in the mention of well-constructed privies on both sides of Waldo's ship. As to provisions on shipboard, Wednesdays there is one-half pound of bacon, daily only one quart of water, as long as the beer is good. In all things *Waldo* wants to watch like a father over his future subjects.

The reader is further made acquainted with the *"Observations of a Friend of the Colonizing Project,"* as being an important and extensive work in spreading the knowledge of the Gospel and the light of faith. *Waldo's* ancestor had been a great war hero in America; his rights date back to 1629 and were newly confirmed in 1732.

An extract from the *Lancaster-Zeitung* in Pennsylvania, Number 6 of the year 1753, gives a description of the new city of Germantown, thirteen miles distant from Boston [Philadelphia]. The city has eight churches and 1800 families. Boards and stones are cheaper than in Philadelphia. All artisans, especially masons and carpenters, are desired. There is a German printery in Philadelphia, where one can also talk with *"Wilhelm" Franklin.*[15] In New York a tanner named *Johann Houtz* can give report.

Waldo presents also a recommendation of his intention in the French language, aimed at the "German" princes of that time, who, as is well known, preferred murdering the French language to devoting themselves to their mother tongue. Here, too, he first of all warns against the "slave-dealers," who have with human beings only the face in common; "moreover they are snakes and malicious monkeys." As the masters — so the servants. The merchants in Rotterdam pay one ducat and more per head:

> Whereas their Serene Highnesses of the Circles of Swabia, Upper and Lower Rhine, and Franconia, and especially of the Landgraviate of Hesse-Darmstadt, the Duchy of Zweibrücken, the Margraviate of Baden-Durlach, the Counties of Erbach and Wertheim, of the Odenwald and the Westerwald, where the agents are swarming on all sides, have obliged this sort of person to present their credentials and to mention the merchants in Rotterdam, in whose name they are acting, etc. . . . they can be admitted, if one finds them authorized by his Britannic Majesty, etc.

Waldo shows his honesty by not turning to people without means, who formed the majority by far, and who generally could not learn to know of his obviously well-meant services.

---

[15]For Franklin's visit to Frankfurt in 1768, see *Altfrankfurt,* Jahrgang II, Nr. 6.

In 1764 we hear also of French agents for New France.[16] The County Government of Erbach at König is informed that it is no doubt aware that many French emissaries have spread themselves through Germany, in order to seduce the inhabitants into going away to the Royal French colonies in America. Through their solicitations many subjects, along with their wives and children, have lost their temporal welfare, and the Holy Roman Empire and its individual governments have lost their subjects. It was resolved to forbid this emigration entirely. People, in whose going nothing is lost, can possibly be dispensed with. And the Village Mayors are at once to cast such "soul-sellers into prison, and turn them over to the County Government." Also, the Burgomaster and Council of the City of Wertheim are warned against the traveling soul-buyers and emissaries — their deceitful representations should be given no hearing. At present there were agents for the French colonies, who already had succeeded with divers subjects of this County. Emigration was forbidden with the penalty of confiscation of goods, which were to be distributed among the guilds. People in poor and poverty-stricken circumstances, who want to seek their fortune and give themselves over to peril, can perhaps receive dispensation on payment of the 20% supplemental tax.

### LETTERS FROM THE NEW LAND

Most of the emigrants had no correct conception of where they were going. They describe the goal of their journey as "the Island of Pennsylvania," the New Land, New England, New Scotland, or even as *"das Bintzel Vannier Land," "die Insul Infania,"* etc.

Very few of them had friends or relatives in the New Land, who could and did report on their own observations. In the great rarity of such letters from that period we will reproduce, in Appendices II and IV, three letters, from the years 1753, 1769,

---

[16]*Rosenberg Archive*, Br. 417, February 11, 1764, Report from the District of Rosenberg: "Many people are desirous of leaving for New France. The Magistrate is ordered to forbid emigration outside Germany with the penalty of confiscation of the emigrant's entire property, allowing, to be sure, dispensation for those in whose going nothing is lost."

and 1780. The one letter from *Johannes Schlessmann* of Nassig remained preserved through the fact that it was presented for the purpose of comparison of the signature with the doubtful Letter of Attorney. In the year 1770, on May 4, there came a messenger of *Schlessmann,* a certain *Nicolaus Zimmermann* from Oxford, Philadelphia County, Pennsylvania, to the relatives, in order to take back *Schlessmann's* inheritance, in the amount of 165 florins.

This Power of Attorney is also found among the *Acta.*[17] It is especially interesting from the fact that the British Notary made use of the German language and German letters both in the printing and in the writing. Also his motto on his official seal, *"suum cuique,"* does not point to an English model. The formerly poor peasant *Schlessmann* had now himself acquired a seal, portraying St. George and the Dragon. No wonder the doubts of the relatives grew, as to whether the thing was quite in order. The Notary himself was named *Peter Miller.* From Oswald Seidensticker's *Geschichte der Deutschen Gesellschaft in Pennsylvanien* (Philadelphia: Kohler, 1876), it appears that *Miller* was Vice President of the German Society from its foundation in 1764. He hailed from Neu-Saarwerden in Nassau-Weilburg, and carried on the business of a notary. In 1769 he announces his moving from Second to Third Street, Philadelphia, where he continues his Notary Office, and prepares all kinds of documents. He also offers books for sale. In 1772 he became Justice of the Peace for the City and County of Philadelphia, and in 1787-1789 was engaged as Judge. During the Revolution he was in Captain *Burkard's* Company of the Third Battalion. For several years he was Register of German emigrants. He died in 1794. Whether he was identical with *Miller* the Printer, is doubtful. In *Schlessmann's* letter, mention is made of the widely known printer *Christoph Sauer,* whose father, of the same name, had established in Germantown in 1738 the first German printery. There he published the first German newspaper and the first German Bible on the American continent. In 1781 there appeared in the *Wertheimer Zeitung* the first book-notice from America:

---

17*Rosenberg Archive,* Br. 387 g.

There has just arrived from Philadelphia, in the Printery of this City, and to be had for nine kreuzer in cash: the *Neumodischer Taschenkalender auf ein ganzes Jahrhundert eingerichtet.*

In 1769 there again appears in Wertheim a messenger from the New World, the Master-Butcher *Michael Hotz,* a Wertheimer, now resident in Philadelphia. He wants to take back the inheritance of *Christian Ernst Beschler,* who has found a new home as schoolmaster in "*Bockhill,*" Bucks County, Province of Pennsylvania.

The Letter of Attorney, brought by *Michael Hotz* to Wertheim in the case of the *Beschler* Estate, was preserved in the Wertheim Archives, and reads as follows:

LETTER OF ATTORNEY

*KNOW ALL MEN BY THESE PRESENTS,* that I, *Christian Ernst Beschler,* resident of *Bockhill* in the County of *Buchs* in the Province of Pennsylvania in North America, have nominated, appointed, and constituted as my true and legal attorney and mandatory, and hereby and by virtue hereof, nominate, appoint, and constitute *Michael Hotz,* Master Butcher and resident of the City of Philadelphia in the said Province of Pennsylvania, [1] to demand and receive, for me and in my name and in my stead, and to my own use and profit all and every sum of money, capital and interests, lands, rents and other effects as named, which are coming to me from any person or persons in the Holy Roman Empire, and in particular that property or legacy which is coming to me from the estate of my late father, *Baltasar Beschler,* and from my late mother, *Maria Catharina Beschler,* née *Weis,* in the Honorable City of Wertheim, in the County of Wertheim, in the Circle of Franconia — which is under the trusteeship of Mr. *Michael Gress* and Mr. *Friedrich Oberdorff* — or wherever else any of my property or inheritance is found; [2] to investigate likewise the pertinent inventories, accounts and other documents, and if circumstances turn out that I am unjustly denied the property, land and effects that are coming to me, to approve likewise in my name and in my stead going to law before all authorized magistracies, courts and tribunals high and low, there to seek and obtain the right to make a settlement, or to let the matter come to a legal verdict, to acquiesce in such legal verdicts or to appeal from them, and to bring the final decision of such case to prosecution and execution; [3] to draw up in my name and complete proper receipts, or other certificates of release, for the actual reception and transfer of my own properties and effects, and especially for the prosecution and successful conclusion of the business herewith laid on him — whether in or out of court, everything to be done legally in my name and in my stead, serviceably and requisitely, and if demanded, on account of some unforeseen circumstances, to have a more specific power of attorney and authority made than is herein expressed, with the same power and validity and to the same legal effect, as if I myself were personally present and had done such or let it be done and delivered; with full power to substitute one or more Attorneys among them or to revoke such substitution again if he thinks best. Then everything that my said Attorney or any person or persons substituted by him in the afore-mentioned business by virtue of this Letter of Attorney legally does or causes to be done and delivered, after this at all times when such is demanded, I approve, and support him and all men who will believe him and act with him in good faith on the basis of this Letter of Attorney, and bind myself herewith in the best legal form to indemnify him completely.

*WITNESS MY HAND SEAL;* done the 17th day of November in the Year of Our Lord One Thousand Seven Hundred and Sixty-eight, in the ninth year of the Reign of His Royal Majesty, George III of Great Britain, France, and Ireland, Defender of the Faith, etc.

(L. S.) CHRISTIAN ERNST BESCHLER

Sealed and delivered
in our presence:
*Henrig Kurtz*
*Vallentin Geiger*

(L.S.) Today, the 17th day of November *Anno Domini* 1768, appeared before me, *Peter Miller,* Royal British *Notarius et Tabularius Publicus* resident in the City of Philadelphia and Province of Pennsylvania, the said *Christian Ernst Beschler* and named the said *Michael Hotz* as his Mandatory, and at once requested me to draw up this Letter of Attorney, and, after I had drawn it up, he signed and sealed the same and delivered it in accordance with English usage. There also appeared with him before me *Henrich Kurtz* and *Valentin Geiger* and subscribed themselves as witnesses: Such have I by virtue of my personal signature attested and authenticated with the Seal of my office on the day and year above given.

PETER MILLER
Royal British *Notarius et Tabularius Publicus.*

* * * *

How to pay over the inheritance was the cause of much pondering. *Platz,* the Director of the Mint, is called into council — he was ready to make over the sum to Pennsylvania through a Letter of Credit drawn on London, and wanted then to deliver a certificate of receipt into the hands of *Beschler's* brother in Wertheim. The money could also be paid in London, so that then "as much of it as remained after deduction of the exchange costs, would be paid over to *Beschler* in Pennsylvania with reimbursement for postage and commission incurred anywhere." Should misfortune arise on the ocean, so that either the letter of credit or the money was lost, then he can take no risk upon himself. The legal judgment is given that "we prefer all the more the exchange through Director of the Mint *Platz,* since *Beschler* in America cannot use the types of money in use here anyway." The County Coregency, however, is of the opinion that the attorney can undertake the exchange with less expense, and in this manner it was then carried out.

## DOWN RIVER TO HOLLAND

The journey from Wertheim to Rotterdam was as a rule made by water. It must not, however, be imagined that one simply got aboard ship and went merrily down the valley. There were more than forty toll-stations to be passed; everywhere there was a delay, many times intentionally, in order to force the people to stay overnight and shell out their money. And when finally, after three or four weeks, the poor devils arrived in Rotterdam, the little money they had with them was already gone. Or they were forced to wait so long in Rotterdam that the people had quite reached the end of their cash and were ready to risk the journey across the wide ocean under any conditions. The trip to Rotterdam in 1754 cost, for every person over fourteen years of age, eight florins and 30 kreuzer; for every person under fourteen years, four florins and 15 kreuzer; for every person under four years, nothing.[18]

An amusing incident, though not amusing to those involved in it, happened in 1773 in Frankfurt. On May 8, there came to Wertheim an announcement from the junior Burgomaster, along with the Municipal Council, of the Free City, that there had yesterday arrived by ship many emigrants from Wertheim bound for America. These had asked entrance into the City, in order to buy bread. He had demanded passes of them, and forbade the continuance of their journey. The boatmen "who had come here with a boatload of colonists," stated that the people had embarked partly at Urfar, partly at Wertheim — altogether eight households and some single women, four households from Urfar, three from Lindelbach, and two from Nassig, among whom were three single women from Nassig. He was to sail them to Frankfurt or Höchst, where they wanted to make further agreements with a boatman from Mainz. The destination of their journey is Pennsylvania. They are all quite poor people, who could not support themselves in their homeland. He is ordered to take the people and their baggage back at once, and have them disembark again at Wertheim. One sergeant and six men to accompany the ship to the High Bridge.[19]

The Wertheim Government received from Frankfurt the following letter:

> Nobly born, Best and Learned, Especially Highly- and Much-Honored Sirs!
>
> Today, through the boatman there, *Johann Jacob Kress,* divers subjects of the principality of Löwenstein-Wertheim arrived here. They are authorized with certificates of manumission, and want to continue their journey to America. These emigrants would indeed not have been molested by us, had not your now reigning Imperial Majesty,—through the public Decree issued for the Empire in the year 1768, a copy of which follows, conformable to the older laws of the Em-

---

[18] *Rosenberg Archive, "Peinliche Sachen,"* Fasc. 57.

[19] *Frankfurt City Archive,* Ugb. A. 9, Nr. 4. On this case, see also Marion Dexter Learned, *Guide to the Manuscript Materials Relating to American History in the German State Archives.* (Washington, D. C.: The Carnegie Institution of Washington, 1912), pp. 310-311. (D. Y.)

> pire, which Decree cannot be unknown to Our Highly and Much Honored Lords—expressly forbidden the departure of imperial subjects outside Germany. Therefore we have no other alternative than to send back the said boatman straightway, with these people he has with him, and to direct him to return them to the country, each to the place where he took them on board. Etc.

The above Decree, much cited in contemporary literature, was printed by the Council of the City of Frankfurt. Emperor Joseph therein forbade emigration, because "through it the dear German Fatherland suffers a noticeable loss of many industrious people." The Imperial Cities and the seaports are strictly forbidden to assist emigration in any way. The sale of property with the prohibited emigration in mind is likewise forbidden. Agents, "seducers" and accomplices are to be punished with corporal and capital punishment; transports are to be sent back and all carriers on water and land are to be informed.

After a fourth of a year the Princely Government of Wertheim — obviously after thorough consideration — writes rather indignantly to the Council of the City of Frankfurt, that the edict in question was to be interpreted in quite another way. It was issued to favor the lords of the land, by hindering the secret departure of their subjects, so detrimental to their interests. In no case are the lords' hands tied, so that they are compelled against their will to keep undesirable people to burden their country. Also in the Decree reference is expressly made to the fact that proper facilitation should continue to be given to emigration. The Imperial City of Frankfurt is not placed as Attorney General over the Estates of the Empire, to remind them to carry out Imperial commands. One should be voluntarily devoted to doing satisfaction to one's obligations as an Estate of the Empire.

Two months later, on September 30, 1773, the Council of the Imperial City writes that it has

> learned with surprise that the Noble Lords President, Chancellor, Secret Court and Government Councilors at Wertheim have become irritated over our utterances, which were in accordance with the law of the Empire, and over the obedience we have shown them. In the most polite manner, the Council

rejects the idea that it wishes to arrogate to itself any sort of Attorney General's office, and still less, that it wanted to interpret the imperial decrees and to make them clear through reasoning. It kept itself solely to the letter of the Decree, according to which such emigrants were to be sent back. In case of a repetition, the affair must be reported to His Imperial Majesty; the Council will then inquire whether emigrations from the principality of Löwenstein-Wertheim are perhaps excepted from the general prohibition.

Now this was a very perplexing case. The Wertheim reviewer felt it best to put the document in the *Acta,* since perhaps the magistrate could not be shaken in his opinion. The emigrants could of course be told to avoid the City of Frankfurt in the future.

### PROVISIONS FOR THE OCEAN VOYAGE

It is not without interest to see what the emigrants took along on their lengthy journey. Mittelberger reports that he embarked at Heilbronn in May, 1750, and took seven weeks getting to Rotterdam. On October 10, he finally arrived in Philadelphia.

The emigrants generally were glad to leave their debts behind. *Thomas Diehm* of Kembach, for example, had as his chief creditor *"die Bonafatur,"* probably the widow of a merchant with the first name *Bonaventura.* Then comes the Jew *Schmul* of Homburg with a claim of 86 florins; the Jew *Fälcklein,* a Wertheimer, with 16 florins; the Jew *Stosel* of Wenkheim, with 25 florins; the Jew *Leyser* of Wenkheim, with 6 florins; the Jew *Zodick* of Wenkheim, with 5 florins; and finally *Itzig* of Bötigheim, with 8 florins. One likes to believe that the good *Diehm* could never have got on in the world with those creditors, and was glad to leave everything in the lurch and go to America.

Of *Philipp Hörner* or Vockenroth, who emigrated in 1786, we have a statement of his preparations for the journey:

| | *Florins* | *Kreuzer* |
|---|---|---|
| White cloth for shirts, for him, his wife and children | 40 | — |
| To a seamstress at Nassig, for making 17 shirts | 1 | 24 |
| For knitting 4 pairs of stockings | — | 50 |

| | | |
|---|---|---|
| To the stocking dealer *Christ,* for more stockings | 2 | — |
| To the clothmaker *Hammelmann,* for 9 yards blue cloth | 10 | 48 |
| To tailor *Wolzen,* for tailoring | 2 | 52 |
| To *Michel Haasen,* for buttons and buckles | — | 39 |
| To *Oesterlein,* for flannel | — | 24 |
| For mohair, buttons and thread | 3 | — |
| A hide (goatskin) for pants | 5 | — |
| One checkered casing for feather-bed | 5 | — |
| Shoemaker work | 8 | — |
| One new cap, 2 florins; one new hat, 1 florin 30 | 3 | 30 |
| One gun | 11 | — |
| One chest | 3 | — |
| One-fourth pail of brandy | 4 | 30 |
| Dried prunes | 3 | — |

Dried prunes and *"schnitz"* are almost always included, at any rate in large quantities according to the above expenditure. Most people also took a Bible along. But how often must it have happened, that their entire baggage was lost on the way, through treachery, theft or violence. The contemporary reports are filled with hair-raising accounts of this. Also the sanitary conditions on shipboard left much to be desired; it is said that only one-fourth of the passengers reached the other shore of the ocean alive.

### EMIGRANTS GOOD AND BAD

Along with this we must correctly portray the nature of the emigrants themselves. Only in a very few cases they were tall, sinewy forms. *Philipp Sührer* of Dietenhan (1752), for example, had for over two years, that is, since the great fire in Bettingen, had the misfortune of wandering about in madness, "from which he is not yet actually free. Besides this he has a lame wife, who is not in condition to manãge any work." *Johann Leonhard Flegler,* a burgher and shoemaker of Wertheim, feels himself in 1752 necessitated on account of deplorable conditions, to leave his fatherland with wife and child. He presents testimony of his poverty, and confesses that "my property is nothing, yes, nothing at all, except myself, as I am." *Adam Schreck* in Steinmark (1753) has worked formerly as a common cowherd, but cannot manage to devote himself any longer to this activity on account of his weak and deformed body, and is scarcely able here to keep himself from beggary.

*Philipp Jacob Oberdorf* of Dertingen (1753) had toward the last herded geese. Already for many years he has had a miserable time supporting himself and has not a kreuzer left. With God's help, he would like to go to America along with some charitable people. *Peter Behringer's* son in Hasloch (1754) had had the misfortune of serving a long imprisonment in Aschaffenburg and Mainz. *Johann Heinrich Ott* of Lindelbach in 1754 complains of hunger: "We have dear bread, when not a load of grain grows for us; the other folks are poor, too, and can give us nothing. Famine is need indeed!" He thanks the Government in advance: "May God be willing to bless Your Subjects, but especially may God be willing to bring dear Lindelbach again to peace and unity, so that blessing may again return to them." He has to leave everything behind, has not a loaf of bread. *Barbara Adelmann* of Höhfeld (1754) is to be released without fees, "in order that we may be rid of this worthless girl." She is poor as a beggar, and beside scandalous in living — "we should gladly be rid of such people." *Johann Adam Ries* of Höhfeld (1785) "belongs in a class of his own with regard to his behavior" — it was the common opinion that nothing would be lost by granting his request for emigration. *Flickert, Hörner,* and *Dosch,* all of Vockenroth (1786), are quite reduced in circumstances — they now want to seek their fortune in America. "*Dosch* is so constituted in his physical and moral circumstances, that the state loses nothing in his emigration."

Naturally more substantial elements appeared also. For instance, *Krank, Seidner,* and *Roos* of Hasselberg (1752). Although poor, they were "young single fellows, who want to offer themselves for menial work in Pennsylvania." *Johann Philipp Weiss,* the tailor, (1753), was driven by need, to solicit his bread elsewhere with God's help, because "as a young man I made up my mind to behave like an honest man." He had no other alternative than to turn his back on his fatherland and put up as a stranger among strangers. *Peter Albert* of Höhfeld went to America seven years ago (1777) with the Hanau Rifle Corps. Meanwhile his wife received four florins every month from his pay. On his return, he sees that he cannot make a go of supporting himself as a cobbler in Höhfeld any more than he could before. Now he wants to go over again with his wife and children. He has seen that he can get ahead better there with his trade.

Artisans were actually sought as colonists. Among our emigrants there are not many, but nevertheless some twenty, among them blacksmiths, a baker, cooper, gunsmith, button-maker, butcher, tanner, saddler, a tailor, cabinet-maker, shoemaker, cartwright, and weaver. And who can say whether *Freudenberger,* the bass-fiddler, was not just as necessary?

### THE COUNTS PROHIBIT EMIGRATION

The Wertheim Government took many pains to restrain its people from rash emigration. On this matter a series of directives were issued. The first came in 1752 — a written order sent out to all the Village Mayors of the County, which reads as follows:

> You are herewith commanded to collect the money realized from the sold properties of the subjects from this County who are departing for New England, and to take from it most expeditiously the outstanding governmental taxes and other indebtedness in vassalage, handwork, and supplemental tax. Secondly, you shall by document satisfy such creditors, who have the customary settlement with their debtors, and the admitted correctness on the part of the latter in their possession. Thirdly, you shall not permit one or the other to depart with the secret sale of his goods and other property to the detriment of the interests of the Coregents and the emigrant's creditors. Fourthly, you shall entirely forbid those young fellows who are considering emigrating there, their free departure without manumission. According to which, etc.

Cause was given for this edict in the complaint of the Village Mayor of Lindelbach over the emigration of so many citizens of the locality, who were selling everything — farms, cattle, and household goods — and letting their fields lie untilled. Since divers ones are heavily indebted, the proceeds from the sale of their lands are to be paid to the Village Mayor. He further inquires whether the single young men are permitted to depart without manumission.

To the parishes there was sent the following decree, which was to be read from the pulpits:

> Since not only this past Spring many subjects . . . let themselves be talked into going to America, through soul-sellers roaming about the country, out of credulity and misrepresentation of its great advantages, but also at the present time . . . other subjects are said to be willing to journey thither, the Noble Government, after the arrest and exile of two such soul-sellers, at whose trial vain falsehoods and trickeries came to light, have, out of their praiseworthy fatherly care for all of their subjects, resolved to issue a warning, namely, that from credible reports it is proved that
>
> (1) The journey is so dangerous and tedious, that of the people, especially the aged or the children, scarcely 20% are able to endure the difficulties of the same, besides the bad and unaccustomed board and water, but the majority are buried in the deep sea, and their little property passes to these soul-sellers, who ply their trade industriously on the sea.
>
> (3) Those with little or no property — since this soon dwindles in the face of the lengthy and costly journey and board — who have the good fortune to endure the evil seasickness besides all other hardships, must then put up wtih being sold as wretched slaves, to earn the money for their costly passage, board, and enlistment money, so that
>
> (3) Parents and children, man and wife, have to travel many miles from each other in service, and indeed often never see, much less speak with each other again their whole life long, besides
>
> (4) The country is not nearly so good, but wretched and a desert . . . and property very high in price.
>
> (5) Public worship is in the most unfortunate state because the majority have no religion at all, but as they say, want to "be Pennsylvania." Etc.
>
> Follow this warning for the welfare of yourselves and your poor, innocent children!

On February 12, 1753, emigration was forbidden with a ten taler fine, and the supplemental tax was raised to 20%. On May 23, Prince *Carl* of Löwenstein issued the following printed decree, which was then a month later adopted *in toto* by the governments on both sides:

The Most Illustrious Prince and Lord,
*Carl,* reigning Prince of the Holy Roman Empire
in Löwenstein-Wertheim, etc. etc.

We, the Authorized Privy Court and Governmental Councilors in your Government.

According to experience, seeing that divers of our subjects are talked into going from here to America, through all sorts of avaricious people traveling about the land, through false and fictitious representations of the great advantages of America, in which solicitation nothing but criminal treachery and slave-trading prevails, as the Government of the Electorate of Hannover itself make known through the following Order, in which warning we can put all the more faith since they are English colonies to which the poor people are being led away, and the Government of the Electorate of Hannover must have the best information on their King's intentions and arrangements:

Our, etc. etc. "We hear that in divers places of this country people, some of whom still have something in property, are letting themselves be talked into going to America, and that in order to influence them thereto, unknown people are going about the country, spreading printed reports which serve their purpose. Although to be sure His Royal Majesty, our Most Gracious Lord, does not regard as vassals those subjects, entrusted to him by God, who are not vassals, and therefore does not deprive any such of their natural freedom, His Highness can, however, on the one hand, not permit His subjects to be seduced from allegiance, or allow them to run out of the country without reasonable causes and authorization. On the other hand, there are connected with this disorder of emigration conditions of such a kind as to necessitate us, on account of His Most Respectful Royal Majesty, for the best interests of those who further let themselves be induced to emigrate in a rash and frivolous manner, to issue this order. As far as the agents or emissaries are concerned, even if they were sent out by the officials or directors of one or another of the English colonies, to seek colonists, they are by no means thereby authorized and warranted to set up agencies in foreign lands without the permission of the government of the country. Moreover, they so sorely lack the proper credentials, that it is reliably known that the English Government and the Directory of Colonial Affairs neither wish for nor provide the transport of new colonists, nor have any part in the dealings of the said emissaries. Then, too, none of these agents were authorized by the Government here, and only one appeared, *Samuel Schröder* by name, who on inquiry into his credentials at once disappeared from sight. So from all this it is possible to gather that very probably on the part of these people, criminal deception and slave-dealing was intended.

"Likewise therefore, we must well and extensively consider in what danger and misery those who let themselves be persuaded by them, place themselves. Therefore you must make this known to the subjects of your district in all possible ways. You must warn and dissuade those who let the lust for emigration take possession of themselves, but favor those, either through passes or in other ways, who are otherwise in circumstances in which permission to emigrate cannot be denied them. But those who stand in any other relation, on account of which they can properly be hindered from emigration, retain by force if necessary.

Hannover, May 1, 1753.

Royal British Councilors,
Authorized for the Government of the
Electorate of Braunschweig-Lüneburg.
G. H. VONMUENCHHAUSEN

Hence we do not only want, in the name of Our Most Gracious Lord, His Princely Majesty, and by virtue of the same herewith to warn all of our subjects from such undertakings, but also we command all officials on this side, Village Mayors and persons connected with Courts, to do the same at every opportunity, with the express addition that through the rigorous use of force they not only restrain expressly from such emigration those who, with some sort of vassalage, are subject to You, Our Most Gracious Prince and Lord's Princely Majesty, but also not to render aid, either through passes or any other way, to anyone, even though vassalage be not attached to him, in making such unconsidered departure; and we shall no less sharply resent it if anyone, by virtue of the offices entrusted to him, attempt to enlist, people to this end. Nor shall a stranger be permitted to put up here with this intention, and the reasons therefore shall, after the arrest of such person has taken place, at once be dutifully announced to this office.

Signed, WERTHEIM, May 23, 1753.[20]

[20]*Rosenberg Archive*, Br. 417.

In the following year, through the order given below, urgent warning was again given against emigration, and emigrating generally forbidden, indeed with the remarkable result that thereupon the emigration from the County so to speak reached its end. The order reads as follows:

*Order of May 20, 1754*

Since daily experience shows that the subjects in this County, despite the well-publicized warnings and dissuasions, under date of October 16, 1752, March 26 and June 23, 1753, springing from the patriarchal solicitude of the rulers, have not let themselves be stopped from emigration; since this frivolous emigration itch [*pruritus emigrandi*] shows itself even among divers well-to-do inhabitants, not without our displeasure, and the abuse is thereby noticed, that not only do such departing persons sell their goods before announcing their emigration, the quicker to bring about, and even to compel, their manumission — but even the Village Mayors do not announce the departure of such persons until after the sale of goods actually has taken place; and since this disorder, amounting to a public disgrace, and to the disadvantage of the High Coregencies, is no longer to be pardoned:

Therefore not only is each and every subject of this County once again warned — not, as happened formerly, to insolently despise the faithful warnings already made so often for their own welfare and that of their innocent children, and in the best interests of the government, and to surrender themselves to those avaricious and deceitful agents and slave-traders to their great hardship, and thus to plunge themselves into an eternal and bitter servitude — but it is herewith generally ordered and made known, that in the future, from the date of this order on, emigration is permitted to no subject vassal, except in quite unusual cases (which move the High Governments of the County to a dispensation), nor shall any subject be allowed to sell his property for the purpose of emigrating, until he has declared before the dual governments the status of his property and debts, on certificate of the Village Mayors and Court of every locality. In such unusual cases, he shall at once receive directly from the dual high governments, the consent to sell his property, as well as manumission. The City Council, Village Mayors, and Courts are, however, earnestly admonished not to allow any burgher and subject to sell his goods, but to announce such intention before the dual governments, and to wait for further decisions. In favorable cases the governmental officials permitting such lapses are without exception to be held repsonsible for the governmental taxes as well as for the debts contracted by the emigrants, and furthermore are to be punished with a governmental penalty.

In case, however, the desired manumission and permission to emigrate are attained directly from the High Governments through a special dispensation, in the face of the above General Prohibition, and the sale of their property is approved, City Council or Village Mayors and Courts are to collect the purchase-shilling, and with it satisfy the governmental officers and other creditors, and faithfully to hand over the remainder to the emigrants, after previous reckoning of the sale money, in return for a receipt. Which therefore everyone is to respect obediently and guard against offenses.

Signed: WERTHEIM, May 20, 1754
From the Dual Governments of Löwenstein-Wertheim.[21]

How very much the emigration was a result of able solicitation, appears best from the numbers which left in various years. Between 1694 and 1749, only five requests for emigration were presented; there followed then: 1750: *6* requests; 1751: *6*; 1752: *85*; 1753: *56*; 1754: *49*; 1755: *4*; 1756-1759: *none*; 1760-1765: *11*; 1766: *11*; 1768-1772: *7*; 1773: *17*; 1774-1779: *10*; 1784: *1*; 1785: *9*; 1786: *7*; 1787-1815: *11*; 1831: *5*; 1832: *15*; 1833: *7*; 1834: *10*; 1836: *8*; 1837: *12*; 1840: *18*.

Even upon a critical approach one finds in the Löwenstein-Wertheim lands no facts leading to the conclusion that the subjects were oppressed and plundered in the intolerable manner authentically reported of the Palatinate, Baden-Durlach, Württemberg, etc. Emigration here had another cause: it was introduced from without by agents.

And so we do not begrudge our contemporaries, that they can move about much more freely and are no longer loaded with ancient customs and burdens. Yet it seems almost like a fabulous tale to us, that there was once a time when every industrious man could find work. Whether our contemporaries are better off with today's tax system, than under the ancient and multiplex taxes of

[21]*Rosenberg Archive,* Br. 417.

the eighteenth century, is a question which our emigrants can no longer answer. And perhaps the golden age will never come again in which the motto has meaning:

*Der Herrschaft den Kopf—*
*Und dem Untertan das Huhn in den Topf!*

---

## NOTE ON THE EDITING

The original German edition of the Langguth List of Wertheimer Emigrants to Colonial America included 250 names; from various sources this list has been enlarged by the American Editor to a totol of 272, through the addition of the following names: *Georg Becker, Barbara Buch, Lorenz Joseph Dennscherz, Nicolaus Detter, Zacharias Endress, Michael Fertig, Regina Fertig, Zacharias Flegler,* [———] *Geiger, Johann Sebastian Hammeter, Anna Elisabetha Heust, Maria Barbara Horn, Johann Adam Kranck, Rosina Kremser, Johann Leonhard Reutlinger, Anna Catharina Schaaf, Leonhard Schoenlein, Anna Catharina Seibert, Anna Catharina Seidner, Johann Wilhelm Strobel,* and *Johann Georg Wild.*

As in the case of the Gerber Lists of Württemberger Emigrants, the American Editor's task has been that of collating the emigrants' names with certain basic Pennsylvania source materials. Of the emigrants, 145 have been more or less positively identified as to date of emigration, in Ralph Beaver Strassburger and William John Hinke, *Pennsylvania German Pioneers,* 3 volumes (Norristown, Pennsylvania: The Pennsylvania German Society, 1934), cited in abbreviated form as "Hinke." The abbreviations "P G S" and "G S P" refer to the Pennsylvania German Society and the Genealogical Society of Pennsylvania respectively. Over 110 of the emigrants have been identified, as to place of settlement, in various Pennsylvania church and cemetery records, or in the Provincial Tax Lists in the Third Series of the *Pennsylvania Archives,* cited as "3PA." It should, however, be pointed out that, as was the case with the Gerber Lists, such identifications are in many cases conjectural, pending further proof.

Our readers who can identify an ancestor among these Wertheimers, and wish to have genealogical research done on their family backgraund in Germany, cannot do better than to write to

OTTO LANGGUTH
Kreuzwertheim-am-Main
Bavaria
American Zone of Germany

either directly, or through the American Editor, who is in constant touch with Dr. Langguth. Dr. Langguth has spent a lifetime of research in the civil and ecclesiastical archives of the Wertheim area, and since the parish registers have been miraculously preserved through two World Wars, he can in many cases trace families to the fifteenth and sixteenth centuries.

It should be pointed out that the frequent variations in the spelling of proper names in this emigrant list are not to be attributed to carelessness on the part of the typesetter or the proof reader, but rather to the zealous endeavors on the part of the American editor to denote the forms as they occurred both in the European and the American sources.

In conclusion, as with the Gerber Lists, the American Editor solicits, from genealogists who can identify ancestors in this List, any additional information about these our Emigrants from the County of Wertheim.

—D. Y.

---

ADELMANN, BARBARA — Höhfeld (1754)

May 19, 1752: single. His father, MARTIN ADELMANN, wants to allow not even able to pay for a petition for manumission. She is to be allowed to leave without fees, "that we may be rid of this worthless girl. She is as poor as a beggar, and dissolute besides. We should like to be rid of her."

ADELMANN, MICHEL — Sonderrieth (1752)

May 19, 1752: single. His father, MARTIN ADELMANN, wants to allow him to go to Pennsylvania. He has borrowed 30 florins for the journey and expenses. // HANS MICHAEL ADELMANN, Ship *Phoenix,* November 22, 1752 (Hinke I, 507), with other Wertheimers.

ADELMANN, [———] — Sonderrieth (1773)

July 5, 1773: SEBASTIAN ADELMANN'S daughter of Sonderrieth, now in New England, has fallen heir to a parental inheritance of 100 florins. From the money, 5 florins are to be collected for manumission and 20% supplemental tax, in case the money is taken out of the country.

ALBERT, CHRISTOF — Oberwittbach (1751)

According to the *Village Mayor's Report* for Oberwittbach (1751), CHRISTOF ALBERT has left for America with wife and children. // CHRISTOF ALBERT, Ship *Duke of Bedford,* September 14, 1751 (Hinke, I, 458), with other Wertheimers. Note also CHRIST-[OPHE]R ALBERT, aged 69, Ship *Patsey Rutledge,* May 23, 1787 (Hinke, III, 23).

ALBERT, LORENZ — Michelrieth (1754)

May 13, 1754: a cartwright, wants to leave the country with wife and children, because his trade does not support him, since every farmer nowadays makes his plow himself. "It is no impertinence or desire of mine, which drives me from the country, but poverty and my uneasiness over wife and child." Mentioned as emigrant also in the *Village Mayor's Report* for Michelrieth (1754): "LORENZ ALBERT, a cartwright, with his wife (HANS ADAM WOLF is his his brother-[father-] in-law)." With them "KUNIGUNDA WOLF, his wife's single sister, likewise a daughter of HANS ADAM WOLF, went without property." In 1761 HANS ADAM WOLF *was* reported dead—"if the Newlanders [i.e., emigrants] come back, or write, his property is to be divided." LORENZ ALBERT is also referred to as an emigrant in the investigation against KIESECKER (q.v.), along with THOMAS ENDRES of Michelrieth. // LORENTZ ALBERTH, with JOHANNES ALBERTH and WILHELM ALBERT, and other Wertheimers, Ship *Phoenix,* October 1, 1754 (Hinke, I, 627ff.). LORENZ ALBERT settled in Huntington Township, York (now Adams) County, Pa., where he was a member of the Lower Bermudian Lutheran Church. For further data on the Alberts, see the Introduction, Appendix III.

## ALBERT, NICOLAUS — Altfeld (1754)

Mentioned in the examination of Kiesecker (q.v.), 1754, along with Michel Teuffel. Both were shepherds. // 3PA, XXIV, 629: Nicholas Albert, Town lot, Cumberland Co., Pa., surveyed 1764. JOHANN NICOLAUS ALBERT and wife Maria were parents of a son Johannes, who was baptized at the Lower Bermudian Union Church in Adams County, Pa., April 11, 1762, i.e., the church of which LORENZ ALBERT first appears as a communicant member in 1765.

## ALBERT, PETER — Höhfeld (1778)

March 6, 1785: from lack of livelihood he went to America with the Hanau Rifle Corps seven years ago, with the consent of his wife; meanwhile his wife has received 4 florins monthly from his pay. On his return, he realizes that unfortunately he cannot support himself as cobbler in Höhfeld any better than formerly. Now he wants to go across the ocean again with his wife and three children. During his seven year stay there he has seen that he can there get on in the world better with his trade. His particular expenditures for his coming journey were as follows:

| | | |
|---|---|---|
| To old *Langguth* in Wertheim, for a short tunic, coat, apron and accessories | 3 florins | 10 kreuzer |
| To the hatmaker *Fleiner,* for 1 hat | 1 florin | 36 kreuzer |
| For 3 yards blue cloth, 12 yards white linen, 16 yards of tow for shirts, striped cloth for apron and coat, and 1½ yards cotton cloth for a short tunic—all from *Philipp Becker* at Wertheim | 13 florins | 10 kreuzer |
| To the leather-worker *Johann Friedrich Garchan* for 3 pairs of sheepskin pants | 6 florins | 10 kreuzer |
| To *Rasp,* the tinner, for tin plates, pots, and cooking utensils | 1 florin | 30 kreuzer |
| To *Bartel Kappes,* cabinetmaker, for 2 chests | 3 florins | 30 kreuzer |
| From the sale of his property, he realizes | 269 florins | 4 kreuzer |
| His expenses and debts amount to | 227 florins | 26½ kreuzer |
| Balance remaining to him for the journey | 41 florins | 37½ kreuzer |

// There were several Peter Alberts in Pennsylvania in the 18th century. Among them were Peter Albert, turner, of Heidelberg Tp., Berks Co., Pa., 1768 (3PA, XVIII, 132), and of Heidelberg Tp., Lancaster Co., Pa., 1772 (3PA, XVII, 313). After 1778 two others appear — Peter Albert of Franklin County, Pa., *(United States Census of 1790 for Pennsylvania,* p. 120), and Peter Albert of Mahanoy Tp., Northumberland Co., Pa., whose will, made 1794 and probated 1799, mentions a wife Anna Regina *("Abstracts of Wills and Administrations of Northumberland County," GSP Proceedings,* XIV, 248). Identification is impossible without further information.

## ARBOURT, CHRISTOPH — Kreuzwertheim (1785)

June 22, 1791: went to Philadelphia some years ago, where he was married to Maria Magdalena Schaefer from Holterbach in the Breuberg region. His father, Conrad Arbourt, meanwhile died and left an estate of 20 florins. In a letter of April 14, 1791, the absent son renounces in favor of his two sisters, since he had taken with him 20 florins for traveling expenses. // CHRISTOPHER ARBORT, Ship *Favourite*, September 5, 1785 (Hinke, III, 8, with other Wertheimers. ANDREAS ARBURTH, who in 1759, was married to ANNA MARGRETHA FRIEDLER, at St. Michaelis and Zion Lutheran Church, Philadelphia, in the presence of HENRICH MUNNICH [of Wertheim], THOMAS LUTZ [of Kreuzwertheim], ANDREAS OBERDORFF and SIMON OBERDORFF [also bearing Wertheim names], (*PGS Proceedings,* XIV, 87) was also very probably a Wertheimer.

## BAUER, BERNHARD — Niclashausen (1752)

May 15, 1752: wants to leave for New England with his wife and 6 children, for the same reasons as JOHANN GEORG DRACH's widow (q.v.). Confirmed in the *Village Mayor's Report:* "BERNHARD BAUER, with wife and children." // JOHANN BERNHARD BAUER, Ship *President,* September 27, 1752 (Hinke, I, 490), with HANNS BAUER.

## BAUER, [———] — Vockenroth (1773)

April 26, 1773: widow of GEORG BAUER, small farmer in Vockenroth. "Oppressed by poverty and almost intolerable misery, in these times of famine and scarcity, she wants to seek abroad, with her son, who is named MICHAEL SCHLESSMANN, the bit of bread necessary for her miserable and — God have mercy on her! — wretched life." Was allowed to leave without the usual fees. She has sold her "house" for 15 florins.

## BAEUSCHLEIN, ANDREAS — Dietenhan (1754)

May 10, 1754: wants to go to America with wife and 1 child; is afraid of becoming a beggar, has only 47 florins left. Has made arrangements with the boatman SELIG for passage to Rotterdam (cf. the investigation of KIESECKER). Mentioned also as emigrant in the *Village Mayor's Report* for Dietenhan (1754): "ANDREAS BEUSCHLEIN and wife." // ANDRES BEUSCHLEIN, Ship *Patience,* September 19, 1749 (Hinke, I, 409), with other Wertheimers. ANDREAS BEUSCHLEIN, Ship *Phoenix,* October 1, 1754 (Hinke, I, 627ff), with other Wertheimers. Since nothing is mentioned in the Wertheim Archives of his having visited the New World previously, the emigrant of 1749 is doubtless another Wertheimer of the same name. If they are different persons, one of them settled in Robeson Tp., Berks Co., Pa., where he is listed in the *Tax Lists* of 1768 and 1781 (3PA, XVIII, 150, 518, 658). In *Will Book* B, p. 67, Berks Co. Courthouse, Reading, is recorded the will of this ANDREW BEISCHLEIN, made 1782 and probated 1783. In it he makes his wife, MARGARET, executrix, and mentions his eldest son MICHAEL BEISCHLEIN. Witnesses were HENRY TREAT and CONRAD MOHR.

## BAEUSCHLEIN, CASPAR — Dietenhan (1752)

May 12, 1752: wants to go to Pennsylvania with wife and 2 children. "The direst need drives me to do it, since there is at the present time no work for daylaborers." Still has 42 florins, which will be spent entirely on his journey. Mentioned also as emigrant in the *Village Mayor's Report* for Dietenhan (1752): "CASPAR BEUSCHLEIN and wife." // CASPER BEUSCHLEIN, Ship *Phoenix,* November 2, 1752 (Hinke, I, 503), with other Wertheimers. He settled in Haycock Tp., Bucks Co., Pa., where as CASPER BISHLINE, he appears in the *Tax Lists* for 1785 and 1787 (3PA, XIII, 557, 797). CASPAR BEUSCHLEIN and wife EVA were parents of a child baptized 1755, by the Lutheran minister of Tohickon Union Church, Bedminster Tp., Bucks Co., Pa. (*PGS Proceedings*, XXXI, 361).

BECK, HANS MICHEL — Sachsenhausen (1752)

May 16, 1752; single, wants to go to Pennsylvania, but his father will not give him a kreuzer to take along. According to the *Village Mayor's Report* for Sachsenhausen (1750-1761): "JACOB BECK's son is not yet manumitted, and still has his inheritance to seek." // HANS MICH*A*L BECK, Ship *Phoenix*, November 2, 1752 (Hinke, I, 502), with other Wertheimers. Several listed in 3PA.

BECK, JOHANNES — Kredenbach (1754)

May 13, 1754: a young fellow 16-17 years old, wants to go to Pennsylvania, but his mother can give him nothing to take along. May 25, 1754: same report. According to the *Village Mayor's Report* for Kredenbach (1754), he left without manumission and without money. On April 16, 1762, it was reported that ANDREAS BECK of Kredenbach has children in America. // JOHANNES BECK, Ship *Phoenix*, October 1, 1754 (Hinke, I, 627ff.), with other Wertheimers. Several listed in 3PA.

BECKER, GEORG — Löwenstein (*ante* 1759)

Added by the American editor. The Historical Society of York County has located, in the Records of the Canadochly Union Church, York County, Pa., the marriage record of CHRISTINA IMENHAEUSSER, on January 28, 1759, to "GEORG BECKER, a single man from Löwenstein."

BEHRINGER, PETER — Hasloch (1754)

May 16, 1754: wants to go with wife and 2 children to Pennsylvania. Has fallen into poverty and is loaded with debts. He does not know how to support himself honestly here. His son suffered an unhappy lot, in being held so long under arrest in Aschaffenburg and Mainz. PETER BEHRINGER has borrowed about 100 *thaler* in Hasloch and paid them out for his son. Finally he had to sell his farm and possessions, to pay his debts. In order not to be forced to go begging, he wants to emigrate, since his son may not remain in the country or let himself be seen there any longer anyhow. The Village Mayor's advice was as follows: BEHRINGER has at most, 5 florins. We should let him go, if only to rid our village of this miscreant. Resolved, that he shall pay 5 florins for his manumission! — But perhaps he got away gratis, for in the *Freudenberg Governmental Protocol*, May 16, 1754, it is reported: has scarcely 10 *thaler* remaining. Manumission should be offered this dangerous man, who has caused so much annoyance for the Electorate of Mainz, and has little or nothing in property, in order to get him out of the country. Cf. the examination of KIESECKER. The *Village Mayor's Report* for Hasloch (1750-1761) mentions him as emigrant also: "PETER BERINGER, with wife and children." // PETER BERRINGER, Ship *Phoenix*, October 1, 1754 (Hinke, I, 627ff.), with other Wertheimers.

BESCHLER, CHRISTIAN ERNST — Wertheim (1764)

March 2, 1769: son of the deceased burgher BALTASAR BESCHLER, and brother of the princely mason BESCHLER in this place. He is now resident at *"Bockhill"* in the County of *"Buchs"* in the Province of

Pennsylvania in North America. He wants to have his parental fortune taken hence to America through MICHAEL HOTZ, Master Butcher and resident of the City of Philadelphia, in the said Province. The administrators, HEINRICH FRIEDRICH OBERDORF and MICHAEL KRESS, ask for permission to hand over the property. The desire of the attorney, MICHAEL HOTZ, who has come hither, shall be granted after deduction of manumission fees and examination of his administrators' accounts. On April 3, the City Bailiff certified the examination of the accounts of CHRISTIAN ERNST BESCHLER, who had settled as resident and schoolmaster in Pennsylvania, to the amount of 625 florins, 27 kreuzer, 3 pfennig. On April 6, the certificate of manumission was issued. On April 11 his brother BESCHLER offered objections to letting HOTZ take the money along, since the latter, although born here, was now living in Philadelphia, and therefore could furnish no security. Something could happen to him on the return trip — then his brother would come into his property. For the rest, see the Introduction. The manumission cost 31 florins, 30 kreuzer. According to the *Burgomaster's Report* of 1768-1769, the Administrator OBERDORF paid as supplemental tax for Schoolmaster BESCHLER who was said to be in America, 20% of the administrator's property of 575 florins, or 115 florins. For the text of the Letter of Attorney, see "Letters from the New Land," in the *Introduction.* // CHRISTIAN ERNST BESCHLER, Ship *Polly,* October 13, 1764 (Hinke, I, 690). The name BESCHLER is uncommon in Pennsylvania. One of the few areas in which it is found is the Mahanoy area of Northumberland County, where one CHRISTIAN BESHLER appears, *circa* 1800, as the witness to the Will of ADAM KEMPEL of Mahanoy Tp. (*GSP, Proceedings* XIV, 250); one HENRY BESHLER was witness to the will of MARTIN KERSTETTER, miller, of Mahanoy Township, in 1798 (*Ibid., XIV,* 159). It is possible therefore that our schoolmaster BESCHLER ended his days in this area, where "a man named BESLER" is said to have taught the first German school in the Mahantango Valley, evidently in the 1790's.

## BETZ, JOHANNES — Lindelbach (1752)

May 12, 1752: belongs to the nine heads of families who together with their 30 children at the same time left everything in the lurch and departed, taking along in all thirty children. They had not even a loaf of bread in their possession, because they could not sell their property and had to leave it behind for their creditors. Were compelled "out of no desire of their own, to seize upon this hard resolution, and like others to go to the so-called New World." Cf. OTT, of Lindelbach, in the List of Emigrants. In the *Freudenberg Governmental Protocol,* March 9, 1753, the Village Mayor of Lindelbach asks to be relieved of the overseeing of the property of the emigrants, left behind and still unsold, on account of his bodily weakness. The substitutes appointed by him, on March 19 excuse themselves saying that they have work enough of their own, and cannot till the abandoned properties besides; also, they find no one who wants to do the necessary work. Betz has four children. // Several other BETZES listed in Hinke.

## BICKH, HANS MARX (MARCUS) — Dertingen (1750)

"HANS MARX BICKH" emigrated in 1750, according to the *Village Mayor's Report,* for Dertingen (1750). // JOHAN MARCUS BECK, Ship *Duke of Bedford,* September 14, 1751 (Hinke, I, 459), with other Wertheimers. One JOHANN MARCUS BECK and wife ANNA ELIZABETH were parents of a child baptized 1753 at Trinity Lutheran Church, Reading, Pa. (*Notes and Queries,* I [1883], p. 104).

## BORGER, HANS MICHEL — Vockenroth (1752)

May 18, 1752: wants to go with wife and 2 children to Pennsylvania. Has only 40 florins left from the sale of his goods, because he had many debts. Mentioned as emigrant also in the *Village Mayor's Report* for Vockenroth (1750-1761): "HANS MICHEL BURGER, with wife and children. BURGER fell heir to property some weeks ago in Grünewörth." // JOHAN[NE]S MICHEL BUERGER, Ship *Phoenix*, November 2, 1752, (Hinke, I, 501), with other Wertheimers. Several listed in 3PA: MICHAEL BORGER, laborer, Heidelberg Tp., Berks Co., Pa., 1768 (3PA, XVIII, 132); and Newberry Tp., York Co., Pa., 1779 (3PA, XXI, 28).

## BORGER, JOHANN NICOLAUS (1) — Nassig (1753)

May 11, 1753: wants to go to New England. Gives Pennsylvania as his destination of emigration with his wife, his poor mother and 3 children. Still has 97 florins. Is to pay 11 florins, 52 kreuzer. Mentioned as emigrant also in the *Village Mayor's Report* for Nassig (1753): "NICOLAUS BURGER, with wife, child, and mother." // JOHANNES NICHOLAS BURGER (BOERGER), aged 33, Ship *Halifax*, September 28, 1753 (Hinke, I, 560), with CHRISTOPHER GETZELMANN. Several NICHOLAS BURGERS in 3PA, including NICH[OLA]S BORGER, Chestnuthill Tp., Northampton Co., Pa., 1772 (3PA, XIX, 75).

## BORGER, JOHANN NICOLAUS (2) — Nassig (1753)

April 12, 1753: of Nassig, still under guardianship, wants to seek his fortune in New England, but does not want to sell his property; wants to take along only some money for the journey. "Because young BURGER has a considerable property and is scarcely 18 years old, one can hardly expect mature consideration on his part, so we should attempt in every way to dissuade him from his hasty decision, and retain him here." Request for emigration was denied.

## BREITENHERD, JOHANN CHRISTOPH — Wertheim (1753)

May 7, 1753: burgher and gunsmith. "Am obliged to leave my Fatherland with my wife and two small children, since I have lost my property in the three years since my marriage, in consequence of bad support and earnings, and do not know what other course to take. But because I am subject to Your Highness through vassalage, and without manumission therefrom, etc." He heard too late, that he must leave behind 20% of his property (*Freudenberg Archive,* "Emigrants of 1753.") Manumission cost him 8 florins, 4 kreuzer, and the supplemental tax, according to the *Burgomaster's Accounts,* amounted to 16 florins. In 1750 he had married in Wertheim the daughter of the gunsmith GROSS. He hailed from Siebeleben near Gotha, had learned his trade with PETER TANNER, Court Gunsmith in Gotha, had been in service in Potsdam, Magdeburg, Cassel and Darmstadt, in Schotten and Herzberg, and through Widow GROSS here in Wertheim, "had frequently the good fortune to present Your Excellencies the Counts some samples of the trade he has learned." (*Freudenberg Archive,* "Correspendence Received.") // JOHAN CHRISTOPH BREITENHERDT, Ship *Neptune,* September 24, 1753 (Hinke, I, 539ff.), with other Wertheimers. CHRISTOPH and DOROTHEA BREITENHEERT settled in Lancaster, Pa., where, in the Records of Trinity Lutheran Church (*PGS Proceedings,* IV, 217), their children's baptisms are listed. In 1773 CHRISTOF BREIDENHART had a "tavern" in Lancaster, in 1782 he is listed with a "shop" (3PA, XVII, 455, 753). Doubtless he was one of the makers of the famous Lancaster or "Kentucky" Rifles for which our Pennsylvania German gunsmiths were famous.

## BUCH, BARBARA — Wertheim (1751)

Added by the American editor. According to the "Register of Members and Their Children Belonging to the Moravian Congregation in Philadelphia, in 1776," *Notes and Queries,* Annual Volume for 1896, p. 214, BARBARA BUCH, born May, 1733, in Wertheim, Germany, who emigrated in 1751, settled in Pennsylvania, where, on June 10, 1755, she was married to JOHN TANNE[N]BERGER, a native of Zauchenthal, Moravia, who had come to Georgia in 1736, and to Pennsylvania in 1737.

## BUCH, PHILIPP — Wertheim (1753)

*Rosenberg Archive,* Br. 417, February 12, 1753: Extract from the Ducal Protocol. BUCH is the son of the boatman PETER BUCH of Wertheim, and went in 1752 to New England and returned a few weeks ago. He is to be regarded as a secret "soul-seller' along with the man from Urfar, whom he brought with him on his return. BUCH has already indirectly enticed very many burghers and subjects, to depart in the Spring. Both BUCH and the Urfar man should possibly be examined on oath as to whether they traveled with the emigrants to the place of their domicile, how they were cared for, what sort of reports they might otherwise have had, whether they were ordered to solicit, by whom they were appointed, and how much they received per head. On April 20 BUCH's father was ordered, at 20 thaler penalty, to produce his son, or to tell where he was staying, and meanwhile not to deliver anything to him. On May 12, 1753, it was reported that perhaps the elder BUCH should be punished, and he should be ordered, under doubled penalty, to produce his son. The young fellow is said to be staying nights outside the Eicheltor, in the dwelling of GEORG MUELLER, the boatman, but at other times he stays at Freudenberg. MUELLER's house is said to be visited at night. BUCH is said to have made an agreement with the boatman, that he should receive 1 florin from every emigrant. Captain-Lieutenant GROSS, the Commandant of the Circle Contingent, is charged to arrest BUCH, and receives permission to search suspect houses with his soldiers. The Wertheim boatmen, BALTASAR LOESCH, LEONHARD STEMMLER, and MICHAEL KRESS are on oath to render a report on their dealings with BUCH. On May 13 it was divulged that young BUCH was in Frankfurt and wanted to join the emigrants there. At any rate he remained unapprehended until the Spring of 1754. Of the further course of Buch's affairs, we have already spoken (cf. Introduction). Buch plied his trade also in the County of Sultzberg; there he wanted to solicit emigrants on the grounds of religious persecution, and promised them he would accompany them to America. The original *Acta* in this case were at the time unfortunately impounded, so that the original letters from America, which contained the main charges against Buch, are no longer to be found. One JOHANNES ICKES and one JACOB MUELLER, the latter from Eberstadt, who let themselves be used likewise as the same kind of agents, were sought out at the same time and brought to trial. // JOHANN PHILLIPP BUCH, Ship *Phoenix,* November 2, 1752 (Hinke, I, 503), with other Wertheimers. According to the Transcript of the "Record of the First Reformed Church, Philadelphia, Pennsylvania," in the William J. Hinke Collection, Historical Society of the Reformed Church, Lancaster, Pa., Vol. I, p. 186, JOHN PHILIP BUCH, from Wertheim, was married on October 21, 1753, to ELIZABETH SCHYNLIN, from Maperche, France. In the "Register of Members and Their Children Belonging to the Moravian Congregation in Philadelphia, in 1766," in *Notes and Queries,* Annual Volume for 1896, 212, the wife's maiden name is given as SCHEINLEIN, and her birthplace as Maynbirnheim [near Würzburg], Germany, where she was born January 19, 1718; she came to Pennsylvania in 1752, and is said to have married PHILIP BUCH in the same year.

## BUEHNER, NICOLAUS — Uettingen (1754)

Named as emigrating with his wife, in the investigation against KIESECKER (q.v.), 1754. // None of the name in Hinke.

## BUEHNER, THOMAS — Wertheim (1754)

Named with his wife as passengers of SELIG, in the Investigation against KIESECKER (q.v.), 1754.

## BUETTEL, BURKARD — Lindelbach (1752)

May 12, 1752: has 2 children, and is emigrating with BETZ (q.v.) and party. January 25, 1754: he still owes his manumission fees. He has gone to America.

## BUETTEL, CHRISTOPH — Dietenhan (1753)

Acording to the *Village Mayor's Report* for Dietenhan (1753), "CHRISTOF BUETTEL and wife" emigrated in 1753. // CHRISTOFF BUETTEL, Ship *Neptune,* September 24, 1753 (Hinke, I, 540ff.), with other Wertheimers.

## BUETTEL, HANS JOERG — Urfar (1752)

May 4, 1752: wants to go to New England with wife and 3 children. Has 326 florins. Since, with his wife and children, he is "related to His Princely Highness by vassalage," he asked to be released from it, which costs him 21 florins. Mentioned also as emigrant in the *Village Mayor's Report* for Urfar (1752): "HANS JOERG BUETTEL, with wife and 3 children." // HANS JOERG BUETTEL, with ANDREAS BUETTEL and other Wertheimers, Ship *Phoenix,* November 2, 1752 (Hinke, I, 502-503). One GEORGE BITTLE, single, appears in the *Tax List* for Germany Tp., York (now Adams) Co., Pa., for 1781 (3PA, XXI, p. 455); another among the Westmoreland County Rangers on the Frontiers, 1778-1783 (3PA, XXIII, p. 324).

## DAMM, HEINRICH — Hasselberg (1754)

May 16, 1754: wants to go to Pennsylvania with his wife, since he is unable to support himself honestly here. "Wants to see whether the Dear Lord will provide a little place elsewhere for him." Has 90 florins. According to the *Village Mayor's Report* for Hasselberg (1754), he is emigrating with his wife. He contracted for passage to Rotterdam with the boatman SELIG (cf. KIESECKER). // HENRICH DANN, Ship *Phoenix,* October 1, 1754, (Hinke, I, 627ff.), with other Wertheimers. Others of the name listed in 3PA.

## DENNSCHERZ, LORENZ JOSEPH — Michelrieth (1752)

Added by the American editor. His name appears, along with very many other Wertheimers, as passenger on the Ship *Phoenix,* November 2, 1752 (Hinke, I, 503). He was a son of Pastor DENNSCHERZ of Michelrieth, mentioned in connection with LORENZ ALBERT, in the

Introduction, Appendix III. If this emigrant settled in Pennsylvania, it was probably around Lebanon, where, in 1779, one ANNA MARGARETHA DAENSCHAEREZ of Heidelberg, was married to JOHANN FRIEDRICH STOEVER, of Lebanon, a son of Pastor JOHANN CASPAR STOEVER, who died the same year. ("Stoever Marriages," *Notes and Queries,* Annual Volume for 1896, p. 114). In 1762 he returned to Michelrieth to visit his aged father. He was a brother-in-law of JOHANN SEBASTIAN HAMMETER (q.v.).

## DETTER, NICOLAUS — Hirschlanden (1749)

Added by the American Editor. Acording to Edna Albert's Translation of the "Church Record of the Reformed and Lutheran Congregation at Lower Bermudian, Latimore Township, Adams County, Pennsylvania," NICOLAUS DETTER, who came to America in 1749 and settled in northeastern Adams County, was born December 20, 1712, at Hirschlanden in Franconia, son of MATTHEIS and MARGARETHA DETTER. His birth certificate, *Zeugniss ehrlicher Geburth, vor Nicolaus Dötter von Hirschlanden* is in the collection of the Historical Society of York County. It reads as follows:

IMMANUEL!
Nicolaus Dötter

Ist von christlichen und ehrlichen Eltern, aus einem reinen und keuschen Ehe-bett, erzeugt und gebohren d. 20ten *Novemb: Anni* 1712. Der Vater is gewesen Matthias Dötter, Einwohner und gemeinsmann allhier; die Mutter aber Margaretha. Die Stelle der gevatterschaft, wurde in der H. Tauff vertretten von dem ehrsamen Nicolaus Keller, Einwohner allhier. Welches auf begehren aus dem hiesigen Tauff-buch, treulich auszeichnen, und mit seinem Namen und Pettschaft bestättigen sollen.

Hirschlanden, d. 12. May, 1749

JOHANNES ANDREAS BULAEUS
Gemein herrschl. Löwenstein-Wertheim.

[Seal] Pfarr.

Perhaps he was a descendant of the MATTHES DOETTER who in 1607 was Village Mayor [Schultheiss] of Hirschlanden, OTTO LANGGUTH, *Die Grafschaft Wertheim,* Heft 4 of *Familiengeschichtlicher Wegweiser durch Stadt und Land,* ed. Dr. Friedrich Wecken (Leipzig: Verlag Degener & Co., Inh. Oswald Spohr, 1936), p. 19.
In 1737 he was married to ANNA CATHARINA BAUMANN, born 1705, daughter of MATTHEIS and MARGARETHA BAUMANN of Hirschlanden. NICOLAUS DOETTER is listed as a passenger on the Ship *Jacob,* October 2, 1749 (Hinke, I, 418), along with MATTIS and MARTIN DOETTER.

## DIEHM, ADAM — Wenkheim (1753)

May 4, 1753: wants to go to New England, with HOERNER, SEMEL, SEUBERT, and MECKELEIN (q.v.), "in return for a tolerable departure fee, because we are not vassals." See Steger, No. 206. They were all loaded with debts. It was resolved, to prepare for each a certificate of free departure and of good conduct, in return for the customary taxes, but according to the new regulation, a supplemental tax of 20% was to be collected. The Certificate reads as follows:

According to the most subservient announcement made by [-----] at Wenkheim to the Coregency of the County, seeing that [he] wanted to go to New England, and fittingly sought therefore for permission and bestowal of a certificate attesting his good conduct, there was found herein no objection to his departure. Therefore not only is the requested permission to depart herewith granted, but it is also certified for his better success abroad, that, the while he was resident at said Wenkheim, he was at all times devoted to an orderly behavior, and has observed the duties of a faithful subject.

In witness whereof, is herein printed the Great Seal of the Government.

[Signature]

// Five ADAM DIEHMS are listed in Hinke, one in 1749 with other Wertheimers (Hinke, I, 409), another in 1751 (Hinke, I, 474), another in 1753 (Hinke, I, 539), and ADAM and HANS ADAM DIEHM (q.v.), in 1754. At least five ADAM DIEMS or DEEMS are listed in 3PA: (1) ADAM DIEM, single; Rading Town, Berks Co., Pa., 1767, with THOMAS, ANDREW, PETER, and THOMAS DIEM (3PA, XVIII, 4, 9); (2) ADAM DIEM, Frederick Town, Derry Tp., Lancaster Co., Pa., 1772 (3PA, XVII, 203); (3) ADAM DEEM, Coventry Tp., Chester Co., 1771, (3PA, XI, 752); and (4), ADAM DEEM, Worcester Tp., Philadelphia Co., Pa., 1779 (3PA, XIV, 735). In addition, an ADAM DIEM had a son HENRIG DIEM, aged 14, and grown daughters confirmed at the New Hanover Lutheran Church in Montgomery Co., Pa., in 1764 (*PGS Proceedings, XX,* 357). Letters of Administration on the estate of ADAM DIHM, of Alsace Tp., Berks Co., were granted in 1781 to BARBARA DIHM, the widow ("Berks County Will Abstracts," GSP, I, 277).

## DIEHM, ANDREAS — Dietenhan (1753)

According to the *Village Mayor's Report* for Dietenhan (1753), "ANDREAS DIEHM and wife" are emigrating. // ANDREAS DIHM, Ship *Richard and Mary,* September 17, 1753 (Hinke, I, 531 ff.), with other Wertheimers. One ANDREW DIEM, single, appears in the Tax Lists of Reading Town, Berks Co., Pa., for 1767, with other Diehms (see ADAM DIEHM) (3PA, XVIII 4, 9).

## DIEHM, ANDREAS — Bettingen (1773)

May 22, 1773: a carpenter, wants to seek his fortune in another part of the world. Has 130 florins property.

## DIEHM, HANS ADAM — Schollbrunn (1754)

1754: made agreement with the boatman SELIG, to emigrate with wife and children (cf. KIESECKER). // HANS ADAM DIHM, Ship *Phoenix,* October 1, 1754 (Hinke, I, 627 ff.), with THOMAS and a second ADAM DIHM. For his possible residence in Pennsylvania, cf. ADAM DIEHM, above.

## DIEHM, JACOB — Dietenhan (1752)

March 16, 1756: went to Pennsylvania four years ago. He is not to be found in the *Acta*; is said to have left in secret on a woman's account. According to the *Village Mayor's Report* for Dietenhan (1754): "JACOB DIEHM, single, son of SIMON DIEHM, went away secretly. His father hopes he will come back soon." According to the *Freudenberg*

*Governmental Protocol*, May 4, 1752, he was charged by ELIZABETH HERMANN with fornication on February 3. JACOB'S father is SIMON DIEHM, who doubts his son's guilt. On May 28 the father further declared that he has not given his son, who went to New England against his will, any marriage portion, nor provided him with any clothes for the journey, nor given him any traveling expenses, and believed in this matter that he should not be required to make amends for his ill-behaved son. However, he is willing to compensate ELISABETH HERMANN of Kembach for the child begotten with her. // JACOB DEEM, West Pennsboro Tp., Cumberland Co., Pa., 1779 (3PA, *XX*, 235).

## DIEHM, JOHANN ADAM — Kembach (1753)

March 26, 1753: is Village Mayor, and on account of debts, wants to go to New England. Has over 400 florins debts and cannot satisfy his creditors with his property. The resolution made in his case was: "It cannot very well be denied a debtor, to depart emptyhanded from the country." // HANS ADAM DIEHM, Ship *Neptune*, September 24, 1753 (Hinke, I, 539 ff.), with other Wertheimers. For residence in Pennsylvania, see ADAM DIEHM, above.

## DIEHM, PETER — Kembach (1752)

May 18, 1752: wants to go to Pennsylvania with his wife and 4 children. Is permitted for the present to take 200 florins along. His holdings were sold for 3200 florins, no debts in evidence. Listed as emigrant in the *Village Mayor's Report* for Kembach (1753): "PETER DIEHM, with wife and children." // JOHANN PETER DIHM, Ship *Windsor*, September 27, 1753. (Hinke, I, 558). In 1758, letters of administration were given to GEORGE DIHM of Amity Tp., Berks Co., Pa., eldest son of PETER DIHM of Reading, in his father's estate (*"Berks County Will Abstracts,"* GSP, I, 28). Another PETER DIEM appears as cordwainer in Reading Town, 1767 (3PA, *XVIII*, 4), with other DIEMS (cf. ADAM DIEM, above). It was probably this PETER DIEHM, of Reading, who made his will in 1793, probated the same year, leaving legacies to his wife HANNAH MARTHA, eldest son WILLIAM, son JOHN, son FREDERICK, daughter CATHARINE, brother-in-law FREDERICK BOHN, executor; witnesses: JOHN GOODHART, GEORGE YOUNG (*Will Book* B, p. 315, Berks County Courthouse, Reading, Pa.). He had evidently made out well in America, for he mentions several town lots he owned in Reading.

## DIEHM, PETER — Urfar (1773)

March 4, 1773: widower, wants to go to New England. Has 130 florins property. Pays 10 florins for manumission, and 24 florins, 6 kreuzer for the supplemental tax of 20% on 120 florins and 30 kreuzer.

## DIEHM, THOMAS — Kembach (1752)

May 19, 1752: wants to go to Pennsylvania with his wife and 3 children, on account of poverty and debts, in the hope that "there he can find his livelihood and his portion of bread." Has sold all that he had in village and field, to THOMAS KRAFT of Buch-am-Ahorn, for 600 florins, and after payment of debts has left 132 florins and 3 kreuzer. Data on his creditors appears in the *Village Mayor's Report*. *Freudenberg Governmental Protocol*, July 1, 1754: the emigrated THOMAS DIEHM of Kembach has left a note behind, from which it is evident how much he was overcharged by both Christians and Jews in excessive taxes and the like, and even was brought to poverty through continuous executions against him. Mr. VACONIUS, the pastor of Dertingen, and the Homburg Jew for four years enforced payment from DIEHM through the agency of Dragoon WOLZ of Eichel, and he could not help himself otherwise than by selling some second mortgages, which were mortgaged elsewhere. Those concerned would have suffered no damage thereby, because there were still other mortgages at hand. According to the *Village Mayor's Report* for Kembach (1753), "HANS THOMAS DIEHM, with wife and children," were among the emigrants of 1753. In the *Village Mayor's Report* for 1755, there is again found a THOMAS DIEHM, who is also said to have gone into bankruptcy, and took nothing along to America; perhaps the two were identical. // From evidence in Hinke and 3PA, it seems more probable that the two THOMAS DIEHMS were not identical. For instance, HANS THOMAS DIHM came over on the Ship *Phoenix*, landing November 2, 1752, with other Wertheimers (Hinke, I, 502); THOMAS DIHM, with ADAM and HANS ADAM DIHM and other Wertheimers, arrived on the Ship *Phoenix*, October 1, 1754 (Hinke, I, 627 ff.). In addition to THOMAS DIEM, and THOMAS DIEM, single, of Reading, Berks Co., in 1767 (3PA, *XVIII*, pp. 4, 9), there were in Pennsylvania THOMAS DEEM of Mahoning Tp., Northumberland Co., Pa., 1778-1780 (3PA, *XIX*, 428); and THOMAS DIEME of Frederick Tp., Philadelphia Co., Pa., 1774 (3PA, *XIV*, 326). The last-mentioned was doubtless the THOMAS THIM (DIEM), member of the Lutheran Church at the Trappe, whose daughter SUSANNA DIEM married JOHAN ADAM STOCK in 1761 (*PGS Proceedings*, VII, 505).

## DILL, J[OHANN] C[ASPAR] — Wertheim

Emigrated to Pennsylvania, where he became a pastor. According to the *Album Lycei Wertheimensis*, he was a student in the Upper Class in 1777. // According to the *Documentary History of the Evangelical Lutheran Ministerium of Pennsylvania and Adjacent States, 1748-1821* (Philadelphia: General Council, 1898), pp. 238-9: "A candidate named DILL, who came here from Germany, applied for admission into the Ministerium" (1791). Despite a few minor accusations against him, "others from the region in which he lives spoke well of him, and as his credentials from Germany also are good," it was resolved that he be licensed for one year. The license was renewed each year until 1802, when he was ordained. At the time he was pastor of Whitehall, Jordan, and other congregations in Lehigh and Berks Counties. According to the *History of Jerusalem Lutheran and Reformed Church of Western Salisbury, Lehigh Co., Penna.* (Allentown: H. Ray Haas and Co., 1911), p. 38: JOHANN CASPAR DILL (1758-1824) served this large parish for twenty-three years, but went to Ohio in 1815 as missionary preacher, and died at Germantown, Ohio, in 1824.

## DILL, JOHANN MICHAEL — Windsheim (1754)

Listed among the emigrants solicited in 1754 for the boatman SELIG (cf. KIESECKER).

## DILL, MICHAEL — Glasofen (1754)

In the *Acta* on KIESECKER (1754): "A young single fellow named MICH[AEL] DILL, is emigrating from Glasofen." // MICHAEL DILL, East Pennsboro Tp., Cumberland Co., Pa., 1778 (3PA, *XX*, 32 ff.).

## DINKEL, MICHAEL — Kreuzwertheim (1752)

May 10, 1752: MICHAEL DINKEL and KACHEL of Dertingen, both formerly musketeers in the Honorable Circle Contingent here, want, in their needy circumstances, to go to New England with wives and children, since they are quite unable here to earn their necessary daily bread. They have served the government faithfully and well as soldiers for 13 years. May 17, 1752: wants to go with KUHN of Urfar, and with his family, to the "Island of Pennsylvania." Is allowed to go without the usual fees. In the case of BUCH (q.v.), the statements of the Musketeer DINKEL and one SCHNEIDER, found in the *Acta,* were to be presented to BUCH to see what excuse he might offer by way of defense. Evidently DINKEL belongs among the victims of the redemptioner trade. His letter is no longer at hand. // MICHAEL DINCKEL, Ship *Phoenix,* November 2, 1752 (Hinke, I, 503), with other Wertheimers. JOHANN MICHAEL DUENCKEL and wife ANNA ELISABETH, two years in America, were parents of a child baptized in 1754 at St. Michaelis and Zion Lutheran Church, Philadelphia, Pa. (*PGS Proceedings,* IX, 457). For this name, cf. also JOHANN PHILIPP WEISS, below.

## DINKEL, NICOLAUS — Kreuzwertheim (1785)

March 22, 1785: wants to go with wife and 4 children to America, since he is reduced almost to beggary to support himself. Still has 30 florins.

## DOSCH, ADAM — Vockenroth (1786)

January 5, 1786: wants to seek his fortune in America, with JOH[ANN] MICH[AEL] FLICKERT and PHILIPP HOERNER, all reduced in property. FLICKERT has a wife and 4 children, HOERNER a wife and 3 children, DOSCH a wife and 1 child. The government's decision was that DOSCH "is so constituted in his physical and moral makeup, that the state loses nothing in letting him emigrate; but the two others perhaps would have been able to keep on paying to the government their taxes paid in lieu of statute labor." The Village Mayor of Vockenroth receives a reprimand for having facilitated the sale of these people's properties, and for trying to drive every other such subject out of the country. DOSCH gives "New Scotland" as his destination, but has nothing at all anymore, and FLICKERT extremely little. So they "take refuge in His Highness as the copious source of grace and mercy, and ask for permission to depart without the usual fees." // ADAM DO*R*SCH, with wife and two children, MARIA SALLEMIE and MARGARIETA DORSCH, along with BARBARA DOSH, PHILIPP HOERNER, MICHAEL FLICKER and CHRISTOPH GERRECHT, Brig *Dispatch,* October 31, 1786 (Hinke, III, 20 ff.).

## DOSCH, ANNA MARGARETHA — Nassig (1773)

April 21, 1773: wants to go to her brother's (name lacking), who went to New England in *1763.*

## DOSCH, CHRISTOPH — Oedengesäss (1752)

*Rosenberg Archive,* Br. 387 b, and Br. 554, Sheet 54 ff., May 8, 1752: has still to pay to JOHANN MICH[AEL] BACH, citizen and tradesman in Wertheim, 50 florins 21 kreuzer, and gave a mortgage on it, but sold his goods to PAUL SCHLESSMANN in Nassig, who also emigrated and went into bankruptcy. // CHRISTOPH DOSCH, Ship *Phoenix,* November 22, 1752 (Hinke, I, 507), with other Wertheimers.

CHRISTOPH DOSCH and wife MARIA ELISABETH evidently settled in or near Lancaster, Pa., where they appear as parents of children baptized 1754-1765, at Trinity Lutheran Church, Lancaster (*PGS Proceedings,* III, 215, 228, 247, etc.). Later in the century, in 1783 and 1785, one CHRISTOPHER DOSH appears with DAN[IEL] DOSH as resident in Shenandoah Co., Va., in 1783 (*Heads of Families at the First Census of the United States Taken in the Year 1790 — Records of the State Enumerations: 1782 to 1785 — Virginia,* pp. 63, 105). One JOSH[UA] DUSH appears as resident in Frederick Co., Va., in 1782 (*Ibid.,* p. 19).

## DOSCH, FRIEDRICH — Nassig (1773)

February 18, 1773: wants to go with PETER DOSCH and their combined families to New England, FRIEDRICH DOSCH having a wife and 2 children. The community of Nassig would like to be rid of them, since they annoy it with their suspicious and dissolute households. They received manumission without the usual fees — are loaded with debts. // JOHAN FRIED*E*RICH D*OE*RSCH, Ship *Minerva,* September 17, 1771 (Hinke, I, 734) is the only one of this name listed in Hinke.

## DOSCH, HANS GEORG — Sachsenhausen (1752)

May 15, 1752: wants to go with wife and 4 children to Pennsylvania. Still has 444 florins property. Mentioned as emigrant in the *Village Mayor's Report* for Sachsenhausen (1750-1761): "JOHANN GEORG DOSCH, with wife and children." // HANS GEORGE (X) DOSH, Ship *Phoenix,* November 22, 1752 (Hinke, I, 508), with other Wertheimers, including CHRISTOPH DOSCH. One GEORGE DOSH was resident of Manor Tp., Lancaster Co., Pa., in 1773 (3PA, *XVII,* 400).

## DOSCH, JOHANN CHRISTOPH — Oedengesäss (1752)

May 8, 1752: wauts to go with wife and 2 children to Pennsylvania. Has only 25 florins. The same report appears in the *Freudenberg Archive.* // See CHRISTOPH DOSCH, above.

## DOSCH, JOHANN MICHAEL — Nassig (1754)

May 24, 1754: the son of the late JACOB DOSCH, has, with his 5 orphaned brothers and sisters, inherited an old dilapidated cottage, and half a little barn worth together 50 florins, yet can find no buyer for them, nor can he sell his share in the house for 10 florins. Wants to seek his fortune in America. According to the *Village Mayor's Report* for Nassig (1753), "JACOB DOSCH's son, single, left with them [the other Nassig emigrants of 1753] also, taking nothing along." // Three of this name appear in Hinke: (1) JOHANN MICHAEL DOSCH, Ship *Neptune,* September 24, 1753 (Hinke, I, 539 ff.) with other Wertheimers; (2) HANS MICH. [?] DOSCH, Ship *Phoenix,* October 1, 1754 (Hinke, I, 627 ff.), with other Wertheimers; and (3) MICHAEL DOSCH, Ship *Minerva,* October 13, 1769 (Hinke, I, 727). One JOHN MICHAEL DOSCH and wife ANNA MARGARET settled in or near Lancaster, Pa., where they appear as parents of children baptized 1754-1756, at Trinity Lutheran Church, Lancaster (*PGS Proceedings,* III, 216 ff.). MICHAEL and CATHARINA DOSCH appear as parents of children baptized in 1762-1768, MICHAEL and ANNA MARIA DOSCH, as parents of children baptized in 1773-1774 (*Ibid.,* III, 236, 244, 262; also IV, 190).

## DOSCH, PETER — Nassig (1773)

Companion of FRIEDRICH DOSCH (q.v.) above. Has a wife and 4 children.

DOSTMANN, [-——] — Nassig (1752)

May 24, 1752: HANS MICHEL DOSTMANN's children, all poor as beggars, want to go to Pennsylvania with some people from Sonderrieth. In the *Village Mayor's Report* for Nassig (1752): "JOHANN MICHEL DOSTMANN's son and daughter, both single, have taken nothing along; nor can they expect anything from their parents." // Perhaps JOHAN MARTIN DOSTMAN, Ship *Phoenix,* November 22, 1752 (Hinke, I, 507), with other Wertheimers, since he is the only one listed in Hinke. In 1778-1783, one JACOB DUSTMAN appears among the Washington County Rangers on the Frontiers (3PA, XXIII, 214), and one HENRY DUSTMAN was resident of Washington Co., Pa., in 1790 (*United States Census of 1790 for Pennsylvania,* p. 257).

DRACH, [———] — Niclashausen (1752)

May 15, 1752: the widow of JOHANN GEORG DRACH wants to go to New England with her 6 children. Has formerly supported herself wretchedly, with hard and unpleasant work on the Bronnbacher Hof, but is afraid that in the end she will get only crippled limbs and the direst poverty from it. "On bended knee, I address to His Princely Highness my most humble, dutiful, and suppliant petition, that out of his noble, inherent, and patriarchal mercy, he may graciously grant to me, poor widow, and to my poor fatherless orphans, manumission from vassalage." Was agreed to, on payment of 13 florins. Mentioned as emigrant in the *Village Mayor's Report* for Niclashausen (1752): "JOHANN GEORG DRACH's widow and children." // Perhaps ANDRES DRACH, with PETTER DRACH and another ANDEREAS ( ) TRAGH, on board, Ship *Phoenix,* November 2, 1752 (Hinke, I, 502), with other Wertheimers. One RUDOLF DRACH followed in 1754.

DRESSLER, [———] — Sachsenhausen (*ca.* 1750-1761)

"WENDEL DRESSLER's son, a tailor's apprentice, emigrated," according to the *Village Mayor's Report* for Sachsenhausen (1750-1761). // Perhaps ANDREAS DRESSLER, Ship *Phoenix,* November 2, 1752 (Hinke, I, 502), with other Wertheimers, although one JOHANN ANDREAS DRESLER had arrived in 1749, (Hinke, I, 393) and others before that. Several listed in 3PA.

EIRICH, ANDREAS — Altfeld (1752)

May 10, 1752: he is an oxherd and wants to go with wife and 6 children to New England. Must pay 20½ florins, on 250 florins property. // ANDREAS EYRICH, Ship *Phoenix,* November 2, 1752 (Hinke, I, 502), with other Wertheimers; ANDERAS EYRICH, with one DAVID OTT, Ship *Minerva,* October 1, 1770 (Hinke, I, 729). One MARGRETHA EIRICHS, widow, married BERNHARD HENKENIUS, widower, in 1753, at the Lutheran Church at New Hanover ("Trappe Records," *PGS Proceedings,* VII, 489). JOHANN GEORG EIRICH married GERTRAUT CLAUSER, 1764, at the New Hanover Lutheran Church (*PGS Proceedings,* XX, 397). GEORG EURICH and wife appear as children of parents baptized 1771-1779 at Hain's Church, Heidelberg Tp., Berks Co., Pa. (*GSP Proceedings,* V, 61 ff.). CONRAD EURICH and wife appear as parents of a child baptized 1774 at the Bern Church, Bern Tp., Berks Co., Pa. (*GSP Proceedings* V, 44).

EIRICH, JOHANN ADAM — Bestenheid (1753-1754)

January 7, 1762: he and his sister ANNA BARBARA went to Pennsylvania 8 or 9 years ago. On June 30, 1762, it was confirmed that they both had gone to America without buying off their vassalage. In the *Freudenberg Governmental Protocol,* May 5, 1752, mention is made of one MARIA BARBARA EIRICH of Bestenheid, daughter of PETER EIRICH, who wants to emigrate. Her father is eventually to be dispossessed. Perhaps she is identical with ANNA BARBARA EIRICH.

## EIRICH, MICHAEL — Sachsenhausen (1786)

February 9, 1786: is a stepson of CHRISTOPH GARRECHT, and is going across the ocean with him. // JOHAN MICHEL ERICH, among the family of CHRISTOPH GARRECHT, Brig *Dispatch,* October 31, 1786 (Hinke, III, 20-21), with other Wertheimers. Another possible Wertheimer, MICHAEL EYRICH, arrived in 1750 with MATHEAS EYRICH, several UTZES and an OESTERLE (Hinke, I, 432), and settled either in York, York County, Pa., where he was taxed in 1779 (3PA, XXI, 4), or in Greenwich Tp., Berks Co., Pa., taxed 1779 (3PA, XVIII, 239).

## EIRICH, PHILIPP — Grünewörth (1752)

A blacksmith, went to America. On June 23, 1780, evidently in consequence of his prolonged absence, his property was divided among relatives. // JOHANN PHILIP EYRICH, Ship *Neptune,* September 24, 1753 (Hinke, I, 539 ff.).

## EITEL, MARGARETHA — Steinmark (1754)

May 20, 1754: single, wants to go to Pennsylvania. Her mother died 14 years ago, and she cannot live with her stepmother without friction. Has formerly had to earn her living as a maid among strangers — is now tired of this and disguted with it. Has learned sewing at Hafenlohr; had to pay 15 florins 30 kreuzer for teaching fees. Is almost propertyless.

## ENDRES, JOHANN — Glasofen (1752)

May 19, 1752: son of PAUL ENDRES, wants to go to Pennsylvania. Mentioned as emigrant in the *Village Mayor's Report* for Glasofen (7150-1761): "Only PAUL ENDRES' son. Has as yet received nothing of his parental inheritance. Left after 1750." // Three of this name appear in Hinke, all of them probably Wertheimers: (1) JOHANNES ENDRES, with (2) JOHANNES ( ) ENDER, JR., sick, and other Wertheimers, Ship *Patience,* September 19, 1749 (Hinke, I, 409); and (3) JOHANNES ENDRES, Ship *Phoenix,* November 2, 1752 (Hinke, I, 503), with other Wertheimers. JOHN ENDRES appears as "inmate" in Heidelberg Tp., Lancaster Co., Pa., in 1772 (3PA, XVI, 151; XVII, 313).

## ENDRES, JOHANNES — Glasofen (1752)

May 19, 1752: son of CARL ENDRES, has saved until now only 10 florins, with which he can hardly meet the expenses of the journey to Rotterdam. The same report appears in the *Freudenberg Governmental Protocol.*

## ENDRES, JOHANN MICHAEL — Remlingen (1753)

*Rosenberg Archive,* Br. 360 a. April 26, 1753: single, son of the late MICH[AEL] ENDRES, wants to go to New England. Is a tailor. // JOHANN MICHEL ENDRES, Ship *Neptune,* September 24, 1753 (Hinke, I, 539 ff.), with other Wertheimers; a second MICHEL ENDRES arrived 1767 (Hinke, I, 716). The MICHAEL ENTRES of Upper Milford Tp., Northampton (now Lehigh) Co., Pa. who made his will 1782, probated 1783, was doubtless of another family, since he mentions a brother, DANIEL ENTRES, "in High Germany, Kyrbrag" [Kirchbracht, Hesse-Darmstadt?] (*Will Book* 1, p. 328, Northampton County Courthouse, Easton, Pa.).

## ENDRES, THOMAS — Michelrieth (1754)

May 9, 1754: wants to go to Pennsylvania, but request was denied. On May 16, he repeated his request, to be permitted to emigrate to Pennsylvania with his wife and 3 children of 11, 13, and 16 years of age. Has 276 florins property. Was permitted to emigrate. Mentioned as emigrant in the *Village Mayor's Report* for Michelrieth (1755): "THOMAS ENDRES, with wife and children, and his total property." See also KIESECKER. In the *Freudenberg Governmental Protocol,* May 6, 1754, he is quite differently described. He is allegedly overburdened with debts, and can no longer support himself. Of the 800 florins *activa* he has about 600 florins debts. Of stock in hand are 3½ florins for books, which he has bought at Bookbinder *Panzer's,* besides 50 florins for clothes and one kettle, which he bought in Heidenfeld. // THOMAS ENDRES, Ship *Phoenix,* October 1 1754 (Hinke, I, 627ff.), with other Wertheimers. THOMAS ENTRESS, Lebanon Tp., Lancaster (now Lebanon) Co., Pa., 1782 (3PA, XVII, 793).

## ENDRESS, ZACHARIAS — Wertheim (1766)

ZACHARIAS ENDRES, who arrived on the Ship *Chance,* September 23, 1766 (Hinke, I, 709), has been added by the American editor as an emigrant from Wertheim. He was the wealthy Philadelphian, "Z. E.," who wrote the letter of 1780, given in Appendix IV, telling of his trials during the Revolutionary War. He was the father of the distinguished Lutheran clergyman, CHRISTIAN F. L. ENDRESS, D.D. (1775-1827). Acording to William B. Sprague's sketch of Dr. Endress, in ANNALS OF THE AMERICAN PULPIT, Vol. IX (New York: Robert Carter & Brothers, 1869), 107-110, CHRISTIAN'S father, "JOHN ZACHARY ENDRESS, was a native of Wortheim-on-the-Main. As an argument with his children not to undervalue their Protestant Evangelical profession of faith, he was accustomed to tell them that he was a descendant of that JACOB ENDRESS, who, as a representative of the city of Nuremburg, in the famous Imperial Diet, held at Augsburg in 1531, subscribed the Augsburg Confession of Faith. His mother was ANNA MARIA HENRICI, of a Huguenot family of that name, who had fled from France to escape persecution, and settled at Neuwied, a town in Rhenish Prussia." The sponsors at CHRISTIAN ENDRESS' baptism in Philadelphia in 1775, "were CHRISTIAN and CATHARINE JAUSCH. FREDERICK LEWIS, one of the Sovereign Counts of Lowenstein-Wertheim had, by letter, a short time before, requested to be considered Godfather to the expected child, and therefore his name is found upon the Baptismal Record of the Church of Zion and St. Michael in Philadelphia, CHRISTIAN FREDERICK LEWIS; but he himself always wrote CHRISTIAN only." The Rev. CHRISTIAN ENDRESS, D.D., after graduation from the University of Pennsylvania, served there as Tutor (1792-1795), then became Principal of the Congregational School of St. Michael's and Zion )1795-1801), serving Frankfort, Pa., Cohansey, N. J., and elsewhere as supply. Licensed in 1799 by the Lutheran Ministerium of Pennsylvania, and ordained in 1802, he served a large parish centering about Easton, Pa. (1801-1814), then succeeded Henry Ernst Muhlenberg in the important Trinity Lutheran Church of Lancaster, Pa. (1815-1827). He was one of the liberal leaders of the Lutheran denomination at this time, an Americanizer in language and a sponsor of the movement to unite the Lutheran and Reformed Synods, and a leader in the formation of the

Lutheran General Synod. He was the author of a commentary on Romans, and other published and unpublished books and pamphlets. CHRISTIAN ENDRESS was certainly one of Wertheim's outstanding contributions to Pennsylvania. See Appendix IV for a full account of the ENDRESS Family.

## ENGLERT, GEORG — Dertingen (1752)

May 19, 1752: single, wants to go to Pennsylvania. Perhaps identical with HANS JOERG ENGLERT, who on May 12, 1752, likewise wants to go to New England. The latter is 18 years old, single, and has divided his parental inheritance with his brother, HANS ADAM ENGLERT. The account of his property is to be preserved in the archive chest at Dertingen. The brother is to pay him 100 florins. In case he should not like it in the above-mentioned country, then he wants to be entitled to receive back his property on payment of 100 florins traveling expenses. The government resolved at the time, that the emifrant must, however, pay for his manumussion, and the 10% supplemental tax besides. At another place mention is made of Pennsylvania as his destination. On May 19 he sold his entire property for 550 florins. Mentioned also as emigrant in the *Village Mayor's Report* for Dertingen (1753): "HANS JOERG ENGLERT, single, with 276 florins property." // Three of this name are listed in Hinke: (1) JOHANN GEORG ENGLERT, Ship *Duke of Wirtenberg,* October 16, 1751 (Hinke, I, 476); (2) JOHANN GEORG ENGLERT, Ship *Forest,* October 10, 1752 (Hinke, I, 494); and (3) HANS JUERG ENGLERT, Ship *Phoenix,* November 2, 1752 (Hinke, I, 503), with other Wertheimers. Perhaps he was the GEORG ENGELER with wife REGINA, listed as parents of a child baptized 1756, at the Williams Township Lutheran Congregation in Northampton Co., Pa. (*PGS Proceedings,* XVIII, 16). GEORGE ENGLER is still resident of Williams Tp. in 1786 (3PA, XIX, 187); while an ADAM ENGLER appears in Chestnuthill Tp., Northampton Co., Pa., in 1785 (3PA, XIX, 178).

## FERTIG, ANDREAS — Altfeld (1749)

*Protocol,* April 16, 1762: the Village Mayor of Kredenbach has acted badly in the division of the property of the weaver ANDREAS FERTIG of Altfeld, who went to America in 1749. The Village Mayor simply appropriated pieces of land worth 375 florins or more belonging to FERTIG, tilled them for his own benefit, and sold of them. But as yet there has come no word from FERTIG — after all, he could still be living. Since the Village Mayor was FERTIG's brother-in-law, the suspicion arises, that he secretly acquired the lands in question from Fertig. // Two men named ANDREAS FERTIG, Ship *Phoenix,* October 1, 1754 (Hinke, I 627 ff.), with other Wertheimers. See the letter of MICHEL FERTIG, 1782, in Introduction, Appendix III, for reference to ANDREAS FERTIG of Tulpehocken and Virginia.

## FERTIG, ANDREAS — Altfeld (1754)

Made an agreement with the boatman SELIG in 1754; evidently other than the emigrant of 1749. According to additional information sent the American editor by Dr. Langguth, the Michelrieth Baptismal Register states on February 25, 1754, that ANDREAS FERTIG of Altfeld, born August 16, 1730, "went to Pennsylvania this year." See KIESECKER. // ANDREAS FERTIG, Ship *Phoenix,* October 1, 1754 (Hinke, I, 627 ff.), with other Wertheimers.

Christian Frederic Lewis Endress, D.D.
Oil Portrait by S. Eichholtz 1816

## FERTIG, HANS — Altfeld (1752)

May 12, 1752: a tailor's son, is indebted to the amount of 200 florins, and wants to go with his wife to New England. // HANS FERTIG, Ship *Phoenix*, November 2, 1752 (Hinke, I, 502), with other Wertheimers. He may have been the JOHANNES FERTIG who in 1762, at the New Hanover Lutheran Church, married ELISABETH DIEM ("Trappe Records," *PGS Proceedings*, VII, 506). JOHANNES and ELISABETH FERTIG are listed as parents of a child baptized 1766, at the New Hanover Lutheran Church (*PGS Proceedings*, XX, 233). Note that a member of the Augustus Church at the Trappe, in the same parish as New Hanover, was one CATHARINA FERTIG, daughter of the late PETER FERTIG, who married ANDREAS DOEROLF in 1761 (*PGS Proceedings*, VII, 505). For JOHANNES FERTIG, of East Nantmeal Tp., Chester Co., Pa., see the MICHEL FERTIG letter of 1782, in the Introduction, Appendix III.

## FERTIG, JOHANN ADAM — Steinmark (1754)

Emigrated 1754. March 3, 1768: HENRICH FUCHS from Pennsylvania, with Power of Attorney, wishes to collect the inheritance of the tailor-apprentice JOHANN ADAM FERTIG of Steinmark, who emigrated 14 years ago (1754), and is now in Philadelphia. Perhaps FERTIG at the time emigrated without manumission. Had at that time received 54 florins, 30 kreuzer. The attorney collects 106 florins, less 10% for delayed manumission from vassalage. // JOHANN ADAM FERTIG married ELISABETH BAUER at the New Hanover Lutheran Church, 1762 ("Trappe Records," *PGS Proceedings*, VII, 506), and they were parents of children baptized there, 1763-1770 (*Ibid.*, XX, 65 ff.).

## FERTIG, MATTHAEUS — Steinmark (*ca.* 1754)

Tailor's son, emigrated *circa* 1754. Mentioned as emigrant in the *Village Mayor's Report* for Steinmark (1750-1757): "HANS FERTIG, the blacksmith's son, a tailor by trade, and MATTHAEUS FERTIG, a tailor's son, who both went abroad, of whom it has been said, they too were in the above-mentioned country [America], but this we do not know for sure."

## FERTIG, JOHANN CHRISTOPH — Grünewörth (1769)

Added by the American editor as a probable emigrant from Wertheim. Dr. Langguth includes him among emigrants to Hungary: "May 8, 1769: has sold his lands, has a balance left over of 415 florins, and wants to go to Hungary. On May 9 he presents the "proper petition seeking early assistance in getting away." Two sureties, Village Mayor SCHWAB and NICOLAUS RAU, confirm his property status. // He very probably came to America instead of Hungary, from the fact that JOHAN CHRISTOFFEL FERDIG appears with HANS GEORG BOPP (POPP), also of Grünewörth, who inquired about emigration to both America and Hungary, on the Ship *Minerva*, October 13, 1769 (Hinke, I, 726). He may have been the JOHN CHRISTOPHER FERTIG, husband of ANNA CATHARINA SEIDNER (q.v.) of Wertheim (1723-1785), who had charge of the Lititz Moravian Church Farm.

## FERTIG, MICHAEL —

Added by the American editor as a probable emigrant from Wertheim. In 1764 he married ANNA MARIA RIES at the New Hanover Lutheran Church (*PGS Proceedings*, XX, 397). See his letter, dated Skippack,

Pa., 1782, to hih cousin *LORENZ* ALBERT, quoted in the Introduction, Appendix III.

## FERTIG, REGINA — Wertheim

Added by the American editor. She was born December 27, 1755, in Wertheim, Germany, was married in 1784 to CHRISTIAN ANDREW KREITER (1751-1824), fulling-miller, and died in 1786 as a member of the Moravian Church at Lititz, Pa., where she is buried (Abraham Reinke Beck, "The Moravian Graveyards of Lititz, Pa., 1744-1905," *Transactions of the Moravian Historical Society* VII, 242, 262). There were no children from this marriage. It is probable that REGINA (FERTIG) KREITER was the daughter of one of the FERTIG emigrants listed above.

## FLATH, PETER — Höchst (1764)

February 11, 1764: PETER FLATH and family, vassals of the Elector Palatine at Höchst in the Odenwald, want to go to South America, a royal French colony. Are to pay 20% supplemental tax, and the usual manumission fee. // He may perhaps have come to Pennsylvania instead, for a PETER FLATT, with JOSEPH, SAMUEL, and JOHN FLATT, were surveyed large tracts of land in Luzerne Co., Pa., in 1788 (3PA, XXIV, 216).

## FIRNHABER, JOHANN NICOLAUS — Wertheim (1773)

November 17, 1787: "JOHANN NICOLAUS FIRNHABER, from here, who is established in Philadelphia, has sold his property in this place to DILL(EN) for 225 florins, 58 kreuzer, from which he still has his manumission fee to pay." // JACOB NICOLAUS FIRNHABER, with JOHANNES FIRNHABER, Ship *Union*, September 27, 1773 (Hinke, I, 752). According to GSP's Transcript of the "Record of St. Michael's Lutheran Church, Germantown, Philadelphia," one JOHANN FERNHABER died in 1777 at the age of 26 (p. 1104), and one JACOB FERNHABER had a child baptized in 1782 (p. 598). Note also that one JOHAN CHRISTOPH FERNHABER (FREIHABER, FREMHABER), arrived September 24, 1753, on the Ship *Neptune*, with very many other Wertheimers (Hinke, I, 539 ff.). Perhaps he was the Notary Public, J. C. FIRNHABER, of Frankfurt-am-Main, whose daughter, MARGARET CATHARINE WEISS (1720-1756), born at Frankfurt, married MATTHIAS WELSS in 1753 and came to America the same year, and died at Bethlehem, Pa., in 1756, where she is buried in the Moravian Cemetery (Augustus Schultze, "Guide to the Old Moravian Cemetery of Bethlehem, Pa., 1742-1910," *PGS Proceedings*, XXI, 58).

Since the name is so unusual, it will be of interest to mention that one of the eighteenth-century Lutheran Superintendents in Wertheim was Magister FRIEDRICH JACOB FIRNHABER; acording to the *Kirchenbuch* for May 12, 1763, his son, JOHANN DAVID FIRNHABER, was a merchant in Lyons, France.

## FITTERLING, VOITH — Dietenhan (1752)

May 8, 1752: wants to go with his wife and 8 children to the so-called "Island of Pennsylvania." From the total sale of his property there remains to him a balance of 333 florins. His name is generally spelled FIEDERLING. Mentioned as emigrant in the *Village Mayor's Report* for Dietenhan (1752): "VOITH FIEDERLING, with wife and children." // VEIT FITTERLING, Ship *Phoenix*, November 2, 1752 (Hinke, I, 502), with other Wertheimers. Among his sons may have been the

MICH'L FITTERLING, of Cumru Tp., Berks Co., Pa., 1779 (3PA, XVIII, 190), and GEO. FIDDERLING, of Brecknock Tp., Berks Co., Pa., 1779 (3PA, XVIII, 206).

## FLEGLER, ANDREAS — Urfar (1773)

January 21, 1775: no one has yet received any word from ANDREAS FLEGLER, who went to Pennsylvania 2 years ago, whether he got across safely. // Perhaps he was the ANDREW FLEGELER, resident in Amity Tp., Berks Co., Pa., 1779 (3PA, XVIII, 183).

## FLEGLER, JOHANN LEONHARD — Wertheim (1752)

May 15, 1752: burgher and shoemaker in Wertheim, feels compelled on account of deplorable conditions, to leave his Fatherland with his wife and one child, and go to Pennsylvania. Brings testimony of his poverty and confesses that "my property is nothing, indeed, nothing at all but myself." In the *Burgomaster's Accounts* of 1751 is the report: "From LEONHARD FLEGLER, nothing produced on the supplemental tax, because his property consists of nothing."

## FLEGLER, MARIA — Kembach (1752)

May 12, 1752: one GARRECHT and a daughter of FLEGLER of Kembach want to go to Pennsylvania. In another place: MARIA FLEGLER, the orphaned daughter of CASPAR FLEGLER of Kembach, wants to go to New England. Has 100 florins.

## FLEGLER, VALENTIN — Niclashausen (1785)

March 11, 1785: VALENTIN FLEGLER, JR., a cooper, wants to go to America with wife and 2 children, since he promised himself more profits from his trade in that part of the world. Balance remaining from his sale, only 23 florins. // VALENTINE FLEGLER, with EVA FLEGLER, DOROTHY FLEGLER, and NICH'S FLEGLER, with KRAFT, ARBORT, the SCHERGERS and the HORNERS, Ship *Favourite*, September 5, 1785 (Hinke, III, 9).

## FLEGLER, ZACHARIAS — Wertheim (1709)

Added by the American editor. He is the earliest Wertheimer on record to come to America. His name appears in the Kocherthal Marriage Register, printed by Otto Lohr as *"Das älteste deutsch-amerikanische Kirchenbuch (1708-1719),"* in the *Jahrbuch für Auslanddeutsche Sippenkunde* I (Stuttgart,1936), 56-57. On August 15, 1710, "ZACHARIAS FLEGLER, of near Wertheim in *Franckenland*, Widower, married ANNA GERTRUDE, orphaned married daughter of the late DIETRICH HUEN[s] of Wallbrühl in the Duchy of Berg." On March 12, 1711, "ZACHARIAS FLEGLER, from Wertheim in *Franckenland*, married ANNA ELISABETHA, widow of the late GEORG SCHULTZ from the Darmstadt region."

## FLICKERT, ADAM — Vockenroth (1785)

March 6, 1785: wants to go to America with his wife and 6 children, since an opportunity is at hand for him to go thither in the Spring. // Perhaps ADAM FLECKER, of the Out Ward of New York City, with a wife and evidently 2 children *(United States Census of 1790 for New York*, p. 131).

## FLICKERT, JOHANN MICHAEL — Vockenroth (1786)

January 5, 1786: same request as ADAM DOSCH (q.v.). In his direct petition to the Prince, he mentions that he has paid the Prince more in rendered hand work and *(Handlohn)* than his whole property has brought him. For 23 years he has been a dutiful subject, gladly paid much in taxes paid in lieu of statute labor, assessment, and other services, etc. May God have mercy on what little he is now able to take away with him. // MICHAEL FLIKER, with wife and 4 children: MARIA DOROTHEA FLIKKER, JOHAN CHRISTOPH FLIKKER, JOHAN MICHEL FLIKKER, and ANNA ELIZABETH FLIKKER, with ADAM DORSCH and other Wertheimers, Brig *Dispatch,* October 31, 1786 (Hinke, III, 21).

FRISCHMUTH, DANIEL — Wertheim (1766)

One FRISCHMUTH from Wertheim, was in Philadelphia in 1780. From a letter published in the *Wertheimer Zeitung* of March 2, 1781: "FRISCHMUTH has as yet suffered little misfortune from the war, and is in good circumstances" (cf. *Introduction,* Appendix IV). September 9, 1784: JACOB FRISCHMUTH, as guardian for the baker's apprentice DANIEL FRISCHMUTH, who has settled in America, pays the manumission fee on an inhertance of 155 florins, which has fallen to DANIEL FRISCHMUTH and his brother and sister. // JOHANN DANIEL FRISCHMUTH, Ship *Chance,* September 23, 1766 (Hinke, I, 709), with JOH. MICHAEL WEINGAERTNER and ZACHARIAS ENDRES. DANIEL FRESHMUTH, City of Philadelphia, Mulberry Ward, 1774 (3PA, XIV, 294); same, listed as "baker," 1780 (3PA, XV, 295). Evidently related to the distinguished orientalist at the University of Jena, Professor Dr. JOHANNES FRISCHMUTHIUS, who was born at Wertheim in 1619 (see Otto Langguth, "Johannes Frischmuthius," *Jahrbuch des Historischen Vereins Alt-Wertheim, 1927,* pp. 46-50).

FROEBER, CATHARINA — Bettingen (1753)

May 4, 1753: single, wants to go to New England. According to the *Village Mayor's Report* for Bettingen (1750-1761), she was the only emigrant from the village in that period.

FUENKNER, DOROTHEA — Niclashausen (1754)

May 16, 1754: single, wants to seek her fortune in New England. Has 43 florins. Pays 1 florin, 9 kreuzer, for her property, and 2 florins for manumission. In the *Village Mayor's Report* for Niclashausen (1754), she is called "ANNA DOROTHEA FUENKNER, single." Possible she is the well-to-do sister in Philadelphia, mentioned in connection with PETER FUENKNER, below.

FUENKNER, PETER — Niclashausen (1769)

April 21, 1769: has for 15 years had a sister living in Philadelphia, who has already written a few times and sought to induce him and their 3 other brothers and sisters to go there too, where she promised them a good livelihood, and because she is in happy and propertied circumstances, promised to provide, and finally even sent them, 4 Louis d'Or for traveling expenses and would at once upon their arrival pay their remaining expenses. He now wants to travel thither with his sister ANNA MARIA, in order to see how they might like it, to stay there or again to make the return journey. He does not yet want to sell any of his property. Is said then to have reconsidered.

GARBEL, EPHRA*HI*M BENEDI*KT* — Wertheim (1753)

April 13, 1753: master-cabinetmaker, wants to go with his wife and child to the so-called New England, on account of poor times, also the overstocking of his trade. GARBEL pays 4 florins, 28 kreuzer for himself, 2 florins for his wife, 1 florin for his child. The City Office and Court examine his *activa* and *passiva* and find 89 florins property. His traveling expenses GARBEL sets as follows: for meat, wine, brandy, bread, lard on the ship and other necessary wares, altogether 24 florins. Destination is Pennsylvania. On May 7, 1753, BREITENHERD and WEINGAERTNER want to join them. According to the *Burgomaster's Accounts* for 1752, he paid 8 florins supplemental tax. // EPHRAIM BENDEDIGT GARBEL, Ship *Neptune,* September 24, 1753 (Hinke, I, 539 ff.), with other Wertheimers. He settled in Lancaster, Pa., along with WEINGAERTNER and BREITENHERD, where EPHRAIM BENEDICT GARBEL and wife ROSINA appear as parents of children baptized at Trinity Lutheran Church, 1756-1758 (*PGS Proceedings,* III, 221, 228).

## GARRECHT, CHRISTOPH — Sachsenhausen (1786)

February 9, 1786: wants to go with wife and 3 children to America. Can no longer raise his taxes and governmental burdens, to say nothing of his own livelihood. Has 1275 florins property and 776 florins debts. Wants to take along 152 florins worth of things. The son of his [wife's] first marriage is named MICHEL EIRICH — his father was a barber — and he is going with them to America. Is taking along a Bible, among other things, which he has bought from CHRISTOPH FLEISCHMANN, with cabinetmaking wares worth 14 florins and 42 kreuzer. The property of 200 florins, secured for the son of the first marriage, in Remlingen, he is to leave here, since it is to be feared that he might cause the son, too, to lose his property. // CHRISTOPH GERRECHT, with wife and 4 children: JOHAN MICHEL ERICH, PIETER WILLEM ANDRIES, CATHARINA and ORCHILLE GARRECHT, and other Wertheimers, Brig *Dispatch,* October 31, 1786 (Hinke, III, 20-21). In 1790, CHRIST[OPHE]R GARRECHT was a resident of Lancaster Borough, Lancaster, Pa. (*U.S. Census of 1790 for Pennsylvania,* p. 137).

## GARRECHT, VEIT — Kembach (1752)

May 12, 1752: wants to go with his wife and 2 children to Philadelphia. Still has 205 florins. Is perhaps identical with [-----] GARRECHT (cf. below), and with the emigrant GARRECHT in the *Village Mayor's Report* for 1753: "VEIT GARRECHT, and his wife's sister." // VEIT GARRECHT, Ship *Phoenix,* November 2, 1752 (Hinke, I, 502), with other Wertheimers. Evidently this family settled in Montgomery Co., Pa., where, in the records of the New Hanover Church, VEIT GARRECHTS and wife appear as sponsors to a child of GEORGE and GERTRAUT WISSNER (*PGS Proceedings,* XX, 337). In the same year, GEORGE GERRICH and wife appear as sponsors; in 1755 GEORGE GERRICH and wife MARGARETHA appear as parents (*Ibid.,* XX, 319, 245).

## GARRECHT, [———] — Kembach (1752)

May 12, 1752: one GARRECHT of Kembach, wants to go to Pennsylvania with Flegler's daughter.

## GEIGER, [———] — Oberschipf

Added by the American editor. On March 28, 1763, CASPAR GEIGER'S wife, née WEINBERGER, from Oberschipf, near Wertheim in Franconia, aged 43 years and 4 months, was buried at St. Michaelis and Zion Lutheran Church, Philadelphia (GSP, "Records of St. Michaelis and Zion Lutheran Church," Burials, p. 148).

## GERBERICH, HANS — Altfeld (1751)

April 6, 1751: has fallen so low in the last 40 years, that he has left out of a once considerable property, only 700 florins. Wants to go to Pennsylvania with his wife CHRISTINE and 6 children: APOLLONIA, MARGARETHA, MARIA MARGARETA, JOHANNES, ANNA BARBARA, and JOHANN MICHAEL. Has yet to pay for freedom from vassalage: 35 florins for his property, and 6 florins for the 6 children. According to KIESECKER's declaration, one GERBERICH of Altfeld turned back again. Boatman SELIG asserts having haerd from him, that in Bingen every boatman is paying fifty kreuzer the head. Perhaps he returned to fetch his daughter APPOLONIA, of whom it is reported in the *Freudenberg Governmental Protocols* of May 16, 1754: APOLLONIA GERBERICH, who already two years ago was bought off by her father and through an unfortunate event was brought into misery, asks for freedom from vassalage. Her property still amounts to 123 florins. // Two of this name are listed in Hinke: (1) HANS GERGERICH, Ship *Brothers,* September 22, 1752 (Hinke, I, 481); and (2) HANS GERBERICH, Ship *Phoenix,* November 2, 1752 (Hinke, I, 503), with other Wertheimers. HANES GERBERICH, Tulpehocken Tp., Berks Co., Pa., 1768 (3PA, XVIII, 164); JOHN GERBERICK, single, Codorus Tp., York Co., Pa., 1782 (3PA, XXI, 549). HANS GERBERICH, the emigrant in question, was the ancestor of Dr. ALBERT HENRY GERBERICH, at present in the U. S. diplomatic corps. Dr. Gerberich is the editor of the *History of the Gerberich Family in America, 1613-1925,* (n. p., 1925) a copy of which can be seen at the Historical Society of York County. According to this valuable work, the Gerberichs of Lebanon, Dauphin and York Counties, in Pennsylvania, and Baltimore County in Maryland, are all descended from one HANS KASPAR GERBERICH (1659-1720) of Michelrieth, and his wife APOLLONIA (VOLZ): Their two sons, (1) JOHANNES [HANS], born June 9, 1701, who in 1727 married CHRISTINA SCHUCH of Remlingen; and (2) HANS MICHAEL, born July 2, 1710, both came to America in 1751, settling in the Tulpehocken Valley. HANS' son ANDREW emigrated in 1754.

On page 231 of the *History* it is stated that "PETER GERBERICH, the oldest of the children of HANS and CHRISTINE GERBERICH, was born at Altfeld bei Marktheidenfeld in the Spessart, Bavaria, Aug. 12, 1730, and was one of the first GERBERICHS to come to America. . . In 1765 he and his brother JOHN are both assessed in Tulpehocken Township, and this is the last we hear of him in Berks County. He probably continued to live there, however, until 1771, and then moved to Codorus Township, York County, Pa." My friend, Mrs. Edith Beard Cannon, Researcher on the Staff of the Historical Society of York County, has found, however, that PETER and MARGARET GERBER'CH had a daughter CATHARINA baptized at St. Jacob's (Stone) Church in York County on the first Sunday after Easter, 1766 — the earliest record of GERBERICHS resident in York County. In some areas of the state the name has been "Dutchified" into "GARVERICK."

## GOETZELMANN, CHRISTOPH, JR. — Nassig (1753)

May 19, 1753: wants to go to Pennsylvania. According to the *Village Mayor's Report* for Nassig (1753): "CHRISTOFF GOETZELMANN, JR. [emigrated] with wife and children; had left many debts behind." // CHRISTOPHER GETZELMAN, aged 34 (on board), Ship *Halifax,* September 28, 1753 (Hinke, I, 559 ff.).

GOETZELMANN, HANS — Wenkheim (1752)

May 19, 1752: with wife and 3 children. Gives his property as 100 florins, but has only 54 florins. Wants to go to New England together with JOERG HOERNER, HANS HOERNER, BARTEL SCHAETZLEIN, MARIA HOERNER, and APOLLONIA KNEUCKER, perhaps also the LIEBLER girl, altogether 4 wives and 13 children. See Steger, No. 232. // JOHANNES GOETZELMAN, with J. JACOB (X) GOETZELMAN and other Wertheimers, Ship *Phoenix,* November 2, 1752 (Hinke, I, 501). "ANDREAS GOETZELMAN, JOHANNES GOETZELMAN'S son, apprenticed in Germantown, aged 17," was confirmed in the New Hanover Lutheran Church, in 1760 (*PGS Proceedings,* XX, 356). JOHN GETZELMAN was a resident of Frankford and New Hanover Township, Philadelphia Co., Pa., 1779 (3PA, XIV, 591). One JOHANN GETZELMANN, of Gernant's Church, near Reading, died December 1, 1803, of *"Brust Krankheit,"* at the age of 83 years, 11 months (Typescript of "Records of First Reformed Church, Reading, 1798-1820, Historical Society of the Reformed Church, Lancaster, Pa., p. 212).

GRAETZ, [———] — Wertheim (1754)

February 21, 1754: the musketeer GRAETZ, who has gone to Pennsylvania, is said to have had an all too intimate relationship with SCHUBERT'S daughter. // Could be ANDREAS GRAETZ, Ship *Two Brothers,* September 21, 1751 (Hinke, I, 465); or CHRISTIAN (X) GRAEZ, Ship *Halifax,* September 22, 1752 (Hinke, I, 482). Several Gretz families are listed in 3PA.

HAMMETER, JOHANN SEBASTIAN — Michelrieth (1753)

Added by the American editor. A tailor in Michelrieth, originally from Gunzenhausen, he was married on June 4, 1748, to MARIA MARGARETHA DENNSCHERZ, daughter of Pastor JOHANN MICHAEL DENNSCHERZ of Michelrieth Parish. When their fourth child, JOHANN ANDREAS JACOB HAMMETER, was baptized on December 26, 1753, Pastor Dennscherz wrote in the Church Register that his son-in-law had "deserted to Pennsylvania" [*nach Pennsylvanien desertiert*], leaving the already overburdened pastor to provide for the wife and family. For further information on the wife's family, see *Introduction,* Appendix III; also "LORENZ JOSEPH DENNSCHERZ," elsewhere in this List. // JOHANN SEBASTIAN HAMMETER, Ship *Neptune,* September 24, 1753 (Hinke, I, 538 ff.).

HENNING, MATTH[AEUS] WILHELM — Michelrieth (1752)

May 20, 1752: a poor, fatherless orphan, son of the late baker, FRIEDRICH HENNING, wants to go to Pennsylvania, in order to learn something and honestly support himself by a trade. // MATTHIAS WILHELM HENNING, Ship *Phoenix,* November 2, 1752 (Hinke, I, 501), with other Wertheimers; other HENNINGS arrived at other times. The MATHIAS HENNING of Bethel Tp., Lancaster Co., Pa., 1771 (3PA, XVII, 157) was a son of one JACOB HENNING, according to the father's will in 1768-1769.

HEUST, ANNA ELISABETHA — Steinbach

Added by the American editor. According to the GSP's Transcript of the "Records of Trinity Lutheran Church, Reading, Pennsylvania," I, 603, ANNA ELISABETHA HEUST, née HAG[E], was born

March 1, 1736, at Steinbach, Franconia, and baptized March 4. Her sponsor, as noted in the Church Register of Michelstadt, was ANNA ELISABETHA GEIST. On March 31, 1750, she was married to GEORG HEUST. She lived with him 45 years, until her death on December 7, 1796, aged 60 years, 8 months and 2 days. She was buried at Reading on December 11. Of their ten children, there were still living at that time, 4 sons and 4 daughters.

## HOH, HANS ADAM — Hasselberg (1752)

May 8, 1752: wants to go with wife and 4 children to Pennsylvania. Still has 100 florins. Mentioned as emigrant in the *Village Mayor's Report* for Hasselberg (1752): "HANS ADAM HOH, with wife and children, to New England." // HANS ADAM HOH, with JOHAN GORG HOH and other Wertheimers, Ship *Phoenix*, November 2, 1752 (Hinke, I, 502-503). Settled in the City of Philadelphia, where he made his will 1784, probated 1785 (*Will Book* T, p. 118, Philadelphia Courthouse), mentioning wife, MARGARET HOH, née SEITNER; son LEONARD; son ADAM; daughter MARGARET HORBIN (?); Executors: MARGARET HOH and ZACHARIAS ENDRES; Witnesses: MICH[AE]L SHUBART and JACOB HIRNEISER.

According to GSP's Transcript of the "Record of St. Michael's Lutheran Church, Germantown, Philadelphia," p. 1117, JOH[ANN] ADAM HOH was buried February 19, 1785, aged 64 years, 10 months and 2 weeks. Perhaps the JOHANN ADAM HOH of Lower Dublin Township, Philadelphia County, who according to the same Record, p| 39, was married on April 23, 1771, to Barbara Wolff of Upper Dublin Township, was his son.

## HOH, [———] — (1752)

May 12, 1752: the widow of HANS ADAM HOH, with 3 children, is on the Lindelbach transport (cf. *Betz*).

## HONECK, MICHAEL — Buch-am-Ahorn (1753)

*Freudenberg Governmental Protocol,* May 24, 1753: MICHAEL HONECK is declared the father of the illegitimate child (born 1749) of MARGARETE HONECK. "But the worthless fellow went to New England." In 1748 he was charged with getting MARIA CATHARINE WOLF of Dietenhan in the family way. "The fugitive has left behind no means for its support." *Governmental Protocol* (1755), p. 223: The father, HANS MICHEL HONECK, is to pay for his son, who went to Pennsylvania, to support an illegitimate child: 18 florins in money besides the usual church fine, 10 Reichstaler to the child's mother *pro defloratione,* and 6 florins yearly to the child, up to his 12th year. It was found, however, that a father cannot be punished for the sins of his son. In consequence of which, the son's inheritance is to be sequestrated.

## HORN, CHRISTOPH, SR. — Eichel (1753)

April 26, 1753: wants to leave for abroad, i.e., New England, with his wife CATHARINE and 5 children. The former years of failure, and other circumstances, have reduced his fortune of 500 florins, and he must leave everything behind for his creditors. There is no hope here of his getting on in the world again. His brother-in-law HERGENHAN is willing to take in his two children, VALENTIN and MARGARETHA — the other 3, EVA, BARBARA, and STEPHAN, he wants to take along. Must pay 10 florins tax. // CHRISTOPH HORN, with SEBASTIAN, JOHANNES, and GEORGE (X) HORN, and other Wertheimers, Ship *Nep-*

*tune,* September 24, 1753 (Hinke, I, 540 ff.). CHRISTOPHER HORN, Bethlehem Tp., Washington Co., Pa., 1781 (3PA, XX, 709); VALENTINE HORNE, land surveyed in Bucks Co., Pa., 1765 (3PA, XXIV, 135).

## HORN, CHRISTOPH, JR. — Eichel (1752)

May 19, 1752: CHRISTOPH HORN, JR., and PHILIPP HORN, two cousins, young fellows, would like to seek their fortune abroad and work as servants in Pennsylvania. // CHRISTOPF [?] HORN, Ship *St. Andrew,* September 23, 1752 (Hinke, I, 484).

## HORN, MARIA BARBARA — Wertheim (1763)

Added by the American editor. According to Augustus Schultze, "Guide to the Old Moravian Cemetery of Bethlehem, Pa., 1742-1910," *PGS Proceedings,* XXI, 90: MARIA BARBARA HORN (1729-1797), a native of Wertheim, Baden, "joined the Moravian Church in 1749 at Herrnhaag, and was 'called' to America in 1763, finding employment as cook in the Sisters' House." She is buried in the Single Sisters' Plot in the Moravian Cemetery at Bethlehem.

## HORN, PHILIPP — Eichel (1752)

May 19, 1752: PHILIPP HORN and CHRISTOPH HORN, JR., two yonug fellows, cousins, would like to seek their fortune abroad and work as servants in Pennsylvania. // Perhaps PHILIPP JACOB HORN, with JOHANN STEPHANUS HORN (q.v.), Ship *Phoenix,* November 2, 1752 (Hinke, I, 501 ff.).

## HORN, SEBASTIAN — Eichel (1753)

April 26, 1753: has only 13 florins and wants to go to New England with his wife, ANNA ROSINA, daughter of GEORG WIESSNER of Lindelbach. Must pay 5 florins. // SEBASTIAN HORN, with CHRISTOPH, JOHANNES, and GEORGE (X) HORN, and other Wertheimers, Ship *Neptune,* September 24, 1753 (Hinke, I, 538 ff.). BASTIAN HORN, Springfield Tp., Bucks Co., Pa., 1779 (3PA, XIII, 32); SEBASTIAN and STEPHIN HORN, Richland Tp., Bucks Co., Pa., 1785 (3PA, XIII, 597). SEBASTIAN HORN of Richland Tp., Bucks Co., Pa., yeoman, made his will 1810, probated 1812, mentioning sons SEBASTIAN and DANIEL, daughters ELIZABETH BARTHOLOMEW, SEVILL CROWMAN, MARY HORN, and BARBARA PRONG, and children of his daughter CATHARINE CHARLES. Executor: DANIEL HORN; witnesses: GEORGE SNYDER, JAMES CHAPMAN (*Will Book* 8, p. 285, Bucks County Courthouse, Doylestown, Pa.).

## HORN, STEPHAN — Eichel (1752)

May 4, 1752: wants to go with his wife and 2 children to Philadelphia. Still has 160 florins. // JOHANN STEPHANUS HORN, with PHILIPP JACOB HORN, Ship *Phoenix,* November 2, 1752 (Hinke, I, 501 ff.). Several STEPHEN HORN[E]s are listed in 3PA: (1) STEPHEN HORN, laborer, Easton, Northampton Co., Pa., 1772 (3PA, XIX, 5); (2) STEVEN HORNE, cordwinder, Richland Tp., Bucks Co., Pa., 1781 (3PA, XIII, 116); and (3) STEPHEN HORN, among Scotch-Irish names, in Turbott Tp., Northumberland Co., Pa., in 1786, and Chillisquaque Tp., Northumberland Co., in 1787 (3PA, XIX, 672, 763). If our emigrant settled in Richland Tp., Bucks Co., Pa., he was doubtless the ancestor of the Rev. ABRAHAM REESER HORNE (1834-1902), D.D., of Allentown, Lutheran minister and editor, and author of *'M Horn Sei Pennsylfawnisch Deitsch Buch,* the dialect classic which went through several editions in Eastern Pennsylvania. According to Dr. Horne's account, he was the great-grandson of STEPHEN HORNE, who emigrated, he thought, from Württemberg about 1755 (*PGS Proceedings*, III, 161).

## HOERNER, ADAM — Höhfeld (1753)

April 30, 1753: son of HANS GEORG HOERNER, wants to go with JACOB ZIMMERMANN'S son to Pennsylvania. In the *Freudenberg Governmental Protocol*, May 11, 1753, is the report: HANS GEORG HOERNER of Höhfeld announces that his son HANS ADAM, single and in his majority, wants to go to New England and would force him to let him go. Now his son is necessary in the field work, but his son would not obey him, and so he wants to do his bidding. At any rate, he must send him away emptyhanded.

## HOERNER, BARBARA — Höhfeld (1753)

April 26, 1753: BARBARA HOERNER, widow of WILHELM HOERNER, wants to leave likewise for New England, with 3 children: MARGARETHA, MARIA, and SEBASTIAN. Has only 22 florins and 25¼ kreuzer. Mentioned as emigrant in the *Village Mayor's Report* for Höhfeld (1750-1761): "BARBARA HOERNER, widow, with 3 children. // Perhaps SEBASTIAN HOENNER, Ship *Neptune*, September 24, 1753 (Hinke, I, 541), with other Wertheimers, including HOERNERS.

## HOERNER, HANS — Wenkheim (1752)

May 19, 1752: wants to go to New England with wife and 2 children, in company with JOERG HOERNER and MARIE HOERNER of Wenkheim, with the Lindelbach Transport (cf. GOETZELMANN). // JOHANS HOERNER, with GEORG, JOHANN MELCHER, and JOHANN JACOB HOERNER, and other Wertheimers, Ship *Phoenix*, November 2, 1752 (Hinke, I, 501).

## HOERNER, HANS ALBERT — Höhfeld (1753)

April 26, 1753: wants to go abroad with his wife, ANNA EVA, daughter of GEORGE KOEHLER of Höhfeld, on account of debts to the amount of 28 florins. Mentioned as emigrant in the *Village Mayor's Report* for Höhfeld (1750-1761): "JOHANN ALBERT HOERNER, wtih wife and 2 little children." // H. ALBERT (X) HOERNER, Ship *Richard and Mary*, September 17, 1753 (Hinke, I, 535), with other Wertheimers.

## HOERNER, JOHANN GEORG — Höhfeld [1752?]

According to the *Village Mayor's Report* for Höhfeld (1750-1761): "JOHANN GEORG HOERNER, a cavalryman's son, went to New England without manumission; took nothing with him except himself." // GEORG HOERNER, with JOHANN MELCHER, JOHANN JACOB, and JOHANS HOERNER, and other Wertheimers, Ship *Phoenix*, November 2, 1752 (Hinke, I, 501). One GEORGE HERNER was resident in Upper Milford Tp., Northampton (now Lehigh Co., Pa., 1785 (3PA, XIX, 97). The name of course would be "Harner' in the Pennsylvania German area today.

## HOERNER, JOHANN JOERG — Eichel (1785)

April 15, 1785: wants to get cash for his goods and go with his wife and 5 children to America, since he can no longer support himself here. Still has 219 florins. Therefore he was taxed as follows: manumission, 10 florins and 57 kreuzer and in addition, 20% supplemental tax, 39 florins and 36 kreuzer; total, 50 florins and 33 kreuzer. // GEO[RGE] HORNER, with ANNA, JNO., JACOB, GEORGE, JR., ANNA

MARG'T, and KUNIGUNDA HORNER, and the FLEGLER Family, Ship *Favourite,* September 5, 1785 (Hinke, III, 9).

## HOERNER, JOERG — Wenkheim (1752)

May 19, 1752; wants to go to New England with wife and 1 child; in company with HANS HOERNER and MARIE HOERNER of Wenkheim, with the Lindelbach Transport (cf. GOETZELMANN); perhaps identical with Steger, No. 245. // See JOHANN GEORG HOERNER, above.

## HOERNER, MARIE — Wenkheim (1752)

May 19, 1752: wants to go to New England with JOERG and HANS HOERNER of Wenkheim, in the Wenkheim Transport (cf. GOETZELMANN). May 5, 1753: MARIA CATHARINA HOERNER is named in company with MECKELEIN, SEUBERT, SEMEL, and DIEHM. It seems that she did not emigrate until a year later.

## HOERNER, MARGARETHA — Dertingen (1754)

May 6, 1754: VALT[IN] HOERNER'S daughter, wants to go to America. Has 222 florins property.

## HOERNER, MICHAEL — Höhfeld (1753)

April 26, 1753: son of CHRISTOPH HOERNER, wants to go to New England with his wife MARIA BARBARA and 2 children, there to seek his living, "which I here find impossible except through begging." Mentioned as emigrant in the *Village Mayor's Report* for Höhfeld (1750-1761): "MICHAEL HOERNER, with wife and 2 little children." // HANS MICHEL HOERNER, Ship *Neptune,* September 24, 1753 (Hinke, I, 539 ff.), with other Wertheimers. Several MICHAEL HARNERS and HORNERS are listed in 3PA. Probably this emigrant settled in Montgomery Co., Pa., where MICHAEL and MARIA BARBARA HOERNER appear as parents of children baptized at the New Hanover Lutheran Church, 1756-1758 (*PGS Proceedings,* XX, 262). At the 1756 baptism, MARIA APOLLONIA FERTIG was sponsor. At the same church, one MICHAEL and ANNA MARIA HORNER appear as parents of children baptized in 1756.

## HOERNER, PHILIPP — Vockenroth (1786)

January 5, 1786: common petition with ADAM DOSCH and others (q.v.). On April 13, 1786, he is still firmly resolved "to emigrate to America." He has turned everything into cash, amounting to 1419 florins, 12 kreuzer, on which rest 764 florins, 14 kreuzer, debts. As to what he takes along on the journey, see *Introduction,* "Provisions for the Ocean Voyage." // JOHANN PHILLIP HOERNER, with wife and 3 children, along with JOHANN HEINERICH HOERNER, the GARRECHTS, DOSCH, etc., Brig *Dispatch,* October 31, 1786 (Hinke, III, 21). The children listed were ORCHIL MARIA, MARIA CATHARINA, MARIA ELIZABETH, CATHARINA, and MARIA DOROTHEA HORNER.

## HOERNER, VALENTIN — Dertingen (1754)

April 29, 1754: wants to go with his wife ANNA KUNIGUNDA and daughter BARBARA, to America. Has 531 florins property. His freedom costs:

| | |
|---|---|
| 20% of 531 florins 15 kreuzer | 26 florins 34 kreuzer |
| for his wife | 2 florins |
| for the daughter | 1 florin |
| TOTAL | 29 florins 34 kreuzer |

The government's decision was as follows: It is very hazardous to grant the right of emigration to subjects who still have so much property and stand in the vassal relation. HOERNER is to be strictly examined, as to the person through whom he was talked into emigrating. It is commanded, without delay, to issue a "General Prohibition of this spreading desire, after the precedent of other German states." The poor and useless subjects we can then perhaps dispense with. In the lands of other lords, where vassalage is not established, similar procedure is observed. Mentioned as emigrant in the *Village Mayor's Report* for Dertingen (1754). "VALT HOERNER made an agreement with the boatman SELIG (cf. KIESECKER). // VALTIN HOERNER, Ship *Phoenix,* October 1, 1754 (Hinke, I, 627 ff.), with other Wertheimers.

## HOTZ, MICHAEL — Wertheim

In 1769 MICHAEL HOTZ, Master Butcher of Philadelphia, returned to his natal city, Wertheim (cf. BESCHLER), then returned to the New World again. May 6, 1769: the son of the late HEINRICH HOTZ, now here for a while, is said not yet to have been manumitted; he emigrated with wife and children. On his marriage, however, nothing can be found in the Wertheim Church Registers. Neither is there any trace of children of his born here. He was born January 30, 1731. His father was in financial difficulties in 1749. See *Introduction,* "Letters from the New Land." // Others of the name in Hinke. MICHAEL HUTZ, butcher, Mulberry Ward, City of Philadelphia, 1774 (3PA, XIV, 294 ff.).

## KACHEL, ANDREAS — Dertingen (1750)

"ANDREAS KACHEL" emigrated, according to the *Village Mayor's Report,* for Dertingen (1750). // HANS ANDREAS KACHEL, Ship *Priscilla,* September 12, 1750 (Hinke, I, 444), with other Wertheimers. The family seems to have settled first in Montgomery, then in Berks County, Pa. ANDREAS and URSULA KACHEL appear as parents of children baptized at the New Hanover Lutheran Church, 1751-1759 (*PGS Proceedings,* XX, 267); the sponsor in 1751 bears a Wertheim name, JOH[ANN] LEONHART WISNER. In 1767 AND[REAS] KOCKEL appears as resident of Cumru Tp., Berks Co., Pa. (3PA, XVIII, 30). ANDREW KACHEL, of Cumry Tp., Berks Co., made his will 1776, probated 1777 (*Will Book* 2, p. 273, Berks County Courthouse, Reading, Pa.), mentioning his wife URSULA and son LEONHARD, whom he makes his executors, and sons SIMON and JOHN; witnesses: CHRIST. WITMAN, VALENTINE ECKERT, and NICHOLAS LOTZ.

## KACHEL, MICHAEL — Dertingen (1752)

May 10, 1752: a musketeer, wants to go to America with the musketeer DINKEL (q.v.), under the same circumstances. // MICHAEL ( ) KOGHILL, sick on board, with MICHAEL DINCKEL and other Wertheimers, Ship *Phoenix,* November 2, 1752 (Hinke, I, 503).

## KELLER, EVA MARGARETHA — Nassig (1763)

April 25, 1763: wants to go to New England. Has 256 florins and a child.

## KIESECKER, JOHANN ERNST — Steinmark (1754)

April 18, 1754: baker, son of the miller, CONRAD KIESECKER, of near Steinmark, reports on sickness and travels; see *Introduction,* "The

Newlander at Work." In the division of the inheritance, there was taken from him:

For learning my trade..............25 florins
For becoming apprenticed and
being freed ......................24 florins
To pay for 2 flasks of wine......... 1 florin
When I went abroad the first time,
I took along and spent...........20 florins
When I lay sick at home, it
cost in money...................16 florins 23 kreuzer
For my clothes in my apprentice
and wander-years ...............29 florins
When I went abroad the second time.33 florins
Spent in the time of my return......24 florins
For clothes for the afore-
mentioned journey ..............32 florins
For some necessary living
expenses on the journey..........15 florins 37 kreuzer

TOTAL.........................220 florins

January 15, 1773, it was reported of him: went to Thüngen and from there to Lancaster, in New England; in 1755 paid for his manumission. April 22, 1754: KIESECKER's property status seems to be incorrectly estimated. He is now 26 years old. In November, 1753, he returned. He now wants to go on foot to Holland, and will have nothing to do with the ship people. In Steinmark no one knows anything of his soliciting activities. On April 23, the ship people LORENZ SELIG and CHRISTOPH HOLLERBACH were charged with cooperating with KIESECKER. SELIG declares having made an agreement for transport to Rotterdam, with the following:

JOHANN CASPAR KNAUER, of Kredenbach
JOHANN GEORG SCHAEFER, of Glasofen, besides wife and children
JOHANN MICHAEL TEUFFEL, of Altfeld, with wife and children
JOHANN MICHAEL DILL, of Windsheim
HANS ADAM SAUER, with and wife children
HANS KNAUER, ANDREAS FERTIG, both of Altfeld
PETER BEHRINGER and LEONHARD OTT, of Hasloch
JOHANN PHILIPP OTT, of Lindelbach
VALT HOERNER, ANDREAS VAITH, and GEORG ADAM KOCH, all of Dertingen
THOMAS BUHNER and wife, of Wertheim
HANS MELCHIOR WEIPPERT, of Uettingen
NICOLAUS BUEHNER and wife, of Uettingen
HEINRICH DAMM and wife, of Hasselberg
HANS ADAM DIEHM and wife and children, of Schollbrunn
ANDREAS BAEUSCHLEIN, of Dietenhan

He presented the Agreement, sealed in Michelrieth on April 11, 1754, and written by the Pastor there. Every person over 14 years old pays 8 florins, 30 kreuzer. Children under 4 years, half. Children under 14 years are to be brought and delivered free, to Rotterdam.
SELIG further declares that yesterday he received an express messenger from Oberleinbach near *P*ossenheim, that he should there and in Schornweissach make agreements with 11 households, who would have nothing to do with any Newlander. They wish the agreement to be made also in Michelrieth, in the presence of the pastor.

In a letter which came from America, they were warned against the Newlanders. The other Wertheim boatmen, BALTASAR LOESCH, LEONHARD STEMMLER, and MICHAEL KRESS, had three Newlanders on their transports. STEMMLER, LOESCH, and KRESS had attached themselves to the Newlanders of Rothenburg and Weikersheim. KIESECKER wanted to take along the persons named in the *Introduction,* (see "The Newlander at Work") and in addition, THOMAS ENDRES and LORENZ ALBERT, a cartwright. KIESECKER is in conclusion to swear to the correctness of his property status. // JOHAN ERNST KIESECKER, aged 20, Ship *Patience,* September 16, 1748 (Hinke, I, 383 ff.). The only member of the family listed in the *United States Census of 1790 for Pennsylvania* (p. 129) is NICHOLAS KISECKER, of Cocalico Tp., Lancaster Co., Pa.

## KIESECKER, JOHANNES — Kredenbach (1754)

According to the *Village Mayor's Report* of 1761, he emigrated to New England in 1754, with his wife and child. Has paid for his manumission, and has nothing to seek anymore in Kredenbach. He was a brother of the Newlander KIESECKER, as also of JOHANN MATTHAEUS KIESECKER, below. // Cf. PHILIP KIESECKER, Ship *Neptune,* September 24, 1753 (Hinke, I, 539 ff.), with other Wertheimers.

## KIESECKER, JOHANN MATTHAEUS — Dertingen (1754)

See the *Introduction,* "The Newlander at Work." Wanted to emigrate with the Newlander KIESECKER, his brother, and his brother JOHANNES KIESECKER, above.

## KLEIN, ANDREAS MICHAEL — Sachsenhausen (1752)

April 28, 1752: wants to go with his wife and 2 children to Pennsylvania. Has 235 florins property. A similar request appears in the *Freudenberg Archive.* Mentioned as emigrant in the *Village Mayor's Report* for Sachsenhausen (1750-1761): "ANDREAS MICHAEL KLEIN, with wife and child; expects something yet from his parents-in-law." // ANDREAS KLEIN, Ship *Beulah,* September 10, 1753 (Hinke, I, 513 ff.); others in 1751 and 1753. Several ANDREW KLEINS in 3PA.

## KLEIN, NICOLAUS — Sachsenhausen (1752)

April 28, 1752: wants to go with wife and 3 children to Pennsylvania. Has only 28 florins property. // JOHAN NICKLES KLEIN, Ship *Phoenix,* November 2, 1752 (Hinke, I, 502), with other Wertheimers; others in 1753 and 1754.

## KNAUER, ANDREAS — Altfeld (1751)

April 17, 1751: is a carpenter, wants to emigrate with his wife MAGDALENA and 9 children as colonist to New England. Has left debts behind, and took nothing along. // ANDREAS KNAUER, with HANS and HANS PETTER KNAUER and JOHANNES and JOHANN MELCHIOR KNOR(R), and other Wertheimers, Ship *Duke of Bedford,* September 14, 1751 (Hinke, I, 458).

## KNAUER, HANS — Altfeld

Among the emigrants solicited by the boatman SELIG (cf. KIESECKER). // HANS KNAUER, with ANDREAS and HANS PETTER KNAUER, JOHANNES and JOHANN MELCHIOR KNOR(E), and other Wertheimers, Ship *Duke of Bedford,* September 14, 1751 (Hinke, I, 458). Doubtless he was the JOHANNES KNAUER who lived in Heidelberg Tp., Lancaster (now Lebanon) Co., Pa., later coming to Allen Tp., Cumberland Co., Pa., with his wife, EVA ANNA KNAUER, and family (1) JACOB KNAUER, married MARIA MAGDALENA STROCK, (2) BARBARA KNAUER, married D. Kishler, (3) CATHARINE KNAUER, and (4) ANNA MARGARETA KNAUER. His daughter, ANNA MARGARETA KNAUER, born in Heidelberg Township, Lancaster Co., Pa., Septemebr 22, 1766, and baptized October 7 by the Rev. JOHANN NICOLAUS KURTZ, married, April 26, 1791, JOHANN CHRISTOPHER ALBERT, born June 25, 1762, son of LORENZ and ANNA BARBARA (WOLFF) ALBERT. So it is evident that these two Wertheimer immigrant families kept in touch with each other in America. JOHANN CHRISTOPHER and ANNA MARGARETA ALBERT lived near the Lower Bermudian Lutheran and Reformed Union Church, in Adams County, Pa., where they are buried, MARGARETA dying on August 11, 1816, CHRISTOPHER on March 1, 1819. They were the ancestors of EDNA ALBERT, novelist and teacher (cf. Introduction).

## KNAUER, JOHANN CASPAR — Kredenbach (1754)

Is listed among the emigrants solicited by the Boatman SELIG (cf. KIESECKER, also the *Introduction,* "The Newlander at Work.")

## KNAUER, [———] — Nassig (1753)

May 11, 1753: in company with SCHUBERT and SCHLESSMANN, who want to sail with the boatman LOESCH.

## KNEUCKER, APOLLONIA — Wenkheim (1752)

May 19, 1752: single, 33 years old, has a child of 2 years, and no property. Wants to travel with the Wenkheim party (cf. GOETZELMANN).

## KOCH, GEORG ADAM — Dertingen (1754)

1754: listed among the emigrants solicited by the boatman SELIG (cf. KIESECKER). // GEORGE ADAM COOK, Washington Tp., Cumberland Co., Pa., 1779 (PA, XX, 244).

## KOELNER, PETER — Höhfeld (1785)

March 3, 1795: also called JOHANN PETER KOELNER. Complains over the impossibility of supporting himself here, wants to sell his property, but is still in doubt whether to go to Hungary or America. On April 7, 1785, he gives America as his destination. The government decided in his case: his conduct in other respects is of such a character that the government loses nothing in him. He realized 985 florins for his property; for cattle, tools, household utensils, etc., 110 florins, 57 kreuzer, he has 590 florins debts, and of the rest he must pay 118 florins, 48 kreuzer, on taxes. Wants to go to America with RIES (q.v.) of Höhfeld, who in respect to behavior is in a class with him. // Cf. MARIA ELIZ[ABE]TH KOELLNER: aged 44, with ANDREW PETER Roos, Ship *Patsey Rutledge,* May 23, 1787 (Hinke, III, 23).

## KRAFT, THOMAS — Kembach (1785)

April 14, 1785: has lost his wife 8 weeks ago through death, and now wants to join the transport of other emigrants which is leaving tomorrow. Was released on the same day. // No THOMAS KRAFT listed in Hinke, but note GEO[RGE] KRAFT, in the same cabin with ANDREAS SCHERGER family and CHRISTOPHER ARBORT, Wertheimers, Ship *Favourite,* September 5, 1785 (Hinke, III, 8).

## KRANK, HANS — Hasselberg (1752)

According to the *Village Mayor's Report* for Hasselberg (1752): "GEORG KRANK [and] HANS KRANCK, single," emigrated. May 20, 1752: perhaps the same as JOHANN JOERG KRANCK, son of JOHANNES KRANCK, the Village Mayor, who wants to emigrate with CASPAR and PETER *R*OOS and JOERG SEIDNER. All are "young single fellows, who want to find menial labor in Pennsylvania." All are in miserable circumstances. // HANS KRANCK, Ship *Phoenix*, November 2, 1752 (Hinke, I, 503), with other Wertheimers. One JOHN KRANCK was listed as "inmate" in Pikeland Tp., Chester Co., Pa., in 1768 (3PA, XI, 446).

## KRAN*C*K, JOHANN ADAM — Hasselberg (1752)

Added by the American editor. According to the "Records of the Lutheran Congregation at Old Goshenhoppen," *The Perkiomen Region*, I, 19: JOHANN ADAM KRANCK, son of JOHANNES KRANCK of Hasselberg and wife MARGARETHA, both Lutherans, was born June 23, 1723, and privately baptized *(genothtauft)*. On February 20, 1752, he married ANNA CATHARINA DAUBENSCHMIDT, born March 3, 1728, daughter of JOHANN GEORG DAUBENSCHMIDT, deceased, of Besterheud [Bestenheid], "of Graff[schaft] Loewenstein, in the district of Wertheim." In 1752 he came to America. He had one child born in Germany: ELISABETHA CATHARINA, born February 2, 1752; the baptisms of his other children are recorded at Old Goshenhoppen, 1754-1761.

## KRANK, JOHANNES — Bestenheid (1752)

May 12, 1752: wants to go to Pennsylvania with his wife and 1 child. Still has 20 florins. // Cf. HANS KRANCK, above, for public identification.

## KREMSER, ROSINA — Kreuzwertheim (1742)

Added by the American editor. According to Augustus Schultze, "Guide to the Old Moravian Cemetery of Bethlehem, Pa., 1742-1910," *PGS Proceedings*, XXI, 105, ROSINA KREMSER (171[-]-1798), born ROSINA OBERDORF at Kreuzwertheim, Franconia, became the wife of ANDREW KREMSER in 1742, "and the same year emigrated with him to Bethlehem. Her husband was steward of the school at Fredericktown, at Nazareth and lastly at Friedensthal, where in 1769 he died. A son JOHN was landlord at Nazareth." For this family, cf. also *Yearbook of the Pennsylvania German Folklore Society*, III, 20.

## KUCH, BURKHARD — Kreuzwertheim (1755)

According to the *Village Mayor's Report* for Kreuzwertheim (1755): "BURKHARD KUCH, a baker, left secretly at night with his wife and children; has nothing at all in property, but left many debts behind." // BURCKHARDT KUCH, Ship *Phoenix*, October 1, 1754 (Hinke, I, 627 ff.), with other Wertheimers.

## KUHN, CHRISTOPH — Urfar (1752)

May 17, 1752: musketeer, wants to go to Pennsylvania with his companion in arms, DINKEL (q.v.). // CHRISTOFF KUHN, *Ship Phoenix*, November 2, 1752 (Hinke, I, 501), with other Wertheimers. Several CHRISTOPHER KUHNS in 3PA. According to the Schlessmann Letters of 1753 and 1769, in Appendix II, JOHANNES SCHLESSMANN of Nassig and Germantown had a brother-in-law named CHRISTOPH KUHN. According to GSP's Transcript of the "Record of St. Michael's

Lutheran Church, Germantown, Philadelphia," p. 316, JOHANNES SCHLESSMANN and wife ANNA BARBARA were godparents at the baptism, on February 2, 1755, of JOHANNES KUHN, son of CHRISTOPH and ANNA ELISABETH KUHN. According to the same Record, p. 38, one CHRISTOPH KUHN of Bristol Township, Philadelphia County, was married, on February 27, 1770, to ELISABETH SCHLOESMANN of Oxford Township.

LEIMEISTER, WENDEL — Niclashausen (1751)

According to the *Village Mayor's Report* for Niclashausen (1751): "WENDEL LAUMEISTER (now written LEIMEISTER), single, has taken along 18 florins servant's wages. His father and mother are dead and were dispossessed and nothing remained to him from his paternal inheritance, except a few pieces of desolate vineyards, which his brother JACOB LAUMEISTER now has." // WENDEL (X) LAWMEISTER, Ship *Priscilla,* September 12, 1750 (Hinke, I, 444), with other Wertheimers. WENDLE LAUMASTER settled in York Borough, York Co., Pa., where he made his will 1797, probated 1797, mentioning ELIZABETH LAUMASTER, and grandson FREDERICK, son of FREDERICK LAUMASTER; Executor: PETER REISINGER (GSP, *"York County Will Abstracts,"* p. 301). The only other emigrant of the name listed in Hinke was JOHANN WILHELM LEYMEISTER, aged 58, who emigrated in 1748 (Hinke, I, 373 ff.) and as HANS WILLIAM LEIMEISTER, appears as farmer in Bern Tp., Berks Co., in 1767 (3PA, XVIII, 83).

LIEBLER, MARGARET*E* — Wenkheim (1752)

May 19, 1752: evidently traveled with the Wenkheim party (cf. GOETZELMANN); she was 20 years old, single, and propertyless.

LUTZ, GEORG MICHAEL — Kreuzwertheim (1752)

April 21, 1752: wants to go with his wife and 2 children to Pennsylvania. Mentioned as emigrant in the *Village Mayor's Report* for Kreuzwertheim (175*1*): "GEORG MICHAEL LUTZ, with wife and 2 children." // JOERG MICHEL LUTZ, Ship *Phoenix,* November 22, 1752 (Hinke, I, 508), with other Wertheimers. Several listed in 3PA, though perhaps this emigrant was the GEORG MICHAEL LUTZ, who, with wife ANNA WALBURGA, was sponsor at a baptism at St. Michael's Lutheran Church of Germantown, Pa. in 1756 (GSP's Transcript of St. Michael's Records, p. 335). Cf. also ANNA CATHARINA SCHAAF, elsewhere in this List.

LUTZ, JOHANN THOMAS — Kreuzwertheim (1755)

May 14, 1755: 14 years musketeer in Wertheim, wants to go with his wife and child to Pennsylvania. Has only 21 florins. // THOMAS LUTZ, Ship *Neptune,* October 7, 1755 (Hinke, I, 677 ff.). Evidently settled in Philadelphia, where, as carpenter, he appears in the Dock Ward in 1774, and the Mulberry Ward in 1782 (3PA, XIV, 239; XVI, 465). Mentioned in records of St. Michaelis and Zion Lutheran Church, Philadelphia, in 1759 (*PGS Proceedings,* XIV, 87), as witness at the wedding of ANDREAS ARBURTH (cf. CHRISTOPH ARBOURT, above).

LUTZ, MICHAEL — Wertheim (1752)

April 17, 1752: the small-farmer MICHAEL LUTZ and wife BARBARA, née SCHLESSMANN, of Nassig, want to go to New England or the "Island of I*n*fania," on account of overcrowded population and lack of food, in hopes there to seek their fortune. Are poor people, destination is Pennsylvania. According to the *Burgomaster's Accounts,* in the City Archives, nothing was reported on the supplemental tax of MICHAEL LUTZ, small farmer, because his property consists of nothing. // JOHANN MICHAEL LUTZ, Ship *Phoenix,* November 2, 1752 (Hinke, I, 502), with other Wertheimers.

## MARX, MAGDALENA and MARIA CATHARINA — Urfar (1752)

May 10, 1752: 24 and 22 years old; want to go to Philadelphia in New England, with the permission of their guardians. Manumission costs them 5 florins and 18 kreuzer. They are the single daughters of MICHEL MARX, according to the *Village Mayor's Report* for Urfar (1752).

## MECKELEIN, JOHANNES — Wenkheim (1753)

May 4, 1753: wants to go to New England with ADAM DIEHM (q.v.) and party. In the *Freudenberg Governmental Protocol,* April 1, 1753, he is called MEGERLIN. He is not permitted to sell his house to the Jews. It is to be put up in open sale and sold as high as possible. The remaining lands remain sequestrated, until the debts are declared and paid. See Steger, Nr. 186. // HANS MECKELEIN, with JOHAN HEINRICH MECKELEIN, and another HANS MECKELEIN, and other Wertheimers, Ship *Neptune,* September 24, 1753 (Hinke, I, 540 ff.). Several JOHN MECKLINS in 3PA. Note that one MARIA CATHARINA MECKLEIN, widow, was married on December 30, 1766, to JOHANNES SCHLOESSMANN of Germantown, according to GSP's Transcript of the "Record of St. Michael's Lutheran Church, Germantown, Philadelphia," p. 34. According to the same Record, p. 1097, she died in 1773, aged 67 years.

## MOENCH, HEINRICH — Wertheim (1751)

*Burgomaster's Accounts* (1751), in the City Archives: nothing from HEINRICH MOENCH, because his property consists of nothing. // JOHAN HENRICH MOENCH, Ship *Phoenix,* November 2, 1752 (Hinke, I, 503), with other Wertheimers. HENRICH MUNNICH, with THOMAS LUTZ [of Kreuzwertheim], and ANDREAS OBERDORFF and SIMON OBERDORFF, was a witness at the wedding of ANDREAS ARBURTH and ANNA MARGARETHA FRIEDLER, in 1759, at St. Michaelis and Zion Lutheran Church, Philadelphia, Pa. (*PGS Proceedings,* XIV, 87).

## MUELLER, ANNA CATHARINA — Kreuzwertheim (1752)

May 24, 1752: daughter of JACOB MUELLER, still single, wants to join the emigrants, but has not a red cent. First name learned from the *Village Mayor's Report* for Kreuzwertheim (1751): "ANNA CATHARINA MUELLER, single daughter of JACOB MUELLER, went emptyhanded from her parents, who are poor."

## NAHM, NICOLAUS — Dertingen (1754)

February 19, 1762: emigrated in 1754 without manumission, and is said to have died in America. Mentioned as emigrant in the *Village Mayor's Report* for Dertingen (1753): "NICOLAUS NAHM, single, took nothing along." In the *Freudenberg Governmental Protocol,* June 10, 1754, it is reported: NICOLAUS NAHM, OBERDORF and VOITH, all of Dertingen, left secretly for Pennsylvania a few days ago, and without receiving their manumission from vassalage.

## NERR, JOHANN PHILIPP — Wertheim (1753)

Buttonmaker. According to the *Burgomaster's Accounts* (1753), in the City Archives: NERR, who went to America, pays 25 florins on supplemental tax. // JOHANN PHILIPP NERN (NEER), Ship *Neptune,* September 24, 1753 (Hinke, I, 539 ff.), with other Wertheimers.

## OBERDORF, ADAM — Kembach (1753)

April 27, 1753: wants to go with his wife ANNA MAGDALENA and 3 children to the Island of Pennsylvania, because the direst need and poverty drives him to it. Is loaded with debts, despite his many pieces of land. Must pay 6 florins. "The government needs not to give anything to the creditors, and is privileged." According to the *Village Mayor's Report,* he went into bankruptcy. In the *Freudenberg Governmental Protocol,* attention is called on March 5, 1753 to the fact that ADAM OBERDORF wants to go to New England, but cannot dispose of his farm, on account of its vulnerability to danger of water and fire. A Catholic (!) from Reicholzheim liked it; he asks for permission to sell it to this foreign subject. On March 9, 1753, he repeats his request through his father, CHRISTOPH OBERDORF, and describes his cot (farmhouse) as old and dilapidated. February 21, 1754: CHRISTOPH OBERDORF inquires whether he should turn over to the creditors the small property of his son ADAM, who last year went to New England, to settle his extensive bankruptcy, since there were 60 florins more debts than the property would pay for. // ADAM OBERDORF, Ship *Richard and Mary,* September 17, 1753 (Hinke, I, 531 ff.), with other Wertheimers.

## OBERDORF, ANDREAS — Lindelbach (1773)

March 30, 1773: widower, with 6 children, wants to go with heads of families RAU and SPIELMANN to New England. In all, 15 children. April 26, 1773: is still to receive 210 florins from his father-in-law. Of this, 10½ florins go for manumission; on the remaining 199½ florins, he must pay a 20% supplemental tax. If he had only had one-half florin more, he would have had to give only 10% supplemental tax! Left behind 819 florins debt. // ANDTERREAS OBERDORFF, with JOHANN MICHEL OBERDORFF, JOHANN BERNHARDT RAU, JOHAN LORENTZ DIHM, etc., Ship *Hope,* October 1, 1773 (Hinke, I, 753). ANDREW OBEBEDORFF *(sic),* 100 acres, Northampton Co., Pa., surveyed 1774 [1775] (3PA, XXVI, 144). Note that the ANDREAS OBERDORFF, who with HANS ANDREAS KACHEL, ANDREAS OETZEL, JOHN SIMON OBERDORFF, WILHELM ADELMANN, and other possible Wertheimers, arrived on the Ship *Priscilla,* September 12, 1750 (Hinke, I, 444), was also probably a Wertheimer emigrant. It was this ANDREAS OBERDORFF who married ANNA MARIA ESTHER VERDION, in 1758, at St. Michaelis and Zion Lutheran Church, Philadelphia, Pa. (*PGS Proceedings,* XIV, 77); witnesses were JACOB OBERDORFF and JOHANN HENRICH MUENNICH, and others.

## OBERDORF, BALTASAR — Dietenhan (*ca.* 1752)

According to the *Village Mayor's Report* for Dietenhan (1752): "BALTZ[ER] OBERDORF and wife, went away as a spendthrift; his 4 children stayed here, [and] must support themselves with servant's wages." // BALTZ OBERDORFF, with JOHAN GORG and JACOB OBERDORFF and VALLENTIN (X) OBERTORF, and other Wertheimers, Ship *Neptune,* September 24, 1753 (Hinke, I, 540 ff.).

## OBERDORF, BARBARA — Lindelbach (1752)

May 12, 1752: listed among the Lindelbach party (cf. BETZ).

## OBERDORF, CASPAR — Dertingen (1754)

May 4, 1762: went to America in 1754, has not yet paid his manumission. No word whether he is dead or alive. Was single, according to the *Village Mayor's Report. Freudenberg Governmental Protocol,* June 10, 1754: CASPAR OBERDORF, NAHM and VOIT, went away secretly some days ago to Pennsylvania, and without manumission from vassalage. According to the *Village Mayor's Report* for Dertingen (1753): "CASPAR OBERDORF, single, [took nothing along]." // CASPER OBERDORF, Ship *Phoenix*, October 1, 1754 (Hinke, I, 672 ff.), with other Wertheimers. Note that the KASPER OBERDORFF who arrived on the Ship *Priscilla,* September 12, 1750 (Hinke, I, 444), with ANDREAS OBERDORFF, JOHAN SIMON ( ) OBERDORFF, on board, and other Wertheimers, was probably also a Wertheimer. According to the Records of St. Michaelis and Zion Lutheran Church, Philadelphia (*PGS Proceedings,* XIV, 130), one CASPAR OBERDORFF was married, in 1763, to MARY CHAMBERS.

## OBERDORF, [JOHANNES] — Kembach (1782)

*Rosenberg Archive,* Br. 387 m, May 3, 1782: called "SCHEUERNHANS." In the 1750's "he was sought as a 'slave-trader' by the criminal jurisdiction of Remlingen, but got away." See the *Introduction,* "The Newlander at Work."

## OBERDORF, JOHANN JACOB — Dietenhan (1752)

May 12, 1752: has incurred many debts through his marriage, and fears that taxes might overwhelm him; feels himself unable to get on in the world with his family, and wants now to go to Pennsylvania with his wife and 4 children. The children were named: MARGARETHA FRIDLIN, 13; CASPAR, 12½; CATHARINA, 7½; and JOHANN CHRISTOPH, 5½. Realized from the sale of his property, 190 florins, 26 kreuzer. According to another reference, the daughter ANNA MARGARETHA FRIDLIN, 17 years old, is said to have remained behind. Mentioned in the *Village Mayor's Report* for Dietenhan (1752): "JACOB OBERDORF, with wife and children." // JACOB OBERDORF, Ship *Phoenix,* November 2, 1752 (Hinke, I, 502), with other Wertheimers. Another JACOB OBERDORFER settled in Douglass Tp., Philadelphia Co., Pa., where he is taxed in 1783. JACOB OBERDORFF of Philadelphia, in his will dated 1758 and probated 1775, mentions sons JACOB and GEORGE, and makes his step-daughter MARGARET, executrix; witnesses, JOHN HENRY MOENCH and JOHN THOS. LUTZ [Wertheimers!] *Will Book* Q, p. 190, Philadelphia County Courthouse, Philadelphia, Pa.). (3PA, XVI, 546).

## OBERDORF, PHILIPP JACOB — Dertingen (1753)

May 4, 1753: has been forced these many years to support himself very meagerly, having in these times of dire need spent his all. Finally he had to herd cattle, and has not a red cent left. Is willing to go to America with his wife and child, with God's help and the chance afforded by beneficent people. Is to pay 5 florins. Brings testimony to his direst need, leaves as a beggar, had at last to herd geese. Was exempted from the tax. // Perhaps JACOB OBERDORFF, with BALTZ, JOHANN GORG OBERDORFF, and VALENTIN (X) OBERTORF, and other Wertheimers, Ship *Neptune,* September 24, 1753 (Hinke, I, 540 ff.). See also JOHANN JACOB OBERDORF, above.

## OBERDORF, [———] — Lindelbach and Dietenhan (1777)

May 15, 1777: of the brothers and sisters named OBERDORF, of Lindelbach and Dietenhan, not all four are said to have gone to New England. BALTASAR is in the Imperial War Service. The legacy in question is said to have been announced in the Frankfurt and Hanau papers, since it is on the one hand possible that some one of them could have returned. On the other hand, this news could very easily reach them, through the present relationship between Germany and the abovementioned part of the world.

## OESTERLEIN, JEREMIAS — Bertingen (1753)

June 26, 1753: bought his freedom in 1751 with VALT. SCHOEFFER, in order to go to Pennsylvania. OESTERLEIN regretted it later, was then in the County of Erbach, but finally went to Pennsylvania with wife and child. Had no property. April 15, 1751: wants to go with wife and 3 children to Pennsylvania. Has 22 florins and must pay 1½ florins for manumission. But meanwhile he laid violent hands on his father, and became a fugitive, with not a farthing's worth of property. // JEREMIAS OESTERLEIN, Ship *Phoenix*, November 2, 1752 (Hinke, I, 502), with other Wertheimers. JEREMIAH ESTERLINE settled in Limerick Tp., Philadelphia (now Montgomery) Co., Pa., where he was taxed in 1769 (3PA, XIV, 53). According to the records of the New Hanover Lutheran Church, JEREMIAS OSTERLEIN married MARIA CATHARINA WEITNER, May 3, 1754 (*PGS Proceedings*, XX, 408), and died March 11, 1775, aged 51 years, 2 months, 2 weeks, and 4 days (*Ibid.*, 436). Children of JEREMIAS and MARIA CATHARINA OESTERLEIN (AESTERLEIN) were baptized from 1755-1767, and there were members of the family still in the community in 1818. JOHANN GOETZELMAN and wife were sponsors of the child born 1762.

## OETZEL, ANDREAS — Dietenhan (1750)

Emigrated with his wife, according to the *Village Mayor's Report* for Dietenhan (1750). // ANDREAS OETZEL, Ship *Priscilla*, September 12, 1750 (Hinke, I, 444), with other Wertheimers. This family seems to have settled in Montgomery Co., Pa., then moved on to Cumru Tp., Berks Co., as did ANDREAS KACHEL of Dertingen. According to the records of the New Hanover Lutheran Church, ANDREW E[T]ZEL and wife CATHARINA were parents of children baptized 1750-1770 (*PGS Proceedings*, XX, 229, 292, etc.) Occasionally persons bearing Wertheim names appear as sponsors, as JUERG WOLF and wife EVA MARIA in 1761, JOH. JOERG WISNER in 1750, ANDREW KACHEL and wife in 1753, LEONHARD WIESNER and wife in 1770. ANDREW ETZEL was taxed in Cumru Tp., Berks Co., Pa., in 1779-1780 (3PA, XVIII, 189, 336), and died there intestate in 1798, letters of administration being granted to CATHARINE, the widow, and a son ANDREW (GSP, "Abstracts of Berks County Wills," II).

## OETZEL, JAKOB — Urfar (1773)

January 21, 1773: wants to go with wife and 3 children to New England in company with STRAUSS's widow, because they can no longer earn their living in Urfar. Their poverty is confirmed in the *Village Mayor's Report*.

## OETZEL, MICHEL — Lindelbach (1752)

May 12, 1752: is listed, with 1 child, among the Lindelbach party (cf. BETZ). // HANS MICHEL OETZEL, Ship *Phoenix*, November 2,

1752 (Hinke, I, 501), with other Wertheimers. According to the GSP's Transcript of the "Records of St. Michael's Lutheran Church of Germantown," p. 1112, MICHAEL ETZEL, of Upper Dublin Township, aged 63 years, was buried March 16, 1782.

## OTT, JOHANN HEINRICH — Lindelbach (1754)

May 20, 1754: is loaded with debts. Now has opportunity to leave the country with his brothers. "Bread is dear for us, when we can raise not a load of grain, and the other people are poor too, and can give us nothing," etc. The government's decision was: manumission costs 3 florins, which he may borrow meanwhile from his companions, and can pay back in Pennsylvania. Is listed among the passengers of the boatman SELIG (cf. KIESECKER). // HEINRICH OTT, with LENHARDT OTT, and other Wertheimers, Ship *Phoenix,* October 1, 1754 (Hinke, I, 627 ff.). One HENRY OTT, farmer, was taxed in Upper Milford Tp., Northampton (now Lehigh) Co., Pa., in 1772 (3PA, XIX, 10); another appears with other Otts, in Bedminster Tp., Bucks Co., Pa., in 1779 (3PA, XIII, 93 ff.).

## OTT, JOHANN NICOLAUS — Hasloch (1752)

May 24, 1752: single, son of HANS BERND OTT's widow, wants to go to New England. His mother wants to him 5 florins to take along. Mentioned as emigrant in the *Village Mayor's Report* for Hasloch (1750-1761): "JOHANN NICOLAUS OTT, single, son of HANS BERND OTT's widow. His mother could give him only 9 florins to take along, because she is a poor widow." // JOHANN NICKOLAUS OTT, Ship *Phoenix,* November 2, 1752 (Hinke, I, 502), with other Wertheimers. NICH'S OTT, Northampton Town, Northampton Co., Pa., 1785 (3PA, XIX, 112 ff.).

## OTT, LEONHARD — Hasloch (1754)

May 10, 1754: has for some years so gone into decline and indebtedness, that he does not know how to help himself anymore, to look after his wife and children in these times of scarce bread. Wants to go to Pennsylvania, with his wife and 5 children in age from 1 to 15 years. Has 463 florins, 23 kreuzer remaining. Owns many fields, vineyards, meadows and gardens. Mentioned as emigrant in the *Village Mayor's Report* for Hasloch (1750-1761): LEONHARD OTT, with wife and children." Is listed among the passengers of the boatman SELIG (cf. KIESECKER). // LENHARDT OTT, with HEINRICH OTT, and other Wertheimers, Ship *Phoenix,* October 1, 1754 (Hinke, I, 627 ff.). It was possibly a son of his, JOHANN PETER OTT, who married SOPHIA CATHARINA KOECHLER, in 1762, at St. Michaelis and Zion Lutheran Church, Philadelphia, Pa. (*PGS Proceedings,* XIV, 124); witnesses were CHRISTOPH ENGLERT, LEONHARDT OTT, and JOH. JAC. OTT.

## PLATZ, JOHANN PAUL — Wertheim (1753)

May 14, 1753: burgher and tanner, wants to go to the New World or to the so-called Island of Pennsylvania, with his two sons. Is propertyless and received manumission gratis. // JOHANN PAULUS PLATZ, with ADAM NICH[OLA]S PLATZ, and other Wertheimers, Ship *Neptune,* September 24, 1752 (Hinke, I, 540 ff.).

## POPP, HANS JOERG — Grünewörth (1768)

April 7, 1768: has about 1200 florins property, with 1000 florins debts, and does not feel able to raise the interest. Wants to go to Pennsylvania. Has 2 children, 14 and 4½ years of age. His fellow citizens can say nothing against his or his wife's conduct. Opinion rendered: It is known that emigrations in foreign lands outside Germany have been forbidden through general Circle-Restrictions and that emigrants from here were interned. The request is to be refused, since the petitioner with wife and children will most probably be plunged into misery, because the little that he takes out of the land, scarcely 140 florins after payment of costs, would hardly pay for his transport to Holland, where he and his would then fall into the hands of the "soul-sellers." It would weigh on our consciences, to let such people bring themselves into misfortune through our indulgence of their wilfulness. Should the petitioner return, as happened often already with others like him, then we could not permit his remaining here, in order not to burden the country with beggars and idlers. POPP then presumably wants to go to Hungary, where the emigration is not forbidden. // HANS GEORG BOPP, with JOHAN CHRISTOFFEL FERDIG, Ship *Minerva,* October 13, 1769 (Hinke, I, 726). Because of the uncertainty of the record, Dr. Langguth included POPP and FERTIG in his list of emigrants to Hungary; this identification in Hinke proves that they went to America. Note also that BERNHART and JOHAN GEORG BOB (POP) arrived on the Ship *Phoenix,* October 1, 1754 (Hinke, I, 627 ff.), with other Wertheimers; perhaps these were members of the same family.

## POEPP, JOERG — Grünewörth (1766)

March 21, 1766: wants to go to New England. // Perhaps identical with HANS JOERG POPP, above.

## RAU, PHILIPP — Lindelbach (1773)

March 20, 1773: wants to go with wife and 6 children to New England, in company with OBERDORF and SPIELMANN. RAU has 466 florins debts, but little or no property — as little as both of the others had. // PHILIPP RAU does not appear in Hinke in 1773, but note JOHANN BERNHARDT RAU, with JOHANN MICHEL OBERDORFF and ANDTERREAS OBERDORFF, Ship *Hope,* October 1, 1773 (Hinke, I, 753).

## REINER, JOHANN GEORG — Nassig (1752)

May 20, 1752: single, wants to go to Pennsylvania with 130 florins. In the *Village Mayor's Report* for Nassig (1753), he is called "HANS GEORG REINER, single." // Perhaps JOHANN GEORG REINHARD, Ship *Queen of Denmark,* November 3, 1752 (Hinke, I, 506). It seems that he was not the GEORGE REINERD, farmer of Upper Milford Tp., Northampton (now Lehigh) Co., Pa., in 1772 (3PA, XIX, 10), who was a Württemberger.

## REUTLINGER, JOHANN LEONHARD — Löwenstein

Added by the American editor. According to the Manuscript "Records of St. Michaelis and Zion Lutheran Church," Philadelphia, Pa., in the Genealogical Society of Pennsylvania, JOHANN LEONHARD REUTLINGER and wife ROSINA, "newcomers from Löwenstein, near Wertheim," had a child baptized in 1754. // Two others are listed in Hinke.

## RIES, JOHANN ADAM — Höhfeld (1785)

March 5, 1785: wants to go with PETER KOELNER to America, since his properties are encumbered with debts. For the government's decision, cf. KOELNER. RIES has a wife and 1 child. Remaining from his sale, 95 florins. Among his provisions for the journey were shoemaker and tinker work, as with ALBERT:

To shoemaker KRITZLER, for 1 pair of woman's shoes ........................................1 florin 4 kreuzer
For dried Schnitz ..........................3 florins
For tow cloth for shirts in Wertheim, paid to MANGER [MANGLER?] WITT in the *Judengasse* ..................................4 florins 20 kreuzer
For 1 pair of man's and 1 pair woman's stockings, to old LANGGUTH....................1 florin 40 kreuzer
For 1 pair of leather pants, paid to the Jew ISRAEL in Neubrunn ......................2 florins 40 kreuzer
To the same Jew for a bodice for his wife....1 florin
For lard and prunes.........................3 florins 15 kreuzer

// ADAM RIESS, with ELIZ., MARG'T, and GEORGE RIESS, along with HORNERS, FLEGLERS, SCHERGERS, ARBORT and KRAFT, Wertheimers, on the Ship *Favourite*, September 5, 1785 (Hinke, III, 8).

## RIES, JOHANN PETER — Wertheim (1753)

May 7, 1753: a saddler, has resolved to go to the so-called Island of Pennsylvania on account of miserable sustenance. In hi hearing at the Town Hall, he swore that he was not saving a red cent, except his good name. Asks for relief from the fee. The government resolved at the time: where there is nothing, the Emperor has lost his right; received manumission without the u ual fee. *Freudenberg Governmental Protocol*, May 11, 1753: PETER RIES, the saddler of this place, wants to leave his children with his father-in-law, the Village Mayor of Eichel, and emigrate alone. // JOHANN PETER RIESS, Ship *Neptune*, September 24, 1753 (Hinke, I, 539 ff.), with other Wertheimers. PETER REES, Bern Tp., Berks Co., Pa., 1779 (3PA, XVIII, 203); PETER RIES, Pinegrove Tp., Berks (now Schuylkill) Co., Pa., 1785 (3PA, XVIII, 777).

## RIES, [———] — Höhfeld (*ca.* 1755)

Son of MARTIN RIES' widow, first name lacking. *Village Mayor's Report* for Höhfeld (1750-1761): "MARTIN RIES' widow's son also took nothing with him. His mother still has the property on hand. Left without manumission." // Perhaps he was the JOHANN LEONHARDT RIES, *"von Höfeld aus Wertheim,"* who according to the GSP's Transcript of the "Record of St. Michael's Lutheran Church, Germantown, Philadelphia," Part I, p. 14, was married, on February 8, 1756, to ELIZABETHA ZEITER, of Schop[f]loch in Württemberg.

## ROOS, CASPAR and PETER — Hasselberg (1752)

May 20, 1752: CASPAR ROOS and PETER ROOS, both sons of the late forester ROOS, want to emigrate with KRANK and SEIDNER, all young single fellows, etc. (cf. KRANK). Mentioned as emigrants in the *Village Mayor's Report* for Hasselberg (1752): "PETER ROOS' widow's 2 sons, emptyhanded and propertyless; they have commissioned their brother trustee of their inheritance." // JOHANN CAS*B*ER ROSS, Ship *Edinburg*, September 14, 1753 (Hinke, I, 521 ff.). PETER ROSS, Ship *Phoenix*, November 2, 1752 (Hinke, I, 502), with other Wertheimers. According to Augustus Schultze, "Guide to the Old Moravian Cemetery of Bethlehem, Pa., 1742-1910," *PGS Proceedings*, XXI, 41: PETER ROSE (1733-1814), born at Hasselberg in Franconia, "came to America when a young man, enlisted in 1755, fought against the French, and was wounded in the right shoulder. After joining the Moravian Church, he worked on the farm at Bethlehem, and in

1773, married A. ROSINA BOECKEL. They removed to North Carolina, but returned to Bethlehem, where, in 1801, he became tollkeeper at the bridge."

RUDOLF, [———] — Altfeld

Mentioned as emigrant in the *Village Mayor's Report* for Altfeld (n.d.): "ANDREAS RUDOLF's daughter, single, has no parents anymore. Still has 100 florins with her brother JUERG RUDOLF in Michelrieth."

SAUER, HANS ADAM — Kredenbach (1754)

April 16, 1762: son of JOHANN THOMAS SAUER, has gone to New England. In 1754 he appears with wife and children, among the passengers of the boatman SELIG (cf. KIESECKER). // Two of the name appear in Hinke: (1) JOHANN ADAM SAUER, with JOHAN LEONHARD SAUER and other Wertheimers, Ship *Neptune,* September 24, 1753 (Hinke, I, 539 ff.); (2) HANS ADAM SAUER, with HANNS MICHEL SAUER and JOHANNES SAUER, and other Wertheimers, Ship *Phoenix,* October 1, 1754 (Hinke, I, 627 ff.). Many listed in 3PA. See the MICHEL FERTIG letter of 1782, *Introduction,* Appendix III, for reference to ADAM SAUR of near Skippack.

SCHAAF, ANNA CATHARINA — Kreuzwertheim (1743)

Added by the American editor. According to Augustus Schultze, "Guide to the Old Moravian Cemetery of Bethlehem, Pa., 1742-1910," *PGS Proceedings,* XXI, 17, 57, ANNA CATHARINA SCHAAF, née LOZE (1722-1748), was "born at Creuz-Wertheim on the Main, Germany. She came to Pennsylvania in November, 1743, with her husband, the weaver, THOMAS SCHAAF." THOMAS SCHAAF (*alias* BOCK!), 1717-1791, was born near Nuremberg, Germany. In Clarence E. Beckel, "Early Marriage Customs of the Moravian Congregation in Bethlehem, Pennsylvania," *Yearbook of the Pennsylvania German Folklore Society,* III, 23-24, her maiden name is given also as LOTZ and LUTZ. Cf. also the several LUTZ emigrants from Kreuzwertheim elsewhere in this List.

SCHABER, JOHANN CHRISTOF — Sachsenhausen (1752)

April 21, 1752: pays 45 florins, 15 kreuzer, for his freedom from vassalage. "Because we do not have reason to give these emigrants undue favors and it was formerly customary to demand 5% of their property, we charge 2 florins for the wife, 1 florin for each child, so these people had to pay, after paying the tax:

| | |
|---|---|
| JOHANN CHRISTOF SCHWAB, | — 45 florins, 15 kreuzer |
| ANDREAS MICHEL KLEIN, | — 15 florins, 45 kreuzer |
| NICLAS KLEIN, | — 7 florins, 30 kreuzer |

// JOHANN CHRISTOPH SCHABER, Ship *Phoenix,* November 2, 1752 (Hinke, I, 503), with other Wertheimers. Two CHRISTOPH[ER] SCHABERS are listed in 3PA: (1) CHRISTOPHER SHABER, Brunswick Tp., Berks (now Schuylkill) Co., Pa., 1779, 1785 (3PA, XVIII, 197 ff.); (2) STOFFEL SCHABER, laborer, Tulpehocken Tp., Berks Co., Pa., 1768 (3PA, XVIII, 169). It was probably this latter CHRISTOPH SCHABER who married MARIA EVA ROSINA STRAUSS of Tulpehocken in 1762 ("Stoever Records," *Notes and Queries.* Annual Volume for 1896, p. 100). CHRISTOPHER and MARIA EVE ROSINA SCHABER removed to Penn's Tp., Northumberland Co., Pa., where his will is dated 1793 ("Abstracts of Wills and Administrations of Northumberland County," *GSP Proceedings,* XIV, 24).

SCHABER, JOHANN CHRISTOPH — Sachsenhausen (1752)

April 28, 1752: asks his "dear and noble magistracy to deign graciously to grant him and wife and children, out of his patriarchal benevolence and mercy, freedom from vassalage, in order that he may go to Pennsylvania." Has 825 florins property, must pay 45 florins, 15 kreuzer for his freedom. Mentioned as emigrant in the *Village Mayor's Report* for Sachsenhausen (1750-1761): "JOHANN CHRISTOF SCHABER, with wife and children." From the *Freudenberg Governmental Protocol,* April 28, 1752, it appears that SCHABER took 2 children along. // For identification in Hinke, and residence in Pennsylvania, see JOHANN CHRISTOF SCHABER, above.

SCHAEFER, GEORG — Dertingen (1752)

May 19, 1752: was 10 years in Bonfeld on the Neckar, then went back again to Dertingen. "Through sickness sent upon me by the Dear Lord, everything was lost, so that little or nohing is left." Because many people are now going to New England, he likewise has resolved to go there, under God, with his wife and 4 children. *Freudenberg Governmental Protocol,* May 19, 1752: asks for a merciful consideration, because he already bought his freedom once, in Bonfeld, but from lack of livelihood he could not stay there either. Now receives manumission *gratis. Ibid.,* October 18, 1754: GEORG SCHAEFER, who went to New England, was a member of the Court Martial of Dertingen. // Perhaps JOH. GEO. SCHEFER, Ship *Queen of Denmark,* September 11, 1753 (Hinke, I, 517).

SCHAEFER, GEORG — Glasofen (1754)

May 6, 1754: GEORG SCHAEFER, his wife BARBARA, sons ANDREAS and JOERG SCHAEFER, and daughters CATHARINA and ANNA SCHAEFER, all of Glasofen, want to go to America. The father, GEORG SCHAEFER, still has 1174 florins and 26 kreuzer remaining from the sale of his property. The Village Mayor SCHAEFER of Hasloch reports that the above GEORG SCHAEFER once had a fortune of 6000 florins and squandered it down to 1174 florins. It is to be feared lest the balance might likewise come to an end in a short time. The government resolved this time, to let all petitioners depart wiithout differentiation, therefore this request, too, is to be approved. There will only be 5% collected out of 1174 florins and 25 kreuzer — amounting to 58 florins and 44 kreuzer. SCHAEFER is listed among the passengers of the boatman SELIG (cf. KIESECKER). *Freudenberg Governmental Protocol:* The emigrant GEORG SCHAEFER of Glasofen still owes the widowed Hospital Inmate ENDRESS, in Wertheim, 83 florins. His property is to be sequestrated. // Perhaps GEORG SCHOEFFER, Brigantine *Mary and Sarah,* October 26, 1754 (Hinke, I, 662 ff.).

SCHAEFER, JOHANN ADAM and PETER — Kredenbach (1752)

May 19, 1752: JOHANN ADAM and PETER SCHAEFFER, both sons of LEONHARD SCHAEFER here, want to go to Pennsylvania, to earn a little money there. Their parents are poor and up in years and can give the sons nothing to take along. The government resolved that for 2 florins per person they can be manumitted, but should they possibly return, they are not to be received as subjects again. In the *Village Mayor's Report* for Kredenbach (1752) is the note: LEONHARD SCHAEFER's two sons left without money. // HANS ADAM SCHAEFFER, with JOHANES (X) and CHRISTIAN SCHAEFFER, and other Wertheimers, Ship *Phoenix,* November 2, 1752 (Hinke, I, 503).

SCHAETZLEIN, BARTEL — Wenkheim (1752)

May 19, 1752: wants to go with his wife and 7 children to New England, in company with HOERNER, GOETZELMANN, etc. His property he sets at 100 florins, but it is found to be 138 florins. See Steger, No. 212. In the Investigation of KIESECKER (q.v.), the latter says he brought a letter from America to GEORG SCHAETZLEIN from his son. But according to Steger, the father's name was NICOLAUS. // BARTHEL SCHAETZLEIN, Ship *Phoenix,* November 2, 1752 (Hinke, I, 503), with other Wertheimers. BARTHOLOMEW SHETZLINE, with ADAM SHETZLINE, Moyamensing, Philadelphia Co., Pa., 1774 (3PA, XIV, 370); BARTH'A SHETZLEIN, Mulberry Ward, Philadelphia, Pa., 1782 (3PA, XVI, 454).

SCHAETZLEIN, JOHANN ANDREAS — Remlingen (1773)

April 23, 1773: wants to go with wife and 2 children to New England. *Rosenberg Archive,* Fascicle Br. 360 a, and Br. 387 i: has 337 florins. In the second case his property is given as 297 florins.

SCHEURICH, JOHANN MATTHES — Nassig (1752)

May 5, 1752: wants to go with his wife to Pennsylvania. Has 50 florins in property. *Village Mayor's Report* for Nassig (1752): "MATH. SCHEURICH, JR., with wife [and] without children." *Village Mayor's Report* for Sachsenhausen (1750-1761): "JOHANN MATTH. SCHEURICH of Nassig, left from here, with his wife." // JOHANN MATTHES SCHEURICH, with VALENTIN, JACOB, and HANS MARTIN SCHEURICH, and other Wertheimers, Ship *Phoenix,* November 22, 1752 (Hinke, I, 507 ff.). These were the only SCHEURICHS listed in Hinke. Settled in or near Lancaster, Pa., where MATTHEUS and CATHARINA SCHAEURICH appear as parents of children baptized 1758-1768, at Trinity Lutheran Church (*PGS Proceedings,* III, 227 ff.). In the same records, JACOB and ANNA MARIA SCHAEURICH (SCHEURIG) appear as parents of baptized children in 1761-1770 (*Ibid.,* III, 241 ff.). MATHEW SHEYRY was taxed in Hempfield Tp., Lancaster Co., Pa., in 1771 (3PA, XVII, 119).

SCHEURICH, MARTIN — Sonderrieth (1752)

May 21, 1752: single, son of the late HANS MICHEL SCHEURICH, wants to go with 300 florins to Pennsylvania. According to the *Village Magistrate's Report* for 1753, he had emigrated by that time. // HANS MARTIN SCHEURICH, with JOHANN MATTHES, VALENTIN, and JACOB SCHEURICH, and other Wertheimers, Ship *Phoenix,* November 22, 1752 (Hinke, I, 507 ff.).

SCHEURICH, VALENTIN — Nassig (1752)

May 5, 1752: wants to go with 5 children to Pennsylvania. Still has 30 florins. Mentioned as emigrant in the *Village Mayor's Report* for Nassig (1752): "VALT. SCHEURICH, widower, and children." // VALENTIN SCHEURICH, with JOHANN MATTHES, JACOB, and HANS MARTIN SCHEURICH, and other Wertheimers, Ship *Phoenix,* November 22, 1752 (Hinke, I, 507 ff.).

SCHLESSMANN, BARBARA — Nassig (1753)

Has one child. Mentioned as emigrant in the *Village Mayor's Report* for Nassig (1753): "BARBARA SCHLESSMANN, with her child." // One

ANNA BARBARA SCHLESSMANN was married, on May 22, 1759, to JOHANN HENRICH HAERDTEL, according to the GSP's Transcript of the "Record of St. Michael's Lutheran Church, Germantown, Philadelphia," Part I, 23. According to the will of JOHANNES SCHLESSMANN (q.v.) of Germantown, BARBARA (SCHLESSMANN) HERDEL was his daughter.

## SCHLESSMANN, HANS CHRISTOF — Nassig (1752)

May 24, 1752: 18 years old, son of JOHANN SCHLESSMANN, wants to go to Pennsylvania; but his father cannot give him a kreuzer to take along. // HANS CHRISTOPH SCHLESSMANN, with JOHANN HEINRICH SCHLESSMANN and JOHANN NICOLAUS SCHLOSSMANN, and other Wertheimers, Ship *Phoenix,* November 2, 1752 (Hinke I, 501 ff.). Note that these are the only SCHLESSMANNS listed in Hinke. According to the Records of St. Michaelis and Zion Lutheran Church, Philadelphia (*PGS Proceedings,* XIV, p. 60), one CHRISTOPH SCHLESSMANN was married, in 1756, to CATHRINA ARS; witnesses were JOHANNES and ANNA CATHARINA SCHLESSMANN, CUNIGUNDA WALFORD, etc.

## SCHLESSMANN, HANS PAUL — Nassig (1752)

May 24, 1752: is still undecided whether to go to Pennsylvania or spend his three journeyman-years as tailor in the Empire. June 9, 1752: HANS PAUL SCHLESSMANN has either to pay for his manumission with 2 florins, or abstain from emigration to New England on penalty of confiscation of his future legacy, as well as his possible reclamation as a fugitive servant. In the first case also his inheritance is to be sequestrated. Mentioned as emigrant in the *Village Mayor's Report* for Nassig (1752): "PAUL SCHLESSMANN's son, a tailor apprentice, also has taken nothing along, and has nothing more to expect here."

## SCHLESSMANN, JOHANNES — Nassig (1753)

May 11, 1753: is going with his wife and 5 children to Pennsylvania. Shall pay 17 florins, 10 kreuzer, out of 203 florins property. May 4, 1770: NICOLAUS ZIMMERMANN of Oxford, County of Philadelphia, by virtue of a Power of Attorney from the British Notary PETER MILLER, wants to take back to America the inheritance of JOHANNES SCHLESSMANN, a native of Nassig. See the Introduction, Appendix II, for the original letters of SCHLESSMANN, preserved in the Wertheim Archives. His relatives are: MICHAEL REINER of Oedengesäss, MICHAEL SCHEURICH of Nassig, and HANS JOERG SCHLESSMANN's widow of Oedengesäss. These question the genuineness of the letter and Power of Attorney, and think "that the money would not get to the right man." On June 27, 1770, it was proved that 16 years ago, SCHLESSMANN had paid his manumission in proper order. The objection of the relatives was set aside, since no doubts arose from the comparison of the handwriting, nor any whatever about the document of the Royal British Officials in Philadelphia. The supplemental tax amounted to 20%, i.e., 33 florins. For the Power of Attorney, see the Introduction, "Letters from the New Land." The witnesses were RICHARD HOXLEY and BENJAMIN MILLER; the seal shows Justice with sword and scales. "JOHANNES SCHLESSMANN, with wife and children," was mentioned as emigrant in the *Village Mayor's Report* for Nassig (1753). May 11, 1753, Fascicle Br. 417: Boatman LOESCH has broken his agreements with Schoolmaster SCHUBERT, SCHLESSMANN of Nassig, and KNAUER of Nassig, who now want to sail with another boatman. // The will of JOHN S*H*LESSMAN, of Oxford, Philadelphia Co.,

Pa. (*Will Book* R, p. 77, Philadelphia County Courthouse, Philadelphia, Pa.), dated 1778, mentions wife ELIZABETH; children: PETER, CHRISTOPHER, BARBARA, JOHN, ELIZABETH, and CATHARINE; stepson: CASPER WEISS; son-in-law: HENRY HERDEL; Executors: GEO. FALKERODT and HENRY HERDEL; and witnesses: FREDERICK ALTEMUS, JACOB MEYER, and ANN-CATHARINE MUTH. The family records of JOHANNES SCHLESSMANN and descendants can be found in the "Record of St. Michael's Lutheran Church, Germantown, Pennsylvania." According to the GSP's Transcript of the Record, 1107, JOHANN SCHLOESSMANN was buried July 22, 1778, aged 68 years and 9 months. The CATHARINA SCHLOESSMANN (*Ibid.*, p. 1097), who died as his wife in 1773, aged 67 years, was evidently his second wife, MARIA CATHARINA (MECKLEIN), who was a widow when she married him on December 30, 1766 (*Ibid.*, p. 34). Perhaps she was the widow of JOHANNES MECKELEIN (q.v.), an emigrant from Wenkheim in 1753.

## SCHLESSMANN, MICHAEL — Vockenroth (1773)

April 26, 1773: cf. GEORG BAUER. // MICHAEL SCHLESSMANN, 330 acres, Northampton Co., Pa., surveyed 1786 (3PA, *26*, p. 175).

## SCHLESSMANN, NICOLAUS — Sachsenhausen (1752)

May 15, 1752: wants to go with his wife and 150 florins property to Pennsylvania. Same report on May 16, 1752. Mentioned as emigrant in the *Village Mayor's Report* for Sachsenhausen (1750-1761): "NICOLAUS SCHLESSMANN and wife, has still an inheritance coming from his father." // JOHANN NICOLAUS SCHL*O*SSMANN, with HANS CHRISTOPH and JOHANN HEINRICH SCHLESSMANN, and other Wertheimers, Ship *Phoenix*, November 2, 1752 (Hinke, I, 501 ff.). NICOLAUS SCHLESSMANN settled in the Tulpehocken Valley, where he appears as father of a child baptized at "Atolhoe" (Rehrersburg) in 1757; one of the sponsors was HANS GEORG DIEMER ("Stoever Records," *Notes and Queries*, Annual Volume for 1896, p. 69). NICH[OLA]S SCHLESMAN was taxed in Tulpehocken Tp., Berks Co., Pa., 1767 (3PA, *18*, 78); and as NICHOLAS SCHLEASMAN, made his will 1786, probated 1787 (*Will Book* B, p. 208, Berks County Courthouse, Reading, Pa.), mentioning wife BARBARA; children JOHN, CATHARINE, ELIZABETH, and PETER; executors: sons JOHN and PETER; witnesses: NICHOLAS KINZER, JOHN LUDWIG.

## SCHLESSMANN, NICOLAUS — Bestenheid (1773)

February 18, 1773: wants to go to New England with his wife and 1 child. Still has 5 florins; is to pay 10 florins for himself, 5 florins for his wife, 2 florins for the child, 1 florin, 15 kreuzer, for certification — total, 18 florins, 15 kreuzer. March 27, 1773: it appears that he has a brother in New England, and wants to go over there also with his old mother. Manumission cost him in all, 28 florins, 41 kreuzer; probably supplemental tax was added to the above. Now he regrets his own proposal, which brought him the deplorable blessing of permission to emigrate from the County. Now he thinks: "Remain at home and support thyself honestly." His mother is old and weak, it's so long a journey for her, involves many expenses and dangers, was strongly advised against it by friends. Would now gladly be inclined, again to enjoy the refreshing protection of his most gracious and noble governments, and trusts too that he will be able to earn his living with the work of his hands. Would therefore like to be received back as subject, and asks that he be favored witn freedom from compulsory service, for the 29 florins. The last request was denied, but possibly be was permitted to remain in Bestenheid.

## SCHLESSMANN, PAUL — Nassig (1753)

May 19, 1753: wants to go to Pennsylvania with NICOLAUS SCHUBERT and CHRISTOF GOETZELMANN, all of Nassig. June 28, 1753: the Village Mayor of Nassig justifies himself on the administration of the sold property of PAUL SCHLESSMANN, who has emigrated; for the creditors there are still 173 florins, 1 kreuzer, 1½ pfennig remaining. *Rosenberg Archive,* Br. 554, on the Bankruptcy of JOHANN PAUL SCHLESSMANN of Nassig (1753-1760:) JOHANN MICHAEL BACH, JOHANN MICHAEL KELLER, and HIERONYMUS WILHELM, all of Wertheim, still have 63, 62, and 8 florins, respectively, to demand, and want to make the Village Magistrate of Nassig responsible for them, because he let SCHLESSMANN go. But the Village Mayor had laid the matter before the Governmental Councilor GREINEISEN and announces that the property will not by any means cover the debts. Councilor GREINEISEN says: if the creditors want to retain SCHLESSMANN here, support him and provide for him, he has nothing against it. To be sure, SCHLESSMANN left before daybreak and at an improper time — the Village Mayor is to blame for this. Of moveable goods he left behind one wagon, which was taken by the Cloister of Bronnbach for outstanding debts; 1 plow, the wheels of which were stolen in the field; and 1 goat, which Keller the baker evidently took. The meager and poor household goods do not reach very far in covering the taxes.

## SCHMITT, ANDREAS — Wenkheim (1754)

May 24, 1754: wants to go to New England with his wife CHRISTINE and little child MARIA MARGARETHA, with 399 florins. Is not a vassal. Has sold his property to his brother-in-law JOHANN GEORG HOERNER, for 500 florins, and realized 38 florins from cattle and goods. Is indebted, among others, to the Jew SAMSON NATHAN for 30 florins, and to the Jew JOELIS 11 florins. May depart on payment of 20% supplemental tax. See Steger, No. 264. // ANDREAS SCHMIT, Ship *Phoenix,* October 1, 1754 (Hinke, I, 627 ff.), with other Wertheimers. One ANDREAS SCHMIDT is listed as parent of a child baptized in 1755 at the "Summer Mountain" ("Stoever Records," *Notes and Queries*, Annual Volume for 1896, p. 65). Another resided in Manchester Tp., York Co., Pa., in 1782 (3PA, XXI, 500). The latter, ANDREW SMITH, SR., made his will 1806, probated 1812 (GSP, "Abstracts of York County Wills," p. 526), mentioning children: ANDREW, JOHN, GEORGE, HENRY, EVE, CATHARINE, BARBARA, and MAGDALENA; Executors were ANDREW SMITH and MICHAEL COPPENHEFFER.

## SCHOBER, JOHANN GEORG — Remlingen (1774)

*Rosenberg Archive,* Br. 360 a, July 2, 1774: is said to have gone to New England in 1773, without manumission.

## SCHOEFFER, VALT — Dertingen (1753)

April 15, 1753: a swineherd, propertyless, went with OESTERLEIN to Pennsylvania. June 26, 1753: has bought his freedom. // VALLENTIN SCHAEFFER, aged 30, Ship *Peggy.* September 24, 1753 (Hinke, I, 546 ff.). Perhaps VALENTINE SHEFFER, farmer, Macungie Tp., Northampton (now Lehigh) Co., Pa., 1772 (3PA, XIX, 46).

## SCHOENLEIN, LEONHARD — Lindelbach

Added by the American editor. According to Abraham Reinke Beck, "The Moravian Graveyards of Lititz, Pa., 1744-1905," in *Transactions of the Moravian Historical Society*, VII, 253, LEONHARD SCHOENLEIN, born April 17, 1746, at "Linnelbach, Earldom of Wertheim," married MARGARET FERTIG (1752-1808), the daughter of JOHN CHRISTOPHER FERTIG, the congregation's farmer. According to GSP's Transcript of the "Record of St. Michael's Lutheran Church, Germantown, Philadelphia," p. 40, LEONHARD SCHOENLEIN, of Upper Merion Township, Philadelphia County, was married, on March 31, 1772, to ANNA MARGARETHE FERTIG, of Roxbury Township. Of their 5 children, ANNA REGINA, born in 1775, married SAMUEL GROSH, merchant, and JOHN, born 1783, became a weaver, like his father. Doubtless LEONHARD was a son of MICHEL SCHOENLEIN, below.

## SCHOENLEIN, MICHEL — Lindelbach (1752)

May 12, 1752: is listed among the Lindelbach party (cf. BETZ). Has 4 children. // MICHILL SCHOENLEIN, Ship *Phoenix,* November 2, 1752 (Hinke, I, 502), with other Wertheimers. He is the only SCHOENLEIN listed in Hinke. Cf. LEONHARD SCHOENLEIN, above. It was perhaps MICHAEL's daughter, CATHARINA SCHOENLEIN, who, as a resident of Upper Merion Township, Philadelphia County, is mentioned in GSP's Transcript of the "Record of St. Michael's Lutheran Church, Germantown, Philadelphia," p. 43, as marrying, on February 22, 1773, the widower JOHANNES FOEMUS, also of Upper Merion. According to the same Record, page 35, one ANDREAS SCHOENLEIN was married, on June 8, 1767, to ELISABETHE BAUER. Additional records of the MICHAEL SCHOENLEIN family can be found in the records of the Lutheran Church at the Trappe (*PGS Proceedings,* VII, 519 ff.).

## SCHOERGER, JEREMIAS — Dertingen (1754)

May 30, 1754: wants to go to America. Is loaded with debts. Has 257 florins *activa* and 371 florins *passiva.* Owes the Jew SAMUEL of Homburg 100 florins, the Jew ERNDLE of Wenkheim 2 florins, and the Jew EISIG of Oberalterheim 40 florins. *Freudenberg Governmental Protocol,* March 13, 1755: the Jew SAMUEL of Homburg demands that SCHOERGER's farm property be signed over to him, for the balance of his outstanding debt. Mentioned as emigrant in the *Village Mayor's Report* for Dertingen (1754): "JEREMIAS SCHUERGER (his debts have exceeded his property)." According to the *Freudenberg Governmental Protocol,* March 13, 1755: the Jew SAMUEL of Homburg still has 92 florins to demand and desires that the farm property be promised to him in writing to settle the debt." // Not in Hinke, but cf., as a possible Wertheimer, ANDREAS SCHERGER, who with MAGDALENE SCHERGER and children: KILIAN, CATH., and BARBARA SCHERGER, along with GEO. KRAFT, CHRISTOPHER ARBORT (q.v.), and other Wertheimers, arrived on the Ship *Favourite,* September 5, 1785 (Hinke, III, 8).

## SCHRECK, ADAM — Steinmark (1753)

April 26, 1753: has formerly served as a common cattle herd, but dares not devote himself to such activity any longer on account of a deformed and weak body. In the face of mounting debts and great poverty he can no longer avoid the wretched beggar's staff, and pay the interest on his debts. Wants now to go to Pennsylvania or New England with wife and 4 children. Yet his property amounts to 277 florins. He shall pay 14 florins for his person and for his 277 florins,

2 florins for his wife, and 4 florins for the 4 children. // ADAM SCHRECK, with JOHANNES SCHRECK and HANS SCHRECK and other Wertheimers, Ship *Neptune*, September 24, 1753 (Hinke, I, 539 ff.). ADAM SCHRECK, 100 acres, Berks Co., Pa., surveyed 1785 (3PA, XXVI, 317). One ADAM SCHRACK appears in Luzerne Co., Pa., in 1794 (3PA, XXIV, 280).

## SCHRECK, NICOLAUS — Steinmark (1750)

Mentioned as emigrant in the *Village Mayor's Report* for Steinmark (1750): "divers persons, among them NICOLAUS SCHRECK, who departed secretly with his children, leaving his wife among us. In property he left nothing behind but a little house, which the wife's brother, KUNKEL, appropriated along with the wife, and provided for her until her death." According to additional information sent the American editor by Dr. Langguth, from the Michelrieth Church Register, there was buried on January 29, 1752, BARBARA, wife of NICOLAUS SCHRECK of Steinmark, "who went secretly to Pennsylvania, three-quarters of a year ago. He took with him his two children (ANNA CATHARINA, born August 2, 1739, and NICOLAUS, born September 18, 1744), and attached himself to a woman — [*eine geborene Teuffelin*]." // NICHOLAS (X) SCHRACH (SHRECK), aged 34, Ship *Peggy*, September 24, 1753 (Hinke, I, 545 ff.).

## SCHUBARTH (SCHUBERT), JOHANN NICOLAUS — Nassig (1753)

May 11, 1753: the schoolmaster, dismissed from his office, asks for freedom from vassalage for wife and children. He himself was free. In order to get out of sight of his enemy, not unknown to the Prince, he wants to go to Pennsylvania, after having to quit his school service, which he had performed as faithfully as possible, though persecuted in every way and manner. Had a trial. Since the dismissal which was sent him would work to his most extreme disadvantage and to the hindrance of his fortune, he asks for a testimony, for which he had to pay further 9 florins, 20 kreuzer. Saves only 49 florins. In Sonderrieth he had an inn valued at 485 florins, and many pieces of land. He paid back to CHRISTOPH LANGGUTH, among others, for loan and interest, 103 florins, further 21 florins and 30 kreuzer. He had two new pairs of pants made by JOHANN CHRISTOPH EICHHORN for 2 florins and 8 kreuzer. The goatskins purchased of EICHHORN the tanner for 8 florins were probably used for that purpose. JOHANN FRIEDRICH LANGGUTH received for tailor work, 6 florins and 4 kreuzer. The bookbinder HELFERICH, for books, 5 florins and 40 kreuzer, and to the same for 2 Bibles, 4 florins. To Advocate KOENIG for trial costs, 33 florins, who remitted him 2 florins and 40 kreuzer. Two guns cost 10 florins, 30 kreuzer. He finally declares his property status "in an oath before Almighty God and in my own soul, etc., so help me God and his Holy Evangel."

Mentioned as emigrant in the *Village Mayor's Report* for Nassig (1753): "JOH. NIC. SCHUBARTH, school master, with wife and children." Is traveling with JOHANNES SCHLESSMANN (q.v.), and KNAUER. *Freudenberg Governmental Protocol,* Septemebr 1, 1752: complaint over the quarrelsome schoolmaster at Nassig, who lives in continual strife with his superior, the pastor, and neglects the school-children. But the pastor was no angel either, as the same record shows. // JOHANN NICOLAUS SCHUBART, with JOHANN MICHAEL SCHUBART and other Wertheimers, Ship *Richard and Mary,* September 17, 1753 (Hinke,

I, 531 ff.). For MICHAEL SCHUBART, who evidently settled in or near Philadelphia, cf. HANS ADAM HOH, above.

## SCHUERGER, SIMON — Dertingen (1750)

Mentioned as emigrant in the *Village Mayor's Report* for Dertingen (1750): "SIMON SCHUERGER." // SIMON SCHIERCHER, Ship *Priscilla*, September 12, 1750 (Hinke, I, 444).

## SEEL, DOROTHEA — Urfar (1752)

May 4, 1752: DOROTHEA SEEL, widow of HANS GEORG SEEL, and her single son HANS JOERG SEEL, want to go to New England. Still have 379 florins. Mentioned as emigrant in the *Village Mayor's Report* for Urfar (1752): "HANS JOERG SELL and mother." // HANS JORG SELL, with ANDRES SELL and other Wertheimers, Ship *Phoenix*, November 2, 1752 (Hinke, I, 503). One GEO[RGE] SELL was taxed in Maxatawny Tp., Berks Co., Pa., in 1767 (3PA, XVIII, 41 ff.).

## SEIBERT, ANNA CATHARINA — Sachsenhausen

Added by the American editor. According to the Ms. "Records of Trinity Lutheran Church, Reading, Pa.," I, 552-3, at the Genealogical Society of Pennsylvania, ANNA CATHARINA SEIBERT was buried September 27, 1783, aged 72 years, 5 months, 7 days. She was born ANNA CATHARINA SCHREINER daughter of JOHANN PETER and ANNA CATHARINE SCHREINER, April 19, 1711, at Sachsenhausen, Wertheim, Franconia. The sponsor at her baptism was AGATHA CATHARINE, wife of CHRISTOPH SCHWAB, the Village Mayor. She was three times married. In her first marriage to [———] SCHABER, 6 children — 4 sons and 2 daughters — were born, 3 of whom died long since, and 2 sons, of whom ANDREAS SCHABER is one, and 1 daughter, survive. She had 26 grandchildren and 5 great-grandchildren. She died of fever and old age, and according to the record, took to her bed on September 15 and never rose from it, dying September 26, 1783. Possibly she was the wife of ANDREAS SEUBERT, listed below.

## SEIDNER, ANNA CATHARINA — Wertheim

Added by the American editor. According to Abraham Reinke Beck, "The Moravian Graveyards of Lititz, Pa., 1744-1905," *Transactions of the Moravian Historical Society*, VII, 242: ANNA CATHARINA SEIDNER, born in Wertheim, Germany, September 24, 1723, married JOHN CHRISTOPHER FERTIG (.qv.). She and her husband had charge of the Church Farm at Lititz, Lancaster Co., Pa., where she died August 23, 1785.

## SEIDNER, JOERG — Hasselberg (1752)

May 20, 1752: the son of the late PHILIPP SEIDNER, wants to go into menial service in Pennsylvania with other single fellows (cf. KRANK). Mentioned as emigrant in the *Village Mayor's Report* for Hasselberg (1754): "MICHAEL SEIDNER, with wife and child, besides PHILIPP SEIDNER'S 3 orphaned children: HANS PHILIPP, GEORG, and APPOLLONIA."

## SEIDNER, JOHANN MICHAEL — Hasselberg (1754)

May 16, 1754: wants to go with wife and 1 child to New England. The direst need and poverty drives him to it. Has indeed learned a trade, but his money was consumed by the time he became master. Still has 60 florins. Mentioned as emigrant in the *Village Mayor's Report* for Hasselberg (1754): "MICHAEL SEIDNER, with wife and child, besides PHILIPP SEIDNER's 3 orphaned children: HANS PHILIPP, GEORG, and APPOLLONIA." // MICHEL SEITTNER, with MARTIN SEITNER and other Wertheimers, Ship *Phoenix*, October 1, 1754 (Hinke, I, 627 ff.). Perhaps MICH'L SIDENER, taxed in Roxborough Tp., Philadelphia Co., Pa., in 1779 (3PA, XIV, 695).

## SEIDNER, MARTIN — Grünewörth (1754)

May 20, 1754: has been left loaded with debts by his father, and wants to go with his wife and child to Pennsylvania. Has been brought to total ruin through so much interest money and now in his advancing years has become a beggar. Wants to see where else the Dear Lord will show him ways and means to earn his daily bread. Had 744 florins property and 657 florins debts. // MARTIN SEITNER, with MICHEL SEITTNER and other Wertheimers, Ship *Phoenix*, October 1, 1754 (Hinke, I, 627 ff.).

## SEIDNER, MARGARETHA BARBARA — Grünewörth (1752)

Added by the American editor. According to Augustus Schultze, "Guide to the Old Moravian Cemetery of Bethlehem, Pa., 1742-1910," *PGS Proceedings*, XXI, 90: MARGARET BARBARA SEIDNER (1714-1796), a native of Grünewörth, near Wertheim, Baden, Germany, "came to Bethlehem in 1752, with ANNA JOH[ANNA] SEIDEL, and was employed on the farm." She is buried in the single sisters' plot in the Moravian Cemetery at Bethlehem.

## SEIDNER, PHILIPP and APPOLLONIA — Hasselberg (1754)

May 16, 1754: children of the late PHILIPP SEIDNER, went to earn their bread in Pennsylvania. Are almost poor as beggars, and were recently deprived of their parents. They do not dare to beg bread from door to door. Must pay together 2 florins for manumission. Cf. the *Village Magistrate's Report* in the case of JOERG SEIDNER, above.

## SELL, ANDREAS — Oberwittbach (1752)

April 11, 1752: Village Mayor has sold everything and is said to have realized 800 florins from it; presumably he went to Pennsylvania. According to the *Freudenberg Governmental Protocol*, April 16, 1752, he was replaced as Village Mayor. On May 17, 1752, he sent the following request to his Lord, Prince CARL:

> "Most Serene Prince of the Empire, Most Gracious Prince and Lord! Fear and shame ought justly to deter me from laying at your feet these lines written with trembling hand. But because according to my confession, it is now too late to justify myself, I will make use of my open confession and ask on my knees, to go with wife and 7 children to '*Pen-Sylvanien*' on May 24th of the present year, because here I cannot very well support myself nor do I want to run around as a spectacle to others, etc. Because of my big family, the shipping charges run high, etc. In my capacity as Village Mayor I have, as much as possible, observed the government's interests. . . In my prayers I will incessantly call upon Almighty God for expected grace, that He may grant Your Princely Highness not only a highly blessed, lengthy reign, but also vouchsafe Your August Highness advanced years with blessings

unto body and soul, and bring my most devoted wish into gracious fulfillment, etc., etc."

The Government's decision was as follows:

Since our Dear Sovereign Cousins have granted manumission without the usual fees to petitioners, so Our Government has to manumit him likewise, because We have graciously granted him release from vassalage.

Signed: CARL, PRINCE OF LOEWENSTEIN

Heubach, May 20, 1752.

Note that this is the only case where the Prince personally signed such a decision. "ANDREAS SELL, Village Mayor, with wife and children," is mentioned as an emigrant in the *Village Mayor's Report* for Oberwittbach (1752). However, according to the *Freudenberg Governmental Protocol,* May 25, 1752: "ANDR[EAS] SELL stayed behind from the Emigrant Transport, with his wife, who has a bad leg, and his children. He is still in Oberwittbach, and wants his money back. He is suspected of wanting to slip away and leave his wife and children behind as a burden on his friends." // Perhaps ANDREAS SELL, with HANS JORG SELL, and other Wertheimers, Ship *Phoenix,* November 2, 1752 (Hinke, I, 503).

## SEMEL, MARTIN — Wenkheim (1753)

May 4, 1753: wants to emigrate with the Wenkheim party (cf. ADAM DIEHM). In the *Village Mayor's Report*, his father is given as PAUL SEMEL. May thus be the MARTIN SEMEL, who in Johannes Steger's famous *Quellenbüchlein zur Kirchen- u. Familiengeschichte des Dorfes Wenkheim,* Nrs. 163, 272, was married on May 16, 1753. In the *Village Mayor's Report* for Wenkheim (1750-1761), "JACOB HOERNER, PAULUS SEMEL, and MARTIN SEUBERTH" are mentioned as fathers of emigrants. // MARTIN SEM*M*EL, Ship *Neptune,* September 24, 1753 (Hinke, I, 540 ff.), with other Wertheimers. Evidently settled in Whitehall Tp., Northampton (now Lehigh) Co., Pa., where a MARTIN SEMEL, with others of the name, was taxed in 1786 (3PA, XIX, 223).

## SEN*F*LEBEN, HANS — Dertingen (1754)

May 19, 1754: wants to go to America with his wife ANNA ELISABETH and 2 daughters. Still has 941 florins. // HANS SENFFTLEBE*R*, Ship *Phoenix* October 1, 1754 (Hinke, I, 627 ff.), with other Wertheimers. He is the only emigrant of the name listed in Hinke.

## SEUBERT, ANDREAS — Wenkheim (1753)

May 4, 1753: among the Wenkheim party (cf. ADAM DIEHM). Possibly No. 263 in Steger. Doubtless the son of MARTIN SEUBERTH of Wenkheim, mentioned in the *Village Mayor's Report* for Wenkheim (1750-1761) as father of an emigrant. // ANDREAS SEUBERTH, with MICHAEL SEUBERT and BALSAR SEUBERTH, and other Wertheimers, Ship *Neptune,* September 24, 1753 (Hinke, I, 540 ff.). Note however that another ANDEREAS SEUBERTH, with HANS SEUBERT and other Wertheimers, arrived on the Ship *Phoenix,* November 2, 1752 (Hinke, I, 501 ff.). One of these, as ANDREAS SEIBERT, appears as resident in Eastern District Tp., Berks Co., Pa., 1767, (3PA, XVIII, 55). Cf. also ANNA CATHARINA SEIBERT, above.

## SPIELMANN, LEONHARD — Lindelbach (1773)

March 30, 1773: widower with 3 children, wants to go to New England with PHILIPP RAU and ANDREAS OBERDORF. Has 550 debts. // Others in 3PA.

## STAPF, JOHANN PETER — Wertheim (1753)

April 12, 1753: born in Sachsenhausen, a shoemaker's apprentice, had resolved with God's help to go to New England, there to seek his fortune. Wants to pay his taxes, but the request is denied without explanation. // FRIEDERICH STAPF, who emigrated in 1768, is the only one of the name listed in Hinke (I, 721).

## STOLBERG, ANDREAS — Lindelbach (1752)

May 12, 1752: among the Lindelbach party (cf. BETZ). Has 4 children. // One of his children, ANDREAS STOLLBERGER, a native of Wertheim, aged 36 years, 3 months less 5 days, was buried at St. Michaelis and Zion Lutheran Church, Philadelphia, Pa., February 15, 1766 (GSP, "Records of St. Michaelis and Zion Lutheran Church," *Burials*, p. 191). According to the same records, pp. 353-4, a daughter, ANNA CATHARINA HUTHMAN, wife of CHRISTIAN FRIEDRICH HUTHMAN of Philadelphia, was buried September 14, 1771, aged 48 years. She was born August 10, 1723, at Lindelbach, in the County of Wertheim, daughter of the late ANDREAS STOLBERGER and wife CATHARINA, who had her baptized. "She came to this land 19 years ago in 1752. Her father died down by New Castle, and her mother died six months afterwards, 16 miles from Philadelphia. The child had to serve. Anno 1759 she was married to CHRISTIAN FRIEDRICH HUTHMAN, a printer, and begat with him 4 children, of whom one died and three sons survive. She was a devout and faithful follower of the Saviour. She longed to depart and be with Christ. Received the Lord's Supper and departed early yesterday between 6 and 7 o'clock." From the same record, p. 231, it appears that another daughter, MARGARETHA HORN, née STOLLBERGER, "from the County of Wertheim," wife of JOHANN ADAM HORN, was buried at Philadelphia, October 18, 1767, aged 42 years.

## STRAUSS, ANNA EVA — Urfar (1753)

May 11, 1753: daughter of MICHAEL STRAUSS, JR., wants to go to New England. Perhaps the same as EVA STRAUSS, sister of NICOLAUS STRAUSS, below.

## STRAUSS, NICOLAUS — Urfar (1753)

April 30, 1753: wants to go to New England with his sister EVA STRAUSS. They do not have a kreuzer, except a few gulden, which the sister saved in service. In the *Freudenberg Governmental Protocol,* May 13, 1754, is the report: the Village Mayor announces that the step-daughter of PHILIPP STRAUSS, a Contingent Musketeer in this place, wants to emigrate. "If, by chance, this woman, who is serving at the time in the City, went away secretly, he would not be answerable for it, although she has no property." In the *Village Mayor's Report* for Urfar (1752), the wife of NICOLAUS STRAUSS is also mentioned among the emigrants, but not the sister. Whether the report in the *Protocol* refers at all to this STRAUSS girl is uncertain, because it is a year later. // NICHOLAS (X) STROUSS, Ship *Richard and Mary,* September 17, 1753 (Hinke, I, 531 ff.), with other Wertheimers. Perhaps NICHOLAS STROUS, who was taxed in Bedminster Tp., Bucks Co., Pa., in 1783 (3PA, XIII, 391). According to his will (*Will Book*

8, p. 31, Bucks County Courthouse, Doylestown, Pa.) made 1808 and probated 1809, NICHOLAS STRAUSS of Bedminster Tp., yeoman, names his wife CHRISTIANA; executors: CONRAD HARPLE and PETER OTT; children MICHAEL, CHRISTOPHER, JOHN, GEORGE, LEONARD, HENRY, JACOB, and ROSINA, the wife of MICHAEL LAMBERT. Witnesses: RALPH STOVER and ABRAHAM FRETZ.

## STRAUSS, NICOLAUS — Urfar (1752)

May 18, 1752: wants to go to New England with his wife and 1 child of 1½ years, has only 38 florins. Perhaps another than the above-mentioned.

## STRAUSS, [———] — Urfar (1753)

April 30, 1753: the widow of HANS MICHEL STRAUSS, has only 21 florins left and wants to go to New England. Pays 2 florins. Mentioned as emigrants in the *Village Mayor's Report* for Urfar (1753): "the widow of HANS MICHEL STRAUSS, SR., [and] the 2 children of the widow of HANS MICHEL STRAUSS, JR. — with empty hand, as poor children, the above persons properly took care of their manumission. The above persons have nothing more to hope for or expect here. Witness: JOHANN CASPAR DIEHM, Village Mayor at Urfar; HANS WOLF RUETTIGER, ANDREAS RAUH, and HANS PETER GEIGER, of the Court."

## STRAUSS, [———] — Urfar (1773)

January 21, 1773: widow of MICHEL STRAUSS wants to go to New England with 3 children, along with JAKOB OETZEL and wife and 3 children, because they cannot earn their living in Urfar. Their poverty is confirmed in the *Village Mayor's Report.*

## STROBEL, JOHANN WILHELM — Wertheim (*ante* 1753)

Added by the American editor. According to the Transcript of the "Church Record of the First Reformed Church, Philadelphia, Pennsylvania" in the William J. Hinke Collection, Historical Society of the Reformed Church, Lancaster, Pa., I, 185, JOHN WILLIAM STROBEL, Lutheran, from Wertheim, widower, was married, on March 6, 1753, to ANNA BARBARA PEEN, widow, both of whom were resident in Philadelphia. In the translation of the same records in *GSP Proceedings*, XIV, 32, the wife's name is given as BARBARA BINS, widow of JOSEPH BINS.

## SUEHRER, ANDREAS — Höhfeld (1754)

February 25, 1754: wants to go to New England. Has 114 florins property and 135 florins debts, among them 30 florins to the Jew LEYSER at Wenkheim. Mentioned as emigrant in the *Village Mayor's Report* for Höhfeld (1750-1761): "ANDREAS SUEHRER, with wife and 3 little children."

## SUEHRER, ANNA EVA — Höhfeld (1753)

April 26, 1753: ANNA EVA SUEHRER, widow of WILHELM SUEHRER, cartwright. Her son JOHANNES WILHELM ("HANS") SUEHRER had already gone to the New Land in 1752. Now she wants to follow her son HANS with her two daughters on account of lack of livelihood. She cannot support herself anymore on her little farm. Mentioned as emigrant in the *Village Mayor's Report* for Höhfeld (1750-1761): "ANNA EVA SUEHRER, widow, with 3 children."

## SUEHRER, JOHANN ADAM — Höhfeld (1753)

*Rosenberg Archive*, Br. 417, May 12, 1753: wants to go to New England, and receives, with permission to depart, a testimony of his good conduct.

## SUEHRER, MARTIN — Höhfeld (1753)

April 26, 1753: parishioner, has only 75 florins and 48 kreuzer, and wants to go to New England with his wife EVA CATHARINA, daughter of HANS MICHEL STRAUSS of Urfar, and a minor child, "in order there to seek my livelihood, which I here can find in almost no other way than begging." Mentioned es emigrant in the *Village Mayor's Report* for Höhfeld (1750-1761): "MARTIN SUEHRER, with wife and 1 small child." // MARTIN SUEHRER, with [GEORGE] NICHOLAS (X) STROUSS and other Wertheimers, Ship *Richard and Mary*, September 17, 1753 (Hinke, I, 531 ff.). One MARTIN (O) SIER is listed in 1749 (Hinke, I, 413).

## SUEHRER, PHILIPP — Dietenhan (1752)

May 12, 1752: a tailor by trade, has these two years and more, since the Bettingen fire, had the misfortune of running around out of his mind, from which he is not yet in fact freed; besides, he has a lame wife, who is not in condition to manage any work, and now wants to make use of the opportunity to take wife and child, also 90 florins, to the Island of Pennsylvania, since many other people are going there, etc. Mentioned as emigrant in the *Village Mayor's Report* for Dietenhan (1752): "PHILIPP SUEHRER and wife, graciously released from vassalage on account of his mad rage and fury." // Perhaps PHILIP SIERER, 100 acres, Berks Co., Pa., surveyed 1763 (3PA, XXVI, 313). Other SIERERS are listed in 3PA, but none bear the names of these Wertheim emigrants.

## SUEHRER, WILHELM — Höhfeld (1752)

*Freudenberg Governmental Protocol*, May 13, 1752: wants to go to Philadelphia on account of direst poverty. The property of his mother is scarcely worth 150 florins. Receives manumission provisionally *gratis*. Perhaps identical with the above HANS SUEHRER.

## TAG, HANS — Lindelbach (1752)

May 12, 1752: has 5 children and wants to go to America with the Lindelbach party (cf. BETZ). On March 6, 1755, it was reported that HANS TAG's widow went to America with her 5 children in 1752. She has not yet paid her manumission fee, and went away emptyhanded. Their bankruptcy is now ended.

## TEUFEL, MICHEL — Steinmark (1754)

April 15, 1751: wanted, too, to go to Pennsylvania, but repented of it, and is now a shepherd at Altfeld. April 19, 1754: MICHEL TEUFEL of Dertingen, now in Steinmark, wants to go to New England. He himself writes his name DEUFFEL. Was a shepherd from his youth, then married in Steinmark ANNA WAMMSER, daughter of PETER WAMMSER, and served further as a shepherd. In the face of approaching old age and great poverty, he fears he cannot support himself without the beggar's staff. Still has 84 florins and often not a bit of bread overnight. With his wife and children, he is listed among the passengers of SELIG (cf. KIESECKER), described however as JOHANN MICHEL TEUFFEL of Altfeld, a neighboring village. KIESECKER declares he wants to take along the two shepherds from Altfeld, NICOLAUS ALBERT and MICHEL TEUFFEL. // [J.] MICHAEL DIEFEL (X) (DIVEL), Ship *Phoenix,* October 1, 1754 (Hinke, I, 627 ff.), with other Wertheimers.

## UTHE, DAVID GOTTFRIED — Wertheim (1751)

*Burgomsater's Accounts,* (1751) City Archives: from DAVID GOTTFRIED UTHE came nothing, because his property consists of nothing. Went to Pennsylvania. // DAVID GOTTFRIED UTHE, Ship *Phoenix,* November 2, 1752 (Hinke, I, 503).

## UTZ, SAMUEL GOTTFRIED — Wertheim (1752)

May 10, 1752: a shoemaker, in poor circumstances, wants to go to Pennsylvania with wife and child. Has spent his fortune through domestic affliction and the sickness of his wife. Must give only 1 florin for himself and his family. Perhaps he is identical with the above DAVID GOTTFRIED UTHE. // The name UTZ is found in York County, and was featured recently in the delightful novel of life in York, Rachel Meisenhelder's *God Bless Our Aunts* (New York: Whittlesey House, 1945). However, one GOTTLIEB UTZ emigrated in 1750 (Hinke, I, 432), and perhaps the York County family are his descendants.

## VAETH (VOITH), ANDREAS — Dertingen (1753)

According to the *Village Mayor's Report,* he went to America in 1753. As ANDREAS VAITH he appears among Selig's passengers (cf. KIESECKER). *Freudenberg Governmental Protocol,* June 10, 1754: ANDREAS VOIT, NICL[AUS] NAHM and CASPAR OBERDORF, all of Dertingen, went away secretly to Pennsylvania some days ago, and without receiving their manumission. *Rosenberg Archive,* May 4, 1762: the same report. Still no news whether he is dead or alive. // Evidently settled in Pennsylvania, since the name ANDREAS FEITH appears in GSP's Transcript of the "Record of St. Michael's Lutheran Church, Germantown, Philadelphia," Part 1, p. 38.

## VERS, CHRISTOPH — Bestenheid (1785)

March 31, 1785: wants to go to America with wife and 2 children. Has only 68 florins. Must sell on account of debts.

## WEIKERT, GEORG — Dertingen (1753)

June 4, 1753: went away secretly to New England with the emigrants, without purchasing his freedom. His wife followed soon after him. Still has money remaining in Dertingen, which is sequestrated. The same report appears in the *Freudenberg Governmental Protocol,* // JOHANN GEORG WEICKERT, with HANS DRIES WEICKERT and other Wertheimers, Ship *Neptune,* September 24, 1753 (Hinke, I, 538 ff.). One GEORG WEICKERT, deceased by 1757, when a married daughter of his is mentioned, appears in the "Records of the Lutheran Congregation at Old Goshenhoppen," *The Perkiomen Region,* II, 20. GEORG WEIKERT and wife MAGDALENA were sponsors at a baptism in 1762, in the same records (*Ibid.,* p. 39). Several other GEORGE WEIKERTS, WEIKERS, and WIKERS are listed in 3PA, one in Northampton Co., another in York Co., another in Bucks Co., Pa.

## WEIMER, GOTTFRIED — Niclashausen (1752)

Mentioned as emigrant in the *Village Mayor's Report* for Niclashausen (1752): "GOTTFRIED WEIMER, single son of GOTTFRIED WEIMER's widow, who is still living. 4 florins were given him by good-hearted people, to take along."

## WEINGAERTNER, GEORG NICOLAUS—Wertheim (1753)

May 7, 1753: tanner, wants to go with GARBEL and BREITENHERD to America. He declares his property status in the Town Hall. "This account WEINGAERTNER swore on his personal oath on May 4." According to the *Burgomaster's Accounts,* he pays 10% supplemental tax—16 florins and 30 kreuzer—and is here mentioned as already having emigrated to America. // GEORG NICOLAUS WEINGAERTNER, Ship *Neptune,* September 24, 1753 (Hinke, I, 538 ff.), with other Wertheimers. Settled in or near Lancaster, Pa., where NICOLAUS and BARBARA WEINGAERTNER were parents of children baptized at Trinity Lutheran Church, 1757-1764 (*PGS Proceedings,* III, 225 ff.). Their son, EPHRAIM BENEDICT WEINGAERTNER, born 1757, was doubtless named for GARBEL (q.v.), who also was a member of the congregation.

## WEINGAERTNER, JOHANN GEORG — Wertheim (1753)

May 7, 1753: burgher and tanner of Wertheim, asks for manumission for himself and his children. Perhaps the same as above GEORG NICOLAUS WEINGAERTNER, since only one is mentioned in the *Burgomaster's Accounts.*

## WEIPPERT, HANS MELCHIOR — Uettingen (1754)

Is listed among the passengers of the boatman SELIG (Cf. KIESECKER). // One THOMAS WEIPERT was resident of Cocalico Tp., Lancaster Co., Pa., in 1790 (*United States Census of 1790 for Pennsylvania,* p. 127). The only member of the family listed in Hinke is JOHAN STEPHAN WEIPERT, aged 19, who emigrated from Enzweihingen, Württemberg, in 1805 (Hinke, III, 174).

## WEISS, GEORG — Hasselberg (1753)

April 9, 1753: wants to go, against his will, with wife and children, to New England, because he has only 72 florins and 32 kreuzer left, and does not know how otherwise to help himself. Taxes: 3 florins and 42 kreuzer, for the man, because he still has 72 florins property; 2 florins for the wife, 4 florins for the 4 children. Mentioned as emigrant in the *Village Mayor's Report* for Hasselberg (1753): "GEORG WEISS, with wife and children." // JOERG WEISS, with PHILIP (W) WEISS, and other Wertheimers, Ship *Neptune,* September 24, 1753 (Hinke, I, 539 ff.). Several listed in 3PA.

## WEISS, JOHANN PHILIPP — Wertheim (1753)

May 11, 1753: a tailor. See Introduction, "Emigrants Good and Bad." Was driven by need, to solicit his bread elsewhere with God's help, because "as a young man I made up my mind to behave like an honest man." He had no other alternative than to turn his back upon his fatherland and put up as a stranger among strangers. // PHILIP (W) WEISS, with JOERG WEISS, and other Wertheimers, Ship *Neptune,* September 24, 1753 (Hinke, I, 539 ff.). According to the GSP's Transcript of the "Records of Trinity Lutheran Church, Reading, Pa.", I, 589: PHILIP WEISS, born in Wertheim, Franconia, died July 2, 1794, and was buried at Reading, July 4, aged 71 years, less two months. He had lived with his second wife, MARIA MAGDALENA WEISS, née MICHEL(E), 11 years. There were no children. According to the same Records, p. 549, his first wife, ANNA ELISABETHA WEISS, née DINCKEL, died March 29, 1782, and was buried March 30, at Reading, aged 70 years, 8 months, 3 weeks. She was born in Kreuzwertheim, Franconia, July 19, 1712, daughter of CHRISTOPH and SALOME DINCKEL, of Kreuzwertheim. Sponsors at her baptism were CHRISTOPH WOLPERT and wife ANNA ELISABETHA, of Kreuzwertheim. In May, 1749, she married PHILIP WEISS, and had one daughter, who died as an infant in Germany.

## WIESLER, HANS MICHEL — Lindelbach (1752)

May 12, 1752: is listed among the Lindelbach party (cf. BETZ). Has 4 children. *Freudenberg Governmental Protocol,* January 12, 1753: JOHANN MICHAEL WIESLER has sold all of his little farm, when he went to Pennsylvania, to JOHANN GEORG HOERNER, for 420 florins and 3 carolin. Now the purchase price is not sufficient to pay his many debts. // JOHAN MICHAEL WISSLER, with JOHAN WOLF and JOHAN CASPER WISSLER, and other Wertheimers, Ship *Phoenix,* November 2, 1752 (Hinke, I, 501). MICHAEL WISSLER was taxed in Providence Tp., Philadelphia Co., Pa., in 1779 (3PA, XIV, 693).

## WIESNER, HANS MICHEL — Dietenhan (1750)

Mentioned as emigrant in the *Village Mayor's Report* for Dietenhan (1750): "HANS MICHAEL WIESNER, a vassal of the Elector of Mainz; his wife and children, vassals in this County." // HANS MICHAEL WISNER, with JOHAN GORG WISSNER, Ship *Priscilla,* September 12, 1750 (Hinke, I, 444). Seems to have settled in Montgomery Co., Pa., where his death is recorded on July 7, 1765, in his 64th year, in the Records of the New Hanover Lutheran Church (*PGS Proceedings,* XX, 444). Others, probably sons of his, are mentioned frequently in the same records (*Ibid.,* XX, 336-7, 416, etc.), often in connection with other Wertheimers. For instance, JOH. JOERG WISNER in 1750 stood sponsor to a child of ANDREW O[E]TZEL (q.v.) JOH. LEONHARDT WIESNER stood sponsor to children of OETZEL and ANDREAS KACHEL (q.v.) LEONHARD WIESNER married in 1761 ROSINA ELIZABETH SCHICK, and their children were baptized at New Hanover, 1762-1778; GEORG WISNER's children were baptized 1754-1774.

## WIESSLER, NICOLAUS — Bestenheid (1752)

May 18, 1752: wants to go to Pennsylvania with wife and 2 children; and, as usual, on account of debts.

## WIESSMAN, HANS — Schollbrunn (1752)

*Preudenberg Governmental Protocol,* June 2, 1752: his brother-in-law HANS LEONHARD EBERT in Schollbrunn complains that HANS WIESSMANN drove his three oxen secretly from the pasture, sold them, stuck the money in his pocket and absconded a week ago with the emigrants, without manumission. The "KELLER CHRIST" is commissioned to take up the property investigation in agreement with the Carthusian Monastery in Grünau. On July 3, 1752, the monastery fined WIESSMANN 9 florins for eating meat at forbidden times, which is not to be conceded on the part of the Counts. The Father Prior is to be given to understand that the demanded ecclesiastic penalty, which, as is well known, one is wont to atone for much more tolerably in another way, can the less be admitted, since a precedent could hardly be found that such punishment had been imposed on the Protestant side.

## WILD, JOHANN GEORG — County of Wertheim

Added by the American editor. According to the GSP's Transcript of the "Records of Christ Church or Bieber Creek Church, Rockland Township, Berks County, Pennsylvania, 1738-1903." JOHANN GEORG WILD, Master Shoemaker in Maxatawny, son of MARTIN WILD *"aus dem Wertheimischen,"* married, on March 6, 1758, MARIA BARBARA ARNOLD, daughter of MICHAEL ARNOLD of Maxatawny.

## WINZENHOELLER, NICOLAUS — Lindelbach (1752)

May 12, 1752: is listed among the Lindelbach party (cf. BETZ). Has 3 children. *Freudenberg Governmental Protocol,* January 11, 1753: the Jew ITZIG of Homburg, for his obligation of 90 florins, wants to gain legal possession of the house of NICOLAUS WINZENHOELLER, who has emigrated. *Ibid.,* October 10, 1754: he still has the mortgage of 90 florins on the property of NICLAS WINZENHOELLER, who 2½ years ago went to New England. Since the house is deteriorating, ISAAC, as he is now called, asks to have the house made over to him. The government resolved, that in case no buyer should be found, the property should be adjudicated to the creditors. // NICKLES WEITZENHOELLER, Ship *Phoenix,* November 2, 1752 (Hinke, I, 502), with other Wertheimers. NICOLAUS WINZENHELLER and wife ANNA MARGRETHA evidently settled in Montgomery Co., Pa., where they appear in 1761 as parents of a child baptized at the Lutheran Church at the Trappe (*PGS Proceedings,* VI, 235). Other records of the family appear in the Records of the New Hanover Lutheran Church (*PGS Proceedings,* XX, 444), where the death of the wife of NICOLAUS WINZENHELLER is recorded on June 20, 1769, aged 40 years, 8 months, and 3 days. JOHANNES and ELIZABETH WENSENKAELER were parents of a child baptized in 1765 at the same church (*Ibid.,* XX, 335).

## WOLF, GEORG — Dietenhan (1753)

According to the *Village Mayor's Report* for Dietenhan (1753), "GEORG WOLF, with wife and children, a poor man," emigrated. *Freudenberg Governmental Protocol,* April 6, 1753: the nationalized Jew FAELKLEIN MEYER receives a mortgage on the house of GEORG WOLF at Dietenhan, who is going to the New Land, to the value of 41 florins. *Ibid.,* March 1, 1754: FAELKLEIN MEYER, the nationalized Jew, petitions right of foreclosure upon the farm of the debtor GEORG WOLF, who has gone to New England. He still has 41 florins to demand. Suitable orders were issued and the Jew permitted to foreclose, yet the residents shall be free to redeem the property for the sum involved. // GERG WOLFF, Ship *Neptune,* September 24, 1753 (Hinke, I, 540 ff.), with other Wertheimers. There was also a second emigrant of this name in 1753 (Hinke, I, 585 ff.).

## WOLF, JACOB — Niclashausen (1752)

May 15, 1752: has, like DRACH's widow and BAUER, all of Niclashausen, worked hard on the Cloister Farm of Bronnbach and now wants to go with wife and 3 children to New England. Still has 448 florins property. Mentioned as emigrant in the *Village Mayor's Report* for Niclashausen (1752): "JACOB WOLF, with wife and child." // FIELIEB JACOB WOLF, with JACOB WOLF and other Wertheimers, Ship *Phoenix,* November 2, 1752 (Hinke, I, 502). There were other JACOB WOLFS in Hinke, later, but this is probably the one. Naturally also there are quite a few JACOB WOLFS listed in 3PA, making identification difficult; but see PHILIPP JACOB WOLF, below.

## WOLF, KUNIGUNDA — Michelrieth (1754)

July 21, 1762: on request of [BARBARA WOLF], the widow of HANS ADAM WOLF, a guardian is appointed for her daughters, who nine years ago went to Pennsylvania. August 11, 1762: the daughters are now spoken of as two sons! June 10, 1763: HANS ADAM WOLF's daughters KUNIGUNDA and BARBARA went to Pennsylvania in 1756 [1754] and secretly took along 110 florins. Mentioned as emigrants in the *Village Mayor's Report* for Michelrieth (1755): "LORENZ ALBERT, a cartwright, with his wife; (HANS ADAM WOLF is his brother [father]-in-law). KUNIGUNDA WOLF, his wife's single sister, likewise a daughter of HANS ADAM WOLF, went without property. HANS ADAM WOLF is now (1761) dead; if the Newlanders [in this case, "emigrants"] come back, or write, his property shall be divided."

## WOLF, MARIA — Dietenhan (1753)

May 14, 1753: single, wants to go to America with the emigrants. Possibly the emigrant referred to in the *Village Mayor's Report* for Dietenhan (1753): "MARIA CATHARINA [——] has not inherited from her father's property over 10 florins, and pays for her manumission out of her servant's wages"

## WOLF, PHILIPP JACOB — Dietenhan (1752)

May 8, 1752: can no longer earn his living here, and wants to go with his wife and 2 children to New England or to the Island of Pennsylvania. Still has 24 florins. Mentioned as emigrant in the *Village Mayor's Report* for Dietenhan (1752): "PHILIPP JACOB WOLF and wife." // FIELIEB JACOB WOLF, with JACOB WOLF and other Wertheimers, Ship *Phoenix,* November 2, 1752 (Hinke, I, 502). There were several Wolff families at the New Hanover Lutheran Church in Montgomery County, Pa., occasionally mentioned in connection with other Wertheimers (*PGS Proceedings,* XX, 338-9). For instance, GEORG and EVA WOLF were parents of a child baptized 1754, the sponsors being ANDREW ETZEL and wife, who were from Dietenhan. JACOB and ELIZABETH WOLF were parents of children baptized in 1764. Others named VEIT and SEBASTIAN WOLF also appear.

## WOLPERT, CHRISTOPH — Vockenroth

Mentioned as emigrant in the *Village Mayor's Report* for Vockenroth (1750-1761): "CHRISTOPH WOLPERT, with wife, without children." // JOHANN CHRISTOPH WALBERT, Ship *Patience,* September 19, 1749 (Hinke I, 409), with other Wertheimers. Perhaps STOPHEL WOLBERT, taxed in Lebanon Tp., Lancaster (now Lebanon) Co., Pa., in 1771 (3PA, XVII, 143 ff.); though CHRISTOPHER WOLFARTS appear in Tulpehocken Tp., Berks Co., in 1781, and York Tp., York Co., Pa., in 1782 (3PA, XVIII, 547 ff.; XXI, 576).

## WOLPERT, PETER — Vockenroth (1773)

March 12, 1773: wants to go to New England with wife and children, because he can no longer earn his living. Has nothing left. Is to pay 19 florins on taxes. // Perhaps PETER WOLFARTH, taxed in Mt. Pleasant Tp., York Co., Pa., in 1782 (3PA, XXI, 553).

## WOLZ, ANNA ELISABETH — Sachsenhausen (1752)

May 4, 1752: widow, wants to go to Pennsylvania with her 4 little and poor children, fatherless orphans. Her late husband was named NICOLAUS. Still has 111 florins. Mentioned as emigrant in the *Village*

*Mayor's Report* for Sachsenhausen (1750-1761): "NICOLAUS WOLZ's widow, with her children." // According to the records of the Lutheran Church at the Trappe, one ANNA MARGRETHA WOLTZ, daughter of "WIDOW WOLTZ," was married, in 1761, to JOHAN JOST BERGER (*PGS Proceedings*, VII, 505).

## WUNDER, JOHANN GEORG — Wertheim (1753)

May 11, 1753: burgher and cabinet-maker, wants to go to New England. Has only 11 florins left, and wants, along with his wife and 2 little children, to be freed from vassalage. "Considering the miserable circumstances of these poor people, only 2 florins tax shall be levied. The Princely Councilor VON OLNHAUSEN is, however, of the opinion that not a "penny" *(Batzen)* less than the tax should be levied, without the Prince's permission. Must pay, therefore, 4 florins and 33 kreuzer. From the *Burgomaster's Accounts* for 1768, in the City Archives, it appears that WUNDER later paid a supplemental tax on 50 florins, which he received to take along on the journey to Pennsylvania, likewise on 30 additional florins, to the amount of 8 florins. // JOHANN GORG WUNDER, Ship *Neptune*, September 24, 1753 (Hinke, I, 539 ff.), with other Wertheimers. Settled in Reading, Pa., where, in the Records of Trinity Lutheran Church (*Notes and Queries,* I [1883], 106), JOH. GEO. and DOROTHEE ELIS. WUNDER are mentioned as parents of a child baptized in 1755. GEORGE WUNDER, born September 7, 1718, at Ebern in Franconia, died September 27, 1803, after a long and tedious illness, aged 85 years, 20 days, and was buried at Reading on September 28, 1803.

## ZIMMERMANN, WILHELM — Höhfeld (1753)

April 30, 1753: wants to go with ADAM HOERNER to Pennsylvania. *Freudenberg Governmental Protocol,* May 24, 1754: WILHELM ZIMMERMAN, of Höhfeld, is said to be willing to go secretly to Pennsylvania. 14 florins were sequestrated. Since his father is still living, his inheritance shall be kept at this time. // WILLIAM ZIMMERMANN was taxed in Worcester Tp., Philadelphia Co., Pa., in 1769, and Norrington Tp., Philadelphia Co., in 1779 (3PA, XIV, 32 ff.; XV, 114 ff.).

# APPENDIX I

## *AGREEMENT FOR TRANSPORT FROM ROTTERDAM TO PHILADELPHIA*

*February 16, 1756*

This contract for transport across the ocean appeared as Appendix IV of the original German edition of this work. The original document, in large folio size (40/27 cm.), printed in German letters on both sides, sealed by the shipowner and signed with the personal signatures of 26 "Pennsylvania German Pioneers," is preserved in the collections of the *Historischer Verein Alt-Wertheim.* Some idea of its importance in Pennsylvania German research can be gained from the fact that it is, so far as the American editor knows, the only extant contract of its kind. It would be nice to think that our emigrant ancestors always received the fair treatment promised in this document!

KNOW ALL MEN BY THESE PRESENTS, especially those whom it may concern, that we, the undersigned passengers, have contracted with Messrs. *Isaac* & *Zacharias Hope,* Merchants in Rotterdam, even as we herewith contract for ourselves and our families in the following manner:

*Firstly,*

The above-mentioned Messrs. *Isaac* & *Zacharias Hope* shall furnish us a good, comfortable, and well-sailing ship, in order with the same to have us transported to

PHILADELPHIA

and to that end there shall be made in the ship firm bunks for each whole freight, six feet long and one and one-half feet wide.

*Secondly,*

The above-mentioned Messrs. *Isaac* & *Zacharias Hope* shall fit out the said ship well with good and proper provisions, namely: good bread, meat, bacon, flour, rice, barley, peas, syrup, butter, cheese, beer, good fresh water, and whatever else is necessary; likewise the ship shall be twice daily cleansed with vinegar and juniper berries, to purify the air; and daily there shall be given out to each whole freight the following:

*Sunday*—one pound of beef cooked with rice
*Monday*—barley and syrup

*Tuesday*—one pound of white wheat flour
*Wednesday*—one pound of bacon with peas
*Thursday*—one pound of beef cooked with rice
*Friday*—one pound of white wheat flour and one pound of butter
*Saturday*—one pound of bacon, one pound of cheese, and six pounds of bread for the entire week.

Besides, every day, one quart of beer (as long as it remains good), and two quarts of water daily, to each whole freight.

If brandy is desired, it shall be given each morning to every person who desires it. Lovers of tobacco, however, shall receive one pound to take along on the journey.

*Thirdly,*

We, the undersigned passengers, want to have freedom (as God's weather permits) to cook a few victuals for ourselves and the little children, and to make use of the fire from six o'clock in the morning till the same time in the evening; also permission to be on deck; yet those who are sick are especially to enjoy the right to help themselves to the fire and water as often as they need it for their refreshment; likewise there shall be provided on the ship all kinds of aromatics and also wine, so that the sick can the better be cared for.

*In Return For Which*

We, the undersigned passengers, promise to pay to the abovementioned Messrs. *Issac & Zacharias Hope* in Rotterdam, or on their order, for transport of our persons, baggage, and household goods, from Rotterdam to Philadelphia,

SEVEN AND ONE-HALF DOUBLOONS for each whole freight, and the goods that we have with us shall be delivered on land there *gratis,* without our being forced to pay anything therefore to the stevedores.

Now the freights shall be reckoned in the following manner: Children under four years old are free; from four to fourteen years, they shall pay half freight; and fourteen years and upwards, full freight.

But if anyone agrees to take them all together for less than the above-mentioned sum, Messrs. *Isaac & Zacharias Hope* promise to do the same, except where it is plainly done as spite work against Messrs. *Isaac & Zacharias Hope,* in which case they release the people from the contract, however in such case those who offer cheaper transportation are to pay Messrs. *Isaac & Zacharias*

*Hope* for the expenses which they incurred before the people arrived at the port.

As proof whereof we vow and promise on both sides to carry out all the above faithfully and uprightly, binding to this end our persons and properties;

IN WITNESS WHEREOF we have validated this Contract with our personal signature.

Done at ROTTERDAM, February 16, 1756.

(Signed) ISAAC & ZACHARIAS HOPE.

P.S. Without prejudice to others we let it be known that this year our agreement has been somewhat altered; the reason WHY and the way IN WHICH it has been improved is this: Because new merchants, who have never made the journey, have had such [an agreement] prepared.

The particular way in which we are now improving ours is as follows:

Inasmuch as we, as experienced merchants, who have been transporting people twenty or more years already, have found that bacon and meat are very heavily salted, from which salted provisions scurvy and other complaints arise, and moreover the High Germans are brought up more on fresh than on salted provisions, we are ready to give two or three fresh meals weekly, which they will judge more fit for them.

[On the margin of the first page, the following prospective emigrants, only a few of whom were Wertheimers, personally subscribed their names, with their proportion in the "freights."]

Johann Philipp Oswald — 1 freight
Balthasar Thorwart — 3½ freights
Johannes Schäfer — 2 freights
Margarete Baumann — 1 bed[?]
Georg Mehrling — 2 freights
Barbara Schlegling — 1 freight
Andon Bock — 11 freights
Christoph Hartlaub — 1 freight
Philipp Stockhammer — 3½ freights
Barbara Schar [Schärin] — 1 freight
Hans Görg Frank — 3 freights
Kaspar Zottelmeyer — 3 freights
Mattes Gröss — 6 freights
Joh[ann] Pet[er] Ziegler — 3½ freights
Caspar Englert — 3 freights

Jak[ob] Kern — 1 freight
Joh[ann] Görg Knobloch — 2 freights
Melcher Landeck — 2 freights
Mattes Stumpf — 1 freight
Joh[ann] Mich[ael] Dosch — 11 freights
Friedr[ich] Ott — 1 freight
Hans Görg Friedert — 1 freight
Barbell Spiell[?] — 3 freights
Görg Jacob Spiell [Sprit?] of Schweinfurt — 3 freights
Mich[ael] Lousser — 1 freight
TOTAL — 71½ freights

---

## APPENDIX II

### *THE JOHANNES SCHLESSMANN LETTERS*

Among eighteenth-century documentation on Pennsylvania German life, letters from the "New Land" to friends or relatives in the old homeland are extremely rare. As Appendices I and II of the original German edition of this work, Dr. Langguth published two such letters from an emigrant from Nassig named *Johannes Schlessmann,* who settled near Germantown, Pennsylvania. The first of these letters, written in the simplest farmer's German a short time after the emigrant's arrival in the "New Land" in 1753, was preserved in the *Rosenberg Archive, Br. 387 h.* It was marked, "This letter is to be given to *Hans Jacob Schlessmann* at Oedengesass and *Hans Scheurich* at Oedengesass or Nassig, near Wertheim, [and] . . . . to *Philipp Stemmler* in Wertheim."

(1) *Letter of Johannes Schlessman, Oxford, Philadelphia County, Pennsylvania, November 26, 1753*

Anno 1753

God greet you! Beloved brother and sister and in-laws and god-parents and sponsor-folk and neighbor people, who have lived near me. I cannot refrain from writing a few lines—if they find you all well, we shall be heartily glad. So we greet you and yours a thousand times. Concerning our long, hard trip, thanks and praise be to God, we all got across the big water safe and sound. We had not the slightest difficulty — great wind, but not a single storm, only nice warm wind, else we would not have been sailing about on the water so long. In nine weeks we saw no land. We arrived in the City of Philadelphia one day before Michaelmas. My brother-in-law, *Christoph Kuhn,* came at once to us on the ship and took us with him into his own house. Since we arrived so late in the country, we will stay with him this winter, but toward spring we will move somewhat further into the country. We met our son Christof at once, but he is not very well—he had the fever during the past summer.

Concerning our work I cannot write you at this time. I and my children and my wife thank and praise God a thousand times, that we are in this healthy country. We expect to support ourselves much better here than in Germany, for this is a free country. One has to give nothing to any government. The first year is free, but thereafter a farmer must give three or four shillings, that amounts to a German gulden, which the poor get. There are no beggars in this country. Grains are as dear here as in Germany, but one can earn five loaves of bread sooner in this country than one in Germany, for the day's wages are very good. In the winter a man gets 18 pence, that is in German money 7 [27?] kreuzer; in summer 11 batzen, but rich board along with it — meat two to three times a day, and a good drink made of apples. A woman gets per day or can earn per day only with spinning, 7 to 8 pence, that is in German money 2 batzen. In this country the women do not work half so hard as in Germany. The English women don't work at all and dress like gentle folk.

Now I ask you, Brother and Sister . . . my Brother *Hans Jakob Schlessmann* and my brother-in-law *Hans Jakob Scheurich,* that you tell all our friends that we cannot write any more at this time. I and my wife and my children do not long anymore to be in Germany. I any my wife and my children are, thanks and praise be to God, all safe, sound and healthy. When we have been in this New Land a year, I will write you more about the country, for it is still unknown to me, because we arrived so late. Then there will be opportunity enough to write, so again we greet you a thousand times, who are our acquaintances. And so we ask you both, Brother and Brother-in-law, to be so good as to write us too in a year what happens in the village and among you, and write me all about *Hans Velten Pahl(en)* [s], our godparents, [......], .... and whatever occurs among you during the year. Both of you can also let both in-laws at Nassig know, *Hans Heinrich Scheurich* and *Hans Jörg Eirich,* that their brother-in-law died last year midway on the ocean. His money was divided by *Hans Jörg Dosch* and the Newlander. These three had bought wares together at Frankfurt and had traded jointly. He had also advanced money to the Newlander on the journey, so it's gone.

Now, you brothers and sisters and all good friends and in-laws, I cannot write you more fully at this time. If you have opportunity in a year, write us news again, and it will be a real joy for us. When I am a year in this country, I will write you more fully about the country — there is opportunity enough over the countryside. But it is a very long journey. We are very far from one another. We are surely about 2000 hours from each another — it can't be emphasized enough how far the journey is. But time, day and hours, sun and moon, stars, day and night, summer and winter, and all creatures under heaven appear here as they do in Germany. It becomes winter just as soon in the *"Bintzel Vannier land"* as in Germany — on Simon and Jude's Day we had such a big snow, cold and rough winds.

Now, remain our most faithful friends unto death, all of you. If we do not meet again in this world, then we will meet in heaven! If you would be so loving as to wish to write us again, it will be a real joy for us. Write to Germantown to *"Dürks Keyser,"* that is six miles from *Viellidelfia,* which is in German two hours. *Türks Keyser* will send me your letter, for my brother-in-law and I are spending the winter in his little house. He is a rich man in *Germandohn* [Germantown].

Done November 26, Anno 1753

(Witness) JOHANNES SCHLESSMANN in *Germandohn*

We present, secondly, a letter from *Johannes Schlessmann,* dated 1769, sent to accompany his Letter of Attorney, drawn up to enable him to receive his paternal inheritance in Wertheim. On the outside appear the words, *"Wertheym.* This Letter to go to *Johann Jakob Scheurich* at Oedengesäss." For additional information on Schlessmann furnishing the background of both these letters, see "Letters from the New Land," in the *Introduction,* also *"Johannes Schlessmann,"* in the List of Emigrants.

### (2) *Letter of Johannes Schlessmann, Oxford, Philadelphia County, Pennsylvania, November 27, 1769*

God greet you, my brother-in-law *Johann Jakob Scheurich* and his wife and children and my brothers and sisters and in-laws, as many of you as are still alive. I can't forego writing you a few lines, and if they find you all well, we shall be heartily glad of it. We are, thanks and praise be to God, still all well, as long as it pleases the Dear Lord. Concerning our children, five of them are married; and the other daughter is about to be engaged. Concerning our life here, we were all this time not far from Philadelphia. Germantown is our locality, where we go to church every Sunday. Whoever wants to write to me and our countrymen, should write to Germantown to *Christof Sauer,* that is the printer, who is known all over the country. That is situated not quite two hours from Philadelphia. I, *Johannes Schlessmann,* have bought me a middling place two good hours from the City of Philadelphia.

Further, we have a great favor to ask of you, brother-in-law *Johann Jakob Scheurich* and of your wife and your children. Because you have written me of my inheritance, I have had a Letter of Attorney made to you by our government, because you wrote me that it was given over to you and that you have taken care of it for me, so I think you will be so good as to take the Letter of Attorney to your government and assist me in getting what is mine. I need it because I have bought my own land, for good land is as dear with us, as in Germany near the city. The man who brings you the Letter of Attorney is from Gelnhausen, his name is *Nicolaus Zimmermann,* a good neighbor in Philadelphia. If you want to show your love to me, give this man the money that is coming to me, and whatever you send me, write on a little paper and send it back with the same man, the amount that is coming to me and what has been deducted. You must not forget your share, for you have had a great deal of trouble over this little money. You must pay yourself what belongs to you. I would have given this Letter of Attorney to *Weingärtner* to take along, but he said he was not coming back again to Pennsylvania. Further I know no better opportunity this time. I ask you once again to assist this man in all things, for which I will thank you indebtedly.

Concerning our countrymen here, we live far scattered from each other. I and my brother-in-law *Christof Kuhn* and *Christoffel Götzelmann* and *Heinrich Schlessmann* and *Johann Michael Schubert, Heinrich Hoffman(?)* and *Hans Michel Schubert* live in Philadelphia. The schoolmaster *(Beschler?)* and the *Borger (Bürger?), Paulus Schlessmann* and *Hans Jörg Dosch's* sons live far away in the bush. Some of them are not getting along so well. My greetings to Mr. *Niclas Schultheiss,* if he is still living, and *Hans Michel Beck* and *Michel Beck* and all my acquaintances and neighbors and sponsor folks. I thought some of our family might be going to Germany once again, but the costs are too great. One must have money enough. Whoever wants to go across the ocean with so little money, it isn't worth the trouble — one piles up so many expenses and loses a whole year's work, for a man can earn and spend much in one year.

Therefore be you commended unto God! I and my wife and my children greet you all a thousand times. If we do not meet in this life, then we will meet in the eternal life. Glory to God in the Highest, peace on earth, good will to men. We two are beginning to get old, yet we can still work so middling.

JOHANNES SCHLESSMANN

---

## APPENDIX III

### *THE LORENZ ALBERT PAPERS*

To highlight our picture of the eighteenth century emigration from Wertheim in terms of one typical emigrant family, the American editor is happy to present, through the courtesy of Miss Edna Albert, M.A., of the Staff of the Pennsylvania Archives, Harrisburg, Pennsylvania, three documents relating to her ancestor *Lorenz Albert,* who emigrated to Pennsylvania in 1754 from Michelrieth in the County of Löwenstein-Wertheim. The documents are the following: (1) Lorenz Albert's Certificate of Manumission, 1754; (2) Lorenz Albert's Baptismal Certificate [Taufschein] and Certificate of Good Conduct [Leumundszeugnis], drawn up by Pastor Dennscherz of Michelrieth, 1754; and (3) The Letter of Michel Fertig of Skippack, Pennsylvania, to his Cousin Lorenz Albert, 1782.

The Albert Family is an ancient one in the County of Wertheim. The earliest available reference to the name in the area dates from 1640, when we find one *Christoph Albert,* a tanner [*Weissgerber*] resident in Wertheim.[1] The ancestors of Lorenz Albert were, however, resident in the village of Altfeld, where he was born in 1719, the son of *Andreas* and *Margaretha Albert.* Doubtless his father was the Andreas Albert listed in the year 1698 as a resident citizen of Altfeld, whose population then numbered forty-six heads of families. According to a document in the Wertheim Archives, Andreas Albert in that year had "no farm-yard [*Hofriethe*], but eighty-five parcels of land — arable

[1]Siegfried Federle, *"Die Bürgerschaft der Stadt Wertheim am Main 1605 und 1640,"* Heft 28, *Flugschriften für Familiengeschichte* (Leipzig: Zentralstelle für deutsche Personen- und Familien-forschung, 1937), p. 7.

fields, meadows, kitchen-garden, clearing(?) [*Reuung*], unproductive vineyards [*böse Weingärten*], also some in the Kredenbach district." Because of its interest to the descendants of the other emigrants of Altfeld in the United States, we present in its entirety Dr. Langguth's list of Andreas Albert's fellow-citizens of Altfeld in 1698:

## RESIDENTS OF ALTFELD 1698

Andreas Fertig
Andreas Freudenberger, Sr. — "has much real estate."
Andreas Gerberich
Hans Caspar Gerberich
Andr[eas] Diehm, Carpenter
Peter Knauer, Carpenter — "has no farmyard, but a poor building site and seventy-two parcels of land.
Johann Endress — to him belongs one-third of the Inn, while the other two-thirds belongs to the children of the Village Mayor, Peter Wolf.
Nicolaus Freudenberger — has a house and half a barn.
Adam Wolf — has real estate also in Michelrieth.
Hans Schöffer, Sr.
Nicol[aus] Wolz — besides house and barn, has also a farm [*Hof*] and press-house and a summer garden.
Peter Wagner, Carpenter
Peter Fertig
Peter Schöffer
Hans Schöffer, Jr.
Hans and Georg Freudenberger
Nicol[aus] Gerberich
Nicol[aus] Diehm, Carpenter — has an old dilapidated house and half a barn.
Andreas Freudenberger, Jr. — has much real estate.
Hans Michel Müller
Hans Reutter, the Linenweaver — has one house and half a barn, besides half of an old house and half a barn.
Hans Hohe
Hans Müller's widow
Andreas Schöffer's widow
Andreas Schwob, widower — has one house, half a barn, and one press-house.
Andreas Fertig, Sr.
Martin Fertig
Peter Gerberich

Hans Fertig, Sr. — besides one house, has three-fourths of a barn.
Philipp Freudenberger — has two houses and two barns, also many parcels of ground, among them thirty-two rods of unproductive vineyards within the bounds of Oberwittbach.
Hans Caspar Fertig, the Blacksmith — besides his house, has one-fourth of a barn.
Hans Georg Fertig
Andreas Albert — see above.
Peter Freudenberger
Hans Albert
Hans Fertig, Jr. — has one house, one old farmer's cottage, one shed and one garden along with it.
Valt[in] Albert
Lorenz Fertig, the Tailor
Hans Seuboth [Seubert]
Nic[olaus] Ruttolf
Hans Diehm, Carpenter — has also an old farmer's cottage.
Linhard Knauer — has one house, half a barn, and another fourth of a barn.
Valt[in] Wolz.
Hans Winzenhöller, Blacksmith — has half of a house, half of a barn, and — by good fortune — one entire smithy!

PETER WOLF
*Village Mayor*[2]

On June 6, 1747, Lorenz Albert was married to *Anna Barbara Wolff,* daughter of *Johann Adam* and *Barbara Wolff,* of Oberwittbach, near Michelrieth. After his marriage, Lorenz Albert removed to Michelrieth, where he carried on his wagon-making business until 1754, when hard times drove him to emigrate to America. In his appearance before the governmental court on May 13, 1754, to request manumission and permission to emigrate, he gives as his reason the hard fact that "his calling no longer supports him, because every farmer makes his own plow himself." Further he states, "It is no impertinence or desire of mine, which drives me from the country, but poverty and uneasiness over wife and child [*"Es ist kein Vorwitz oder Lust, der mich aus dem Land*

[2]Otto Langguth, *"Einiges aus der Geschichte von Altfeld," Beiträge zur Heimatkunde,* Heft 1, (Kreuzwertheim-am-Main: Heimatverlag, 1932), p. 4.

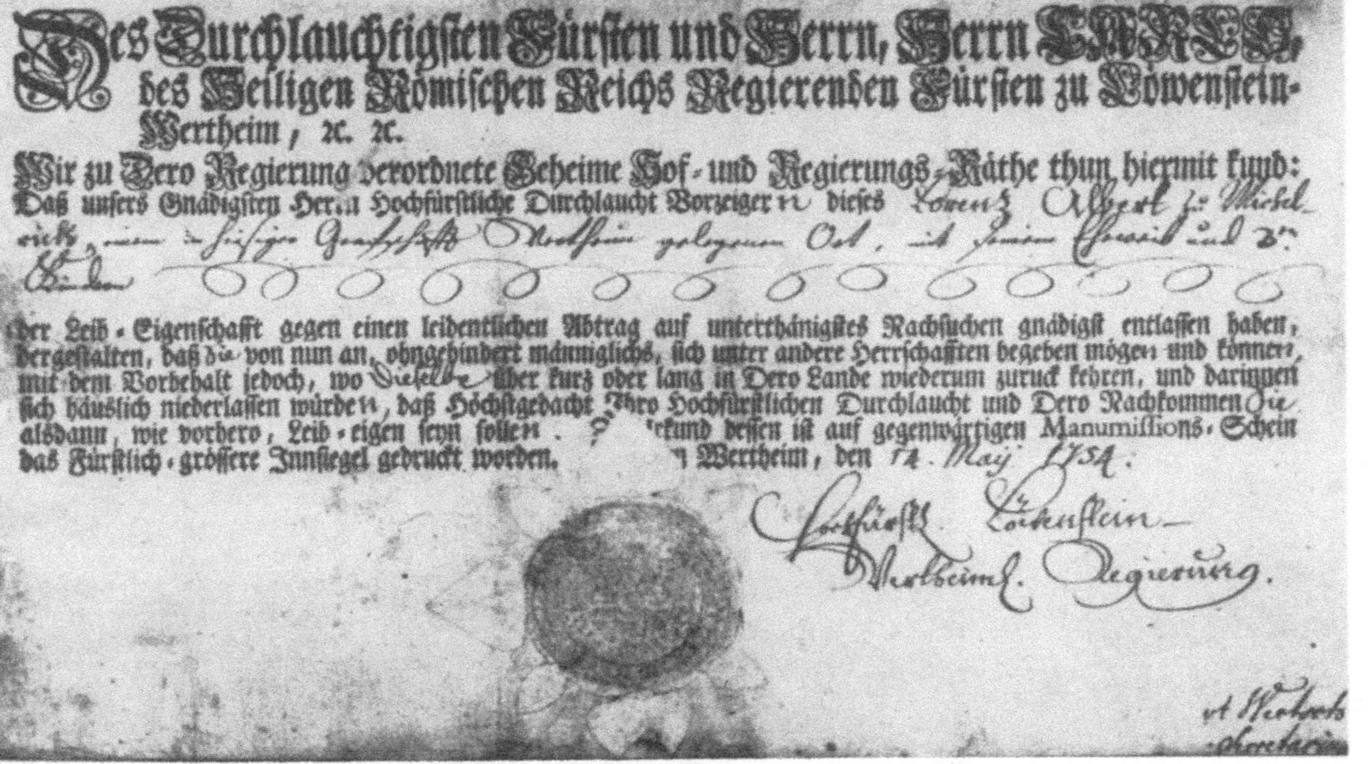

Des Durchlauchtigsten Fürsten und Herrn, Herrn CARLS, des Heiligen Römischen Reichs Regierenden Fürsten zu Löwenstein-Wertheim, rc. rc.

Wir zu Dero Regierung verordnete Geheime Hof- und Regierungs-Räthe thun hiermit kund: Daß unsers Gnädigsten Herrn Hochfürstliche Durchlaucht Vorzeigern dieses Lorenz Albert [illegible]

der Leib-Eigenschafft gegen einen leidentlichen Abtrag auf unterthänigstes Nachsuchen gnädigst entlassen haben, dergestalten, daß die von nun an, ohngehindert männiglichs, sich unter andere Herrschafften begeben mögen und können, mit dem Vorbehalt jedoch, wo dieselbe über kurz oder lang in Dero Lande wiederum zuruck kehren, und darinnen sich häuslich niederlassen würden, daß Höchstgedacht Ihro Hochfürstlichen Durchlaucht und Dero Nachkommen sie alsdann, wie vorhero, Leib-eigen seyn sollen. [illegible]rkund dessen ist auf gegenwärtigen Manumissions-Schein das Fürstlich-grössere Innsiegel gedruckt worden. [illegible] Wertheim, den 14. May 1754.

Hochfürstl. Löwenstein-Wertheim. Regierung.

Lorenz Albert's Certificate of Manumission, issued May 14, 1754

*treibt, sondern die Armut und die Sorge für Weib und Kind."*][3] Which could have been the words of most of our emigrant ancestors who left the old homeland for Pennsylvania in the 1750's.

The first document illustrating Lorenz Albert's emigration to Pennsylvania is the "Certificate of Manumission from Vassalage," without which he was not free to leave the territories of his sovereign lords, the Counts of Löwenstein-Wertheim.

(1) *Certificate of Manumission from Vassalage for Lorenz Albert, 1754*

HIS HIGHNESS PRINCE AND LORD, SIR CARL, REIGNING PRINCE OF LOEWENSTEIN-WERTHEIM IN THE HOLY ROMAN EMPIRE, ETC., ETC.

We, the Privy Court and Governmental Councilors authorized for this government, announce herewith: that our Gracious Lord, His Highness the Prince, has, after a most humble petition, and in return for a tolerable sum, graciously released from vassalage the bearer hereof, *Lorenz Albert* of Michelrieth, a locality situate in this County of Wertheim, with his wife and three children, in such wise that henceforth, without hindrance from any one, they may and can place themselves under other governments, with the proviso, however, that if sooner or later, they return again to this country, and want to take up residence therein, they shall be then, as heretofore, vassals to His Respected Princely Highness and His Descendants.

In witness whereof, the Great Princely Seal is imprinted upon this Certificate of Manumission.

Done at Wertheim, May 14, 1754

[SEAL] PRINCELY GOVERNMENT OF LOEWENSTEIN-WERTHEIM

Our second document is the elaborate *Tauff-Schein für den Ehrsamen Meister Wagnern Lorentz Albert zu Michelrieth, und dessen Weib mit dreyen Kindern, 1754,* prepared by Pastor *Johann Michael Dennscherz* of Michelrieth for Lorenz Albert and his family, as a testimony to their legitimate birth and descent, and

---

[3]Otto Langguth, *"Auswanderer aus der Grafschaft Wertheim," Jahrbuch des Historischen Vereins Alt-Wertheim,* 1935, Pt. 2, p. 15; also Otto Langguth, *"Auswanderer aus der Grafschaft Wertheim," Beiträge zur Heimatkunde,* Heft 3 (Kreuzwertheim am Main: Heimatverlag, 1932), p. 65.

their Christian conduct while they were his parishioners in the Parish of Michelrieth. It is to be compared with the *Tauf-, Ehe- und Toden-Schein für Sebastian Schweicker, Bürger und Schreiner in Bodelshausen, Tübinger Ober-Amts,* which we reproduced in connection with the Gerber Lists of Württemberger Emigrants.[4]

(2) *"Baptismal Certificate for the Honorable Master Cartwright Lorentz Albert at Michelrieth, His Wife and Three Children, 1754"*

A BLESSING, READER,

FROM THE FOUNT OF BLESSING, JESUS CHRIST, AMEN!

The bearer hereof, the Honorable [*Ehrsam*] Master *Lorentz* Al*bert,* by trade a free cartwright [*Wagner*], with his dear wife *Anna Barbara,* and three children, *Maria Apollonia, Susanna,* and *Andreas,* all vassal subjects of Michelrieth, in the Honorable County of Löwenstein-Wertheim, have, with God's blessing and the permission of our High Conjoint Government, resolved to go to Pennsylvania, there to settle under the protection of His Royal Majesty of England and seek their fortune. On this account the aforesaid *Lorentz Albert* has respectfully requested of me, pastor of the parish, as denoted below, a certified statement of the legitimate descent and birth of himself and his household, as also of their Christian conduct, to be furnished to him. Since there could nor would be any objection to such a just demand, may the following by virtue of my office and my conscience serve his purpose:

Firstly, that he, *Lorentz Albert,* was conceived in lawful wedlock and born into the world at Altfeldt, October 22, Anno Domini 1719. His father was the late Honorable [*Andreas*] *Albert,* resident in that neighborhood, his mother was named *Margaretha.* These two beloved parents, on the very same day, had this beloved and loving son whom God had granted them, brought to Holy Baptism, at which there stood as godfather the then young apprentice *Lorenz Reuter,* legitimate son of the late Honorable *Hanss Reuter,* weaver and member of the Court of Altfeld.

He was married to the former Miss *Anna Barbara Wolff* of Michelrieth, with the Christian marriage ceremony, on June 6, 1747, and then came to Michelrieth to live. Her dear parents, of whom she was likewise conceived and born in lawful wedlock,

[4]Don Yoder (ed.), "Emigrants from Württemberg: The Adolf Gerber Lists," *The Pennsylvania German Folklore Society,* Vol. X (1945), pp. 120-121.

and who had her baptized, on November 22, 1722, were the Honorable *Johann Adam Wolff,* then at Oberwittbach, now however resident in Michelrieth, and his wife *Barbara.* The sponsor at her baptism was Miss *Anna Barbara Schaffer,* legitimate daughter of *Hanss Schaffer* of Altfeld.

This married couple produced, with God's blessing, the following children:

(1) A daughter named *Maria Apol[l]onia,* who was born and baptized on March 10, 1748; her sponsor [*Tauffpathe*] was Miss *Maria Apollonia,* legitimate daughter of the Honorable *Andreas Hoh,* neighbor at Oberwittbach.

(2) A daughter named *Susanna,* born and baptized on December 26, 1750, whose sponsor was *Susanna Albert,* wife of the Honorable *Johann Georg Albert,* blacksmith and innkeeper at Michelrieth.

(3) A son, named *Andreas,* born and baptized April 20, 1753, whose sponsor was the young apprentice, *Johann Andreas Iessberger,* legitimate son of the Honorable *Sebastian Iessberger,* resident of Michelrieth.

All of which has been extracted from the Church Register [*Kirchen-Matricul*], and recorded on request.

Secondly, that the aforementioned have, one and all, conducted themselves in an honest, pious, unobtrusive and Christian manner, that they have been with all people of their kind — as with me their father-confessor — popular, beloved, and praised. Therefore they also have left behind them a Christian memory of their praiseworthy conduct. Which all the more can be attested of them, by *Lorenz Albert,* and asserted of him, as true, just as above said — all such is according to the precious truth. So every reader of this, in whatever station of life, please put full faith in this my given testimony.

Herewith I most humbly and heartily beg of God the All-High, that He may further be and remain with them with His grace and blessing, and pray: "O dear Father in Heaven, guard and protect them in body and soul! Keep them in good health! Guard them against all evil! Provide for them like a father! Guide them like a faithful escort! Protect them in all danger! Bless all their actions and labor! And because Satan is wandering about through cities and all lands, and is lying in wait especially for travelers and wayfarers, for whom he sets a trap, desiring to overthrow them — so protect them, O powerful God, against all cunning attacks on the ways and by-paths of loathsome Satan and his accursed train. O Lord of Hosts, command Thy holy angels, that they may encamp round about them and watch them on all their paths. May Thy Good Spirit guide them on their course, on the paths of Thy commandments, of pure evangelical doctrine, and of holy and blessed life and conduct. Preserve them in the true faith. When they stumble and fall, work true repentance in them. Plant in them the Cross and humility and Christian patience. Strengthen their hope, and grant that they may complete the pilgrimage of their mortal life comforted and with conscience inviolate, may die blessedly, and at last enter into the Heavenly Fatherland, for Jesus Christ's sake, Amen!"

Done at Michelrieth, May 23, 1754
M[*agister*] JOHANN MICHEL DENNSCHERZ
Thirty-eight years Pastor there

Armed with his Certificate of Manumission and his *Taufschein,* Lorenz Albert with other Wertheimers, joined the Kiesecker party of emigrants and sailed down the Main and Rhein Rivers to Rotterdam, where they took ship on the *Phoenix,* which arrived at the port of Philadelphia on October 1, 1754.[5] A mute witness to the perilous ocean voyage is preserved to us in the words of Pastor Lucas Rauss, who, when he was preparing the Albert Family Record for the Register of the Lutheran and Reformed Union Church on the Bermudian Creek, in what is now Adams County, Pennsylvania, where Lorenz Albert settled, had to write after the name of little Susanna Albert — *"gestorben auf der See 1754."* Other children were born in America: (1) *Johann Jacob Albert,* born September 24, 1757; (2) *Maria Margaretha Albert,* born January 7, 1760; and (3) *Johann Christoph Albert,* born June 26, 1762.[6]

---

[5]Ralph Beaver Strassburger and William John Hinke, *Pennsylvania German Pioneers* (Norristown, Pennsylvania: The Pennsylvania German Society, 1934), I, 627 ff. It is of interest to note that while several Alberts came to America from the County of Löwenstein-Wertheim in the eighteenth century, others were going to the German settlements in Eastern Europe. According to the information on emigrants to other lands than America, in the original German edition of this work, we find that *Leonhard Albert* of Altfeld emigrated to Hungary in 1724, and in 1766 a "poor orphan" named *Margarete Albert,* of Höhfeld, "still young," is described in the manumission records as wanting to "seek her fortune in Russia."

[6]The Family Record by Pastor Rauss can be found in the Register of the Lower Bermudian Lutheran and Reformed Church, Volume I (1745-1864), the original of which is preserved at Gettysburg Lutheran Seminary. Typed translations by Miss Edna Albert can be consulted at the Genealogical Society of Pennsylvania, or the Historical Society of York County.

The third Albert document is a letter written by *Michel Fertig* of Skippack, a Wertheimer emigrant, to his cousin *Lorenz Albert,* June 30, 1782, inquiring about the Alberts and their friends and relatives from Wertheim in the "New Land." As in the Schlessmann and Endres letters given in Appendices II and IV, a deeply religious note pervades the message. We are happy to report that this letter was actually received by Lorenz Albert. He lived in the Bermudian Valley of Northeastern Adams County, and the letter was addressed to "To Mr. Lorentz Albert, in the neighborhood of Fredericktown [Maryland]!"

(3) *Letter of Michel Fertig of Skippack, to Lorenz Albert, June 30, 1782*

Beloved Friend and Esteemed Cousin *Lorentz Albert,* to you, your wife and children, as to all those of your household — my greeting and the greeting of all of us! Because Providence has ordained that we are so far removed from each other in this western land, where we are now spending our pilgrimage, I have often felt sorry that we are not able to visit each other, even if not in person, yet to write to each other, but even this is sometimes impossible, even with a safe opportunity [to send a letter], though sometimes it may have been negligence. And because we now are so eager to hear from you, I could not resist writing you a few lines. If I were as ready for traveling as for writing, I would visit you personally, but my bodily weakness keeps me from it. From the bearer, [——— ———] by name, a traveling preacher around here and a good friend, we learn that you are in good circumstances, which we are happy to hear. Concerning ourselves, we are, thank God, still well here, and our circumstances are briefly as follows:

I, *Michael Fertig,* and my wife and six children and mother-in-law, live in *Schipbach* Township, Philadelphia County, and have a house and 50 acres of land, which however is so poor that we can scarcely support ourselves on it, and although I work constantly at my trade, we cannot live otherwise than *van den handen to den tanten,* i.e., according to a Dutch proverb, "from hand to mouth." Consequently I have often wished I were farther up country with my family, but no opportunity has opened. My stepbrother *Adam Saur* lives nearby here, and his father with him. Mother has been dead two years. He has a wife and three children, a place of 75 acres, and they are able to make out well there. Besides them I have no [Wertheimer] friends hereabouts. My brother, *Johannas Fertig,* lives in Chester County, about 18 miles from me, in *Est Nentmel* [East Nantmeal] Township, has a wife and six children, 100 or more acres of land, but is not getting on.

This little in regard to our worldly circumstances I wanted to tell you, and hope, dear friend, it will not be unpleasant news. Besides, I wanted to inquire of you, if I may, whether you could not give me some news of our cousin *Andreas Fertig*. We are able to hear nothing at all of him and his family. It is already about 20 years since I visited him in *Tolpenhacken,* but we have heard that they moved away from there and are somewhere in *Virgini*[*a*] and so, then, we are scattered in this desert of the West like sheep who have no shepherd, and if we never get to see each other again on this stage, the world, may God grant that we see each other in that world where no one will complain anymore of need and pain, where no one will hear anyone say that he wants to be redeemed.

*Wer in Mesech mit Vertruss*
*Und in Kedar wohnen muss.*
*Der wird dort wie Petrus bitten*
*Herr lass uns hier bauen Hütten.*

Concerning the times — we are living here quietly, thank God, on account of the war, except that we are somewhat oppressed by expenses, and everything is very dear, except that the precious bread is cheap, because not much is exported.

And now, beloved friend, I commend you, one and all, along with my former hearty greeting, into the protection of Almighty God, who will so guide and direct us all that at the end of our mortal lives we can say

*Welt, adjeu, ich bin dein müde*
*Fahren will ich hin in Friede*
*Wo man recht sanfte schläft und ruht.*

And herewith remain in all sincerity

Your friend and most devoted servant

MICHEL FERTIG

Schipbach, June 30, A. D. 1782

The Albert family, whom Pastor Dennscherz commended to God, did not fail their good pastor. *Lorenz* and *Anna Barbara Albert,* their children, grandchildren, and great-grandchildren appear in the records as faithful communicant members of the Lower Bermudian Lutheran Church, near York Springs, Adams County, Pennsylvania. Of Lorenz Albert's descendants, his grandson

*Johann E. Albert* became a Lutheran minister.[7] His great-grandson, *Professor Frank Albert,* taught mathematics at Millersville and Indiana State Teachers' Colleges, and his great-great-granddaughter, Miss *Edna Albert,* M.A., was a professor at the Dover Academy in Delaware and at Williamsport Dickinson Seminary, now Lycoming College, at Williamsport, Pennsylvania.

Miss Albert is the author of the splendid children's novel of the eighteenth-century German emigration, *Little Pilgrim to Penn's Woods* (New York: Longmans, Green and Company, 1930). In this book she has effectively used the story of her own family, the Alberts of Michelrieth in the County of Löwenstein-Wertheim, who, for obvious reasons, become in her story the "Reinhardts of Rosenrieth in the County of Altenstein-Wertheim." Her delightful pen describes in fascinating fashion and with historically accurate detail the life in the storybook villages of eighteenth-century Germany, the trip down the Main and Rhine to Rotterdam, the tedious sea voyage, and the building of new homes in Penn's Woods. It is all there — the interview with Prince Carl, the family conferences preparatory to leaving, the blessing of Pastor Dennscherz, the last long backward looks at the old homes they were leaving forever. *Little Pilgrim to Penn's Woods* is one the most charming fictional accounts of life among the Pennsylvania Germans in the eighteenth century, ranking with Elsie Singmaster's *A High Wind Rising* and Conrad Richter's *The Free Man.*

### THE PASTOR OF MICHELRIETH PARISH

The sainted pastor who wrote the lovely prayer contained in the Albert *Taufschein* deserves a few lines here by way of biography before we leave the Albert Family. According to Dr.

---

[7]Another family of Alberts in Pennsylvania which produced several Lutheran ministers, including the Reverends *John Jacob Albert,* D.D. (1798-1875) and his sons *Luther Endress Albert,* D.D. (1828-1908 and *Charles Stanley Albert,* D.D. (1847-1912), had settled around Elizabethtown, Lancaster County, Pennsylvania, where *John Jacob Albert* was born. *Charles S. Albert* was pastor at Lancaster, Carlisle, and Baltimore, a writer and editor, President of the General Synod (1893-1895), and for 18 years President of the General Synod's Home Mission Board. See E. H. Delk (ed.), *Life and Works of Charles S. Albert* (Philadelphia: Lutheran Publication Society, 1915).

Langguth's researches, generously communicated to the American editor in letter form especially for this work, Pastor *Dennscherz* was an interesting character. Magister *Johann Michael Dennscherz,* Pastor of the Evangelical Lutheran Parish of Michelrieth, was born in Wertheim, May 1, 1691, son of the tailor *Joseph Dennscherz* in Wertheim, originally from Schwarzenau, and his wife *Anna Margaretha,* née *Volk.* The sponsor [*Pate*] at his baptism was *Johann Michael Platz,* Tanner [*Rotgerber*] in Wertheim.

After the usual university education leading to the Master of Arts degree, whence came his highly-prized title of "*Magister,*" he was installed as pastor at Michelrieth and vicinity. In his marriage record in 1718, in the Church Register, Pastor Dennscherz described himself as "Pastor of the Six Congregations on the Mountain" [*Pfarrer der 6 Gemeinden auf dem Berg*] — which sounds surprisingly like an Eastern Pennsylvania Lutheran or Reformed parish! The villages connected with this extensive parish were Altfelt and Eichenfürst (counted as one congregation), Credenbach, Michelrieth, Oberwittbach, Steinmark, and Glasofen. The remaining villages of that neighborhood were Catholic and under episcopal supervision.

In 1765 the aging pastor was transferred to Bettingen, where he received the honor of being "*Ministerii Senior,*" i.e., the eldest of all Wertheimer pastors, having served forty-nine years at Michelrieth. These last years were hard for him, according to the Church Records, since the rough peasants denied him — as a decrepit old preacher! — water and pasture rights! At a great age, and even after a stroke which left him lame the rest of his life, he received no vicar to aid him in his work, and his cries for help died away unheard! After a long and useful ministry, he finally retired, dying in 1772, and was buried in Wertheim, May 16, 1772, aged 81 years and 16 days.

According to a German proverb, those who leave literary remains for posterity to read have the best chance of attaining immortality — *Wer schreibt, der bleibt!* The Wertheimer historian Rommel calls Dennscherz "a very learned man" and poet, the compiler of a Prayerbook which appeared at Wertheim in 1760. He was also the author of a Prayerbook, entitled *Einer andächtigen Seelen, wöchentliche Morgen- und Abend-Andachten. . . .* (Wertheim, 1741), a copy of which Lorenz Albert brought to America with him, perhaps as a parting gift from his good pastor. A copy of this rare volume, not listed in either the British Museum or the Library of Congress Catalogues, is in the possession of Miss Edna Albert. Of Pastor Dennscherz's poems, the *Historischer Verein Alt-Wertheim* possesses a few, mostly *Carmina* written for the birthdays of government officials, though they are, writes Dr. Langguth in a letter to the American editor, *"nach heutigen Begriffen geschmackloses Zeug."!* A sample of his poetry is his rhymed petition for payments of wine, a part of his official state salary which was not being delivered:

Ich stehe hier dreyssig Jahr un habs nie gross geachtet,
Ob bey dem Wasserkrug ich halber bin verschmachtet,
Der Magen wird sehr schlapp, die Kräfte nehmen ab,
Weil keinen Tropfen Wein — ich zur Besoldung hab'."

Prince Carl of Löwenstein-Wertheim fulfilled his request in a government order which was likewise in rhyme.[8]

Since several of the pastor's family came to Pennsylvania, some account of his descendants can be given at this point. In Michelrieth, on February 15, 1718, young Pastor Dennscherz was married to *Anna Barbara Endres,* second daughter of *Lorenz Endres,* Master of the Hospital [*Spitalmeister*] in Wertheim, originally from Credenbach, and his wife *Johanna Catharina Schürer,* of an old family of Wertheim officials. *Anna Barbara* was born in Wertheim, March 26, 1698, and was buried there July 9, 1772, at the age of seventy-six. The following children were born in the parsonage at Michelrieth:

(1) *Catharina Margaretha Dennscherz,* born in Michelrieth, June 29, 1719, died the same day.

(2) *Lorenz Joseph Dennscherz,* born in Michelrieth, July 8, 1720; sponsors at his baptism, both grandfathers. In 1731 he himself stood as sponsor [*Pate*] at the baptism of a child of Schoolmaster *Rosenkranz,* and again in 1740 for Schoolmaster *Klein.* In 1752 he emigrated to Pennsylvania [cf. his name in the List of Emigrants], and according to the

[8]Otto Langguth, *"Auswanderer aus der Grafschaft Wertheim," Jahrbuch des Historischen Vereins Alt Wertheim, 1935,* Pt. 2, p. 22.

Church Register of Michelrieth, he again stood sponsor at a baptism on September 10, 1762, having returned to Michelrieth on July 7, from *"Pen-Sylvanien,"* to visit Pastor Dennscherz there.

(3) *Sophia Dorothea Dennscherz,* born in Michelrieth, July 30, 1722, died December 16, 1722; sponsors at baptism, *Barbara Sophia Neumesius,* daughter of *Leonhard Neumesius,* Pastor at Uettingen, also *Maria Dorothea Günther,* daughter of *Wilhelm Ezard Günther,* Pastor at Hasloch.

(4) *Maria Margaretha Dennscherz,* born in Michelrieth, January 7, 1725; sponsors at baptism, *Catharina Maria Assum,* daughter of *Ludwig Heinrich Assum,* Merchant in Wertheim, also *Catharina Margaretha Endres,* daughter of *Georg Michael Endres,* Landlord at the "Golden Chain" Tavern in Wertheim. On June 4, 1748, *Maria Margaretha Dennscherz* was married in Michelrieth to *Johann Sebastian Hammeter,* a tailor of Michelrieth, originally from Gunzenhausen. When their fourth child, *Johann Andreas Jacob Hammeter,* was baptized, on December 26, 1753, Pastor Dennscherz had to write in the Church Register that his son-in-law had "deserted to Pennsylvania" [*nach Pensylvanien desertiert*], leaving the already overburdened pastor to provide for the wife and family.

---

## APPENDIX IV

### *THE ZACHARIAS ENDRES PAPERS*

In contrast to the *Lorenz Albert* family, which was a typical rural emigrant family, the story of *Zacharias Endres* — who emigrated in 1766 from Kredenbach, near Wertheim, and settled in Philadelphia, where he became a wealthy brewer and Revolutionary patriot — stands out as a rare exception among our Pennsylvania German Pioneers. With a university education and the social advantages brought by wealth and travel and close friendship with the Counts of Löwenstein-Wertheim, he was naturally not an average Pennsylvania German emigrant, but this does not make his story any the less interesting.

In the original German edition of "Emigrants from the County of Wertheim," Dr. Langguth included, as Appendix III, a

"Letter from a Wealthy Wertheimer in Philadelphia to his Friends in Wertheim," dated 1780, and printed in the *Wertheimer Intelligenzblatt*, No. 9, March 2, 1781. This valuable letter, which we reproduce in translated form below, tells of the sufferings of a Philadelphia brewer and landowner at the hands of the British during the Revolution. Simply signed "Z. E.," this letter called forth all the latent detective talents of the American editor, to identify the writer. Since the name *Endres* appears frequently in the List of Emigrants, and knowing that one of the most distinguished American Lutheran clergymen in the first quarter of the nineteenth century was the Reverend *Christian Endress,* D.D., he was enabled to discover that *Christian Endress* was the son of one *"John Zachary Endress,"* who, according to his son's biographer, was born at "Wortheim-on-the-Main."[1]

Other investigations in Philadelphia have conclusively proved that Dr. Langguth's "Z. E." was this *Zacharias Endress,* a wealthy brewer and landowner in Philadelphia, and a leader in the Revolutionary cause. The fascinating story of his life was written in manuscript form by his grandson, Judge *Isaac L. Endress* of Dansville, New York, in 1855-1860, and published, in part, by Judge *Endress*'s son and grandson in 1926, in the volume entitled *Endress Im Hof — A Genealogical History of the Endress Family.*[2] Except where otherwise indicated, this *Endress Im Hof* volume is the source of the following biography of *Zacharias Endress,* which, in abbreviated form, can be reconstructed as follows.

In the late Middle Ages, the family of *Im Hof,* of which one branch came to be known as *Endress Im Hof,* and later simply as

---

[1]William B. Sprague (ed.), *Annals of the American Pulpit,* Volume IX. (New York: Robert Carter & Brothers, 1869), pp. 107-110.

[2]This volume of 112 pages, compiled by William Fries Endress and his son William Fitzhugh Endress, was published by the Knickerbocker Press in 1926, and distributed to libraries and others interested without being put up to sale. We are indebted to both of its compilers for the privilege of using facts from their biography of Zacharias Endress, and the letters from the Counts of Löwenstein-Wertheim given below, as well as for the excellent reproductions of their photograph of Wertheim-on-the-Main, and the portraits of the Reverend Christian Endress, done by Jacob Eichholz of Lancaster in 1816, and still in the possession of the Endress family of Jamestown, N. Y.

*Endres* or *Endress,* rose into prominence in the City of Nürnberg, where they produced several burgomasters and erected the *Im Hof* Monument in the famous Church of St. Lorenz. One of them, according to Dr. *Christian Endress'* account, was "*Jacob Endress,* who, as a representative of the city of Nuremberg, in the famous Imperial Diet held at Augsburg in 1531, subscribed the Augsburg Confession of Faith."[3] From Nürnberg, around the year 1560, a member of this family named *Nicholaus Endres* removed to the Protestant territory around Kreuzwertheim. His direct descendant, *Philipp Jacob Endress* (1682-1762), a native and resident of Kredenbach, who married *Eva Dorothea Schaffer* of Dertingen, had three sons: (1) *Philipp Jacob,* (2) *Georg,* and (3) *Johann Zacharias.* The father died in 1762 and was buried in the Endress family burial place in Michelrieth.[4]

*Johann Zacharias Endres,* the emigrant, was born at Kredenbach, in the County of Löwenstein-Wertheim, August 1, 1726. Educated at the University of Tübingen in Württemberg, he set out as a young man on extensive travels, described as follows by his son Christian:

> When my father was young, an uncle, a nobleman, Frey Herr (Baron) von Hof, took him for a few years to Frankfort, and from thence sent him to Geneva where he stayed about fourteen months, and, together with the young Count of Löwenstein-Wertheim, studied Jurisprudence under the charge and direction of the famous French writer and philosopher, Voltaire. He was sent hence upon a tour through Italy, and up the Mediterranean, where he was taken prisoner and carried to Algiers.
>
> From this captivity he was redeemed by a Venetian merchant who had come to Barbary for the purpose of purchasing mules. The Venetian made him overseer of his affairs, took him to Tunis, and thence to Turkey in Europe, where he set him free and sent him off to Marseilles. From Marseilles he went to Lyons and remained there with a relative for some

---

[3]Sprague, *op. cit., loc. cit.*

[4]In a letter of April 18, 1948, Dr. Langguth informed the American editor that the "principal residence of the Endres family was Credenbach, where they collected the toll, changed travelers' horses, housed guests overnight and managed a widely known public house. Credenbach lay along the single road which led through the wild Spessart Forest."

years, until obliged to flee from religious persecution. . . . He went to Paris and from there returned home after an absence of many years. . . . Soon after, his father died, and he was disappointed in receiving any part of the estate."[5]

On his return to his homeland, he was taken under the protection of his friend, the Count of Löwenstein-Wertheim. In 1761 he married and had one child, *Andreas Philipp,* who later was to come to America, and died in Kentucky about 1790, while agent for his father's land interests. In 1764 *Zacharias Endres'* wife died, and having lost all of his property in a lawsuit with a nobleman, he decided to seek his fortune in the New World. Aided financially by the Count, he set off for America in August, 1766, at the age of forty, landing at Philadelphia on September 23, 1766, on the Ship *Chance.*[6]

Having learned the brewer's trade with his relatives in Lyons, France, he set himself up in the business in Philadelphia, on a property on Vine and Callowhill, Second and Third Streets, which is today worth millions of dollars. Again he became wealthy, and on December 14, 1768, he was married to *Anna Maria (Henrici) Sänsfelt* (1738-1798), a native of Diedorff near Neuwied, of Huguenot descent, the widow of *Philip Sänsfelt. Zacharias* and *Anna Maria Endress* had the following children, whose births are recorded in the Baptismal Register of St. Michaelis and Zion Lutheran Church, Philadelphia, of which the family were prominent members:

(1) *Johann Zacharias,* born October 2, 1769, died 1811.
(2) *Philipp Jacob,* born March 20, 1771, died 1772.
(3) *Maria Dorothea (Ralston),* born November 1, 1772, died 1849.
(4) *Christian Friedrich Ludwig,* born March 17, 1775, died 1827.
(5) *Johann Philipp Heinrich,* born July 17, 1777, died 1795.

---

[5]According to his grandson, Judge Endress' account, in the *Endress Im Hof* history, when the Romanist officers were after him at Lyons, his friends hid him in the attic of their home, between the ceiling and the roof. One officer stuck a short sword through the thin boards and gave the young Lutheran a severe wound in the thigh, the scar of which he carried to the grave.

[6]Ralph B. Strassburger and William J. Hinke. *Pennsylvania German Pioneers,* I (Norristown, Pennsylvania: The Pennsylvania German Society, 1934), p. 709.

(6) *Anna Magdalena (Evans),* born November 12, 1779, died *ca.* 1865.

(7) *Susanna Catharina,* born July 8, 1782, died 1831.

Meanwhile the Revolutionary movement was arising. Despite his great wealth, which made many other well-established Philadelphians become Tories, *Zacharias Endress* identified himself fully with the colonial interests. To continue *Christian Endress'* narrative of his father's life:

> At the commencement of the war in 1774 he was the owner of 10 houses and 2 or 3 small places in Kensington. He took an active part in the events leading up to and in the Revolution, and was at first a member, then Captain, of the Philadelphia Guards, a Volunteer company. He discovered a plot of the Tories to deliver Philadelphia into the hands of the British and published it to Congress through John Hancock. When Philadelphia was taken by the British he fled to Northampton County. Although there was little destruction of property generally, the British, because of his previous activities, destroyed all his properties and buildings. He returned to Philadelphia about 1778 and determined to rebuild.

From this period comes the letter of *Zacharias Endres* written to his brother-in-law and sister in Wertheim, describing his losses during the American Revolution. The child about whose welfare he inquires may be either (1) his own son of his first marriage, *Andreas Philipp Endres,* who was left with his mother's people in Wertheim, or (2) a child named for *Zacharias Endress* in baptism, about whose progress he had heard nothing due to the interrupted foreign mail service of the Revolutionary period. The letter, which was printed in the *Wertheimer Intelligenzblatt* of March 2, 1781, reads as follows:

### LETTER OF ZACHARIAS ENDRESS OF PHILADELPHIA TO RELATIVES IN WERTHEIM, MAY 22, 1870

God's Grace and Blessing to you in greeting!

Dearly beloved Brother-in-law and Sister! For three years I have had no opportunity to write to you on account of the war, but I heard from an Anspach soldier that you were still well, which was joyous news to me![7]

---

[7]On November 3, 1777, there was lodged at the Ox Tavern at Wertheim "*Herr von Diskau,* Captain among the Anspach Troops who passed through here on their way to America." This transport evidently followed the water route to Holland.—O. L.

My wife and child and I are, thank God, all well, but have endured very much during this time — twice we fled from house and farm. For about two years we lived 50 miles from the City, and spent much money. During this time, the English and Hessians nearly ruined me. When we came back again to the City, my brewhouse, malthouse, and four new houses built of cedar, had been torn down and quite destroyed, so that I estimate my loss at 18,000 gulden.[8] We found some of our houses still standing, but ruined. My orchard, in which all kinds of the best trees stood, I found quite empty. Yes, it was almost over with me! I had nothing left but six children. The merciful God however looked on my misery, and helped me again according to His great goodness, for which I cannot thank Him enough in eternity. When I regard all the misery of my neighbors, I forget mine, because it is indescribable. One sees many orphans, who lost their fathers, crying for bread. Many parents, who were robbed of their children, now have no support and consolation in their old age. Here one hears a widow crying over the loss of her husband; and there one sees old men in direst need and want. The farmer was forced to bear the sword, and his plow stands idle. Need and near-hunger oppress the land — enemies from within and without harass it, and we cannot see the end of it.

Despite this I wanted to write you, how I wish to satisfy you for your many pains in my behalf. Many still have their inheritance to get, and it is dangerous to bring it over here. So inquire as to whether the property of *Förster* of *Urfel* (Urfar) is still safe. From it you can draw the 200 gulden for which I was surety, and then send it when he sends a Letter of Attorney. Already he has asked me here, to take care of it, but I have not yet spoken with him on your account. *M. Frischmuth* here is sending his godfather to Wertheim, otherwise would have had no opportunity. He will give you more news of it. *Frischmuth* has as yet suffered little misfortune from the war, and is in good circumstances. *Catharina Müller,* sister of the innkeeper in Creutzwertheim, is still living, and often comes to see me. *Sauer's* wife of Altfeld died a short time ago, which her youngest son asked me to tell her friends. The war made many of our countrymen here quite rich. With my wife's permission I would doubtless have sent you some money, upon the gracious Document of His Excellency the Count, of June 3, 1772, or had it paid through a

---

[8] 1 gulden=60 kreuzer=40 cents. But at thet time one could buy for 1 gulden 12 pounds of beef. For 60 kreuzer a hard worker had to labor for three days, from sunup to sunset One cow then cost about 16 gulden; for the above sum one could thus have bought in Germany over 1000 head of cattle –O. L.

Letter of Attorney, but on the advice of *Zimmermann's* wife here and all my friends, dared not out of fear. If my enemies got wind of it you would have to pay out constantly.

Dear Sister and Brother-in-law! Do not worry yourselves on my account. I will provide for you. It is my intent that neither you nor anybody else will lose anything because of me. The Lord has struck me, but He will bind me up again. He will provide for me. Only please remember my poor child with you. Write me, when was it baptized? What is its name? Where is it? And whether it is being raised in the fear of God. I wish that he were with me, or that before my end I might yet write to him. Give him my greetings and tell him of my concern about him. May the Almighty, before whom my fathers also have walked, bless him and His angel protect him from all evil paths. May God requite, richly and eternally, those who do him good. Give hearty greetings to all my friends and acquaintances. Ask my cousin *Kraft,* the bookbinder, to give me in a letter a full account of my child, your circumstances, and those of all my friends. And if my child can write, he should do so as soon as possible, which concerns me most. Lastly, I commend you unto the protection of the Most High, and remain, Honored Brother-in-law and Dear Sister,

Your faithful Friend and Brother,

Z[ACHARIAS] E[NDRES].

Philadelphia, May 22, 1780
Written in haste

[P.S.] For this letter I shall pay the esteemed friend who delivers it — may God go with him! Because of lack of time I have ended the letter, and send with a page from the Almanac, to show you how things look now in and around the fair City of Philadelphia.

In the hard times of 1786-1787, *Zacharias Endress* again lost his fortune, his creditors forcing a sale which left him penniless at the age of 61, with a family of six children to support. Until 1789 they struggled on in Philadelphia, then moved to Elkton, in Cecil County, Maryland. Here they lived for a decade, and the father again gradually recouped his finances. In 1798 when his wife died, *Zacharias Endress* was 72, and his son wrote that this last sorrow broke him in health and spirit. He lost most of his property and lived thenceforth with his family at Lancaster and

Easton. He died at the home of his daughter, Mrs. *Mary Ralston*, at Easton, in 1810, where he is buried in the Lutheran cemetery. It is recorded that though all his life he had used German with his family, in his last hours he lived almost entirely in his colorful past and spoke only in French.

It is strange that the story of *Zarachias Endress* has escaped our Pennsylvania German historians. The reason is not hard to find — the valuable Endress Family Papers have not as yet been copied and deposited in one of our Pennsylvania research libraries, and the extracts from them published in the *Endress Im Hof* history have been overlooked because many social historians, devoted exclusively to the steam-shovel technique of research in the broader topics of American history, have missed the occasional vein of treasure turned up by the hoe or mattock of an untrained local historian or genealogist.

At any rate, a Pennsylvania German who had studied with Voltaire, and who was on the most intimate terms with his former sovereigns, the Counts of Löwenstein-Wertheim, and who moved in the highest circles of Philadelphia society, is something new under the sun. And the Endress influence in America did not end with *Zacharias Endress*. Despite his undoubtedly nationalistic education, he valued his Lutheran heritage — his connection with St. Michaelis and Zion Lutheran Church, and the deeply religious note of his Letter of 1780 are sufficient proof of that! — and in his son, the Reverend *Christian F. L. Endress*, D.D. (1775-1827), he contributed to the infant Lutheran Church in America one of its most outstanding early leaders. His grandson, Judge *Isaac L. Endress*, was a founder of St. Peter's Episcopal Church in Dansville, New York, and the judge's son and grandson, *William Fries Endress* and *William Fitzhugh Endress*, were noted military men and industrial engineers in Cuba, Panama, and western New York State. Surely *Zacharias Endress*, the Wertheimer emigrant, who could have had every honor in the Old World of his birth and education, has, in his own and his posterity's contribution to our society, greatly enriched the New World of his adoption.

His son's biographer in Sprague's *Annals of the American*

*Pulpit* records the interesting fact tht a short time before the birth of *Zacharias'* son *Christian Endress,* "Frederick Lewis, one of the Sovereign Counts of Lowenstein-Wertheim, had, by letter . . . . requested to be considered Godfather to the expected child, and therefore his name is found upon the Baptismal Record of the Church of Zion and St. Michael in Philadelphia, *Christian Frederick Lewis,* but he himself always wrote *Christian* only." The American editor is happy to be able to include three letters of the Counts of Wertheim to *Zacharias Endress,* who corresponded regularly with his former sovereigns.[9] The first two are from *Carl Ludwig* (1712-1779), who had become Prince when his lands were mediatized or incorporated into Bavaria. The third, dated 1784, was by his brother, *Frederic Ludwig* (1706-1796), for whom *Zacharias Endress'* son *Christian* had been named.

(1) *Letter of Carl Ludwig, Count of Löwenstein-Wertheim, to Zacharias Endress, June 30, 1770*

First, our Regards, dear Zachary.

Having learnt that your good friend, *N. Zimmerman,* is about to return to Philadelphia, I send by him this line to you to express to you the pleasure with which I have received the news of your welfare, and of your happy marriage in that distant country.

At the same time I return my thanks for the handsome present that you sent to me, of a fine hat of American manufac-

[9]As the letters show, Zacharias Endress exchanged gifts frequently with the Counts. In addition to the medals sent by Counts, others of their gifts preserved in the Endress family were a ring, a snuff-box, and a wax bust. Of interest also in this connection is the "Legend of the White Nun," a story associated with Zacharias Endress and his friend the Count. According to family tradition, at a dinner party in 1763 at which their ancestor was present, the Count offered to give an old convent and the lands belonging to it, to any man in the party who dared to spend the night alone in the deserted building, which had the reputation of being haunted. Characteristically, Zacharias Endress agreed, and used to like to relate to any credulous audience the following ghost-story. The ghost of a nun, he said, directed him to the tower stairs, where, with his sword, he found a secret place in the wall, and on investigation next morning, the Count found a baby's skeleton, which he promptly had buried in Holy Ground. The tale ends happily, the nun's soul at last finding welcome in Heaven! This story, as told by Zacharias Endress' daughter, Mrs. Mary Ralston, was early published in America, in (1) Margaret Junkin, "The Ankle-chain, a Veritable Ghost-Story," *Philadelphia Evening Bulletin,* August 28, 1852; and in poetic form by the Reverend Joseph Few Smith, D.D., as "The Convent of Vardoun," *Yale Literary Magazine,* Volume V, Number 7, June, 1840, and reprinted in the *Endress Im Hof* history, pp. 24-35.

ture; and as I am at a loss what to send over to you in return, I have concluded to present to you as a token of Remembrance, and in Reciprocal acknowledgement, a gold medal, which I had struck at my mint and for my own use only (the value of the gold and hard metal in the same is a Ducat and three gulden.)

I will add that I shall ever feel an interest in your good-fortune and wish that the same may be enduring and perfect, and with the assurance of my continual grace, I am,

Your Well-affectioned

CARL LUDWIG
Count of Löwenstein-Wertheim, &c.
June 30, 1770.

(2) *Letter of Carl Ludwig, Count of Löwenstein-Wertheim, to Zacharias Endress, June 3, 1772*

Dear Endress.

From your letter of the 12th of last December I received with pleasure the information of your steady continued prosperity and steady faithful allegiance towards your former sovereignty,— and likewise the due receipt by you of my letter forwarded by Mr. Zimmerman. If there is any favor or kindness which I can do for you in this country, you may at all times depend upon me.

In your letter you inform me that you can obtain for me from the Government of your country a site for building a city, without difficulty and upon a moderate payment, — and that 100 mechanics and farmers would be sufficient to accomplish the enterprise, — and that such a colony would yield an income of £1000 Sterling.

But, notwithstanding that the execution of such a Project may seem among your citizens a work of easy accomplishment, I cannot bring myself to think that in its actual working out it may not, as the sure consequence thereof, be attended with endless difficulties and considerable expenses. For in this country men are slow in determining to emigrate to the East or West Indies, unless they can no longer support themselves here at home, and such sort of persons seldom take means with them when they go, greater than to meet the expenses of the journey only. If these men are to be preserved from the most unfortunate condition in a strange country, then the Lord of the Colony would be obliged to provide for the settlement of the Colonists at his own expense, and this would amount to several thousand gulden. Whereby the profits would always be rendered inconsiderable; unless the owner of the Colony were a merchant and personally present to give constant attention to the management of the Colony, and afterwards upon a commerce upon the product of the Colonists. Nevertheless, I do not reject the project which, in your affectionate regard for me, you have proposed, but I will consider upon the matter. But you must send a circumstantial plan prepared by a prudent merchant experienced in such matters, whereby one may judge how such an enterprise is to be commenced and carried along, — how and wherewith a commerce is to be built up, — into whose direction the same is to be committed, — what amount of disbursement will be required, and what profit may be reasonably expected, — and I will then write to you further upon the subject. In conclusion, I wish you constant good health and the happy continuance of your prosperity, and remain, with the favorable regards of my beloved Consort, who, as well as myself and my family, by the Blessing of God, continue in good health.

Your well-affectioned,

CARL LUDWIG, Count, etc. —
*Wertheim,* the 3rd of June, 1772

(3) *Letter of Frederic Ludwig, Count of Löwenstein-Wertheim, to Zacharias Endress, August 20, 1784*

First, my friendly regards. Your letter of 18th of April of this year came to my hand on the 20th of the past month of July, together with the enclosed printed article — and several weeks thereafter I received likewise two leather-bound volumes of the Constitution of the Government of the Republic of Pennsylvania, one of them, directed to my Lord, my nephew Count John Carl L. W. &c., I sent to himself, at the same time [retaining] the one which you directed to me, with a letter of dedication, written in red ink upon the inside of the cover.

All these printed articles are very acceptable to me, and I am the more gratified in the receipt of your letter because I learn from it that you did happily during the long and painful American War, and after suffering many dangers and losses of property, not only preserve your life and health, but even unto this time continue in good health and circumstances and reputation in your country.

After such disturbances and devastations, which are unavoidable in any war, but especially in such as America has passed through, there is nothing more for its inhabitants to desire than a right long-continuing Peace, and Rest, from without and within, and no one can intend this wish more earnestly than I, who take a sympathetic interest in every war and bloodshed[d]ing, which extends to all, however innocent. Particularly I hope for you and yours, and for all Wertheimers and Germans, that in a long-continuing peace, you may soon make up what losses you have suffered by the War, and that God may keep you and yours in permanent happiness and prosperity.

I am now in the 79th year of my life, and upon the 14th of March[,] 1781, celebrated the Jubilee of my Fifty-years-Reign,—and as I desired to preserve the memory of this rare circumstance to posterity in a medal, so likewise I judge that I will make to you an agreeable present in sending to you with this letter a like silver coinage, together with two printed explanations thereof, for Remembrance and as a Token of the Warm Regard with which I am Ever

Your Well-wisher,

FREDERIC LUDWIG
Count *in* Löwenstein-Wertheim, etc.
*Wertheim*, Aug[ust] 20, 1874

A LIST OF

# German Immigrants

TO THE AMERICAN COLONIES
FROM ZWEIBRUECKEN
IN THE PALATINATE

1728 - 1749

*Edited by*

*WILLIAM JOHN HINKE*

*and*

*JOHN BAER STOUDT*

THE PALATINATE AND THE MIDDLE RHINE
The district of Zweibrücken lies mainly to the north and east of the City of Zweibrücken.

# Immigrants from Zweibruecken

HEN the Provincial Council of Pennsylvania issued in 1727 the order that in future all masters of vessels landing in Philadelphia and importing foreigners, should hand in lists of all the people they were importing, the order called for three things: (1) the names of all the arrivals, to be submitted by the captains, (2) their several occupations, (3) the places from which they had come. The first point of the order was carried out by the captains, but the other two points were completely ignored, to the great chagrin and disappointment of all historians and genealogists of later generations. Unless these pioneers brought with them passports or other documents, revealing their former places of residences, or unless they brought family Bibles which contained information about their origin, and unless these precious documents survived to the present time, it was thus far impossible to ascertain the birthplaces of the newcomers.

As a result of this state of affairs, the hope has frequently been expressed, most recently by Professor Albert B. Faust of Cornell University[1], that lists of emigrants might be discovered in German and Swiss archives, which would throw light upon the original homes, from which the early German pioneers came to Pennsylvania. Such lists would be a fitting and most welcome supplement to the lists, preserved by the State of Pennsylvania, which at first promised this information, but did not actually contain it.

This hope was partially realized by Professor Faust himself, when he brought to light such lists in the archives of Switzerland. They were published by him in 1920 and 1925, in two volumes, entitled *Lists of Swiss Emigrants in the Eighteenth Century to the American Colonies*[2].

About the same time other important sources were made available, from which the homes of the emigrants could be ascertained. These were church records in Germany, in which many pastors had noted the departure of their parishioners to the New World. In 1928, Dr. Adolf Gerber published two pamphlets: *Beiträge zur Auswanderung nach Amerika im 18. Jahrhundert aus altwürttembergischen Kirchenbüchern,* i. e., "Contributions to the emigration to America in the 18th century from old Wurttemberg church records", and also *"Neue Beiträge zur Auswanderung nach Amerika"*, i. e., "New Contributions to emigration to America", published in Stuttgart in 1928. These publications showed clearly that the German church records preserved the names of hundreds of persons, who emigrated to America in the 18th century and indicated at the same time the places from which the emigrants had started.

The list which we publish below is the first to be derived from the German archives. It was extracted from a document in the Bavarian State Archives at Speyer, Germany, and was communicated to the editors by Dr. Albert Pfeiffer, Chief Archivist at

1—In his review of "Pennsylvania German Pioneers", in the *Pennsylvania Magazine of Historw and Biography,* vol. 69 (1935), p. 436.

2—Vol. I, contains lists from Zurich, 1734-1744; Vol. II, lists from Bern, 1706-1795; and lists from Basel, 1734-1794. Compiled and edited by A. B. Faust and Gaius M. Brumbaugh, National Genealogical Society, Washington, 1920 and 1925.

Speyer. It is taken from a document, marked "Zweibruecken III,2035." Unfortunately, no detailed description of this document is at present available, as it is reserved for the publication of the original German text. Meanwhile we offer a literal English rendering, in which the spelling of all proper names, names of persons as well as of places, has been carefully presented as given in the original transcript, furnished by Dr. Pfeiffer, to whom our heartiest thanks are due for allowing us to place this important document before American readers.

The list which we publish treats of emigrants who left the former duchy of Zweibruecken, during the years 1728-1749. It is not a complete list of all the emigrants who left Zweibruecken during this period, as is plain from the lists of pioneers in Pennsylvania, but we must be grateful for the information which it contains.

The Duchy of Zweibruecken had become a part of the Palatinate in 1685, when the Zweibruecken-Neuburg line of Dukes fell heir to the Electoral Palatinate upon the extinction of the Palatinate-Simmern line of princes, who had ruled the Palatinate from 1559 to 1685. The Zweibruecken-Neuburg line of Dukes were Catholics, and by their oppressive measures, which they adopted against their Protestant subjects, contributed their share to setting the emigration of their subjects to America in motion.

The territory of Zweibruecken contained what is now comprised in the "Bayerische Rheinpfaltz", i. e., the Bavarian Rhenish Palatinate, a district lying on the left bank of the Rhine, also the principality of Birkenfeld, to which the Nohefelden belonged, also those parts of Hesse, that lie on the left bank of the Rhine and parts of the Rhineprovince, which now belong to Prussia. The distribution of the various districts to Bavaria, Hesse, Oldenburg and Prussia, goes back to the Congress of Vienna in 1815.

The list which we present covers four Oberämter, or governmental districts. That of Bargzabern, in the south-east, Zweibruecken in the south-west, Meisenheim and Lichtenberg in the north-west. The accompanying map will show the location of the chief places named. Many of the places, however, that appear in the list, are so insignificant, that they are not located on an ordinary map. Still, the general district, under which they are named, locates them approximately.

There are 404 names in our list, although the number of persons covered is considerably larger. But, as the exact number of persons in each family is not always given, it is impossible to state the total number of persons included in the list. Of the 404 persons at least 30 are women. Of the rest, 374 men, 190 are found in the Pennsylvania lists of pioneers. That is, more than half can actually be traced as having come to Pennsylvania. The others may have died on the way, or some of them may have gone to other American colonies, notably to Carolina, for which many were headed in the beginning.

In order to make the list more useful, the exact name as found in the Pennsylvania lists and the time of arrival in Philadelphia are given in smaller print immediately below the names, while statements as to their places of settlement in Pennsylvania, are given in footnotes. Let us hope that other, similar lists may soon be found, which will identify more homes, from which these sturdy pioneers came forth to venture upon the long and difficult journey to the New World, where they made a noteworthy contribution to American civilization.

# LIST OF EMIGRANTS FROM ZWEIBRUECKEN

## 1728-1749

OBERAMT[1] BERGZABERN.

1732. Adam Armbruster of Edisheim leaves for a foreign country.

1741. Philips Krum of Pleisweiler leaves for America.

CLEEBURG.

1731. Hans Adam Edelman of Rott leaves the country.
Hans Martin and Hans Adam Weiss of Hundsbach leave.

1733. Michel Weiss of Hundsbach, David and Philip Edelmann, Michel Hammer and Peter Scheib of Steinselz leave with wives and children for America.

Michael Wise and Philip Jacob Edelman arrived at Philadelphia, Sept. 28, 1733, on the Brigantine Richard and Elizabeth. Hans Michael Hammer, Sept. 29, 1733, Pink Mary.

Johann Schlabbach and Christian Suder leave for Pennsylvania.

Johannes Slabach and Christian Sooter, Sept. 29, 1733, pink Mary.

1738. Michel Bayerfalck of Steinselz leaves for Pennsylvania.
Caspar Dirry of Cleeburg leaves for America.

1740. Johann Jakob Stambach of Bürlenbach leaves the country.

Hans Jacob Stambach, Sept. 26, 1741, ship St. Mark.

1749. Hermann Lorentz of Hundsbach leaves the country.
Peter Kehler of Oberhofen leaves the country.
Michel Rummel of Cleeburg leaves for America.
Blasius Hauck of Ingelsheim with wife and children, and

[1]—Oberamt corresponds to Regierungsbezirk, a governmental district, in other parts of Germany.

Margaret Hauck, of the same place, leave for America.
Blasius Hauch, Sept. 28, 1749, ship Ann.

1749. Sebastian Späth, miller of the Zellbrück mill, Hofner[4] Bannes, with wife and five children, leave for Weissenburg.
Hofner Bannes, perhaps identical with Johann Jacob Banutz, Sept. 13, 1749, ship Christian. Hofner is not a Christian name.
Johann Jakob Rummel of Cleeburg leaves for America.
Jakob Schumacher, Daniel Schumacher, Barthel Schumacher, and Anna Barbara Schumacher, all of Cleeburg, leave for America.
Jakob Clor of Bremmelbach, with wife and one child, leaves for America.

FALKENBURG.

1737. Georg Schiessler of Hinterweidenthal leaves for America.
George Shissler, Sept. 26, 1737, ship St. Andrew Galley.

1741. Hans Adam Stock of Willgartswiesen leaves for America.
Hans Adam Stock, Oct. 2, 1741, ship St. Andrew.

LANDSBERG.

1740. Justus Lindemann, Görg Conrad, Anna Catharina Conradin, Peter Tielmann Bohn, Veltin Grimm, these five of Unkenbach,
Justus Linteman, Yearig Conarad, Hendryk Dealbone and Feltin Krimm, Nov. 25, 1741, ship Loyal Judith.
Ulerich Hart of Alsenz, all six leave for America.
Ulrich Hartman, Nov. 25, 1740, ship Loyal Judith.
Johann Görg Dornberger of Niedermoschel leaves for America.

1741. Johann Philips Fett of Niedermoschel leaves for America.

1748. Peter Thomas of Niedermoschel leaves with wife and six children for America.

OBERAMT LICHTENBERG.

1733. Georg Pfaffenberg of Ulmet and John Riegel of Pfeffelbach leave with wives and children for America.
Georg Pfaffenberger, Sept. 29, 1733, Pink Mary, and Johannes Riegel, Sept. 18, 1733, ship Pennsylvania Merchant.

1737. Adam Drumm of Ulmet leaves with his wife for Carolina.

---

4—Hofner, more correctly Hafner or Haefner (from hafen, pot) means potter.

Wilhelm Rabenalt[5] of the valley of Lichtenberg leaves with his wife and children for America.

Jakob Wolf of Ronneberg leaves with wife and children for America.

Andreas Aulenbacher[6] of Reichweiler leaves for America.

Adam Mohr of Russberg leaves with three sons for Holland.

Christian Doll of Irtzweiler leaves for Carolina.

1738. Konrad Reppmann of Ulmet leaves for America.

Nickel Holl of Liebensthal leaves for America.

Adam Albert of Ulmet leaves for Carolina.

Peter Pontius' widow of Langenbach and Nickel Simon of Pfeffelbach, both leave for America.

Nickel Klee, Theobald Klee, Nickel Fischer, Michel Hartmann, Daniel Schneider, Erhard Hofmann, all from Rehweiler, leave for Carolina.

Stephan Clär of Diedelkopf leaves for Carolina.

Daniel Staud of Essweiler leaves for America.

Johann Cuntz and Peter Jost of Mannbächel leave for Carolina.

1738. Michel Clemens of Grünbach leaves for Carolina.

Peter Heyderich of Oberalben leaves for Pennsylvania.

Michel Müller of Essweiler leaves for Carolina.

Peter Staud of Essweiler leaves for Carolina.

Theobald Diel of Etschberg and widow of Matheis Theiss of Grünbach leave for Carolina.

Johann Huntzinger of Rammelsbach leaves for Carolina.

Nickel Müller of Pfeffelbach leaves for America.

Jakob Mack's widow of Oberalben and her son-in-law Jakob Mann leave for America.

Stephan Braun of Ruschberg, Johann Friedrich Bartz of Reichweiler, Jakob Schwartz of Ohmbach leave for Carolina.

Johann Friedrich Bartz, Oct. 25, 1738, ship Davy.

Hans Adam Schad of Russberg leaves for America.

5—Wilhelm Raubennalt settled in Lowhill Township, Lehigh County, where his widow Magdalena in 1749 took out a warrant for land.

6—Andrew Aulenbacher was an elder in the Tulpenhocken Reformed congregation in 1739.

1739. Christian Schuch[7] and his son-in-law Jakob Kochert of Rathsweiler leave for America.

Paul Samstel or Samsel[8], of the same place [Rathsweiler], leaves for America.

Simon Drum of Frützweiler leaves for America.

Nickel Helfenstein of the valley of Lichtenberg leaves for America.

1739. Stoffel Doll and his son-in-law Peter Monbauer of Irtzweiler leave for America.

Hans Otto Ridy of the same place [Irtzweiler] leaves for America.

Henrich Fress, of the valley of Lichtenberg, aged 20 years, leaves for America.

Henrich Heyderich of Irtzweiler leaves for America.

Nickel Monbauer of Irtzweiler leaves for America.

Lorentz Ming of Hintzweiler leaves for America.

Peter Becker of Friedelhausen leaves for America.

Melchior Faust's widow, her son and his wife, leave for America.

This is very likely Abraham Faust, who arrived Aug. 27, 1739, on the ship Samuel.

Daniel Burger of Hachenbach leaves for America.

Simon Geres of Horschbach leaves for America.

Jakob Hauch and Johann Nickel Schiehl, both of Langenbach, leave for America.

Jacob Kockert's widow Catharina leaves for America.

Johann Nickel Bollmann of Aulenbach leaves for America.

Johann Friedrich Gubel, a serf of the cloister Offenbach,

---

7—Christian Schug settled in Springfield township, Bucks County. On October 3, 1739, John, Richard and Thomas Penn granted to Christian Shook a tract of land on a branch of Cook's Creek, near Durham. On June 30, 1747, Rev. Michael Schlatter preached "at a place called Springfield or Schuggenhaus", to a congregation of Reformed people, served by John Conrad Wirtz, which shows that the first place of worship was either in the house of Christian Schug or in a house built on land given by him. On Sept. 29, 1747, Christian Schug was present at the first meeting of the Coetus of Pennsylvania, held in Philadelphia. On November 12, 1763, Christian Schuck, of Springfield township, conveyed to the trustees of the Springfield church one acre and 56 perches. The cornerstone of the first stone building erected in 1763, which is still preserved in the front wall of the present building, contains the initials of the building committee, one of them being C. H. S., which is supposed to stand for Christian H. Schug. He was one of the leading Reformed elders in the first period of the Pennsylvania Coetus.

8—Paul Samsel and his wife Margaret, settled at Great Swamp, Lower Milford township, Lehigh county. About 1758, Paul Samsel was a member of the Reformed congregation at Great Swamp. (See *History of the Goshenhoppen Charge*, p. 277.) Some of his children appear in the Great Swamp Reformed Record.

leaves for America.

1739. Sebastian Albert, son of a subject of Baldwein from Eckersweiler, leaves for America.

Bast Doll, of Oberweiler, leaves for America.

Peter Linn of Hachenbach leaves for America.

1740. Peter Tascher of Altenglan leaves for America.

1741. Friedrich Freess, from the valley of Lichtenberg, leaves for America.

Johann Jakob Schreiner of Selchenbach,

Friedrich Meyer of Bedesbach,

George Ruth of Oberalben,

Johan Friederich Frees, Friederich Meyer, Georg Ruth, Sept. 23, 1741, ship Marlborough.

Hans Adam Sonntag of Pfeffelbach,

Hans Adam Sonntag, Oct. 26, 1741, Snow Molly.

Peter Burgay of Schellweiler,

Henrich Christmann of Quirnbach,

Peter Weber, of the same place,

Heinrich Christmann, Nov. 20, 1741, ship Europa, and Peter Weber, Oct. 26, 1741, Snow Molly.

Wilhelm Osswald, all eight of them leave for America.

Jakob Simon of Pfeffelbach leaves for America.

Jacob Simon, Oct. 12, 1741, ship Friendship.

Maria Catharina Doll, widow of the late Peter Doll, of Oberweiler, leaves for America.

Johannes Emmerich's widow of Schellweiler and her little daughter Maria Magdalena leave for America.

Michel Diehl of Hintzweiler leaves for America.

Jakob Benedick of Hintzweiler leaves for America.

1742. Jakob Weber of Hintzweiler leaves for America.

Henrich Staud of Bosenbach leaves for America.

Michel Weiss of Hintzweiler,

Simon Peter Dhiel, of the same place,

Arnold Guckert of Oberweiler,

Peter Gerres of Horsbach, all leave for America.

Johann Leonhard Fuhr, schoolmaster of Herschweiler,

Johann Lehnhart Fuhr, Sept. 3, 1742, ship Loyal Judith.

Simon Jakob Diel, of Oberweiler,

Jakob Dhiel and his brother Wilhelm Dhiel of Horspach, all leave for America.

Anna Magdalena Staud and his sister Catharina Christina Staud, of Bosenbach, both leave for America.

1744. Anna Catharina, widow of Daniel Werner of Oberweiler leaves with her three children for America.

Peter Hahn of Oberweiler leaves for America.

Petter Hann, Nov. 2, 1744, ship Friendship.

Wilhelm Müller, formerly shepherd at Pettersheim, leaves for America.

Daniel Bender of Herschweiler leaves for America.

Daniel Dhiel of Oberweiler, with wife and six children,

Philipp Dhiel of Horspach, single,

Thomas Gilcher, of Nertzweiler, with his wife and six children,

Hans Jakob Gilcher, of the same place, the aged father of the last, leave together for America.

1746. Anna Eva Thonauer of Essweiler marries Jobann Abraham Heyl, of the Electoral Palatinate, and intends to go with him to Holland.

1747. Maria Dorothea Geibel of Konken-Langenbach leaves for Carolina.

1748. Johann Nickel Müller of Hof in the Osterthal leaves with wife and two children for America.

Either identical with Johannes Müller, Sept. 15, 1748, ship Two Brothers, or with John Nicklas Miller, arrived Sept. 15, 1749, ship Phoenix. The latter is more probably the man.

Margaretha Catharina Theiss of Wahnwegen leaves for America.

Friedrich Hörth from the valley Lichtenberg leaves with wife and six children for America.

Hans Adam Klein of Bupach emigrated to Pennsylvania in 1709, but was only now [1748] manumitted.

Hans Nickel Clementz, the miller at the Haasen mill near Konken, leaves with wife and four children for America.

Nickelaus Clementz, Sept. 15, 1748, ship Two Brothers.

1749. Nickel Nickum, Senior, with his wife,

Nickel Nickum, Junior, with wife and four children,

Nickel Nickum, Senr, Nicklas Necum and Peter Nickum, Aug. 24, 1749, ship Elliot.

Peter Nickum with wife and two children, all from Irtzweiler, leave for America.

Lorenz Loch's widow of Rusperg with five chidren,

Hans Nickel Kemmer of Mannbächel, with wife and two children, leave for America.

Theobald Schneider of Saal in Osterthal leaves with wife and four children for America.

Jakob Strauss of Rehweiler leaves for America.

Jacob Straus, Oct. 7, 1749, ship Leslie.

Henrich Schmitt of Rusperg leaves with his wife and four children for America.

Henrich Schmitt, Sept. 26, 1749, ship Dragon.

Jakob Hamman of Rusperg leaves with wife and four children for America.

Jacob Hamman[9], Sept. 15, 1749, ship Edinburgh.

Peter Klein of Irtzweiler leaves with his wife for America.

Peter Klein and Jacob Meyer, Oct. 7, 1749, ship Leslie.

Jakob Meyer of Rohrbach leaves with wife and five children for America.

Margaretha Schmitt of Pfeffelbach with her child leaves for America.

OBERAMT MEISENHEIM.

1738. Johann Georg Mill of Heiligenmoschel leaves for America.

Johann Bartholmae, Bernhard Rauch, Görg Gebhard, Johann Dreher, all of Desloch,

Carl Neumann, Christoph Bernhard of Gallbach,

Nickel Bauer of Jeckenbach, all seven leave for Pennsylvania.

Henrich Böhmer of Roth leaves for Pennsylvania.

Daniel Carile and Nickel Wolf, both of Cronenberg, leave for America.

Peter Heyl, miller of Adenbach, leaves for Pennsylvania.

Petter Heyel, Sept. 11, 1738, ship Robert & Alice.

1739. Mattheiss Velten of Ransweiler, a tenant-farmer, leaves for America.

---

9—Jacob Hamman is probably a member of the Hamman family which settled in Lehigh county and were there members of the Jordan Lutheran congregation. A Balthasar Hamman came to Pennsylvania on the Snow Molly, landing at Philadelphia, October 26, 1741. He was then 19 years of age. In 1752 a son, Jacob Hamman, was born to him. It is, therefore, possible that this Jacob Hamman, who arrived in 1749, was the father or uncle of Balthasar Hamman and that his son Jacob was named after his grandfather, or his uncle.

1739. Peter Wolf of Reifenbach leaves for America.
Astmus Frantz of Ransweiler leaves for America.
Philipp Hasselberger of Ransweiler leaves for America.
Nikolaus Klein of Becherbach and Peter Mohr, of the same place, both leave for America.
Johann Adam Becker of Seelen leaves for America.
Johann Nickel Schotto of Lettweiler leaves for America.

1740. Jakob Theobald of Meddard leaves for America.
Johann Henrich Geib of Meddard leaves for America.
Adam Bischof of Oberhausen, Görg Krieger of Duchrodt,
Philipp Schuster's four children of Oberhausen,
David Knöchermann, of the same place, and
David Zimmermann of Duchrodt, all leave for America.
Johann Nikolaus Zell of Rehborn leaves for America.
Johann Adam Maurer of Becherbach,
Philips Schneider of Odenbach,
Joseph Küchler of Gallbach,
Leonhard Gerhard of Lettweiler,
Johann Peter Hegener of Dessloch,
Peter Hegner, Dec. 3, 1740, ship Samuel.
Johann Abraham Haass of Meddard and
Johannes Wolf of Gangloff, all seven families leave for America.

1740. Gerhard Zimmermann of Duchrodt leaves with his wife and children for America.
Gerhard Zimmerman, Dec. 3, 1740, ship Samuel.
Antoni Keller, with his wife and children,
Adam Maurer, with his wife and children, both of Lettweiler, leave for America.
Isaac Dietrich of Biesterschied leoves for America.

1741. Johann Friedrich Bayer of Staudernheim leaves for America.
Johann Philips Daum of Niederhausen, and
Philibs Daum, Oct. 17, 1741, ship Molly.
Johann Henrich Schmitt, of the same place, leave for America.
Maria Unger of Rehborn and her daughter Otilia leave for America.

Erasmus Keim of Finkenbach leaves for America,
Aschmes Keim, Sept. 23, 1741, ship Marlborough.

Peter Horbach of Jeckenbach,
Johan Peter Herbach, Oct. 26, 1741, Snow Molly.

Sebastian Hepp, of Odenbach,
Peter Kiefer of Odenbach,
Peter Keeffer, Sept. 23, 1741, ship Marlborough.

Peter Reidenbach of Odenbach,
Henrich Grimm of Lettweiler,
Michel Hergesheimer, of the same place,
Johann Philips Plott of Niederhausen,
Michel Meyer of Dantesbergerhof,
Simon Meyer of Rehborn, all leave for America.

Philips Kallbach of Duchrodt leaves for America.
Filib Kalbach, Sept. 26, 1741, ship St. Mark.

**1741.** Johannes Schaum of Duchrodt leaves for America.

Johannes Maurer of Becherbach leaves for America.

Görg Plott, Adam Gerhard, Görg Funck, Wilhelm Neumann, of Kallbach, Martin Lamb, Jacob Bernhard of Reifelbach,
George Funk, Oct. 26, 1741, Snow Molly, Martin Lamp, Oct. 12, 1741, ship Friendship, List A.

Peter Bartholme, Peter Gebhard, Nickel Gebhard, Peter Hüll and Johann Hüll, absconded at night, all of Dessloch.
Peter Bartholoma, Sept. 23, 1741, ship Marlborough, Peter Gebhart, Sept. 26, 1741, ship St. Mark.

Jakob Rempy, Daniel Gilmann of Breitenheim,
Konrad Stoltz, Jakob Gerhard, Peter Hofmann of Jeckenbach, all sixteen leave for America.
Jacob Rimbi, Daniel Gillmann, Oct. 17, 1741, ship Molly.
Conrad Stoltz, Jacob Gerhartt, Sept. 26, 1741, ship St. Mark.

Adam Beyer of Duchrodt,
Peter Fuchs of Staudernheim, both leave for America.

**1742.** Johann Nickel Heyel of Meddard leaves for America.

Maria Sophia Dietrich of Bisterschied leaves for America.

**1747.** Frantz Schuster, Peter Conrad, Eleanora Catharina, widow of Henrich Köster, Adolf Mey, all four of Niederhausen, leave for America.
Johann Peter Conradt, Adolff May, Oct. 13, 1747, ship Two Brothers.

Anna Catharina Bischoff of Oberhausen leaves with her three children for America.

1748. Peter Engel of Becherbach leaves for America.

Johann Peter Engel, Sept. 15, 1748, ship Two Brothers.

Leonhard Mey of Niederhausen leaves for America.

Daniel Mey, Franz Peter Mey, Maria Elisabetha Mey, Anna Margaretha Mey, all four of Niederhausen, leave for America.

Michel König of Seelen leaves for America.

Michael König, Sept. 7, 1748, Mary Galley.

Maria Catharina Mey, Johann Jakob Lorentz, Philips Lorentz, Anna Maria Lorentz, all four of Niederhausen, leave for America.

1749. Jakob Schuster of Rehborn leaves with his wife and two children for America.

Henrich Weber of Seelen leaves with his wife and four children for America.

Johann Henrich Weber, Sept. 26, 1749, ship Dragon.

Philip Hoynsinger of Seelen leaves with his wife and four children for America.

Andreas Glipp of Reichstahl leaves with his wife and four children for America.

Maria Katharina König of Seelen leaves for America.

Johann Ritscher von Dessloch leaves wtih his wife and three children for America.

Johann Hermann Metz of Dessloch leaves with his family for America.

Anna Margaretha and her sister Anna Catharina Fuchs of Duchroth leave for America.

Balthasar Schmitt of Reifelbach leaves with his wife and four children for America.

Friedrich Mey of Reifelbach leaves with his wife and three children for America.

Philips Mayerer of Reifelbach leaves with his wife and three children for America.

Johann Görg Redenbach of Duchroth leaves for America.

Johann Henrich Schmitt of Duchroth leaves with his wife for America.

NOHEFELDEN.

1728. Maria Cunigunda and Angelica Meiss of Ellweiler leave the country.

1733. Peter Ruth[10] of Wallhausen leaves for Pennsylvania.
Christian Ruth[11] of Wallhausen and Philips Schmeyer[12] of Wolfersweiler leave with wives and children for Pennsylvania.

1737. Four different persons leave for America.
Peter Hujet of Achtelsbach and
Christian Ruth of Wallhausen leave for America.

1738. Jakob Fenstermacher, Mathias Fenstermacher, Hans Adam Miller, Peter Thomas and Elisabetha Fautz from the district of Nohefelden leave for America.

Jacob Fenstermacher, Philip Fenstermacher, Mathes Fenstermacher, Sept. 9, 1738, ship Glasgow, Peter Thomas, Jan. 10, 1739, Bellinder London.

Melchior Zwinn of Wolfersweiler leaves for America.
Catharina Baum of Wolfersweiler leaves for America.
Anna Barbara Staud[12], daughter of Abraham Staud, of Gimbsweiler, leave for America.

1739. Peter Marcker, a tenant-farmer of Wallhausen, leaves for America.

---

10—Peter Ruth settled on the Cacoosing Creek in Cumru township, Berks County, Pa. At the time of his death in 1771 he was possessed upwards of nine hundred acres of land. He was survived by his wife Catharine, and children, Michael, Jacob, Christian, Peter, George, John, Henry, Francis, Catharine, Mary, Barbara, Eva, Magdalena, Margaret. Jane Addams of Hull House fame, was a granddaughter of Barbara Ruth and a great-granddaughter of Peter Ruth. The family were members of the nearby Hain's Reformed Church, in the records of which the name Ruth appears more frequently than that of any other family. Mrs. Tillie R. Reber, West Reading, is family historian.

11—Christian Ruth settled in Macungie township, Lehigh County. He was a member of the Consistory of the Longswamp Reformed Congregation in 1748.

12—Philip Schmeyer settled at Spring Creek, Lower Macungie township, Lehigh County. He died in 1750, leaving widow Marie and children Johann, Elizabeth, Peter, Daniel, Christian, Anna, Margretha, Michael, John Philip. Rev. Melville B. C. Schmoyer, Allentown, family historian.
Mathias, Jacob and Philip Fenstermaker were residents of Longswamp township, Berks County, in 1752. The names of the latter two are found in the list of members of the Longswamp Reformed congregation of 1748.

Johann Nickel Klee and

Abraham Staud[13], both of Gimbsweiler, leave for America.

David Fortune of Gimbsweiler leaves for America.

Johann Nickel Doll of Steinberg leaves for America.

Peter Marker, Hans Nichall Kley, Abraham Staudt, Johan Jerg Staudt, David Fordney, Johan Nickell Doll, Sept. 3, 1739, ship Loyal Judith.

1740. Anna Ottilia Zimmermann of Hahnweiler leaves the country.

Johann Caspar Brey of Ellweiler leaves for America.

Philips Cuntz, the shepherd of Reichweiler,

Perhaps Philipp Kuntz, Sept. 23, 1741, ship Marlborough.

Theobald Schank, tenant-farmer of Wallhausen,

Dewalt Shank, Nov. 20, 1741, ship Europa.

Jakob Geis of Wolfersweiler,

Anna Margaretha Geiss, daughter of the late mayor Geiss, of Wolfersweiler, all for leave for America.

---

13—Abraham Staudt, of Gimbweiler, was born at Herschweiler April 5, 1672. He was the son of Tilghman Staudt, a member of the town council of Herschweiler, and the censor or ruling elder in the Reformed congregation. He was married to Engel Becker, a daughter of Wilhelm Becker, of Ilbheim. Seven of their children reached majority: Abraham, Hans, Andreas, Johannes, Katharina, Hans Nickel, juror of the Court of Justice, who was married to Anna Katrina Sontag; and Agnes, the wife of Johannes Geiss, of Gimbweiler. Three of the sons, Abraham, Andreas, and Nickel, ended their days in Pennsylvania.

Abraham Staudt was married on February 8, 1701, to Anna Katharina Geiss, a daughter of Hans Georg Geiss. She was born at Gimbweiler, February 28, 1684, and died there April 28, 1734. They were the parents of three sons and eight daughters, of whom the three sons and five of the daughters came to Pennsylvania. Abraham settled with his son George in Salisbury township, Lehigh County. The latter was a member of Zion Reformed congregation.

Jacob Staudt, born at Wolfersweiler, October 13, 1710, died at Perkasie, Bucks County, April 30, 1779. The home he erected is still standing. He was a member of the Tohicken Reformed congregation. He has many descendants. A son Abraham was a member of the Constitutional Convention of Pennsylvania at the time of the American Revolution. Jacob was the first of the family of Abraham Staudt to come to Pennsylvania. On the same ship in 1737 were two of his kinsmen, John Staudt, aged 30 years, and Hans Adam Staudt, aged 19 years. Anna Katherina, baptized October 21, 1701; Anna Elizabeth, baptized April 18, 1718; and Anna Barbara, born April 7, 1722, followed their brother to Pennsylvania the following year. They probably sailed on the ship Glasglow, which landed at Philadelphia on September 9, 1738. Quite a few of the passengers on the ship were from Zweibruecken, among these were Daniel Staudt, aged 45 years, and Peter Staudt, aged 17 years. The latter was a member of the Tohicken Reformed church in Bucks County, where a gravestone marks his place of burial. Lisa Margaret, born in 1715, was married on February 11, 1738, to Johan Nickel Klee, of Wohrbach. The year following the marriage they accompanied her father Abraham Staudt to Pennsylvania. Mattheis Staudt, the younger son of Abraham Staudt, was born December 26, 1725. Tradition has it that he came with his father to Pennsylvania. Margareth Katharina, baptized April 19, 1724, is believed to have also been in the party sailing for the land of hope and promise. Matthias being only 14 years of age his name does not appear among the passengers. He settled in Bern township, Berks County, where his cousin Michael Staudt had settled in 1733. A head-stone at the Bern Reformed church marks his place of burial. Dr. Calvin K. Staudt, missionary at Bagdad, is a descendant.

1742. Maria Barbara, widow of Jakob Schweich, of Wolfersweiler, leaves for America.

Maria Catharina, widow of Michael Seybert, of Wolfersweiler, leaves for America.

1743. Matheiss Gisch of Answeiler leaves for America.

Anna Elisabetha Neumann from the district of Nohefelden, leaves for America.

1744. Jakob Stephan of Wolfersweiler leaves with wife and one child for America.

Jacob Stephen, Oct. 20, 1744, ship Phoenix.

1748. Johann Adam Schreyer of Nohefelden leaves for America.

1749. Jakob Britius"[14] widow of Wolfersweiler, leaves with four children for America.

Jakob Hornberger of the same place, with his wife, leaves for America.

Michel Hujet of Hanweiler leaves with his wife and four children for America.

Michel Schmeyer of Wallhausen leaves with his wife and seven children for America.

Johannes Staud[14], of Wolfersweiler, leaves for America.

Michel Staud[14], of the same place, leaves for America.

---

14—Johannes Michel Staudt, a nephew of Abraham Staudt, was born October 9, 1712. He was the son of Johannes Staudt, a member of the Select Council of Wolfersweiler, and a grandson of Tilman Staudt. The father Johannes Staudt was born at Hirschweiler January 9, 1678, and died at Wolfersweiler October 6, 1755. He was married at Wolfersweiler July 16, 1699, to Maria Engel Britzius, a daughter of Johan Nickel Britzius, of Achtelbach, Juror of the Court of Justice. At the baptism of Johannes Michel Staudt, Michel Bruck and Johannes Geiss, of Gimbweiler, were godfathers, hence the name Johannes Michel. The godmother was the mother's sister Christina Britzius. Michel Staudt was the first of the family to make his home in Pennsylvania. He sailed on the good ship Merchant of London, which landed at Philadelphia September 18th, 1733. On October 25, 1737, there was surveyed unto him a tract of 180 acres on the west bank of the Schuylkill River opposite "the flat meadows." He was already seated on this land at the time of survey. He apparently returned to Zweibruecken in 1749 to visit his parents and friends at Wolfersweiler. Upon his return his brother Johannes accompanied him. In the same company most likely was the widow of Jacob Britzius of Wolfersweiler who "with her four children left for America in 1749." Johannes Staudt resided for a time with his brother Michel, and then removed to Brunswick, Schuylkill County, where he died. Michel Staudt died at Stoudts Ferry on the Schuylkill May 3, 1776, and was buried at the Bern Reformed church, of which he was one of the founders. He was the father of 12 children.

George Wilhelm Staudt, who qualified at Philadelphia on October 20, 1744, and Johan Nickel Staudt, who landed at Philadelphia September 18, 1773, were probably brothers of Michel Staudt. It is known that he had brothers of those names. The several notes on the Staudt family are rather extended. The purpose is obvious. To make this information available to the many descendants, and to show by this cross section, as it were, how these families that emmigrated from Zweibruecken were related by ties of kinship.

WEGELBURG.

1731. Johannes Stöhr of Rumbach goes abroad.

1737. Georg Kern[15], and
Friedrich Neuhard[15], of Rumbach, leave with their wives and children for Carolina.
Georg Hefft of Nothweiler and
Philip Stephan of Hirschthal leave with their wives and children for Pennsylvania.

1738. Ulerich Stöchel of Hirschthal leaves for America.
Johann Wein Müller of Rumbach leaves for Carolina.
Johannes Weinmüller, Sept. 19, 1738, ship Thistle.

OBERAMT ZWEIBRUECKEN.

1736. Johann Nickel Agné of Einöth leaves for America.
Jacob Hollinger of Waldmohr leaves with wife and child for America.
Jacob Hollinger, Sept. 24, 1737, ship Virtuous Grace.
Michel Ehrmannstraut, with wife and six children,
Hans Adam Haas, with wife and two children,
Christoph Christmann, with wife and five children, leave the country.
Jakob Schüler of Krähenberg, with wife and eight children, leaves for Carolina.
Theobald Kiefer[16] of Kirkel leaves with wife and children for Carolina.
Christian Bollinger of Winterbach leaves for Carolina.
Christn Bullinger, Sept. 24, 1737, ship Virtuous Grace.

1736. Michel Herth of Kirkel, Barthel Remy of Webenheim, Hans Georg Hoch, Barbara Schwartz, Adam Diehl and Friedrich Kiefer[17] of Einöd leave for Carolina.
Bartel Reme, Friedrich Kiefer, Sept. 24, 1737, ship Virtuous Grace.
Sixteen different persons from Zweibrücken leave for Carolina.

---

15—George Frederick Neihart, Georg Neihart, and Michel Neihart settled in Whitehall township, Lehigh County. Georg Kern and Frederick jointly took out warrant for 400 acres of land on the Coplay Creek. Nicolas Kern resided in Whitehall township in 1734. He came to Pennsylvania in 1727. The names of the above appear on the records of the Egypt Reformed congregation. Charles R. Roberts is historian for the Newhard family.

16—Dewald Kieffer settled in Maxatawny township, Berks County.

17—Frederick Kieffer died in Longswamp, Berks County, in 1758. In his will he mentions his wife Mary Catharine, and children: Peter, Barthol, Anna Elizabeth, Anna Mary, and Abraham.

Ludwig Born[18] of Dellfeld leaves with his wife and children for Pennsylvania.

Ludwig Born, Sept. 24, 1737, ship Virtuous Grace.

Johannes Drachsel, miller at Duntzweiler, leaves with his wife and children for Pennsylvania.

Johannes Drachsell, Aug. 30, 1737, ship Samuel.

Hans Georg Tilemann Degen of Niederauerbach leaves with his wife and children for Pennsylvania.

Perhaps identical with Hans Jörg, Dillman, Sept. 24, 1737, ship Virtuous Grace.

Daniel Kiefer of Bierbach leaves with his wife and children for America.

Johannes Heyel of Waldmohr, Hans Georg Schüler of Waldmohr, leave for America.

Henrich Fritz leaves with wife and children for America.

Jakob Bollinger of Biedershausen leaves for Carolina.

Jacob Bullinger, Sept. 24, 1737, ship Virtuous Grace.

1738. Philip Henrich Andrié and Henrich Andrié of Reischweiler leave for Carolina.

Martin Grimm of Böckweiler leaves for America.

Michel Schmöltzer and Paul Schöffer of Rimschweiler leave for Carolina.

Martin Grim and Paulus Schiffer, Sept. 19, 1738, ship Thistle.

Philip Jakob of Niederauerbach leaves for America.

Hans Peter Lantz of Winsberg leaves for Carolina.

Hans Peter Lans, Oct. 28, 1738, Billender Thistle.

Jakob Rauch of Brenschelbach and

Henrich Galetta of Brenschelbach leave for Carolina.

Nickel Leiner of Rimschweiler, Johann Kopp of Niederbexbach leave for Carolina.

Henrich Schwartz of Einöd leaves for America.

Johann Henrich Degen, warrant officer of Zweibrücken, leaves for Carolina.

Johann Schleich of Wattweiler, Jakob Landsmann of

18—Ludwig Born, a tailor, was born in 1702 at Rimschweiler, in Zweibruecken. He and his wife Anna Maria, settled at the Swatara, in the present Lebanon county. He was an elder of the Swatara Reformed congregation. On February 12, 1745, Jacob Lichty and Christian Rauch preached in the Swatara church, and went "to Ludwig Born, a Reformed elder of this congregation, to stay over night with him." In 1749, he joined the Moravian congregation at the Swatara. See "Catalogus of the Members at Swatara", a document in the Moravian Archives at Bethlehem.

Kleinsteinhausen, Jakob Dietz of Ernstweiler, Caspar Scheck of Contwig, Johann Schmitt of Contwig, all leave for America.

Johann Jacob Dietz, Oct. 28, 1738, ship Thistle, Caspar Scheck, Sept. 11, 1738, ship Robert & Alice, Johann Peter Schmidt, Sept. 16, 1738, ship Queen Elizabeth.

Hans Georg Dietz of Hochetschweiler leaves for Carolina.

Hans Georg Dietz, Oct. 28, 1738, ship Thistle.

Georg Braher of Rimschweiler leaves for America. He belongs with his son-in-law Philip Gohn.

Conrad Dietz of Althornbach, Jakob Clother of Rimschweiler,

Philipp Gohn of Rimschweiler, Friedrich Cromer of Rimschweiler, Barthel Cransdorf, of the same place, and Nickel Cransdorf, of that place, all six leave with their wives and children for America.

Fielip Gohn, Sept. 19, 1738, ship Thistle.

Michel Diehl of Hengsbach leaves for Carolina.

Elisabeth Panther of Breitenfelder Hof, Michel Dielmann of Contwig, Paul Büffel of Contwig, Ulrich Seegässer of Wolfersheim, leave for America.

Paulus Buffel, Sept. 11, 1738, ship Robert & Alice.

Hans Adam Huber of Rieschweiler leaves for Carolina.

Philipp Stockheimer of Limbach leaves with wife and children for Carolina.

1739. Adam Ditz[19] of Hoheneschweiler [Höhetschweiler] leaves for America.

Balthasar Husson of Limbach leaves for America.

Christoph Doll and his sister, born in Thallichtenberg, wife of Joseph Bier, miller at Limbach, leave for America.

Christopher Doll, Aug. 27, 1739, ship Samuel.

1740. Nickel Zoller of Webenheim leaves for America.

Nicklas Zöller, Dec. 3, 1740, ship Samuel.

Johann Daniel Hock of Waibenheim [Webenheim], Nickel Göltzer's, late member of the community of Mimbach,

---

19—Adam Dietz and Georg Dietz settled in Plainfield township, Northampton county. On October 18, 1750, a warrant for 25 acres, "near George Berringer at the Blue Mountain, above the Forks of the Delaware, in trust for the Calvinist Congregation there", was issued to Adam Deeds. In 1763, Adam Dietz was an elder and Georg Dietz a deacon of the Plainfield Reformed congregation.

daughter; Andreas Schmitt's daughter of Mimbach, and Jakob Clar of Mimbach, all four leave for America.

Anna Catharina Kuntz and her brother Johann Nickel Kuntz leave for America.

Nicklas Kuntz, Dec. 3, 1740, ship Samuel.

1741. Johann Jakob Klein of Höchem leaves for America.

Michel Haberstich of Böckweiler absconded at night and surreptitiously left for America.

Michel Haberstüch, Nov. 20, 1741, ship Europa.

1742. Johannes Koch and Christian Seibert of Gutenbrunnen leave for America.

Perhaps identified with Johannes Koch, Sept. 5, 1743, Snow Charlotta.

1743. Nickel Schwartz of Waibenheim leaves for America.

Bernhard Mader of Limbach leaves for Carolina.

Jakob Brabänder of Limbach leaves for America.

Görg Huber of Walshausen leaves for America.

Maria Elisabetha Fortibauer of Limbach leaves for America.

Catharina Ber, nee Wengert, of Böckweiler, leaves with her husband, Christoph Ber[20], for America.

Christopher Bär, Melchior Bär, Melcher Bär and Johannes Bär, Sept. 30, 1743, ship Phoenix.

1744. Jakob Steigner of Niederbexbach leaves for America.

1746. Theobald Agné and his sister Magdalena Agné of Lambsborn leave for America.

1748. Maria Barbara Decker of Breidenbach leaves for America.

Caspar and Abraham Kiefer of Breitenbach leave with their wives and chidren for America.

Abraham Kieffer, Sept. 15, 1748, ship Two Brothers.

Jörg Müller of Oberhausen leaves with his wife and six children for America.

1749. Isaac Schäfer of Waldmohr leaves for America.

Jakob Schramm of Waldmohr leaves with his wife and three children for America.

Johann Nickel Schäfer of Waldmohr leaves with his wife and four children for America.

Johan Nicklas Shaffer, George Jacob Shaffer, Sept. 26, 1749, ship Dragon.

---

20—Melchior Baer, Sr., Melchior Baer, Jr., Johannes Baer, and Christopher Baer, settled in Lehigh county.

Melchior Riess of Mausbach leaves with his wife and four children for America.

Peter Bergmann of Mausbach leaves with his wife and two children for America.

Görg Theobald Hofstätt of Niederauerbach leaves for America.

Philipp Jakob Schmitt of Schmittshausen leaves with his wife and one child for America.

Filb Jacob Schmitt, Sept. 26, 1749, ship Dragon.

Martin Andreas of Waldmohr leaves with his wife and two children for America.

Martin Andereas, Oct. 7, 1749, ship Leslie.

Jakob Bliess of Waldmohr leaves for America.

Jakob Müller of Schmittshausen leaves with his wife and five children for America.

Nickel and Christoph Eich, brothers, of Vogelbach, leave for America.

Joh. Nickel Eich and Christoph Eich, Sept. 26, 1749, ship Dragon.

Matheiss Müller of Schmittshausen leaves with his wife for America.

Mathias Müller, Sept. 19, 1749, Ship Lydia.

# A List of German Immigrants to the American Colonies from Zweibruecken in the PALATINATE 1750-1771

Edited by Dr. Friedrich Krebs, *Archivist*

Speyer-am-Rhein, Germany

With an Introduction by Dr. Don Yoder

# INTRODUCTION

IT has always been difficult for Pennsylvania German genealogists to discover the European homelands of their emigrant forefathers. For so few of our emigrants left any record of the villages whence they came, that in most cases our transition back into the past from that Pennsylvania farm in the shadow of the Blue Mountain to the half-timbered and stork-nested village in the Rhineland vineyard country has been almost impossible.

It was therefore a major contribution to Pennsylvania German scholarship when in 1936 there appeared, in Volume I of the Yearbook of the then newly-founded Pennsylvania German Folklore Society, "A List of German Immigrants to the American Colonies from Zweibruecken in the Palatinate, 1728-1749." This list, discovered in the Archives at Speyer by Chief Archivist Dr. Albert Pfeiffer, was brought to America by Bryant Wiest of Elizabethville, Pa., who published the German text of the document in the *Valley Citizen* (Valley View, Pennsylvania) in 1933, was translated and edited by Drs. William John Hinke and John Baer Stoudt. The editors identified a certain proportion of the emigrants in the Pennsylvania ship lists, and added other historical and genealogical notes. This list represented the second area to be heard from geographically in Germanic Europe, following as it did upon the Faust and Brumbaugh Lists of Swiss Emigrants to the American Colonies.

Several years ago Dr. Friedrich Krebs, of the Palatinate Archives at Speyer, brought to light from the *Kirchschaffnei Archiv* in Zweibrücken, a continuation of the Zweibrücken List, covering the years 1750-1771. This second Zweibrücken List offers us 152 names of emigrants, of whom 45 were identified by Dr. Krebs in the lists of *Pennsylvania German Pioneers,* edited by Strassburger and Hinke. The emigrant's name and his time of arrival in Philadelphia, and the name of the ship he arrived on, are given below each name. The majority of these emigrants seem to have left their homeland in the years 1750-1754, the intervention of the Seven Years War between France and England being responsible for drying the stream of emigration down to a trickle after 1755. The geographical names in the list are given as in the original document, succeeded in brackets by the present spelling.

The Krebs List has already been published in Germany, as "Eine Liste deutscher Auswanderer nach den amerikanischen Kolonien aus Zweibrücken in der Pfalz 1750-1771," edited by Dr. Friedrich Krebs, in *Familie und Volk,* Volume I, Number 1 (January-February, 1952).

Principally of genealogical interest, this list will enable many Pennsylvania German families to identify their emigrant ancestors and trace them to a home village in the former Duchy of Zweibrücken in the western part of the Palatinate. Will those readers who can identify an American ancestor in the list please contact the American editor?

DON YODER, Ph.D.

Pennsylvania Dutch Folklore Center
Franklin & Marshall College
Lancaster, Pennsylvania

# LIST OF EMIGRANTS FROM ZWEIBRUECKEN
## 1750 - 1771
### OBERAMT BERGZABERN

1750—JACOB JAUTER of Winden leaves with wife and children for America.

HENRICH BRUNCK of Dierbach also leaves with wife and two children for America.

1751—CATHARINA KESSLER, née Hausswurth, of Winden, leaves with her husband and four children for America.

JOHANN JACOB HAUSSWURTH of Winden leaves for America.

(JACOB HAUSWIRD, Octob. 7, 1751, ship *Janet*)

1752—ABRAHAM SONTAG of Edigkoben [Edenkoben], JACOB SCHUSTER of Edigkoben [Edenkoben] with wife and three children, Maria Barbara, née Acker, wife of Philipp Jacob Schenckel, of Edigkoben [Edenkoben] with one child, all three families leave for America.

(ABRAHAM SONTAG, Octob. 16, 1752, ship *Snow Ketty.*

JACOB SCHUSTER, Octob. 16, 1752, ship *Snow Ketty.*)

1753—JACOB CLEMENTZ with his wife, BERNHARD WUERTENBECHER with his wife and two children, FRANTZ KOST with his wife and four children, GEORG CLEMENTZ, all persons of Ilbesheim, all four families leave for America.

JOHANN ADAM WURTENBERGER of Ilbesheim leaves for America.

JOHANN GORG KURTZ of Dierbach leaves with wife and three children for America.

1754—VALENTIN CLEMENTZ of Ilbesheim leaves for America.

(VALENTINE CLEMENTZ, Sept. 30, 1754, ship *Neptune*)

VALENTIN ZAHNEISSEN'S wife, née Clementz, of Ilbesheim, leaves with two children for America.

1757—HANSS GEORG KASTEN of Illwesheim [Ilbesheim] has left for America in the year 1749.

1771—JOHANN ALTSCHUH of Göcklingen of the Oberamt Germersheim of the Electoral Palatinate intends to leave for America.

## CLEE- and CATHARINENBURG

1750—JOHANN JACOB RUMMEL of Cleeburg [Kleeburg], his wife and one child leave for America.

(JACOB RUMEL, Nov. 30, 1750, ship *Sandwich*)

JACOB BRUECKER of Cleeburg [Kleeburg] leaves with wife and seven daughetrs for America.

(This is perhaps J. JACOB BRUKER, Sept. 22, 1752, ship *Halifax.*)

PETER SCHMIDT of Ingelsheim [Ingolsheim] leaves with wife and six children for America.

(This is either PETER SHMIT, Aug. 13, 1750, ship *Edinburgh,* or PETER SCHMITT, Aug. 28, 1750, ship *Phoenix,* or PETER SHMIT, Nov. 30, 1750, ship *Sandwich*)

1751—ABRAHAM KOENIG of Hooffen [Hofen] leaves with his family, wife and six children for America.

(ABRAHAM KONIG, Octob. 7, 1751, ship *Janet.*)
PHILIPS ENES of Cleeburg [Kleeburg] leaves with wife and one child for America.

(PHILIB ENES, Octob. 7, 1751, ship *Janet.*)

1752—JOHANN GORG DOERRMANN, PHILIPS JACOB LEHMANN, JOHANN PHILIPSS FISCHER, all of Hunspach, JACOB KOHLER of Ingelsheim [Ingolsheim], THEOBALD NIESS of Hoffen [Hofen], leave all for America.

RUDOLPH SCHUMACHER of Cleeburg [Kleeburg] leaves also there.

BALTHASER KERN of Rott, his wife and three children leave for America.

JACOB JUNG of Ingelsheim [Ingolsheim] leaves with wife and two children for America.

MARTIN HAUCK with wife and two children, MARTIN HUELLER with wife and four children, THEOBALD

BILLMANN, JOHANN KOEHLER with wife and one child, all of Ingolsheim, leave for America.

(MARTI HAUG, Octob. 20, 1752, ship *Duke of Wirtenburg*. H. DEWALT BILLMAN, Sept. 23, 1752, ship *St. Andrew*.)

1752—The two daughters left behind by their father, JOHANNES MUELLER of Cleeburg [Kleeburg] leave for America. CATHARINA HAGELBERGER of Rott leaves for America.

FRANTZ SPECK with wife and three children, JOHANNES DOPPERT with wife and one child, all of Ingelsheim [Ingolsheim], APOLLONIA ZIMMERMANN, of Rott, widow of the late Görg Bronner, with four children, MICHEL HARR of Rott with wife and one child, MARTIN WITTERICH of Hunspach, JACOB DIERY with wife and five children, PHILIPS DIERY with wife and three children, BALTHASAR MUELLER with wife and three children, JACOB RUBB with wife and three children, all of Oberhoffen [Oberhofen], JACOB KERN'S old widow of Rott, HENRICH KERN with wife and three children, JACOB KERN with wife and five children, all of Rott, JACOB SEYLER of Birlenbach with wife and five children, BENJAMIN HAGELBERGER with wife and five children, ANNA ELISABETHA BARTHEL with one child, ANNA MARIA SCHMITT and BARBARA HERRMANN, all four of Rott, all seventeen families leave for America.

JOHANNES SCHMITT of Steinseltz [Steinselz], his wife and four children leave for America.

SEYFRIED SCHNEIDER of Cleeburg [Kleeburg], his wife and his eight children leave for America.

JOHANNES SCHUBAR of Hunspach leaves for America with wife and one child.

1753—MICHEL HUMMEL of Birlenbach leaves for America with his wife.

1754—MICHEL STEINMANN of Breidenacker [Breitenacker] leaves with wife and six children for America.

(MICKEL STEINMAN, Sept. 14, 1754, ship *Barclay*.)

JOHANNES DAERENDINGER of Ingelsheim [Ingolsheim] leaves with his family, one son and two daughters, for America.

(JOHANNES DAERENDINGER, Nov. 7, 1754, ship *John and Elizabeth.*)

JACOB GANTHER of Keffenach leaves with his wife for America, too.

(JACOB GANDER, Nov. 7, 1754, ship *John and Elizabeth.*)

LUDWIG HAASS, the young, of Cleeburg [Kleeburg] leaves with his wife and his child for America.

(LUDWIG HAAS, Sept. 14, 1754, ship *Barclay.*)

CATHARINA, widow of HENRICH HECKMANN of Steinseltz [Steinselz] leaves with her four children for America.

GOERG HECHLER of Ingelsheim [Ingolsheim] leaves with his five children for America.

NICKEL HOFMANN of Cleeburg [Kleeburg] leaves with his wife and three children for America.

(JOHANN NICOLAUS HOFFMANN, Octob. 23, 1754, ship *Good Intent.*)

NICOLAUS ESCH of Hunspach leaves for America.

MARGARETHA DREHER of Graszerslocher Hof leaves for America.

## AMT LANDSBERG

1751—HENRICH VALENTIN BERNHARD of Unckenbach [Unkenbach] leaves for America.

1752—BARBARA RHEINHARD of Hallgarten and PHILIPS RHEINHARD of the same place, have left for Philadelphia.

PETER GRIMM of Unckenbach [Unkenbach] leaves with wife and three children for America.

1754—JOHANNES HENRICHS of Sitters leaves with wife and three children for America.

JOHANNES HENRICHS, Octob. 1st, 1754, ship *Phoenix.*)

WENDEL GRIMM of Unckenbach [Unkenbach] leaves with wife and six children for America.

1755—BERNHARD and PHILIPP RAPP of Alsentz [Alsenz] have already left for America in 1749.

JOHANNES and MATTHEISS WAGNER of Alsentz [Alsenz] have already left for America in 1749.

(JOHANNES and MATTEIS WAGNER, Sept. 26, 1749, ship *Dragon.*)

## OBERAMT LICHTENBERG

1750—ANNA MARGARETHA, widow of PHILIPP WOLLSCHLAEGER, her unmarried son and her son-in-law JACOB BRANG, his wife and one child, [all] of Oberweiller [Oberweiler] leave for America.

(JOHANN JACOB BRANG, August 13, 1750, ship *Edinburgh.*)

JOHANN PETER FAUST of Manbächel [Mambächel] leaves for America.

1751—ABRAHAM SCHREINER of Ulmeth [Ulmet] leaves for America.

NICKEL HENRICH of Aulenbach leaves with his wife, her mother and his father for America.

MICHEL BURGER of Aulenbach leaves with his wife and his unmarried daughter for America.

(MICHAEL BURGER, Sept. 16, 1751, ship *Edinburgh.*)

JOHANNES GOETTGEN of Rüsperg [Rüschberg] leaves with his wife and six children for America.

(JOHANNES GOETTGEN, Sept. 16, 1751, ship *Edinburgh.*)

1752—MATTHEISS BOLLINGER of Bossenbach [Bosenbach] leaves with wife and two children for America.

CHRISTIAN WEISS of Bossenbach [Bosenbach] leaves with wife and four children for America.

(CHRISTIAN WEISS, Sept. 27, 1753, ship *Windsor.*)

1753—JOHANN JACOB CREUTZ of Eissenbach [Eisenbach] leaves for America.

JACOB ZUMBRO of Ronnenberg leaves for America.

(JACOB ZOMBRO, Sept. 14, 1753, ship *Edinburgh.*)

JACOB TREIN of Ronnenberg leaves for America.

JOHANN NICKEL LINN of Hachenbach leaves for America.

(JOHANN NICKEL LIN, Sept. 27, 1753, ship *Windsor.*)

PETER SCHUG of Ulmeth [Ulmet] leaves with wife and children for America.
(This is probably PETER SCHUCH, Sept. 14, 1753, ship *Edinburgh.*)

JACOB WOLFF of the same place leaves also there.
(JACOB WOLF, Sept. 30, 1754, ship *Richard and Mary.*)

1754—SIMON DRUMM of Quirnbach has already left for America 13 years ago.
(This is probably SIMON DRUM, August 27, 1739, ship *Samuel and Snow Betsie.*)

1756—PHILIPP EDINGER of Bledesbach has left for America.

1766—The candidate of theology POMP of Mannbächel [Mambächel] has been called to North-America as a clergyman.

1770—HENRICH BENEDUM of Ullmet [Ulmet] has left for America in 1753 without having been manumitted.

## OBERAMT MEISENHEIM

1750—ANNA MARIA WEISS of Niederkirchen leaves for America.

## AMT NOHFELDEN

1754—WENDEL PRITZIUS of Wolffersweiler [Wolfersweiler] leaves for America.
(WENDEL PRITZIUS, Nov. 7, 1754, ship *John and Elizabeth.*)

NICKEL CUNTZER of Anssweiller [Asweiler] has left for America many years ago.
(NICKEL CUNTZER, Aug. 29, 1730, ship *Thistle of Glasgow.*)

## WEGELBURG

1751—NICKEL WOLFF of Hirschthal leaves with wife and three

children for America.
(NICKOLAS WOLFF, Sept. 9, 1751, ship *Patience*.)

1753—ADAM BLEY of Rumbach leaves with wife and two children for America.

The children of SCHNEIDER of Rumbach: i.e. MARTIN SCHNEIDER, MARIA ELISABETHA SCHNEIDER, HENRICH BALTHASAR SCHNEIDER and GOERG FRIDERICH SCHNEIDER with wife and two children leave for America.
(MARTIN SCHNEIDER, Octob. 21, 1754, ship *Friendship*.)

MAGDALENA WEBER of Schönau leaves for America.

1755—JACOB SCHNEIDER and his wife Maria Elisabetha, née Scheel, of Nothweiler, leave with their two children for America.

## OBERAMT ZWEIBRUECKEN

1750—JOHANN JACOB KUNTZ, FRANTZ KUNTZ and ANNA ELISABETHA KUNTZ, all three of Waldmohr, leave for America.
(FRANTZ CUNTZ, August 13, 1750, ship *Edinburgh*.)

GOERG PETER FUNCK of Mittelbach leaves with his wife for America.
(This is probably PETER FUNCK, August 13, 1750, ship *Bennet Gally*.)

LOUISA WERNER of Wattweiler leaves for America.

JOHANNES SCHMITT, hitherto a hereditary tenant-farmer of the Bliesberger Hof, leaves with his family for America.

OTTILIA ROTH of Walssheim [Walsheim] leaves for America.

SUSANNA MARIA HABERSTICH of Böckweiler leaves for America.

CHRISTOPH KRAENDLER of Kirckel [Kirkel] leaves with his wife and one child for America.

CHRISTIAN BRENNESHOLTZ of the same place leaves with wife and four children for America.

1751—ANNA MARIA STRUBEL of Contwig leaves for America.

ANDREAS FICHTHORN of Nünschweiler leaves with wife and one child for America.

1752—THEOBALD SCHWARTZ, of Contwig, his wife and his one child leave for America.

BALTHASAR SCHWARTZ of Contwig and his wife leave for America.

ELISABETHA SCHWAB of Mittelbach and her two sons leave for America.

HANSS GOERG KUHN and MARGARETHA KUHN of Webenheim, JACOB KILL of Contwig with wife and four children, ANGELICA RINCK of Rohrbach, all three families leave for America.

(JOHANN GEORG KUHN, Sept. 14, 1753, ship *Edinburgh.*)

1753—JACOB HAMM of Bierbach leaves with his wife for America.
(JOHAN JACOB HAM, Sept. 14, 1753, ship *Edinburgh.*)

THEOBALD ANGNE of Lambsborn leaves with his wife for America.
(THEOBALT ANGENE, Sept. 14, 1753, ship *Edinburgh.*)

1754—DANIEL SCHWARTZ of Webenheim leaves with his wife for America.

ANDREAS HOCK of Webenheim leaves with wife and several of his children for Pennsylvania.

CHRISTINA KLEIN of the same place leaves also for Pennsylvania.

CHRISTIAN BRENGEL of Wolffersheim [Wolfersheim] leaves also for Pennsylvania.
(CHRISTIAN BRENGEL, Octob. 1st, 1754, ship *Phoenix.*)

DANIEL HAMM of Waibenheim [Webenheim] leaves with his wife for America.

PETER SPIRY of Wolffersheim [Wolfersheim] leaves with wife and seven children for America.

THOMAS HUNTZICKER of Wolffersheim [Wolfersheim] leaves with wife and eight children for America.
(THOMAS HUNSICKER, Octob. 1st, 1754, ship *Phoenix.*)

PETER GUTH of Wolffersheim [Wolfersheim] leaves with his family for America.

(PETER GUTH, Octob. 1st, 1754, ship *Phoenix.*)

GOERG DESSLOCH of Hengstpach [Hengstbach] leaves with wife and five children for America.

(JERG DESLOCH, Sept. 14, 1754, ship *Nancy.*)

VALENTIN HOFMANN of the Fauster mill leaves for America.

MARGARETHA FELL of Kirckel [Kirkel] leaves with her fiancé PETER NEU of the territory of Nassau-Weilburg for America.

(PETER NEU, Octob. 1st, 1754, ship *Phoenix.*)

HANSS PETER SCHOTT of Schwartzenacker [Schwarzenacker], DANIEL DITTLO of the cloister Wörschweiler, JOHANNES KAUFFMANN of Gutenbrunnen, ELISABETHA KAUFFMANN of the same place, ADAM JAQUES' widow of Schwartzenacker, all five leave for America.

(HANS PETER SCHOTT, Oct. 1st, 1754, ship *Phoenix.*)

(DANIEL DITLOH, Octob. 1st, 1754, ship *Phoenix.*)

(JOHANNES KAUFFMANN, Octob. 1st, 1754, ship *Phoenix.*)

1763—JOHANN JACOB BERGMANN of Mittelbach intends to leave for America with his wife and his five children.

(JACOB BERGMAN, Octob. 5, 1763, ship *Richmond.*)

1769—The children of PHILIPP HENRICH ANDRIES of Dellfeld, i.e. MATTHEIS, ANNA APPOLONIA, CATHARINA MARGARETHA and MARIA URSULA, have left for America.

## CUSEL

1759—The son of NICKEL SEIBERT of Eitzweiler [Eizweiler] has left for America twenty years ago.

# A List of Eighteenth-Century Emigrants from the Canton of Schaffhausen to the American Colonies 1734-1752

Edited by Dr. Ernst Steinemann

Schaffhausen, Switzerland

With an Introduction by Dr. Don Yoder

# INTRODUCTION

THE Swiss contingent among the eighteenth-century emigrants to Pennsylvania has been more fully evaluated than that from any other Germanic area. The first emigrant lists from European sources to be published in America were the Faust and Brumbaugh *Lists of Swiss Emigrants in the Eighteenth Century to the American Colonies,* two volumes covering the Cantons of Bern, Basel and Zürich, published at Washington, D. C., 1921-1925, by the National Genealogical Society. In addition, our Mennonite historians and genealogists have added invaluable bibliographical items to our American shelf list of books on the Swiss influences among the Palatine and Pennsylvania Mennonites.

At last another Swiss area is heard from. We are happy to present to our American readers the valuable Steinemann List of Emigrants from the Swiss Canton of Schaffhausen, containing 122 names of heads of families and others who emigrated in the period 1734-1752, from the Canton of Schaffhausen, in north-central Switzerland, at the Falls of the Rhine.

Lacking the intensely human source materials presented in my editions of the Gerber Lists of Württemberg Emigrants, published in the Yearbook of the Pennsylvania German Folklore Society, Volume X (1945), and the Langguth List of Emigrants from the County of Wertheim, Volume XII (1947), the Steinemann Lists will be principally of genealogical interest. The List has been alphabetized, and the name of the home village and the year of emigration have been placed after the emigrant's name. However, the original documents do furnish us a few hints as to the personalities, lives and work of these long-dead and long-forgotten Swiss emigrant forefathers of ours. Occasionally the emigrant's nickname is given; and in several instances, where the emigrant was something other than a farmer, his occupation is indicated — carpenter, huntsman, mason, cartwright, bailiff. The few "Separatists" mentioned were of course Mennonites.

The emigration from Schaffhausen was directed toward three of the American colonies. Pennsylvania was the expressed destination of the majority of the emigrants in this field. Second in preference was Halifax (Nova Scotia), and third, Carolina. Since only a few of these names appear in the Strassburger and Hinke *Pennsylvania German Pioneers,* our standard "blue book" of eighteenth-century Germanic emigrants to Pennsylvania, it is difficult to know how many reached their destinations. The fact, however, that a name does not appear in the *Pioneers,* is no indication that the person did not arrive and settle in Pennsylvania. In many cases names which do not appear in the emigrant lists turn up in the registers of the Reformed Churches of Eastern Pennsylvania, as for instance the Bringolf, Demuth and Dunkel Families, which appear in the records of First Reformed Church, Lancaster.

Readers who can identify their emigrant ancestors from this list should contact the American editor, who is preparing at the Pennsylvania Dutch Folklore Center at Lancaster, Pennsylvania, a card index of all eighteenth-century Germanic emigrants to Pennsylvania, with information from church registers and burial records as to their place of settlement in Pennsylvania.

Historians who wish to read further from the Swiss sources on the Schaffhausen emigration, should consult Ernst Steinemann's "Die Schaffhauserische Auswanderung und ihre Ursachen. Ein Beitrag zur Wirtschaftsgeschichte," in *Zeitschrift für Schweizerische Geschichte,* Volume XIV, Numbers 3-4, 1934; also "Zur Schaffhauserischen Auswanderung," in the *Beiträge zur vaterländischen Geschichte Herausgegeben vom Historisch-antiquarischen Verein des Kantons Schaffhausen,* Number 13 (1936). The Steinemann List of Schaffhausen Emigrants appears in the second of these articles.

DON YODER, Ph.D.

Pennsylvania Dutch Folklore Center
Franklin & Marshall College
Lancaster, Pennsylvania

# EMIGRANTS FROM THE CANTON OF SCHAFFHAUSEN

BRINGOLF, HANS — Hallau (1744)
To Pennsylvania. Demanded his inheritance in 1770.

BRINGOLF, KASPAR — Hallau (1751)
To Pennsylvania, with wife and two children.

BRINGOLF, MELCHIOR — Hallau (1748)
Weaver. To Pennsylvania, with wife and children.

BRUEHLINGER, ADAM — Merishausen (1742)
To Pennsylvania, with wife and children.

BRUEHLINGER, PETER — Merishausen (1742)
To Pennsylvania, with wife and children.

BRUEHLINGER, PETER — Merishausen (1751)
To Pennsylvania, with daughter. // Peter Breilinger, with Peter Wehrner, also of Merishausen, on Ship *Anderson,* 1751.

BRUELLMANN, JACOB — Lohn (1747)
To Pennsylvania, with wife and children.

BRUEHLMANN, JOHANNES — Lohn (1742)
With wife, two children, and son-in-law. Destination unknown.

BRUEHLMANN, JOHANNES — Lohn (1752)
With wife. Destination unknown.

BUCHTER, HANS CONRAD — Thayngen (1744)
To Pennsylvania, with wife and children.

BUCHTER, MARTIN — Thayngen (1751)
To Carolina.

BUERER, HANS JAKOB — Buettenhardt (1742)
To Pennsylvania, with wife and children.

BUERER, HANS MARTIN — Opfertshofen (1751)
Bailiff [Vogt]. To Pennsylvania, with wife and children.

BUSENHARD, HANS ULRICH — Lohn (1747)
To Pennsylvania, with wife and children.

DEMUTH, HEINRICH — Buettenhardt (1742).
To Pennsylvania, with wife and children.

DUNKEL, HANS — Merishausen (1748)
To Carolina, with wife and children.

DUNKEL, HANS — Merishausen (1749)
To Pennsylvania, with wife and two sons.

DUNKEL, MELCHIOR — Merishausen (1742)
To Pennsylvania, with wife and children.

DUNKEL, BARBARA — Merishausen (1742)
To Pennsylvania.

DUNKEL, JERG — Merishausen (1742)
To Pennsylvania, with wife and children.

FOTSCH, HANS — Hallau (1744)
Weaver. To Pennsylvania, with wife, five children and three stepchildren.

GASSER, VERENA — Hallau (1744)
Single. To Pennsylvania.

GOEPFERT, HANS — Merishausen (1738)
To Carolina, with wife and children.

GOEPFERT, JERG — Merishausen (1742)
To Pennsylvania, with wife and children.

GRIESHABER, HANS — Hallau (1751)
To Pennsylvania — with wife and one child.

GRUETMANN, MELCHIOR — Beggingen (1751)
To Pennsylvania, with wife and four children.

GRUETMANN, JAKOB'S DAUGHTER — Beggingen (1751)
To Pennsylvania.

GRUETMAN, HANS ULRICH — Beggingen (1751)
To Pennsylvania.

HATT, ADAM — Hemmenthal (1751)
To Halifax, with his mother, Anna.

HATT, JAKOB — Hemmenthal (1751)
To Halifax, with wife.

HATT, HANS CONRAD — Hemmenthal (1750)
Wants to go to Pennsylvania.

HATT, JAKOB — Hemmenthal (1750)
Wants to go to Pennsylvania.

HATT, KONRAD — Hemmenthal (1751)
To Halifax, with wife and children.

HEER, HANS — Hallau (1751)
To Pennsylvania, with wife and one child.

HUEBSCHER, HANS — Thayngen (1751)
Shoemaker. To Pennsylvania, with wife and one child.

IRMEL, HEINRICH — Schleitheim (1742)
Separatist. Destination unknown.

KELLER, HANS JAKOB — Hallau (1744)
Mason. To Pennsylvania.

KELLER, HANS JAKOB — Hallau (1748)
Mason. To Pennsylvania, with wife and children.

KELLER, JOSEF — Buchberg (1738)
To Carolina, with wife and children. // Joseph Keller, Ship *Thistle,* 1738.

KELLER, URSULA — Hallau (1748)
To Pennsylvania, with one fatherless child.

KIHM, ADAM — Buettenhardt (1742)
To Pennsylvania, with wife and children.

KRAPF, JAKOB — Beggingen (1751)
To Pennsylvania, with wife and two children.

KUELLING, JERG — Wilchingen (1748)
To Pennsylvania, with wife and children.

KUMMER, JOHANNES — Thayngen (1751)
Locksmith, later missionary of the Unitas Fratrum.
To Pennsylvania, with wife and three children.

KUSTER, JERG — Merishausen (1742)
To Pennsylvania, with wife and children.

KUSTER, THEBIS — Merishausen (1742)
To Pennsylvania, with wife and children.

LEU, HANS — Merishausen (1742)
Mason. To Pennsylvania, with wife and children.

LEU, HANS JERG — Merishausen (1742)
To Pennsylvania, with wife and children.

LEU, HANS JAKOB — Merishausen (1742)
To Pennsylvania, with wife and children.

LOEW, JOSEF — Hemmenthal (1751)
To Halifax, with wife, children, and father.

LOEW, MICHEL — Hemmenthal (1751)
Cabinetmaker. To Halifax, with wife and children.

MEIER, HANS — Merishausen (1742)
To Pennsylvania, with wife and children.

METTLER, ALEXANDER — Hemmenthal (1751)
To Halifax.

METTLER, BARBARA — Hemmenthal (1751)
To Halifax.

MEYER, GEORG — Schleitheim (1742)
Separatist. Destination unknown.

NUEKUM, HANS — Hallau (1751)
To Pennsylvania, with wife and three children.

PEYER, SAMUEL — Schleitheim (1742)
Separatist. Destination unknown.

PFEIFFER, HANS — Beggingen (1747)
To Pennsylvania, with wife and children.

PFEIFFER, HANS JAKOB — Neunkirch (1741)
Huntsman. To Pennsylvania, with wife and children.
// Jacob Pfeiffer, Ship *St. Andrew,* 1741.

PFISTER (PFEIFFER?), ANDREAS — Beggingen (1751)
To Pennsylvania.

PFUND, ADAM — Hallau (1751)
To Pennsylvania, with two adult daughters.

PFUND, JAKOB — Hallau (1748)
To Pennsylvania, with wife and three children. Described as "Jakob Pfund, who lives at the Butcher Shop."

PFUND, MORITZ — Hallau (1744)
Agent. To Pennsylvania, with wife, three children, and one stepchild.

RAHM, ELISABETH — Hallau (1748)
Wants to go with her brother in Pennsylvania.

RAHM, BARBARA — Hallau (1748)
Wants to go to her brother's in Pennsylvania.

RAHM, GEORG — Hallau (1751)

Single. To Pennsylvania.

RAHM, HANS JAKOB — Hallau (1751)
To Pennsylvania, with wife and one daughter.

RAHM, KASPER — Hallau (1744)
Carpenter. To Pennsylvania, with wife and two children. His son Alexander came over in 1760 for his inheritance and returned.

REGLI, ANNA — Hallau (1744)
Had her inheritance sent to Philadelphia in 1772.

ROESCHLI, BALTHASAR — Buchberg (1738)
Weaver. To Carolina, with wife and children.

ROOST, HANS CONRAD — Beringen (1742)
To Halifax, with wife and children.

ROOST, HANS JAKOB — Beringen (1752)
To Halifax, with wife, Eva Bollinger.

RUEGER, THEBIS — Merishausen (1738)
To Carolina, with wife and children.

RUSSENBERGER, MICHEL — Schleitheim (1742)
Separatist. Destination unknown.

RUSSENBERGER, HANS — Schleitheim (1742)
Separatist. Destination unknown.

SCHLATTER, JOSEF — Hemmenthal (1751)
To Pennsylvania, with Jerg Wehrner.

SCHLATTER, MICHEL — Hemmenthal (1751)
To Pennsylvania, with Jerg Wehrner.

SCHNEZLER, MARIA — Gaechlingen (1744)
Single. To Pennsylvania.

SCHOETTLIN, MELCHIOR — Hallau (1748)
To Pennsylvania, with wife.

SCHOETTLY, HANS — Hallau (1744)
To Pennsylvania, with wife and five children.

SCHOETTLY, HANS JAKOB — Hallau (1744)
To Pennsylvania. Described as "Schwarzen Sohn."

SCHUDEL, HANS — Beggingen (1751)
To Pennsylvania. Andreas Schudel's son.

SCHWYTZER, HANS — Hallau (1751)
To Pennsylvania, with wife and three children.

SIGG, CASPAR — Herblingen (1742)
To Pennsylvania, with wife and children.

STAMM, JERG — Thayngen (1751)
To Carolina, with four children.

STEINIMANN, ANDREAS — Opfertshofen (1738)
With wife and children. Departure uncertain, but probably to Carolina.

STEINIMANN, JAKOB — Opfertshofen (1738)
With wife and children. Departure uncertain, but probably to Carolina.

STOCKER, ALEXANDER — Thayngen (1751)
To Carolina.

STOCKER, ULRICH — Thayngen (1742)
To Pennsylvania, with two single and two married children.

STRASSER, PETER — Merishausen (1738)
With wife and children. Departure uncertain, but probably to Carolina.

TANNER, HANS JAKOB — Bargen (1749)
To Carolina, with wife and three children.

TANNER, HANS — Bargen (1744)
With wife and children. Allegedly to Carolina, but probably Halifax.

TANNER, HANS JAKOB — Bargen (1744)
To Halifax, with wife and daughter-in-law.

TANNER, JERG — Bargen (1744)
Allegedly to Carolina, but probably Halifax.

THANNER, ANNA — Bargen (1742)
To Pennsylvania. Described as "Urban's" [wife, widow?]

THANNER, HANS GEORG — Bargen (1751)
Blacksmith. To Carolina, with wife and daughter.

THANNER, HANS JAKOB — Bargen (1750)
To Pennsylvania, with wife and children.
Nicknamed "Juck."

THANNER, MICHEL — Bargen (1751)
To Carolina, with wife and six children. Two unnamed families

also went from Bargen to Pennsylvania in 1751. // Michel Danner, Ship *Forest,* 1752.

UHLMANN, JOHANN (MELCHIOR?) — Beringen (1742)
Cabinetmaker. To Halifax, with wife and children.

VOGEL, HEINRICH — Schaffhausen (1734)
Cooper. To Carolina, with wife and two children.

VOGELSANGER, MICHEL — Beggingen (1747)
To Pennsylvania, with wife and children.

WALDVOGEL, HANS MARTIN — Stetten (1747)
To Pennsylvania, with wife and children.

WALDVOGEL, HANS MARTIN — Stetten (1747)
Goes to his brother in London.

WALDVOGEL, HANS ULRICH — Stetten (1742)
To Pennsylvania, with wife and children.

WALDVOGEL, JOHANNES — Stetten (1742)
To Pennsylvania, with wife and children.

WALTER, JAKOB — Loehningen (1751)
Cartwright. To Carolina, with wife and children.
// Perhaps the Jacob (X) Walder who arrived on the Ship *Phoenix,* 1751, with members of the Demuth and Hübscher families, which bear Schaffhausen names.

WEBER, [——] — Siblingen (1751)
To Pennsylvania. Daughter of Magdalena Weber.

WEHRNER, HANS JERG — Merishausen (1742)
Cartwright. Single. Agent. To Pennsylvania.

WEHRNER, ANNA — Merishausen (1742)
"Forster's" Anna. To Pennsylvania.

WEHRNER, KASPAR — Merishausen (1742)
To Pennsylvania.

WEHRNER, BARBARA — Merishausen (1742)
To Pennsylvania.

WEHRNER, PETER — Merishausen (1751)
To Pennsylvania, with wife and mother.
// Peter Wehrner, with Peter Bruehlinger, Ship *Anderson,* 1751.

WEHRNER, WILHELM — Beggingen (1751)
To Pennsylvania, with wife and three children.

WERNER, HANS — Beringen (1747)
To Pennsylvania, with children.

WILDBERGER, HEINRICH — Neunkirch (1744)
To Pennsylvania, with wife and three children.

WIPF, DANIEL — Lohn (1752)
With wife. Destination unknown.

WOLF, MAGDALENA — Beringen (1742)
To Halifax.

ZIEGLER, HANS — Stetten (1751)
To Pennsylvania, with wife and children.

ZIEGLER, HANS JAKOB — Neunkirch (1741)
Carpenter. To Pennsylvania, with wife and children.

ZIMMERLIN, JERG — Hallau (1751)
To Pennsylvania, with wife and two children.

ZIMMERMANN, JERG — Hallau (1744)
To Pennsylvania, with wife, two children, and one stepdaughter.

ZIMMERMANN, SEBASTIAN — Trasadingen (1744)
To Pennsylvania, with wife and six children.

INDEXES TO

# PENNSYLVANIA GERMAN IMMIGRANTS, 1709-1786

Prepared by
ELIZABETH PETTY BENTLEY

# Index to Personal Names

--- C ---

--- E ---

--- G ---

--- M ---

--- N ---

--- O ---

--- P ---

# Index to Ships

www.ingramcontent.com/pod-product-compliance
Lightning Source LLC
Chambersburg PA
CBHW070538270326
41926CB00013B/2140

* 9 7 8 0 8 0 6 3 0 8 9 2 0 *